Information Retrieval

Information Retrieval

Implementing and Evaluating Search Engines

Stefan Büttcher

Charles L. A. Clarke

Gordon V. Cormack

The MIT Press
Cambridge, Massachusetts
London, England

First MIT Press paperback edition, 2016

© 2010 Massachusetts Institute of Technology.

Typeset by the authors using LATEX.

Library of Congress Cataloging-in-Publication Data
Büttcher, Stefan.
Information retrieval : implementing and evaluating search engines / Stefan Büttcher, Charles L.A. Clarke, and Gordon V. Cormack.
    p.   cm.
Includes bibliographical references and index.
ISBN 978-0-262-02651-2 (hardcover : alk. paper)
ISBN 978-0-262-52887-0 (paperback)
1. Search engines—Programming. 2. Information retrieval. I. Clarke, Charles L. A., 1964–. II. Cormack, Gordon V. III. Title.
TK5105.884.B98 2010
025.5'24—dc22   2009048455

to our families

Contents

III Retrieval and Ranking   *257*

VI *Appendix*   *591*

Foreword

An academic dynasty has come together to write an excellent textbook on information retrieval. Stefan Büttcher, Charles Clarke, and Gordon Cormack make up three generations of stellar information retrieval researchers with over fifty years of combined experience. Büttcher was Clarke's doctoral student, and Clarke was Cormack's doctoral student. All three are known for their deep research insights and their passion for building real search systems, a rare combination in a field rich with world-class researchers.

The book covers the major components of a search engine, from crawling to indexing to query processing. Major sections are devoted to the core topics of indexing, retrieval methods, and evaluation. Emphasis is put on implementation and experimentation, allowing the reader to learn about the low-level details of information retrieval systems, including index compression and index update strategies, and to understand which methods work well in practice. Two chapters on evaluation provide the methodological and the statistical foundations for evaluating search engines, enabling the reader to decide, for instance, whether a change to the search engine's ranking formula has a positive effect on the quality of the search results. A chapter on classification provides an introduction to machine learning techniques that are useful for advanced search operations, such as limiting one's query to documents in a specific language, or filtering offensive material from the search results. Chapters on parallel information retrieval and on Web search describe the changes necessary to transform a basic IR system into a large-scale search service covering billions of documents and serving hundreds or thousands of users at the same time.

The authors provide a tutorial overview of current information retrieval research, with hundreds of references into the research literature, but they go well beyond the typical survey. Using a running set of examples and a common framework, they describe in concrete terms the important methods underlying each component — why they work, how they may be implemented, and how they may be shown to work. For the purpose of this book, the authors have implemented and tested nearly every important method, conducting hundreds of experiments whose results augment the exposition. Exercises at the end of each chapter encourage you to build and explore on your own.

This book is a must-read for all search academics and practitioners!

Amit Singhal, Google Fellow

Preface

Information retrieval forms the foundation for modern search engines. In this textbook we provide an introduction to information retrieval targeted at graduate students and working professionals in computer science, computer engineering, and software engineering. The selection of topics was chosen to appeal to a wide audience by providing a broad foundation for future studies, with coverage of core topics in algorithms, data structures, indexing, retrieval, and evaluation. Consideration is given to the special characteristics of established and emerging application environments, including Web search engines, parallel systems, and XML retrieval.

We aim for a balance between theory and practice that leans slightly toward the side of practice, emphasizing implementation and experimentation. Whenever possible, the methods presented in the book are compared and validated experimentally. Each chapter includes exercises and student projects. Wumpus, a multi-user open-source information retrieval system written by one of the co-authors, provides model implementations and a basis for student work. Wumpus is available at `www.wumpus-search.org`.

Organization of the Book

The book is organized into five parts, with a modular structure. Part I provides introductory material. Parts II to IV each focus on one of our major topic areas: indexing, retrieval, and evaluation. After reading Part I, each of these parts may be read independently of the others. The material in Part V is devoted to specific application areas, building on material in the previous parts.

Part I covers the basics of information retrieval. Chapter 1 discusses foundational concepts including IR system architecture, terminology, characteristics of text, document formats, term distributions, language models, and test collections. Chapter 2 covers the fundamentals of our three major topics: indexing, retrieval, and evaluation. Each of these three topics is expanded upon in its own separate part of the book (Parts II to IV). The chapter provides a foundation that allows each topic to be treated more or less independently. The final chapter of Part I, Chapter 3, continues some of the topics introduced in Chapter 1, bookending Chapter 2. It covers problems associated with specific natural (i.e., human) languages, particularly *tokenization* — the process of converting a document into a sequence of terms for indexing and retrieval. An IR system must be able to handle documents written in a mixture of natural languages, and the chapter discusses the important characteristics of several major languages from this perspective.

Part II is devoted to the creation, access, and maintenance of inverted indices. Chapter 4 examines algorithms for building and accessing *static* indices, which are appropriate for document collections that change infrequently, where time is available to rebuild the index from scratch when changes do occur. Index access and query processing are discussed in Chapter 5. The chapter introduces a lightweight approach to handling document structure and applies this approach to support Boolean constraints. Chapter 6 covers index compression. Chapter 7 presents algorithms for maintaining *dynamic* collections, in which updates are frequent relative to the number of queries and updates must be applied quickly.

Part III covers retrieval methods and algorithms. Chapters 8 and 9 introduce and compare two major approaches to ranked retrieval based on document content: the probabilistic and language modeling approaches. The effectiveness of these approaches may be improved upon by considering explicit relevance information, by exploiting document structure, and through feedback and query expansion. We discuss the details with respect to each approach. Chapter 10 introduces techniques for document categorization and filtering, including basic machine learning algorithms for classification. Chapter 11 introduces techniques for combining evidence and parameter tuning, along with metalearning algorithms and their application to ranking.

IR evaluation forms the topic of Part IV, with separate chapters devoted to effectiveness and efficiency. Chapter 12 presents basic effectiveness measures, explores the statistical foundations for evaluating effectiveness, and discusses some recent measures, proposed over the past decade, that extend beyond the traditional IR evaluation methodology. Chapter 13 develops a methodology for the evaluation of IR system performance in terms of response time and throughput.

The chapters in Part V, the final part of the book, cover a small number of specific application areas, drawing upon and extending the more general material in one or more of the first four parts. The architecture and operation of parallel search engines is covered in Chapter 14. Chapter 15 discusses topics specific to Web search engines, including link analysis, crawling, and duplicate detection. Chapter 16 covers information retrieval over collections of XML documents.

Each chapter of the book concludes with a section providing references for further reading and with a small set of exercises. The exercises are generally intended to test and extend the concepts introduced in the chapter. Some require only a few minutes with pencil and paper; others represent substantial programming projects. These references and exercises also provide us with an opportunity to mention important concepts and topics that could not covered in the main body of the chapter.

The diagram on the next page shows the relationships between the parts and chapters of this book. Arrows indicate dependencies between chapters. The organization of the book allows its readers to focus on different aspects of the subject. A course taught from a database systems implementation perspective might cover Chapters 1–2, 4–7, 13, and 14. A more traditional information retrieval course, with a focus on IR theory, might cover Chapters 1–3, 8–12, and 16. A course on the basics of Web retrieval might cover Chapters 1–2, 4–5, 8, and 13–15. Each of these sequences represents one-half to two-thirds of the book, and could be completed in a single three-to-four month graduate course.

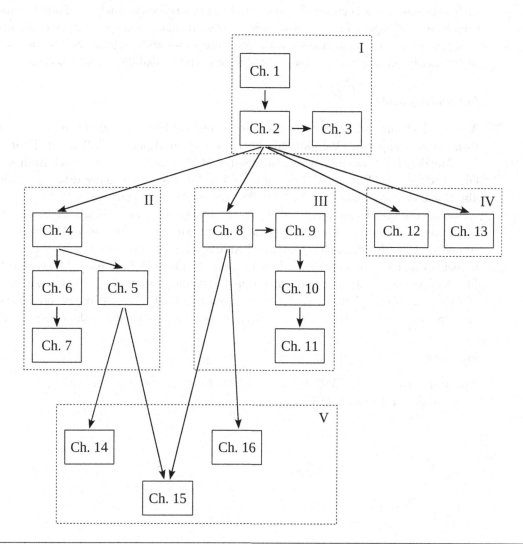

Organization of the book. Arrows between the individual chapters indicate dependencies.

Background

We assume that the reader possesses basic background knowledge consistent with an under-graduate degree in computer science, computer engineering, software engineering, or a related discipline. This background should include familiarity with: (1) basic data structuring concepts, such as linked data structures, B-trees, and hash functions; (2) analysis of algorithms and time complexity; (3) operating systems, disk devices, memory management, and file systems. In addition, we assume some fluency with elementary probability theory and statistics, including such concepts as random variables, distributions, and probability mass functions.

Acknowledgments

A number of our colleagues took the time to review drafts of individual chapters related to their areas of expertise. We particularly thank Eugene Agichtein, Alina Alt, Lauren Griffith, Don Metzler, Tor Myklebust, Fabrizio Silvestri, Mark Smucker, Torsten Suel, Andrew Trotman, Olga Vechtomova, William Webber, and Justin Zobel for their many valuable comments. We also thank our anonymous referees for their positive reviews and feedback.

Several classes of graduate students were subjected to early drafts of this material. We thank them for their patience and tolerance. Four students — Mohamad Hasan Ahmadi, John Akinyemi, Chandra Prakash Jethani, and Andrew Kane — read drafts with great care, helping to identify and fix many problems. Three other students — Azin Ashkan, Maheedhar Kolla, and Ian MacKinnon — volunteered to run our first attempt at an in-class evaluation effort in the fall of 2007, thus contributing to many of the exercises in Part I. Jack Wang proofread the material on CJK languages in Chapter 3. Kelly Itakura provided input on the Japanese language.

Web site

The authors maintain a Web site of material related to the book, including errata and links to cited papers, at `ir.uwaterloo.ca/book`.

Notation

For convenient reference, the list below summarizes notation that occurs frequently in the book. Additional notation is introduced as needed.

$\mathcal{C}$	a text collection
d	a document
$E[X]$	the expected value of the random variable X
$f_{t,d}$	the number of occurrences of the term t within the document d
l_{avg}	the average length of all documents in the collection
$l_{\mathcal{C}}$	the size of the collection $\mathcal{C}$, measured in tokens
l_d	the length of the document d, measured in tokens
l_t	the length of t's postings list (i.e., number of occurrences)
$\mathcal{M}$	a probability distribution; usually a language model or a compression model
N	the number of documents in the collection
N_t	the number of documents that contain the term t
n_r	the number of relevant documents
$n_{t,r}$	the number of relevant documents that contain the term t
$\Pr[x]$	the probability of the event x
$\Pr[x\,|\,y]$	the conditional probability of x, given y
q	a query
q_t	the number of times term t appears in the query q
t	a term
$\mathcal{V}$	the vocabulary of a text collection
$\vec{x}$	a vector
$|\vec{x}|$	the length of the vector $\vec{x}$
$|\mathcal{X}|$	the cardinality of the set $\mathcal{X}$

I Foundations

1 Introduction

1.1 What Is Information Retrieval?

Information retrieval (IR) is concerned with representing, searching, and manipulating large collections of electronic text and other human-language data. IR systems and services are now widespread, with millions of people depending on them daily to facilitate business, education, and entertainment. Web search engines — Google, Bing, and others — are by far the most popular and heavily used IR services, providing access to up-to-date technical information, locating people and organizations, summarizing news and events, and simplifying comparison shopping. Digital library systems help medical and academic researchers learn about new journal articles and conference presentations related to their areas of research. Consumers turn to local search services to find retailers providing desired products and services. Within large companies, enterprise search systems act as repositories for e-mail, memos, technical reports, and other business documents, providing corporate memory by preserving these documents and enabling access to the knowledge contained within them. Desktop search systems permit users to search their personal e-mail, documents, and files.

1.1.1 Web Search

Regular users of Web search engines casually expect to receive accurate and near-instantaneous answers to questions and requests merely by entering a short query — a few words — into a text box and clicking on a search button. Underlying this simple and intuitive interface are clusters of computers, comprising thousands of machines, working cooperatively to generate a ranked list of those Web pages that are likely to satisfy the information need embodied in the query. These machines identify a set of Web pages containing the terms in the query, compute a score for each page, eliminate duplicate and redundant pages, generate summaries of the remaining pages, and finally return the summaries and links back to the user for browsing.

In order to achieve the subsecond response times expected from Web search engines, they incorporate layers of caching and replication, taking advantage of commonly occurring queries and exploiting parallel processing, allowing them to scale as the number of Web pages and users increases. In order to produce accurate results, they store a "snapshot" of the Web. This snapshot must be gathered and refreshed constantly by a *Web crawler*, also running on a cluster of hundreds or thousands of machines, and downloading periodically — perhaps once a week — a fresh copy of each page. Pages that contain rapidly changing information of high quality, such as news services, may be refreshed daily or hourly.

Consider a simple example. If you have a computer connected to the Internet nearby, pause for a minute to launch a browser and try the query "information retrieval" on one of the major commercial Web search engines. It is likely that the search engine responded in well under a second. Take some time to review the top ten results. Each result lists the URL for a Web page and usually provides a title and a short snippet of text extracted from the body of the page. Overall, the results are drawn from a variety of different Web sites and include sites associated with leading textbooks, journals, conferences, and researchers. As is common for *informational* queries such as this one, the Wikipedia article[1] may be present. Do the top ten results contain anything inappropriate? Could their order be improved? Have a look through the next ten results and decide whether any one of them could better replace one of the top ten results.

Now, consider the millions of Web pages that contain the words "information" and "retrieval". This set of pages includes many that are relevant to the subject of information retrieval but are much less general in scope than those that appear in the top ten, such as student Web pages and individual research papers. In addition, the set includes many pages that just happen to contain these two words, without having any direct relationship to the subject. From these millions of possible pages, a search engine's ranking algorithm selects the top-ranked pages based on a variety of features, including the content and structure of the pages (e.g., their titles), their relationship to other pages (e.g., the hyperlinks between them), and the content and structure of the Web as a whole. For some queries, characteristics of the user such as her geographic location or past searching behavior may also play a role. Balancing these features against each other in order to rank pages by their expected relevance to a query is an example of *relevance ranking*. The efficient implementation and evaluation of relevance ranking algorithms under a variety of contexts and requirements represents a core problem in information retrieval, and forms the central topic of this book.

1.1.2 Other Search Applications

Desktop and file system search provides another example of a widely used IR application. A desktop search engine provides search and browsing facilities for files stored on a local hard disk and possibly on disks connected over a local network. In contrast to Web search engines, these systems require greater awareness of file formats and creation times. For example, a user may wish to search only within their e-mail or may know the general time frame in which a file was created or downloaded. Since files may change rapidly, these systems must interface directly with the file system layer of the operating system and must be engineered to handle a heavy update load.

---

[1] en.wikipedia.org/wiki/Information_retrieval

Lying between the desktop and the general Web, enterprise-level IR systems provide document management and search services across businesses and other organizations. The details of these systems vary widely. Some are essentially Web search engines applied to the corporate intranet, crawling Web pages visible only within the organization and providing a search interface similar to that of a standard Web search engine. Others provide more general document- and content-management services, with facilities for explicit update, versioning, and access control. In many industries, these systems help satisfy regulatory requirements regarding the retention of e-mail and other business communications.

Digital libraries and other specialized IR systems support access to collections of high-quality material, often of a proprietary nature. This material may consist of newspaper articles, medical journals, maps, or books that cannot be placed on a generally available Web site due to copyright restrictions. Given the editorial quality and limited scope of these collections, it is often possible to take advantage of structural features — authors, titles, dates, and other publication data — to narrow search requests and improve retrieval effectiveness. In addition, digital libraries may contain electronic text generated by *optical character recognition* (OCR) systems from printed material; character recognition errors associated with the OCR output create yet another complication for the retrieval process.

1.1.3   Other IR Applications

While search is the central task within the area of information retrieval, the field covers a wide variety of interrelated problems associated with the storage, manipulation, and retrieval of human-language data:

- Document *routing*, *filtering*, and *selective dissemination* reverse the typical IR process. Whereas a typical search application evaluates incoming queries against a given document collection, a routing, filtering, or dissemination system compares newly created or discovered documents to a fixed set of queries supplied in advance by users, identifying those that match a given query closely enough to be of possible interest to the users. A news aggregator, for example, might use a routing system to separate the day's news into sections such as "business," "politics," and "lifestyle," or to send headlines of interest to particular subscribers. An e-mail system might use a spam filter to block unwanted messages. As we shall see, these two problems are essentially the same, although differing in application-specific and implementation details.

- Text *clustering* and *categorization* systems group documents according to shared properties. The difference between clustering and categorization stems from the information provided to the system. Categorization systems are provided with *training data* illustrating the various classes. Examples of "business," "politics," and "lifestyle" articles might be provided to a categorization system, which would then sort unlabeled articles into the same categories. A clustering system, in contrast, is not provided with training examples. Instead, it sorts documents into groups based on patterns it discovers itself.

- *Summarization* systems reduce documents to a few key paragraphs, sentences, or phrases describing their content. The snippets of text displayed with Web search results represent one example.

- *Information extraction* systems identify named entities, such as places and dates, and combine this information into structured records that describe relationships between these entities — for example, creating lists of books and their authors from Web data.

- *Topic detection and tracking* systems identify events in streams of news articles and similar information sources, tracking these events as they evolve.

- *Expert search* systems identify members of organizations who are experts in a specified area.

- *Question answering* systems integrate information from multiple sources to provide concise answers to specific questions. They often incorporate and extend other IR technologies, including search, summarization, and information extraction.

- *Multimedia information retrieval* systems extend relevance ranking and other IR techniques to images, video, music, and speech.

Many IR problems overlap with the fields of library and information science, as well as with other major subject areas of computer science such as natural language processing, databases, and machine learning.

Of the topics listed above, techniques for categorization and filtering have the widest applicability, and we provide an introduction to these areas. The scope of this book does not allow us to devote substantial space to the other topics. However, all of them depend upon and extend the basic technologies we cover.

1.2 Information Retrieval Systems

Most IR systems share a basic architecture and organization that is adapted to the requirements of specific applications. Most of the concepts discussed in this book are presented in the context of this architecture. In addition, like any technical field, information retrieval has its own jargon. Words are sometimes used in a narrow technical sense that differs from their ordinary English meanings. In order to avoid confusion and to provide context for the remainder of the book, we briefly outline the fundamental terminology and technology of the subject.

1.2.1 Basic IR System Architecture

Figure 1.1 illustrates the major components in an IR system. Before conducting a search, a user has an *information need*, which underlies and drives the search process. We sometimes refer to this information need as a *topic*, particularly when it is presented in written form as part

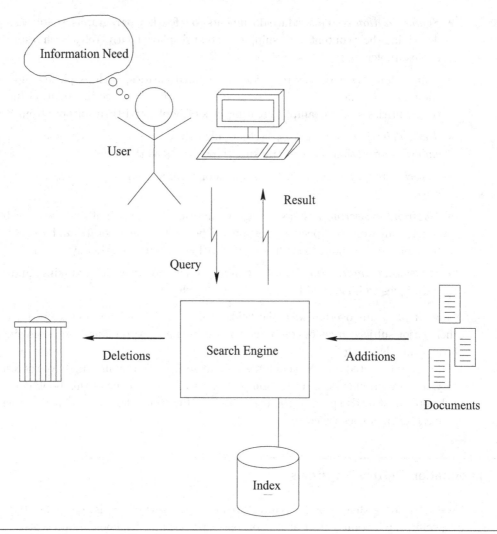

Figure 1.1   Components of an IR system.

of a test collection for IR evaluation. As a result of her information need, the user constructs
and issues a *query* to the IR system. Typically, this query consists of a small number of *terms*,
with two to three terms being typical for a Web search. We use "term" instead of "word",
because a query term may in fact not be a word at all. Depending on the information need,
a query term may be a date, a number, a musical note, or a phrase. Wildcard operators and
other partial-match operators may also be permitted in query terms. For example, the term
"inform*" might match any word starting with that prefix ("inform", "informs", "informal",
"informant", "informative", etc.).

Although users typically issue simple keyword queries, IR systems often support a richer query syntax, frequently with complex Boolean and pattern matching operators (Chapter 5). These facilities may be used to limit a search to a particular Web site, to specify constraints on fields such as author and title, or to apply other *filters*, restricting the search to a subset of the collection. A user interface mediates between the user and the IR system, simplifying the query-creation process when these richer query facilities are required.

The user's query is processed by a *search engine*, which may be running on the user's local machine, on a large cluster of machines in a remote geographic location, or anywhere in between. A major task of a search engine is to maintain and manipulate an *inverted index* for a *document collection*. This index forms the principal data structure used by the engine for searching and relevance ranking. As its basic function, an inverted index provides a mapping between terms and the locations in the collection in which they occur. Because the size of an inverted list is on the same order of magnitude as the document collection itself, care must be taken that index access and update operations are performed efficiently.

To support relevance ranking algorithms, the search engine maintains collection statistics associated with the index, such as the number of documents containing each term and the length of each document. In addition, the search engine usually has access to the original content of the documents, in order to report meaningful results back to the user.

Using the inverted index, collection statistics, and other data, the search engine accepts queries from its users, processes these queries, and returns ranked lists of results. To perform relevance ranking, the search engine computes a *score*, sometimes called a *retrieval status value* (RSV), for each document. After sorting documents according to their scores, the result list may be subjected to further processing, such as the removal of duplicate or redundant results. For example, a Web search engine might report only one or two results from a single host or domain, eliminating the others in favor of pages from different sources. The problem of scoring documents with respect to a user's query is one of the most fundamental in the field.

1.2.2 Documents and Update

Throughout this book we use "document" as a generic term to refer to any self-contained unit that can be returned to the user as a search result. In practice, a particular document might be an e-mail message, a Web page, a news article, or even a video. When predefined components of a larger object may be returned as individual search results, such as pages or paragraphs from a book, we refer to these components as *elements*. When arbitrary text passages, video segments, or similar material may be returned from larger objects, we refer to them as *snippets*.

For most applications, the update model is relatively simple. Documents may be added or deleted in their entirety. Once a document has been added to the search engine, its contents are not modified. This update model is sufficient for most IR applications. For example, when a Web crawler discovers that a page has been modified, the update may be viewed as a deletion of the old page and an addition of the new page. Even in the context of file system search, in which individual blocks of a file may be arbitrarily modified, most word processors and other applications dealing with textual data rewrite entire files when a user saves changes. One important exception is e-mail applications, which often append new messages to the ends of mail folders. Because mail folders can be large in size and can grow quickly, it may be important to support append operations.

1.2.3 Performance Evaluation

There are two principal aspects to measuring IR system performance: *efficiency* and *effectiveness.* Efficiency may be measured in terms of time (e.g., seconds per query) and space (e.g., bytes per document). The most visible aspect of efficiency is the *response time* (also known as *latency*) experienced by a user between issuing a query and receiving the results. When many simultaneous users must be supported, the query *throughput,* measured in queries per second, becomes an important factor in system performance. For a general-purpose Web search engine, the required throughput may range well beyond tens of thousands of queries per second. Efficiency may also be considered in terms of storage space, measured by the bytes of disk and memory required to store the index and other data structures. In addition, when thousands of machines are working cooperatively to generate a search result, their power consumption and carbon footprint become important considerations.

Effectiveness is more difficult to measure than efficiency, since it depends entirely on human judgment. The key idea behind measuring effectiveness is the notion of *relevance*: A document is considered relevant to a given query if its contents (completely or partially) satisfy the information need represented by the query. To determine relevance, a human *assessor* reviews a document/topic pair and assigns a relevance value. The relevance value may be *binary* ("relevant" or "not relevant") or *graded* (e.g., "perfect", "excellent", "good", "fair", "acceptable", "not relevant", "harmful").

The fundamental goal of relevance ranking is frequently expressed in terms of the *Probability Ranking Principle* (PRP), which we phrase as follows:

> If an IR system's response to each query is a ranking of the documents in the collection in order of decreasing probability of relevance, then the overall effectiveness of the system to its users will be maximized.

This assumption is well established in the field of IR and forms the basis of the standard IR evaluation methodology. Nonetheless, it overlooks important aspects of relevance that must be considered in practice. In particular, the basic notion of relevance may be extended to consider the size and scope of the documents returned. The *specificity* of a document reflects the degree to which its contents are focused on the information need. A highly specific document consists primarily of material related to the information need. In a marginally specific document, most of the material is not related to the topic. The *exhaustivity* of a document reflects the degree to which it covers the information related to the need. A highly exhaustive document provides full coverage; a marginally exhaustive document may cover only limited aspects. Specificity and exhaustivity are independent dimensions. A large document may provide full coverage but contain enough extraneous material that it is only marginally specific.

When relevance is viewed in the context of a complete ranked document list, the notion of *novelty* comes to light. Once the user examines the top-ranked document and learns its relevant content, her information need may shift. If the second document contains little or no novel information, it may not be relevant with respect to this revised information need.

1.3   Working with Electronic Text

Human-language data in the form of electronic text represents the raw material of information retrieval. Building an IR system requires an understanding of both electronic text formats and the characteristics of the text they encode.

1.3.1   Text Formats

The works of William Shakespeare provide a ready example of a large body of English-language text with many electronic versions freely available on the Web. Shakespeare's canonical works include 37 plays and more than a hundred sonnets and poems. Figure 1.2 shows the start of the first act of one play, *Macbeth*.

This figure presents the play as it might appear on a printed page. From the perspective of an IR system, there are two aspects of this page that must be considered when it is represented in electronic form, and ultimately when it is indexed by the system. The first aspect, the *content* of the page, is the sequence of words in the order they might normally be read: "Thunder and lightning. Enter three Witches First Witch When shall we..." The second aspect is the *structure* of the page: the breaks between lines and pages, the labeling of speeches with speakers, the stage directions, the act and scene numbers, and even the page number.

The content and structure of electronic text may be encoded in myriad document formats supported by various word processing programs and desktop publishing systems. These formats include Microsoft Word, HTML, XML, XHTML, LaTeX, MIF, RTF, PDF, PostScript, SGML, and others. In some environments, such as file system search, e-mail formats and even program source code formats would be added to this list. Although a detailed description of these formats is beyond our scope, a basic understanding of their impact on indexing and retrieval is important.

Two formats are of special interest to us. The first, HTML (HyperText Markup Language), is the fundamental format for Web pages. Of particular note is its inherent support for hyperlinks, which explicitly represent relationships between Web pages and permit these relationships to be exploited by Web search systems. Anchor text often accompanies a hyperlink, partially describing the content of the linked page.

Thunder and lightning. Enter three Witches   I.1

FIRST WITCH

    When shall we three meet again

    In thunder, lightning, or in rain?

SECOND WITCH

    When the hurlyburly's done,

    When the battle's lost and won.

THIRD WITCH

    That will be ere the set of sun.

FIRST WITCH

    Where the place?

SECOND WITCH   Upon the heath.

THIRD WITCH

    There to meet with Macbeth.

FIRST WITCH

    I come Grey-Malkin!

SECOND WITCH   Padock calls.

THIRD WITCH   Anon!

ALL

    Fair is foul, and foul is fair.

    Hover through the fog and filthy air.   *Exeunt*   10

Alarum within   I.2

Enter King Duncan, Malcolm, Donalbain, Lennox,

with Attendants, meeting a bleeding Captain

KING

    What bloody man is that? He can report,

53

Figure 1.2   The beginning of the first act of Shakespeare's *Macbeth*.

The second format, XML (eXtensible Markup Language), is not strictly a document format but rather a *metalanguage* for defining document formats. Although we leave a detailed discussion of XML to later in the book (Chapter 16), we can begin using it immediately. XML possesses the convenient attribute that it is possible to construct human-readable encodings that are reasonably self-explanatory. As a result, it serves as a format for examples throughout the remainder of the book, particularly when aspects of document structure are discussed. HTML and XML share a common ancestry in the Standard Generalized Markup Language (SGML) developed in the 1980s and resemble each other in their approach to tagging document structure.

Figure 1.3 presents an XML encoding of the start of *Macbeth* taken from a version of Shakespeare's plays. The encoding was constructed by Jon Bosak, one of the principal creators of the XML standard. Tags of the form <*name*> represent the start of a structural element and tags of the form </*name*> represent the end of a structural element. Tags may take other forms, and they may include attributes defining properties of the enclosed text, but these details are left for Chapter 16. For the bulk of the book, we stick to the simple tags illustrated by the figure.

In keeping with the traditional philosophy of XML, this encoding represents only the *logical structure* of the document — speakers, speeches, acts, scenes, and lines. Determination of the *physical structure* — fonts, bolding, layout, and page breaks — is deferred until the page is actually rendered for display, where the details of the target display medium will be known.

Unfortunately, many document formats do not make the same consistent distinction between logical and physical structure. Moreover, some formats impede our ability to determine a document's content or to return anything less than an entire document as the result of a retrieval request. Many of these formats are *binary formats*, so called because they contain internal pointers and other complex organizational structures, and cannot be treated as a stream of characters.

For example, the content of a PostScript document is encoded in a version of the programming language Forth. A PostScript document is essentially a program that is executed to render the document when it is printed or displayed. Although using a programming language to encode a document provides for maximum flexibility, it may also make the content of the document difficult to extract for indexing purposes. The PDF format, PostScript's younger sibling, does not incorporate a complete programming language but otherwise retains much of the flexibility and complexity of the older format. PostScript and PDF were originally developed by Adobe Systems, but both are now open standards and many third-party tools are available to create and manipulate documents in these formats, including open-source tools.

Various conversion utilities are available to extract content from PostScript and PDF documents, and they may be pressed into service for indexing purposes. Each of these utilities implements its own heuristics to analyze the document and guess at its content. Although they often produce excellent output for documents generated by standard tools, they may fail when faced with a document from a more unusual source. At an extreme, a utility might render a document into an internal buffer and apply a pattern-matching algorithm to recognize characters and words.

```
<STAGEDIR>Thunder and lightning. Enter three Witches</STAGEDIR>

<SPEECH>
<SPEAKER>First Witch</SPEAKER>
<LINE>When shall we three meet again</LINE>
<LINE>In thunder, lightning, or in rain?</LINE>
</SPEECH>

<SPEECH>
<SPEAKER>Second Witch</SPEAKER>
<LINE>When the hurlyburly's done,</LINE>
<LINE>When the battle's lost and won.</LINE>
</SPEECH>

<SPEECH>
<SPEAKER>Third Witch</SPEAKER>
<LINE>That will be ere the set of sun.</LINE>
</SPEECH>

<SPEECH>
<SPEAKER>First Witch</SPEAKER>
<LINE>Where the place?</LINE>
</SPEECH>

<SPEECH>
<SPEAKER>Second Witch</SPEAKER>
<LINE>Upon the heath.</LINE>
</SPEECH>

<SPEECH>
   <SPEAKER>Third Witch</SPEAKER>
   <LINE>There to meet with Macbeth.</LINE>
</SPEECH>
```

Figure 1.3   An XML encoding of Shakespeare's *Macbeth*.

Moreover, identifying even the simplest logical structure in PostScript or PDF poses a significant challenge. Even a document's title may have to be identified entirely from its font, size, location in the document, and other physical characteristics. In PostScript, extracting individual pages can also cause problems because the code executed to render one page may have an impact on later pages. This aspect of PostScript may limit the ability of an IR system to return a range of pages from a large document, for example, to return a single section from a long technical manual.

Other document formats are proprietary, meaning they are associated with the products of a single software manufacturer. These proprietary formats include Microsoft's "doc" format. Until recently, due to the market dominance of Microsoft Office, this format was widely used for document exchange and collaboration. Although the technical specifications for such proprietary formats are often available, they can be complex and may be modified substantially from version to version, entirely at the manufacturer's discretion. Microsoft and other manufacturers have now shifted toward XML-based formats (such as the OpenDocument format or Microsoft's OOXML), which may ameliorate the complications of indexing.

In practice, HTML may share many of the problems of binary formats. Many HTML pages include scripts in the JavaScript or Flash programming languages. These scripts may rewrite the Web page in its entirety and display arbitrary content on the screen. On pages in which the content is generated by scripts, it may be a practical impossibility for Web crawlers and search engines to extract and index meaningful content.

1.3.2 A Simple Tokenization of English Text

Regardless of a document's format, the construction of an inverted index that can be used to process search queries requires each document to be converted into a sequence of *tokens*. For English-language documents, a token usually corresponds to a sequence of alphanumeric characters (A to Z and 0 to 9), but it may also encode structural information, such as XML tags, or other characteristics of the text. Tokenization is a critical step in the indexing process because it effectively limits the class of queries that may be processed by the system.

As a preliminary step before tokenization, documents in binary formats must be converted to *raw text* — a stream of characters. The process of converting a document to raw text generally discards font information and other lower-level physical formatting but may retain higher-level logical formatting, perhaps by re-inserting appropriate tags into the raw text. This higher-level formatting might include titles, paragraph boundaries, and similar elements. This preliminary step is not required for documents in XML or HTML because these already contain the tokens in the order required for indexing, thus simplifying the processing cost substantially. Essentially, these formats are in situ raw text.

For English-language documents, characters in the raw text may be encoded as seven-bit ASCII values. However, ASCII is not sufficient for documents in other languages. For these languages, other coding schemes must be used, and it may not be possible to encode each character as a single byte. The UTF-8 representation of Unicode provides one popular method for encoding these characters (see Section 3.2). UTF-8 provides a one-to-four byte encoding for the characters in most living languages, as well as for those in many extinct languages, such as Phoenician and Sumerian cuneiform. UTF-8 is backwards compatible with ASCII, so that ASCII text is automatically UTF-8 text.

To tokenize the XML in Figure 1.3, we treat each XML tag and each sequence of consecutive alphanumeric characters as a token. We convert uppercase letters outside tags to lowercase in order to simplify the matching process, meaning that "FIRST", "first" and "First" are treated

...

745396	745397	745398	745399	745400
`<STAGEDIR>`	thunder	and	lightning	enter

745401	745402	745403	745404	745405
three	witches	`</STAGEDIR>`	`<SPEECH>`	`<SPEAKER>`

745406	745407	745408	745409	745410
first	witch	`</SPEAKER>`	`<LINE>`	when

745411	745412	745413	745414	745415
shall	we	three	meet	again

745416	745417	745418	745419	745420
`</LINE>`	`<LINE>`	in	thunder	lightning

745421	745422	745423	745424	745425
or	in	rain	`</LINE>`	`</SPEECH>`

745426	745427	745428	745429	745430
`<SPEECH>`	`<SPEAKER>`	second	witch	`</SPEAKER>`

...

Figure 1.4   A tokenization of Shakespeare's *Macbeth*.

as equivalent. The result of our tokenization is shown in Figure 1.4. Each token is accompanied by an integer that indicates its position in a collection of Shakespeare's 37 plays, starting with position 1 at the beginning of *Antony and Cleopatra* and finishing with position 1,271,504 at the end of *The Winter's Tale*. This simple approach to tokenization is sufficient for our purposes through the remainder of Chapters 1 and 2, and it is assumed where necessary. We will reexamine tokenization for English and other languages in Chapter 3.

The set of distinct tokens, or *symbols*, in a text collection is called the *vocabulary*, denoted as $\mathcal{V}$. Our collection of Shakespeare's plays has $|\mathcal{V}| = 22{,}987$ symbols in its vocabulary.

$$\mathcal{V} = \{\text{a}, \text{aaron}, \text{abaissiez}, ..., \text{zounds}, \text{zwaggered}, ..., \text{<PLAY>}, ..., \text{<SPEAKER>}, ..., \text{</PLAY>}, ...\}$$

Table 1.1 The twenty most frequent terms in Bosak's XML version of Shakespeare.

Rank	Frequency	Token		Rank	Frequency	Token
1	107,833	<LINE>		11	17,523	of
2	107,833	</LINE>		12	14,914	a
3	31,081	<SPEAKER>		13	14,088	you
4	31,081	</SPEAKER>		14	12,287	my
5	31,028	<SPEECH>		15	11,192	that
6	31,028	</SPEECH>		16	11,106	in
7	28,317	the		17	9,344	is
8	26,022	and		18	8,506	not
9	22,639	i		19	7,799	it
10	19,898	to		20	7,753	me

For Shakespeare, the vocabulary includes 22,943 words and 44 tags, in which we consider any string of alphanumeric characters to be a word. In this book, we usually refer to symbols in the vocabulary as "terms" because they form the basis for matching against the terms in a query. In addition, we often refer to a token as an "occurrence" of a term. Although this usage helps reinforce the link between the tokens in a document and the terms in a query, it may obscure the crucial difference between a symbol and a token. A symbol is an abstraction; a token is an instance of that abstraction. In philosophy, this difference is called the "type-token distinction." In object-oriented programming, it is the difference between a class and an object.

1.3.3 Term Distributions

Table 1.1 lists the twenty most frequent terms in the XML collection of Shakespeare's plays. Of these terms, the top six are tags for lines, speakers, and speeches. As is normally true for English text, "the" is the most frequent word, followed by various pronouns, prepositions, and other function words. More than one-third (8,336) of the terms, such as "abaissiez" and "zwaggered", appear only once.

The frequency of the tags is determined by the structural constraints of the collection. Each start tag <*name*> has a corresponding end tag </*name*>. Each play has exactly one title. Each speech has at least one speaker, but a few speeches have more than one speaker, when a group of characters speak in unison. On average, a new line starts every eight or nine words.

While the type and relative frequency of tags will be different in other collections, the relative frequency of words in English text usually follows a consistent pattern. Figure 1.5 plots the frequency of the terms in Shakespeare in rank order, with tags omitted. Logarithmic scales are used for both the x and the y axes. The points fall roughly along a line with slope −1, although both the most frequent and the least frequent terms fall below the line. On this plot, the point

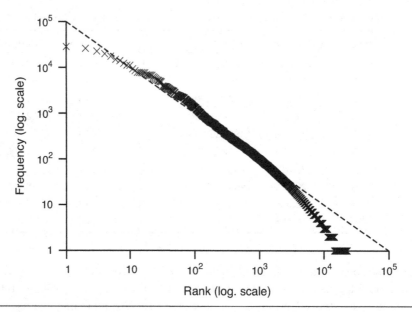

Figure 1.5 Frequency of words in the Shakespeare collection, by rank order. The dashed line corresponds to Zipf's law with $\alpha = 1$.

corresponding to "the" appears in the upper left. The point corresponding to "zwaggered" appears in the lower right, together with the other words that appear exactly once.

The relationship between frequency and rank represented by this line is known as *Zipf's law*, after the linguist George Zipf, who developed it in the 1930s and used it to model the relative frequencies of data across a number of areas in the social sciences (Zipf, 1949). Mathematically, the relationship may be expressed as

$$\log(\text{frequency}) \; = \; C - \alpha \cdot \log(\text{rank}) \,, \tag{1.1}$$

or equivalently as

$$\mathcal{F}_i \sim \frac{1}{i^\alpha} \,, \tag{1.2}$$

where $\mathcal{F}_i$ is the frequency of the ith most frequent term. For English text, the value of α may vary, but it is usually close to 1. Zipf's law is known to apply to the relative word frequencies in other natural languages, as well as to other types of data. In Chapter 4, it motivates the use of a certain data structure for indexing natural language text. In Chapter 15, we apply Zipf's law to model the relative frequency of search engine queries.

1.3.4 Language Modeling

There are 912,052 tokens in Bosak's XML version of Shakespeare's plays, excluding tags (but including some front matter that does not appear in the original versions). If we pick a token uniformly at random from these plays, the probability of picking "the" is $28,317/912,052 \approx 3.1\%$, whereas the probability of picking "zwaggered" is only $1/912,052 \approx 0.00011\%$. Now, imagine that a previously unknown Shakespearean play is discovered. Can we predict anything about the content of this play from what we know of the existing plays? In making these predictions, we redefine the vocabulary $\mathcal{V}$ to exclude tags. An unknown Shakespearean play is unlikely to be encoded in XML (at least when it is first discovered).

Predictions concerning the content of unseen text may be made by way of a special kind of probability distribution known as a *language model*. The simplest language model is a fixed probability distribution $\mathcal{M}(\sigma)$ over the symbols in the vocabulary:

$$\sum_{\sigma \in \mathcal{V}} \mathcal{M}(\sigma) \; = \; 1. \tag{1.3}$$

A language model is often based on an existing text. For example, we might define

$$\mathcal{M}(\sigma) \; = \; \frac{\text{frequency}(\sigma)}{\sum_{\sigma' \in \mathcal{V}} \text{frequency}(\sigma')} \tag{1.4}$$

where frequency(σ) represents the number of occurrences of the term σ in Shakespeare's plays. Thus, we have $\mathcal{M}(\text{"the"}) \approx 3.1\%$ and $\mathcal{M}(\text{"zwaggered"}) \approx 0.00011\%$.

If we pick a token uniformly at random from Shakespeare's known plays, the probably of picking the term σ is $\mathcal{M}(\sigma)$. Based on this knowledge of Shakespeare, if we pick a token uniformly at random from the previously unseen play, we might assume that the probably of picking σ is also $\mathcal{M}(\sigma)$. If we start reading the unseen play, we can use the language model to make a prediction about the next term in the text, with $\mathcal{M}(\sigma)$ giving the probability that the next term is σ. For this simple language model, we consider each term in isolation. The language model makes the same independent prediction concerning the first term, and the next, and the next, and so on. Based on this language model, the probability that the next six terms are "to be or not to be" is:

$$2.18\% \times 0.76\% \times 0.27\% \times 0.93\% \times 2.18\% \times 0.76\% \; = \; 0.000000000069\%.$$

Equation 1.4 is called the *maximum likelihood estimate* (MLE) for this simple type of language model. In general, maximum likelihood is the standard method for estimating unknown parameters of a probability distribution, given a set of data. Here, we have a parameter corresponding to each term — the probability that the term appears next in the unseen text. Roughly speaking, the maximum likelihood estimation method chooses values for the parameters that make the data set most likely. In this case, we are treating the plays of Shakespeare as providing the necessary data set. Equation 1.4 is the assignment of probabilities that is most likely to produce

Shakespeare. If we assume that the unseen text is similar to the existing text, the maximum likelihood model provides a good starting point for predicting its content.

Language models can be used to quantify how close a new text fragment is to an existing corpus. Suppose we have a language model representing the works of Shakespeare and another representing the works of the English playwrightJohn Webster. A new, previously unknown, play is found; experts debate about who might be its author. Assuming that our two language models capture salient characteristics of the two writers, such as their preferred vocabulary, we may apply the language models to compute the probability of the new text according to each. The language model that assigns the higher probability to the new text may indicate its author.

However, a language model need not use maximum likelihood estimates. Any probability distribution over a vocabulary of terms may be treated as a language model. For example, consider the probability distribution

$$\mathcal{M}(\text{"to"}) = 0.40 \quad \mathcal{M}(\text{"be"}) = 0.30 \quad \mathcal{M}(\text{"or"}) = 0.20 \quad \mathcal{M}(\text{"not"}) = 0.10.$$

Based on this distribution, the probability that the next six words are "to be or not to be" is

$$0.40 \times 0.30 \times 0.20 \times 0.10 \times 0.40 \times 0.30 = 0.029\%.$$

Of course, based on this model, the probability that the next six words are "the lady doth protest too much" is zero.

In practice, unseen text might include unseen terms. To accommodate these unseen terms, the vocabulary might be extended by adding an UNKNOWN symbol to represent these "out-of-vocabulary" terms.

$$\mathcal{V}' = \mathcal{V} \cup \{\text{UNKNOWN}\} \tag{1.5}$$

The corresponding extended language model $\mathcal{M}'(\sigma)$ would then assign a positive probability to this UNKNOWN term

$$\mathcal{M}'(\text{UNKNOWN}) = \beta, \tag{1.6}$$

where $0 \leq \beta \leq 1$. The value β represents the probability that the next term does not appear in the existing collection from which the model $\mathcal{M}$ was estimated. For other terms, we might then define

$$\mathcal{M}'(\sigma) = \mathcal{M}(\sigma) \cdot (1 - \beta), \tag{1.7}$$

where $\mathcal{M}(\sigma)$ is the maximum likelihood language model. The choice of a value for β might be based on characteristics of the existing text. For example, we might guess that β should be roughly half of the probability of a unique term in the existing text:

$$\beta = 0.5 \cdot \frac{1}{\sum_{\sigma' \in \mathcal{V}} \text{frequency}(\sigma')}. \tag{1.8}$$

Fortunately, out-of-vocabulary terms are not usually a problem in IR systems because the complete vocabulary of the collection may be determined during the indexing process.

Index and text compression (Chapter 6) represents another important area for the application of language models. When used in compression algorithms, the terms in the vocabulary are usually individual characters or bits rather than entire words. Language modeling approaches that were invented in the context of compression are usually called *compression models*, and this terminology is common in the literature. However, compression models are just specialized language models. In Chapter 10, compression models are applied to the problem of detecting e-mail spam and other filtering problems.

Language models may be used to generate text, as well as to predict unseen text. For example, we may produce "random Shakespeare" by randomly generating a sequence of terms based on the probability distribution $\mathcal{M}(\sigma)$:

> strong die hat circumstance in one eyes odious love to our the wrong wailful would all sir you to babies a in in of er immediate slew let on see worthy all timon nourish both my how antonio silius my live words our my ford scape

Higher-order models

The random text shown above does not read much like Shakespeare, or even like English text written by lesser authors. Because each term is generated in isolation, the probability of generating the word "the" immediately after generating "our" remains at 3.1%. In real English text, the possessive adjective "our" is almost always followed by a common noun. Even though the phrase "our the" consists of two frequently occurring words, it rarely occurs in English, and never in Shakespeare.

Higher-order language models allow us to take this context into account. A *first-order* language model consists of conditional probabilities that depend on the previous symbol. For example:

$$\mathcal{M}_1(\sigma_2 \,|\, \sigma_1) \;=\; \frac{\text{frequency}(\sigma_1\sigma_2)}{\sum_{\sigma' \in \mathcal{V}} \text{frequency}(\sigma_1\sigma')} \,. \tag{1.9}$$

A first-order language model for terms is equivalent to the zero-order model for term *bigrams* estimated using the same technique (e.g., MLE):

$$\mathcal{M}_1(\sigma_2 \,|\, \sigma_1) \;=\; \frac{\mathcal{M}_0(\sigma_1\sigma_2)}{\sum_{\sigma' \in \mathcal{V}} \mathcal{M}_0(\sigma_1\sigma')} \,. \tag{1.10}$$

More generally, every nth-order language model may be expressed in terms of a zero-order $(n+1)$-gram model:

$$\mathcal{M}_n(\sigma_{n+1} \,|\, \sigma_1 \ldots \sigma_n) \;=\; \frac{\mathcal{M}_0(\sigma_1 \ldots \sigma_{n+1})}{\sum_{\sigma' \in \mathcal{V}} \mathcal{M}_0(\sigma_1 \ldots \sigma_n \,\sigma')} \,. \tag{1.11}$$

As an example, consider the phrase "first witch" in Shakespeare's plays. This phrase appears a total of 23 times, whereas the term "first" appears 1,349 times. The maximum likelihood bigram model thus assigns the following probability:

$$\mathcal{M}_0(\text{"first witch"}) = \frac{23}{912{,}051} \approx 0.0025\%$$

(note that the denominator is 912,051, not 912,052, because the total number of bigrams is one less than the total number of tokens). The corresponding probability in the first-order model is

$$\mathcal{M}_1(\text{"witch"} \mid \text{"first"}) = \frac{23}{1349} \approx 1.7\%.$$

Using Equations 1.9 and 1.10, and ignoring the difference between the number of tokens and the number of bigrams, the maximum likelihood estimate for "our the" is

$$\mathcal{M}_0(\text{"our the"}) = \mathcal{M}_0(\text{"our"}) \cdot \mathcal{M}_1(\text{"the"} \mid \text{"our"}) = 0\%,$$

which is what we would expect, because the phrase never appears in the text. Unfortunately, the model also assigns a zero probability to more reasonable bigrams that do not appear in Shakespeare, such as "fourth witch". Because "fourth" appears 55 times and "witch" appears 92 times, we can easily imagine that an unknown play might contain this bigram. Moreover, we should perhaps assign a small positive probability to bigrams such as "our the" to accommodate unusual usage, including archaic spellings and accented speech. For example, *The Merry Wives of Windsor* contains the apparently meaningless bigram "a the" in a speech by the French physician Doctor Caius: "If dere be one or two, I shall make-a the turd." Once more context is seen, the meaning becomes clearer.

Smoothing

One solution to this problem is to *smooth* the first-order model $\mathcal{M}_1$ with the corresponding zero-order model $\mathcal{M}_0$. Our smoothed model $\mathcal{M}_1'$ is then a linear combination of $\mathcal{M}_0$ and $\mathcal{M}_1$:

$$\mathcal{M}_1'(\sigma_2 \mid \sigma_1) = \gamma \cdot \mathcal{M}_1(\sigma_2 \mid \sigma_1) + (1 - \gamma) \cdot \mathcal{M}_0(\sigma_2) \tag{1.12}$$

and equivalently

$$\mathcal{M}_0'(\sigma_1 \sigma_2) = \gamma \cdot \mathcal{M}_0(\sigma_1 \sigma_2) + (1 - \gamma) \cdot \mathcal{M}_0(\sigma_1) \cdot \mathcal{M}_0(\sigma_2), \tag{1.13}$$

where γ in both cases is a smoothing parameter ($0 \leq \gamma \leq 1$). For example, using maximum likelihood estimates and setting $\gamma = 0.5$, we have

$$
\begin{aligned}
\mathcal{M}_0'(\text{"first witch"}) &= \gamma \cdot \mathcal{M}_0(\text{"first witch"}) + (1 - \gamma) \cdot \mathcal{M}_0(\text{"first"}) \cdot \mathcal{M}_0(\text{"witch"}) \\
&= 0.5 \cdot \frac{23}{912{,}051} + 0.5 \cdot \frac{1{,}349}{912{,}052} \cdot \frac{92}{912{,}052} \approx 0.0013\%
\end{aligned}
$$

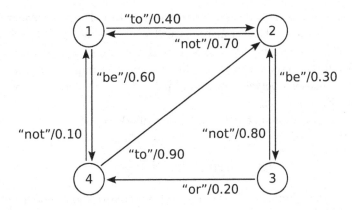

Figure 1.6 A Markov model.

and

$$\mathcal{M}_0'(\text{``fourth witch''}) = \gamma \cdot \mathcal{M}_0(\text{``fourth witch''}) + (1-\gamma) \cdot \mathcal{M}_0(\text{``fourth''}) \cdot \mathcal{M}_0(\text{``witch''})$$
$$= 0.5 \cdot \frac{0}{912,051} + 0.5 \cdot \frac{55}{912,052} \cdot \frac{92}{912,052} \approx 0.00000030\%.$$

First-order models can be smoothed using zero-order models; second-order models can be smoothed using first-order models; and so forth. Obviously, for zero-order models, this approach does not work. However, we can follow the same approach that we used to address out-of-vocabulary terms (Equation 1.5). Alternatively (and more commonly), the zero-order model $\mathcal{M}_{S,0}$ for a small collection S can be smoothed using another zero-order model, built from a larger collection L:

$$\mathcal{M}_{S,0}' = \gamma \cdot \mathcal{M}_{S,0} + (1-\gamma) \cdot \mathcal{M}_{L,0}, \tag{1.14}$$

where L could be an arbitrary (but large) corpus of English text.

Markov models

Figure 1.6 illustrates a *Markov model*, another important method for representing term distributions. Markov models are essentially finite-state automata augmented with transition probabilities. When used to express a language model, each transition is labeled with a term, in addition to the probability. Following a transition corresponds to predicting or generating that term. Starting in state 1, we may generate the string "to be or not to be" by following the state sequence $1 \to 2 \to 3 \to 4 \to 1 \to 2 \to 3$, with the associated probability

$$0.40 \times 0.30 \times 0.20 \times 0.10 \times 0.40 \times 0.30 = 0.029\%.$$

Missing transitions (e.g., between state 1 and state 4) are equivalent to transitions with zero probability. Because these transitions will never be taken, it is pointless to associate a term with them. For simplicity, we also assume that there is at most one transition between any two states. We do not sacrifice anything by making this simplification. For any Markov model with multiple transitions between the same pair of states, there is a corresponding model without them (see Exercise 1.7).

The probability predicted by a Markov model depends on the starting state. Starting in state 4, the probability of generating "to be or not to be" is

$$0.90 \times 0.30 \times 0.20 \times 0.10 \times 0.40 \times 0.30 \; = \; 0.065\%.$$

Markov models form the basis for a text compression model introduced for filtering in Chapter 10.

We may represent a Markov model with n states as an $n \times n$ *transition matrix* M, where $M[i][j]$ gives the probability of a transition from state i to state j. The transition matrix corresponding to the Markov model in Figure 1.6 is

$$M \; = \; \begin{pmatrix} 0.00 & 0.40 & 0.00 & 0.60 \\ 0.70 & 0.00 & 0.30 & 0.00 \\ 0.00 & 0.80 & 0.00 & 0.20 \\ 0.10 & 0.90 & 0.00 & 0.00 \end{pmatrix}. \tag{1.15}$$

Note that all of the values in the matrix fall in the range $[0, 1]$ and that each row of M sums to 1. An $n \times n$ matrix with these properties is known as a *stochastic matrix*.

Given a transition matrix, we can compute the outcome of a transition by multiplying the transition matrix by a *state vector* representing the current state. For example, we can represent an initial start state of 1 by the vector (1 0 0 0). After one step, we have

$$\begin{pmatrix} 1 & 0 & 0 & 0 \end{pmatrix} \begin{pmatrix} 0.00 & 0.40 & 0.00 & 0.60 \\ 0.70 & 0.00 & 0.30 & 0.00 \\ 0.00 & 0.80 & 0.00 & 0.20 \\ 0.10 & 0.90 & 0.00 & 0.00 \end{pmatrix} = \begin{pmatrix} 0.00 & 0.40 & 0.00 & 0.60 \end{pmatrix}.$$

That is, after one step, the probability of being in state 2 is 0.40 and the probability of being in state 4 is 0.60, as expected. Multiplying again, we have

$$\begin{pmatrix} 0.00 & 0.40 & 0.00 & 0.60 \end{pmatrix} \begin{pmatrix} 0.00 & 0.40 & 0.00 & 0.60 \\ 0.70 & 0.00 & 0.30 & 0.00 \\ 0.00 & 0.80 & 0.00 & 0.20 \\ 0.10 & 0.90 & 0.00 & 0.00 \end{pmatrix} = \begin{pmatrix} 0.34 & 0.54 & 0.12 & 0.00 \end{pmatrix}.$$

This result tells us, for example, that the probability of being in state 2 after two steps is 0.54. In general, the state vector may be any n-dimensional vector whose elements sum to 1. Multiplying the state vector by the transition matrix k times gives the probability of being in each state after k steps.

A stochastic matrix together with an initial state vector is known as a *Markov chain*. Markov chains are used in the presentation of Web link analysis algorithms in Chapter 15. Markov chains — and by extension Markov models — are named after the Russian statistician Andrey Markov (1856–1922), who stated and proved many of their properties.

1.4   Test Collections

Although *Macbeth* and Shakespeare's other plays provide an excellent source of examples for simple IR concepts, researchers have developed more substantial test collections for evaluation purposes. Many of these collections have been created as part of TREC[2] (Text REtrieval Conference), a series of experimental evaluation efforts conducted annually since 1991 by the U.S. National Institute of Standards and Technology (NIST). TREC provides a forum for researchers to test their IR systems on a broad range of problems. For example, more than 100 groups from universities, industry, and government participated in TREC 2007.

In a typical year, TREC experiments are structured into six or seven *tracks*, each devoted to a different area of information retrieval. In recent years, TREC has included tracks devoted to enterprise search, genomic information retrieval, legal discovery, e-mail spam filtering, and blog search. Each track is divided into several tasks that test different aspects of that area. For example, at TREC 2007, the enterprise search track included an e-mail discussion search task and a task to identify experts on given topics. A track typically operates for three or more years before being retired.

TREC provides at least two important benefits to the IR community. First, it focuses researchers on common problems, using common data, thus providing a forum for them to present and discuss their work and facilitating direct inter-system comparisons. What works and what does not work can be determined quickly. As a result, considerable progress and substantial performance improvements are often seen immediately following the introduction of a new track into TREC. As a second benefit, TREC aims to create *reusable* test collections that can be used by participating groups to validate further improvements and by non-participating groups to evaluate their own work. In addition, since its inception, TREC has formed the inspiration for a number of similar experimental efforts throughout the world. These include the European INEX effort for XML retrieval, the CLEF effort for multi-lingual information retrieval, the Japanese NTCIR effort for Asian language information retrieval, and the Indian FIRE effort.

---

[2] `trec.nist.gov`

```
<DOC>
<DOCNO> LA051990-0141 </DOCNO>

<HEADLINE> COUNCIL VOTES TO EDUCATE DOG OWNERS </HEADLINE>

<P>
The City Council stepped carefully around enforcement of a dog-curbing
ordinance this week, vetoing the use of police to enforce the law.
</P>

...

</DOC>
```

Figure 1.7   Example TREC document (LA051990-0141) from disk 5 of the TREC CDs.

1.4.1   TREC Tasks

Basic search tasks — in which systems return a ranked list from a static set of documents using previously unseen topics — are referred to as "adhoc" tasks in TREC jargon (often written as one word). Along with a set of documents, a test collection for an adhoc task includes sets of topics, from which queries may be created, and sets of relevance judgments (known as "qrel files" or just "qrels"), indicating documents that are relevant or not relevant to each topic. Over the history of TREC, adhoc tasks have been a part of tracks with a number of different research themes, such as Web retrieval or genomic IR. Despite differences in themes, the organization and operation of an adhoc task is basically the same across the tracks and is essentially unchanged since the earliest days of TREC.

Document sets for older TREC adhoc tasks (before 2000) were often taken from a set of 1.6 million documents distributed to TREC participants on five CDs. These disks contain selections of newspaper and newswire articles from publications such as the *Wall Street Journal* and the *LA Times*, and documents published by the U.S. federal government, such as the *Federal Register* and the *Congressional Record*. Most of these documents are written and edited by professionals reporting factual information or describing events.

Figure 1.7 shows a short excerpt from a document on disk 5 of the TREC CDs. The document appeared as a news article in the *LA Times* on May 19, 1990. For the purposes of TREC experiments, it is marked up in the style of XML. Although the details of the tagging schemes vary across the TREC collections, all TREC documents adhere to the same tagging convention for identifying document boundaries and document identifiers. Every TREC document is surrounded by <DOC>...</DOC> tags; <DOCNO>...</DOCNO> tags indicate its unique identifier. This identifier is used in qrels files when recording judgments for the document. This convention simplifies the indexing process and allows collections to be combined easily. Many research IR systems provide out-of-the-box facilities for working with documents that follow this convention.

```
<top>

<num> Number: 426
<title> law enforcement, dogs

<desc> Description:
Provide information on the use of dogs worldwide for
law enforcement purposes.

<narr> Narrative:
Relevant items include specific information on the
use of dogs during an operation. Training of dogs
and their handlers are also relevant.

</top>
```

Figure 1.8   TREC topic 426.

Document sets for newer TREC adhoc tasks are often taken from the Web. Until 2009, the largest of these was the 426GB GOV2 collection, which contains 25 million Web pages crawled from sites in the U.S. government's gov domain in early 2004. This crawl attempted to reach as many pages as possible within the gov domain, and it may be viewed as a reasonable snapshot of that domain within that time period. GOV2 contains documents in a wide variety of formats and lengths, ranging from lengthy technical reports in PDF to pages of nothing but links in HTML. GOV2 formed the document set for the Terabyte Track from TREC 2004 until the track was discontinued at the end of 2006. It also formed the collection for the Million Query Track at TREC 2007 and 2008.

Although the GOV2 collection is substantially larger than any previous TREC collection, it is still orders of magnitude smaller than the collections managed by commercial Web search engines. TREC 2009 saw the introduction of a billion-page Web collection, known as the ClueWeb09 collection, providing an opportunity for IR researchers to work on a scale comparable to commercial Web search.[3]

For each year that a track operates an adhoc task, NIST typically creates 50 new topics. Participants are required to freeze development of their systems before downloading these topics. After downloading the topics, participants create queries from them, run these queries against the document set, and return ranked lists to NIST for evaluation.

A typical TREC adhoc topic, created for TREC 1999, is shown in Figure 1.8. Like most TREC topics, it is structured into three parts, describing the underlying information need in several forms. The *title* field is designed to be treated as a keyword query, similar to a query that might be entered into a search engine. The *description* field provides a longer statement of the topic requirements, in the form of a complete sentence or question. It, too, may be used

---

[3] boston.lti.cs.cmu.edu/Data/clueweb09

Table 1.2 Summary of the test collections used for many of the experiments described in this book.

Document Set	Number of Docs	Size (GB)	Year	Topics
TREC45	0.5 million	2	1998	351–400
			1999	401–450
GOV2	25.2 million	426	2004	701–750
			2005	751–800

as a query, particularly by research systems that apply natural language processing techniques as part of retrieval. The *narrative*, which may be a full paragraph in length, supplements the other two fields and provides additional information required to specify the nature of a relevant document. The narrative field is primarily used by human assessors, to help determine if a retrieved document is relevant or not.

Most retrieval experiments in this book report results over four TREC test collections based on two document sets, a small one and a larger one. The small collection consists of the documents from disks 4 and 5 of the TREC CDs described above, excluding the documents from the *Congressional Record*. It includes documents from the *Financial Times*, the U.S. *Federal Register*, the U.S. Foreign Broadcast Information Service, and the *LA Times*. This document set, which we refer to as *TREC45*, was used for the main adhoc task at TREC 1998 and 1999.

In both 1998 and 1999, NIST created 50 topics with associated relevance judgments over this document set. The 1998 topics are numbered 351–400; the 1999 topics are numbered 401–450. Thus, we have two test collections over the TREC45 document set, which we refer to as *TREC45 1998* and *TREC45 1999*. Although there are minor differences between our experimental procedure and that used in the corresponding TREC experiments (which we will ignore), our experimental results reported over these collections may reasonably be compared with the published results at TREC 1998 and 1999.

The larger one of the two document sets used in our experiments is the GOV2 corpus mentioned previously. We take this set together with topics and judgments from the TREC Terabyte track in 2004 (topics 701–750) and 2005 (751–800) to form the GOV2 2004 and GOV2 2005 collections. Experimental results reported over these collections may reasonably be compared with the published results for the Terabyte track of TREC 2004 and 2005.

Table 1.2 summarizes our four test collections. The TREC45 collection may be obtained from the NIST Standard Reference Data Products Web page as Special Databases 22 and 23.[4] The GOV2 collection is distributed by the University of Glasgow.[5] Topics and qrels for these collections may be obtained from the TREC data archive.[6]

---

[4] `www.nist.gov/srd`

[5] `ir.dcs.gla.ac.uk/test_collections`

[6] `trec.nist.gov`

1.5   Open-Source IR Systems

There exists a wide variety of open-source information retrieval systems that you may use for exercises in this book and to start conducting your own information retrieval experiments. As always, a (non-exhaustive) list of open-source IR systems can be found in Wikipedia.[7]

Since this list of available systems is so long, we do not even try to cover it in detail. Instead, we restrict ourselves to a very brief overview of three particular systems that were chosen because of their popularity, their influence on IR research, or their intimate relationship with the contents of this book. All three systems are available for download from the Web and may be used free of charge, according to their respective licenses.

1.5.1   Lucene

Lucene is an indexing and search system implemented in Java, with ports to other programming languages. The project was started by Doug Cutting in 1997. Since then, it has grown from a single-developer effort to a global project involving hundreds of developers in various countries. It is currently hosted by the Apache Foundation.[8] Lucene is by far the most successful open-source search engine. Its largest installation is quite likely Wikipedia: All queries entered into Wikipedia's search form are handled by Lucene. A list of other projects relying on its indexing and search capabilities can be found on Lucene's "PoweredBy" page.[9]

Known for its modularity and extensibility, Lucene allows developers to define their own indexing and retrieval rules and formulae. Under the hood, Lucene's retrieval framework is based on the concept of *fields*: Every document is a collection of fields, such as its title, body, URL, and so forth. This makes it easy to specify structured search requests and to give different weights to different parts of a document.

Due to its great popularity, there is a wide variety of books and tutorials that help you get started with Lucene quickly. Try the query "lucene tutorial" in your favorite Web search engine.

1.5.2   Indri

Indri[10] is an academic information retrieval system written in C++. It is developed by researchers at the University of Massachusetts and is part of the Lemur project,[11] a joint effort of the University of Massachusetts and Carnegie Mellon University.

---

[7] `en.wikipedia.org/wiki/List_of_search_engines`

[8] `lucene.apache.org`

[9] `wiki.apache.org/lucene-java/PoweredBy`

[10] `www.lemurproject.org/indri/`

[11] `www.lemurproject.org`

Indri is well known for its high retrieval effectiveness and is frequently found among the top-scoring search engines at TREC. Its retrieval model is a combination of the language modeling approaches discussed in Chapter 9. Like Lucene, Indri can handle multiple fields per document, such as title, body, and anchor text, which is important in the context of Web search (Chapter 15). It supports automatic query expansion by means of pseudo-relevance feedback, a technique that adds related terms to an initial search query, based on the contents of an initial set of search results (see Section 8.6). It also supports query-independent document scoring that may, for instance, be used to prefer more recent documents over less recent ones when ranking the search results (see Sections 9.1 and 15.3).

1.5.3 Wumpus

Wumpus[12] is an academic search engine written in C++ and developed at the University of Waterloo. Unlike most other search engines, Wumpus has no built-in notion of "documents" and does not know about the beginning and the end of each document when it builds the index. Instead, every part of the text collection may represent a potential unit for retrieval, depending on the structural search constraints specified in the query. This makes the system particularly attractive for search tasks in which the ideal search result may not always be a whole document, but may be a section, a paragraph, or a sequence of paragraphs within a document.

Wumpus supports a variety of different retrieval methods, including the proximity ranking function from Chapter 2, the BM25 algorithm from Chapter 8, and the language modeling and divergence from randomness approaches discussed in Chapter 9. In addition, it is able to carry out real-time index updates (i.e., adding/removing files to/from the index) and provides support for multi-user security restrictions that are useful if the system has more than one user, and each user is allowed to search only parts of the index.

Unless explicitly stated otherwise, all performance figures presented in this book were obtained using Wumpus.

1.6 Further Reading

This is not the first book on the topic of information retrieval. Of the older books providing a general introduction to IR, several should be mentioned. The classic books by Salton (1968) and van Rijsbergen (1979) continue to provide insights into the foundations of the field. The treatment of core topics given by Grossman and Frieder (2004) remains relevant. Witten et al. (1999) provide background information on many related topics that we do not cover in this book, including text and image compression.

---

[12] www.wumpus-search.org

Several good introductory texts have appeared in recent years. The textbook by Croft et al. (2010) is intended to give an undergraduate-level introduction to the area. Baeza-Yates and Ribeiro-Neto (2010) provide a broad survey of the field, with experts contributing individual chapters on their areas of expertise. Manning et al. (2008) provide another readable survey.

Survey articles on specific topics appear regularly as part of the journal series *Foundations and Trends in Information Retrieval*. The *Encyclopedia of Database Systems* (Özsu and Liu, 2009) contains many introductory articles on topics related to information retrieval. Hearst (2009) provides an introduction to user interface design for information retrieval applications. The field of natural language processing, particularly the sub-field of statistical natural language processing, is closely related to the field of information retrieval. Manning and Schütze (1999) provide a thorough introduction to that area.

The premier research conference in the area is the *Annual International ACM SIGIR Conference on Research and Development in Information Retrieval* (SIGIR), now well into its fourth decade. Other leading research conferences and workshops include the *ACM Conference on Information and Knowledge Management* (CIKM), the *Joint Conference on Digital Libraries* (JCDL), the *European Conference on Information Retrieval* (ECIR), the *ACM International Conference on Web Search and Data Mining* (WSDM), the conference on *String Processing and Information Retrieval* (SPIRE), and the *Text REtrieval Conference* (TREC). Important IR research also regularly appears in the premier venues of related fields, such as the *World Wide Web Conference* (WWW), the *Annual Conference on Neural Information Processing Systems* (NIPS), the *Conference on Artificial Intelligence* (AAAI), and the *Knowledge Discovery and Data Mining Conference* (KDD). The premier IR journal is *ACM Transactions on Information Systems*. Other leading journals include *Information Retrieval* and the venerable *Information Processing & Management*.

Many books and Web sites devoted to learning and using XML are available. One important resource is the XML home page of the World Wide Web Consortium (W3C),[13] the organization responsible for defining and maintaining the XML technical specification. Along with extensive reference materials, the site includes pointers to introductory tutorials and guides. Jon Bosak's personal Web page[14] contains many articles and other information related to the early development and usage of XML, including Shakespeare's plays.

---

[13] www.w3.org/XML/

[14] www.ibiblio.org/bosak

1.7   Exercises

Exercise 1.1   Record the next ten queries you issue to a Web search engine (or check your Web history if your search engine allows it). Note how many are *refinements* of previous queries, adding or removing terms to narrow or broaden the focus of the query. Choose three commercial search engines, including the engine you normally use, and reissue the queries on all three. For each query, examine the top five results from each engine. For each result, rate on it a scale from -10 to +10, where +10 represents a perfect or ideal result and -10 represents a misleading or harmful result (spam). Compute an average score for each engine over all ten queries and results. Did the engine you normally use receive the highest score? Do you believe that the results of this exercise accurately reflect the relative quality of the search engines? Suggest three possible improvements to this experiment.

Exercise 1.2   Obtain and install an open-source IR system, such as one of those listed in Section 1.5. Create a small document collection from your e-mail, or from another source. A few dozen documents should be enough. Index your collection. Try a few queries.

Exercise 1.3   Starting in state 3 of the Markov model in Figure 1.6, what is the probability of generating "not not be to be"?

Exercise 1.4   Starting in an unknown state, the Markov model in Figure 1.6 generates "to be". What state or states could be the current state of the model after generating this text?

Exercise 1.5   Is there a finite n, such that the current state of the Markov model in Figure 1.6 will always be known after it generates a string of length n or greater, regardless of the starting state?

Exercise 1.6   For a given Markov model, assume there is a finite n so that the current state of the model will always be known after it generates a string of length n or greater. Describe a procedure for converting such a Markov model into an nth-order finite-context model.

Exercise 1.7   Assume that we extend Markov models to allow multiple transitions between pairs of states, where each transition between a given pair of states is labeled with a different term. For any such model, show that there is an equivalent Markov model in which there is no more than one transition between any pair of states. (*Hint*: Split target states.)

Exercise 1.8   Outline a procedure for converting an nth-order finite-context language model into a Markov model. How many states might be required?

Exercise 1.9 (project exercise) This exercise develops a test corpus, based on Wikipedia, that will be used in a number of exercises throughout Part I.

To start, download a current copy of the English-language Wikipedia. At the time of writing, its downloadable version consisted of a single large file. Wikipedia itself contains documentation describing the format of this download.[15]

Along with the text of the articles themselves, the download includes *redirection records* that provide alternative titles for articles. Pre-process the download to remove these records and any other extraneous information, leaving a set of individual articles. Wikipedia-style formatting should also be removed, or replaced with XML-style tags of your choosing. Assign a unique identifier to each article. Add <DOC> and <DOCNO> tags. The result should be consistent with TREC conventions, as described in Section 1.4 and illustrated in Figure 1.7.

Exercise 1.10 (project exercise) Following the style of Figure 1.8, create three to four topics suitable for testing retrieval performance over the English-language Wikipedia. Try to avoid topics expressing an information need that can be completely satisfied by a single "best" article. Instead, try to create topics that require multiple articles in order to cover all relevant information. (*Note*: This exercise is suitable as the foundation for a class project to create a Wikipedia test collection, with each student contributing enough topics to make a combined set of 50 topics or more. (See Exercise 2.13 for further details.)

Exercise 1.11 (project exercise) Obtain and install an open-source IR system (see Exercise 1.2). Using this IR system, index the collection you created in Exercise 1.9. Submit the titles of the topics you created in Exercise 1.10 as queries to the system. For each topic, judge the top five documents returned as either relevant or not. Does the IR system work equally well on all topics?

Exercise 1.12 (project exercise) Tokenize the collection you created in Exercise 1.9, following the procedure of Section 1.3.2. For this exercise, discard the tags and keep only the words (i.e., strings of alphanumeric characters). Wikipedia text is encoded in UTF-8 Unicode, but you may treat it as ASCII text for the purpose of this exercise. Generate a log-log plot of frequency vs. rank order, equivalent to that shown in Figure 1.5. Does the data follow Zipf's law? If so, what is an approximate value for α?

Exercise 1.13 (project exercise) Create a trigram language model based on the tokenization of Exercise 1.12. Using your language model, implement a random Wikipedia text generator. How could you extend your text generator to generate capitalization and punctuation, making your text look more like English? How could you extend your text generator to generate random Wikipedia articles, including tagging and links?

---

[15] en.wikipedia.org/wiki/Wikipedia:Database_download

1.8   Bibliography

Baeza-Yates, R. A., and Ribeiro-Neto, B. (2010). *Modern Information Retrieval* (2nd ed.). Reading, Massachusetts: Addison-Wesley.

Croft, W. B., Metzler, D., and Strohman, T. (2010). *Search Engines: Information Retrieval in Practice*. London, England: Pearson.

Grossman, D. A., and Frieder, O. (2004). *Information Retrieval: Algorithms and Heuristics* (2nd ed.). Berlin, Germany: Springer.

Hearst, M. A. (2009). *Search User Interfaces*. Cambridge, England: Cambridge University Press.

Manning, C. D., Raghavan, P., and Schütze, H. (2008). *Introduction to Information Retrieval*. Cambridge, England: Cambridge University Press.

Manning, C. D., and Schütze, H. (1999). *Foundations of Statistical Natural Language Processing*. Cambridge, Massachusetts: MIT Press.

Özsu, M. T., and Liu, L., editors (2009). *Encyclopedia of Database Systems*. Berlin, Germany: Springer.

Salton, G. (1968). *Automatic Information Organziation and Retrieval*. New York: McGraw-Hill.

van Rijsbergen, C. J. (1979). *Information Retrieval* (2nd ed.). London, England: Butterworths.

Witten, I. H., Moffat, A., and Bell, T. C. (1999). *Managing Gigabytes: Compressing and Indexing Documents and Images* (2nd ed.). San Francisco, California: Morgan Kaufmann.

Zipf, G. K. (1949). *Human Behavior and the Principle of Least-Effort*. Cambridge, Massachusetts: Addison-Wesley.

2 Basic Techniques

As a foundation for the remainder of the book, this chapter takes a tour through the elements of information retrieval outlined in Chapter 1, covering the basics of indexing, retrieval and evaluation. The material on indexing and retrieval, constituting the first two major sections, is closely linked, presenting a unified view of these topics. The third major section, on evaluation, examines both the efficiency and the effectiveness of the algorithms introduced in the first two sections.

2.1 Inverted Indices

The inverted index (sometimes called *inverted file*) is the central data structure in virtually every information retrieval system. At its simplest, an inverted index provides a mapping between terms and their locations of occurrence in a text collection $\mathcal{C}$. The fundamental components of an inverted index are illustrated in Figure 2.1, which presents an index for the text of Shakespeare's plays (Figures 1.2 and 1.3). The *dictionary* lists the terms contained in the vocabulary $\mathcal{V}$ of the collection. Each term has associated with it a *postings list* of the positions in which it appears, consistent with the positional numbering in Figure 1.4 (page 14).

If you have encountered inverted indices before, you might be surprised that the index shown in Figure 2.1 contains not document identifiers but "flat" word positions of the individual term occurrences. This type of index is called a *schema-independent index* because it makes no assumptions about the structure (usually referred to as *schema* in the database community) of the underlying text. We chose the schema-independent variant for most of the examples in this chapter because it is the simplest. An overview of alternative index types appears in Section 2.1.3.

Regardless of the specific type of index that is used, its components — the dictionary and the postings lists — may be stored in memory, on disk, or a combination of both. For now, we keep the precise data structures deliberately vague. We define an inverted index as an abstract data type (ADT) with four methods:

- **first**(t) returns the first position at which the term t occurs in the collection;
- **last**(t) returns the last position at which t occurs in the collection;
- **next**$(t, current)$ returns the position of t's first occurrence after the *current* position;
- **prev**$(t, current)$ returns the position of t's last occurrence before the *current* position.

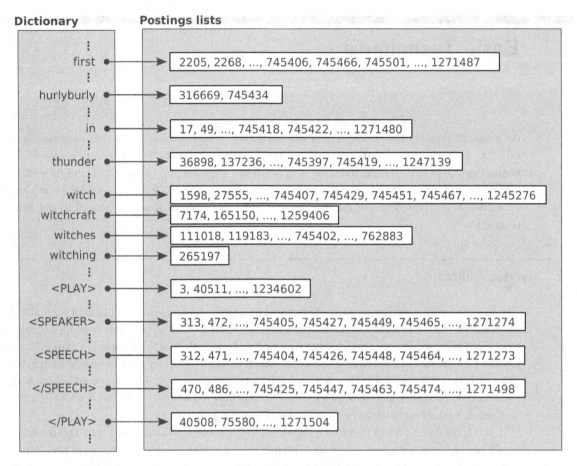

Figure 2.1 A schema-independent inverted index for Shakespeare's plays. The dictionary provides a mapping from terms to their positions of occurrence.

In addition, we define l_t to represent the total number of times the term t appears in the collection (i.e., the length of its postings list). We define $l_\mathcal{C}$ to be the length of the collection, so that $\sum_{t \in \mathcal{V}} l_t = l_\mathcal{C}$ (where $\mathcal{V}$ is the collection's vocabulary).

For the inverted index in Figure 2.1, we have:

first("hurlyburly") = 316669   **last**("thunder") = 1247139

first("witching") = 265197   **last**("witching") = 265197

$$\mathbf{next}(\text{"witch"}, 745429) = 745451 \qquad \mathbf{prev}(\text{"witch"}, 745451) = 745429$$

$$\mathbf{next}(\text{"hurlyburly"}, 345678) = 745434 \qquad \mathbf{prev}(\text{"hurlyburly"}, 456789) = 316669$$

$$\mathbf{next}(\text{"witch"}, 1245276) = \infty \qquad \mathbf{prev}(\text{"witch"}, 1598) = -\infty$$

$$l_{<\text{PLAY}>} = 37 \qquad l_{\mathcal{C}} = 1271504$$

$$l_{\text{witching}} = 1$$

The symbols $-\infty$ and ∞ act as beginning-of-file and end-of-file markers, representing positions beyond the beginning and the end of the term sequence. As a practical convention we define:

$$\mathbf{next}(t, -\infty) = \mathbf{first}(t) \qquad \mathbf{next}(t, \infty) = \infty$$

$$\mathbf{prev}(t, \infty) = \mathbf{last}(t) \qquad \mathbf{prev}(t, -\infty) = -\infty$$

The methods of our inverted index permit both sequential and random access into postings lists, with a sequential scan of a postings list being a simple loop:

```
current ← −∞
while current < ∞ do
    current ← next(t, current)
    do something with the current value
```

However, many algorithms require random access into postings lists, including the phrase search algorithm we present next. Often, these algorithms take the result of a method call for one term and apply it as an argument to a method call for another term, skipping through the postings lists nonsequentially.

2.1.1 Extended Example: Phrase Search

Most commercial Web search engines, as well as many other IR systems, treat a list of terms enclosed in double quotes ("...") as a phrase. To process a query that contains a phrase, the IR system must identify the occurrences of the phrase in the collection. This information may then be used during the retrieval process for filtering and ranking — perhaps excluding documents that do not contain an exact phrase match.

Phrase search provides an excellent example of how algorithms over inverted indices operate. Suppose we wish to locate all occurrences of the phrase "first witch" in our collection of Shakespeare's plays. Perhaps we wish to identify all speeches by this character. By visually scanning the postings lists in Figure 2.1, we can locate one occurrence starting at 745406 and ending at 745407. We might locate other occurrences in a similar fashion by scanning the postings lists for an occurrence of "first" immediately followed by an occurrence of "witch". In this section we

nextPhrase $(t_1t_2...t_n, position) \equiv$
1    $v \leftarrow position$
2   **for** $i \leftarrow 1$ **to** n **do**
3        $v \leftarrow \textbf{next}(t_i, v)$
4   **if** $v = \infty$ **then**
5   **return** $[\infty, \infty]$
6    $u \leftarrow v$
7   **for** $i \leftarrow n-1$ **down to** 1 **do**
8        $u \leftarrow \textbf{prev}(t_i, u)$
9   **if** $v - u = n - 1$ **then**
10   **return** $[u, v]$
11   **else**
12   **return nextPhrase**$(t_1t_2...t_n, u)$

Figure 2.2   Function to locate the first occurrence of a phrase after a given position. The function calls the **next** and **prev** methods of the inverted index ADT and returns an interval in the text collection as a result.

present an algorithm that formalizes this process, efficiently locating all occurrences of a given phrase with the aid of our inverted index ADT.

We specify the location of a phrase by an interval $[u,v]$, where u indicates the start of the phrase and v indicates the end of the phrase. In addition to the occurrence at $[745406, 745407]$, the phrase "first witch" may be found at $[745466, 745467]$, at $[745501, 745502]$, and elsewhere. The goal of our phrase searching algorithm is to determine values of u and v for all occurrences of the phrase in the collection.

We use the above interval notation to specify retrieval results throughout the book. In some contexts it is also convenient to think of an interval as a stand-in for the text at that location. For example, the interval $[914823, 914829]$ might represent the text

O Romeo, Romeo! wherefore art thou Romeo?

Given the phrase "$t_1t_2...t_n$", consisting of a sequence of n terms, our algorithm works through the postings lists for the terms from left to right, making a call to the **next** method for each term, and then from right to left, making a call to the **prev** method for each term. After each pass from left to right and back, it has computed an interval in which the terms appear in the correct order and as close together as possible. It then checks whether the terms are in fact adjacent. If they are, an occurrence of the phrase has been found; if not, the algorithm moves on.

Figure 2.2 presents the core of the algorithm as a function **nextPhrase** that locates the next occurrence of a phrase after a given position. The loop over lines 2–3 calls the methods of the inverted index to locate the terms in order. At the end of the loop, if the phrase occurs in the interval $[position,v]$, it ends at v. The loop over lines 7–8 then shrinks the interval to the smallest size possible while still including all terms in order. Finally, lines 9–12 verify that the terms are adjacent, forming a phrase. If they are not adjacent, the function makes a tail-recursive call. On line 12, note that u (and not v) is passed as the second argument to the recursive call. If the terms in the phrase are all different, then v could be passed. Passing u correctly handles the case in which two terms t_i and t_j are equal ($1 \leq i < j \leq n$).

As an example, suppose we want to find the first occurrences of the phrase "first witch": **nextPhrase**("first witch", $-\infty$). The algorithm starts by identifying the first occurrence of "first":

$$\textbf{next}(\text{"first"}, -\infty) = \textbf{first}(\text{"first"}) = 2205.$$

If this occurrence of "first" is part of the phrase, then the next occurrence of "witch" should immediately follow it. However,

$$\textbf{next}(\text{"witch"}, 2205) = 27555;$$

that is, it does not immediately follow it. We now know that the first occurrence of the phrase cannot end before position 27555, and we compute

$$\textbf{prev}(\text{"first"}, 27555) = 26267.$$

In jumping from 2205 to 26267 in the postings list for "first", we were able to skip 15 occurrences of "first". Because interval [26267, 27555] has length 1288, and not the required length 2, we move on to consider the next occurrence of "first" at

$$\textbf{next}(\text{"first"}, 26267) = 27673.$$

Note that the calls to the **prev** method in line 8 of the algorithm are not strictly necessary (see Exercise 2.2), but they help us to analyze the complexity of the algorithm.

If we want to generate all occurrences of the phrase instead of just a single occurrence, an additional loop is required, calling **nextPhrase** once for each occurrence of the phrase:

$$u \leftarrow -\infty$$
$$\textbf{while } u < \infty \textbf{ do}$$
$$\quad [u,v] \leftarrow \textbf{nextPhrase}(\text{"}t_1 t_2 ... t_n\text{"}, u)$$
$$\quad \textbf{if } u \neq \infty \textbf{ then}$$
$$\quad\quad \text{report the interval } [u,v]$$

The loop reports each interval as it is generated. Depending on the application, reporting $[u,v]$ might involve returning the document containing the phrase to the user, or it might involve storing the interval in an array or other data structure for further processing. Similar to the code in Figure 2.2, u (and not v) is passed as the second argument to **nextPhrase**. As a result, the function can correctly locate all six occurrences of the phrase "spam spam spam" in the follow passage from the well-known Monty Python song:

Spam spam spam spam
Spam spam spam spam

To determine the time complexity of the algorithm, first observe that each call to **nextPhrase** makes $O(n)$ calls to the **next** and **prev** methods of the inverted index (n calls to **next**, followed by $n-1$ calls to **prev**). After line 8, the interval $[u,v]$ contains all terms in the phrase in order, and there is no smaller interval contained within it that also contains all the terms in order. Next, observe that each occurrence of a term t_i in the collection can be included in no more than one of the intervals computed by lines 1–8. Even if the phrase contains two identical terms, t_i and t_j, a matching token in the collection can be included in only one such interval as a match to t_i, although it might be included in another interval as a match to t_j. The time complexity is therefore determined by the length of the shortest postings list for the terms in the phrase:

$$l = \min_{1 \leq i \leq n} l_{t_i}. \tag{2.1}$$

Combining these observations, in the worst case the algorithm requires $O(n \cdot l)$ calls to methods of our ADT to locate all occurrences of the phrase. If the phrase includes both common and uncommon terms ("Rosencrantz and Guildenstern are dead"), the number of calls is determined by the least frequent term ("Guildenstern") and not the most frequent one ("and").

We emphasize that $O(n \cdot l)$ represents the number of method calls, not the number of steps taken by the algorithm, and that the time for each method call depends on the details of how it is implemented. For the access patterns generated by the algorithm, there is a surprisingly simple and efficient implementation that gives good performance for phrases containing any mixture of frequent and infrequent terms. We present the details in the next section.

Although the algorithm requires $O(n \cdot l)$ method calls in the worst case, the actual number of calls depends on the relative location of the terms in the collection. For example, suppose we are searching for the phrase "hello world" and the text in the collection is arranged:

hello ... hello ... hello ... hello world ... world ... world ... world

with all occurrences of "hello" before all occurrences of "world". Then the algorithm makes only four method calls to locate the single occurrence of the phrase, regardless of the size of the text or the number of occurrences of each term. Although this example is extreme and artificial, it illustrates the *adaptive* nature of the algorithm — its actual execution time is determined by characteristics of the data. Other IR problems may be solved with adaptive algorithms, and we exploit this approach whenever possible to improve efficiency.

To make the adaptive nature of the algorithm more explicit, we introduce a measure of the characteristics of the data that determines the actual number of method calls. Consider the interval $[u,v]$ just before the test at line 9 of Figure 2.2. The interval contains all the terms in the phrase in order, but does not contain any smaller interval containing all the terms in order. We call an interval with this property a *candidate phrase* for the terms. If we define κ to be the number of candidate phrases in a given document collection, then the number of method calls required to locate all occurrences is $O(n \cdot \kappa)$.

2.1.2 Implementing Inverted Indices

It moves across the blackness that lies between stars, and its mechanical legs move slowly. Each step that it takes, however, crossing from nothing to nothing, carries it twice the distance of the previous step. Each stride also takes the same amount of time as the prior one. Suns flash by, fall behind, wink out. It runs through solid matter, passes through infernos, pierces nebulae, faster and faster moving through the starfall blizzard in the forest of the night. Given a sufficient warm-up run, it is said that it could circumnavigate the universe in a single stride. What would happen if it kept running after that, no one knows.

— Roger Zelazny, *Creatures of Light and Darkness*

When a collection will never change and when it is small enough to be maintained entirely in memory, an inverted index may be implemented with very simple data structures. The dictionary may be stored in a hash table or similar structure, and the postings list for each term t may be stored in a fixed array $P_t[]$ with length l_t. For the term "witch" in the Shakespeare collection, this array may be represented as follows:

1	2		31	32	33	34		92
1598	27555	$\cdots$	745407	745429	745451	745467	$\cdots$	1245276

The **first** and **last** methods of our inverted index ADT may be implemented in constant time by returning $P_t[1]$ and $P_t[l_t]$, respectively. The **next** and **prev** methods may be implemented by a binary search with time complexity $O(\log(l_t))$. Details for the **next** method are provided in Figure 2.3; the details for the **prev** method are similar.

Recall that the phrase searching algorithm of Section 2.1.1 requires $O(n \cdot l)$ calls to the **next** and **prev** methods in the worst case. If we define

$$L = \max_{1 \leq i \leq n} l_{t_i}, \tag{2.2}$$

then the time complexity of the algorithms becomes $O(n \cdot l \cdot \log(L))$ because each call to a method may require up to $O(\log(L))$ time. When expressed in terms of κ, the number of candidate phrases, the time complexity becomes $O(n \cdot \kappa \cdot \log(L))$.

When a phrase contains both frequent and infrequent terms, this implementation can provide excellent performance. For example, the term "tempest" appears only 49 times in the works of Shakespeare. As we saw in Section 1.3.3, the term "the" appears 28,317 times. However, when

```
     next (t, current) ≡
1        if l_t = 0 or P_t[l_t] ≤ current then
2            return ∞
3        if P_t[1] > current then
4            return P_t[1]
5        return P_t[binarySearch (t, 1, l_t, current)]

     binarySearch (t, low, high, current) ≡
6        while high − low > 1 do
7            mid ← ⌊(low + high)/2⌋
8            if P_t[mid] ≤ current then
9                low ← mid
10           else
11               high ← mid
12       return high
```

Figure 2.3   Implementation of the **next** method through a binary search that is implemented by a separate function. The array $P_t[]$ (of length l_t) contains the postings list for term t. The **binarySearch** function assumes that $P_t[low] \leq current$ and $P_t[high] > current$. Lines 1–4 establish this precondition, and the loop at lines 6–11 maintains it as an invariant.

searching for the phrase "the tempest", we access the postings list array for "the" less than two thousand times while conducting at most $2 \cdot 49 = 98$ binary searches.

On the other hand, when a phrase contains terms with similar frequencies, the repeated binary searches may be wasteful. The terms in the phrase "two gentlemen" both appear a few hundred times in Shakespeare (702 and 225 times, to be exact). Identifying all occurrences of this phrase requires more than two thousand accesses to the postings list array for "two". In this case, it would be more efficient if we could scan sequentially through both arrays at the same time, comparing values as we go. By changing the definition of the **next** and **prev** methods, the phrase search algorithm can be adapted to do just that.

To start with, we note that as the phrase search algorithm makes successive calls to the **next** method for a given term t_i, the values passed as the second argument strictly increase across calls to **nextPhrase**, including the recursive calls. During the process of finding all occurrences of a given phrase, the algorithm may make up to l calls to **next** for that term (where l, as before, is the length of the shortest postings list):

$$\mathbf{next}(t_i, v_1), \ \mathbf{next}(t_i, v_2), \ ..., \ \mathbf{next}(t_i, v_l)$$

with

$$v_1 < v_2 < ... < v_l \, .$$

Moreover, the results of these calls also strictly increase:

$$\mathbf{next}(t_i, v_1) < \mathbf{next}(t_i, v_2) < ... < \mathbf{next}(t_i, v_l) \, .$$

next $(t,\ current) \equiv$
1   **if** $l_t = 0$ **or** $P_t[l_t] \leq current$ **then**
2   **return** ∞
3   **if** $P_t[1] > current$ **then**
4        $c_t \leftarrow 1$
5   **return** $P_t[c_t]$
6   **if** $c_t > 1$ **and** $P_t[c_t - 1] > current$ **then**
7        $c_t \leftarrow 1$
8   **while** $P_t[c_t] \leq current$ **do**
9        $c_t \leftarrow c_t + 1$
10   **return** $P_t[c_t]$

Figure 2.4 Implementation of the **next** method through a linear scan. This implementation updates a cached index offset c_t for each term t, where $P_t[c_t]$ represents the last noninfinite result returned from a call to **next** for this term. If possible, the implementation starts its scan from this cached offset. If not, the cached offset is reset at lines 6–7.

For example, when searching for "first witch" in Shakespeare, the sequence of calls for "first" begins:

$$\textbf{next}(\text{"first"},\ -\infty),\ \ \textbf{next}(\text{"first"},\ 26267),\ \ \textbf{next}(\text{"first"},\ 30608),\ \ ...$$

returning the values

$$2205 < 27673 < 32995 < ...$$

Of course, the exact values for v_1, v_2, ... and the actual number of calls to **next** depend on the locations of the other terms in the phrase. Nonetheless, we know that these values will increase and that there may be l of them in the worst case.

To implement our sequential scan, we remember (or cache) the value returned by a call to **next** for a given term. When the function is called again (for the same term), we continue our scan at this cached location. Figure 2.4 provides the details. The variable c_t caches the array offset of the value returned by the previous call, with a separate value cached for each term in the phrase (e.g., c_{first} and c_{witch}). Because the method may be used in algorithms that do not process postings lists in a strictly increasing order, we are careful to reset c_t if this assumption is violated (lines 6–7).

If we take a similar approach to implementing **prev** and maintain corresponding cached values, the phrase search algorithm scans the postings lists for the terms in the phrase, accessing each element of the postings list arrays a bounded number of times ($O(1)$). Because the algorithm may fully scan the longest postings list (of size L), and all postings lists may be of this length, the overall time complexity of the algorithm is $O(n \cdot L)$. In this case the adaptive nature of the algorithm provides no benefit.

We now have two possible implementations for **next** and **prev** that in effect produce two implementations of **nextPhrase**. The first implementation, with overall time complexity $O(n \cdot l \cdot \log(L))$, is particularly appropriate when the shortest postings list is considerably

```
     next (t, current) ≡
1        if lₜ = 0 or Pₜ[lₜ] ≤ current then
2            return ∞
3        if Pₜ[1] > current then
4            cₜ ← 1
5            return Pₜ[cₜ]
6        if cₜ > 1 and Pₜ[cₜ − 1] ≤ current then
7            low ← cₜ − 1
8        else
9            low ← 1
10       jump ← 1
11       high ← low + jump
12       while high < lₜ and Pₜ[high] ≤ current do
13           low ← high
14           jump ← 2 · jump
15           high ← low + jump
16       if high > lₜ then
17           high ← lₜ
18       cₜ ← binarySearch (t, low, high, current)
19       return Pₜ[cₜ]
```

Figure 2.5 Implementation of the **next** method through a galloping search. Lines 6–9 determine an initial value for *low* such that $P_t[low] \leq current$, using the cached value if possible. Lines 12–17 gallop ahead in exponentially increasing steps until they determine a value for *high* such that $P_t[high] > current$. The final result is determined by a binary search (from Figure 2.3).

shorter than the longest postings list ($l \ll L$). The second implementation, with time complexity $O(n \cdot L)$, is appropriate when all postings lists have approximately the same length ($l \approx L$).

Given this dichotomy, we might imagine choosing between the algorithms at run-time by comparing l with L. However, it is possible to define a third implementation of the methods that combines features of both algorithms, with a time complexity that explicitly depends on the relative sizes of the longest and shortest lists (L/l). This third algorithm is based on an *exponential* or *galloping search*. The idea is to scan forward from a cached position in exponentially increasing steps ("galloping") until the answer is passed. At this point, a binary search is applied to the range formed by the last two steps of the gallop to locate the exact offset of the answer. Figure 2.5 provides the details.

Figure 2.6 illustrates and compares the three approaches for a call to **prev**("witch", 745429) over the Shakespeare collection. Using a binary search (part a), the method would access the array seven times, first at positions 1 and 92 to establish the invariant required by the binary search (not shown), and then at positions 46, 23, 34, 28, and 31 during the binary search itself. Using a sequential scan (part b) starting from an initial cached offset of 1, the method would access the array 34 times, including the accesses required to check boundary conditions (not shown). A galloping search (part c) would access positions 1, 2, 4, 8, 16, and 32 before

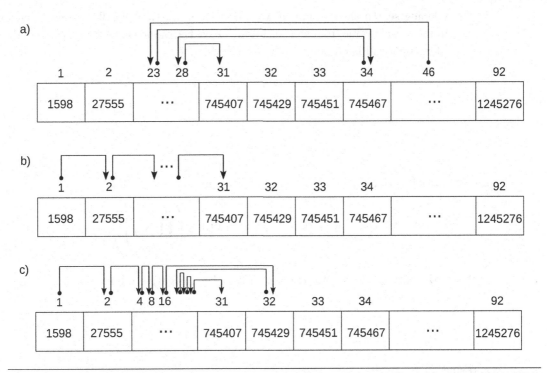

Figure 2.6 Access patterns for three approaches to solving **prev**("witch", 745429) = 745407: (a) binary search, (b) sequential scan, and (c) galloping. For (b) and (c), the algorithms start at an initial cached position of 1.

establishing the conditions for a binary search, which would then access positions 24, 28, 30, and 31, for a total of twelve accesses to the postings list array (including checking the boundary conditions). At the end of both the scanning and the galloping methods, the cached array offset would be updated to 31.

To determine the time complexity of galloping search, we return to consider the sequence of calls to **next** that originally motivated the sequential scanning algorithm. Let c_t^j be the cached value after the jth call to **next** for term t during the processing of a given phrase search.

$$P_t[c_t^1] = \mathbf{next}\ (t, v_1)$$
$$P_t[c_t^2] = \mathbf{next}\ (t, v_2)$$
$$\cdots$$
$$P_t[c_t^l] = \mathbf{next}\ (t, v_l)$$

For a galloping search the amount of work done by a particular call to **next** depends on the change in the cached value from call to call. If the cached value changes by Δc, then the amount of work done by a call is $O(\log(\Delta c))$. Thus, if we define

$$
\begin{aligned}
\Delta c_1 &= c_t^1 \\
\Delta c_2 &= c_t^2 - c_t^1 \\
&\cdots \\
\Delta c_l &= c_t^l - c_t^{l-1},
\end{aligned}
$$

then the total work done by calls to **next** for term t is

$$
\sum_{j=1}^{l} O(\log(\Delta c_j)) = O\left(\log\left(\prod_{j=1}^{l} \Delta c_j\right)\right). \tag{2.3}
$$

We know that the arithmetic mean of a list of nonnegative numbers is always greater than its geometric mean

$$
\frac{\sum_{j=1}^{l} \Delta c_j}{l} \geq \sqrt[l]{\prod_{j=1}^{l} \Delta c_j}, \tag{2.4}
$$

and since $\sum_{j=1}^{l} \Delta c_j \leq L$, we have

$$
\prod_{j=1}^{l} \Delta c_j \leq (L/l)^l. \tag{2.5}
$$

Therefore, the total work done by calls to **next** (or **prev**) for the term t is

$$
O\left(\log\left(\prod_{j=1}^{l} \Delta c_j\right)\right) \subseteq O\left(\log\left((L/l)^l\right)\right) \tag{2.6}
$$

$$
= O\left(l \cdot \log(L/l)\right). \tag{2.7}
$$

The overall time complexity for a phrase with n terms is $O(n \cdot l \cdot \log(L/l))$. When $l \ll L$, this performance is similar to that of binary search; when $l \approx L$, it is similar to scanning. Taking the adaptive nature of the algorithm into account, a similar line of reasoning gives a time complexity of $O(n \cdot \kappa \cdot \log(L/\kappa))$.

Although we have focused on phrase searching in our discussion of the implementation of inverted indices, we shall see that galloping search is an appropriate technique for other problems, too. Part II of the book extends these ideas to data structures stored on disk.

2.1.3 Documents and Other Elements

Most IR systems and algorithms operate over a standard unit of retrieval: the document. As was discussed in Chapter 1, requirements of the specific application environment determine exactly what constitutes a document. Depending on these requirements, a document might be an e-mail message, a Web page, a newspaper article, or similar element.

In many application environments, the definition of a document is fairly natural. However, in a few environments, such as a collection of books, the natural unit (an entire book) may sometimes be too large to return as a reasonable result, particularly when the relevant material is limited to a small part of the text. Instead, it may be desirable to return a chapter, a section, a subsection, or even a range of pages.

In the case of our collection of Shakespeare's plays, the most natural course is probably to treat each play as a document, but acts, scenes, speeches, and lines might all be appropriate units of retrieval in some circumstances. For the purposes of a simple example, assume we are interested in speeches and wish to locate those spoken by the "first witch".

The phrase "first witch" first occurs at $[745406, 745407]$. Computing the speech that contains this phrase is reasonably straightforward. Using the methods of our inverted index ADT, we determine that the start of a speech immediately preceding this phrase is located at

$$\mathbf{prev}(\text{``<SPEECH>''}, 745406) = 745404.$$

The end of this speech is located at

$$\mathbf{next}(\text{``</SPEECH>''}, 754404) = 745425.$$

Once we confirm that the interval $[745406, 745407]$ is contained in the interval $[745404, 745425]$, we know we have located a speech that contains the phrase. This check to confirm the containment is necessary because the phrase may not always occur as part of a speech. If we wish to locate all speeches by the "first witch", we can repeat this process with the next occurrence of the phrase.

A minor problem remains. Although we know that the phrase occurs in the speech, we do not know that the "first witch" is the speaker. The phrase may actually appear in the lines spoken. Fortunately, confirming that the witch is the speaker requires only two additional calls to methods of the inverted index (Exercise 2.4). In fact, simple calls to these methods are sufficient to compute a broad range of structural relationships, such as the following:

1. Lines spoken by any witch.

2. The speaker who says, "To be or not to be".

3. Titles of plays mentioning witches and thunder.

In a broader context, this flexible approach to specifying retrieval units and filtering them with simple containment criteria has many applications. In Web search systems, simple filtering can restrict retrieval results to a single domain. In enterprise search, applying constraints to the sender field allows us to select messages sent by a particular person. In file system search, structural constraints may be used to determine if file permissions and security restrictions allow a user to search a directory.

Because a requirement for "lightweight" structure occurs frequently in IR applications, we adopt a simple and uniform approach to supporting this structure by incorporating it directly into the inverted index, making it part of the basic facilities an inverted index provides. The examples above illustrate our approach. Complete details will be presented in Chapter 5, in which the approach forms the basis for implementing the advanced search operators, which are widely used in domain-specific IR applications, such as legal search. The approach may be used to implement the differential field weighting described in Section 8.7, which recognizes that the presence of a query term in a document's title may be a stronger indicator of relevance than its presence in the body. The approach may also be used to provide a foundation for the implementation of the more complex index structures required to fully support XML retrieval (see Chapter 16).

Notwithstanding those circumstances in which lightweight structure is required, most IR research assumes that the text collection naturally divides into documents, which are considered to be atomic units for retrieval. In a system for searching e-mail, messages form this basic retrieval unit. In a file system, files do; on the Web, Web pages. In addition to providing a natural unit of retrieval, documents also provide natural divisions in the text, allowing a collection to be partitioned into multiple subcollections for parallel retrieval and allowing documents to be reordered to improve efficiency, perhaps by grouping all documents from a single source or Web site.

Document-Oriented Indices

Because document retrieval represents such an important special case, indices are usually optimized around it. To accommodate this optimization, the numbering of positions in a document collection may be split into two components: a document number and an offset within the document.

We use the notation $n{:}m$ to indicate positions within a document-oriented index in which n is a document identifier (or *docid*) and m is an *offset*. Figure 2.7 presents an inverted index for Shakespeare's plays that treats plays as documents. The methods of our inverted index ADT continue to operate as before, but they accept *docid:offset* pairs as arguments and return them as results.

Dictionary **Postings lists**

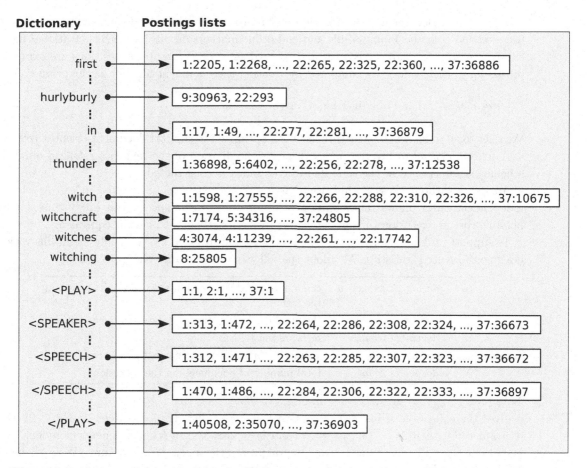

Figure 2.7 A document-centric index for Shakespeare's plays equivalent to the one shown in Figure 2.1 (page 34). Each posting is of the form *docid:within-document-position*.

For example,

$$\textbf{first}(\text{``hurlyburly''}) = 9{:}30963 \qquad\qquad \textbf{last}(\text{``thunder''}) = 37{:}12538$$
$$\textbf{first}(\text{``witching''}) = 8{:}25805 \qquad\qquad \textbf{last}(\text{``witching''}) = 8{:}25805$$

$$\textbf{next}(\text{``witch''}, 22{:}288) = 22{:}310 \qquad\quad \textbf{prev}(\text{``witch''}, 22{:}310) = 22{:}288$$
$$\textbf{next}(\text{``hurlyburly''}, 9{:}30963) = 22{:}293 \qquad \textbf{prev}(\text{``hurlyburly''}, 22{:}293) = 9{:}30963$$
$$\textbf{next}(\text{``witch''}, 37{:}10675) = \infty \qquad\qquad \textbf{prev}(\text{``witch''}, 1{:}1598) = -\infty$$

Offsets within a document start at 1 and range up to the length of the document. We continue to use $-\infty$ and ∞ as beginning-of-file and end-of-file markers despite the slight notational inconsistency, with $-\infty$ read as $-\infty{:}{-}\infty$ and ∞ read as $\infty{:}\infty$. When term positions are expressed in this form, their values are compared by treating the document number as the primary key:

$$n{:}m < n'{:}m' \text{ if and only if } (n < n' \text{ or } (n = n' \text{ and } m < m')).$$

We refer to an index whose structure has been optimized to support document-oriented retrieval as a *schema-dependent* inverted index, because the division of the text into retrieval units (its schema) is determined at the time its inverted index is constructed.

An index without these optimizations is a *schema-independent* inverted index. A schema-independent index allows the definition of a document to be specified at query time, with a possible cost in execution time in comparison with its schema-dependent equivalent.

To support ranking algorithms, a schema-dependent inverted index usually maintains various document-oriented statistics. We adopt the following notation for these statistics:

N_t	*document frequency*	the number of documents in the collection containing the term t
$f_{t,d}$	*term frequency*	the number of times term t appears in document d
l_d	*document length*	measured in tokens
l_{avg}	*average length*	average document length across the collection
N	*document count*	total number of documents in the collection

Note that $\sum_{d \in \mathcal{C}} l_d = \sum_{t \in \mathcal{V}} l_t = l_{\mathcal{C}}$, and $l_{avg} = l_{\mathcal{C}}/N$.

Over the collection of Shakespeare's plays, $l_{avg} = 34363$. If $t = $ "witch" and $d = 22$ (i.e., $d = Macbeth$), then $N_t = 18$, $f_{t,d} = 52$, and $l_d = 26805$. In a schema-dependent index, these statistics are usually maintained as an integral part of the index data structures. With a schema-independent index, they have to be computed at query time with the methods of our inverted index ADT (see Exercise 2.5).

To help us write algorithms that operate at the document level, we define additional methods of our inverted index ADT. The first two break down positions into separate docids and offsets:

docid(*position*)   returns the docid associated with a *position*

offset(*position*)   returns the within-document offset associated with a *position*

When a posting takes the form $[u{:}v]$, these methods simply return u and v, respectively. They may also be implemented on top of a schema-independent index, albeit slightly less efficiently.

We also define document-oriented versions of our basic inverted index methods that will prove useful in later parts of this chapter:

firstDoc(t)	returns the docid of the first document containing the term t
lastDoc(t)	returns the docid of the last document containing the term t
nextDoc(t, *current*)	returns the docid of the first document after *current* that contains the term t
prevDoc(t, *current*)	returns the docid of the last document before *current* that contains the term t

In a schema-dependent index, many postings may now share a common prefix in their docids. We can separate out these docids to produce postings of the form

$$(d, f_{t,d}, \langle p_0, ..., p_{f_{t,d}} \rangle)$$

where $\langle p_0, ..., p_{f_{t,d}} \rangle$ is the list of the offsets of all $f_{t,d}$ occurrences of the term t within document d. Besides eliminating unnecessary repetition, this notation better reflects how the postings are actually represented in an implementation of a schema-dependent index. Using this notation, we would write the postings list for the term "witch" as

$$(1, 3, \langle 1598, 27555, 31463 \rangle), \ ..., \ (22, 52, \langle 266, 288, ... \rangle), \ ..., \ (37, 1, \langle 10675 \rangle)$$

In specialized circumstances it may not be necessary for positional offsets to be maintained by an inverted index. Basic keyword search is sufficient for some applications, and effective ranking can be supported with document-level statistics. For the simplest ranking and filtering techniques, these document-level statistics are not even required.

Based on the type of information found in each postings list, we can distinguish four types of inverted indices, the first three of which are schema-dependent:

- A *docid index* is the simplest index type. For each term, it contains the document identifiers of all documents in which the term appears. Despite its simplicity, this index type is sufficient to support filtering with basic Boolean queries (Section 2.2.3) and a simple form of relevance ranking known as coordination level ranking (Exercise 2.7).

- In a *frequency index*, each entry in an inverted list consists of two components: a document ID and a term frequency value. Each posting in a frequency index is of the form $(d, f_{t,d})$. Frequency indices are sufficient to support many effective ranking methods (Section 2.2.1), but are insufficient for phrase searching and advanced filtering.

- A *positional index* consists of postings of the form $(d, f_{t,d}, \langle p_1, ..., p_{f_{t,d}} \rangle)$. Positional indices support all search operations supported by a frequency index. In addition, they can be used to realize phrase queries, proximity ranking (Section 2.2.2), and other query types that take the exact position of a query term within a document into account, including all types of structural queries.

- A *schema-independent index* does not include the document-oriented optimizations found in a positional index, but otherwise the two may be used interchangeably.

Table 2.1 Text fragment from Shakespeare's *Romeo and Juliet*, act I, scene 1.

Document ID	Document Content
1	Do you quarrel, sir?
2	Quarrel sir! no, sir!
3	If you do, sir, I am for you: I serve as good a man as you.
4	No better.
5	Well, sir.

Table 2.2 Postings lists for the terms shown in Table 2.1. In each case the length of the list is appended to the start of the actual list.

Term	Docid List	Positional List	Schema-Independent
a	1; 3	1; $(3,1,\langle 13\rangle)$	1; 21
am	1; 3	1; $(3,1,\langle 6\rangle)$	1; 14
as	1; 3	1; $(3,2,\langle 11,15\rangle)$	2; 19, 23
better	1; 4	1; $(4,1,\langle 2\rangle)$	1; 26
do	2; 1, 3	2; $(1,1,\langle 1\rangle),(3,1,\langle 3\rangle)$	2; 1, 11
for	1; 3	1; $(3,1,\langle 7\rangle)$	1; 15
good	1; 3	1; $(3,1,\langle 12\rangle)$	1; 20
i	1; 3	1; $(3,2,\langle 5,9\rangle)$	2; 13, 17
if	1; 3	1; $(3,1,\langle 1\rangle)$	1; 9
man	1; 3	1; $(3,1,\langle 14\rangle)$	1; 22
no	2; 2, 4	2; $(2,1,\langle 3\rangle),(4,1,\langle 1\rangle)$	2; 7, 25
quarrel	2; 1, 2	2; $(1,1,\langle 3\rangle),(2,1,\langle 1\rangle)$	2; 3, 5
serve	1; 3	1; $(3,1,\langle 10\rangle)$	1; 18
sir	4; 1, 2, 3, 5	4; $(1,1,\langle 4\rangle),(2,2,\langle 2,4\rangle),(3,1,\langle 4\rangle),(5,1,\langle 2\rangle)$	5; 4, 6, 8, 12, 28
well	1; 5	1; $(5,1,\langle 1\rangle)$	1; 27
you	2; 1, 3	2; $(1,1,\langle 2\rangle),(3,3,\langle 2,8,16\rangle)$	4; 2, 10, 16, 24

Table 2.1 shows an excerpt from Shakespeare's *Romeo and Juliet*. Here, each line is treated as a document — we have omitted the tags to help shorten the example to a reasonable length. Table 2.2 shows the corresponding postings lists for all terms that appear in the excerpt, giving examples of docid lists, positional postings lists, and schema-independent postings lists.

Of the four different index types, the docid index is always the smallest one because it contains the least information. The positional and the schema-independent indices consume the greatest space, between two times and five times as much space as a frequency index, and between three times and seven times as much as a docid index, for typical text collections. The exact ratio depends on the lengths of the documents in the collection, the skewedness of the term distribution, and the impact of compression. Index sizes for the four different index types and

Table 2.3 Index sizes for various index types and three test collections, with and without applying index compression techniques. In each case the first number refers to an index in which each component is stored as a simple 32-bit integer, and the second number refers to an index in which each entry is compressed using a byte-aligned encoding method.

	Shakespeare	TREC	GOV2
Docid index	n/a	578 MB/200 MB	37751 MB/12412 MB
Frequency index	n/a	1110 MB/333 MB	73593 MB/21406 MB
Positional index	n/a	2255 MB/739 MB	245538 MB/78819 MB
Schema-independent index	5.7 MB/2.7 MB	1190 MB/533 MB	173854 MB/65960 MB

our three example collections are shown in Table 2.3. Index compression has a substantial effect on index size, and it is discussed in detail in Chapter 6.

With the introduction of document-oriented indices, we have greatly expanded the notation associated with inverted indices from the four basic methods introduced at the beginning of the chapter. Table 2.4 provides a summary of this notation for easy reference throughout the remainder of the book.

2.2 Retrieval and Ranking

Building on the data structures of the previous section, this section presents three simple retrieval methods. The first two methods produce ranked results, ordering the documents in the collection according to their expected relevance to the query. Our third retrieval method allows Boolean filters to be applied to the collection, identifying those documents that match a predicate.

Queries for ranked retrieval are often expressed as *term vectors*. When you type a query into an IR system, you express the components of this vector by entering the terms with white space between them. For example, the query

william   shakespeare   marriage

might be entered into a commercial Web search engine with the intention of retrieving a ranked list of Web pages concerning Shakespeare's marriage to Anne Hathaway. To make the nature of these queries more obvious, we write term vectors explicitly using the notation $\langle t_1, t_2, ..., t_n \rangle$. The query above would then be written

$\langle$ "william", "shakespeare", "marriage" $\rangle$.

You may wonder why we represent these queries as vectors rather than sets. Representation as a vector (or, rather, a *list*, since we do not assume a fixed-dimensional vector space) is useful when terms are repeated in a query and when the ordering of terms is significant. In ranking formulae, we use the notation q_t to indicate the number of times term t appears in the query.

Table 2.4   Summary of notation for inverted indices.

Basic inverted index methods	
first(*term*)	returns the first position at which the *term* occurs
last(*term*)	returns the last position at which the *term* occurs
next(*term, current*)	returns the next position at which the *term* occurs after the *current* position
prev(*term, current*)	returns the previous position at which the *term* occurs before the *current* position

Document-oriented equivalents of the basic methods	
firstDoc(*term*), **lastDoc**(*term*), **nextDoc**(*term, current*), **lastDoc**(*term, current*)	

Schema-dependent index positions	
n:m	$n = docid$ and $m = offset$
docid(*position*)	returns the docid associated with a *position*
offset(*position*)	returns the within-document offset associated with a *position*

Symbols for document and term statistics	
l_t	the length of t's postings list
N_t	the number of documents containing t
$f_{t,d}$	the number of occurrences of t within the document d
l_d	length of the document d, in tokens
l_{avg}	the average document length in the collection
N	the total number of documents in the collection

The structure of postings lists	
docid index	$d_1, d_2, \ldots, d_{N_t}$
frequency index	$(d_1, f_{t,d_1}), (d_2, f_{t,d_2}), \ldots$
positional index	$(d_1, f_{t,d_1}, \langle p_1, \ldots, p_{f_{t,d_1}} \rangle), \ldots$
schema-independent	$p_1, p_2, \ldots, p_{l_t}$

Boolean predicates are composed with the standard Boolean operators (AND, OR, NOT). The result of a Boolean query is a set of documents matching the predicate. For example, the Boolean query

"william" AND "shakespeare" AND NOT ("marlowe" OR "bacon")

specifies those documents containing the terms "william" and "shakespeare" but not containing either "marlowe" or "bacon". In later chapters we will extend this standard set of Boolean operators, which will allow us to specify additional constraints on the result set.

There is a key difference in the conventional interpretations of term vectors for ranked retrieval and predicates for Boolean retrieval. Boolean predicates are usually interpreted as strict filters — if a document does not match the predicate, it is not returned in the result set. Term vectors, on the other hand, are often interpreted as summarizing an information need. Not all the terms in the vector need to appear in a document for it to be returned. For example, if we are interested in the life and works of Shakespeare, we might attempt to create an exhaustive (and exhausting) query to describe our information need by listing as many related terms as we can:

> william shakespeare stratford avon london plays sonnets poems tragedy comedy poet playwright players actor anne hathaway susanna hamnet judith folio othello hamlet macbeth king lear tempest romeo juliet julius caesar twelfth night antony cleopatra venus adonis willie hughe wriothesley henry ...

Although many relevant Web pages will contain some of these terms, few will contain all of them. It is the role of a ranked retrieval method to determine the impact that any missing terms will have on the final document ordering.

Boolean retrieval combines naturally with ranked retrieval into a two-step retrieval process. A Boolean predicate is first applied to restrict retrieval to a subset of the document collection. The documents contained in the resulting subcollection are then ranked with respect to a given topic. Commercial Web search engines follow this two-step retrieval process. Until recently, most of these systems would interpret the query

> william   shakespeare   marriage

as both a Boolean conjunction of the terms — "william" AND "shakespeare" AND "marriage" — and as a term vector for ranking — ⟨"william", "shakespeare", "marriage"⟩. For a page to be returned as a result, each of the terms was required to appear in the page itself or in the anchor text linking to the page.

Filtering out relevant pages that are missing one or more terms may have the paradoxical effect of harming performance when extra terms are added to a query. In principle, adding extra terms should improve performance by serving to better define the information need. Although some commercial Web search engines now apply less restrictive filters, allowing additional documents to appear in the ranked results, this two-step retrieval process still takes place. These systems may handle longer queries poorly, returning few or no results in some cases.

In determining an appropriate document ranking, basic ranked retrieval methods compare simple features of the documents. One of the most important of these features is *term frequency*, $f_{t,d}$, the number of times query term t appears in document d. Given two documents d_1 and d_2, if a query term appears many more times in d_1 than in d_2, this may suggest that d_1 should be ranked higher than d_2, other factors being equal. For the query ⟨"william", "shakespeare", "marriage"⟩, the repeated occurrence of the term "marriage" throughout a document may suggest that it should be ranked above one containing the term only once.

Another important feature is *term proximity*. If query terms appear closer together in document d_1 than in document d_2, this may suggest that d_1 should be ranked higher than d_2, other factors being equal. In some cases, terms form a phrase ("william shakespeare") or other collocation, but the importance of proximity is not merely a matter of phrase matching. The co-occurrence of "william", "shakespeare", and "marriage" together in a fragment such as

> ... while no direct evidence of the **marriage** of Anne Hathaway and **William Shakespeare** exists, the wedding is believed to have taken place in November of 1582, while she was pregnant with his child ...

suggests a relationship between the terms that might not exist if they appeared farther apart.

Other features help us make trade-offs between competing factors. For example, should a thousand-word document containing four occurrences of "william", five of "shakespeare", and two of "marriage" be ranked before or after a five-hundred-word document containing three occurrences of "william", two of "shakespeare", and seven of "marriage"? These features include the lengths of the documents (l_d) relative to the average document length (l_{avg}), as well as the number of documents in which a term appears (N_t) relative to the total number of documents in the collection (N).

Although the basic features listed above form the core of many retrieval models and ranking methods, including those discussed in this chapter, additional features may contribute as well. In some application areas, such as Web search, the exploitation of these additional features is critical to the success of a search engine.

One important feature is document structure. For example, a query term may be treated differently if it appears in the title of a document rather than in its body. Often the relationship between documents is important, such as the links between Web documents. In the context of Web search, the analysis of the links between Web pages may allow us to assign them a query-independent ordering or *static rank*, which can then be a factor in retrieval. Finally, when a large group of people make regular use of an IR system within an enterprise or on the Web, their behavior can be monitored to improve performance. For example, if results from one Web site are clicked more than results from another, this behavior may indicate a user preference for one site over the other — other factors being equal — that can be exploited to improve ranking. In later chapters these and other additional features will be covered in detail.

2.2.1   The Vector Space Model

The *vector space model* is one of the oldest and best known of the information retrieval models we examine in this book. Starting in the 1960s and continuing into 1990s, the method was developed and promulgated by Gerald Salton, who was perhaps the most influential of the early IR researchers. As a result, the vector space model is intimately associated with the field as a whole and has been adapted to many IR problems beyond ranked retrieval, including document clustering and classification, in which it continues to play an important role. In recent years, the

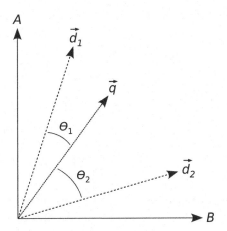

Figure 2.8 Document similarity under the vector space model. Angles are computed between a query vector $\vec{q}$ and two document vectors $\vec{d_1}$ and $\vec{d_2}$. Because $\theta_1 < \theta_2$, d_1 should be ranked higher than d_2.

vector space model has been largely overshadowed by probabilistic models, language models, and machine learning approaches (see Part III). Nonetheless, the simple intuition underlying it, as well as its long history, makes the vector space model an ideal vehicle for introducing ranked retrieval.

The basic idea is simple. Queries as well as documents are represented as vectors in a high-dimensional space in which each vector component corresponds to a term in the vocabulary of the collection. This query vector representation stands in contrast to the term vector representation of the previous section, which included only the terms appearing in the query. Given a query vector and a set of document vectors, one for each document in the collection, we rank the documents by computing a similarity measure between the query vector and each document vector, comparing the angle between them. The smaller the angle, the more similar the vectors. Figure 2.8 illustrates the basic idea, using vectors with only two components (A and B).

Linear algebra provides us with a handy formula to determine the angle θ between two vectors. Given two $|\mathcal{V}|$-dimensional vectors $\vec{x} = \langle x_1, x_2, ..., x_{|\mathcal{V}|} \rangle$ and $\vec{y} = \langle y_1, y_2, ..., y_{|\mathcal{V}|} \rangle$, we have

$$\vec{x} \cdot \vec{y} = |\vec{x}| \cdot |\vec{y}| \cdot \cos(\theta). \tag{2.8}$$

where $\vec{x} \cdot \vec{y}$ represents the *dot product* (also called the *inner product* or *scalar product*) between the vectors; $|\vec{x}|$ and $|\vec{y}|$ represent the lengths of the vectors. The dot product is defined as

$$\vec{x} \cdot \vec{y} = \sum_{i=1}^{|\mathcal{V}|} x_i \cdot y_i \tag{2.9}$$

and the length of a vector may be computed from the Euclidean distance formula

$$|\vec{x}| = \sqrt{\sum_{i=1}^{|\mathcal{V}|} x_i{}^2} \, .$$

(2.10)

Substituting and rearranging these equations gives

$$\cos(\theta) = \frac{\vec{x}}{|\vec{x}|} \cdot \frac{\vec{y}}{|\vec{y}|} = \frac{\sum_{i=1}^{|\mathcal{V}|} x_i \, y_i}{\left(\sqrt{\sum_{i=1}^{|\mathcal{V}|} x_i{}^2}\right)\left(\sqrt{\sum_{i=1}^{|\mathcal{V}|} y_i{}^2}\right)} \, .$$

(2.11)

We could now apply arccos to determine θ, but because the cosine is monotonically decreasing with respect to the angle θ, it is convenient to stop at this point and retain the cosine itself as our measure of similarity. If $\theta = 0°$, then the vectors are colinear, as similar as possible, with $\cos(\theta) = 1$. If $\theta = 90°$, then the vectors are orthogonal, as dissimilar as possible, with $\cos(\theta) = 0$.

To summarize, given a document vector $\vec{d}$ and a query vector $\vec{q}$, the cosine similarity $sim(\vec{d}, \vec{q})$ is computed as

$$sim(\vec{d}, \vec{q}) = \frac{\vec{d}}{|\vec{d}|} \cdot \frac{\vec{q}}{|\vec{q}|} \, ,$$

(2.12)

the dot product of the document and query vectors normalized to unit length. Provided all components of the vectors are nonnegative, the value of this *cosine similarity measure* ranges from 0 to 1, with its value increasing with increasing similarity.

Naturally, for a collection of even modest size, this vector space model produces vectors with millions of dimensions. This high-dimensionality might appear inefficient at first glance, but in many circumstances the query vector is sparse, with all but a few components being zero. For example, the vector corresponding to the query ⟨"william", "shakespeare", "marriage"⟩ has only three nonzero components. To compute the length of this vector, or its dot product with a document vector, we need only consider the components corresponding to these three terms. On the other hand, a document vector typically has a nonzero component for each unique term contained in the document, which may consist of thousands of terms. However, the length of a document vector is independent of the query. It may be precomputed and stored in a frequency or positional index along with other document-specific information, or it may be applied to normalize the document vector in advance, with the components of the normalized vector taking the place of term frequencies in the postings lists.

Although queries are usually short, the symmetry between how documents and queries are treated in the vector space model allows entire documents to be used as queries. Equation 2.12 may then be viewed as a formula determining the similarity between two documents. Treating a document as a query is one possible method for implementing the "Similar pages" and "More like this" features seen in some commercial search engines.

As a ranking method the cosine similarity measure has intuitive appeal and natural simplicity. If we can appropriately represent queries and documents as vectors, cosine similarity may be used to rank the documents with respect to the queries. In representing a document or query as a vector, a *weight* must be assigned to each term that represents the value of the corresponding component of the vector. Throughout the long history of the vector space model, many formulae for assigning these weights have been proposed and evaluated. With few exceptions, these formulae may be characterized as belonging to a general family known as *TF-IDF weights*.

When assigning a weight in a document vector, the TF-IDF weights are computed by taking the product of a function of term frequency $(f_{t,d})$ and a function of the inverse of document frequency $(1/N_t)$. When assigning a weight to a query vector, the within-query term frequency (q_t) may be substituted for $f_{t,d}$, in essence treating the query as a tiny document. It is also possible (and not at all unusual) to use different TF and IDF functions to determine weights for document vectors and query vectors.

We emphasize that a TF-IDF weight is a product of *functions* of term frequency and inverse document frequency. A common error is to use the raw $f_{t,d}$ value for the term frequency component, which may lead to poor performance.

Over the years a number of variants for both the TF and the IDF functions have been proposed and evaluated. The IDF functions typically relate the document frequency to the total number of documents in the collection (N). The basic intuition behind the IDF functions is that a term appearing in many documents should be assigned a lower weight than a term appearing in few documents. Of the two functions, IDF comes closer to having a "standard form",

$$\text{IDF} \; = \; \log(N/N_t), \qquad\qquad\qquad (2.13)$$

with most IDF variants structured as a logarithm of a fraction involving N_t and N.

The basic intuition behind the various TF functions is that a term appearing many times in a document should be assigned a higher weight for that document than for a document in which it appears fewer times. Another important consideration behind the definition of a TF function is that its value should not necessarily increase linearly with $f_{t,d}$. Although two occurrences of a term should be given more weight than one occurrence, they shouldn't necessarily be given twice the weight. The following function meets these requirements and appears in much of Salton's later work:

$$\text{TF} \; = \; \begin{cases} \log(f_{t,d}) + 1 & \text{if } f_{t,d} > 0, \\ 0 & \text{otherwise.} \end{cases} \qquad\qquad (2.14)$$

When this equation is used with a query vector, $f_{t,d}$ is replaced by q_t the query term frequency of t in q. We use this equation, along with Equation 2.13, to compute both document and query weights in the example that follows.

Consider the *Romeo and Juliet* document collection in Table 2.1 (page 50) and the corresponding postings lists given in Table 2.2. Because there are five documents in the collection and "sir" appears in four of them, the IDF value for "sir" is

$$\log(N/f_{\mathrm{sir}}) \;=\; \log(5/4) \;\approx\; 0.32.$$

In this formula and in other TF-IDF formulae involving logarithms, the base of the logarithm is usually unimportant. As necessary, for purposes of this example and others throughout the book, we assume a base of 2.

Because "sir" appears twice in document 2, the TF-IDF value for the corresponding component of its vector is

$$(\log(f_{\mathrm{sir},2}) + 1) \cdot (\log(N/f_{\mathrm{sir}})) \;=\; (\log(2)+1) \cdot (\log(5/4)) \;\approx\; 0.64.$$

Computing TF-IDF values for the remaining components and the remaining documents, gives the following set of vectors:

$$\vec{d_1} \;\approx\; \langle 0.00, 0.00, 0.00, 0.00, 1.32, 0.00, 0.00, 0.00, 0.00, 0.00, 0.00, 1.32, 0.00, 0.32, 0.00, 1.32 \rangle$$
$$\vec{d_2} \;\approx\; \langle 0.00, 0.00, 0.00, 0.00, 0.00, 0.00, 0.00, 0.00, 0.00, 0.00, 1.32, 1.32, 0.00, 0.64, 0.00, 0.00 \rangle$$
$$\vec{d_3} \;\approx\; \langle 2.32, 2.32, 4.64, 0.00, 1.32, 2.32, 2.32, 4.64, 2.32, 2.32, 0.00, 0.00, 2.32, 0.32, 0.00, 3.42 \rangle$$
$$\vec{d_4} \;\approx\; \langle 0.00, 0.00, 0.00, 2.32, 0.00, 0.00, 0.00, 0.00, 0.00, 0.00, 1.32, 0.00, 0.00, 0.00, 0.00, 0.00 \rangle$$
$$\vec{d_5} \;\approx\; \langle 0.00, 0.00, 0.00, 0.00, 0.00, 0.00, 0.00, 0.00, 0.00, 0.00, 0.00, 0.00, 0.00, 0.32, 2.32, 0.00 \rangle$$

where the components are sorted alphabetically according to their corresponding terms. Normalizing these vectors, dividing by their lengths, produces:

$$\vec{d_1}/|\vec{d_1}| \;\approx\; \langle 0.00, 0.00, 0.00, 0.00, 0.57, 0.00, 0.00, 0.00, 0.00, 0.00, 0.00, 0.57, 0.00, 0.14, 0.00, 0.57 \rangle$$
$$\vec{d_2}/|\vec{d_2}| \;\approx\; \langle 0.00, 0.00, 0.00, 0.00, 0.00, 0.00, 0.00, 0.00, 0.00, 0.00, 0.67, 0.67, 0.00, 0.33, 0.00, 0.00 \rangle$$
$$\vec{d_3}/|\vec{d_3}| \;\approx\; \langle 0.24, 0.24, 0.48, 0.00, 0.14, 0.24, 0.24, 0.48, 0.24, 0.24, 0.00, 0.00, 0.24, 0.03, 0.00, 0.35 \rangle$$
$$\vec{d_4}/|\vec{d_4}| \;\approx\; \langle 0.00, 0.00, 0.00, 0.87, 0.00, 0.00, 0.00, 0.00, 0.00, 0.00, 0.49, 0.00, 0.00, 0.00, 0.00, 0.00 \rangle$$
$$\vec{d_5}/|\vec{d_5}| \;\approx\; \langle 0.00, 0.00, 0.00, 0.00, 0.00, 0.00, 0.00, 0.00, 0.00, 0.00, 0.00, 0.00, 0.00, 0.14, 0.99, 0.00 \rangle$$

If we wish to rank these five documents with respect to the query $\langle$ "quarrel", "sir" $\rangle$, we first construct the query vector, normalized by length:

$$\vec{q}/|\vec{q}| \;\approx\; \langle 0.00, 0.00, 0.00, 0.00, 0.00, 0.00, 0.00, 0.00, 0.00, 0.00, 0.00, 0.97, 0.00, 0.24, 0.00, 0.00 \rangle$$

rankCosine $(\langle t_1, ..., t_n \rangle, \text{k}) \equiv$
1   $j \leftarrow 1$
2   $d \leftarrow \min_{1 \leq i \leq n} \textbf{nextDoc}\ (t_i, -\infty)$
3   **while** $d < \infty$ **do**
4       $Result[j].docid \leftarrow d$
5       $Result[j].score \leftarrow \frac{\vec{d}}{|\vec{d}|} \cdot \frac{\vec{q}}{|\vec{q}|}$
6       $j \leftarrow j + 1$
7       $d \leftarrow \min_{1 \leq i \leq n} \textbf{nextDoc}\ (t_i, d)$
8   sort *Result* by *score*
9   **return** $Result[1..k]$

Figure 2.9   Query processing for ranked retrieval under the vector space model. Given the term vector $\langle t_1, ..., t_n \rangle$ (with corresponding query vector $\vec{q}$), the function identifies the top k documents.

Computing the dot product between this vector and each document vector gives the following cosine similarity values:

Document ID	1	2	3	4	5
Similarity	0.59	0.73	0.01	0.00	0.03

The final document ranking is 2, 1, 5, 3, 4.

Query processing for the vector space model is straightforward (Figure 2.9), essentially performing a merge of the postings lists for the query terms. Docids and corresponding scores are accumulated in an array of records as the scores are computed. The function operates on one document at a time. During each iteration of the **while** loop, the algorithm computes the score for document d (with corresponding document vector $\vec{d}$), stores the docid and score in the array of records *Result*, and determines the next docid for processing. The algorithm does not explicitly compute a score for documents that do not contain any of the query terms, which are implicitly assigned a score of zero. At the end of the function, *Result* is sorted by *score* and the top k documents are returned.

For many retrieval applications, the entire ranked list of documents is not required. Instead we return at most k documents, where the value of k is determined by the needs of the application environment. For example, a Web search engine might return only the first $k = 10$ or 20 results on its first page. It then may seem inefficient to compute the score for every document containing any of the terms, even a single term with low weight, when only the top k documents are required. This apparent inefficiency has led to proposals for improved query processing methods that are applicable to other IR models as well as to the vector space model. These query processing methods will be discussed in Chapter 5.

Of the document features listed at the start of this section — term frequency, term proximity, document frequency, and document length — the vector space model makes explicit use of only term frequency and document frequency. Document length is handled implicitly when the vectors are normalized to unit length. If one document is twice as long as another but contains the same terms in the same proportions, their normalized vectors are identical. Term proximity is not considered by the model at all. This property has led to the colorful description of the vector space model (and other IR models with the same property) as a "bag of words" model.

We based the version of the vector space model presented in this section on the introductory descriptions given in Salton's later works. In practice, implementations of the vector space model often eliminate both length normalization and the IDF factor in document vectors, in part to improve efficiency. Moreover, the Euclidean length normalization inherent in the cosine similarity measure has proved inadequate to handle collections containing mixtures of long and short documents, and substantial adjustments are required to support these collections. These efficiency and effectiveness issues are examined in Section 2.3.

The vector space model may be criticized for its entirely heuristic nature. Beyond intuition, its simple mathematics, and the experiments of Section 2.3, we do not provide further justification for it. IR models introduced in later chapters (Chapters 8 and 9) are more solidly grounded in theoretical frameworks. Perhaps as a result, these models are more adaptable, and are more readily extended to accommodate additional document features.

2.2.2 Proximity Ranking

The vector space ranking method from the previous section explicitly depends only on TF and IDF. In contrast, the method detailed in this section explicitly depends only on term proximity. Term frequency is handled implicitly; document frequency, document length, and other features play no role at all.

When the components of a term vector $\langle t_1, t_2, \ldots, t_n \rangle$ appear in close proximity within a document, it suggests that the document is more likely to be relevant than one in which the terms appear farther apart. Given a term vector $\langle t_1, t_2, \ldots, t_n \rangle$, we define a *cover* for the vector as an interval in the collection $[u, v]$ that contains a match to all the terms without containing a smaller interval $[u', v']$, $u \leq u' \leq v' \leq v$, that also contains a match to all the terms. The candidate phrases defined on page 39 are a special case of a cover in which all the terms appear in order.

In the collection of Table 2.1 (page 50), the intervals [1:2, 1:4], [3:2, 3:4], and [3:4, 3:8] are covers for the term vector $\langle$"you", "sir"$\rangle$. The interval [3:4, 3:16] is not a cover, even though both terms are contained within it, because it contains the cover [3:4, 3:8]. Similarly, there are two covers for the term vector $\langle$"quarrel", "sir"$\rangle$: [1:3, 1:4] and [2:1, 2:2].

Note that covers may overlap. However, a token matching a term t_i appears in at most $n \cdot l$ covers, where l is the length of the shortest postings list for the terms in the vector. To see that there may be as many as $n \cdot l$ covers for the term vector $\langle t_1, t_2, \ldots, t_n \rangle$, consider a collection in which all the terms occur in the same order the same number of times:

... t_1 ... t_2 ... t_3 ... t_n ... t_1 ... t_2 ... t_3 ... t_n ... t_1 ...

nextCover $(\langle t_1, ..., t_n \rangle,\ position) \equiv$

1     $v \leftarrow \max_{1 \le i \le n}(\mathbf{next}(t_i,\ position))$

2   **if** $v = \infty$ **then**

3   **return** $[\infty, \infty]$

4     $u \leftarrow \min_{1 \le i \le n}(\mathbf{prev}(t_i,\ v + 1))$

5   **if** $\mathbf{docid}(u) = \mathbf{docid}(v)$ **then**

6   **return** $[u, v]$

7   **else**

8   **return** nextCover$(\langle t_1, ..., t_n \rangle,\ u)$

Figure 2.10   Function to locate the next occurrence of a cover for the term vector $\langle t_1, ..., t_n \rangle$ after a given position.

We leave the demonstration that there may be no more than $n \cdot l$ covers to Exercise 2.8. A new cover starts at each occurrence of a term from the vector. Thus, the total number of covers for a term vector is constrained by $n \cdot l$ and does not depend on the length of the longest postings list L. With respect to proximity ranking, we define κ to be the number of covers for a term vector occurring in a document collection where $\kappa \le n \cdot l$.

Perhaps not surprisingly, our algorithm to compute covers is a close cousin of the phrase searching algorithm in Figure 2.2 (page 36). The function in Figure 2.10 locates the next occurrence of a cover after a given position. On line 1, the algorithm determines the smallest position v such that the interval $[position, v]$ contains all the terms in the vector. A cover starting after u cannot end before this position. On line 4, the algorithm shrinks the interval ending at v, adjusting u so that no smaller interval ending at v contains all the terms. The check at line 5 determines whether u and v are contained in the same document. If not, **nextCover** is called recursively.

This last check is required only because the cover will ultimately contribute to a document's score for ranking. Technically, the interval [1:4, 2:1] is a perfectly acceptable cover for the term vector $\langle$ "quarrel", "sir"$\rangle$. However, in a schema-dependent index, a cover that crosses document boundaries is unlikely to be meaningful.

Ranking is based on two assumptions: (1) the shorter the cover, the more likely that the text containing the cover is relevant, and (2) the more covers contained in a document, the more likely that the document is relevant. These assumptions are consistent with intuition. The first assumption suggests that a score for an individual cover may be based on its length. The second assumption suggests that a document may be assigned a score by summing the individual scores of the covers contained within it. Combining these ideas, we score a document d containing covers $[u_1, v_1]$, $[u_2, v_2]$, $[u_3, v_3]$, ... using the formula

$$score(d) \;=\; \sum \left(\frac{1}{v_i - u_i + 1} \right). \qquad (2.15)$$

rankProximity $(\langle t_1, ..., t_n \rangle, \text{k}) \equiv$

1    $[u, v] \leftarrow$ **nextCover**$(\langle t_0, t_1, ..., t_n \rangle, -\infty)$

2    $d \leftarrow$ **docid**(u)

3    $score \leftarrow 0$

4    $j \leftarrow 0$

5   **while** $u < \infty$ **do**

6   **if** $d <$ **docid**(u) **then**

7        $j \leftarrow j + 1$

8        $Result[j].docid \leftarrow d$

9        $Result[j].score \leftarrow score$

10        $d \leftarrow$ **docid**(u)

11        $score \leftarrow 0$

12      $score \leftarrow score + 1/(v - u + 1)$

13      $[u, v] \leftarrow$ **nextCover**$(\langle t_1, ..., t_n \rangle, u)$

14   **if** $d < \infty$ **then**

15      $j \leftarrow j + 1$

16      $Result[j].docid \leftarrow d$

17      $Result[j].score \leftarrow score$

18   sort $Result[1..j]$ by $score$

19   **return** $Result[1..k]$

Figure 2.11   Query processing for proximity ranking. The **nextCover** function from Figure 2.10 is called to generate each cover.

Query processing for proximity ranking is presented in Figure 2.11. Covers are generated by calls to the **nextCover** function and processed one by one in the while loop of lines 5–13. The number of covers κ in the collection is exactly equal to the number of calls to **nextCover** at line 13. When a document boundary is crossed (line 6), the score and docid are stored in an array of records *Result* (lines 8–9). After all covers are processed, information on the last document is recorded in the array (lines 14–17), the array is sorted by score (line 18), and the top k documents are returned (line 19).

As the **rankProximity** function makes calls to the **nextCover** function, the position passed as its second argument strictly increases. In turn, as the **nextCover** function makes successive calls to the **next** and **prev** methods, the values of their second arguments also strictly increase. As we did for the phrase searching algorithm of Section 2.1.1, we may exploit this property by implementing **next** and **prev** using galloping search. Following a similar argument, when galloping search is used, the overall time complexity of the **rankProximity** algorithm is $O\left(n^2 l \cdot \log\left(L/l\right)\right)$.

Note that the time complexity is quadratic in n, the size of the term vector, because there may be $O(n \cdot l)$ covers in the worst case. Fortunately, the adaptive nature of the algorithm comes to our assistance again, giving a time complexity of $O\left(n \cdot \kappa \cdot \log\left(L/\kappa\right)\right)$.

For a document to receive a nonzero score, all terms must be present in it. In this respect, proximity ranking shares the behavior exhibited until recently by many commercial search engines. When applied to the document collection of Table 2.1 to rank the collection with respect to the query ⟨"you", "sir"⟩, proximity ranking assigns a score of 0.33 to document 1, a score of 0.53 to document 3, and a score of 0 to the remaining documents.

When applied to rank the same collection with respect to the query ⟨"quarrel","sir"⟩, the method assigns scores of 0.50 to documents 1 and 2, and a score of 0.00 to documents 3 to 5. Unlike cosine similarity, the second occurrence of "sir" in document 2 does not contribute to the document's score. The frequency of individual terms is not a factor in proximity ranking; rather, the frequency and proximity of their co-occurrence are factors. It is conceivable that a document could include many matches to all the terms but contain only a single cover, with the query terms clustered into discrete groups.

2.2.3 Boolean Retrieval

Apart from the implicit Boolean filters applied by Web search engines, explicit support for Boolean queries is important in specific application areas such as digital libraries and the legal domain. In contrast to ranked retrieval, Boolean retrieval returns sets of documents rather than ranked lists. Under the Boolean retrieval model, a term t is considered to specify the set of documents containing it. The standard Boolean operators (AND, OR, and NOT) are used to construct Boolean queries, which are interpreted as operations over these sets, as follows:

A AND B intersection of A and B ($A \cap B$)

A OR B union of A and B ($A \cup B$)

NOT A complement of A with respect to the document collection ($\bar{A}$)

where A and B are terms or other Boolean queries. For example, over the collection in Table 2.1, the query

("quarrel" OR "sir") AND "you"

specifies the set $\{1, 3\}$, whereas the query

("quarrel" OR "sir") AND NOT "you"

specifies the set $\{2, 5\}$.

Our algorithm for solving Boolean queries is another variant of the phrase searching algorithm of Figure 2.2 and the cover finding algorithm of Figure 2.10. The algorithm locates *candidate solutions* to a Boolean query where each candidate solution represents a *range* of documents that together satisfy the Boolean query, such that no smaller range of documents contained within it also satisfies the query. When the range represented by a candidate solution has a length of 1, this single document satisfies the query and should be included in the result set.

The same overall method of operation appears in both of the previous algorithms. In the phrase search algorithm, lines 1–6 identify a range containing all the terms in order, such that no smaller range contained within it also contains all the terms in order. In the cover finding algorithm, lines 1–4 similarly locate all the terms as close together as possible. In both algorithms an additional constraint is then applied.

To simplify our definition of our Boolean search algorithm, we define two functions that operate over Boolean queries, extending the **nextDoc** and **prevDoc** methods of schema-dependent inverted indices.

$$\textbf{docRight}(Q, u) —$$ end point of the first candidate solution to Q starting after document u

$$\textbf{docLeft}(Q, v) —$$ start point of the last candidate solution to Q ending before document v

For terms we define:

$$\textbf{docRight}(t, u) \equiv \textbf{nextDoc}(t, u)$$
$$\textbf{docLeft}(t, v) \equiv \textbf{prevDoc}(t, v)$$

and for the AND and OR operators we define:

$$\textbf{docRight}(A \textbf{ AND } B, u) \equiv \max(\textbf{docRight}(A, u), \textbf{docRight}(B, u))$$
$$\textbf{docLeft}(A \textbf{ AND } B, v) \equiv \min(\textbf{docLeft}(A, v), \textbf{docLeft}(B, v))$$
$$\textbf{docRight}(A \textbf{ OR } B, u) \equiv \min(\textbf{docRight}(A, u), \textbf{docRight}(B, u))$$
$$\textbf{docLeft}(A \textbf{ OR } B, v) \equiv \max(\textbf{docLeft}(A, v), \textbf{docLeft}(B, v))$$

To determine the result for a given query, these definitions are applied recursively. For example:

$$\textbf{docRight}((\text{``quarrel'' OR ``sir''}) \text{ AND ``you''}, 1)$$
$$\equiv \max(\textbf{docRight}(\text{``quarrel'' OR ``sir''}, 1), \textbf{docRight}(\text{``you''}, 1))$$
$$\equiv \max(\min(\textbf{docRight}(\text{``quarrel''}, 1), \textbf{docRight}(\text{``sir''}, 1)), \textbf{nextDoc}(\text{``you''}, 1))$$
$$\equiv \max(\min(\textbf{nextDoc}(\text{``quarrel''}, 1), \textbf{nextDoc}(\text{``sir''}, 1)), 3)$$
$$\equiv \max(\min(2, 2), 3)$$
$$\equiv 3$$

$$\textbf{docLeft}((\text{``quarrel'' OR ``sir''}) \text{ AND ``you''}, 4)$$
$$\equiv \min(\textbf{docLeft}(\text{``quarrel'' OR ``sir''}, 4), \textbf{docLeft}(\text{``you''}, 4))$$
$$\equiv \min(\max(\textbf{docLeft}(\text{``quarrel''}, 4), \textbf{docLeft}(\text{``sir''}, 4)), \textbf{prevDoc}(\text{``you''}, 4))$$
$$\equiv \min(\max(\textbf{prevDoc}(\text{``quarrel''}, 4), \textbf{prevDoc}(\text{``sir''}, 4)), 3)$$
$$\equiv \min(\max(2, 3), 3)$$
$$\equiv 3$$

nextSolution (Q, *position*) ≡
1    $v \leftarrow$ **docRight**(Q, *position*)
2   if $v = \infty$ then
3   return ∞
4    $u \leftarrow$ **docLeft**(Q, v + 1)
5   if $u = v$ then
6   return u
7   else
8   return **nextSolution** (Q, v)

Figure 2.12 Function to locate the next solution to the Boolean query Q after a given position. The function **nextSolution** calls **docRight** and **docLeft** to generate a candidate solution. These functions make recursive calls that depend on the structure of the query.

Definitions for the NOT operator are more problematic, and we ignore the operator until after we present the main algorithm.

Figure 2.12 presents the **nextSolution** function, which locates the next solution to a Boolean query after a given position. The function calls **docRight** and **docLeft** to generate a candidate solution. Just after line 4, the interval [u,v] contains this candidate solution. If the candidate solution consists of a single document, it is returned. Otherwise, the function makes a recursive call. Given this function, all solutions to Boolean query Q may be generated by the following:

$$u \leftarrow -\infty$$
$$\textbf{while } u < \infty \textbf{ do}$$
$$u \leftarrow \textbf{nextSolution}(Q, u)$$
$$\textbf{if } u < \infty \textbf{ then}$$
$$\text{report } \textbf{docid}(u)$$

Using a galloping search implementation of nextDoc and prevDoc, the time complexity of this algorithm is $O(n \cdot l \cdot \log(L/l))$, where n is the number of terms in the query. If a docid or frequency index is used, and positional information is not recorded in the index, l and L represent the lengths of the shortest and longest postings lists of the terms in the query as measured by the number of documents. The reasoning required to demonstrate this time complexity is similar to that of our phrase search algorithm and proximity ranking algorithm. When considered in terms of the number of candidate solutions κ, which reflects the adaptive nature of the algorithm, the time complexity becomes $O(n \cdot \kappa \cdot \log(L/\kappa))$. Note that the call to the **docLeft** method in line 4 of the algorithm can be avoided (see Exercise 2.9), but it helps us to analyze the complexity of the algorithm, by providing a clear definition of a candidate solution.

We ignored the NOT operator in our definitions of **docRight** and **docLeft**. Indeed, it is not necessary to implement general versions of these functions in order to implement the NOT operator. Instead, De Morgan's laws may be used to transform a query, moving any NOT operators inward until they are directly associated with query terms:

$$\textbf{NOT } (A \textbf{ AND } B) \equiv \textbf{NOT } A \textbf{ OR } \textbf{NOT } B$$

$$\textbf{NOT } (A \textbf{ OR } B) \equiv \textbf{NOT } A \textbf{ AND } \textbf{NOT } B$$

For example, the query

"william" AND "shakespeare" AND NOT ("marlowe" OR "bacon")

would be transformed into

"william" AND "shakespeare" AND (NOT "marlowe" AND NOT "bacon").

This transformation does not change the number of AND and OR operators appearing in the query, and hence does not change the number of terms appearing in the query (n). After appropriate application of De Morgan's laws, we are left with a query containing expressions of the form **NOT** t, where t is a term. In order to process queries containing expressions of this form, we require corresponding definitions of **docRight** and **docLeft**. It is possible to write these definitions in terms of **nextDoc** and **prevDoc**.

$$\textbf{docRight}(\textbf{NOT } t, u) \equiv$$
$$u' \leftarrow \textbf{nextDoc}(t, u)$$
$$\textbf{while } u' = u + 1 \textbf{ do}$$
$$u \leftarrow u'$$
$$u' \leftarrow \textbf{nextDoc}(t, u)$$
$$\textbf{return } u + 1$$

Unfortunately, this approach introduces potential inefficiencies. Although this definition will exhibit acceptable performance when few documents contain the term t, it may exhibit unacceptable performance when most documents contain t, essentially reverting to the linear scan of the postings list that we avoided by introducing galloping search. Moreover, the equivalent implementation of **docLeft**(**NOT** t, v) requires a scan *backward* through the postings list, violating the requirement necessary to realize the benefits of galloping search.

Instead, we may implement the NOT operator directly over the data structures described in Section 2.1.2, extending the methods supported by our inverted index with explicit methods for **nextDoc**(**NOT** t, u) and **prevDoc**(**NOT** t, v). We leave the details for Exercise 2.5.

2.3   Evaluation

Our presentation of both cosine similarity and proximity ranking relies heavily on intuition. We appeal to intuition to justify the representation of documents and queries as vectors, to justify the determination of similarity by comparing angles, and to justify the assignment of higher weights when terms appear more frequently or closer together. This reliance on intuition can be accepted only when the methods are effective in practice. Moreover, an implementation of a retrieval method must be efficient enough to compute the results of a typical query in adequate time to satisfy the user, and possible trade-offs between efficiency and effectiveness must be considered. A user may not wish to wait for a longer period of time — additional seconds or even minutes — in order to receive a result that is only slightly better than a result she could have received immediately.

2.3.1 Recall and Precision

Measuring the effectiveness of a retrieval method depends on human assessments of relevance. In some cases, it might be possible to infer these assessments implicitly from user behavior. For example, if a user clicks on a result and then quickly backtracks to the result page, we might infer a negative assessment. Nonetheless, most published information retrieval experiments are based on manual assessments created explicitly for experimental purposes, such as the assessments for the TREC experiments described in Chapter 1. These assessments are often binary — an assessor reads the document and judges it *relevant* or *not relevant* with respect to a topic. TREC experiments generally use these binary judgments, with a document being judged relevant if any part of it is relevant.

For example, given the information need described by TREC topic 426 (Figure 1.8 on page 25), a user might formulate the Boolean query

(("law" AND "enforcement") OR "police") AND ("dog" OR "dogs").

Running this query over the TREC45 collection produces a set of 881 documents, representing 0.17% of the half-million documents in the collection.

In order to determine the effectiveness of a Boolean query such as this one, we compare two sets: (1) the set of documents returned by the query, *Res*, and (2) the set of relevant documents for the topic contained in the collection, *Rel*. From these two sets we may then compute two standard effectiveness measures: *recall* and *precision*.

$$\text{recall} \quad = \quad \frac{|Rel \cap Res|}{|Rel|} \tag{2.16}$$

$$\text{precision} \quad = \quad \frac{|Rel \cap Res|}{|Res|} \tag{2.17}$$

In a nutshell, recall indicates the fraction of relevant documents that appears in the result set, whereas precision indicates the fraction of the result set that is relevant.

According to official NIST judgments, there are 202 relevant documents in the TREC45 test collection for topic 426. Our query returns 167 of these documents, giving a precision of 0.190 and a recall of 0.827. A user may find this result acceptable. Just 35 relevant documents are outside the result set. However, in order to find a relevant document, the user must read an average of 4.28 documents that are not relevant.

You will sometimes see recall and precision combined into a single value known as an *F-measure*. The simplest F-measure, F_1, is the harmonic mean of recall and precision:

$$F_1 \;=\; \frac{2}{\frac{1}{R}+\frac{1}{P}} \;=\; \frac{2\cdot R\cdot P}{R+P}\,, \tag{2.18}$$

where R represents recall and P represents precision. In comparison with the arithmetic mean $((R+P)/2)$, the harmonic mean enforces a balance between recall and precision. For example, if we return the entire collection as the result of a query, recall will be 1 but precision will almost always be close to 0. The arithmetic mean gives a value greater than 0.5 for such a result. In contrast, the harmonic mean gives a value of $2P/(1+P)$, which will be close to 0 if P is close to 0.

This formula may be generalized through a *weighted harmonic mean* to allow greater emphasis to be placed on either precision or recall,

$$\frac{1}{\alpha\frac{1}{R}+(1-\alpha)\frac{1}{P}}\,. \tag{2.19}$$

where $0 \le \alpha \le 1$. For $\alpha = 0$, the measure is equivalent to precision. For $\alpha = 1$, it is equivalent to recall. For $\alpha = 0.5$ it is equivalent to Equation 2.18. Following standard practice (van Rijsbergen, 1979, Chapter 7), we set $\alpha = 1/(\beta^2 + 1)$ and define the F-measure as

$$F_\beta \;=\; \frac{(\beta^2+1)\cdot R\cdot P}{\beta^2\cdot R+P}\,, \tag{2.20}$$

where β may be any real number. Thus, F_0 is recall and F_∞ is precision. Values of $|\beta| < 1$ place emphasis on recall; values of $|\beta| > 1$ place emphasis on precision.

recall—)precision—)

2.3.2   Effectiveness Measures for Ranked Retrieval

If the user is interested in reading only one or two relevant documents, ranked retrieval may provide a more useful result than Boolean retrieval. To extend our notions of recall and precision to the ordered lists returned by ranked retrieval algorithms, we consider the top k documents returned by a query, $Res[1..k]$, and define:

$$\text{recall@}k \;=\; \frac{|Rel \cap Res[1..k]|}{|Rel|} \tag{2.21}$$

$$\text{precision@}k \;=\; \frac{|Rel \cap Res[1..k]|}{|Res[1..k]|}\,, \tag{2.22}$$

where precision@k is often written as P@k. If we treat the title of topic 426 as a term vector for ranked retrieval, ⟨"law", "enforcement", "dogs"⟩, proximity ranking gives P@10 = 0.400 and recall@10 = 0.0198. If the user starts reading from the top of the list, she will find four relevant documents in the top ten.

By definition, recall@k increases monotonically with respect to k. Conversely, if a ranked retrieval method adheres to the Probability Ranking Principle defined in Chapter 1 (i.e., ranking documents in order of decreasing probability of relevance), then P@k will tend to decrease as k increases. For topic 426, proximity ranking gives

k	10	20	50	100	200	1000
P@k	0.400	0.450	0.380	0.230	0.115	0.023
recall@k	0.020	0.045	0.094	0.114	0.114	0.114

Since only 82 documents contain all of the terms in the query, proximity ranking cannot return 200 or 1,000 documents with scores greater than 0. In order to allow comparison with other ranking methods, we compute precision and recall at these values by assuming that the empty lower ranks contain documents that are not relevant. All things considered, a user may be happier with the results of the Boolean query on page 67. But of course the comparison is not really fair. The Boolean query contains terms not found in the term vector, and perhaps required more effort to craft. Using the same term vector, cosine similarity gives

k	10	20	50	100	200	1000
P@k	0.000	0.000	0.000	0.060	0.070	0.051
recall@k	0.000	0.000	0.000	0.030	0.069	0.253

Cosine ranking performs surprisingly poorly on this query, and it is unlikely that a user would be happy with these results.

By varying the value of k, we may trade precision for recall, accepting a lower precision in order to identify more relevant documents and vice versa. An IR experiment might consider k over a range of values, with lower values corresponding to a situation in which the user is interested in a quick answer and is willing to examine only a few results. Higher values correspond to a situation in which the user is interested in discovering as much information as possible about a topic and is willing to explore deep into the result list. The first situation is common in Web search, where the user may examine only the top one or two results before trying something else. The second situation may occur in legal domains, where a case may turn on a single precedent or piece of evidence and a thorough search is required.

As we can see from the example above, even at $k = 1000$ recall may be considerably lower than 100%. We may have to go very deep into the results to increase recall substantially beyond this point. Moreover, because many relevant documents may not contain any of the query terms at

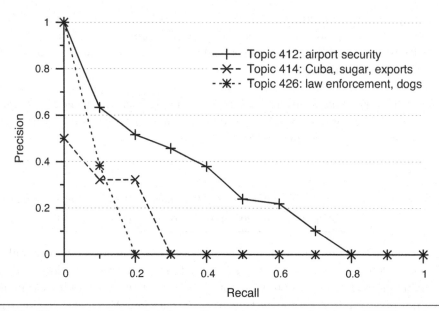

Figure 2.13 Eleven-point interpolated recall-precision curves for three TREC topics over the TREC45 collection. Results were generated with proximity ranking.

all, it is usually not possible to achieve 100% recall without including documents with 0 scores. For simplicity and consistency, information retrieval experiments generally consider only a fixed number of documents, often the top $k = 1000$. At higher levels we simply treat precision as being equal to 0. When conducting an experiment, we pass this value for k as a parameter to the retrieval function, as shown in Figures 2.9 and 2.11.

In order to examine the trade-off between recall and precision, we may plot a *recall-precision curve*. Figure 2.13 shows three examples for proximity ranking. The figure plots curves for topic 426 and two other topics taken from the 1998 TREC adhoc task: topic 412 ("airport security") and topic 414 ("Cuba, sugar, exports"). For 11 recall points, from 0% to 100% by 10% increments, the curve plots the maximum precision achieved at that recall level or higher. The value plotted at 0% recall represents the highest precision achieved at any recall level. Thus, the highest precision achieved for topic 412 is 80%, for topic 414 is 50%, and for topic 426 is 100%. At 20% or higher recall, proximity ranking achieves a precision of up to 57% for topic 412, 32% for topic 414, but 0% for topic 426. This technique of taking the maximum precision achieved at or above a given recall level is called *interpolated precision*. Interpolation has the pleasant property of producing monotonically decreasing curves, which may better illustrate the trade-off between recall and precision.

As an indication of effectiveness across the full range of recall values, we may compute an *average precision* value, which we define as follows:

$$\frac{1}{|Rel|} \cdot \sum_{i=1}^{k} \text{relevant}(i) \times \text{P@}i \qquad (2.23)$$

where relevant$(i) = 1$ if the document at rank i is relevant (i.e., if $Res[i] \in Rel$) and 0 if it is not. Average precision represents an approximation of the area under a (noninterpolated) recall-precision curve. Over the top one thousand documents returned for topic 426, proximity ranking achieves an average precision of 0.058; cosine similarity achieves an average precision of 0.016.

So far, we have considered effectiveness measures for a single topic only. Naturally, performance on a single topic tells us very little, and a typical IR experiment will involve fifty or more topics. The standard procedure for computing effectiveness measures over a set of topics is to compute the measure on individual topics and then take the arithmetic mean of these values. In the IR research literature, values stated for P@k, recall@k, and other measures, as well as recall-precision curves, generally represent averages over a set of topics. You will rarely see values or plots for individual topics unless authors wish to discuss specific characteristics of these topics. In the case of average precision, its arithmetic mean over a set of topics is explicitly referred to as *mean average precision* or *MAP*, thus avoiding possible confusion with averaged P@k values.

Partly because it encapsulates system performance over the full range of recall values, and partly because of its prevalence at TREC and other evaluation forums, the reporting of MAP values for retrieval experiments was nearly ubiquitous in the IR literature until a few years ago. Recently, various limitations of MAP have become apparent and other measures have become more widespread, with MAP gradually assuming a secondary role.

Unfortunately, because it is an average of averages, it is difficult to interpret MAP in a way that provides any clear intuition regarding the actual performance that might be experienced by the user. Although a measure such as P@10 provides less information on the overall performance of a system, it does provide a more understandable number. As a result, we report both P@10 and MAP in experiments throughout the book. In Part III, we explore alternative effectiveness measures, comparing them with precision, recall, and MAP.

For simplicity, and to help guarantee consistency with published results, we suggest you do not write your own code to compute effectiveness measures. NIST provides a program, `trec_eval`[1] that computes a vast array of standard measures, including P@k and MAP. The program is the standard tool for computing results reported at TREC. Chris Buckley, the creator and maintainer of `trec_eval`, updates the program regularly, often including new measures as they appear in the literature.

---

[1] `trec.nist.gov/trec_eval`

Table 2.5   Effectiveness measures for selected retrieval methods discussed in this book.

| Method | TREC45 | | | | GOV2 | | | |
| | 1998 | | 1999 | | 2004 | | 2005 | |
	P@10	MAP	P@10	MAP	P@10	MAP	P@10	MAP
Cosine (2.2.1)	0.264	0.126	0.252	0.135	0.120	0.060	0.194	0.092
Proximity (2.2.2)	0.396	0.124	0.370	0.146	0.425	0.173	0.562	0.230
Cosine (raw TF)	0.266	0.106	0.240	0.120	0.298	0.093	0.282	0.097
Cosine (TF docs)	0.342	0.132	0.328	0.154	0.400	0.144	0.466	0.151
BM25 (Ch. 8)	0.424	0.178	0.440	0.205	0.471	0.243	0.534	0.277
LMD (Ch. 9)	0.450	0.193	0.428	0.226	0.484	0.244	0.580	0.293
DFR (Ch. 9)	0.426	0.183	0.446	0.216	0.465	0.248	0.550	0.269

Effectiveness results

Table 2.5 presents MAP and P@10 values for various retrieval methods over our four test collections. The first row provides values for the cosine similarity ranking described in Section 2.2.1. The second row provides values for the proximity ranking method described in Section 2.2.2.

As we indicated in Section 2.2.1, a large number of variants of cosine similarity have been explored over the years. The next two lines of the table provide values for two of them. The first of these replaces Equation 2.14 (page 57) with raw TF values, $f_{t,d}$, the number of occurrences of each term. In the case of the TREC45 collection, this change harms performance but substantially improves performance on the GOV2 collection. For the second variant (the fourth row) we omitted both document length normalization and document IDF values (but kept IDF in the query vector). Under this variant we compute a score for a document simply by taking the inner product of this unnormalized document vector and the query vector:

$$score(q, d) \; = \; \sum_{t \in (q \cap d)} q_t \cdot \log \left(\frac{N}{N_t} \right) \cdot (\log(f_{t,d}) + 1) . \tag{2.24}$$

Perhaps surprisingly, this change substantially improves performance to roughly the level of proximity ranking.

How can we explain this improvement? The vector space model was introduced and developed at a time when documents were of similar length, generally being short abstracts of books or scientific articles. The idea of representing a document as a vector represents the fundamental inspiration underlying the model. Once we think of a document as a vector, it is not difficult to take the next step and imagine applying standard mathematical operations to these vectors, including addition, normalization, inner product, and cosine similarity. Unfortunately, when it is applied to collections containing documents of different lengths, vector normalization does

Table 2.6 Selected ranking formulae discussed in later chapters. In these formulae the value q_t represents query term frequency, the number of times term t appears in the query. b and k_1, for BM25, and μ, for LMD, are free parameters set to $b = 0.75$, $k_1 = 1.2$, and $\mu = 1000$ in our experiments.

Method	Formula
BM25 (Ch. 8)	$\sum_{t \in q} q_t \cdot (f_{t,d} \cdot (k_1 + 1))/(k_1 \cdot ((1 - b) + b \cdot (l_d/l_{avg})) + f_{t,d}) \cdot \log(N/N_t)$
LMD (Ch. 9)	$\sum_{t \in q} q_t \cdot (\log(\mu + f_{t,d} \cdot l_C/l_t) - \log(\mu + l_d))$
DFR (Ch. 9)	$\sum_{t \in q} q_t \cdot (\log(1 + l_t/N) + f'_{t,d} \cdot \log(1 + N/l_t))/(f'_{t,d} + 1)$,
	where $f'_{t,d} = f_{t,d} \cdot \log(1 + l_{avg}/l_d)$

not successfully adjust for these varying lengths. For this reason, by the early 1990s this last variant of the vector space model had become standard.

The inclusion of the vector space model in this chapter is due more to history than anything else. Given its long-standing influence, no textbook on information retrieval would be complete without it. In later chapters we will present ranked retrieval methods with different theoretical underpinnings. The final three rows of Table 2.5 provide results for three of these methods: a method based on probabilistic models (BM25), a method based on language modeling (LMD), and a method based on divergence from randomness (DFR). The formulae for these methods are given in Table 2.6. As can be seen from the table, all three of these methods depend only on the simple features discussed at the start of Section 2.2. All outperform both cosine similarity and proximity ranking.

Figure 2.14 plots 11-point interpolated recall-precision curves for the 1998 TREC adhoc task, corresponding to the fourth and fifth columns of Table 2.5. The LM and DFR methods appear to slightly outperform BM25, which in turn outperforms proximity ranking and the TF docs version of cosine similarity.

2.3.3 Building a Test Collection

Measuring the effectiveness of a retrieval method depends on human assessments of relevance. Given a topic and a set of documents, an assessor reads each document and makes a decision: Is it relevant or not? Once a topic is well understood, assessment can proceed surprisingly quickly. Once up to speed, an assessor might be able to make a judgment in 10 seconds or less. Unfortunately, even at a rate of one judgment every ten seconds, an assessor working eight-hour days with breaks and holidays would spend nearly a year judging a single topic over the half-million documents in TREC45, and her entire career judging a topic over the 25 million documents in GOV2.

Given the difficulty of judging a topic over the entire collection, TREC and other retrieval efforts depend on a technique known as *pooling* to limit the number of judgments required. The standard TREC experimental procedure is to accept one or more experimental *runs* from each group participating in an adhoc task. Each of these runs consists of the top 1,000 or 10,000

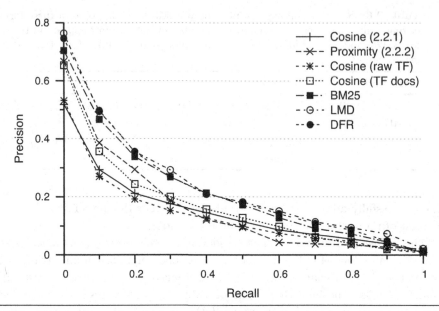

Figure 2.14 11-point interpolated recall-precision curves for various basic retrieval methods on the 1999 TREC adhoc task (topics 401–450, TREC45 document collection).

documents for each topic. Under the pooling method, the top 100 or so documents from each run are then *pooled* into a single set and presented to assessors in random order for judging. Even with dozens of participants the size of this pool may be less than a thousand documents per topic, because the same document may be returned by multiple systems. Even if assessment is done very carefully, with each judgment taking several minutes on average, it is possible for an assessor to work through this pool in less than a week. Often, less time is required.

The goal of the pooling method is to reduce the amount of assessment effort while retaining the ability to make reasonable estimates of precision and recall. For runs contributing to a pool, the values for P@k and recall@k are accurate at least down to the pool depth. Beyond this depth many documents will still be judged, because other runs will have ranked these documents above the pool depth. MAP is still calculated over the entire 1,000 or 10,000 documents in each run, with *unjudged documents treated as not relevant*. Because the top documents have the greatest impact on MAP, estimates made in this way are still acceptably accurate.

Armed with the pooling method, the creation of a test collection at TREC and similar evaluation efforts generally proceed as follows:

1. Obtain an appropriate document set either from public sources or through negotiation with its owners.

2. Develop at least 50 topics, the minimum generally considered acceptable for a meaningful evaluation.

3. Release the topics to the track participants and receive their experimental runs.

4. Create the pools, judge the topics, and return the results to the participants.

When developing a topic, a preliminary test of the topic on a standard IR system should reveal a reasonable mixture of relevant and non-relevant documents in the top ranks. With many relevant documents it may be too easy for systems to achieve a MAP value close to 1.0, making it difficult to distinguish one system from another. With few relevant documents, many systems will fail to achieve a MAP value above 0.0, again making it difficult to distinguish between them. Borrowing our criteria from Goldilocks in the story of the three bears, we want not too many, not too few, but just right.

Ideally, a test collection would be reusable. A researcher developing a new retrieval method could use the documents, topics, and judgments to determine how the new method compares with previous methods. Although the pooling method allows us to create a test collection in less than a lifetime, you may have some legitimate concern regarding its ability to create such reusable collections. A truly novel retrieval method might surface many relevant documents that did not form part of the original pool and are not judged. If unjudged documents are treated as nonrelevant for the purposes of computing evaluation measures, this novel method might receive an unduly harsh score. Tragically, it might even be discarded by the researcher and lost to science forever. Alternative effectiveness measures to address this and related issues are covered in Chapter 12.

2.3.4 Efficiency Measures

In addition to evaluating a system's retrieval effectiveness, it is often necessary to evaluate its efficiency because it affects the cost of running the system and the happiness of its users. From a user's perspective the only efficiency measure of interest is *response time*, the time between entering a query and receiving the results. *Throughput*, the average number of queries processed in a given period of time, is primarily of interest to search engine operators, particularly when the search engine is shared by many users and must cope with thousands of queries per second. Adequate resources must be available to cope with the query load generated by these users without compromising the response time experienced by each. Unacceptably long response times may lead to unhappy users and, as a consequence, fewer users.

A realistic measurement of throughput and its trade-off against response time requires a detailed simulation of query load. For the purposes of making simple efficiency measurements, we may focus on response time and consider the performance seen by a single user issuing one query at a time on an otherwise unburdened search engine. Chapter 13 provides a more detailed discussion of throughput along with a broader discussion of efficiency.

A simple but reasonable procedure for measuring response time is to execute a full query set, capturing the start time from the operating system at a well-defined point just before the first query is issued, and the end time just after the last result is generated. The time to execute the full set is then divided by the number of queries to give an *average response time* per query.

Table 2.7   Average time per query for the Wumpus implementation of Okapi BM25 (Chapter 8), using two different index types and four different query sets.

Index Type	TREC45		GOV2	
	1998	1999	2004	2005
Schema-independent index	61 ms	57 ms	1686 ms	4763 ms
Frequency index	41 ms	41 ms	204 ms	202 ms

Results may be discarded as they are generated, rather than stored to disk or sent over a network, because the overhead of these activities can dominate the response times, particularly with small collections.

Before executing a query set, the IR system should be restarted or reset to clear any information precomputed and stored in memory from previous queries, and the operating system's I/O cache must be flushed. To increase the accuracy of the measurements, the query set may be executed multiple times, with the system reset each time and an average of the measured execution times used to compute the average response time.

An an example, Table 2.7 compares the average response time of a schema-independent index versus a frequency index, using the Wumpus implementation of the Okapi BM25 ranking function (shown in Table 2.6). We use Okapi BM25 for this example, because the Wumpus implementation of this ranking function has been explicitly tuned for efficiency.

The efficiency benefits of using the frequency index are obvious, particularly on the larger GOV2 collection. The use of a schema-independent index requires the computation at run-time of document and term statistics that are precomputed in the frequency index. To a user, a 202 ms response time would seem instantaneous, whereas a 4.7 sec response time would be a noticeable lag. However, with a frequency index it is not possible to perform phrase searches or to apply ranking functions to elements other than documents.

The efficiency measurements shown in the table, as well as others throughout the book, were made on a rack-mounted server based on an AMD Opteron processor (2.8 GHz) with 2 GB of RAM. A detailed performance overview of the computer system is in Appendix A.

2.4   Summary

This chapter has covered a broad range of topics, often in considerable detail. The key points include the following:

- We view an inverted index as an abstract data type that may be accessed through the methods and definitions summarized in Table 2.4 (page 52). There are four important variants — docid indices, frequency indices, positional indices, and schema-independent indices — that differ in the type and format of the information they store.

- Many retrieval algorithms — such as the phrase searching, proximity ranking, and Boolean query processing algorithms presented in this chapter — may be efficiently implemented using galloping search. These algorithms are adaptive in the sense that their time complexity depends on characteristics of the data, such as the number of candidate phrases.

- Both ranked retrieval and Boolean filters play important roles in current IR systems. Reasonable methods for ranked retrieval may be based on simple document and term statistics, such as term frequency (TF), inverse document frequency (IDF), and term proximity. The well-known cosine similarity measure represents documents and queries as vectors and ranks documents according to the cosine of the angle between them and the query vector.

- Recall and precision are two widely used effectiveness measures. A trade-off frequently exists between them, such that increasing recall leads to a corresponding decrease in precision. Mean average precision (MAP) represents a standard method for summarizing the effectiveness of an IR system over a broad range of recall levels. MAP and P@10 are the principal effectiveness measures reported throughout the book.

- Response time represents the efficiency of an IR system as experienced by a user. We may make reasonable estimates of minimum response time by processing queries sequentially, reading them one at a time and reporting the results of one query before starting the next query.

2.5   Further Reading

Inverted indices have long been the standard data structure underlying the implementation of IR systems (Faloutsos, 1985; Knuth, 1973, pages 552–554). Other data structures have been proposed, generally with the intention of providing more efficient support for specific retrieval operations. However, none of these data structures provide the flexibility and generality of inverted indices, and they have mostly fallen out of use.

Signature files were long viewed as an important competitor to inverted indices, particularly when disk and memory were at a premium (Faloutsos, 1985; Faloutsos and Christodoulakis, 1984; Zobel et al., 1998). Signature files are intended to provide efficient support for Boolean queries by quickly eliminating documents that do not match the query. They provide one method for implementing the filtering step of the two-step retrieval process described on page 53. Unfortunately, false matches can be reported by signature files, and they cannot be easily extended to support phrase queries and ranked retrieval.

A suffix tree (Weiner, 1973) is a search tree in which every path from the root to a leaf corresponds to a unique suffix in a text collection. A suffix array (Gonnet, 1987; Manber and Myers, 1990) is an array of pointers to unique suffixes in the collection that is sorted in lexicographical order. Both suffix trees and suffix arrays are intended to support efficient phrase searching, as well as operations such as lexicographical range searching and structural retrieval (Gonnet et al., 1992). Unfortunately, both data structures provide poor support for ranked retrieval.

Galloping search is described and evaluated by Bentley and Yao (1976). The algorithms presented in this chapter for phrase searching, proximity ranking, and Boolean retrieval may all be viewed as variants of algorithms for computing set operations over sorted lists. The term "galloping" was coined by Demaine et al. (2000), who present and analyze adaptive algorithms for set union, intersection and difference. Other algorithms for computing the intersection of sorted lists are described by Barbay and Kenyon (2002) and by Baeza-Yates (2004). Our abstraction of an inverted index into an ADT accessed through a small number of simple methods is based on Clarke et al. (2000). The proximity ranking algorithm presented in this chapter is a simplified version of the algorithm presented in that paper.

The vector space model was developed into the version presented in this chapter through a long process that can be traced back at least to the work of Luhn in the 1950s (Luhn, 1957, 1958). The long-standing success and influence of the model are largely due to the efforts of Salton and his research group at Cornell, who ultimately made the model a key element of their SMART IR system, the first version of which became operational in the fall of 1964 (Salton, 1968, page 422). Until the early 1990s SMART was one of a small number of platforms available for IR research, and during that period it was widely adopted by researchers outside Salton's group as a foundation for their own work.

By the time of the first TREC experiments in the early 1990s, the vector space model had evolved into a form very close to that presented in this chapter (Buckley et al., 1994). A further development, introduced at the fourth TREC in 1995, was the addition of an explicit adjustment for document length, known as *pivoted document length normalization* (Singhal et al., 1996). This last development has been accepted as an essential part of the vector space model for ranked retrieval but not for other applications, such as clustering or classification. After Salton's death in 1995, development of the SMART system continued under the supervision of Buckley, and it remained a competitive research system more than ten years later (Buckley, 2005).

Latent Semantic Analysis (LSA) is an important and well-known extension of the vector space model (Deerwester et al., 1990) that we do not cover in this book. LSA applies singular value decomposition, from linear algebra, to reduce the dimensionality of the term-vector space. The goal is to reduce the negative impact of synonymy — multiple terms with the same meaning — by merging related words into common dimensions. A related technique, Probabilistic Latent Semantic Analysis (PLSA), approaches the same goal by way of a probabilistic model (Hofmann, 1999). Unfortunately, the widespread application of LSA and PLSA to IR systems has been limited by the difficulty of efficient implementation.

The Spam song (page 38) has had perhaps the greatest influence of any song on computer terminology. The song was introduced in the twelfth episode of the second season of *Monty Python's Flying Circus*, which first aired on December 15, 1970, on BBC Television.

2.6   Exercises

Exercise 2.1   Simplify **next**("the", **prev**("the", **next** ("the", $-\infty$))).

Exercise 2.2   Consider the following version of the phrase searching algorithm shown in Figure 2.2 (page 36).

> **nextPhrase2** ($t_1 t_2 ... t_n$, *position*) $\equiv$
> $u \leftarrow$ **next**(t_1, *position*)
> $v \leftarrow u$
>   **for** $i \leftarrow 2$ **to** n **do**
> $v \leftarrow$ **next**(t_i, v)
>   **if** $v = \infty$ **then**
>   **return** $[\infty, \infty]$
>   **if** $v - u = n - 1$ **then**
>   **return** $[u, v]$
>   **else**
>   **return nextPhrase2**($t_1 t_2 ... t_n$, $v - n$)

It makes the same number of calls to **next** as the version shown in the figure but does not make any calls to **prev**. Explain how the algorithm operates. How does it find the next occurrence of a phrase after a given position? When combined with galloping search to find all occurrences of a phrase, would you expect improved efficiency compared to the original version? Explain.

Exercise 2.3   Using the methods of the inverted index ADT, write an algorithm that locates all intervals corresponding to speeches (<SPEECH>...</SPEECH>). Assume the schema-independent indexing shown in Figure 2.1, as illustrated by Figure 1.3.

Exercise 2.4   Using the methods of the inverted index ADT, write an algorithm that locates all speeches by a witch in Shakespeare's plays. Assume the schema-independent indexing shown in Figure 2.1, as illustrated by Figure 1.3.

Exercise 2.5   Assume we have a schema-independent inverted index for Shakespeare's plays. We decide to treat each PLAY as a separate document.

(a) Write algorithms to compute the following statistics, using only the **first**, **last**, **next**, and **prev** methods: (i) N_t, the number of documents in the collection containing the term t; (ii) $f_{t,d}$, the number of times term t appears in document d; (iii) l_d, the length of document d; (iv) l_{avg}, average document length; and (v) N, total number of documents.

(b) Write algorithms to implement the **docid**, **offset**, **firstDoc**, **lastDoc**, **nextDoc**, and **prevDoc** methods, using only the **first**, **last**, **next**, and **prev** methods.

For simplicity, you may treat the position of each ⟨PLAY⟩ tag as the document ID for the document starting at that position; there's no requirement for document IDs to be assigned sequentially. For example, *Macbeth* would be assigned docid 745142 (with an initial occurrence of "first witch" at [745142:265, 745142:266]).

Exercise 2.6 When postings lists are stored on disk rather than entirely in memory, the time required by an inverted index method call can depend heavily on the overhead required for accessing the disk. When conducting a search for a phrase such as "Winnie the Pooh", which contains a mixture of frequent and infrequent terms, the first method call for "winnie" (**next**("winnie", $-\infty$)) might read the entire postings list from disk into an array. Further calls would return results from this array using galloping search. Similarly, the postings list for "pooh" could be read into memory during its first method call. On the other hand, the postings list for "the" may not fit into memory in its entirety, and only a very small number of these postings may form part of the target phrase.

Ideally, all of the postings for "the" would not be read from disk. Instead, the methods might read a small part of the postings list at a time, generating multiple disk accesses as the list is traversed and skipping portions of the list as appropriate.

Because each method call for "the" may generate a disk access, it may be preferable to search for the phrase "Winnie the Pooh" by immediately checking for an occurrence of "pooh" (two positions away) after locating each occurrence of "winnie". If "pooh" does not occur in the expected location, we may abandon this occurrence of "winnie" and continue to another occurrence without checking for an occurrence of "the" between the two. Only when we have located an occurrence of "winnie" and "pooh" correctly spaced ("winnie ___ pooh") do we need to make a method call for "the".

To generalize, given a phrase "$t_1 t_2 ... t_n$", a search algorithm might work from the least frequent term to the most frequent term, abandoning a potential phrase once a term is found to be missing and thus minimizing the number of calls for the most frequent terms. Using the basic definitions and methods of our inverted index ADT, complete the details of this algorithm. What is the time complexity of the algorithm in terms of calls to the **next** and **prev** methods? What is the overall time complexity if galloping search is used to implement these methods?

Can the algorithm be considered adaptive? (*Hint:* Consider a search in the "hello world" collection on page 38. How many method calls must be made?)

Exercise 2.7 Coordination level is the number of terms from a vector $\langle t_1, ..., t_n \rangle$ that appear in a document. Coordination level may range from 1 to n. Using the methods of our inverted index ADT, write an algorithm that ranks documents according to their coordination level.

Exercise 2.8 Demonstrate that the term vector $\langle t_1, ..., t_n \rangle$ may have at most $n \cdot l$ covers (see Section 2.2.2), where l is the length of the shortest postings list for the terms in the vector.

Exercise 2.9 Taking a hint from Exercise 2.2, design a version of the algorithm shown in Figure 2.10 (page 61) that does not make a call to the **docLeft** method.

Exercise 2.10 If $\alpha = 1/(\beta^2 + 1)$, show that Equations 2.19 and 2.20 are equivalent.

Exercise 2.11 (project exercise) Implement the in-memory array-based version of inverted indices presented in Section 2.1.2, including all three versions of the **next** method: binary search, sequential scan and galloping search. Using your implementation of inverted indices, implement the phrase searching algorithm of Section 2.1.1.

To test your phrase searching implementation, we suggest a corpus 256MB or larger that fits comfortably in the main memory of your computer. The corpus created in Exercise 1.9 (or a subset) would be suitable. Select at least 10,000 phrases of various lengths from your corpus and verify that your implementation successfully locates these phrases. Your selection should include short phrases of length 2–3, longer phrases of length 4–10, and very long phrases with length 100 or greater. Include phrases containing both frequent and infrequent terms. At least half of the phrases should contain a least one very common term, such as an article or a preposition.

Following the guidelines of Section 2.3.4, compare the efficiency of phrase searching, using your three versions of the **next** method. Compute average response times. Plot response time against phrase length for all three versions. For clarity, you may need to plot the results for linear scan separately from those of the other two methods.

Select another set of phrases, all with length 2. Include phrases containing combinations of frequent and infrequent terms. Plot response time against L (the length of the longest postings list) for all three versions. Plot response time against l (the length of the shortest postings list) for all three versions.

Optional extension: Implement the phrase searching algorithm described in Exercise 2.6. Repeat the performance measurements using this new implementation.

Exercise 2.12 (project exercise) Implement cosine similarity ranking, as described in Section 2.2.1. Test your implementation using the test collection developed in Exercise 2.13 or with any other available collection, such as a TREC collection.

Exercise 2.13 (project exercise) As a class project, undertake a TREC-style adhoc retrieval experiment, developing a test collection based on Wikipedia. Continuing from Exercises 1.9 and 1.10, each student should contribute enough topics to make a combined set of 50 topics or more. Each student should implement their own retrieval system, perhaps by starting with an open-source IR system and extending it with techniques from later chapters, or with techniques of their own invention. Each student should then run the titles of the topics as queries to their system. Pool and judge the results, with each student judging the topics they created. The design and implementation of an interactive judging interface might be undertaken as a sub-project by a group of interested students. Use `trec_eval` to compare runs and techniques.

2.7   Bibliography

Baeza-Yates, R. (2004). A fast set intersection algorithm for sorted sequences. In *Proceedings of the 15th Annual Symposium on Combinatorial Pattern Matching*, pages 400–408. Istanbul, Turkey.

Barbay, J., and Kenyon, C. (2002). Adaptive intersection and t-threshold problems. In *Proceedings of the 13th Annual ACM-SIAM Symposium on Discrete Algorithms*, pages 390–399. San Francisco, California.

Bentley, J. L., and Yao, A. C. C. (1976). An almost optimal algorithm for unbounded searching. *Information Processing Letters*, 5(3):82–87.

Buckley, C. (2005). The SMART project at TREC. In Voorhees, E. M., and Harman, D. K., editors, *TREC — Experiment and Evaluation in Information Retrieval*, chapter 13, pages 301–320. Cambridge, Massachusetts: MIT Press.

Buckley, C., Salton, G., Allan, J., and Singhal, A. (1994). Automatic query expansion using SMART: TREC 3. In *Proceedings of the 3rd Text REtrieval Conference*. Gaithersburg, Maryland.

Clarke, C. L. A., Cormack, G. V., and Tudhope, E. A. (2000). Relevance ranking for one to three term queries. *Information Processing & Management*, 36(2):291–311.

Deerwester, S. C., Dumais, S. T., Landauer, T. K., Furnas, G. W., and Harshman, R. A. (1990). Indexing by latent semantic analysis. *Journal of the American Society of Information Science*, 41(6):391–407.

Demaine, E. D., López-Ortiz, A., and Munro, J. I. (2000). Adaptive set intersections, unions, and differences. In *Proceedings of the 11th Annual ACM-SIAM Symposium on Discrete Algorithms*, pages 743–752. San Francisco, California.

Faloutsos, C. (1985). Access methods for text. *ACM Computing Surveys*, 17(1):49–74.

Faloutsos, C., and Christodoulakis, S. (1984). Signature files: An access method for documents and its analytical performance evaluation. *ACM Transactions on Office Information Systems*, 2(4):267–288.

Gonnet, G. H. (1987). PAT *3.1 — An Efficient Text Searching System — User's Manual.* University of Waterloo, Canada.

Gonnet, G. H., Baeza-Yates, R. A., and Snider, T. (1992). New indices for text — PAT trees and PAT arrays. In Frakes, W. B., and Baeza-Yates, R., editors, *Information Retrieval — Data Structures and Algorithms*, chapter 5, pages 66–82. Englewood Cliffs, New Jersey: Prentice Hall.

Hofmann, T. (1999). Probabilistic latent semantic indexing. In *Proceedings of the 22nd Annual International ACM SIGIR Conference on Research and Development in Information Retrieval*, pages 50–57. Berkeley, California.

Knuth, D. E. (1973). *The Art of Computer Programming*, volume 3. Reading, Massachusetts: Addison-Wesley.

Luhn, H. P. (1957). A statistical approach to mechanized encoding and searching of literary information. *IBM Journal of Research and Development*, 1(4):309–317.

Luhn, H. P. (1958). The automatic creation of literature abstracts. *IBM Journal of Research and Development*, 2(2):159–165.

Manber, U., and Myers, G. (1990). Suffix arrays: A new method for on-line string searches. In *Proceedings of the 1st Annual ACM-SIAM Symposium on Discrete Algorithms*, pages 319–327. San Francisco, California.

Salton, G. (1968). *Automatic Information Organziation and Retrieval.* New York: McGraw-Hill.

Singhal, A., Salton, G., Mitra, M., and Buckley, C. (1996). Document length normalization. *Information Processing & Management*, 32(5):619–633.

van Rijsbergen, C. J. (1979). *Information Retrieval* (2nd ed.). London, England: Butterworths.

Weiner, P. (1973). Linear pattern matching algorithm. In *Proceedings of the 14th Annual IEEE Symposium on Switching and Automata Theory*, pages 1–11. Iowa City, Iowa.

Zobel, J., Moffat, A., and Ramamohanarao, K. (1998). Inverted files versus signature files for text indexing. *ACM Transactions on Database Systems*, 23(4):453–490.

3 Tokens and Terms

Tokens provide the link between queries and documents. During indexing, the IR system divides each document into a sequence of tokens and inserts these tokens into an inverted index for searching. At query time, a corresponding tokenization is applied to the query. The resulting query terms are then matched against the inverted index to effect retrieval and ranking.

Chapter 1 introduced simple rules for tokenizing raw text: Tokens are sequences of alphanumeric characters separated by nonalphanumeric characters. The tokens are *case normalized* by converting uppercase letters to lowercase. In addition — ignoring the complexities of full XML — we treat simple XML tags of the form <*name*> and </*name*> as tokens.

Although these simple rules are sufficient for the purposes of the experiments reported in this book, more complex tokenization rules may be required in practice. For example, under our simple rules, contractions such as "didn't" are represented by the pair of tokens "didn t", which would not match a search for the phrase "did not". The number "10,000,000" would be represented by the three tokens "10 000 000", the first of which would incorrectly match the query term "10".

Moreover, in applying these simple rules we explicitly assume that the raw text is written in the English language, perhaps encoded as ASCII values. Under these rules the definition of "alphanumeric" does not include the letter β or the number 八 because these characters cannot be represented in ASCII. Even the English word "naïve" cannot be properly represented using ASCII values.

In most practical environments, IR systems must provide appropriate support for languages other than English. Supporting a broad range of human languages requires us to take into account specific properties of the individual languages, including their character sets and rules for tokenization. Crudely speaking, tokenization splits documents into *words*. Although the concept of a word is essentially universal in human language (Trask, 2004), the characteristics of words vary greatly from language to language. Not every word makes a good token; not every token is a word.

In this chapter we revisit the problem of tokenization and term matching for English, and extend our discussion to other languages. We focus on the content of documents, leaving the complexities of XML and other document structure for Chapters 5 and 16. Relatively minor details of tokenization can have a substantial impact on retrieval effectiveness for specific queries. Getting it right requires careful consideration of these specific queries, as well as measuring overall retrieval effectiveness.

Section 3.1 covers English, including a discussion of two traditional IR topics closely associated with tokenization: *stemming* and *stopping*. Stemming provides a way for the query term "orienteering" to match an occurrence of "orienteers" by reducing both terms to their common root. Stopping reflects the observation that many common words, such as "the" and "I", may have little value for retrieval purposes. Ignoring these *stopwords* may improve retrieval efficiency and reduce the size of the inverted index.

Section 3.2 discusses character encodings, covering the basics of Unicode and UTF-8. Section 3.3 describes character n-gram indexing, which can provide a baseline for supporting new languages. Character n-gram indexing can also serve as a method for tokenizing noisy text, such as that produced by OCR (optical character recognition) systems. The final sections of the chapter discuss tokenization for a number of European and Asian languages, providing a sketch of the difficulties associated with them.

3.1 English

English provides a good starting point for understanding tokenization and term matching. The language is, by necessity, familiar to you as a reader of this book. It is one of the most widely spoken languages, with hundreds of millions of native speakers. Hundreds of millions more learn it as a second or third language. Content in the English language continues to comprise a disproportionate share of the Web. As a result, the ability to provide effective support for English is a fundamental requirement for many IR systems.

3.1.1 Punctuation and Capitalization

English contains a number of features that create minor tokenization problems. Many of them are related to punctuation and capitalization. In English a particular punctuation mark may be used for multiple unrelated purposes. The use of the apostrophe in contractions such as "I'll" and "it's" has already been mentioned, and it might be reasonable to tokenize these as "I will" and "it is" rather than "I ll" and "it s". However, the apostrophe is also used in constructions such as "o'clock" and "Bill's". The first might best be treated as a single token rather than two, because a match against "clock" may not be appropriate. On the other hand, if a match against "bill" is desirable, the second must be indexed as two tokens.

Periods end sentences. However, the same character appears in acronyms, numbers, initials, Internet addresses, and other contexts. Acronyms such as "I.B.M." and "U.S." may alternatively be written as "IBM" and "US". An IR system might recognize and tokenize such acronyms consistently, so that a query for "IBM" matches both forms. Punctuation marks may also appear as an integral part of the names of companies and organizations, such as "Yahoo!" and the band "Panic! At the Disco". For a small set of terms, the improper treatment of punctuation characters may render the search results completely useless. Examples include "C++", "C#", and "\index" (a LaTeX command). For the vast majority of queries, however, punctuation may safely be ignored.

Case normalization (i.e., converting all characters to lowercase in the index and in each query), on the other hand, affects almost every query. In many languages the first character of the word that starts a given sentence is always capitalized, and we want to be able to find those words even if the user types her query in lowercase (as most users do). Unfortunately, case normalization has the potential to cause great harm because capitalization is essential to preserve the meaning of many terms. Only capitalization distinguishes the acronym "US" from the pronoun "us", or the acronym "THE"[1] from the English definite article "the".

A simple heuristic to handle acronyms and similar tokenization problems is to *double index* these terms. For example, the acronym "US" would be indexed twice at each position at which it occurs. The inverted index would include postings lists for both "us" and "US". An occurrence of the acronym would appear in both lists, whereas an occurrence of the pronoun would appear only in the first list. A query containing the term "us" would be processed with the first list; a query containing the term "US" (and possibly "U.S.") would be processed with the second. Double indexing may also provide support for proper names, allowing the personal name "Bill" to be distinguished from an itemized invoice.

We must be cautious when adjusting our tokenization procedure to account for capitalization and punctuation. Adjustments to a tokenization procedure can negatively impact some queries while having a positive impact on others. Fans of the movie *The Terminator* (1984) will immediately recognize the quote "I'll be back", and a match against "I will be back" would not be appropriate. Occasionally, text is WRITTEN ENTIRELY IN CAPITAL LETTERS, perhaps accidentally or as a method for communicating the emotional state of the writer. Such text should not be treated as a long series of acronyms and abbreviations. The term "IN" in this sentence does not refer to the US state of Indiana, and this document does not discuss its capital. As with any information retrieval technique, tokenization must be evaluated with respect to its overall impact on effectiveness and efficiency.

3.1.2 Stemming

Stemming allows a query term such as "orienteering" to match an occurrence of "orienteers", or "runs" to match "running". Stemming considers the *morphology*, or internal structure, of terms, reducing each term to a *root form* for comparison. For example, "orienteering" and "orienteers" might reduce to the root form "orienteer"; "runs" and "running" might reduce to "run".

In an IR system a *stemmer* may be applied at both indexing time and query time. During indexing each token is passed through the stemmer and the resulting root form is indexed. At query time, the query terms are passed through the same stemmer and matched against the index terms. Thus the query term "runs" would match an occurrence of "running" by way of their common root form "run".

---

[1] The THE operating system, a pioneering multiprogramming system, was created at the Technische Universiteit Eindhoven by Turing award winner Edsger Dijkstra and colleagues in the mid-1960's.

Original

To be, or not to be: that is the question:
Whether 'tis nobler in the mind to suffer
The slings and arrows of outrageous fortune,
Or to take arms against a sea of troubles,
And by opposing end them? To die: to sleep;
No more; and by a sleep to say we end
The heart-ache and the thousand natural shocks
That flesh is heir to, 'tis a consummation
Devoutly to be wish'd. To die, to sleep;
To sleep: perchance to dream: ay, there's the rub;

Normalized	**Normalized and stemmed**
to be or not to be that is the question	to be or not to be that is the question
whether tis nobler in the mind to suffer	whether ti nobler in the mind to suffer
the slings and arrows of outrageous fortune	the sling and arrow of outrag fortun
or to take arms against a sea of troubles	or to take arm against a sea of troubl
and by opposing end them to die to sleep	and by oppos end them to die to sleep
no more and by a sleep to say we end	no more and by a sleep to sai we end
the heart ache and the thousand natural shocks	the heart ach and the thousand natur shock
that flesh is heir to tis a consummation	that flesh is heir to ti a consumm
devoutly to be wish d to die to sleep	devoutli to be wish d to die to sleep
to sleep perchance to dream ay there s the rub	to sleep perchanc to dream ay there s the rub

Figure 3.1 The opening lines of Hamlet's soliloquy. At the top is the original text. The bottom-left version has been case normalized and stripped of punctuation. The bottom-right version is stemmed with the Porter stemmer.

Stemming is related to the concept of *lemmatization* from linguistics. Lemmatization reduces a term to a *lexeme*, which roughly corresponds to a word in the sense of a dictionary entry. For each lexeme a particular form of the word, or *lemma*, is chosen to represent it. The lemma is the form of a word you look up in a dictionary. For example, the form "run" is conventionally chosen to represent the group that includes "runs", "running", and "ran".

Stemming and lemmatization are sometimes equated, but this view is misleading. Stemming is strictly an operational process. When a stemmer transforms a term into its root form, we are not directly concerned with the linguistic validity of this transformation, but only with its measurable impact on retrieval effectiveness for specific queries.

The Porter stemmer, developed by Martin Porter in the late 1970s, is one of the best-known stemmers for the English language (Porter, 1980). Figure 3.1 shows the opening lines of Hamlet's famous soliloquy before and after application of the Porter stemmer. The text was stripped of punctuation and case normalized before applying the stemmer. As you can see in the figure, the stemmer may produce root forms that are not English words. For example, "troubles" stems down to "troubl". This behavior does not cause problems in practice because these root forms are never seen by a user. The term "troubling" in a query would also stem down to "troubl", providing a correct match.

Table 3.1   Impact of stemming. The table lists effectiveness measures for selected retrieval methods discussed in this book. The results in this table may be compared with those in Table 2.5 on page 72.

| | TREC45 | | | | GOV2 | | | |
| | 1998 | | 1999 | | 2004 | | 2005 | |
Method	P@10	MAP	P@10	MAP	P@10	MAP	P@10	MAP
Proximity (2.2.2)	0.418	0.139	0.430	0.184	0.453	0.207	0.576	0.283
BM25 (Ch. 8)	0.440	0.199	0.464	0.247	0.500	0.266	0.600	0.334
LMD (Ch. 9)	0.464	0.204	0.434	0.262	0.492	0.270	0.600	0.343
DFR (Ch. 9)	0.448	0.204	0.458	0.253	0.471	0.252	0.584	0.319

The Porter stemmer may sometimes appear to be overly aggressive. Both "orienteering" and "orienteers" stem down to "orient" rather than "orienteer". The term "oriental" also stems down to "orient", incorrectly conflating these terms. Moreover, the stemmer does not handle irregular verbs and pluralizations correctly. Both "runs" and "running" stem down to "run", but the irregular form "ran" stems (unchanged) to "ran". Similarly, "mouse" stems to "mous", but "mice" stems to "mice". In addition, the stemmer handles only suffixes. Prefixes such as "un" and "re" are not removed.

The stemmer operates by applying lists of rewrite rules organized into a sequence of steps. For example, the first list of rewrite rules (constituting step 1a) handles plural forms as follows:

sses → ss
ies → i
ss → ss
s →

To apply a rule, the pattern on the left-hand side of the rule is matched against the current suffix of the term. If the suffix matches, the suffix is rewritten by removing it and replacing it with the pattern on the right-hand side. Thus, the first of these rules rewrites "caresses" into "caress", and the second rewrites "ponies" into "poni" (not "pony"). Only the first matching rule in a list is applied. The third rule, which appears to do nothing, exists to prevent the "ss" suffix on words such as "caress" from being rewritten by the fourth rule. This last rule simply removes a final "s", rewriting "cats" to "cat". Overall, the algorithm has five main steps, some of which have sub-steps. In total there are nine lists of rules, the longest of which contains twenty rules.

The application of a stemmer may improve recall by allowing more documents to be retrieved but may also harm precision by allowing inappropriate matches, assigning high scores to non-relevant documents. Nonetheless, when averaged over the topics in a typical TREC experiment, stemming often produces a noticable improvement. Table 3.1 shows the impact of applying the Porter stemmer to the test collections discussed in Chapter 1. The values in this table may be directly compared with those in Table 2.5 on page 72. For all four data sets, stemming has a positive impact on retrieval effectiveness. These results suggest that the application of a stemmer is an excellent idea if you are participating in a TREC-style experiment.

When stemming goes wrong, however, it can have a strongly negative impact. For example, the title of TREC topic 314, "marine vegetation", stems down to "marin veget" under the Porter stemmer. Unfortunately, "marinated vegetables" stems down to the same root form. A user issuing this query may be surprised and confused if the IR system retrieves recipes and restaurant reviews along with (or instead of) articles on aquatic botany. A user may have no idea why such documents would be retrieved by her query. To her, the system may appear broken or buggy. Even if she understands the cause of the problem, she may not know how to solve it unless a method for explicitly disabling the stemmer is provided.

In research contexts, stemming may often be appropriate. For participants in an experimental effort such as TREC, stemming may substantially improve performance with little additional effort on the part of the researchers. However, in more realistic settings, any tokenization method that has the potential to produce inexplicably erroneous results should be treated with caution. Before integrating a stemmer into an operational IR system, the downside should be considered carefully.

3.1.3   Stopping

Function words are words that have no well-defined meanings in and of themselves; rather, they modify other words or indicate grammatical relationships. In English, function words include prepositions, articles, pronouns and articles, and conjunctions. Function words are usually among the most frequently occurring words in any language. All of the words (as opposed to XML tags) appearing in Figure 1.1 on page 15 are function words.

When documents are viewed as unstructured "bags of words", as they are under the vector space model, the inclusion of function words in a query may appear to be unnecessary. Even under a proximity model, the close proximity of a particular function word to other query terms is hardly surprising, given the frequency of all function words in ordinary text. As a result IR systems traditionally define a list of *stopwords*, which usually include the function words. At query time these stopwords are stripped from the query, and retrieval takes place on the basis of the remaining terms alone.

Consider the appearance of the term "the" in a query. Roughly 6% of tokens in English text will match this term. Similarly, roughly 2% of tokens will match the term "of". Nearly every English-language document contains both terms. If a user is searching for information on "the marriage of William Shakespeare", reducing this information need to the query ⟨"marriage", "william", "shakespeare"⟩ — treating "of" and "the" as stopwords — should have no negative impact on retrieval effectiveness.

In addition to function words, a list of stopwords might include single letters, digits, and other common terms, such as the state-of-being verbs. In the specific environment of the Web, the stopword list might include terms such as "www", "com", and "http", which are essentially meaningless in this context. Depending on the IR system and its environment, the stopword

list might range from less than a dozen terms to many hundreds of terms. After the removal of
typical stopwords, the text of Figure 3.1 (page 87) reduces to:

question
ti nobler mind suffer
sling arrow outrag fortun
take arm sea troubl
oppos end die sleep
sleep sai end
heart ach thousand natur shock
flesh heir ti consumm
devoutli wish die sleep
sleep perchanc dream ay rub

Because stopwords are usually frequent terms with relatively long postings lists, their elimination
may substantially reduce query execution times by avoiding the processing of these longer lists.
Furthermore, if stopwords are consistently stripped from all queries, they do not need to be
included in the index at all. In early IR systems, this elimination of stopwords provided the
benefit of reducing index sizes, an important consideration when disks and memory were small
and expensive.

Unfortunately, a small number of queries are adversely affected by stopword elimination,
usually because stopwords form an essential part of a phrase. The start of Hamlet's soliloquy,
"to be or not to be that is the", provides a well-known example. Although we may immediately
recognize this quote, it is composed entirely of terms that are traditionally stopwords. The
name of the band "The The" provides another example — as well as further demonstrating the
importance of capitalization. Although you might view these examples as extreme cases — and
they are — they still should be handled in a reasonable way by a search engine.

In order to handle cases such as these, we recommend the inclusion of all stopwords in
the index. Depending on the retrieval algorithm, it may be possible to selectively eliminate
them from queries when the positive impact of their presence is expected to be minimal. With
stopwords present in the index, the IR system can make a decision on a query-by-query basis.
Ranking methods in a modern commercial search engine will incorporate many ranking features,
including features based on term frequency and proximity. For features that do not consider
proximity between query terms, stopwords may be elminated. For features that do consider
proximity between query terms, particularly to match their occurrence in phrases, it may be
appropriate to retain stopwords.

3.2 Characters

Tokenizing raw text requires an understanding of the characters it encodes. So far in the book, we have tacitly assumed an encoding of the text as 7-bit ASCII values. ASCII is sufficient to encode most characters in English text, including uppercase and lowercase letters, digits, and many punctuation characters.

Although ASCII encoding is acceptable for English, it is wholly inadequate for most other languages. ASCII was standardized in 1963, at a time when memory was at a premium, networking was a dream, and English-speaking countries represented the major market for computing equipment. Support for other languages was undertaken as needed, on a country-by-country or region-by-region basis. Often, these specialized character encodings provided incomplete support for their target languages. For some languages, incompatible encodings were developed for different countries or regions, or by different hardware manufacturers. Even for English, IBM's Extended Binary Coded Decimal Interchange Code (EBCDIC) provided a widely implemented competitor to ASCII.

Progress came slowly, but by the late 1980s efforts were under way to create a single unified character encoding that encompassed all living languages (and eventually many extinct ones). This Unicode[2] standard now provides encodings for the characters from a large and growing set of languages. Except for simple experimental IR systems, support for Unicode is essential. Although many documents still use other encodings, these can be handled by conversion to Unicode. Providing native support for Unicode allows an IR system to grow and accommodate new languages as required.

Unicode assigns a unique value, called a *codepoint*, to each character but does not specify how these values are represented as raw text. A codepoint is written in the form U+*nnnn*, where *nnnn* indicates the value of the codepoint in hexadecimal. For example, the character β is represented by the codepoint U+03B2. Unicode currently supports more than 100,000 characters, with codepoints ranging beyond U+2F800.

An associated standard, UTF-8, provides a convenient method for representing these codepoints as raw text. Although there are competing methods for representing Unicode, UTF-8 has several advantages, including backward compatibility with ASCII. UTF-8 represents each codepoint with one to four bytes. Each character appearing in the ASCII character set is encoded as a single byte having the same value as the corresponding ASCII character. Thus, raw text in ASCII is automatically raw text in UTF-8.

Although UTF-8 uses a variable-length encoding for a character, the interpretation of this encoding is straightforward, with the high-order bits of the first byte indicating the length of the encoding. If the most significant bit is 0 — so that the byte has the form 0xxxxxxx — the length of the encoding is one byte. This byte represents the codepoint having the value indicated

---

[2] www.unicode.org

by the lower seven bits, which represents the character having the same seven-bit ASCII value. For example, the UTF-8 byte 01100101 represents the character "e" (U+0065), just as it does in ASCII.

If the most significant bit of the first byte is 1, the length of the encoding is two to four bytes, with the length encoded in unary by the bits that follow. Thus, the first byte of a two-byte encoding has the form 110xxxxx, the first byte of three-byte encoding has the form 1110xxxx, and the first byte of a four-byte encoding has the form 11110xxx. The second and subsequent bytes of a multibyte encoding all have the form 10xxxxxx. By examining the two most significant bits of any byte, we can determine whether it starts an encoding.

The value of the codepoint for a two-to-four-byte encoding is taken from the remaining unspecified bits, with the most significant bit being taken from the first byte. A two-byte encoding can represent codepoints in the range U+0080 to U+07FF, a three-byte encoding can represent codepoints in the range U+0800 to U+FFFF, and a four-byte encoding can represent codepoints with values U+10000 and above. For example, a three-byte encoding has the overall form

1110xxxx 10yyyyyy 10zzzzzz

and represents the 16-bit value xxxxyyyyyyzzzzzz. The character 八 is assigned the codepoint U+516B, which is 01010001 01101011 in binary. In UTF-8, the character would be encoded by the three bytes 11100101 10000101 10101011.

3.3   Character N-Grams

The difficulty of translating a sequence of characters into a sequence of tokens for indexing depends on the details of the underlying language. The process of recognizing and stemming words differs greatly from language to language. Character n-grams represent an alternative to complex language-specific tokenization. In this section we illustrate the technique with English. In later sections we apply it to other languages.

Using this technique, we simply treat overlapping sequences of n characters as tokens. For example, if $n = 5$, the word "orienteering" would be split into the following 5-grams:

＿orie orien rient iente entee nteer teeri eerin ering ring＿

The "＿" character indicates the beginning or end of a word. Indexing then proceeds with each distinct n-gram given its own postings list. At query time the query is similarly split into n-grams for retrieval. Under this technique a three-character word such as "the" would be indexed with the 5-gram "＿the＿". For two-character and one-character words, we cheat a little, indexing "of" as "＿of＿" and "a" as "＿a＿".

In principle, n-gram indexing need not account for punctuation, capitalization, white space, or other language characteristics. Although the optimal value for n varies from language to

Table 3.2 Impact of 5-gram indexing. The table lists effectiveness measures for selected retrieval methods discussed in this book. The results in this table may be compared with those in Tables 2.5 and 3.1.

| Method | TREC45 | | | | GOV2 | | | |
| | 1998 | | 1999 | | 2004 | | 2005 | |
	P@10	MAP	P@10	MAP	P@10	MAP	P@10	MAP
Proximity (2.2.2)	0.392	0.125	0.388	0.149	0.431	0.171	0.552	0.233
BM25 (Ch. 8)	0.410	0.177	0.446	0.214	0.463	0.226	0.522	0.296
LMD (Ch. 9)	0.416	0.186	0.438	0.222	0.404	0.188	0.502	0.276
DFR (Ch. 9)	0.440	0.203	0.444	0.230	0.478	0.243	0.540	0.284

language, the approach is otherwise language-independent. We just split documents into n-grams, construct an index, and issue queries. In practice, n-gram indexing typically takes into account basic language characteristics. For English, we might strip punctuation and apply case normalization.

N-grams can substitute for a stemmer when no stemmer is available. For many languages, morphology is reflected in the number of n-grams shared by two terms. More of the 5-grams in "orienteers" are matched by 5-grams from "orienteering" than by 5-grams from "oriental".

For English, n-gram indexing has no strong impact. Table 3.2 shows the effectiveness results for 5-gram indexing over our standard experimental collections. The results in the table may be compared with those in Tables 2.5 and 3.1. Compared with those in Table 2.5, the results are mixed. Some are a little better; some are a little worse. As we show in the next section, the outcome may be different for other languages.

N-gram indexing comes at the price of increased index size and decreased efficiency. The compressed indices for the collections in Table 3.2 require up to six times as much storage as the corresponding indices for word-based tokens (in a typical corpus of English text, an average word consists of six characters). Query execution time may be expected to increase by a factor of thirty or more because we increase the number of terms in each query (after tokenization) as well as the lengths of the postings lists.

N-gram indexing can be further extended. Even when words are delimited by white space and punctuation, as they are in English, n-grams may be allowed to cross word boundaries, thus potentially allowing phrasal relationships to be captured. For example, the fragment "...perchance to dream..." would be split into the following 5-grams:

⎵perc perch ercha rchan chanc hance ance⎵ nce⎵t ce⎵to e⎵to⎵ ⎵to⎵d to⎵dr o⎵dre ⎵drea dream ream⎵

where the "⎵" character indicates an interword space. Although this technique generally has a slightly negative impact on the retrieval methods and English-language collections used in our experiments, it may be of benefit for other methods and languages.

3.4   European Languages

In this section we broaden our discussion of tokenization from English to other European languages. Into this category we place a broad range of languages belonging to several distinct language families. For example, French and Italian are Romance languages; Dutch and Swedish are Germanic languages; Russian and Polish are Slavic languages. The Romance, Germanic, and Slavic languages are related to each other, but Finnish and Hungarian belong to a fourth, unrelated family. Irish and Scottish Gaelic belong to a fifth family. Basque, spoken by more than a million people in Spain and France, is an *isolate*, related to no other living language.

Although the category "European language" has little or no meaning from a linguistics perspective, from an IR perspective we can consider these languages as a group. Due to the shared history of the continent, these languages use similar conventions in their *orthography*, the rules by which they are written. Each uses an alphabet of a few dozen letters with uppercase and lowercase forms. Punctuation provides structure. Most usefully, letters are divided into words by white space and punctuation.

There are a number of tokenization issues common to many European languages that are not shared by English. Accents and other diacritical marks are almost nonexistent in English, with "naïve" being a rare exception. In many other European languages, diacritics are essential for pronunciation and may be required to distinguish one word from another. In Spanish, "cuna" is a cradle but "cuña" is a wedge. In Portuguese, "nó" is a knot but "no" is a function word meaning "in the" or "at the". Although carefully edited text will have correct diacritics, these marks may be missing in queries and more casual writing, thus preventing a match.

One solution is to remove the accent marks during tokenization, so that "cuna" and "cuña" are treated as the same term. Another solution is to double index such terms, with and without diacritics. During query processing, the IR system would determine when diacritics are essential and when they are not. Specialized retrieval methods might consider both forms, allowing a match either way. The best solution depends on details of the specific language and the IR environment.

Other tokenization issues are specific to individual languages or language families. In many Germanic languages compound nouns are written as single words. For example, the Dutch equivalent of "bicycle wheel" is "fietswiel". During tokenization this compound noun might be *broken* or *segmented* into two terms, allowing the query term "fiets" to match. Similarly, the German word "Versicherungsbetrug" is a compound of "Versicherung" ("insurance") and "Betrug" ("fraud"). Note that in this case, it is not sufficient simply to split the word into two parts; we also need to take care of the "s" character that connects the two components. Other problems occur when IR systems contain documents in a mixture of languages. Only the acute accent distinguishes the French "thé" ("tea") from the English definite article.

Table 3.3 Comparison of tokenization techniques for several European languages (based on McNamee, 2008). The table lists mean average precision values for tokenizations based on unstemmed words, the Snowball stemmer, character 4-grams, and character 5-grams.

Language	Words	Stemmer	4-grams	5-grams
Dutch	0.416	0.427	0.438	0.444
English	0.483	0.501	0.441	0.461
Finnish	0.319	0.417	0.483	0.496
French	0.427	0.456	0.444	0.440
German	0.349	0.384	0.428	0.432
Italian	0.395	0.435	0.393	0.422
Spanish	0.427	0.467	0.447	0.438
Swedish	0.339	0.376	0.424	0.427

Stemmers are available for most European languages. Of particular note is the Snowball stemmer, which provides support for more than a dozen European languages, including Turkish.[3] Snowball is the creation of Martin Porter, the developer of the Porter stemmer for English, and it shares the algorithmic approach of his older stemmer. N-gram character tokenization also works well for European languages, with values of $n = 4$ or $n = 5$ being optimal.

Table 3.3 compares tokenization techniques for eight European languages, using TREC-style test collections. For all languages the Snowball stemmer outperforms unstemmed words. For Dutch, Finnish, German, and Swedish, character 5-grams give the best overall performance.

3.5 CJK Languages

Chinese, Japanese, and Korean form what are called the *CJK languages*. Like the European languages, the written forms of these languages are linked by shared orthographic conventions deriving from their common history, although they are not members of a single language family. Compared with the European languages, their character sets are enormous. A typical Chinese-language newspaper contains thousands of distinct characters. Moreover, Chinese and Japanese words are not separated by spaces. As a result, segmentation is an essential part of tokenization for these languages.

The complexity of the character sets poses substantial problems. Japanese uses three main scripts. In two of these, each character represents a syllable in the spoken language. The third script is derived from Chinese characters and shares Unicode codepoints with them. In principle,

---

[3] snowball.tartarus.org

a word may be written in any of the three scripts. A query term written in one script may be expected to match against a document term written in another.

Many Chinese characters have a traditional form and a simplified form. For historical reasons, different forms dominate in different regions of the Chinese-speaking world. For example, traditional characters are common in Hong Kong and Macau, whereas simplified characters are standard elsewhere in China. It may be appropriate to return a document in one form in response to a query in the other form. Many people can read text written in either form. Software tools such as browser plugins are also available to automatically translate from one form to the other.

The Chinese language is unusual in that it assigns a meaning to each character, but this property does not imply that each character may be treated as a word. Moreover, the meaning of a word is not consistently linked to the meanings of its characters; a word is not just the sum of its parts. For instance, the Chinese word for "crisis" (危機) is often described as being composed of the character for "danger" followed by the character for "opportunity" (Gore, 2006). However, in this context the second character means something closer to "crucial point", and it often means "machine" in other contexts. The same character appears as the first character in "airport" (機場) in which the second character means "field". Connecting the parts correctly is essential to preserve meaning. An airport is not a "machine field". Freedom (自由) is not just another word for "self cause".

Although some Chinese words, including many function words, consist of a single character, most words are longer. A large proportion of these words are bigrams: two characters in length. Segmenting a sequence of characters into words is a difficult process. Consider the following English sentence written without spaces: "Wegotogethertogether.". The correct segmentation ("We go to get her together.") requires a knowledge of English grammar as well as English vocabulary. In Chinese a character may form a word with both the character that proceeds it and the character that follows it. The correct segmentation depends on the context. Nonetheless, word segmentation is not absolutely essential for Chinese-language information retrieval. Perhaps because of the predominance of bigrams, 2-gram character indexing works well for Chinese, providing a simple baseline for evaluating automatic word segmentation.

The CJK languages all have standardized conventions for their transliteration into the Roman alphabet. For Chinese the modern transliteration standard is *Hanyu Pinyin* (or just *Pinyin*). In Pinyin, 危機 becomes "wēijī" and 機場 becomes "jīchǎng". The diacritical marks indicate *tonality*, the changes in pitch used when pronouncing the syllable.

Pinyin provides a convenient alternative for expressing Chinese-language queries. Unfortunately, the use of Pinyin introduces a certain level of ambiguity. For example, about six common characters are transliterated as "jī". Moreover, Pinyin queries are commonly entered without diacritics, giving rise to additional ambiguity. With tone marks omitted, some thirty common characters are transliterated as "yi", and even more are transliterated as "shi". The query term "shishi" could mean "current event" (時事), "implementation" (實施), and several other things. To address this ambiguity, a search engine might present alternative interpretations to users, allowing them to choose the correct one.

3.6   Further Reading

Simplistically, tokenization attempts to split a document into words. Trask (2004) provides a readable discussion of the concept of "a word" from a linguistics standpoint. Additional discussion of tokenization and lemmatization from an NLP perspective is given in Chapter 4 of Manning and Schütze (1999).

Most programming languages and operating systems now provide support for Unicode and UTF-8. Details of the Unicode standard are given on its official Web site.[4] The UTF-8 encoding for Unicode codepoints was invented by Rob Pike and Ken Thompson as part of their Plan-9 Operating System effort (Pike and Thompson, 1993). Since the time of Pike and Thompson's invention, UTF-8 has been modified to accommodate changes and extensions to Unicode. It is defined as an Internet standard by RFC 3639.[5]

In addition to the Porter stemmer (Porter, 1980), early stemmers for English include those by Lovins (1968), Frakes (1984), and Paice (1990). Harman (1991) describes a simple *S stemmer*, designed to reduce plural words to their singular forms. She compared the performance of this S stemmer with those of the Porter and Lovins stemmers but found no significant improvement in retrieval performance over unstemmed words for any of the stemmers. Through a more extensive evaluation using larger test collections, Hull (1996) demonstrates that stemming can significantly improve average effectiveness measures. However, he cautions that aggressive stemming may degrade the performance of many queries while still improving average effectiveness by greatly improving the performance of a few queries.

The Snowball[6] stemmer provides an algorithmic framework for creating stemmers. Nonetheless, the creation and validation of a stemmer for a new language remains a labor-intensive process. As a result, several attempts have been made to automatically create stemmers by using large corpora to provide language examples. Creutz and Lagus (2002) describe a method for segmenting words by minimizing a cost function and compare their method with existing stemmers for English and Finnish. Majumder et al. (2007) describe a method that clusters words into equivalence classes based on a morphological analysis. They evaluate their method over several languages, including Bengali.

McNamee and Mayfield (2004) provide an overview of character n-gram tokenization for information retrieval. McNamee et al. (2008) and McNamee (2008) compare n-gram indexing with the Snowball stemmer and with the method of Creutz and Lagus (2002). In addition, character n-grams provide one method for coping with errors introduced by optical character recognition (OCR). Beitzel et al. (2002) provide a short survey of this area.

---

[4] www.unicode.org

[5] tools.ietf.org/html/rfc3629

[6] snowball.tartarus.org

Spanish IR was the subject of an experimental track at TREC from 1994 to 1996; Chinese was the subject of a track in 1996 and 1997 (Voorhees and Harman, 2005). A multilingual track that considered Arabic along with other languages ran from 1997 until 2002 (Gey and Oard, 2001). Starting in 2000 the Cross-Language Evaluation Forum (CLEF[7]) conducted multilingual and crosslingual experiments on European languages. The results in Table 3.3 are derived from CLEF test collections. Since 2001 the Japanese National Institute of Informatics Test Collection for IR Systems project (NTCIR[8]) has provided a similar experimental forum for Asian languages. The Indian Forum for Information Retrieval Evaluation (FIRE[9]) conducts experiments on languages of the Indian subcontinent.

Computer processing for Asian languages presents difficult and complex problems, and it remains the subject of substantial ongoing research. A major journal, *ACM Transactions on Asian Language Information Processing* is devoted entirely to the topic. Luk and Kwok (2002) provide an extensive overview of word segmentation and tokenization techniques for Chinese information retrieval. Peng et al. (2002) explore the importance of word segmentation for Chinese information retrieval, evaluating and comparing a number of competing techniques. Braschler and Ripplinger (2004) consider word segmentation (also called *decompounding*) for German. Kraaij and Pohlmann (1996) consider decompounding for Dutch. A special issue of the *Information Retrieval Journal* is devoted to non-English Web retrieval (Lazarinis et al., 2009).

Tokenization for a new language requires careful consideration of both its orthography and its morphology. Fujii and Croft (1993) cover the basics of tokenization for Japanese. Asian et al. (2005) discuss Indonesian. Larkey et al. (2002) discuss Arabic. Nwesri et al. (2005) present and evaluate an algorithm for removing affixes representing conjunctions and prepositions from Arabic words.

Spelling correction is closely related to tokenization. Because tokens provide the link between queries and documents, matching becomes harder when misspellings are present. Kukich (1992) provides a survey of foundational work on the detection and correction of spelling errors. Brill and Moore (2000) present an error model for spelling correction. Ruch (2002) examines the impact of spelling errors on a basic adhoc retrieval task. Both Cucerzan and Brill (2004) and Li et al. (2006) describe spell checkers created by identifying spelling errors and their corrections from the query logs of a commercial Web search engine. Jain et al. (2007) describe related methods for expanding acronyms using query logs.

---

[7] www.clef-campaign.org

[8] research.nii.ac.jp/ntcir

[9] www.isical.ac.in/~clia

3.7 Exercises

Exercise 3.1 Try the following queries on at least two commercial search engines:

(a) to be or not to be
(b) U.S.
(c) US
(d) THE
(e) The The
(f) I'll be back
(g) R-E-S-P-E-C-T

Each query has a peculiar meaning that may be lost through tokenization. Judge the top five results. Which are relevant?

Exercise 3.2 In the content of the Web certain terms appear so frequently that they may viewed as stopwords. Try the following queries on at least two commercial search engines:

(a) www
(b) com
(c) http

Judge the top five results. Which are relevant?

Exercise 3.3 Unicode assigns the character β a codepoint of U+03B2. What is its binary UTF-8 representation?

Exercise 3.4 (project exercise) Tokenize the collection you created in Exercise 1.9. For this exercise, keep only the tokens consisting entirely of characters from the English alphabet. Ignore tags and tokens containing non-ASCII characters. Generate character 5-grams from these tokens, following the procedure of Section 3.3. Generate a log-log plot of frequency vs. rank order, similar to the plot in Figure 1.5 or the plot generated for Exercise 1.12. Do the 5-grams follow Zipf's law? If so, what is an approximate value for α?

Exercise 3.5 (project exercise) Repeat Exercise 3.4 using Chinese-language text from Wikipedia, tokenized as character bigrams.

Exercise 3.6 (project exercise) Obtain a copy of the Porter stemmer or another stemmer for English. Tokenize the collection you created in Exercise 1.9. As you did in Exercise 3.4, keep only the tokens consisting entirely of characters from the English alphabet. Eliminate duplicate tokens to create a vocabulary for the collection. Execute the stemmer over the terms in the vocabulary to create sets of equivalent terms, all of which stem to the same root form. Which set (or sets) is the largest? Identify at least three sets containing terms that are inappropriately conflated by the stemmer.

Exercise 3.7 (project exercise) If you are familiar with a language other than English for which a stemmer is available, repeat Exercise 3.6 for that language. You may use Wikipedia as a source of text.

3.8 Bibliography

Asian, J., Williams, H. E., and Tahaghoghi, S. M. M. (2005). Stemming Indonesian. In *Proceedings of the 28th Australasian Computer Science Conference*, pages 307–314. Newcastle, Australia.

Beitzel, S., Jensen, E., and Grossman, D. (2002). Retrieving OCR text: A survey of current approaches. In *Proceedings of the SIGIR 2002 Workshop on Information Retrieval and OCR: From Converting Content to Grasping Meaning*. Tampere, Finland.

Braschler, M., and Ripplinger, B. (2004). How effective is stemming and decompounding for German text retrieval? *Information Retrieval*, 7(3-4):291–316.

Brill, E., and Moore, R. C. (2000). An improved error model for noisy channel spelling correction. In *Proceedings of the 38th Annual Meeting on Association for Computational Linguistics*, pages 286–293. Hong Kong, China.

Creutz, M., and Lagus, K. (2002). Unsupervised discovery of morphemes. In *Proceedings of the ACL-02 Workshop on Morphological and Phonological Learning*, pages 21–30.

Cucerzan, S., and Brill, E. (2004). Spelling correction as an iterative process that exploits the collective knowledge of Web users. In *Proceedings of the Conference on Empirical Methods in Natural Language Processing*, pages 293–300.

Frakes, W. B. (1984). Term conflation for information retrieval. In *Proceedings of the 7th Annual International ACM SIGIR Conference on Research and Development in Information Retrieval*, pages 383–389. Cambridge, England.

Fujii, H., and Croft, W. B. (1993). A comparison of indexing techniques for Japanese text retrieval. In *Proceedings of the 16th Annual International ACM SIGIR Conference on Research and Development in Information Retrieval*, pages 237–246. Pittsburgh, Pennsylvania.

Gey, F. C., and Oard, D. W. (2001). The TREC-2001 cross-language information retrieval track: Searching Arabic using English, French or Arabic queries. In *Proceedings of the 10th Text REtrieval Conference*, pages 16–25. Gaithersburg, Maryland.

Gore, A. (2006). *An Inconvenient Truth*. Emmaus, Pennsylvania: Rodale.

Harman, D. (1991). How effective is suffixing? *Journal of the American Society for Information Science*, 42(1):7–15.

Hull, D. A. (1996). Stemming algorithms: A case study for detailed evaluation. *Journal of the American Society for Information Science*, 47(1):70–84.

Jain, A., Cucerzan, S., and Azzam, S. (2007). Acronym-expansion recognition and ranking on the Web. In *Proceedings of the IEEE International Conference on Information Reuse and Integration*, pages 209–214. Las Vegas, Nevada.

Kraaij, W., and Pohlmann, R. (1996). *Using Linguistic Knowledge in Information Retrieval*. Technical Report OTS-WP-CL-96-001. Research Institute for Language and Speech, Utrecht University.

Kukich, K. (1992). Technique for automatically correcting words in text. *ACM Computing Surveys*, 24(4):377–439.

Larkey, L. S., Ballesteros, L., and Connell, M. E. (2002). Improving stemming for Arabic information retrieval: Light stemming and co-occurrence analysis. In *Proceedings of the 25th Annual International ACM SIGIR Conference on Research and Development in Information Retrieval*, pages 275–282. Tampere, Finland.

Lazarinis, F., Vilares, J., Tait, J., and Efthimiadis, E. N. (2009). Introduction to the special issue on non-English Web retrival. *Information Retrieval*, 12(3).

Li, M., Zhu, M., Zhang, Y., and Zhou, M. (2006). Exploring distributional similarity based models for query spelling correction. In *Proceedings of the 21st International Conference on Computational Linguistics and the 44th Annual Meeting of the Association for Computational Linguistics*, pages 1025–1032. Sydney, Australia.

Lovins, J. B. (1968). Development of a stemming algorithm. *Mechanical Translation and Computational Linguistics*, 11(1–2):22–31.

Luk, R. W. P., and Kwok, K. L. (2002). A comparison of Chinese document indexing strategies and retrieval models. *ACM Transactions on Asian Language Information Processing*, 1(3):225–268.

Majumder, P., Mitra, M., Parui, S. K., Kole, G., Mitra, P., and Datta, K. (2007). YASS: Yet another suffix stripper. *ACM Transactions on Information Systems*, 25(4):article 18.

Manning, C. D., and Schütze, H. (1999). *Foundations of Statistical Natural Language Processing*. Cambridge, Massachusetts: MIT Press.

McNamee, P. (2008). Retrieval experiments at Morpho Challenge 2008. In *Cross-Language Evaluation Forum*. Aarhus, Denmark.

McNamee, P., and Mayfield, J. (2004). Character n-gram tokenization for European language text retrieval. *Information Retrieval*, 7(1-2):73–97.

McNamee, P., Nicholas, C., and Mayfield, J. (2008). Don't have a stemmer?: Be un+concern+ed. In *Proceedings of the 31st Annual International ACM SIGIR Conference on Research and Development in Information Retrieval*, pages 813–814. Singapore.

Nwesri, A. F. A., Tahaghoghi, S. M. M., and Scholer, F. (2005). Stemming Arabic conjunctions and prepositions. In *Proceedings of the 12th International Conference on String Processing and Information Retrieval*, pages 206–217. Buenos Aires, Agentina.

Paice, C. D. (1990). Another stemmer. *ACM SIGIR Forum*, 24(3):56–61.

Peng, F., Huang, X., Schuurmans, D., and Cercone, N. (2002). Investigating the relationship between word segmentation performance and retrieval performance in Chinese IR. In *Proceedings of the 19th International Conference on Computational Linguistics*. Taipei, Taiwan.

Pike, R., and Thompson, K. (1993). Hello world. In *Proceedings of the Winter 1993 USENIX Conference*, pages 43–50. San Diego, California.

Porter, M. F. (1980). An algorithm for suffix stripping. *Program*, 14(3):130–137.

Ruch, P. (2002). Information retrieval and spelling correction: An inquiry into lexical disambiguation. In *Proceedings of the 2002 ACM Symposium on Applied Computing*, pages 699–703. Madrid, Spain.

Trask, L. (2004). *What is a Word?* Technical Report LxWP11/04. Department of Linguistics and English Language, University of Sussex, United Kingdom.

Voorhees, E. M., and Harman, D. K. (2005). The Text REtrieval Conference. In Voorhees, E. M., and Harman, D. K., editors, *TREC — Experiment and Evaluation in Information Retrieval*, chapter 1, pages 3–20. Cambridge, Massachusetts: MIT Press.

II Indexing

4 Static Inverted Indices

In this chapter we describe a set of index structures that are suitable for supporting search queries of the type outlined in Chapter 2. We restrict ourselves to the case of static text collections. That is, we assume that we are building an index for a collection that never changes. Index update strategies for dynamic text collections, in which documents can be added to and removed from the collection, are the topic of Chapter 7.

For performance reasons, it may be desirable to keep the index for a text collection completely in main memory. However, in many applications this is not feasible. In file system search, for example, a full-text index for all data stored in the file system can easily consume several gigabytes. Since users will rarely be willing to dedicate the most part of their available memory resources to the search system, it is not possible to keep the entire index in RAM. And even for dedicated index servers used in Web search engines it might be economically sensible to store large portions of the index on disk instead of in RAM, simply because disk space is so much cheaper than RAM. For example, while we are writing this, a gigabyte of RAM costs around $40 (U.S.), whereas a gigabyte of hard drive space costs only about $0.20 (U.S.). This factor-200 price difference, however, is not reflected by the relative performance of the two storage media. For typical index operations, an in-memory index is usually between 10 and 20 times faster than an on-disk index. Hence, when building two equally priced retrieval systems, one storing its index data on disk, the other storing them in main memory, the disk-based system may actually be faster than the RAM-based one (see Bender et al. (2007) for a more in-depth discussion of this and related issues).

The general assumption that will guide us throughout this chapter is that main memory is a scarce resource, either because the search engine has to share it with other processes running on the same system or because it is more economical to store data on disk than in RAM. In our discussion of data structures for inverted indices, we focus on hybrid organizations, in which some parts of the index are kept in main memory, while the majority of the data is stored on disk. We examine a variety of data structures for different parts of the search engine and evaluate their performance through a number of experiments. A performance summary of the computer system used to conduct these experiments can be found in the appendix.

4.1 Index Components and Index Life Cycle

When we discuss the various aspects of inverted indices in this chapter, we look at them from two perspectives: the structural perspective, in which we divide the system into its components and examine aspects of an individual component of the index (e.g., an individual postings list); and the operational perspective, in which we look at different phases in the life cycle of an inverted index and discuss the essential index operations that are carried out in each phase (e.g., processing a search query).

As already mentioned in Chapter 2, the two principal components of an inverted index are the *dictionary* and the *postings lists*. For each term in the text collection, there is a postings list that contains information about the term's occurrences in the collection. The information found in these postings lists is used by the system to process search queries. The dictionary serves as a lookup data structure on top of the postings lists. For every query term in an incoming search query, the search engine first needs to locate the term's postings list before it can start processing the query. It is the job of the dictionary to provide this mapping from terms to the location of their postings lists in the index.

In addition to dictionary and postings lists, search engines often employ various other data structures. Many engines, for instance, maintain a *document map* that, for each document in the index, contains document-specific information, such as the document's URL, its length, PageRank (see Section 15.3.1), and other data. The implementation of these data structures, however, is mostly straightforward and does not require any special attention.

The life cycle of a static inverted index, built for a never-changing text collection, consists of two distinct phases (for a dynamic index the two phases coincide):

1. *Index construction*: The text collection is processed sequentially, one token at a time, and a postings list is built for each term in the collection in an incremental fashion.

2. *Query processing*: The information stored in the index that was built in phase 1 is used to process search queries.

Phase 1 is generally referred to as *indexing time*, while phase 2 is referred to as *query time*. In many respects these two phases are complementary; by performing additional work at indexing time (e.g., precomputing score contributions — see Section 5.1.3), less work needs to be done at query time. In general, however, the two phases are quite different from one another and usually require different sets of algorithms and data structures. Even for subcomponents of the index that are shared by the two phases, such as the search engine's dictionary data structure, it is not uncommon that the specific implementation utilized during index construction is different from the one used at query time.

The flow of this chapter is mainly defined by our bifocal perspective on inverted indices. In the first part of the chapter (Sections 4.2–4.4), we are primarily concerned with the query-time aspects of dictionary and postings lists, looking for data structures that are most suitable for supporting efficient index access and query processing. In the second part (Section 4.5) we focus on aspects of the index construction process and discuss how we can efficiently build the data structures outlined in the first part. We also discuss how the organization of the dictionary and the postings lists needs to be different from the one suggested in the first part of the chapter, if we want to maximize their performance at indexing time.

For the sake of simplicity, we assume throughout this chapter that we are dealing exclusively with *schema-independent* indices. Other types of inverted indices, however, are similar to the schema-independent variant, and the methods discussed in this chapter apply to all of them (see Section 2.1.3 for a list of different types of inverted indices).

4.2 The Dictionary

The *dictionary* is the central data structure that is used to manage the set of terms found in a text collection. It provides a mapping from the set of index terms to the locations of their postings lists. At query time, locating the query terms' postings lists in the index is one of the first operations performed when processing an incoming keyword query. At indexing time, the dictionary's lookup capability allows the search engine to quickly obtain the memory address of the inverted list for each incoming term and to append a new posting at the end of that list.

Dictionary implementations found in search engines usually support the following set of operations:

1. Insert a new entry for term T.
2. Find and return the entry for term T (if present).
3. Find and return the entries for all terms that start with a given prefix P.

When building an index for a text collection, the search engine performs operations of types 1 and 2 to look up incoming terms in the dictionary and to add postings for these terms to the index. After the index has been built, the search engine can process search queries, performing operations of types 2 and 3 to locate the postings lists for all query terms. Although dictionary operations of type 3 are not strictly necessary, they are a useful feature because they allow the search engine to support *prefix queries* of the form "inform*", matching all documents containing a term that begins with "inform".

Table 4.1   Index sizes for various index types and three example collections, with and without applying index compression techniques. In each case the first number refers to an index in which each component is stored as a simple 32-bit integer, while the second number refers to an index in which each entry is compressed using a byte-aligned encoding method.

	Shakespeare	**TREC45**	**GOV2**
Number of tokens	1.3×10^6	3.0×10^8	4.4×10^{10}
Number of terms	2.3×10^4	1.2×10^6	4.9×10^7
Dictionary (uncompr.)	0.4 MB	24 MB	1046 MB
Docid index	n/a	578 MB/200 MB	37751 MB/12412 MB
Frequency index	n/a	1110 MB/333 MB	73593 MB/21406 MB
Positional index	n/a	2255 MB/739 MB	245538 MB/78819 MB
Schema-ind. index	5.7 MB/2.7 MB	1190 MB/532 MB	173854 MB/63670 MB

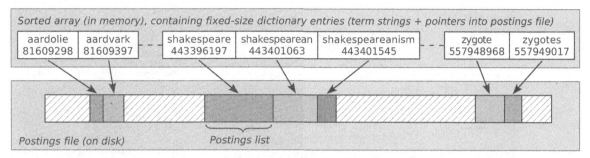

Figure 4.1 Dictionary data structure based on a sorted array (data extracted from a schema-independent index for TREC45). The array contains fixed-size dictionary entries, composed of a zero-terminated string and a pointer into the postings file that indicates the position of the term's postings list.

For a typical natural-language text collection, the dictionary is relatively small compared to the total size of the index. Table 4.1 shows this for the three example collections used in this book. The size of the uncompressed dictionary is only between 0.6% (GOV2) and 7% (Shakespeare) of the size of an uncompressed schema-independent index for the respective collection (the fact that the relative size of the dictionary is smaller for large collections than for small ones follows directly from Zipf's law — see Equation 1.2 on page 16). We therefore assume, at least for now, that the dictionary is small enough to fit completely into main memory.

The two most common ways to realize an in-memory dictionary are:

- A *sort-based* dictionary, in which all terms that appear in the text collection are arranged in a sorted array or in a search tree, in lexicographical (i.e., alphabetical) order, as shown in Figure 4.1. Lookup operations are realized through tree traversal (when using a search tree) or binary search (when using a sorted list).

- A *hash-based* dictionary, in which each index term has a corresponding entry in a hash table. Collisions in the hash table (i.e., two terms are assigned the same hash value) are resolved by means of *chaining* — terms with the same hash value are arranged in a linked list, as shown in Figure 4.2.

Storing the dictionary terms

When implementing the dictionary as a sorted array, it is important that all array entries are of the same size. Otherwise, performing a binary search may be difficult. Unfortunately, this causes some problems. For example, the longest sequence of alphanumeric characters in GOV2 (i.e., the longest term in the collection) is 74,147 bytes long. Obviously, it is not feasible to allocate 74 KB of memory for each term in the dictionary. But even if we ignore such extreme outliers and truncate each term after, say, 20 bytes, we are still wasting precious memory resources. Following the simple tokenization procedure from Section 1.3.2, the average length of a term

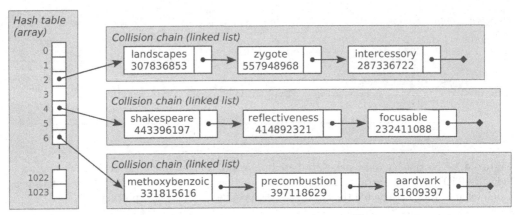

Figure 4.2 Dictionary data structure based on a hash table with $2^{10} = 1024$ entries (data extracted from schema-independent index for TREC45). Terms with the same hash value are arranged in a linked list (*chaining*). Each term descriptor contains the term itself, the position of the term's postings list, and a pointer to the next entry in the linked list.

in GOV2 is 9.2 bytes. Storing each term in a fixed-size memory region of 20 bytes wastes 10.8 bytes per term on average (*internal fragmentation*).

One way to eliminate the internal fragmentation is to not store the index terms themselves in the array, but only pointers to them. For example, the search engine could maintain a *primary* dictionary array, containing 32-bit pointers into a *secondary* array. The secondary array then contains the actual dictionary entries, consisting of the terms themselves and the corresponding pointers into the postings file. This way of organizing the search engine's dictionary data is shown in Figure 4.3. It is sometimes referred to as the *dictionary-as-a-string approach*, because there are no explicit delimiters between two consecutive dictionary entries; the secondary array can be thought of as a long, uninterrupted string.

For the GOV2 collection, the dictionary-as-a-string approach, compared to the dictionary layout shown in Figure 4.1, reduces the dictionary's storage requirements by $10.8 - 4 = 6.8$ bytes per entry. Here the term 4 stems from the pointer overhead in the primary array; the term 10.8 corresponds to the complete elimination of any internal fragmentation.

It is worth pointing out that the term strings stored in the secondary array do not require an explicit termination symbol (e.g., the "\0" character), because the length of each term in the dictionary is implicitly given by the pointers in the primary array. For example, by looking at the pointers for "shakespeare" and "shakespearean" in Figure 4.3, we know that the dictionary entry for "shakespeare" requires $16629970 - 16629951 = 19$ bytes in total: 11 bytes for the term plus 8 bytes for the 64-bit file pointer into the postings file.

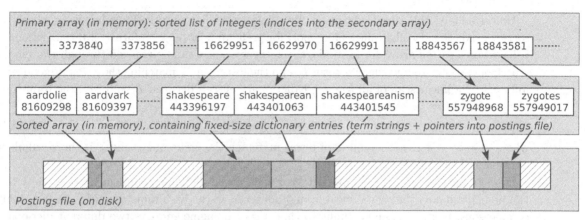

Figure 4.3 Sort-based dictionary data structure with an additional level of indirection (the so-called *dictionary-as-a-string* approach).

Sort-based versus hash-based dictionary

For most applications a hash-based dictionary will be faster than a sort-based implementation, as it does not require a costly binary search or the traversal of a path in a search tree to find the dictionary entry for a given term. The precise speed advantage of a hash-based dictionary over a sort-based dictionary depends on the size of the hash table. If the table is too small, then there will be many collisions, potentially reducing the dictionary's performance substantially. As a rule of thumb, in order to keep the lengths of the collision chains in the hash table small, the size of the table should grow linearly with the number of terms in the dictionary.

Table 4.2 Lookup performance at query time. Average latency of a single-term lookup for a sort-based (shown in Figure 4.3) and a hash-based (shown in Figure 4.2) dictionary implementation. For the hash-based implementation, the size of the hash table (number of array entries) is varied between 2^{18} ($\approx$ 262,000) and 2^{24} ($\approx$ 16.8 million).

	Sorted	Hashed (2^{18})	Hashed (2^{20})	Hashed (2^{22})	Hashed (2^{24})
Shakespeare	0.32 μs	0.11 μs	0.13 μs	0.14 μs	0.16 μs
TREC45	1.20 μs	0.53 μs	0.34 μs	0.27 μs	0.25 μs
GOV2	2.79 μs	19.8 μs	5.80 μs	2.23 μs	0.84 μs

Table 4.2 shows the average time needed to find the dictionary entry for a random index term in each of our three example collections. A larger table usually results in a shorter lookup time, except for the *Shakespeare* collection, which is so small (23,000 different terms) that the effect of decreasing the term collisions is outweighed by the less efficient CPU cache utilization. A bigger hash table in this case results in an increased lookup time. Nonetheless, if the table size is chosen properly, a hash-based dictionary is usually at least twice as fast as a sort-based one.

Unfortunately, this speed advantage for single-term dictionary lookups has a drawback: A sort-based dictionary offers efficient support for prefix queries (e.g., "inform*"). If the dictionary is based on a sorted array, for example, then a prefix query can be realized through two binary search operations, to find the first term T_j and the last term T_k matching the given prefix query, followed by a linear scan of all $k - j + 1$ dictionary entries between T_j and T_k. The total time complexity of this procedure is

$$\Theta(\log(|\mathcal{V}|)) + \Theta(m), \qquad (4.1)$$

where $m = k - j + 1$ is the number of terms matching the prefix query and $\mathcal{V}$ is the vocabulary of the search engine.

If prefix queries are to be supported by a hash-based dictionary implementation, then this can be realized only through a linear scan of all terms in the hash table, requiring $\Theta(|\mathcal{V}|)$ string comparisons. It is therefore not unusual that a search engine employs two different dictionary data structures: a hash-based dictionary, used during the index construction process and providing efficient support of operations 1 (insert) and 2 (single-term lookup), and a sort-based dictionary that is created after the index has been built and that provides efficient support of operations 2 (single-term lookup) and 3 (prefix lookup).

The distinction between an indexing-time and a query-time dictionary is further motivated by the fact that support for high-performance single-term dictionary lookups is more important during index construction than during query processing. At query time the overhead associated with finding the dictionary entries for all query terms is negligible (a few microseconds) and is very likely to be outweighed by the other computations that have to be performed while processing a query. At indexing time, however, a dictionary lookup needs to be performed for every token in the text collection — 44 billion lookup operations in the case of GOV2. Thus, the dictionary represents a major bottleneck in the index construction process, and lookups should be as fast as possible.

4.3 Postings Lists

The actual index data, used during query processing and accessed through the search engine's dictionary, is stored in the index's postings lists. Each term's postings list contains information about the term's occurrences in the collection. Depending on the type of the index (docid, frequency, positional, or schema-independent — see Section 2.1.3), a term's postings list contains more or less detailed, and more or less storage-intensive, information. Regardless of the actual type of the index, however, the postings data always constitute the vast majority of all the data in the index. In their entirety, they are therefore usually too large to be stored in main memory and have to be kept on disk. Only during query processing are the query terms' postings lists (or small parts thereof) loaded into memory, on a by-need basis, as required by the query processing routines.

To make the transfer of postings from disk into main memory as efficient as possible, each term's postings list should be stored in a contiguous region of the hard drive. That way, when accessing the list, the number of disk seek operations is minimized. The hard drives of the computer system used in our experiments (summarized in the appendix) can read about half a megabyte of data in the time it takes to perform a single disk seek, so discontiguous postings lists can reduce the system's query performance dramatically.

Random list access: The per-term index

The search engine's list access pattern at query time depends on the type of query being processed. For some queries, postings are accessed in an almost strictly sequential fashion. For other queries it is important that the search engine can carry out efficient random access operations on the postings lists. An example of the latter type is phrase search or — equivalently — conjunctive Boolean search (processing a phrase query on a schema-independent index is essentially the same as resolving a Boolean AND on a docid index).

Recall from Chapter 2 the two main access methods provided by an inverted index: **next** and **prev**, returning the first (or last) occurrence of the given term after (or before) a given index address. Suppose we want to find all occurrences of the phrase "iterative binary search" in GOV2. After we have found out that there is exactly one occurrence of "iterative binary" in the collection, at position [33,399,564,886, 33,399,564,887], a single call to

$$\textbf{next}(\text{``search''}, \; 33,399,564,887)$$

will tell us whether the phrase "iterative binary search" appears in the corpus. If the method returns 33,399,564,888, then the answer is yes. Otherwise, the answer is no.

If postings lists are stored in memory, as arrays of integers, then this operation can be performed very efficiently by conducting a binary search (or galloping search — see Section 2.1.2) on the postings array for "search". Since the term "search" appears about 50 million times in GOV2, the binary search requires a total of

$$\lceil \log_2(5 \times 10^7) \rceil = 26$$

random list accesses. For an on-disk postings list, the operation could theoretically be carried out in the same way. However, since a hard disk is not a true random access device, and a disk seek is a very costly operation, such an approach would be prohibitively expensive. With its 26 random disk accesses, a binary search on the on-disk postings list can easily take more than 200 milliseconds, due to seek overhead and rotational latency of the disk platter.

As an alternative, one might consider loading the entire postings list into memory in a single sequential read operation, thereby avoiding the expensive disk seeks. However, this is not a good solution, either. Assuming that each posting requires 8 bytes of disk space, it would take our computer more than 4 seconds to read the term's 50 million postings from disk.

list header	per-term index (5 postings)				
TF: 27	239539	242435	248080	255731	281080
239539	239616	239732	239765	240451	242395
242435	242659	243223	243251	245282	247589
248080	248526	248803	249056	254313	254350
255731	256428	264780	271063	272125	279107
281080	281793	284087			

Figure 4.4   Schema-independent postings list for "denmark" (extracted from the Shakespeare collection) with per-term index: one synchronization point for every six postings. The number of synchronization points is implicit from the length of the list: $\lceil 27/6 \rceil = 5$.

In order to provide efficient random access into any given on-disk postings list, each list has to be equipped with an auxiliary data structure, which we refer to as the *per-term index*. This data structure is stored on disk, at the beginning of the respective postings list. It contains a copy of a subset of the postings in the list, for instance, a copy of every 5,000th posting. When accessing the on-disk postings list for a given term T, before performing any actual index operations on the list, the search engine loads T's per-term index into memory. Random-access operations of the type required by the **next** method can then be carried out by performing a binary search on the in-memory array representing T's per-term index (identifying a candidate range of 5,000 postings in the on-disk postings list), followed by loading up to 5,000 postings from the candidate range into memory and then performing a random access operation on those postings.

This approach to random access list operations is sometimes referred to as *self-indexing* (Moffat and Zobel, 1996). The entries in the per-term index are called *synchronization points*. Figure 4.4 shows the postings list for the term "denmark", extracted from the Shakespeare collection, with a per-term index of granularity 6 (i.e., one synchronization point for every six postings in the list). In the figure, a call to **next**(250,000) would first identify the postings block starting with 248,080 as potentially containing the candidate posting. It would then load this block into memory, carry out a binary search on the block, and return 254,313 as the answer. Similarly, in our example for the phrase query "iterative binary search", the random access operation into the list for the term "search" would be realized using only 2 disk seeks and loading a total of about 15,000 postings into memory (10,000 postings for the per-term index and 5,000 postings from the candidate range) — translating into a total execution time of approximately 30 ms.

Choosing the granularity of the per-term index, that is, the number of postings between two synchronization points, represents a trade-off. A greater granularity increases the amount of data between two synchronization points that need to be loaded into memory for every random access operation; a smaller granularity, conversely, increases the size of the per-term index and thus the amount of data read from disk when initializing the postings list (Exercise 4.1 asks you to calculate the optimal granularity for a given list).

In theory it is conceivable that, for a very long postings list containing billions of entries, the optimal per-term index (with a granularity that minimizes the total amount of disk activity) becomes so large that it is no longer feasible to load it completely into memory. In such a situation it is possible to build an index for the per-term index, or even to apply the whole procedure recursively. In the end this leads to a multi-level static B-tree that provides efficient random access into the postings list. In practice, however, such a complicated data structure is rarely necessary. A simple two-level structure, with a single per-term index for each on-disk postings list, is sufficient. The term "the", for instance, the most frequent term in the GOV2 collection, appears roughly 1 billion times in the collection. When stored uncompressed, its postings list in a schema-independent index consumes about 8 billion bytes (8 bytes per posting). Suppose the per-term index for "the" contains one synchronization point for every 20,000 postings. Loading the per-term index with its 50,000 entries into memory requires a single disk seek, followed by a sequential transfer of 400,000 bytes ($\approx$ 4.4 ms). Each random access operation into the term's list requires an additional disk seek, followed by loading 160,000 bytes ($\approx$ 1.7 ms) into RAM. In total, therefore, a single random access operation into the term's postings list requires about 30 ms (two random disk accesses, each taking about 12 ms, plus reading 560,000 bytes from disk). In comparison, adding an additional level of indexing, by building an index for the per-term index, would increase the number of disk seeks required for a single random access to at least three, and would therefore most likely decrease the index's random access performance.

Compared to an implementation that performs a binary search directly on the on-disk postings list, the introduction of the per-term index improves the performance of random access operations quite substantially. The true power of the method, however, lies in the fact that it allows us to store postings of variable length, for example postings of the form (*docid, tf,* ⟨*positions*⟩), and in particular compressed postings. If postings are stored not as fixed-size (e.g., 8-byte) integers, but in compressed form, then a simple binary search is no longer possible. However, by compressing postings in small chunks, where the beginning of each chunk corresponds to a synchronization point in the per-term index, the search engine can provide efficient random access even for compressed postings lists. This application also explains the choice of the term "synchronization point": a synchronization point helps the decoder establish synchrony with the encoder, thus allowing it to start decompressing data at an (almost) arbitrary point within the compressed postings sequence. See Chapter 6 for details on compressed inverted indices.

Prefix queries

If the search engine has to support prefix queries, such as "inform∗", then it is imperative that postings lists be stored in lexicographical order of their respective terms. Consider the GOV2 collection; 4,365 different terms with a total of 67 million occurrences match the prefix query "inform∗". By storing lists in lexicographical order, we ensure that the inverted lists for these 4,365 terms are close to each other in the inverted file and thus close to each other on disk. This decreases the seek distance between the individual lists and leads to better query performance. If lists were stored on disk in some random order, then disk seeks and rotational latency alone would account for almost a minute (4,365 × 12 ms), not taking into account any of the other operations that need to be carried out when processing the query. By arranging the inverted lists in lexicographical order of their respective terms, a query asking for all documents matching "inform*" can be processed in less than 2 seconds when using a frequency index; with a schema-independent index, the same query takes about 6 seconds. Storing the lists in the inverted file in some predefined order (e.g., lexicographical) is also important for efficient index updates, as discussed in Chapter 7.

A separate positional index

If the search engine is based on a document-centric positional index (containing a docid, a frequency value, and a list of within-document positions for each document that a given term appears in), it is not uncommon to divide the index data into two separate inverted files: one file containing the docid and frequency component of each posting, the other file containing the exact within-document positions. The rationale behind this division is that for many queries — and many scoring functions — access to the positional information is not necessary. By excluding it from the main index, query processing performance can be increased.

4.4   Interleaving Dictionary and Postings Lists

For many text collections the dictionary is small enough to fit into the main memory of a single machine. For large collections, however, containing many millions of different terms, even the collective size of all dictionary entries might be too large to be conveniently stored in RAM. The GOV2 collection, for instance, contains about 49 million distinct terms. The total size of the concatenation of these 49 million terms (if stored as zero-terminated strings) is 482 MB. Now suppose the dictionary data structure used in the search engine is based on a sorted array, as shown in Figure 4.3. Maintaining for each term in the dictionary an additional 32-bit pointer in the primary sorted array and a 64-bit file pointer in the secondary array increases the overall memory consumption by another 12×49 = 588 million bytes (approximately), leading to a total memory requirement of 1046 MB. Therefore, although the GOV2 collection is small enough to be managed by a single machine, the dictionary may be too large to fit into the machine's main memory.

To some extent, this problem can be addressed by employing dictionary compression techniques (discussed in Section 6.4). However, dictionary compression can get us only so far. There exist situations in which the number of distinct terms in the text collection is so enormous that it becomes impossible to store the entire dictionary in main memory, even after compression. Consider, for example, an index in which each postings list represents not an individual term but a term bigram, such as "information retrieval". Such an index is very useful for processing

Table 4.3 Number of unique terms, term bigrams, and trigrams for our three text collections. The number of unique bigrams is much larger than the number of unique terms, by about one order of magnitude.

	Tokens	Unique Words	Unique Bigrams	Unique Trigrams
Shakespeare	1.3×10^6	2.3×10^4	2.9×10^5	6.5×10^5
TREC45	3.0×10^8	1.2×10^6	2.5×10^7	9.4×10^7
GOV2	4.4×10^{10}	4.9×10^7	5.2×10^8	2.3×10^9

phrase queries. Unfortunately, the number of unique bigrams in a text collection is substantially larger than the number of unique terms. Table 4.3 shows that GOV2 contains only about 49 million distinct terms, but 520 million distinct term bigrams. Not surprisingly, if trigrams are to be indexed instead of bigrams, the situation becomes even worse — with 2.3 billion different trigrams in GOV2, it is certainly not feasible to keep the entire dictionary in main memory anymore.

Storing the entire dictionary on disk would satisfy the space requirements but would slow down query processing. Without any further modifications an on-disk dictionary would add at least one extra disk seek per query term, as the search engine would first need to fetch each term's dictionary entry from disk before it could start processing the given query. Thus, a pure on-disk approach is not satisfactory, either.

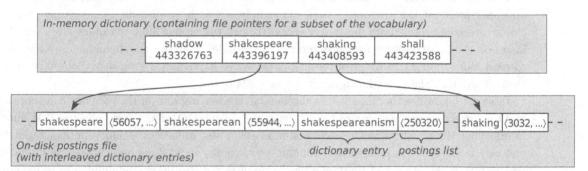

Figure 4.5 Interleaving dictionary and postings lists: Each on-disk inverted list is immediately preceded by the dictionary entry for the respective term. The in-memory dictionary contains entries for only *some* of the terms. In order to find the postings list for "shakespeareanism", a sequential scan of the on-disk data between "shakespeare" and "shaking" is necessary.

A possible solution to this problem is called *dictionary interleaving*, shown in Figure 4.5. In an interleaved dictionary all entries are stored on disk, each entry right before the respective postings list, to allow the search engine to fetch dictionary entry and postings list in one sequential read operation. In addition to the on-disk data, however, copies of *some* dictionary entries

Table 4.4 The impact of dictionary interleaving on a schema-independent index for GOV2 (49.5 million distinct terms). By choosing an index block size $B = 16,384$ bytes, the number of in-memory dictionary entries can be reduced by over 99%, at the cost of a minor query slowdown: 1 ms per query term.

Index Block Size (in bytes)	1,024	4,096	16,384	65,536	262,144
No. of in-memory dict. entries ($\times 10^6$)	3.01	0.91	0.29	0.10	0.04
Avg. index access latency (in ms)	11.4	11.6	12.3	13.6	14.9

(but not all of them) are kept in memory. When the search engine needs to determine the location of a term's postings list, it first performs a binary search on the sorted list of in-memory dictionary entries, followed by a sequential scan of the data found between two such entries. For the example shown in the figure, a search for "shakespeareanism" would first determine that the term's postings list (if it appears in the index) must be between the lists for "shakespeare" and "shaking". It would then load this index range into memory and scan it in a linear fashion to find the dictionary entry (and thus the postings list) for the term "shakespeareanism".

Dictionary interleaving is very similar to the self-indexing technique from Section 4.3, in the sense that random access disk operations are avoided by reading a little bit of extra data in a sequential manner. Because sequential disk operations are so much faster than random access, this trade-off is usually worthwhile, as long as the additional amount of data transferred from disk into main memory is small. In order to make sure that this is the case, we need to define an upper limit for the amount of data found between each on-disk dictionary entry and the closest preceding in-memory dictionary entry. We call this upper limit the *index block size*. For instance, if it is guaranteed for every term T in the index that the search engine does not need to read more than 1,024 bytes of on-disk data before it reaches T's on-disk dictionary entry, then we say that the index has a block size of 1,024 bytes.

Table 4.4 quantifies the impact that dictionary interleaving has on the memory consumption and the list access performance of the search engine (using GOV2 as a test collection). Without interleaving, the search engine needs to maintain about 49.5 million in-memory dictionary entries and can access the first posting in a random postings list in 11.3 ms on average (random disk seek + rotational latency). Choosing a block size of $B = 1,024$ bytes, the number of in-memory dictionary entries can be reduced to 3 million. At the same time, the search engine's list access latency (accessing the first posting in a randomly chosen list) increases by only 0.1 ms — a negligible overhead. As we increase the block size, the number of in-memory dictionary entries goes down and the index access latency goes up. But even for a relatively large block size of $B = 256$ KB, the additional cost — compared with a complete in-memory dictionary — is only a few milliseconds per query term.

Note that the memory consumption of an interleaved dictionary with block size B is quite different from maintaining an in-memory dictionary entry for every B bytes of index data. For example, the total size of the (compressed) schema-independent index for GOV2 is 62 GB. Choosing an index block size of $B = 64$ KB, however, does not lead to 62 GB / 64 KB $\approx$ 1 million

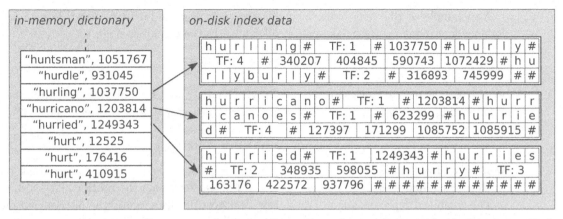

Figure 4.6 Combining dictionary and postings lists. The index is split into blocks of 72 bytes. Each entry of the in-memory dictionary is of the form (*term, posting*), indicating the first term and first posting in a given index block. The "#" symbols in the index data are record delimiters that have been inserted for better readability.

dictionary entries, but 10 times less. The reason is that frequent terms, such as "the" and "of", require only a single in-memory dictionary entry each, even though their postings lists each consume far more disk space than 64 KB (the compressed list for "the" consumes about 1 GB).

In practice, a block size between 4 KB and 16 KB is usually sufficient to shrink the in-memory dictionary to an acceptable size, especially if dictionary compression (Section 6.4) is used to decrease the space requirements of the few remaining in-memory dictionary entries. The disk transfer overhead for this range of block sizes is less than 1 ms per query term and is rather unlikely to cause any performance problems.

Dropping the distinction between terms and postings

We may take the dictionary interleaving approach one step further by dropping the distinction between terms and postings altogether, and by thinking of the index data as a sequence of pairs of the form (*term, posting*). The on-disk index is then divided into fixed-size index blocks, with each block perhaps containing 64 KB of data. All postings are stored on disk, in alphabetical order of their respective terms. Postings for the same term are stored in increasing order, as before. Each term's dictionary entry is stored on disk, potentially multiple times, so that there is a dictionary entry in every index block that contains at least one posting for the term. The in-memory data structure used to access data in the on-disk index then is a simple array, containing for each index block a pair of the form (*term, posting*), where *term* is the first term in the given block, and *posting* is the first posting for *term* in that block.

An example of this new index layout is shown in Figure 4.6 (data taken from a schema-independent index for the Shakespeare collection). In the example, a call to

$$\textbf{next}(\text{``hurried''},\ 1{,}000{,}000)$$

would load the second block shown (starting with "hurricano") from disk, would search the block for a posting matching the query, and would return the first matching posting (1,085,752). A call to

$$\textbf{next}(\text{``hurricano''},\ 1{,}000{,}000)$$

would load the first block shown (starting with "hurling"), would not find a matching posting in that block, and would then access the second block, returning the posting 1,203,814.

The combined representation of dictionary and postings lists unifies the interleaving method explained above and the self-indexing technique described in Section 4.3 in an elegant way. With this index layout, a random access into an arbitrary term's postings list requires only a single disk seek (we have eliminated the initialization step in which the term's per-term index is loaded into memory). On the downside, however, the total memory consumption of the index is higher than if we employ self-indexing and dictionary interleaving as two independent techniques. A 62-GB index with block size $B = 64$ KB now in fact requires approximately 1 million in-memory entries.

4.5   Index Construction

In the previous sections of this chapter, you have learned about various components of an inverted index. In conjunction, they can be used to realize efficient access to the contents of the index, even if all postings lists are stored on disk, and even if we don't have enough memory resources to hold a complete dictionary for the index in RAM. We now discuss how to efficiently construct an inverted index for a given text collection.

From an abstract point of view, a text collection can be thought of as a sequence of term occurrences — tuples of the form (*term, position*), where *position* is the word count from the beginning of the collection, and *term* is the term that occurs at that position. Figure 4.7 shows a fragment of the Shakespeare collection under this interpretation. Naturally, when a text collection is read in a sequential manner, these tuples are ordered by their second component, the position in the collection. The task of constructing an index is to change the ordering of the tuples so that they are sorted by their first component, the term they refer to (ties are broken by the second component). Once the new order is established, creating a proper index, with all its auxiliary data structures, is a comparatively easy task.

In general, index construction methods can be divided into two categories: in-memory index construction and disk-based index construction. In-memory indexing methods build an index for a given text collection entirely in main memory and can therefore only be used if the collection

Text fragment:

⟨SPEECH⟩

⟨SPEAKER⟩ JULIET ⟨/SPEAKER⟩

⟨LINE⟩ O Romeo, Romeo! wherefore art thou Romeo? ⟨/LINE⟩

⟨LINE⟩ ...

Original tuple ordering (collection order):

..., ("⟨speech⟩", 915487), ("⟨speaker⟩", 915488), ("juliet", 915489),

("⟨/speaker⟩", 915490), ("⟨line⟩", 915491), ("o", 915492), ("romeo", 915493),

("romeo", 915494), ("wherefore", 915495), ("art", 915496), ("thou", 915497),

("romeo", 915498), ("⟨/line⟩", 915499), ("⟨line⟩", 915500), ...

New tuple ordering (index order):

..., ("⟨line⟩", 915491), ("⟨line⟩", 915500), ...,

("romeo", 915411), ("romeo", 915493), ("romeo", 915494), ("romeo", 915498),

..., ("wherefore", 913310), ("wherefore", 915495), ("wherefore", 915849), ...

Figure 4.7 The index construction process can be thought of as reordering the tuple sequence that constitutes the text collection. Tuples are rearranged from their original *collection order* (sorted by position) to their new *index order* (sorted by term).

is small relative to the amount of available RAM. They do, however, form the basis for more sophisticated, disk-based index construction methods. Disk-based methods can be used to build indices for very large collections, much larger than the available amount of main memory.

As before, we limit ourselves to schema-independent indices because this allows us to ignore some details that need to be taken care of when discussing more complicated index types, such as document-level positional indices, and lets us focus on the essential aspects of the algorithms. The techniques presented, however, can easily be applied to other index types.

4.5.1 In-Memory Index Construction

Let us consider the simplest form of index construction, in which the text collection is small enough for the index to fit entirely into main memory. In order to create an index for such a collection, the indexing process needs to maintain the following data structures:

- a dictionary that allows efficient single-term lookup and insertion operations;
- an extensible (i.e., dynamic) list data structure that is used to store the postings for each term.

Assuming these two data structures are readily available, the index construction procedure is straightforward, as shown in Figure 4.8. If the right data structures are used for dictionary and extensible postings lists, then this method is very efficient, allowing the search engine to build

buildIndex (*inputTokenizer*) ≡
1   *position* ← 0
2   **while** *inputTokenizer.hasNext*() **do**
3   *T* ← *inputTokenizer.getNext*()
4   obtain dictionary entry for *T*; create new entry if necessary
5   append new posting *position* to *T*'s postings list
6   *position* ← *position* + 1
7   sort all dictionary entries in lexicographical order
8   **for each** term *T* in the dictionary **do**
9   write *T*'s postings list to disk
10   write the dictionary to disk
11   **return**

Figure 4.8 In-memory index construction algorithm, making use of two abstract data types: in-memory dictionary and extensible postings lists.

an index for the Shakespeare collection in less than one second. Thus, there are two questions that need to be discussed: 1. What data structure should be used for the dictionary? 2. What data structure should be used for the extensible postings lists?

Indexing-time dictionary

The dictionary implementation used during index construction needs to provide efficient support for single-term lookups and term insertions. Data structures that support these kinds of operations are very common and are therefore part of many publicly available programming libraries. For example, the C++ Standard Template Library (STL) published by SGI[1] provides a `map` data structure (binary search tree), and a `hash_map` data structure (variable-size hash table) that can carry out the lookup and insert operations performed during index construction. If you are implementing your own indexing algorithm, you might be tempted to use one of these existing implementations. However, it is not always advisable to do so.

We measured the performance of the STL data structures on a subset of GOV2, indexing the first 10,000 documents in the collection. The results are shown in Table 4.5. At first sight, it seems that the lookup performance of STL's `map` and `hash_map` implementations is sufficient for the purposes of index construction. On average, `map` needs about 630 ns per lookup; `hash_map` is a little faster, requiring 240 ns per lookup operation.

Now suppose we want to index the entire GOV2 collection instead of just a 10,000-document subset. Assuming the lookup performance stays at roughly the same level (an optimistic assumption, since the number of terms in the dictionary will keep increasing), the total time spent on

[1] www.sgi.com/tech/stl/

hash_map lookup operations, one for each of the 44 billion tokens in GOV, is:

$$44 \times 10^9 \times 240 \text{ ns } = 10{,}560 \text{ sec } \approx 3 \text{ hrs.}$$

Given that the fastest publicly available retrieval systems can build an index for the same collection in about 4 hours, including reading the input files, parsing the documents, and writing the (compressed) index to disk, there seems to be room for improvement. This calls for a custom dictionary implementation.

When designing our own dictionary implementation, we should try to optimize its performance for the specific type of data that we are dealing with. We know from Chapter 1 that term occurrences in natural-language text data roughly follow a Zipfian distribution. A key property of such a distribution is that the vast majority of all tokens in the collection correspond to a surprisingly small number of terms. For example, although there are about 50 million different terms in the GOV2 corpus, more than 90% of all term occurrences correspond to one of the 10,000 most frequent terms. Therefore, the bulk of the dictionary's lookup load may be expected to stem from a rather small set of very frequent terms. If the dictionary is based on a hash table, and collisions are resolved by means of chaining (as in Figure 4.2), then it is crucial that the dictionary entries for those frequent terms are kept near the beginning of each chain. This can be realized in two different ways:

1. **The insert-at-back heuristic**

   If a term is relatively frequent, then it is likely to occur very early in the stream of incoming tokens. Conversely, if the first occurrence of a term is encountered rather late, then chances are that the term is not very frequent. Therefore, when adding a new term to an existing chain in the hash table, it should be inserted at the end of the chain. This way, frequent terms, added early on, stay near the front, whereas infrequent terms tend to be found at the end.

2. **The move-to-front heuristic**

   If a term is frequent in the text collection, then it should be at the beginning of its chain in the hash table. Like insert-at-back, the move-to-front heuristic inserts new terms at the end of their respective chain. In addition, however, whenever a term lookup occurs and the term descriptor is not found at the beginning of the chain, it is relocated and moved to the front. This way, when the next lookup for the term takes place, the term's dictionary entry is still at (or near) the beginning of its chain in the hash table.

We evaluated the lookup performance of these two alternatives (using a handcrafted hash table implementation with a fixed number of hash slots in both cases) and compared it against a third alternative that inserts new terms at the beginning of the respective chain (referred to as the *insert-at-front* heuristic). The outcome of the performance measurements is shown in Table 4.5.

The insert-at-back and move-to-front heuristics achieve approximately the performance level (90 ns per lookup for a hash table with 2^{14} slots). Only for a small table size does move-to-front have a slight edge over insert-at-back (20% faster for a table with 2^{10} slots). The insert-at-front

Table 4.5 Indexing the first 10,000 documents of GOV2 ($\approx$ 14 million tokens; 181,334 distinct terms). Average dictionary lookup time per token in microseconds. The rows labeled "Hash table" represent a handcrafted dictionary implementation based on a fixed-size hash table with chaining.

Dictionary Implementation	Lookup Time	String Comparisons
Binary search tree (STL `map`)	0.63 μs per token	18.1 per token
Variable-size hash table (STL `hash_map`)	0.24 μs per token	2.2 per token
Hash table (2^{10} entries, insert-at-front)	6.11 μs per token	140 per token
Hash table (2^{10} entries, insert-at-back)	0.37 μs per token	8.2 per token
Hash table (2^{10} entries, move-to-front)	0.31 μs per token	4.8 per token
Hash table (2^{14} entries, insert-at-front)	0.32 μs per token	10.1 per token
Hash table (2^{14} entries, insert-at-back)	0.09 μs per token	1.5 per token
Hash table (2^{14} entries, move-to-front)	0.09 μs per token	1.3 per token

heuristic, however, exhibits a very poor lookup performance and is between 3 and 20 times slower than move-to-front. To understand the origin of this extreme performance difference, look at the table column labeled "String Comparisons". When storing the 181,344 terms from the 10,000-document subcollection of GOV2 in a hash table with $2^{14} = 16,384$ slots, we expect about 11 terms per chain on average. With the insert-at-front heuristic, the dictionary — on average — performs 10.1 string comparisons before it finds the term it is looking for. Because the frequent terms tend to appear early on in the collection, insert-at-front places them at the end of the respective chain. This is the cause of the method's dismal lookup performance. Incidentally, STL's `hash_map` implementation also inserts new hash table entries at the beginning of the respective chain, which is one reason why it does not perform so well in this benchmark.

A hash-based dictionary implementation employing the move-to-front heuristic is largely insensitive to the size of the hash table. In fact, even when indexing text collections containing many millions of different terms, a relatively small hash table, containing perhaps 2^{16} slots, will be sufficient to realize efficient dictionary lookups.

Extensible in-memory postings lists

The second interesting aspect of the simple in-memory index construction method, besides the dictionary implementation, is the implementation of the extensible in-memory postings lists. As suggested earlier, realizing each postings list as a singly linked list allows incoming postings to be appended to the existing lists very efficiently. The disadvantage of this approach is its rather high memory consumption: For every 32-bit (or 64-bit) posting, the indexing process needs to store an additional 32-bit (or 64-bit) pointer, thus increasing the total space requirements by 50–200%.

Various methods to decrease the storage overhead of the extensible postings lists have been proposed. For example, one could use a fixed-size array instead of a linked list. This avoids the

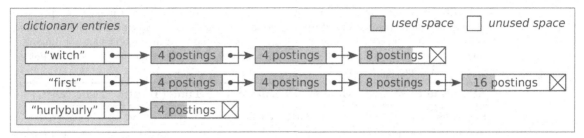

Figure 4.9   Realizing per-term extensible postings list by linking between groups of postings (*unrolled linked list*). Proportional pre-allocation (here with pre-allocation factor $k = 2$) provides an attractive trade-off between space overhead due to **next** pointers and space overhead due to internal fragmentation.

storage overhead associated with the **next** pointers in the linked list. Unfortunately, the length of each term's postings list is not known ahead of time, so this method requires an additional pass over the input data: In the first pass, term statistics are collected and space is allocated for each term's postings list; in the second pass, the pre-allocated arrays are filled with postings data. Of course, reading the input data twice harms indexing performance.

Another solution is to pre-allocate a postings array for every term in the dictionary, but to allow the indexing process to change the size of the array, for example, by performing a call to **realloc** (assuming that the programming language and run-time environment support this kind of operation). When a novel term is encountered, *init* bytes are allocated for the term's postings (e.g., *init* = 16). Whenever the capacity of the existing array is exhausted, a **realloc** operation is performed in order to increase the size of the array. By employing a proportional pre-allocation strategy, that is, by allocating a total of

$$s_{\text{new}} = \max\{s_{\text{old}} + init, k \times s_{\text{old}}\} \tag{4.2}$$

bytes in a reallocation operation, where s_{old} is the old size of the array and k is a constant, called the *pre-allocation factor*, the number of calls to **realloc** can be kept small (logarithmic in the size of each postings list). Nonetheless, there are some problems with this approach. If the pre-allocation factor is too small, then a large number of list relocations is triggered during index construction, possibly affecting the search engine's indexing performance. If it is too big, then a large amount of space is wasted due to allocated but unused memory (internal fragmentation). For instance, if $k = 2$, then 25% of the allocated memory will be unused on average.

A third way of realizing extensible in-memory postings lists with low storage overhead is to employ a linked list data structure, but to have multiple postings share a **next** pointer by linking to *groups* of postings instead of individual postings. When a new term is inserted into the dictionary, a small amount of space, say 16 bytes, is allocated for its postings. Whenever the space reserved for a term's postings list is exhausted, space for a new group of postings is

Table 4.6 Indexing the TREC45 collection. Index construction performance for various memory allocation strategies used to manage the extensible in-memory postings lists (32-bit postings; 32-bit pointers). Arranging postings for the same term in small groups and linking between these groups is faster than any other strategy. Pre-allocation factor used for both `realloc` and *grouping*: $k = 1.2$.

Allocation Strategy	Memory Consumption	Time (Total)	Time (CPU)
Linked list (simple)	2,312 MB	88 sec	77 sec
Two-pass indexing	1,168 MB	123 sec	104 sec
`realloc`	1,282 MB	82 sec	71 sec
Linked list (grouping)	1,208 MB	71 sec	61 sec

allocated. The amount of space allotted to the new group is

$$s_{\text{new}} = \min\{limit, \max\{16, (k-1) \times s_{\text{total}}\}\}, \tag{4.3}$$

where *limit* is an upper bound on the size of a postings group, say, 256 postings, s_{total} is the amount of memory allocated for postings so far, and k is the pre-allocation factor, just as in the case of `realloc`.

This way of combining postings into groups and having several postings share a single `next` pointer is shown in Figure 4.9. A linked list data structure that keeps more than one value in each list node is sometimes called an *unrolled linked list*, in analogy to loop unrolling techniques used in compiler optimization. In the context of index construction, we refer to this method as *grouping*.

Imposing an upper limit on the amount of space pre-allocated by the grouping technique allows to control internal fragmentation. At the same time, it does not constitute a performance problem; unlike in the case of `realloc`, allocating more space for an existing list is a very lightweight operation and does not require the indexing process to relocate any postings data.

A comparative performance evaluation of all four list allocation strategies — simple linked list, two-pass, `realloc`, and linked list with grouping — is given by Table 4.6. The two-pass method exhibits the lowest memory consumption but takes almost twice as long as the grouping approach. Using a pre-allocation factor $k = 1.2$, the `realloc` method has a memory consumption that is about 10% above that of the space-optimal two-pass strategy. This is consistent with the assumption that about half of the pre-allocated memory is never used. The grouping method, on the other hand, exhibits a memory consumption that is only 3% above the optimum. In addition, grouping is about 16% faster than `realloc` (61 sec vs. 71 sec CPU time).

Perhaps surprisingly, linking between groups of postings is also faster than linking between individual postings (61 sec vs. 77 sec CPU time). The reason for this is that the unrolled linked list data structure employed by the grouping technique not only decreases internal fragmentation, but also improves CPU cache efficiency, by keeping postings for the same term close

buildIndex_sortBased (*inputTokenizer*) ≡
1   *position* ← 0
2   **while** *inputTokenizer.hasNext*() **do**
3   *T* ← *inputTokenizer.getNext*()
4   obtain dictionary entry for *T*; create new entry if necessary
5   *termID* ← unique term ID of *T*
6   write record $R_{position}$ ≡ (*termID, position*) to disk
7   *position* ← *position* + 1
8   *tokenCount* ← *position*
9   sort $R_0 \ldots R_{tokenCount-1}$ by first component; break ties by second component
10   perform a sequential scan of $R_0 \ldots R_{tokenCount-1}$, creating the final index
11   **return**

Figure 4.10   Sort-based index construction algorithm, creating a schema-independent index for a text collection. The main difficulty lies in efficiently sorting the on-disk records $R_0 \ldots R_{tokenCount-1}$.

together. In the simple linked-list implementation, postings for a given term are randomly scattered across the used portion of the computer's main memory, resulting in a large number of CPU cache misses when collecting each term's postings before writing them to disk.

4.5.2   Sort-Based Index Construction

Hash-based in-memory index construction algorithms can be extremely efficient, as demonstrated in the previous section. However, if we want to index text collections that are substantially larger than the available amount of RAM, we need to move away from the idea that we can keep the entire index in main memory, and need to look toward disk-based approaches instead. The sort-based indexing method presented in this section is the first of two disk-based index construction methods covered in this chapter. It can be used to index collections that are much larger than the available amount of main memory.

Recall from the beginning of this section that building an inverted index can be thought of as the process of reordering the sequence of term-position tuples that represents the text collection — transforming it from collection order into index order. This is a sorting process, and sort-based index construction realizes the transformation in the simplest way possible. Consuming tokens from the input files, a sort-based indexing process emits records of the form (*termID, position*) and writes them to disk immediately. The result is a sequence of records, sorted by their second component (*position*). When it is done processing the input data, the indexer sorts all tuples written to disk by their first component, using the second component to break ties. The result is a new sequence of records, sorted by their first component (*termID*). Transforming this new sequence into a proper inverted file, using the information found in the in-memory dictionary, is straightforward.

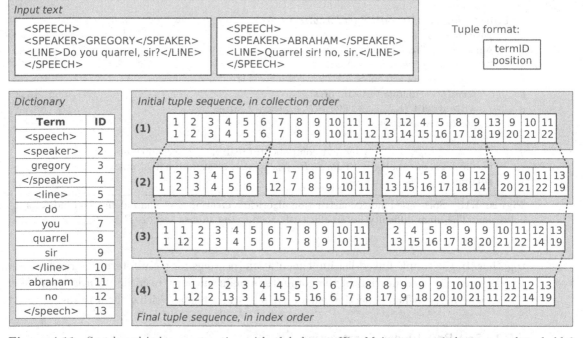

Figure 4.11 Sort-based index construction with global term IDs. Main memory is large enough to hold 6 (*termID*, *position*) tuples at a time. (1)→(2): sorting blocks of size ≤ 6 in memory, one at a time. (2)→(3) and (3)→(4): merging sorted blocks into bigger blocks.

The method, shown as pseudo-code in Figure 4.10, is very easy to implement and can be used to create an index that is substantially larger than the available amount of main memory. Its main limitation is the available amount of disk space.

Sorting the on-disk records can be a bit tricky. In many implementations, it is performed by loading a certain number of records, say n, into main memory at a time, where n is defined by the size of a record and the amount of available main memory. These n records are then sorted in memory and written back to disk. The process is repeated until we have $\lceil \frac{tokenCount}{n} \rceil$ blocks of sorted records. These blocks can then be combined, in a *multiway merge operation* (processing records from all blocks at the same time) or in a *cascaded merge operation* (merging, for example, two blocks at a time), resulting in a sorted sequence of *tokenCount* records. Figure 4.11 shows a sort-based indexing process that creates the final tuple sequence by means of a cascaded merge operation, merging two tuple sequences at a time. With some additional data structures, and with the *termID* component removed from each posting, this final sequence can be thought of as the index for the collection.

Despite its ability to index text collections much larger than the available amount of main memory, sort-based indexing has two essential limitations:

- It requires a substantial amount of disk space, usually at least 8 bytes per input token (4 bytes for the term ID + 4 bytes for the position), or even 12 bytes (4 + 8) for larger text collections. When indexing GOV2, for instance, the disk space required to store the temporary files is at least $12 \times 44 \times 10^9$ bytes ($= 492$ GB) — more than the uncompressed size of the collection itself (426 GB).

- To be able to properly sort the (*termID*, *docID*) pairs emitted in the first phase, the indexing process needs to maintain globally unique term IDs, which can be realized only through a complete in-memory dictionary. As discussed earlier, a complete dictionary for GOV2 might consume more than 1 GB of RAM, making it difficult to index the collection on a low-end machine.

There are various ways to address these issues. However, in the end they all have in common that they transform the sort-based indexing method into something more similar to what is known as *merge-based index construction*.

4.5.3   Merge-Based Index Construction

In contrast to sort-based index construction methods, the merge-base method presented in this section does not need to maintain any global data structures. In particular, there is no need for globally unique term IDs. The size of the text collection to be indexed is therefore limited only by the amount of disk space available to store the temporary data and the final index, but not by the amount of main memory available to the indexing process.

Merge-based indexing is a generalization of the in-memory index construction method discussed in Section 4.5.1, building inverted lists by means of hash table lookup. In fact, if the collection for which an index is being created is small enough for the index to fit completely into main memory, then merge-based indexing behaves exactly like in-memory indexing. If the text collection is too large to be indexed completely in main memory, then the indexing process performs a *dynamic partitioning* of the collection. That is, it starts building an in-memory index. As soon as it runs out of memory (or when a predefined memory utilization threshold is reached), it builds an on-disk inverted file by transferring the in-memory index data to disk, deletes the in-memory index, and continues indexing. This procedure is repeated until the whole collection has been indexed. The algorithm is shown in Figure 4.12.

The result of the process outlined above is a set of inverted files, each representing a certain part of the whole collection. Each such subindex is referred to as an *index partition*. In a final step, the index partitions are merged into the final index, representing the entire text collection. The postings lists in the index partitions (and in the final index) are usually stored in compressed form (see Chapter 6), in order to keep the disk I/O overhead low.

The index partitions written to disk as intermediate output of the indexing process are completely independent of each other. For example, there is no need for globally unique term IDs; there is not even a need for numerical term IDs. Each term is its own ID; the postings lists in each partition are stored in lexicographical order of their terms, and access to a term's list can

buildIndex_mergeBased (*inputTokenizer*, *memoryLimit*) ≡
1    $n \leftarrow 0$ // initialize the number of index partitions
2    $position \leftarrow 0$
3    $memoryConsumption \leftarrow 0$
4   **while** *inputTokenizer.hasNext*() **do**
5        $T \leftarrow inputTokenizer.getNext()$
6   obtain dictionary entry for T; create new entry if necessary
7   append new posting *position* to T's postings list
8        $position \leftarrow position + 1$
9        $memoryConsumption \leftarrow memoryConsumption + 1$
10   **if** $memoryConsumption \geq memoryLimit$ **then**
11   **createIndexPartition**()
12   **if** $memoryConsumption > 0$ **then**
13   **createIndexPartition**()
14   merge index partitions $I_0 \ldots I_{n-1}$, resulting in the final on-disk index I_{final}
15   **return**

createIndexPartition () ≡
16   create empty on-disk inverted file I_n
17   sort in-memory dictionary entries in lexicographical order
18   **for each** term T in the dictionary **do**
19   add T's postings list to I_n
20   delete all in-memory postings lists
21   reset the in-memory dictionary
22   $memoryConsumption \leftarrow 0$
23   $n \leftarrow n + 1$
24   **return**

Figure 4.12   Merge-based indexing algorithm, creating a set of independent sub-indices (*index partitions*). The final index is generated by combining the sub-indices via a multiway merge operation.

be realized by using the data structures described in Sections 4.3 and 4.4. Because of the lexicographical ordering and the absence of term IDs, merging the individual partitions into the final index is straightforward. Pseudo-code for a very simple implementation, performing repeated linear probing of all subindices, is given in Figure 4.13. If the number of index partitions is large (more than 10), then the algorithm can be improved by arranging the index partitions in a priority queue (e.g., a heap), ordered according to the next term in the respective partition. This eliminates the need for the linear scan in lines 7–10.

Overall performance numbers for merge-based index construction, including all components, are shown in Table 4.7. The total time necessary to build a schema-independent index for GOV2 is around 4 hours. The time required to perform the final merge operation, combining the n index partitions into one final index, is about 30% of the time it takes to generate the partitions.

mergeIndexPartitions $(\langle I_0, \ldots, I_{n-1} \rangle) \equiv$

1   create empty inverted file I_{final}

2   **for** $k \leftarrow 0$ **to** $n - 1$ **do**

3   open index partition I_k for sequential processing

4      $currentIndex \leftarrow 0$

5   **while** $currentIndex \neq nil$ **do**

6          $currentIndex \leftarrow nil$

7   **for** $k \leftarrow 0$ **to** $n - 1$ **do**

8   **if** I_k still has terms left **then**

9   **if** $(currentIndex = nil) \lor (I_k.currentTerm < currentTerm)$ **then**

10                      $currentIndex \leftarrow I_k$

11                      $currentTerm \leftarrow I_k.currentTerm$

12   **if** $currentIndex \neq nil$ **then**

13              $I_{\text{final}}.addPostings(currentTerm, currentIndex.getPostings(currentTerm))$

14              $currentIndex.advanceToNextTerm()$

15   delete $I_0 \ldots I_{n-1}$

16   **return**

Figure 4.13   Merging a set of n index partitions $I_0 \ldots I_{n-1}$ into an index I_{final}. This is the final step in merge-based index construction.

The algorithm is very scalable: On our computer, indexing the whole GOV2 collection (426 GB of text) takes only 11 times as long as indexing a 10% subcollection (43 GB of text).

There are, however, some limits to the scalability of the method. When merging the index partitions at the end of the indexing process, it is important to have at least a moderately sized read-ahead buffer, a few hundred kilobytes, for each partition. This helps keep the number of disk seeks (jumping back and forth between the different partitions) small. Naturally, the size of the read-ahead buffer for each partition is bounded from above by M/n, where M is the amount of available memory and n is the number of partitions. Thus, if n becomes too large, merging becomes slow.

Reducing the amount of memory available to the indexing process therefore has two effects. First, it decreases the total amount of memory available for the read-ahead buffers. Second, it increases the number of index partitions. Thus, reducing main memory by 50% decreases the size of each index partition's read-ahead buffer by 75%. Setting the memory limit to $M = 128$ MB, for example, results in 3,032 partitions that need to be merged, leaving each partition with a read-ahead buffer of only 43 KB. The general trend of this effect is depicted in Figure 4.14. The figure shows that the performance of the final merge operation is highly dependent on the amount of main memory available to the indexing process. With 128 MB of available main memory, the final merge takes 6 times longer than with 1,024 MB.

There are two possible countermeasures that could be taken to overcome this limitation. The first is to replace the simple multiway merge by a cascaded merge operation. For instance, if 1,024 index partitions need to be merged, then we could first perform 32 merge operations

Table 4.7 Building a schema-independent index for various text collections, using merge-based index construction with 512 MB of RAM for the in-memory index. The indexing-time dictionary is realized by a hash table with 2^{16} entries and move-to-front heuristic. The extensible in-memory postings lists are unrolled linked lists, linking between groups of postings, with a pre-allocation factor $k = 1.2$.

	Reading, Parsing & Indexing	Merging	Total Time
Shakespeare	1 sec	0 sec	1 sec
TREC45	71 sec	11 sec	82 sec
GOV2 (10%)	20 min	4 min	24 min
GOV2 (25%)	51 min	11 min	62 min
GOV2 (50%)	102 min	25 min	127 min
GOV2 (100%)	205 min	58 min	263 min

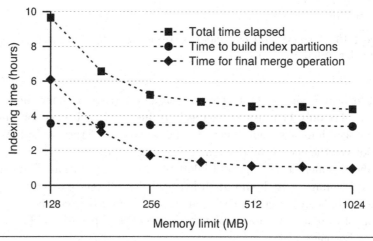

Figure 4.14 The impact of available RAM on the performance of merge-based indexing (data set: GOV2). The performance of phase 1 (building index partitions) is largely independent of the amount of available main memory. The performance of phase 2 (merging partitions) suffers severely if little main memory is available.

involving 32 partitions each, and then merge the resulting 32 new partitions into the final index. This is a generalization of the process shown in Figure 4.11, which depicts a cascaded merge operation that works on 2 partitions at a time. The second countermeasure is to decrease the space consumed by the postings lists, by means of compressed in-memory inversion. Compressing postings on-the-fly, as they enter the in-memory index, allows the indexing process to accumulate more postings before it runs out of memory, thus decreasing the number of on-disk index partitions created.

In conclusion, despite some problems with the final merge operation, merge-based index construction lets us build an inverted file for very large text collections, even on a single PC. Its advantage over the sort-based method is that it does not require globally unique term IDs. It is therefore especially attractive if the number of dictionary terms is very large. Another great advantage of this index construction algorithm over the sort-based method is that it produces an in-memory index that is immediately queriable. This feature is essential when the search engine needs to deal with dynamic text collections (see Chapter 7).

4.6   Other Types of Indices

In our discussion of index data structures, we have limited ourselves to the case of inverted indices. However, an inverted index is just one possible type of index that can be used as part of a search engine.

A *forward index* (or *direct index*) is a mapping from document IDs to the list of terms appearing in each document. Forward indices complement inverted indices. They are usually not used for the actual search process, but to obtain information about per-document term distributions at query time, which is required by query expansion techniques such as pseudo-relevance feedback (see Chapter 8), and to produce result *snippets*. Compared to extracting this information from the raw text files, a forward index has the advantage that the text has already been parsed, and the relevant data can be extracted more efficiently.

Signature files (Faloutsos and Christodoulakis, 1984) are an alternative to docid indices. Similar to a Bloom filter (Bloom, 1970), a signature file can be used to obtain a list of documents that *may* contain the given term. In order to find out whether the term actually appears in a document, the document itself (or a forward index) needs to be consulted. By changing the parameters of the signature file, it is possible to trade time for speed: A smaller index results in a greater probability of false positives, and vice versa.

Suffix trees (Weiner, 1973) and *suffix arrays* (Manber and Myers, 1990) can be used to efficiently find all occurrences of a given n-gram sequence in a given text collection. They can be used either to index character n-grams (without tokenizing the input text) or to index word n-grams (after tokenization). Suffix trees are attractive data structures for phrase search or regular expression search, but are usually larger than inverted indices and provide less efficient search operations when stored on disk instead of in RAM.

4.7 Summary

In this chapter we have covered the essential algorithms and data structures necessary to build and access inverted indices. The main points of the chapter are:

- Inverted indices are usually too large to be loaded completely into memory. It is therefore common to keep only the dictionary, which is relatively small compared to the size of the entire index, in memory, while storing the postings lists on disk (Section 4.2).
- For a large text collection even the dictionary might be too large to fit into RAM. The memory requirements of the dictionary can be substantially decreased by keeping an incomplete dictionary in memory, interleaving dictionary entries with on-disk postings lists, and exploiting the fact that all lists in the index are sorted in lexicographical order (Section 4.4).
- A sort-based dictionary implementation should be used, and postings lists should be stored on disk in lexicographical order, if prefix queries are to be supported by the search engine (Sections 4.2 and 4.3).
- For each on-disk postings list, a per-term index, containing a subset of the term's postings, can be used to realize efficient quasi-random access into the list (Section 4.3).
- Highly efficient in-memory index construction can be realized by employing a hash-based in-memory dictionary with move-to-front heuristic and by using grouped linked lists to implement extensible in-memory postings lists (Section 4.5.1).
- If the amount of main memory available to the indexing process is too small to allow the index to be built completely in RAM, then the in-memory index construction method can be extended to a merge-based method, in which the text collection is divided into subcollections, dynamically and based on the available amount of main memory. An index for each subcollection is built using the in-memory indexing method. After the entire collection has been indexed, the indices for the individual subcollections are merged in a single multiway merge operation or a cascaded merge process (Section 4.5.3).
- The performance of merge-based index construction is essentially linear in the size of the collection. However, the final merge operation may suffer severely if too little main memory is available for the subindices' read buffers (Section 4.5.3).

4.8 Further Reading

Good entry points for an in-depth understanding of the architecture and performance of inverted indices are provided by Witten et al. (1999, chapters 3 and 5) and Zobel and Moffat (2006). A high-level overview of the index data structures employed by Google around 1998 is given by Brin and Page (1998).

Moffat and Zobel (1996) discuss query-time efficiency issues of inverted files, including the per-term index data structure ("self-indexing") used for random list access that is outlined in Section 4.3. Rao and Ross (1999, 2000) demonstrate that random access issues arise not only in the context of on-disk indices but also for in-memory inverted files. They show that binary search is *not* the best way to realize random access for in-memory postings lists.

Heinz and Zobel (2003) discuss single-pass merge-based index construction and its advantages over the sort-based method. They also examine the efficiency of various in-memory dictionary implementations, including the move-to-front heuristic described in Section 4.5.1 (Zobel et al., 2001), and propose a new dictionary data structure, the *burst trie* (Heinz et al., 2002), which achieves a single-term lookup performance close to a hash table but — unlike a hash table — can also be used to resolve prefix queries.

Memory management strategies for extensible in-memory postings lists (e.g., unrolled linked lists) are examined by Büttcher and Clarke (2005) and, more recently, by Luk and Lam (2007).

With a naïve implementation of the final merge procedure in merge-based index construction (and variants of sort-based indexing), the total storage requirement is twice as large as the size of the final index. Moffat and Bell (1995) describe a clever technique that can be used to realize the merge in situ, re-using the disk space occupied by already processed parts of the input partitions to store the final index.

Faloutsos and Christodoulakis (1984) give a nice overview of signature files, including some theoretical properties. Zobel et al. (1998) discuss the relative performance of inverted files and signature files in text search. They come to the conclusion that, for many applications, inverted files are the better choice. Carterette and Can (2005) argue that, under certain circumstances, signature files can be almost as fast as inverted files.

Suffix trees made their first appearance under the name *position trees* in a paper by Weiner (1973). Ukkonen (1995) presents a linear-time construction method for suffix trees. Clark and Munro (1996) discuss a variant of suffix trees that allows efficient search operations when stored on disk instead of main memory.

4.9 Exercises

Exercise 4.1 In Section 4.3 we introduced the concept of the *per-term index* as a means to improve the index's random access performance. Suppose the postings list for some term consists of 64 million postings, each of which consumes 4 bytes. In order to carry out a single random access into the term's postings list, the search engine needs to perform two disk read operations:

1. Loading the per-term index (list of synchronization points) into RAM.

2. Loading a block B of postings into RAM, where B is identified by means of binary search on the list of synchronization points.

Let us call the number of postings per synchronization point the *granularity* of the per-term index. For the above access pattern, what is the optimal granularity (i.e., the one that minimizes disk I/O)? What is the total number of bytes read from disk?

Exercise 4.2 The introduction of the per-term index in Section 4.3 was motivated by the performance characteristics of typical hard disk drives (in particular, the high cost of disk seeks). However, the same method can also be used to improve the random access performance of in-memory indices. To confirm this claim, you have to implement two different data structures for in-memory postings lists and equip them with a **next** access method (see Chapter 2). The first data structure stores postings in a simple array of 32-bit integers. Its **next** method operates by performing a binary search on that array. In the second data structure, an auxiliary array is used to store a copy of every 64th posting in the postings list. The **next** method first performs a binary search on the auxiliary array, followed by a *sequential scan* of the 64 candidate postings in the postings list. Measure the average single-element lookup latency of both implementations, working with lists of n postings, for $n = 2^{12}, 2^{16}, 2^{20}, 2^{24}$. Describe and analyze your findings.

Exercise 4.3 Building an inverted index is essentially a sorting process. The lower bound for every general-purpose sorting algorithm is $\Omega(n \log(n))$. However, the merge-based index construction method from Section 4.5.3 has a running time that is linear in the size of the collection (see Table 4.7, page 130). Find at least two places where there is a hidden logarithmic factor.

Exercise 4.4 In the algorithm shown in Figure 4.12, the memory limit is expressed as the number of postings that can be stored in RAM. What is the assumption that justifies this definition of the memory limit? Give an example of a text collection or an application in which the assumption does not hold.

Exercise 4.5 In Section 4.5.1 we discussed the performance characteristics of various dictionary data structures. We pointed out that hash-based implementations offer better performance for single-term lookups (performed during index construction), while sort-based solutions are more appropriate for multi-term lookups (needed for prefix queries). Design and implement a data structure that offers better single-term lookup performance than a sort-based dictionary and better prefix query performance than a hash-based implementation.

Exercise 4.6 (project exercise) Design and implement an index construction method that creates a schema-independent index for a given text collection. The result of the index construction process is an on-disk index. The index does not need to use any of the optimizations discussed in Sections 4.3 and 4.4.

- Implement the in-memory index construction method described in Section 4.5.1. When run on typical English text, your implementation should be able to build an index for a collection containing approximately $\frac{M}{8}$ tokens, where M is the amount of available main memory, in bytes.

- Extend your implementation so that the size of the text collection is no longer limited by the amount of main memory available to the indexing process. This will probably require you to write a module that can merge two or more on-disk indices into a single index.

4.10 Bibliography

Bender, M., Michel, S., Triantafillou, P., and Weikum, G. (2007). Design alternatives for large-scale Web search: Alexander was great, Aeneas a pioneer, and Anakin has the force. In *Proceedings of the 1st Workshop on Large-Scale Distributed Systems for Information Retrieval (LSDS-IR)*, pages 16–22. Amsterdam, The Netherlands.

Bloom, B. H. (1970). Space/time trade-offs in hash coding with allowable errors. *Communications of the ACM*, 13(7):422–426.

Brin, S., and Page, L. (1998). The anatomy of a large-scale hypertextual Web search engine. *Computer Networks and ISDN Systems*, 30(1-7):107–117.

Büttcher, S., and Clarke, C. L. A. (2005). *Memory Management Strategies for Single-Pass Index Construction in Text Retrieval Systems*. Technical Report CS-2005-32. University of Waterloo, Waterloo, Canada.

Carterette, B., and Can, F. (2005). Comparing inverted files and signature files for searching a large lexicon. *Information Processing & Management*, 41(3):613–633.

Clark, D. R., and Munro, J. I. (1996). Efficient suffix trees on secondary storage. In *Proceedings of the 7th Annual ACM-SIAM Symposium on Discrete Algorithms*, pages 383–391. Atlanta, Georgia.

Faloutsos, C., and Christodoulakis, S. (1984). Signature files: An access method for documents and its analytical performance evaluation. *ACM Transactions on Information Systems*, 2(4):267–288.

Heinz, S., and Zobel, J. (2003). Efficient single-pass index construction for text databases. *Journal of the American Society for Information Science and Technology*, 54(8):713–729.

Heinz, S., Zobel, J., and Williams, H. E. (2002). Burst tries: A fast, efficient data structure for string keys. *ACM Transactions on Information Systems*, 20(2):192–223.

Luk, R. W. P., and Lam, W. (2007). Efficient in-memory extensible inverted file. *Information Systems*, 32(5):733–754.

Manber, U., and Myers, G. (1990). Suffix arrays: A new method for on-line string searches. In *Proceedings of the 1st Annual ACM-SIAM Symposium on Discrete Algorithms*, pages 319–327. San Francisco, California.

Moffat, A., and Bell, T. A. H. (1995). In-situ generation of compressed inverted files. *Journal of the American Society for Information Science*, 46(7):537–550.

Moffat, A., and Zobel, J. (1996). Self-indexing inverted files for fast text retrieval. *ACM Transactions on Information Systems*, 14(4):349–379.

Rao, J., and Ross, K. A. (1999). Cache conscious indexing for decision-support in main memory. In *Proceedings of 25th International Conference on Very Large Data Bases*, pages 78–89. Edinburgh, Scotland.

Rao, J., and Ross, K. A. (2000). Making B$^+$-trees cache conscious in main memory. In *Proceedings of the 2000 ACM SIGMOD International Conference on Management of Data*, pages 475–486. Dallas, Texas.

Ukkonen, E. (1995). On-line construction of suffix trees. *Algorithmica*, 14(3):249–260.

Weiner, P. (1973). Linear pattern matching algorithm. In *Proceedings of the 14th Annual IEEE Symposium on Switching and Automata Theory*, pages 1–11. Iowa City, Iowa.

Witten, I. H., Moffat, A., and Bell, T. C. (1999). *Managing Gigabytes: Compressing and Indexing Documents and Images* (2nd ed.). San Francisco, California: Morgan Kaufmann.

Zobel, J., Heinz, S., and Williams, H. E. (2001). In-memory hash tables for accumulating text vocabularies. *Information Processing Letters*, 80(6):271–277.

Zobel, J., and Moffat, A. (2006). Inverted files for text search engines. *ACM Computing Surveys*, 38(2):1–56.

Zobel, J., Moffat, A., and Ramamohanarao, K. (1998). Inverted files versus signature files for text indexing. *ACM Transactions on Database Systems*, 23(4):453–490.

5 Query Processing

In Chapter 4 we explored the fundamental data structures that make up an inverted index. We now discuss how to realize efficient search operations on top of these data structures. Details of the search process and its implementation can vary from search engine to search engine. However, the essential ideas and algorithms are usually the same, regardless of whether we are dealing with a single-user desktop search system or a large-scale Web search engine.

The most basic retrieval model is quite likely the Boolean model that we have already discussed in Section 2.2. In the Boolean model, each term represents the set of documents in which it appears. Document sets may be combined by using the standard operators AND (set intersection), OR (union), and NOT (inversion). In this chapter we explore two popular alternatives to the Boolean model. The first one, ranked retrieval (Section 5.1), allows the search engine to rank search results according to their predicted relevance to the query. The second one, lightweight structure (Section 5.2), is a natural extension of the Boolean model to the sub-document level. Instead of restricting the search process to entire documents, it allows the user to search for arbitrary text passages satisfying Boolean-like constraints (e.g., "show me all passages that contain 'apothecary' and 'drugs' within 10 words").

Although we will occasionally refer to effectiveness measures, such as mean average precision (MAP), the focus of this chapter is not so much on the quality of the search results as on the efficiency of the search process. Quality aspects of various retrieval functions are covered in Chapters 8 and 9.

5.1 Query Processing for Ranked Retrieval

As pointed out in Section 2.2, Boolean retrieval and ranked retrieval are not mutually exclusive, but complementary: The search engine may use a Boolean interpretation of the user's query to determine the set of matching documents. For instance, given the query

$$Q = \langle \text{"greek"}, \text{"philosophy"}, \text{"stoicism"} \rangle \tag{5.1}$$

(TREC topic 433), the search engine may retrieve all documents that match the *conjunctive* Boolean query

$$\text{"greek" AND "philosophy" AND "stoicism"} \tag{5.2}$$

or the *disjunctive* Boolean query

$$\text{"greek" OR "philosophy" OR "stoicism"} \tag{5.3}$$

and then rank those documents according to their similarity to Q, for example, using the cosine measure (Equation 2.12 on page 56).

Traditional information retrieval systems usually follow the disjunctive approach, while Web search engines often employ conjunctive query semantics. The conjunctive retrieval model leads to faster query processing than the disjunctive model, because fewer documents have to be scored and ranked. However, this performance advantage comes at the cost of a lower recall: If a relevant document contains only two of the three query terms, it will never be returned to the user. This limitation is quite obvious for the query Q shown above. Of the half-million documents in the TREC collection, 7,834 match the disjunctive interpretation of the query, whereas only a single document matches the conjunctive version. Incidentally, that document is not even relevant (it is about a Mexican actor and his latest film projects).

The failure of the conjunctive approach for the above query can be explained as follows: Authors familiar with the concept of Stoicism do not feel the need to mention that it is a philosophy or that it originated in Greece; both details seem obvious to them. The user might think that she helps the search engine by providing the additional keywords "philosophy" and "greek", when in fact adding these terms makes the search results worse. This effect becomes even more pronounced for longer queries, in which the presence of a single unwisely chosen (or misspelled) query term can completely ruin the search results.

We hold the view that adding relevant terms to the query should not hurt the search results. Throughout the following sections, we assume that the search engine follows the disjunctive approach, retrieving all documents that contain at least one of the query terms, and leaving it to the ranking function to determine which of these documents best match the user's query. Of course, there is no doubt that the conjunctive model usually allows more efficient query processing than the disjunctive model. Therefore, many of the optimizations covered in this section share the same common goal: to narrow the performance gap between the AND interpretation and the OR interpretation of a given query.

Okapi BM25

For the purpose of our discussion, we assume that the search engine employs the Okapi BM25 scoring function (Equation 8.48 on page 272) to rank documents based on their predicted relevance to the query. For convenience, we repeat the ranking formula here:

$$\text{Score}_{\text{BM25}}(q, d) \quad = \quad \sum_{t \in q} \log\left(\frac{N}{N_t}\right) \cdot \text{TF}_{\text{BM25}}(t, d), \tag{5.4}$$

$$\text{TF}_{\text{BM25}}(t, d) \quad = \quad \frac{f_{t,d} \cdot (k_1 + 1)}{f_{t,d} + k_1 \cdot ((1 - b) + b \cdot (l_d/l_{avg}))}. \tag{5.5}$$

The formula has two free parameters: k_1 (default value: $k_1 = 1.2$), which regulates how fast the TF component saturates, and b (default value: $b = 0.75$), which controls the degree of document length normalization. All other variables have the standard semantics, as listed in the "Notation" table at the beginning of this book.

If you are interested in the theory underlying the BM25 formula, you can find a derivation and in-depth discussion in Chapter 8. In order to follow the material covered in this section, a full understanding of BM25 is not required. We do, however, want to focus briefly on the role of the parameter k_1, as it interacts closely with various query optimizations for ranked retrieval. k_1 caps the score contribution of an individual query term:

$$\lim_{f_{t,d} \to \infty} \text{TF}_{\text{BM25}}(t, d) \;=\; k_1 + 1. \tag{5.6}$$

For the default value $k_1 = 1.2$, the TF contribution of any given query term can never exceed 2.2. Because of this rather tight upper bound, a document that contains two different query terms is far more likely to be ranked highly than a document that contains only a single query term, even if the latter contains that term many times.

Suppose we are given the query $q = \langle t_1, t_2 \rangle$, with $N_{t_1} \approx N_{t_2}$, and we want to score two documents d_1 and d_2 of average length (i.e., $l_{d_1} = l_{d_2} = l_{avg}$). Further suppose that d_1 contains one occurrence of each t_1 and t_2, while d_2 contains 10 occurrences of t_1 and no occurrence of t_2. Then we have:

$$\text{Score}_{\text{BM25}}(q, d_1) \;\approx\; \log\left(\frac{N}{N_{t_1}}\right) \cdot \left(2 \cdot \frac{1 \cdot (k_1 + 1)}{1 + k_1}\right) \;\approx\; 2 \cdot \log\left(\frac{N}{N_{t_1}}\right), \tag{5.7}$$

$$\text{Score}_{\text{BM25}}(q, d_2) \;\approx\; \log\left(\frac{N}{N_{t_1}}\right) \cdot \frac{10 \cdot (k_1 + 1)}{10 + k_1} \;\approx\; 1.95 \cdot \log\left(\frac{N}{N_{t_1}}\right) \tag{5.8}$$

(for $k_1 = 1.2$). Later in this section we will use the upper bounds provided by k_1 to ignore postings for which we know a priori that they cannot push the corresponding document into the top search results.

5.1.1   Document-at-a-Time Query Processing

The most common form of query processing for ranked retrieval is called the *document-at-a-time* approach. In this method all matching documents are enumerated, one after the other, and a score is computed for each of them. At the end all documents are sorted according to their score, and the top k results (where k is chosen by the user or the application) are returned to the user.

Figure 5.1 shows a document-at-a-time algorithm for BM25. The algorithm — except for the score computation — is the same as the **rankCosine** algorithm in Figure 2.9 (page 59). The overall time complexity of the algorithm is

$$\Theta(m \cdot n + m \cdot \log(m)), \tag{5.9}$$

rankBM25_DocumentAtATime $(\langle t_1, ..., t_n \rangle, k) \equiv$

1    $m \leftarrow 0$ // m is the total number of matching documents
2    $d \leftarrow \min_{1 \le i \le n} \{\textbf{nextDoc}(t_i, -\infty)\}$
3   **while** $d < \infty$ **do**
4        $results[m].docid \leftarrow d$
5        $results[m].score \leftarrow \sum_{i=1}^{n} \log(N/N_{t_i}) \cdot \text{TF}_{\text{BM25}}(t_i, d)$
6        $m \leftarrow m + 1$
7        $d \leftarrow \min_{1 \le i \le n} \{\textbf{nextDoc}(t_i, d)\}$
8   sort $results[0..(m-1)]$ in decreasing order of $score$
9   **return** $results[0..(k-1)]$

Figure 5.1   Document-at-a-time query processing with BM25.

where n is the number of query terms and m is the number of matching documents (containing at least one query term). The term $m \cdot n$ corresponds to the loop starting in line 3 of the algorithm. The term $m \cdot \log(m)$ corresponds to the sorting of the search results in line 8.

It is sometimes difficult to use Equation 5.9 directly, because the value of m is not known without running the algorithm and enumerating all search results. Depending on how often the query terms co-occur in a document, m can be anywhere between N_q/n and N_q, where $N_q = N_{t_1} + \cdots + N_{t_n}$ is the total number of postings of all query terms. In the worst case, each matching document contains only a single query term. The time complexity of the algorithm in Figure 5.1 is then

$$\Theta(N_q \cdot n + N_q \cdot \log(N_q)). \tag{5.10}$$

In practice the vast majority of all matching documents do in fact contain only one query term. For instance, for our earlier example query $\langle$"greek", "philosophy", "stoicism"$\rangle$ we have $m = 7835$ and $N_q = 7921$. Thus, Equation 5.10 is usually a good approximation of Equation 5.9.

The basic document-at-a-time algorithm shown in Figure 5.1 has two major sources of inefficiency:

- The computations carried out in lines 5 and 7 need to iterate over all n query terms, regardless of whether they actually appear in the current document or not. If n is large, then this can become a problem. Consider the extreme case in which we have ten query terms, and each matching document contains exactly one of them. Then the algorithm performs ten times as much work as it would if it processed each term individually.

- The final sorting step in line 8 sorts all documents in the *results* array. Of course, sorting the whole array is a waste of resources, given that we are interested in only the top k results. The $\Theta(m \cdot \log(m))$ complexity of the sorting process might not seem so bad. But keep in mind that we are potentially dealing with a few million matching documents, so the $m \cdot \log(m)$ term in Equation 5.9 may in fact outweigh the $m \cdot n$ term corresponding to the score computation.

We can address both problems in the same way: by employing a data structure known as *heap*. If you already know what a heap is, feel free to skip ahead to the section "Efficient query processing with heaps" (page 142).

Binary heaps

A heap (or, more precisely, a *binary min-heap*) is a binary tree that satisfies the following definition:

1. Every empty binary tree is a heap.

2. A nonempty binary tree $\mathcal{T}$ is a heap if all of the following hold:
   (a) $\mathcal{T}$ is completely filled on all levels, except possibly the deepest one.
   (b) $\mathcal{T}$'s deepest level is filled from left to right.
   (c) For each node v, the value stored in v is smaller than the values stored in any of v's children.

Requirements (a) and (b), in combination, are sometimes referred to as the *shape property*. Because of the shape property, a heap may be represented not only as a tree but also as an array. The tree's root node is then stored in position 0, and the children for a node in position i are stored in position $2i + 1$ and $2i + 2$, respectively. Figure 5.2(a) shows the tree representation of a heap for the set $\{1, 2, 3, 4, 5, 6\}$. Figure 5.2(b) shows the equivalent array representation.

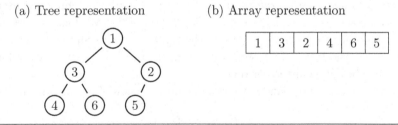

Figure 5.2   A heap for $\{1, 2, 3, 4, 5, 6\}$, in tree representation and equivalent array representation.

In practical implementations the array representation is almost always preferred over the tree representation because it is more space efficient (no child pointers) and also faster (better data locality). In the array representation, requirement 2(c) from above translates into

$$\forall i \in \{0, 1, 2, \ldots, len - 1\}:$$
$$(2i + 1 \geq len \ \vee \ A[i] \leq A[2i + 1]) \ \wedge \ (2i + 2 \geq len \ \vee \ A[i] \leq A[2i + 2]), \quad (5.11)$$

where *len* is the length of the array A. In particular, every sorted array is a heap (but not every heap is a sorted array).

Heaps support a variety of interesting operations. The only operation we are interested in here is called REHEAP. Consider the heap from Figure 5.2. Suppose we want to replace the root's value, 1, with a new value, say 9, while maintaining the heap property. The REHEAP algorithm would do this by replacing 1 with 9, then swapping 9 with 2 and finally swapping 9 with 5, resulting in the new array $\langle 2, 3, 5, 4, 6, 9 \rangle$, which again has the heap property. More formally, REHEAP takes a binary tree that meets all requirements for being a heap except for 2(c), and transforms it into a heap by moving the root's value down the tree until the heap property is established.

What is the time complexity of this algorithm? Consider a heap $\mathcal{T}$ containing n elements. Because every heap is a balanced binary tree, we know that each of $\mathcal{T}$'s leaves has either height $\lfloor \log_2(n) \rfloor$ or height $\lfloor \log_2(n) - 1 \rfloor$. Therefore, REHEAP will finish in $O(\log(n))$ steps.

Efficient query processing with heaps

We can use REHEAP to overcome the limitations of the algorithm in Figure 5.1. In the revised version of the algorithm, we employ two heaps: one to manage the query terms and, for each term t, keep track of the next document that contains t; the other one to maintain the set of the top k search results seen so far.

The resulting algorithm is shown in Figure 5.3. The *terms* heap contains the set of query terms, ordered by the next document in which the respective term appears (*nextDoc*). It allows us to perform an efficient multiway merge operation on the n postings lists. The *results* heap contains the top k documents encountered so far, ordered by their scores. It is important to note that *results*'s root node (i.e., *results*[0] in the array representation employed by the algorithm) does not contain the best document seen so far, but the kth-best document seen so far. This allows us to maintain and continually update the top k search results by replacing the lowest-scoring document in the top k (and restoring the heap property) whenever we find a new document that scores better than the old one.

The worst-case time complexity of the revised version of the document-at-a-time algorithm is

$$\Theta(N_q \cdot \log(n) + N_q \cdot \log(k)), \tag{5.12}$$

where $N_q = N_{t_1} + \cdots + N_{t_n}$ is the total number of postings for all query terms. The first term ($N_q \cdot \log(n)$) corresponds to REHEAP operations carried out on the *terms* heap, restoring the heap property after every posting. The second term ($N_q \cdot \log(k)$) corresponds to REHEAP operations carried out on the *results* heap, restoring the heap property whenever a new document is added to the set of top k results.

Compared to Equation 5.10, the revised algorithm constitutes a substantial improvement, primarily because of the speedup achieved by restricting the final sorting procedure to the top k documents instead of all matching documents. Moreover, although maintaining the top-k set has indeed a worst-case complexity of $\Theta(N_q \cdot \log(k))$, this worst-case complexity plays no role in practice; the algorithm's average-case complexity is even better than what is shown in Equation 5.12 (see Exercise 5.1).

rankBM25_DocumentAtATime_WithHeaps $(\langle t_1, ..., t_n \rangle, k) \equiv$

1   **for** $i \leftarrow 1$ **to** k **do**   // create a min-heap for the top k search results
2       $results[i].score \leftarrow 0$
3   **for** $i \leftarrow 1$ **to** n **do**   // create a min-heap for the n query terms
4       $terms[i].term \leftarrow t_i$
5       $terms[i].nextDoc \leftarrow \textbf{nextDoc}(t_i, -\infty)$
6   sort $terms$ in increasing order of $nextDoc$ // establish heap property for $terms$
7   **while** $terms[0].nextDoc < \infty$ **do**
8       $d \leftarrow terms[0].nextDoc$
9       $score \leftarrow 0$
10   **while** $terms[0].nextDoc = d$ **do**
11          $t \leftarrow terms[0].term$
12          $score \leftarrow score + \log(N/N_t) \cdot \text{TF}_{\text{BM25}}(t, d)$
13          $terms[0].nextDoc \leftarrow \textbf{nextDoc}(t, d)$
14   **reheap**($terms$)   // restore heap property for $terms$
15   **if** $score > results[0].score$ **then**
16          $results[0].docid \leftarrow d$
17          $results[0].score \leftarrow score$
18   **reheap**($results$)   // restore heap property for $results$
19 remove from $results$ all items with $score = 0$
20 sort $results$ in decreasing order of $score$
21 **return** $results$

Figure 5.3   Document-at-a-time query processing with BM25, using binary heaps for managing the set of terms and managing the set of top-k documents.

MaxScore

Although the algorithm in Figure 5.3 already achieves reasonable query processing performance, there is still room for improvement. Recall from our earlier discussion that the BM25 TF contribution can never exceed $k_1 + 1 = 2.2$. Thus, the overall score contribution of a term t is bounded from above by $2.2 \cdot \log(N/N_t)$. This bound is called the term's *MaxScore*. Now consider again the query

$$Q = \langle \text{ "greek", "philosophy", "stoicism" } \rangle. \tag{5.13}$$

The query terms' document frequencies, IDF weights, and corresponding MaxScore values are:

Term	N_t	$\log_2(N/N_t)$	MaxScore
"greek"	4,504	6.874	15.123
"philosophy"	3,359	7.297	16.053
"stoicism"	58	13.153	28.936

Table 5.1 Total time per query and CPU time per query, with and without MaxScore. Data set: 10,000 queries from TREC TB 2006, evaluated against a frequency index for GOV2.

	Without MaxScore			With MaxScore		
	Wall Time	**CPU**	**Docs Scored**	**Wall Time**	**CPU**	**Docs Scored**
OR, k=10	400 ms	304 ms	$4.4 \cdot 10^6$	188 ms	93 ms	$2.8 \cdot 10^5$
OR, k=100	402 ms	306 ms	$4.4 \cdot 10^6$	206 ms	110 ms	$3.9 \cdot 10^5$
OR, k=1000	426 ms	329 ms	$4.4 \cdot 10^6$	249 ms	152 ms	$6.2 \cdot 10^5$
AND, k=10	160 ms	62 ms	$2.8 \cdot 10^4$	n/a	n/a	n/a

Suppose the user who entered the query is interested in the top $k = 10$ search results. After scoring a few hundred documents, we may encounter the situation in which the 10th-best result found so far exceeds the maximum score contribution of the term "greek". That is,

$$results[0].score > \text{MaxScore}(\text{"greek"}) = 15.123. \qquad (5.14)$$

When this happens, we know that a document that only contains "greek", but neither "philosophy" nor "stoicism", can never make it into the top 10 search results. Thus, there is no need even to score any documents that contain only "greek". We may remove the term from the *terms* heap and look at its postings only when we find a document that contains one of the other two query terms.

As we compute scores for more and more documents, we may at some point encounter the situation in which

$$results[0].score > \text{MaxScore}(\text{"greek"}) + \text{MaxScore}(\text{"philosophy"}) = 31.176. \qquad (5.15)$$

At that point, we know that a document can make it into the top 10 only if it contains the term "stoicism", and we can remove "philosophy" from the *terms* heap, just as we did for "greek".

The strategy outlined above is called MaxScore. It is due to Turtle and Flood (1995). MaxScore is guaranteed to produce the same set of top k results as the algorithm in Figure 5.3, but to do so much faster because it ignores all documents for which we know a priori that they cannot be part of the final top k.

Note that, even though MaxScore removes some terms from the heap, it still uses them for scoring. This is done by maintaining two data structures, one for terms that are still on the heap and the other for terms that have been removed from the heap. Whenever we find a document d that contains one of the terms still on the heap, we iterate over the set of terms removed from the heap, and for each term t we call **nextDoc**$(t, d - 1)$ to determine whether t appears in d. If it does, we compute t's score contribution and add it to the score for d.

Table 5.1 lists the average time per query and average CPU time per query for 10,000 queries from the TREC 2006 Terabyte track, run against an on-disk frequency index for the GOV2 collection (containing postings of the form $(d, f_{t,d})$). For $k = 10$, the default setting of many search engines, MAXSCORE decreases the total time per query by 53% and the CPU time per query by 69%, compared to the algorithm in Figure 5.3. It does this by reducing the total number of documents scored by the search engine, from 4.4 million to 280,000 documents per query on average. Note that, even with MAXSCORE, the search engine still has to score an order of magnitude more documents than it would if it employed a conjunctive retrieval model (Boolean AND). However, in terms of overall performance, Boolean OR with MAXSCORE is not very far from Boolean AND. The average CPU time per query, for instance, is only 50% higher: 93 ms per query versus 62 ms.

5.1.2   Term-at-a-Time Query Processing

As an alternative to the document-at-a-time approach, some search engines process queries in a *term-at-a-time* fashion. Instead of merging the query terms' postings lists by using a heap, the search engine examines, in turn, all (or some) of the postings for each query term. It maintains a set of document score *accumulators*. For each posting inspected, it identifies the corresponding accumulator and updates its value according to the posting's score contribution to the respective document. When all query terms have been processed, the accumulators contain the final scores of all matching documents, and a heap may be used to collect the top k search results.

One of the motivations behind the term-at-a-time approach is that the index is stored on disk and that the query terms' postings lists may be too large to be loaded into memory in their entirety. In that situation a document-at-a-time implementation would need to jump back and forth between the query terms' postings lists, reading a small number of postings into memory after each such jump, and incurring the cost of a nonsequential disk access (disk seek). For short queries, containing two or three terms, this may not be a problem, as we can keep the number of disk seeks low by allocating an appropriately sized read-ahead buffer for each postings list. However, for queries containing more than a dozen terms (e.g., after applying pseudo-relevance feedback — see Section 8.6), disk seeks may become a problem. A term-at-a-time implementation does not exhibit any nonsequential disk access pattern. The search engine processes each term's postings list in a linear fashion, moving on to term t_{i+1} when it is done with term t_i.

Because the term-at-a-time paradigm processes each postings list separately, it is typically used only for scoring functions that are of the form

$$\text{score}(q, d) \ = \ \text{quality}(d) + \sum_{t \in q} \text{score}(t, d). \tag{5.16}$$

In this equation, quality(d) is an optional, query-independent score component, for example, PageRank (Equation 15.8 on page 518). Most traditional scoring functions, including VSM (Equation 2.12 on page 56), BM25 (Equation 8.48 on page 272) and LMD (Equation 9.32 on page 295), are of this (or an equivalent) form. They are sometimes referred to as *bag-of-words*

rankBM25_TermAtATime $(\langle t_1, ..., t_n \rangle,\ k) \equiv$

1   sort $\langle t_1, ..., t_n \rangle$ in increasing order of N_{t_i}

2    $acc \leftarrow \{\},\ acc' \leftarrow \{\}$ // initialize two empty accumulator sets

3    $acc[0].docid \leftarrow \infty$ // end-of-list marker

4   **for** $i \leftarrow 1$ **to** n **do**

5      $inPos \leftarrow 0$ // current position in acc

6      $outPos \leftarrow 0$ // current position in acc'

7   **for each** document d in t_i's postings list **do**

8   **while** $acc[inPos] < d$ **do**   // copy accumulators from acc to acc'

9          $acc'[outPos\,\texttt{++}] \leftarrow acc[inPos\,\texttt{++}]$

10       $acc'[outPos].docid \leftarrow d$

11       $acc'[outPos].score \leftarrow \log(N/N_{t_i}) \cdot \mathrm{TF}_{\mathrm{BM25}}(t_i, d)$

12   **if** $acc[inPos].docid = d$ **then**   // term and accumulator coincide

13         $acc'[outPos].score \leftarrow acc'[outPos].score + acc[inPos\,\texttt{++}].score$

14       $d \leftarrow \textbf{nextDoc}(t_i, acc'[outPos])$

15       $outPos \leftarrow outPos + 1$

16   **while** $acc[inPos] < \infty$ **do**   // copy remaining accumulators from acc to acc'

17        $acc'[outPos\,\texttt{++}] \leftarrow acc[inPos\,\texttt{++}]$

18      $acc'[outPos].docid \leftarrow \infty$ // end-of-list marker

19   swap acc and acc'

20   **return** the top k items of acc // use a heap to select the top k

Figure 5.4   Term-at-a-time query processing with BM25. Document scores are stored in accumulators. The accumulator array is traversed co-sequentially with the current term's postings list.

methods. Scoring functions that take into account the proximity of query terms in the document, including phrase queries, are incompatible with Equation 5.16. In theory, they may still be implemented within a term-at-a-time query processing framework. However, the per-document accumulators maintained by the search engine would need to hold some extra information (e.g., term positions) in addition to the documents' scores, thus increasing their size substantially.

Figure 5.4 shows a possible term-at-a-time query processing algorithm for BM25. In the figure, the score accumulators are kept in the array acc. For each query term t_i, the array is traversed co-sequentially with t_i's postings list, creating a new array acc' that contains the updated accumulators. The worst-case time complexity of this algorithm is

$$\Theta\left(\sum_{i=1}^{n}(N_q/n \cdot i) + N_q \cdot \log(k)\right) = \Theta(N_q \cdot n + N_q \cdot \log(k)), \tag{5.17}$$

where $N_q = N_{t_1} + \cdots + N_{t_n}$ is the total number of postings for all query terms. The worst case occurs when $N_{t_i} = N_q/n$ for $1 \leq i \leq n$.

By comparing Equation 5.17 with Equation 5.12, we see that the term-at-a-time algorithm, at least in the form presented in Figure 5.4, is actually slightly slower than the document-at-a-time algorithm ($N_q \cdot n$ instead of $N_q \cdot \log(n)$), due to the necessity to traverse the entire accumulator set for every query term t_i. In theory, we could eliminate this bottleneck by replacing the array implementation for *acc* with a hash table so that each accumulator update is an $O(1)$ operation. This would result in an overall complexity of $\Theta(N_q + N_q \cdot \log(k)) = \Theta(N_q \cdot \log(k))$. In practice, however, the array implementation seems to be superior to the hash-based implementation, for two reasons. First, an array is very cache-efficient; a hash table, due to the nonsequential access pattern, could potentially lead to a large number of CPU cache misses. Second, and more important, real-world implementations following the term-at-a-time approach usually do not keep the full set of accumulators, but instead employ a strategy known as *accumulator pruning*.

Accumulator pruning

As mentioned before, one motivation behind term-at-a-time query processing is that the query terms' postings lists may be too large to be completely loaded into memory. Of course, this implies that the accumulator set *acc* is also too large to be kept in memory. Thus, the algorithm in Figure 5.4 is incompatible with its initial motivation. To overcome this inconsistency, we have to revise the algorithm so that it requires only a fixed amount of memory for its accumulator set. That is, we have to impose an upper limit a_{max} on the number of accumulators that may be created.

The two classic accumulator pruning strategies are the QUIT and CONTINUE methods due to Moffat and Zobel (1996). With the QUIT strategy, the search engine — whenever it is done with the current query term — tests whether $|acc| \geq a_{max}$. If this is the case, query processing is terminated immediately, and the current accumulator set represents the final search results. If CONTINUE is used instead, the search engine may continue to process postings lists and to update existing accumulators, but may no longer create any new accumulators.

Unfortunately, since a term's postings list may contain more than a_{max} entries, neither QUIT nor CONTINUE actually enforces a hard limit, and for small values of a_{max} it is in fact quite likely that the limit is exceeded greatly. Our discussion of accumulator pruning is based on more recent work conducted by Lester et al. (2005). Lester's algorithm guarantees that the number of accumulators created stays within a constant factor of a_{max}. In the variant presented here, it is guaranteed that the accumulator limit is never exceeded.

Similar to the MAXSCORE heuristic for document-at-a-time query evaluation, the basic idea behind accumulator pruning is that we are not interested in the full set of matching documents, but only in the top k, for some small k. In contrast to MAXSCORE, however, accumulator pruning strategies are not guaranteed to return the same result set that an exhaustive evaluation would generate. They produce only an approximation; the quality of this approximation depends on the pruning strategy that is used and on the value of a_{max}.

In the algorithm shown in Figure 5.4, the query terms are processed in order of frequency, from least frequent to most frequent. While this is generally beneficial for unpruned term-at-a-time query processing, because fewer accumulators have to be copied from *acc* to *acc'*, it is crucial if accumulator pruning is employed. The main insight is the following: If we are allowed only a limited number of accumulators, we should spend them on documents that are most likely to make it into the top k. All other things being equal, if query term t has a greater weight than query term t', then a document containing t is more likely to be among the top k than a document containing t'. In the context of BM25 (or any other IDF-based ranking formula), this means that less frequent terms (with shorter postings lists) should be processed first.

In order to define the actual pruning strategy, we have to devise a rule that tells us for a given posting whether it deserves its own accumulator or not. Suppose the search engine, after processing the first $i-1$ query terms, has piled up a set of $a_{current}$ accumulators and is about to start working on t_i. Then we can distinguish three possible cases:

1. $a_{current} + N_{t_i} \leq a_{max}$. In this case we have enough free accumulators for all of t_i's postings, and no pruning is required.

2. $a_{current} = a_{max}$. In this case the accumulator limit has already been reached. None of t_i's postings will be allowed to create new accumulators.

3. $a_{current} < a_{max} < a_{current} + N_{t_i}$. In this case we may not have sufficient accumulator quota to create new accumulators for all of t_i's postings. Pruning may be required.

Cases 1 and 2 are straightforward. For case 3, a possible (simplistic) pruning strategy is to allow new accumulators for the first $a_{max} - a_{current}$ postings whose documents do not yet have accumulators, but not for the remaining ones. The problem with this approach is that it favors documents that appear early on in the collection. This seems inappropriate, as there is no evidence that such documents are more likely to be relevant to the given query (unless documents are sorted according to some query-independent quality measure, such as PageRank).

Ideally, we would like to define a threshold ϑ such that exactly $a_{max} - a_{current}$ postings from t_i's postings list have a score contribution greater than ϑ. Postings whose score exceeds ϑ would then be allowed to create a new accumulator, but lower-scoring postings would not. Taken literally, this approach necessitates a two-pass query processing strategy: In the first pass, score contributions for all of t_i's postings are scored and sorted to obtain the threshold ϑ. In the second pass, all of t_i's postings are scored again, and compared to the threshold. As t_i's postings list may be long, the computational cost of this approach can be substantial. We address this problem in two steps:

1. The necessity to score all of t_i's postings can be eliminated by employing a slightly different threshold value ϑ_{TF} and using it as a proxy for the original threshold ϑ. The new threshold value is compared directly to each posting's TF component, not to its score contribution, thus reducing the overall computational cost.

2. The second pass over t_i's postings can be avoided by using an approximate value of ϑ_{TF} instead of the exact value. The approximate value is computed on the fly and is updated periodically, based on the TF distribution of the postings that have already been processed.

rankBM25_TermAtATimeWithPruning $(\langle t_1, ..., t_n \rangle, k, a_{max}, u) \equiv$
1   sort $\langle t_1, ..., t_n \rangle$ in increasing order of N_{t_i}
2    $acc \leftarrow \{\}, \ acc' \leftarrow \{\}$ // initialize two empty accumulator sets
3    $acc[0].docid \leftarrow \infty$ // end-of-list marker
4   **for** $i = 1$ **to** n **do**
5        $quotaLeft \leftarrow a_{max} - length(acc)$ // the remaining accumulator quota
6   **if** $N_{t_i} \leq quotaLeft$ **then**   // Case 1: no pruning required
7   do everything as in Figure 5.4
8   **else if** $quotaLeft = 0$ **then**   // Case 2: no unused accumulators left
9   **for** $j = 1$ **to** $length(acc)$ **do**
10               $acc[j].score \leftarrow acc[j].score + \log(N/N_{t_i}) \cdot \mathrm{TF}_{\mathrm{BM25}}(t_i, acc[j].docid)$
11   **else**   // Case 3: some accumulators left; pruning may be required
12           $tfStats[j] \leftarrow 0 \quad \forall j$ // initialize TF statistics used for pruning
13           $\vartheta_{TF} \leftarrow 1$ // initialize TF threshold for new accumulators
14           $postingsSeen \leftarrow 0$ // the number of postings seen from t_i's postings list
15           $inPos \leftarrow 0$ // current position in acc
16           $outPos \leftarrow 0$ // current position in acc'
17   **for each** document d in t_i's postings list **do**
18   **while** $acc[inPos] < d$ **do**   // copy accumulators from acc to acc'
19                   $acc'[outPos\texttt{++}] \leftarrow acc[inPos\texttt{++}]$
20   **if** $acc[inPos].docid = d$ **then**   // term and accumulator coincide
21                   $acc'[outPos].docid \leftarrow d$
22                   $acc'[outPos\texttt{++}].score \leftarrow acc[inPos\texttt{++}].score + \log(N/N_{t_i}) \cdot \mathrm{TF}_{\mathrm{BM25}}(t_i, d)$
23   **else if** $quotaLeft > 0$ **then**
24   **if** $f_{t_i,d} \geq \vartheta_{TF}$ **then**   // $f_{t_i,d}$ exceeds the threshold; create a new accumulator
25                       $acc'[outPos].docid \leftarrow d$
26                       $acc'[outPos\texttt{++}].score \leftarrow \log(N/N_{t_i}) \cdot \mathrm{TF}_{\mathrm{BM25}}(t_i, d)$
27                       $quotaLeft \leftarrow quotaLeft - 1$
28                       $tfStats[f_{t_i,d}] \leftarrow tfStats[f_{t_i,d}] + 1$
29                   $postingsSeen \leftarrow postingsSeen + 1$
30   **if** $(postingsSeen \bmod u = 0)$ **then**   // recompute ϑ_{TF} based on $tfStats$
31                       $q \leftarrow (N_{t_i} - postingsSeen)/postingsSeen$
32                       $\vartheta_{TF} \leftarrow \mathrm{argmin}_x \{ x \in \mathbb{N} \mid \sum_{j=1}^{x} (tfStats[j] \cdot q) \geq quotaLeft \}$
33   copy the remaining accumulators from acc to acc', as in Figure 5.4
34   swap acc and acc'
35   **return** the top k items of acc // use a heap to select the top k

Figure 5.5   Term-at-a-time query processing with BM25 and accumulator pruning. Input parameters: the query terms $t_1, \ldots, t_n$; the number k of documents to be returned; the accumulator limit a_{max}; the threshold update interval u.

The resulting algorithm is shown in Figure 5.5. In addition to the query terms and the parameter k that specifies the number of search results to return, the algorithm takes two arguments: the accumulator limit a_{max} and the update interval u used for the approximation of ϑ_{TF}. The algorithm uses the array *tfStats* to record the number of postings with a given TF value that,

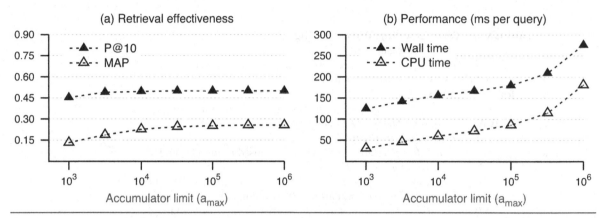

Figure 5.6   Retrieval effectiveness and query processing performance for term-at-a-time query evaluation with accumulator pruning. Data set: 10,000 queries from TREC TB 2006, run against a frequency index for GOV2.

when they were encountered, did not yet have a corresponding accumulator. By extrapolating these statistics to the remaining postings, we can predict how many postings we will see for a given TF value, thus allowing us to compute an estimate for ϑ_{TF}. This computation takes place in lines 31–32 of the algorithm.

The update interval parameter u is used to limit the computational cost of the periodic recomputation of ϑ_{TF}. From our experience, $u = 128$ seems to be a good trade-off between approximation accuracy and computational overhead. As an alternative to a fixed update interval, Lester et al. (2005) suggest exponentially increasing intervals, taking into account the fact that, as we progress, our approximation of the optimal threshold ϑ_{TF} becomes more accurate and requires less frequent corrections.

Regarding the efficiency of the threshold computation in line 32, it is worth pointing out that it is not necessary to have an entry for every possible TF value in the *tfStats* array. Most $f_{t_i,d}$ values are very small (less than 4 or 5), so it makes sense to group larger values together, to avoid maintaining a *tfStats* array in which most entries are 0. For example, changing line 28 of the algorithm to

$$tfStats[\min\{15, f_{t_i,d}\}] \leftarrow tfStats[\min\{15, f_{t_i,d}\}] + 1$$

has rarely any effect on the value of ϑ_{TF}, but allows us to recompute ϑ_{TF} in line 32 very efficiently.

Figure 5.6 shows the retrieval effectiveness and query processing performance of our implementation of the accumulator pruning algorithm in Figure 5.5. Effectiveness was measured by retrieving the top $k = 10,000$ documents for short queries generated for the 99 adhoc topics from TREC Terabyte 2004 and 2005. Query processing performance was measured by retrieving the top $k = 10$ documents for each of the 10,000 efficiency topics from TREC Terabyte 2006.

Retrieval effectiveness is quite stable, even for small values of a_{max}. Mean average precision (MAP) starts degrading at $a_{max} \approx 10^5$. Precision at 10 documents (P@10) shows signs of deterioration only for very aggressive pruning ($a_{max} < 10^4$). The performance of the algorithm, measured in seconds per query, is in the same ballpark as the performance of the document-at-a-time algorithm (with MAXSCORE). For $a_{max} = 10^5$, both methods require approximately the same amount of time and achieve roughly the same level of effectiveness. For larger values of a_{max}, the term-at-a-time method loses to document-at-a-time due to the overhead associated with traversing the whole accumulator array for every query term.

Interestingly, for aggressive pruning ($a_{max} \leq 10^4$), the term-at-a-time algorithm is actually faster than the Boolean AND approach (comparing Figure 5.6 with Table 5.1). This is not entirely unexpected. According to Table 5.1, if the search engine follows a conjunctive query interpretation (Boolean AND), it has to score 28,000 matching documents per query on average. Thus, under certain conditions the conjunctive approach may in fact be less efficient than the disjunctive approach with accumulator pruning. Of course, this comparison is not completely fair, as conjunctive query evaluation is also amenable to accumulator pruning (see Exercise 5.2).

5.1.3   Precomputing Score Contributions

It should have become clear by now that the computation of the final document scores, for example, according to the BM25 formula (Equation 5.5 on page 138), is a major bottleneck of the search engine's query processing routines. Both MAXSCORE and accumulator pruning obtain their performance gains from limiting score computations to documents that are likely to make it into the top k search results.

For scoring algorithms that follow the bag-of-words paradigm (Equation 5.16), it is not necessary to compute the query term's score contributions at query time. Instead, we may precompute each posting's score contribution during index construction and store it in the index, along with the docid, leading to postings of the form (*docid*, *score*) instead of (*docid*, *tf*). Precomputing score contributions can dramatically reduce the search engine's CPU cost during query processing. Of course, if TF values are replaced with precomputed score contributions, it will be impossible to make any changes to the scoring functions after the index has been built. In many applications this may not be a problem. But it makes it difficult to experiment with new scoring functions.

A perhaps more serious problem is posed by the space requirements of precomputed scores. To reduce their space requirements (and, in the case of on-disk indices, the disk I/O overhead), inverted indices are usually stored in compressed form. The details of how index compression works are not important here (they are described in Chapter 6), but the basic idea is that small integer values should be stored using a small number of bits. The vast majority of the TF values in an inverted index, for example, are very small (less than 4). Thus, they can be compressed extremely well and require only between 2 and 3 bits per posting in the index. Precomputed

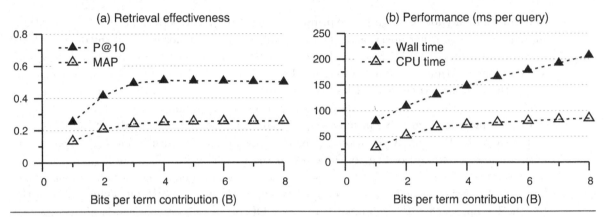

Figure 5.7   Retrieval effectiveness and query processing performance for document-at-a-time query evaluation with precomputed term contributions and MAXSCORE heuristic. Data set: 10,000 queries from TREC TB 2006, run against a frequency index for GOV2.

term scores, on the other hand, are essentially incompressible. If term scores are represented as 32-bit floating point numbers, they will require between 24 and 32 bits in the index.[1]

If we want to speed up the scoring process by using precomputed term contributions, then it is crucial that we discretize the range of possible scores into a predefined set of buckets. Let B denote the number of bits (uncompressed) that we are willing to reserve for each score contribution. Then a possible discretization could be

$$score' = \left\lfloor \frac{score}{score_{max}} \cdot 2^B \right\rfloor,$$

(5.18)

where $score_{max}$ is the maximum score contribution allowed by the scoring function. In the case of standard BM25, we have $score_{max} = k_1 + 1 = 2.2$ (ignoring the IDF component of the scoring formula).

Because the discretized $score'$ values are usually not uniformly distributed across all 2^B possible values, they are likely to be amenable to compression, such as Huffman coding (Section 6.2.2), and can be expected to consume slightly less than B bits each.

Figure 5.7 depicts experimental results (retrieval effectiveness and time per query) for a document-at-a-time implementation based on precomputed score contributions. It can be seen that, with as little as 4 bits per precomputed score (uncompressed), we can achieve a retrieval effectiveness that is on par with the original implementation that computes all term scores on the fly. At the same time the average time per query is reduced from 188 ms to 148 ms (-21%).

---

[1] The IEEE standard for floating point arithmetic divides a 32-bit floating point number into a 24-bit significand and an 8-bit exponent. The significand is virtually incompressible.

Increasing the number of bits per score makes the search engine slower, up to a point where the revised implementation, using precomputed scores, requires more time per query than the original implementation (e.g., 207 ms per query for $B = 8$, up from 188 ms). Note, however, that the slowdown stems almost exclusively from the increased disk I/O overhead, as the average CPU time per query remains approximately constant. Thus, the effect will not be observed if the index is kept in memory instead of on disk.

5.1.4   Impact Ordering

In the inverted index data structure described in Chapter 4, postings are stored in the index in the order in which they appear in the collection. This way of organizing the postings lists has the advantage that the index is easy to build and that query operations (such as intersecting postings lists) can be carried out relatively efficiently. However, the original document order is not necessarily the best ordering for the postings in a given postings list. In the term-at-a-time algorithm with accumulator pruning (Figure 5.5), for instance, we had to resort to a few tricks to efficiently obtain an approximation of the top-scoring postings in t_i's postings list. If the postings in that list had been sorted by their score contributions, this would have been much easier; we could have selected the first few postings from the list and ignored the rest.

An index in which the postings in each list are sorted according to their respective score contributions is called an *impact-ordered* index. Impact-ordered indices usually contain precomputed scores instead of TF values, as the ordering of the postings already implies a certain scoring function.

When implemented naïvely, impact ordering can have a devastating effect on the complexity of basic index access functions. For instance, the **next** method from Chapter 2 no longer has logarithmic, but linear complexity! To avoid this, postings in an impact-ordered index are usually not ordered by their exact score contribution, but — similar to what we did in the previous section — according to a quantized impact value. As before, we can group impact values into 2^B discrete buckets, where B is typically between 3 and 5. The postings in a given term's postings list are then sorted by their discretized impact value. Within each bucket, however, postings are sorted according to docid, as in the standard index organization from Chapter 4.

Following this hybrid approach, the computational overhead of random access operations, compared to a strictly document-ordered index, becomes tolerable. And the advantages of having quick access to a term's top postings are quite obvious, especially within a term-at-a-time query processing framework.

5.1.5   Static Index Pruning

The accumulator pruning technique from Section 5.1.2, with or without impact ordering, achieves its performance gains by ignoring a large portion of the query terms' postings. For instance, with an accumulator limit $a_{max} = 1,000$, the search engine never scores more than

1,000 documents. Unfortunately, even though many postings do not contribute anything to the scoring process, most of them still need to be read from the index and decompressed in order for the search engine to be able to access the "interesting" postings that do make a contribution.

If we want to squeeze the last bit of query processing performance out of our search engine, we can try to predict — at indexing time — which postings are likely to be used during query processing and which are not. Based on this prediction, we can remove from the index all postings which we don't think will play an important role in the search process. This strategy is referred to as *static index pruning*. It can yield substantial performance improvements due to the shorter postings lists in the index.

Static index pruning has several obvious limitations. First, when processing queries from a pruned index, we can no longer guarantee that the search engine returns the top-scoring documents for a given query. Second, it breaks down if we allow the users to define structural query constraints or to issue phrase queries. For instance, if a user searches for the phrase "to be or not to be" in the Shakespeare collection, and the index pruning algorithm has decided that the occurrence of "not" in act III, scene 2 of Shakespeare's *Hamlet* is unimportant, then the user will not be able to find the scene that she is looking for. Nonetheless, despite being inappropriate for certain types of queries, index pruning has proven to be quite successful for traditional bag-of-words query processing algorithms.

Index pruning algorithms usually come in one of two flavors:

- In *term-centric* index pruning, each term in the index is treated independently. From each term's postings list, the pruning algorithm selects the most important postings, according to some predefined criteria, and discards the rest.

- A *document-centric* pruning algorithm, in contrast, looks at individual documents. Given a document, the algorithm tries to predict which query terms are most important and most representative of that document. If a term is considered important, a posting is added to the index; otherwise, the term is discarded and treated as if it did not appear in the document at all.

Term-centric pruning

Term-centric index pruning was first studied by Carmel et al. (2001). In their paper they examine several different pruning algorithms that are, however, all relatively similar. Here we limit ourselves to their top-(K,ε) term-centric pruning algorithm.

Consider a term t with associated postings list L_t, and an unknown query q that contains the term t. Everything else being equal, the probability that a given posting P in L_t corresponds to one of the top k documents for the query q is monotonic in P's score contribution. Therefore, the term-centric pruning algorithm operates by sorting all postings in L_t according to their score contribution for the chosen scoring function (e.g., BM25). It selects the top K_t postings for inclusion in the index, discarding all other elements of L_t.

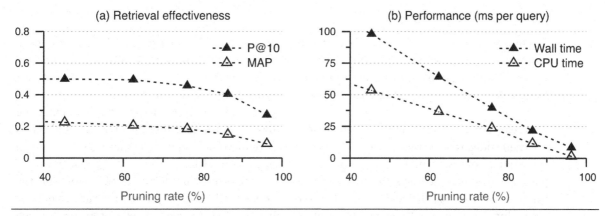

Figure 5.8   Term-centric index pruning with $K = 1{,}000$ and ε between 0.5 and 1. Data set for efficiency evaluation: 10,000 queries from TREC TB 2006. Data set for effectiveness evaluation: TREC topics 701–800.

There are various ways in which the cutoff parameter K_t can be chosen. One possibility is to use the same value K_t for all terms in the index. Alternatively, an index-wide score contribution threshold ϑ may be chosen, such that all postings whose score contribution exceeds ϑ are included in the index, while all other postings are discarded. A third variant is to guarantee each term at least K postings in the index. If a term t appears in more than K documents, its postings limit K_t depends on the distribution of score contributions in its postings list. This is the top-(K,ε) pruning method:

- Choose two parameters $K \in \mathbb{N}$ and $\varepsilon \in [0, 1]$.

- If a term t appears in fewer than K documents, store all of t's postings in the index.

- If a term t appears in more than K documents, compute $\vartheta_t = score(L_t[K]) \cdot \varepsilon$, where $score(L_t[K])$ is the score contribution of t's Kth-highest-scoring posting. Discard all postings with a score contribution below ϑ_t. Include the remaining postings in the index.

In general, it is unclear how K and ε should be chosen. However, once one parameter has been fixed, the other one can be varied freely until the desired index size, performance, or search result quality is reached.

In our experiments (Figure 5.8) we arbitrarily set $K = 1000$ and measured both retrieval effectiveness and query performance for various values of ε between 0.5 and 1. As can be seen from the figure, for $\varepsilon = 0.5$ (pruning rate: $\approx 50\%$) there is no noticeable difference in result quality between the pruned and the unpruned index (P@10 = 0.500, down from 0.503; MAP = 0.238, down from 0.260). The average time per query, however, decreases from 188 ms to 118 ms (-37%). For more aggressive pruning parameters, the performance gains are even more pronounced. However, if more than 70% of all postings are removed from the index, the quality of the search results begins to suffer markedly.

Document-centric pruning

Document-centric index pruning is motivated by document-based pseudo-relevance feedback methods (see Section 8.6). Pseudo-relevance feedback is a two-pass query processing strategy in which, in a first pass, the search engine identifies the set of k' top-scoring documents for the given query. It then assumes that these k' documents are all relevant to the query (*pseudo-relevance*) and selects a set of terms that it considers most representative of these documents. The selection is usually based on a statistical analysis of term distributions. The selected terms are then added to the original query (usually with a reduced weight, so that they do not outweigh the original query terms), and the augmented query is used for scoring in a second retrieval pass. It turns out that the set of terms selected by pseudo-relevance feedback often contains the original query terms. Hence, it is possible to run a query-independent pseudo-relevance feedback algorithms on individual documents — at indexing time! — to select a set of terms for which the given document is likely to rank highly.

Inspired by a pseudo-relevance feedback mechanism studied by Carpineto et al. (2001), Büttcher and Clarke (2006) propose the following document-centric pruning algorithm:

- Select a pruning parameter $\lambda \in (0, 1]$.

- For each document d, sort all n unique terms in d according to the following function:

$$score(t, d) \;=\; p_d(t) \cdot \log\left(\frac{p_d(t)}{p_{\mathcal{C}}(t)}\right), \tag{5.19}$$

where $p_d(t) = f_{t,d}/l_d$ is t's probability of occurrence according to the unigram language model of the document d, and $p_{\mathcal{C}}(t) = l_t/l_{\mathcal{C}}$ is the term's probability of occurrence according to the unigram language model of the text collection $\mathcal{C}$. Select the top $\lceil \lambda \cdot n \rceil$ terms for inclusion in the index; discard the rest.

If you are familiar with the concepts of information theory, Equation 5.19 might remind you of the *Kullback-Leibler divergence* (*KL divergence*) between two probability distributions. Given two discrete probability distributions f and g, their KL divergence is defined as

$$\sum_x f(x) \cdot \log\left(\frac{f(x)}{g(x)}\right). \tag{5.20}$$

KL divergence is often used to measure how different two probability distributions are. It plays an important role in various areas of information retrieval. In Section 9.4 it is used to compute document scores in a language modeling framework for ranked retrieval.

In the context of index pruning, we can use KL divergence to quantify how different a given document is from the rest of the collection. The pruning criterion from Equation 5.19 can then be viewed as selecting the terms that make the greatest contribution to the document's KL divergence and thus are, in some sense, most representative of what makes the document

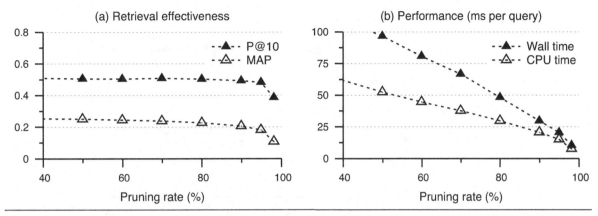

Figure 5.9 Document-centric index pruning with λ between 0.05 and 0.6. Data set for efficiency evaluation: 10,000 queries from TREC TB 2006. Data set for effectiveness evaluation: TREC topics 701–800.

unique. Note that this pruning criterion is independent of the scoring function employed by the search engine.

Figure 5.9 shows experimental results obtained for document-centric pruning. You can see that moderate levels of pruning have virtually no impact on retrieval effectiveness. For instance, after removing 70% of the postings from the index ($\lambda = 0.3$), MAP is still at 0.238 (down from 0.260). P@10 is almost unaffected and is even slightly higher than for an unpruned index (0.508 vs. 0.503). Only if we prune very aggressively ($\lambda < 0.1$), we will start to see an impact on early precision (P@10).

If you compare Figures 5.8 and 5.9, you will see that, at any given pruning rate, the term-centric method leads to lower response times than the document-centric approach. This can be explained by the fact that term-centric pruning selects postings for all terms in the index. Many of those terms are content generation artifacts (e.g., document time stamps) that never show up in search queries. The document-centric method detects that these terms are not important within their respective documents (because they usually appear only a single time in the document). It excludes them from the index, which increases the average length of the postings lists for the remaining terms. Therefore, at the same pruning level, the document-centric approach leads to more work for the search engine.

Figure 5.10 shows a head-to-head comparison between term-centric and document-centric pruning. For moderate performance levels (> 60 ms per query), there is not much of a difference between the two methods; both achieve almost the same precision as the original unpruned index. As we push for higher performance, however, the difference becomes quite visible. For example, at a fixed precision level of P@10=0.45, document-centric pruning is about twice as fast as the term-centric variant.

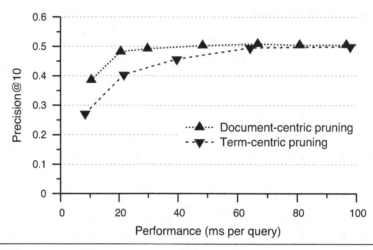

Figure 5.10   Efficiency-vs.-effectiveness trade-offs for document-centric and term-centric static index pruning.

Correctness guarantees

Although the static index pruning methods discussed above have interesting properties and allow the operator of a search engine to make efficiency-versus-effectiveness trade-offs by changing the parameters of the pruning algorithm, they are often not very attractive in real-world settings. In the Web search market, for instance, competition is fierce, and even small reductions in result quality represent a competitive disadvantage that may lead to a reduced market share. Performance improvements are welcome, but only as long as they don't have a negative impact on retrieval effectiveness.

Ntoulas and Cho (2007) present a method that can be used to decide whether the search results obtained from a pruned index are identical with the search results an unpruned index would have produced. Their work is based on the assumption that the ranking function employed by the search engine follows a bag-of-words scoring model (see Equation 5.16 on page 145).

For simplicity, our presentation of Ntoulas's method is based on a modified version of Equation 5.16 that lacks the quality component:

$$\mathrm{score}(q, d) \;=\; \sum_{t \in q} \mathrm{score}(t, d). \tag{5.21}$$

Now suppose that the search engine uses a scoring function that is of the form shown above, and that it processes queries from a pruned index, with some postings missing. Further suppose that the term-centric top-(K, ε) pruning mechanism from page 154 was used to prune the index. Then, for each term t in the index, there is a threshold value ϑ_t, such that all of t's postings

rankBM25_DocumentAtATimeWithCorrectnessGuarantee $(\langle t_1, ..., t_n \rangle, k) \equiv$
1     $m \leftarrow 0$ // m is the total number of matching documents
2     $d \leftarrow \min_{1 \le i \le n} \{\textbf{nextDoc}(t_i, -\infty)\}$
3   **while** $d < \infty$ **do**
4         $results[m].docid \leftarrow d$
5         $results[m].score \leftarrow 0$
6         $results[m].numHits \leftarrow 0$
7   **for** $i \leftarrow 1$ **to** n **do**
8   **if** $\textbf{nextDoc}(t_i, d-1) = d$ **then**
9                 $results[m].score \leftarrow results[m].score + \log(N/N_{t_i}) \cdot \text{TF}_{\text{BM25}}(t_i, d)$
10                $results[m].numHits \leftarrow results[m].numHits + 1$
11   **else**
12                $results[m].score \leftarrow results[m].score + \vartheta_{t_i}$
13        $m \leftarrow m + 1$
14        $d \leftarrow \min_{1 \le i \le n} \{\textbf{nextDoc}(t_i, d)\}$
15   sort $results[0..(m-1)]$ in decreasing order of $score$
16   **if** $results[i].numHits = n$ for $0 \le i < k$ **then**
17   **return** $(results[0..(k-1)], true)$ // results are guaranteed to be correct
18   **else**
19   **return** $(results[0..(k-1)], false)$ // results may be incorrect

Figure 5.11   Document-at-a-time query processing based on a pruned index. Depending on whether the correctness of the top k search results can be guaranteed or not, the function returns either *true* or *false*.

with a term contribution in excess of ϑ_t are in the index, while all postings with a smaller contribution have been dropped.

We may use this fact to determine whether the results produced by the pruned index are the same as the results that an unpruned index would have produced or whether they might be different. Consider a three-word query $q = \langle t_1, t_2, t_3 \rangle$ and a document d that, according to the pruned index, contains t_1 and t_2, but not t_3. From the index alone, it is impossible to tell whether d actually contains t_3 or not, as the posting may have been pruned. However, we do know that, if d contains t_3, then score(t_3, d) cannot be larger than ϑ_{t_3}. This gives us an upper bound for d's final score:

$$\text{score}(q, d) \le \text{score}(t_1, d) + \text{score}(t_2, d) + \vartheta_{t_3}. \tag{5.22}$$

We can take into account the incomplete nature of the pruned index by ranking the document d not according to its computed score but according to this upper bound. The resulting algorithm, a revised version of the algorithm in Figure 5.1, is shown in Figure 5.11. In the algorithm, when a document does not have a hit for query term t, the pruning cutoff ϑ_t is used in place of the actual score contribution. At the end of the computation, if we have complete information for each of the top k results ($results[i].numHits = n$ in line 16), we know that the ranking is correct.

The algorithm in Figure 5.11 can be used as part of a two-tiered query processing architecture in which the first tier consists of a pruned index and the second tier contains the original, unpruned index. Queries are first sent to the pruned index. If we can guarantee the correctness of the results produced by the pruned index, we are done. Otherwise, we process the query again, this time using the unpruned index. Depending on the relative performance of the pruned index compared to the full index, and on the fraction of queries that can be answered without consulting the full index, this approach has the potential to reduce the average amount of work done per query without sacrificing the quality of the search results. However, note that the algorithm in Figure 5.11 cannot be used in conjunction with document-centric pruning, because the latter does not provide an upper bound ϑ_t for the score contribution of pruned term occurrences. Thus, although document-centric pruning often does not reduce the quality of the search results, the index does not contain enough information for us to prove it.

5.2   Lightweight Structure

At the start of Chapter 2 we presented a simple abstract data type (ADT) for inverted indices. We demonstrated how this ADT could be used for phrase searching and for computing simple relationships involving structural elements, such as identifying all speeches spoken by a particular character in Shakespeare's plays (page 45). In that example we explicitly used the methods of the ADT to find occurrences of the character's name, and then the speeches containing them. We now extend and generalize this approach through the presentation of a *region algebra*.

Region algebras provide operators and functions for combining and manipulating text intervals (or *regions*) in support of lightweight structure. They represent an intermediate point between basic document retrieval and the complexity of full XML retrieval (see Chapter 16). They also provide a method for unifying many of the *advanced search* features supported by search engines and digital libraries. A number of region algebras have been described in the literature, dating back to the PAT region algebra, created for the *New Oxford English Dictionary* project in the early 1980s (Gonnet, 1987; Salminen and Tompa, 1994). The particular region algebra we present in this chapter is representative of the group, but is relatively simple and builds directly on the techniques introduced in Chapter 2 (Clarke et al., 1995a, 1995b; Clarke and Cormack, 2000).

5.2.1   Generalized Concordance Lists

Broadly speaking, region algebras work with sets of text intervals. Each interval may be expressed as a pair $[u, v]$, where u indicates the start of the interval and v indicates its end. Our particular region algebra places a simple but important requirement on the sets of intervals it manipulates: *No interval in the set may have another interval from the set nested within it.* We refer to a set of intervals with this property as a *generalized concordance list*, or *GC-list*.

The GC-list takes its name from a *concordance*, an alphabetical listing of the words in a document along with the context in which they appear. Prior to the advent of computer-based retrieval, paper-based concordances provided a tool for searching major works such as Shakespeare's. Essentially, they were an early form of an inverted index.

We use the notation $[u, v] \sqsubset [u', v']$ to indicate that $[u, v]$ is nested in $[u', v']$. Similarly, the notation $[u, v] \not\sqsubset [u', v']$ indicates that $[u, v]$ is not nested in $[u', v']$. If $[u, v]$ and $[u', v']$ are both part of a set manipulated by our region algebra, then $[u, v] \not\sqsubset [u', v']$ — either $u < u'$ and $v < v'$, or $u > u'$ and $v > v'$. For example, the set of intervals

$$S = \{[1, 10], [5, 9], [8, 12], [15, 20]\} \qquad (5.23)$$

is not a GC-list because $[5, 9] \sqsubset [1, 10]$. We could reduce this set to a GC-list by, for example, removing $[1, 10]$ to produce

$$\{[5, 9], [8, 12], [15, 20]\}. \qquad (5.24)$$

Note that $[5, 9]$ *overlaps* $[8, 12]$. Unlike nesting intervals, overlapping intervals are acceptable. Indeed, overlaps are essential to the correct operation of the region algebra. Note that we could also reduce S to a GC-list by removing the interval $[5, 9]$. For reasons that will become apparent later in this section, eliminating the larger interval is preferred.

We formalize the reduction of a set of intervals to a GC-list as follows: Let S be a set of intervals. We define the function $\mathcal{G}(S)$ as

$$\mathcal{G}(S) = \{a \mid a \in S \text{ and } \nexists\, b \in S \text{ such that } b \sqsubset a\} \qquad (5.25)$$

Given a set of text intervals, this function eliminates those that have other members of the set nested within them, thus reducing the set to a GC-list. Therefore, a set S is a GC-list if and only if $\mathcal{G}(S) = S$ and $\mathcal{G}(S) = \mathcal{G}(\mathcal{G}(S))$. GC-lists arise naturally from our implementation of the region algebra. While our implementation never explicitly reduces a set of intervals to a GC-list, the function helps us to provide a concise explanation for the behavior of the algebra.

GC-lists possess a number of important properties. Since intervals cannot nest, no two intervals in a GC-list may start at the same position. Thus, given two intervals $[u, v]$ and $[u', v']$, either $u < u'$ or $u > u'$. Similarly, no two intervals may end at the same position; if $u < u'$, then $v < v'$. Thus, ordering the intervals in a GC-list by either their start positions or their end positions produces the same ordering. Finally, because each position can form the start position for no more than one interval, the size of a GC-list is bounded by the total length of the collection.

A schema-independent postings list may be viewed as a GC-list by treating each entry as an interval of length 1, starting and ending at the same position. Thus, the postings list for "first" in Figure 2.1 on page 34 may be viewed as the GC-list

$$\text{"first"} = \{[2205, 2205], [2268, 2268], ..., [1271487, 1271487]\}. \qquad (5.26)$$

Table 5.2   Definitions for the binary operators in the region algebra.

Containment Operators

  Contained In:
  $$A \lhd B = \{a \mid a \in A \text{ and } \exists \, b \in B \text{ such that } a \sqsubset b\}$$

  Containing:
  $$A \rhd B = \{a \mid a \in A \text{ and } \exists \, b \in B \text{ such that } b \sqsubset a\}$$

  Not Contained In:
  $$A \ntriangleleft B = \{a \mid a \in A \text{ and } \nexists \, b \in B \text{ such that } a \sqsubset b\}$$

  Not Containing:
  $$A \ntriangleright B = \{a \mid a \in A \text{ and } \nexists \, b \in B \text{ such that } b \sqsubset a\}$$

Combination Operators

  Both Of:
  $$A \bigtriangleup B = \mathcal{G}(\{c \mid \exists \, a \in A \text{ such that } a \sqsubset c \text{ and } \exists \, b \in B \text{ such that } b \sqsubset c\})$$

  One Of:
  $$A \bigtriangledown B = \mathcal{G}(\{c \mid \exists \, a \in A \text{ such that } a \sqsubset c \text{ or } \exists \, b \in B \text{ such that } b \sqsubset c\})$$

Ordering Operator

  Before:
  $$A \ldots B = \mathcal{G}(\{c \mid \exists \, [u, v] \in A \text{ and } \exists \, [u', v'] \in B \text{ where } v < u' \text{ and } [u, v'] \sqsubset c\})$$

The answer to a phrase query may also be viewed as a GC-list, with the start and end positions of each phrase forming an interval in the GC-list. For example, the GC-list corresponding to the phrase "first witch" over the Shakespeare collection is

$$\text{"first witch"} \;=\; \{[745406, 745407], [745466, 745467], [745501, 745502], ...\}. \tag{5.27}$$

5.2.2 Operators

Our region algebra has seven binary operators, presented in Table 5.2. Each operator is defined over GC-lists and evaluates to a GC-list. The operators fall into three classes: containment, combination, and ordering.

The *containment operators* select the intervals in a GC-list that are contained in, not contained in, contain, or do not contain the intervals in a second GC-list. The containment operators are used to formulate queries that refer to the hierarchical characteristics of structural elements in the collection. The expression on the right-hand side of a containment operator acts as a filter to restrict the expression on the left-hand side — the result of the operation is a subset of the GC-list on the left-hand side.

The two *combination operators* are similar to the standard Boolean operators AND and OR. The "both of" operator is similar to AND: Each interval in the result contains an interval from both operands. The $\mathcal{G}()$ function is applied to ensure the result is a GC-list. The "one of" operator merges two GC-lists: Each interval in the result is an interval from one of the operands.

The *ordering operator* generalizes concatenation. Each interval in the result starts with an interval from the first operand and ends with an interval from the second operand. The interval from the first operand will end before the starting position of the interval from the second operand. The ordering operator may be used, for example, to connect tags that delineate structural elements, producing GC-lists in which each interval corresponds to one occurrence of the structural element. Examples showing the use of all seven binary operators are given in the next section.

In addition to the binary operators, there are two unary *projection operators*, π_1 and π_2. If A is a GC-list, we define

$$\pi_1(A) \;=\; \{[u,u] \mid \exists v \text{ with } [u,v] \in A\}, \tag{5.28}$$

$$\pi_2(A) \;=\; \{[v,v] \mid \exists u \text{ with } [u,v] \in A\}. \tag{5.29}$$

For example,

$$\pi_1(\{[5,9],[8,12],[15,20]\}) \;=\; \{[5,5],[8,8],[15,15]\}, \tag{5.30}$$

$$\pi_2(\{[5,9],[8,12],[15,20]\}) \;=\; \{[9,9],[12,12],[20,20]\}. \tag{5.31}$$

We also define GC-lists that include all intervals of a fixed size as

$$[i] \;=\; \{[u,v] \mid v - u + 1 = i\}. \tag{5.32}$$

For example,

$$[10] \;=\; \{...,[101,110],[102,111],[103,112],...\}. \tag{5.33}$$

5.2.3 Examples

The region algebra may be used to solve the queries given on page 45 of Chapter 2, as follows:

1. *Lines spoken by any witch.*

    ("⟨LINE⟩"   ...   "⟨/LINE⟩")
    ◁ (("⟨SPEECH⟩"   ...   "⟨/SPEECH⟩")
    ▷ (("⟨SPEAKER⟩"   ...   "⟨/SPEAKER⟩") ▷ "witch"))

    Brackets group the expressions, indicating the order in which the operations are to be applied. The query first locates speakers that are witches. The lines within their speeches are then extracted. All intermediate results, as well as the final result, are GC-lists.

2. *The speaker who says, "To be or not to be".*

("⟨SPEAKER⟩"   ...   "⟨/SPEAKER⟩")

◁ (("⟨SPEECH⟩"   ...   "⟨/SPEECH⟩")

▷ (("⟨LINE⟩"   ...   "⟨/LINE⟩") ▷ "to be or not to be"))

Lines containing the quote are located, the corresponding speeches are identified, and their speakers are extracted. Since this phrase appears only once in Shakespeare's plays, the resulting GC-list contains only a single interval.

3. *Titles of plays mentioning witches and thunder.*

("⟨TITLE⟩"   ...   "⟨/TITLE⟩")

◁ (("⟨PLAY⟩"   ...   "⟨/PLAY⟩") ▷ ("witch" △ "thunder"))

The query first identifies fragments of text that include both "witch" and "thunder", expressing the result as a GC-list. Titles are then extracted from plays containing these fragments.

In these examples we make reasonable assumptions about the structure of the XML used to encode Shakespeare's plays: Elements such as titles, scenes, plays, and lines are surrounded by appropriate tags; all plays contain a title; all speeches contain a speaker and one or more lines. In addition, we assume that structural elements do not nest (i.e., speeches don't contain other speeches).

A unique property of the region algebra is its ability to assign a meaning to a Boolean query such as "witch" △ "thunder", without reference to an explicit universe such as plays or lines, since its solution be may expressed as a GC-list. Over Shakespeare's plays,

$$\text{"witch"} \triangle \text{"thunder"} \ = \ \{[31463, 36898], [36898, 119010], [125483, 137236], ...\}. \tag{5.34}$$

Intervals in this GC-list overlap, and some intervals extend across multiple plays. Since no interval may have another nested within it, each interval starts with either the term "witch" or the term "thunder", and ends with the other term. Locating plays, scenes, lines, or structural elements that satisfy the Boolean expression is a matter of filtering one GC-list against another.

The combination operators are sufficient for Boolean expression requiring only AND and OR. For example, the query

$$(\text{"witch"} \triangledown \text{"king"}) \triangle (\text{"thunder"} \triangledown \text{"dagger"})$$

identifies fragments of text that contain either "witch" or "king" and either "thunder" or "dagger". Intervals in the resulting GC-list do not have intervals contained within them that also satisfy the Boolean expression. Any larger interval that satisfies the Boolean expression will have an interval from the GC-list contained within it. In our definition of $\mathcal{G}(S)$ in Equation 5.25, we chose to remove the larger of two nesting intervals rather than the smaller. The reasoning underlying this choice may now be more apparent. At least in the case of Boolean expressions, nothing is gained by explicitly computing these larger intervals.

Boolean NOT requires an explicit universe. For example, a query for plays not mentioning witches or thunder could be expressed as

$$(\text{ ``$\langle$PLAY$\rangle$''} \ \ldots \ \text{``$\langle$/PLAY$\rangle$''}) \not\rhd (\text{``witch''} \ \triangledown \ \text{``thunder''}).$$

Our region algebra may be used as one method for implementing the advanced search features supported by many search engines and digital libraries. It is fairly common for these IR systems to support Boolean queries that are restricted to specific fields, such as titles, authors, or abstracts. These queries naturally map into the facilities of the region algebra. Many Web search engines support a feature that allows a search to be restricted to a particular site. Including the query term "site:uwaterloo.ca" restricts the search to pages at the University of Waterloo. Assuming appropriate tagging and indexing, this query might be translated into the expression

$$(\text{``$\langle$PAGE$\rangle$''} \ \ldots \ \text{``$\langle$/PAGE$\rangle$''}) \rhd ((\text{``$\langle$SITE$\rangle$''} \ \ldots \ \text{``$\langle$/SITE$\rangle$''}) \rhd \text{``uwaterloo.ca''}).$$

5.2.4   Implementation

The implementation of our region algebra generalizes the algorithms for phrase searching, proximity ranking, and Boolean queries presented in Chapter 2. As we demonstrated earlier, the start positions and the end positions of each interval order the elements of a GC-list in exactly the same way. We exploit this ordering to develop a framework for efficiently implementing the region algebra. The approach involves indexing into GC-lists using an ADT similar to the one we defined for inverted indices on page 33. The ordering of intervals in a GC-list is used as the basis for defining this ADT. Given a GC-list and a position in the collection, we index into the GC-list to find the interval that is in some sense "closest to" that position. We begin with an example and follow it with a formal exposition of the framework.

Consider evaluating the expression $A \ldots B$ (see Figure 5.12). An interval from the resultant GC-list starts with an interval from A and ends with an interval from B. Suppose $[u,v]$ is the first interval in A. If $[u',v']$ is the first interval from B with $u' > v$, then v' must be the end of the first interval of $A \ldots B$. We index into B to find the first interval with $u' > v$. The last interval from A that ends before u' starts the first interval of $A \ldots B$. We index into A to find the last interval $[u'',v'']$ where $v'' < u'$. The interval $[u'',v']$ is then the first solution to $A \ldots B$. Indexing first into A, then into B, and again into A, gives us the first interval in $A \ldots B$ in three steps. The next solution to $A \ldots B$ begins after u''. We index into A to produce the first interval after u''. This procedure of successively indexing into A and B can be continued to find the remaining intervals in $A \ldots B$.

The implementation framework consists of four methods that allow indexing into GC-lists in various ways. Each of the methods represents a variation on the notion of "closest interval"

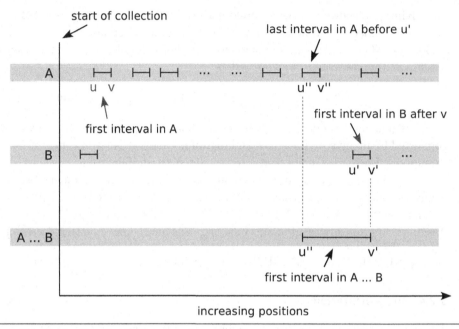

Figure 5.12   Evaluating the GCL expression $A \ldots B$.

in a GC-list to a specified position in the collection. We implement the four methods for each operator in the region algebra, using the methods of its operands.

- The method $\tau(S, k)$ returns the first interval in the GC-list S starting at or after the position k:

$$\tau(S, k) = \begin{cases} [u, v] & \text{if } \exists \, [u, v] \in S \text{ such that } k \leq u \\ & \text{and } \not\exists \, [u', v'] \in S \text{ such that } k \leq u' < u \\ [\infty, \infty] & \text{if } \not\exists \, [u, v] \in S \text{ such that } k \leq u \end{cases} \qquad (5.35)$$

- The method $\rho(S, k)$ returns the first interval in S ending at or after the position k:

$$\rho(S, k) = \begin{cases} [u, v] & \text{if } \exists \, [u, v] \in S \text{ such that } k \leq v \\ & \text{and } \not\exists \, [u', v'] \in S \text{ such that } k \leq v' < v \\ [\infty, \infty] & \text{if } \not\exists \, [u, v] \in S \text{ such that } k \leq v \end{cases} \qquad (5.36)$$

$$\tau(t,k) \equiv$$
1 **if** $k = \infty$ **then**
2     $u \leftarrow \infty$
3 **else if** $k = -\infty$ **then**
4     $u \leftarrow -\infty$
5 **else**
6     $u \leftarrow \textbf{next}(t, k-1)$
7 **return** $[u, u]$

$$\tau'(t,k) \equiv$$
8 **if** $k = \infty$ **then**
9     $v \leftarrow \infty$
10 **else if** $k = -\infty$ **then**
11     $v \leftarrow -\infty$
12 **else**
13     $v \leftarrow \textbf{prev}(t, k+1)$
14 **return** $[v, v]$

Figure 5.13   Pseudo-code for $\tau(t,k)$ and $\tau'(t,k)$, where t is a term.

- The method $\tau'(S, k)$ is the converse of τ. It returns the last interval in S ending at or before the position k:

$$\tau'(S,k) = \begin{cases} [u,v] & \text{if } \exists\, [u,v] \in S \text{ such that } k \geq v \\ & \quad \text{and } \not\exists\, [u',v'] \in S \text{ such that } k \geq v' > v \\ [\text{-}\infty,\text{-}\infty] & \text{if } \not\exists\, [u,v] \in S \text{ such that } k \geq v \end{cases} \quad (5.37)$$

- The method $\rho'(S, k)$ is the converse of ρ. It returns the last interval in S starting at or before the position k:

$$\rho'(S,k) = \begin{cases} [u,v] & \text{if } \exists\, [u,v] \in S \text{ such that } k \geq u \\ & \quad \text{and } \not\exists\, [u',v'] \in S \text{ such that } k \geq u' > u \\ [\text{-}\infty,\text{-}\infty] & \text{if } \not\exists\, [u,v] \in S \text{ such that } k \geq u \end{cases} \quad (5.38)$$

For example, if $S = \{[5,9], [8,12], [15,20]\}$ and $k = 10$, we have:

$$\tau(\{[5,9], [8,12], [15,20]\}, 10) = [15,20]$$
$$\rho(\{[5,9], [8,12], [15,20]\}, 10) = [8,12]$$
$$\tau'(\{[5,9], [8,12], [15,20]\}, 10) = [5,9]$$
$$\rho'(\{[5,9], [8,12], [15,20]\}, 10) = [8,12]$$

Just as they do for our inverted index ADT, the symbols ∞ and $-\infty$ act as end-of-file and beginning-of-file markers.

The methods $\tau(S,k)$, $\rho(S,k)$, $\tau'(S,k)$, and $\rho'(S,k)$ are closely related to our inverted index ADT of Chapter 2. For individual query terms these methods may be defined using that ADT, as shown in Figure 5.13 for $\tau(t,k)$ and $\tau'(t,k)$. Thus, for the inverted index of Figure 2.1 (page 34) we have

$$\tau(\text{``first''}, 745466) = [745501, 745501]. \quad (5.39)$$

$\tau(A \ldots B, k) \equiv$		$\tau(A \lhd B, k) \equiv$		$\rho(A \rhd B, k) \equiv$	
1	**if** $k = \infty$ **then**	13	**if** $k = \infty$ **then**	27	**if** $k = \infty$ **then**
2	**return** $[\infty, \infty]$	14	**return** $[\infty, \infty]$	28	**return** $[\infty, \infty]$
3	**if** $k = -\infty$ **then**	15	**if** $k = -\infty$ **then**	29	**if** $k = -\infty$ **then**
4	**return** $[-\infty, -\infty]$	16	**return** $[\,\infty, -\infty]$	30	**return** $[-\infty, -\infty]$
5	$[u, v] \leftarrow \tau(A, k)$	17	$[u, v] \leftarrow \tau(A, k)$	31	$[u, v] \leftarrow \rho(A, k)$
6	**if** $[u, v] = [\infty, \infty]$ **then**	18	**if** $[u, v] = [\infty, \infty]$ **then**	32	**if** $[u, v] = [\infty, \infty]$ **then**
7	**return** $[\infty, \infty]$	19	**return** $[\infty, \infty]$	33	**return** $[\infty, \infty]$
8	$[u', v'] \leftarrow \tau(B, v + 1)$	20	$[u', v'] \leftarrow \rho(B, v)$	34	$[u', v'] \leftarrow \tau(B, u)$
9	**if** $[u', v'] = [\infty, \infty]$ **then**	21	**if** $[u', v'] = [\infty, \infty]$ **then**	35	**if** $[u', v'] = [\infty, \infty]$ **then**
10	**return** $[\infty, \infty]$	22	**return** $[\infty, \infty]$	36	**return** $[\infty, \infty]$
11	$[u'', v''] \leftarrow \tau'(A, u' - 1)$	23	**if** $u' \le u$ **then**	37	**if** $v' \le v$ **then**
12	**return** $[u'', v']$	24	**return** $[u, v]$	38	**return** $[u, v]$
		25	**else**	39	**else**
		26	**return** $\tau(A \lhd B, u')$	40	**return** $\rho(A \rhd B, v')$

Figure 5.14 Implementation of $\tau(A \ldots B, k)$, $\tau(A \lhd B, k)$, and $\rho(A \rhd B, k)$, where A and B are GC-lists.

The definition of $\rho(t, k)$ is similar to that of $\tau(t, k)$; the definition of $\rho'(t, k)$ is similar to that of $\tau'(t, k)$. For fixed-size intervals $[i]$, implementation of the GC-list methods is even more straightforward, because the solution may be computed directly from k (see Exercise 5.5).

The methods for the binary operators are built upon the methods of their operands. Figure 5.14 provides some examples. In the implementation of $\tau(A \ldots B, k)$, most of the lines handle boundary cases associated with ∞ and $-\infty$. The core of the algorithm is expressed by lines 5, 8, and 11, reflecting the idea illustrated by Figure 5.12. On line 5, the first interval in A starting at or after k is computed. On line 8, the first interval in B starting at or after the interval from A is computed. The end position of this interval is the end position of the solution to $\tau(A \ldots B, k)$. Finally, on line 11 the start position of the solution is computed.

The methods are amenable to implementation by galloping search (see Figure 2.5 on page 42). To generate all solutions to a query Q, we call $\tau(Q, k)$ iteratively:

$$k \leftarrow 0$$
$$\textbf{while } k < \infty \textbf{ do}$$
$$[u, v] \leftarrow \tau(Q, k)$$
$$\textbf{if } k \neq \infty \textbf{ then}$$
$$\text{output } [u, v]$$
$$k \leftarrow u + 1$$

5.3   Further Reading

At the beginning of Section 5.1, we implied that a query processor for ranked retrieval has to follow either the conjunctive or the disjunctive Boolean model. However, combinations are possible. For example, it is possible to initially evaluate the query according to a conjunctive interpretation and then switch to a disjunctive interpretation if the conjunctive one matches too few documents. A more general version of this "weak-AND" approach is described by Broder et al. (2003).

The MAXSCORE heuristic (Section 5.1.1) is due to Turtle and Flood (1995). A similar algorithm was proposed in earlier work by Smith (1990). More recently, Strohman et al. (2005) presented an improved version of MAXSCORE that uses precomputed topdocs lists (you may think of these lists as a very aggressively pruned index) to obtain a lower bound for the score of the kth-best search result. This lower bound can then be used to remove query terms from the heap before a single document is scored. Strohman et al. (2005) report time savings of 23% compared to the original MAXSCORE algorithm. Zhu et al. (2008) propose a variation of MAXSCORE that can be used for ranking functions that have a term proximity component. Their method is similar to Strohman's approach but uses a phrase index to compute proximity-aware topdocs.

Impact ordering (Section 5.1.4) was first studied by Persin et al. (1996) under the label "frequency-sorted indexes". Refinements of this basic method were explored in a series of publications by Anh et al. (2001, 2004, 2006). The final paper in this series is of particular interest, because it demonstrates the suitability of the impact-ordered index organization for document-at-a-time query processing strategies — something that is not immediately obvious.

The PAT region algebra (Gonnet, 1987; Salminen and Tompa, 1994), initially developed to meet the needs of the *New Oxford English Dictionary* project, was later commercialized by Open Text Corporation as an integral part of their search engine (Open Text Corporation, 2001). Tim Bray, the sole author of the first version of that engine, went on to become a co-creator of the XML Standard. Later versions of the engine provided search services for Yahoo! during the mid-1990s and continue to power the company's enterprise content management products.

The success of PAT inspired a number of extensions and improvements. The PADRE system (Hawking and Thistlewaite, 1994) provided a parallel implementation of PAT. Burkowski (1992) presents containment and set operators for a hierarchical region algebra. The region algebra presented in this chapter is based on Clarke et al. (1995a, 1995b) and may be viewed as an extension (and simplification) of Burkowski's region algebra. Dao et al. (1996) and Jaakkola and Kilpeläinen (1999) present further extensions in support of recursive structure (e.g., speeches that contain speeches). Consens and Milo (1995) explore theoretical aspects and limitations of region algebras. The region algebra described by Navarro and Baeza-Yates (1997) organizes regions into multiple hierarchies, supporting direct ancestor/child relationships and recursive structure.

Additional information on the efficient implementation of the combination operators can be found in Clarke and Cormack (2000). Zhang et al. (2001) discuss algorithms for efficiently implementing containment queries in the context of a relational database system. Young-Lai and Tompa (2003) describe a bottom-up, one-pass approach to implementation. Boldi and Vigna (2006) explore efficient implementation through lazy evaluation.

5.4 Exercises

Exercise 5.1 Equation 5.12 on page 142 states that the worst-case complexity of the document-at-a-time algorithm with heaps is $\Theta(N_q \cdot \log(n) + N_q \cdot \log(k))$.

(a) Characterize the kind of input (i.e., document score distribution) that represents the worst case.

(b) Prove that, on average, the complexity of the algorithm is strictly better than $\Theta(N_q \cdot \log(k))$. You may assume that $k > n$ and that document scores are distributed uniformly, that is, every document is equally likely to have the highest score, second-highest score, and so forth.

Exercise 5.2 Design a term-at-a-time query processing algorithm for conjunctive queries (Boolean AND) that supports accumulator pruning.

Exercise 5.3 Figure 5.7(b) shows that the average CPU time per query drops sharply if less than $B = 3$ bits are used per precomputed score contribution. This is a side effect of the MAXSCORE heuristic employed by the query processing algorithm. Explain why MAXSCORE is more effective for smaller values of B.

Exercise 5.4 Given the assumptions of Section 5.2.3, express the following queries in the region algebra:

(a) Find plays that contain "Birnam" followed by "Dunsinane".
(b) Find fragments of text that contain "Birnam" and "Dunsinane".
(c) Find plays in which the word "Birnam" is spoken by a witch.
(d) Find speeches that contain "toil" or "trouble" in the first line, and do not contain "burn" or "bubble" in the second line.
(e) Find a speech by an apparition that contains "fife" and that appears in a scene along with the line "Something wicked this way comes".

Exercise 5.5 Write pseudo-code implementing the four GC-list methods for fixed-length intervals: $\tau([i], k)$, $\rho([i], k)$, $\tau'([i], k)$, and $\rho'([i], k)$.

Exercise 5.6 Write pseudo-code implementing the GC-list methods for the two projection operators: $\tau(\pi_1(A), k)$, $\rho(\pi_1(A), k)$, $\tau'(\pi_1(A), k)$, $\rho'(\pi_1(A), k)$, $\tau(\pi_2(A), k)$, $\rho(\pi_2(A), k)$, $\tau'(\pi_2(A), k)$, and $\rho'(\pi_2(A), k)$.

Exercise 5.7 Following the pattern of the algorithms shown in Figure 5.14 (page 168), write pseudo-code for the following methods:

(a) $\rho(A \ldots B, k)$
(b) $\tau(A \triangle B, k)$
(c) $\tau(A \triangledown B, k)$
(d) $\tau(A \not\triangleright B, k)$
(e) $\rho(A \triangleleft B, k)$
(f) $\tau'(A \triangleleft B, k)$

Exercise 5.8 Write pseudo-code implementing the four GC-list methods for phrases: $\tau(t_1...t_n, k)$, $\rho(t_1...t_n, k)$, $\tau'(t_1...t_n, k)$, and $\rho'(t_1...t_n, k)$. (*Hint:* As a starting point, consider the implementation of the **nextPhrase** function in Figure 2.2 on page 36).

Exercise 5.9 (project exercise) Implement the BM25 ranking formula (Equation 8.48 on page 272), using a document-at-a-time evaluation strategy. Your implementation should use the MaxScore heuristic to reduce the number of document scores computed.

5.5 Bibliography

Anh, V.N., de Kretser, O., and Moffat, A. (2001). Vector-space ranking with effective early termination. In *Proceedings of the 24th Annual International ACM SIGIR Conference on Research and Development in Information Retrieval*, pages 35–42. New Orleans, Louisiana.

Anh, V.N., and Moffat, A. (2004). Collection-independent document-centric impacts. In *Proceedings of the 9th Australasian Document Computing Symposium*, pages 25–32. Melbourne, Australia.

Anh, V.N., and Moffat, A. (2006). Pruned query evaluation using pre-computed impacts. In *Proceedings of the 29th Annual International ACM SIGIR Conference on Research and Development in Information Retrieval*, pages 372–379. Seattle, Washington.

Boldi, P., and Vigna, S. (2006). Efficient lazy algorithms for minimal-interval semantics. In *String Processing and Information Retrieval, 13th International Conference*, pages 134–149. Glasgow, Scotland.

Broder, A.Z., Carmel, D., Herscovici, M., Soffer, A., and Zien, J. (2003). Efficient query evaluation using a two-level retrieval process. In *Proceedings of the 12th International Conference on Information and Knowledge Management*, pages 426–434. New Orleans, Louisiana.

Burkowski, F. J. (1992). An algebra for hierarchically organized text-dominated databases. *Information Processing & Management*, 28(3):333–348.

Büttcher, S., and Clarke, C. L. A. (2006). A document-centric approach to static index pruning in text retrieval systems. In *Proceedings of the 15th ACM International Conference on Information and Knowledge Management*, pages 182–189. Arlington, Virginia.

Carmel, D., Cohen, D., Fagin, R., Farchi, E., Herscovici, M., Maarek, Y., and Soffer, A. (2001). Static index pruning for information retrieval systems. In *Proceedings of the 24th Annual International ACM SIGIR Conference on Research and Development in Information Retrieval*, pages 43–50. New Orleans, Louisiana.

Carpineto, C., de Mori, R., Romano, G., and Bigi, B. (2001). An information-theoretic approach to automatic query expansion. *ACM Transactions on Information Systems*, 19(1):1–27.

Clarke, C. L. A., and Cormack, G. V. (2000). Shortest-substring retrieval and ranking. *ACM Transactions on Information Systems*, 18(1):44–78.

Clarke, C. L. A., Cormack, G. V., and Burkowski, F. J. (1995a). An algebra for structured text search and a framework for its implementation. *Computer Journal*, 38(1):43–56.

Clarke, C. L. A., Cormack, G. V., and Burkowski, F. J. (1995b). Schema-independent retrieval from heterogeneous structured text. In *Proceedings of the 4th Annual Symposium on Document Analysis and Information Retrieval*, pages 279–289. Las Vegas, Nevada.

Consens, M. P., and Milo, T. (1995). Algebras for querying text regions. In *Proceedings of the 14th ACM SIGACT-SIGMOD-SIGART Symposium on Principles of Database Systems*, pages 11–22. San Jose, California.

Dao, T., Sacks-Davis, R., and Thom, J. A. (1996). Indexing structured text for queries on containment relationships. In *Proceedings of the 7th Australasian Database Conference*, pages 82–91. Melbourne, Australia.

Gonnet, G. H. (1987). PAT 3.1 — An Efficient Text Searching System — User's Manual. University of Waterloo, Canada.

Hawking, D., and Thistlewaite, P. (1994). Searching for meaning with the help of a PADRE. In *Proceedings of the 3rd Text REtrieval Conference (TREC-3)*, pages 257–267. Gaithersburg, Maryland.

Jaakkola, J., and Kilpeläinen, P. (1999). *Nested Text-Region Algebra*. Technical Report CC-1999-2. Department of Computer Science, University of Helsinki, Finland.

Lester, N., Moffat, A., Webber, W., and Zobel, J. (2005). Space-limited ranked query evaluation using adaptive pruning. In *Proceedings of the 6th International Conference on Web Information Systems Engineering*, pages 470–477. New York.

Moffat, A., and Zobel, J. (1996). Self-indexing inverted files for fast text retrieval. *ACM Transactions on Information Systems*, 14(4):349–379.

Navarro, G., and Baeza-Yates, R. (1997). Proximal nodes: A model to query document databases by content and structure. *ACM Transactions on Information Systems*, 15(4):400–435.

Ntoulas, A., and Cho, J. (2007). Pruning policies for two-tiered inverted index with correctness guarantee. In *Proceedings of the 30th Annual International ACM SIGIR Conference on Research and Development in Information Retrieval*, pages 191–198. Amsterdam, The Netherlands.

Open Text Corporation (2001). *Ten Years of Innovation*. Waterloo, Canada: Open Text Coporation.

Persin, M., Zobel, J., and Sacks-Davis, R. (1996). Filtered document retrieval with frequency-sorted indexes. *Journal of the American Society for Information Science*, 47(10):749–764.

Salminen, A., and Tompa, F. W. (1994). PAT expressions — An algebra for text search. *Acta Linguistica Hungarica*, 41(1–4):277–306.

Smith, M. E. (1990). *Aspects of the P-Norm Model of Information Retrieval: Syntactic Query Generation, Efficiency, and Theoretical Properties*. Ph.D. thesis, Cornell University, Ithaca, New York.

Strohman, T., Turtle, H., and Croft, W. B. (2005). Optimization strategies for complex queries. In *Proceedings of the 28th Annual International ACM SIGIR Conference on Research and Development in Information Retrieval*, pages 219–225. Salvador, Brazil.

Turtle, H., and Flood, J. (1995). Query evaluation: Strategies and optimization. *Information Processing & Management*, 31(1):831–850.

Young-Lai, M., and Tompa, F. W. (2003). One-pass evaluation of region algebra expressions. *Information Systems*, 28(3):159–168.

Zhang, C., Naughton, J., DeWitt, D., Luo, Q., and Lohman, G. (2001). On supporting containment queries in relational database management systems. In *Proceedings of the 2001 ACM SIGMOD International Conference on Management of Data*, pages 425–436. Santa Barbara, California.

Zhu, M., Shi, S., Yu, N., and Wen, J. R. (2008). Can phrase indexing help to process non-phrase queries? In *Proceedings of the 17th ACM Conference on Information and Knowledge Management*, pages 679–688. Napa, California.

6   Index Compression

An inverted index for a given text collection can be quite large, especially if it contains full positional information about all term occurrences in the collection. In a typical collection of English text there is approximately one token for every 6 bytes of text (including punctuation and whitespace characters). Hence, if postings are stored as 64-bit integers, we may expect that an uncompressed positional index for such a collection consumes between 130% and 140% of the uncompressed size of the original text data. This estimate is confirmed by Table 6.1, which lists the three example collections used in this book along with their uncompressed size, their compressed size, and the sizes of an uncompressed and a compressed schema-independent index. An uncompressed schema-independent index for the TREC45 collection, for instance, consumes about 331 MB, or 122% of the raw collection size.[1]

Table 6.1   Collection size, uncompressed and compressed (`gzip --best`), and size of schema-independent index, uncompressed (64-bit integers) and compressed (vByte), for the three example collections.

	Collection Size		Index Size	
	Uncompressed	Compressed	Uncompressed	Compressed
Shakespeare	7.5 MB	2.0 MB	10.5 MB (139%)	2.7 MB (36%)
TREC45	1904.5 MB	582.9 MB	2331.1 MB (122%)	533.0 MB (28%)
GOV2	425.8 GB	79.9 GB	328.3 GB (77%)	62.1 GB (15%)

An obvious way to reduce the size of the index is to not encode each posting as a 64-bit integer but as a $\lceil \log(n) \rceil$-bit integer, where n is the number of tokens in the collection. For TREC45 ($\lceil \log(n) \rceil = 29$) this shrinks the index from 2331.1 MB to 1079.1 MB — 57% of the raw collection size. Compared to the naïve 64-bit encoding, this is a major improvement. However, as you can see from Table 6.1, it is not even close to the 533 MB that can be achieved if we employ actual index compression techniques.

Since an inverted index consists of two principal components, the dictionary and the postings lists, we can study two different types of compression methods: dictionary compression and postings list compression. Because the size of the dictionary is typically very small compared

---

[1] The numbers for GOV2 are lower than for the other two collections because its documents contain a nontrivial amount of JavaScript and other data that are not worth indexing.

to the total size of all postings lists (see Table 4.1 on page 106), researchers and practitioners alike usually focus on the compression of postings lists. However, dictionary compression can sometimes be worthwhile, too, because it decreases the main memory requirements of the search engine and allows it to use the freed resources for other purposes, such as caching postings lists or search results.

The remainder of this chapter consists of three main parts. In the first part (Sections 6.1 and 6.2) we provide a brief introduction to general-purpose, symbolwise data compression techniques. The second part (Section 6.3) treats the compression of postings lists. We discuss several compression methods for inverted lists and point out some differences between the different types of inverted indices. We also show how the effectiveness of these methods can be improved by applying document reordering techniques. The last part (Section 6.4) covers compression algorithms for dictionary data structures and shows how the main memory requirements of the search engine can be reduced substantially by storing the in-memory dictionary entries in compressed form.

6.1 General-Purpose Data Compression

In general, a data compression algorithm takes a chunk of data A and transforms it into another chunk of data B, such that B is (hopefully) smaller than A, that is, it requires fewer bits to be transmitted over a communication channel or to be stored on a storage medium. Every compression algorithm consists of two components: the *encoder* (or *compressor*) and the *decoder* (or *decompressor*). The encoder takes the original data A and outputs the compressed data B. The decoder takes B and produces some output C.

A particular compression method can either be *lossy* or *lossless*. With a lossless method, the decoder's output, C, is an exact copy of the original data A. With a lossy method, C is not an exact copy of A but an approximation that is somewhat similar to the original version. Lossy compression is useful when compressing pictures (e.g., JPEG) or audio files (e.g., MP3), where small deviations from the original are invisible (or inaudible) to the human senses. However, in order to estimate the loss of quality introduced by those small deviations, the compression algorithm needs to have some a priori knowledge about the structure or the meaning of the data being compressed.

In this chapter we focus exclusively on lossless compression algorithms, in which the decoder produces an exact copy of the original data. This is mainly because it is not clear what the value of an approximate reconstruction of a given postings list would be (except perhaps in the case of positional information, where it may sometimes be sufficient to have access to approximate term positions). When people talk about *lossy index compression*, they are often not referring to data compression methods but to index pruning schemes (see Section 5.1.5).

6.2 Symbolwise Data Compression

When compressing a given chunk of data A, we are usually less concerned with A's actual appearance as a bit string than with the *information* contained in A. This information is called the *message*, denoted as M. Many data compression techniques treat M as a sequence of *symbols* from a symbol set $\mathcal{S}$ (called the *alphabet*):

$$M = \langle \sigma_1, \sigma_2, \ldots, \sigma_n \rangle, \quad \sigma_i \in \mathcal{S}. \tag{6.1}$$

Such methods are called *symbolwise* or *statistical*. Depending on the specific method and/or the application, a symbol may be an individual bit, a byte, a word (when compressing text), a posting (when compressing an inverted index), or something else. Finding an appropriate definition of what constitutes a symbol can sometimes be difficult, but once a definition has been found, well-known statistical techniques can be used to re-encode the symbols in M in order to decrease their overall storage requirements. The basic idea behind symbolwise data compression is twofold:

1. Not all symbols in M appear with the same frequency. By encoding frequent symbols using fewer bits than infrequent ones, the message M can be represented using a smaller number of bits in total.

2. The i-th symbol in a symbol sequence $\langle \sigma_1, \sigma_2, \ldots, \sigma_i, \ldots, \sigma_n \rangle$ sometimes depends on the previous symbols $\langle \ldots, \sigma_{i-2}, \sigma_{i-1} \rangle$. By taking into account this interdependence between the symbols, even more space can be saved.

Consider the task of compressing the text found in the Shakespeare collection (English text with XML markup), stored in ASCII format and occupying 8 bytes per character. Without any special effort we can decrease the storage requirements from 8 to 7 bits per character because the collection contains only 86 distinct characters. But even among the characters that do appear in the collection, we can see that there is a large gap between the frequencies with which they appear. For example, the six most frequent and the six least frequent characters in the Shakespeare collection are:

1. " ":	742,018	4. "⟨":	359,452		81. "(":	2	84. "8":	2
2. "E":	518,133	5. "⟩":	359,452	...	82. ")":	2	85. "$":	1
3. "e":	410,622	6. "t":	291,103		83. "5":	2	86. "7":	1

If the most frequent character (the whitespace character) is re-encoded using 1 bit less (6 instead of 7), and the two least frequent characters are re-encoded using 1 bit more (8 instead of 7), a total of 742,016 bits is saved.

Moreover, there is an interdependence between consecutive characters in the text collection. For example, the character "u", appearing 114,592 times in the collection, is located somewhere in the middle of the overall frequency range. However, every occurrence of the character "q" is followed by a "u". Thus, every "u" that is preceded by a "q" can be encoded using 0 bits because a "q" is never followed by anything else!

6.2.1 Modeling and Coding

Symbolwise compression methods usually work in two phases: modeling and coding. In the modeling phase a probability distribution $\mathcal{M}$ (also referred to as the *model*) is computed that maps symbols to their probability of occurrence. In the coding phase the symbols in the message M are re-encoded according to a code $\mathcal{C}$. A code is simply a mapping from each symbol σ to its codeword $\mathcal{C}(\sigma)$, usually a sequence of bits. $\mathcal{C}(\sigma)$ is chosen based on σ's probability according to the compression model $\mathcal{M}$. If $\mathcal{M}(\sigma)$ is small, then $\mathcal{C}(\sigma)$ will be long; if $\mathcal{M}(\sigma)$ is large, then $\mathcal{C}(\sigma)$ will be short (where the length of a codeword σ is measured by the number of bits it occupies).

Depending on how and when the modeling phase takes place, a symbolwise compression method falls into one of three possible classes:

- In a **static method** the model $\mathcal{M}$ is independent of the message M to be compressed. It is assumed that the symbols in the message follow a certain predefined probability distribution. If they don't, the compression results can be quite disappointing.

- **Semi-static methods** perform an initial pass over the message M and compute a model $\mathcal{M}$ that is then used for compression. Compared with static methods, semi-static methods have the advantage that they do not blindly assume a certain distribution. However, the model $\mathcal{M}$, computed by the encoder, now needs to be transmitted to the decoder as well (otherwise, the decoder will not know what to do with the encoded symbol sequence) and should therefore be as compact as possible. If the model itself is too large, a semi-static method may lose its advantage over a static one.

- The encoding procedure of an **adaptive compression method** starts with an initial static model and gradually adjusts this model based on characteristics of the symbols from M that have already been coded. When the compressor encodes σ_i, it uses a model $\mathcal{M}_i$ that depends only on the previously encoded symbols (and the initial static model):

$$\mathcal{M}_i = f(\sigma_1, \ldots, \sigma_i - 1).$$

When the decompressor needs to decode σ_i, it has already seen $\sigma_1, \ldots, \sigma_i - 1$ and thus can apply the same function f to reconstruct the model $\mathcal{M}_i$. Adaptive methods, therefore, have the advantage that no model ever needs to be transmitted from the encoder to the decoder. However, they require more complex decoding routines, due to the necessity to continuously update the compression model. Because of that, decoding is usually somewhat slower than with a semi-static method.

The probabilities in the compression model $\mathcal{M}$ do not need to be unconditional. For example, it is quite common to choose a model in which the probability of a symbol σ depends on the $1, 2, 3, \ldots$ previously coded symbols (we have seen this in the case of the Shakespeare collection, where the occurrence of a "q" is enough information to know that the next character is going to be a "u"). Such models are called *finite-context* models or *first-order, second-order, third-order,* ... models. A model $\mathcal{M}$ in which the probability of a symbol is independent of the previously seen symbols is called a *zero-order* model.

Compression models and codes are intimately connected. Every compression model $\mathcal{M}$ has a code (or a family of codes) associated with it: the code (or codes) that minimizes the average codeword length for a symbol sequence generated according to $\mathcal{M}$. Conversely, every code has a corresponding probability distribution: the distribution for which the code is optimal. For example, consider the zero-order compression model $\mathcal{M}_0$:

$$\mathcal{M}_0(\text{``a''}) = 0.5, \ \mathcal{M}_0(\text{``b''}) = 0.25, \ \mathcal{M}_0(\text{``c''}) = 0.125, \ \mathcal{M}_0(\text{``d''}) = 0.125. \qquad (6.2)$$

A code $\mathcal{C}_0$ that is optimal with respect to the model $\mathcal{M}_0$ has the following property:

$$|\mathcal{C}_0(\text{``a''})| = 1, \ |\mathcal{C}_0(\text{``b''})| = 2, \ |\mathcal{C}_0(\text{``c''})| = 3, \ |\mathcal{C}_0(\text{``d''})| = 3 \qquad (6.3)$$

(where $|\mathcal{C}_0(X)|$ denotes the bit length of $\mathcal{C}_0(X)$). The following code meets this requirement:[2]

$$\mathcal{C}_0(\text{``a''}) = \overline{0}, \ \mathcal{C}_0(\text{``b''}) = \overline{11}, \ \mathcal{C}_0(\text{``c''}) = \overline{100}, \ \mathcal{C}_0(\text{``d''}) = \overline{101}. \qquad (6.4)$$

It encodes the symbol sequence "aababacd" as

$$\mathcal{C}_0(\text{``aababacd''}) = \overline{00110110100101}. \qquad (6.5)$$

An important property of the code $\mathcal{C}_0$ is that it is *prefix-free*, that is, there is no codeword $\mathcal{C}_0(x)$ that is a prefix of another codeword $\mathcal{C}_0(y)$. A prefix-free code is also referred to as a *prefix code*. Codes that are not prefix-free normally cannot be used for compression (there are some exceptions to this rule; see Exercise 6.3). For example, consider the alternative code $\mathcal{C}_1$, with

$$\mathcal{C}_1(\text{``a''}) = \overline{1}, \ \mathcal{C}_1(\text{``b''}) = \overline{01}, \ \mathcal{C}_1(\text{``c''}) = \overline{101}, \ \mathcal{C}_1(\text{``d''}) = \overline{010}. \qquad (6.6)$$

Based on the lengths of the codewords, this code also appears to be optimal with respect to $\mathcal{M}_0$. However, the encoded representation of the sequence "aababacd" now is

$$\mathcal{C}_1(\text{``aababacd''}) = \overline{11011011101010}. \qquad (6.7)$$

---

[2] To avoid confusion between the numerals "0" and "1" and the corresponding bit values, we denote the bit values as $\overline{0}$ and $\overline{1}$, except where it is obvious that the latter meaning is intended.

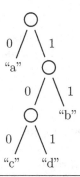

Figure 6.1 Binary tree associated with the prefix code C_0. Codewords: $C_0(\text{``a''}) = \overline{0}$, $C_0(\text{``b''}) = \overline{11}$, $C_0(\text{``c''}) = \overline{100}$, $C_0(\text{``d''}) = \overline{101}$.

When the decoder sees this sequence, it has no way of knowing whether the original symbol sequence was "aababacd" or "accaabd". Hence, the code is ambiguous and cannot be used for compression purposes.

A prefix code C can be thought of as a binary tree in which each leaf node corresponds to a symbol σ. The labels encountered along the path from the tree's root to the leaf associated with σ define the symbol's codeword, $C(\sigma)$. The depth of a leaf equals the length of the codeword for the respective symbol.

The code tree for the code C_0 is shown in Figure 6.1. The decoding routine of a compression algorithm can translate a bit sequence back into the original symbol sequence by following the edges of the tree, outputting a symbol — and jumping back to the root node — whenever it reaches a leaf, thus essentially using the tree as a binary decision diagram. The tree representation of a binary code also illustrates why the prefix property is so important: In the tree for a code that is not prefix-free, some codewords are assigned to internal nodes; when the decoder reaches such a node, it does not know whether it should output the corresponding symbol and jump back to the root, or keep following edges until it arrives at a leaf node.

Now consider a compression model $\mathcal{M}$ for a set of symbols $\{\sigma_1, \ldots, \sigma_n\}$ such that the probability of each symbol is an inverse power of 2:

$$\mathcal{M}(\sigma_i) = 2^{-\lambda_i} \; ; \; \lambda_i \in \mathbb{N} \text{ for } 1 \leq i \leq n. \tag{6.8}$$

Because $\mathcal{M}$ is a probability distribution, we have

$$\sum_{i=1}^{n} \mathcal{M}(\sigma_i) = \sum_{i=1}^{n} 2^{-\lambda_i} = 1. \tag{6.9}$$

Let us try to find an optimal code tree for this distribution. Every node in the tree must be either a leaf node (and have a codeword associated with it) or an internal node with exactly two children. Such a tree is called a *proper binary tree*. If the tree had an internal node with only one child, then it would be possible to improve the code by removing that internal node, thus reducing the depths of its descendants by 1. Hence, the code would not be optimal.

For the set $\mathcal{L} = \{L_1, \ldots, L_n\}$ of leaf nodes in a proper binary tree, the following equation holds:

$$\sum_{i=1}^{n} 2^{-d(L_i)} = 1, \tag{6.10}$$

where $d(L_i)$ is the depth of node L_i and is also the length of the codeword assigned to the symbol associated with L_i. Because of the similarity between Equation 6.9 and Equation 6.10, it seems natural to assign codewords to symbols in such a way that

$$|\mathcal{C}(\sigma_i)| = d(L_i) = \lambda_i = -\log_2(\mathcal{M}(\sigma_i)) \ \text{ for } 1 \leq i \leq n. \tag{6.11}$$

The resulting tree represents an optimal code for the given probability distribution $\mathcal{M}$. Why is that? Consider the average number of bits per symbol used by $\mathcal{C}$ if we encode a sequence of symbols generated according to $\mathcal{M}$:

$$\sum_{i=1}^{n} \Pr[\sigma_i] \cdot |\mathcal{C}(\sigma_i)| = -\sum_{i=1}^{n} \mathcal{M}(\sigma_i) \cdot \log_2(\mathcal{M}(\sigma_i)) \tag{6.12}$$

because $|\mathcal{C}(\sigma_i)| = -\log_2(\mathcal{M}(S_i))$. According to the following theorem, this is the best that can be achieved.

Source Coding Theorem (Shannon, 1948)
Given a symbol source S, emitting symbols from an alphabet $\mathcal{S}$ according to a probability distribution $\mathcal{P}_S$, a sequence of symbols cannot be compressed to consume less than

$$\mathcal{H}(S) = -\sum_{\sigma \in \mathcal{S}} \mathcal{P}_S(\sigma) \cdot \log_2(\mathcal{P}_S(\sigma))$$

bits per symbol on average. $\mathcal{H}(S)$ is called the *entropy* of the symbol source S.

By applying Shannon's theorem to the probability distribution defined by the model $\mathcal{M}$, we see that the chosen code is in fact optimal for the given model. Therefore, if our initial assumption that all probabilities are inverse powers of 2 (see Equation 6.8) holds, then we know how to quickly find an optimal encoding for symbol sequences generated according to $\mathcal{M}$. In practice, of course, this will rarely be the case. Probabilities can be arbitrary values from the interval $[0, 1]$. Finding the optimal prefix code $\mathcal{C}$ for a given probability distribution $\mathcal{M}$ is then a little more difficult than for the case where $\mathcal{M}(\sigma_i) = 2^{-\lambda_i}$.

6.2.2 Huffman Coding

One of the most popular bitwise coding techniques is due to Huffman (1952). For a given probability distribution $\mathcal{M}$ on a finite set of symbols $\{\sigma_1, \ldots, \sigma_n\}$, Huffman's method produces a prefix code $\mathcal{C}$ that minimizes

$$\sum_{i=1}^{n} \mathcal{M}(\sigma_i) \cdot |\mathcal{C}(\sigma_i)|. \tag{6.13}$$

A Huffman code is guaranteed to be optimal among all codes that use an integral number of bits per symbol. If we drop this requirement and allow codewords to consume a fractional number of bits, then there are other methods, such as arithmetic coding (Section 6.2.3), that may achieve better compression.

Suppose we have a compression model $\mathcal{M}$ with $\mathcal{M}(\sigma_i) = \Pr[\sigma_i]$ (for $1 \leq i \leq n$). Huffman's method constructs an optimal code tree for this model in a bottom-up fashion, starting with the two symbols of smallest probability. The algorithm can be thought of as operating on a set of trees, where each tree is assigned a probability mass. Initially there is one tree T_i for each symbol σ_i, with $\Pr[T_i] = \Pr[\sigma_i]$. In each step of the algorithm, the two trees T_j and T_k with minimal probability mass are merged into a new tree T_l. The new tree is assigned a probability mass $\Pr[T_l] = \Pr[T_j] + \Pr[T_k]$. This procedure is repeated until there is only a single tree T_{Huff} left, with $\Pr[T_{\text{Huff}}] = 1$.

Figure 6.2 shows the individual steps of the algorithm for the symbol set $\mathcal{S} = \{\sigma_1, \sigma_2, \sigma_3, \sigma_4, \sigma_5\}$ with associated probability distribution

$$\Pr[\sigma_1] = 0.18, \; \Pr[\sigma_2] = 0.11, \; \Pr[\sigma_3] = 0.31, \; \Pr[\sigma_4] = 0.34, \; \Pr[\sigma_5] = 0.06. \tag{6.14}$$

After the tree has been built, codewords may be assigned to symbols in a top-down fashion by a simple traversal of the code tree. For instance, σ_3 would receive the codeword $\overline{01}$; σ_2 would receive the codeword $\overline{110}$.

Optimality

Why are the codes produced by this method optimal? First, note that an optimal prefix code $\mathcal{C}_{opt}$ must satisfy the condition

$$\Pr[x] < \Pr[y] \Rightarrow |\mathcal{C}_{opt}(x)| \geq |\mathcal{C}_{opt}(y)| \quad \text{for every pair of symbols } (x, y) \tag{6.15}$$

(otherwise, we could simply swap the codewords for x and y, thus arriving at a better code). Furthermore, because an optimal prefix code is always represented by a proper binary tree, the codewords for the two least likely symbols must always be of the same length d (their nodes are siblings, located at the lowest level of the binary tree that represents $\mathcal{C}_{opt}$; if they are not siblings, we can rearrange the leaves at the lowest level in such a way that the two nodes become siblings).

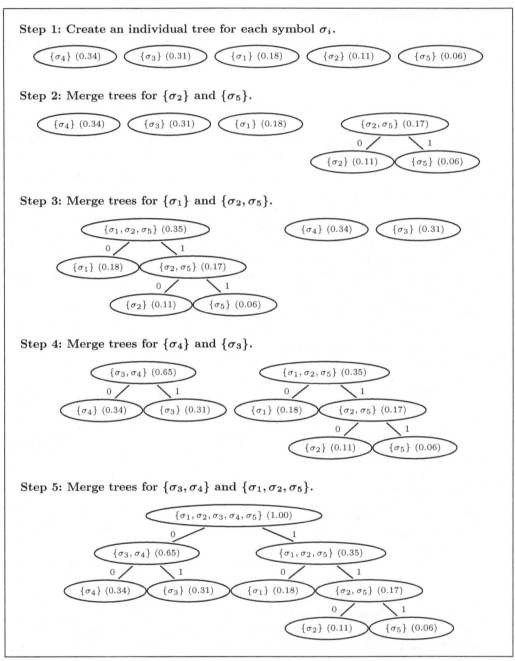

Figure 6.2 Building a Huffman code tree for the symbol set $\{\sigma_1, \sigma_2, \sigma_3, \sigma_4, \sigma_5\}$ with associated probability distribution $\Pr[\sigma_1] = 0.18$, $\Pr[\sigma_2] = 0.11$, $\Pr[\sigma_3] = 0.31$, $\Pr[\sigma_4] = 0.34$, $\Pr[\sigma_5] = 0.06$.

We can now prove the optimality of Huffman's algorithm by induction on the number of symbols n for which a prefix code is built. For $n = 1$, the method produces a code tree of height 0, which is clearly optimal. For the general case consider a symbol set $\mathcal{S} = \{\sigma_1, \ldots, \sigma_n\}$. Let σ_j and σ_k denote the two symbols with least probability ($j < k$ w.l.o.g.). Their codewords have the same length d. Thus, the expected codeword length for a sequence of symbols from $\mathcal{S}$ is

$$\mathrm{E}[\mathrm{Huff}(\mathcal{S})] = d \cdot (\Pr[\sigma_j] + \Pr[\sigma_k]) + \sum_{x \in (\mathcal{S} \setminus \{\sigma_j, \sigma_k\})} \Pr[x] \cdot |\mathcal{C}(x)| \qquad (6.16)$$

(bits per symbol). Consider the symbol set

$$\mathcal{S}' = \{\sigma_1, \ldots, \sigma_{j-1}, \sigma_{j+1}, \ldots, \sigma_{k-1}, \sigma_{k+1}, \ldots, \sigma_n, \sigma'\} \qquad (6.17)$$

that we obtain by removing σ_j and σ_k and replacing them by a new symbol σ' with

$$\Pr[\sigma'] = \Pr[\sigma_j] + \Pr[\sigma_k]. \qquad (6.18)$$

Because σ' is the parent of σ_j and σ_k in the Huffman tree for $\mathcal{S}$, its depth in the tree for $\mathcal{S}'$ is $d - 1$. The expected codeword length for a sequence of symbols from $\mathcal{S}'$ then is

$$\mathrm{E}[\mathrm{Huff}(\mathcal{S}')] = (d - 1) \cdot (\Pr[\sigma_j] + \Pr[\sigma_k]) + \sum_{x \in (\mathcal{S}' \setminus \{\sigma'\})} \Pr[x] \cdot |\mathcal{C}(x)|. \qquad (6.19)$$

That is, $\mathrm{E}[\mathrm{Huff}(\mathcal{S}')] = \mathrm{E}[\mathrm{Huff}(\mathcal{S})] - \Pr[\sigma_j] - \Pr[\sigma_k]$.

By induction we know that the Huffman tree for $\mathcal{S}'$ represents an optimal prefix code (because $\mathcal{S}'$ contains $n - 1$ elements). Now suppose the Huffman tree for $\mathcal{S}$ is not optimal. Then there must be an alternative, optimal tree with expected cost

$$\mathrm{E}[\mathrm{Huff}(\mathcal{S})] - \varepsilon \quad (\text{for some } \varepsilon > 0). \qquad (6.20)$$

By collapsing the nodes for σ_j and σ_k in this tree, as before, we obtain a code tree for the symbol set $\mathcal{S}'$, with expected cost

$$\mathrm{E}[\mathrm{Huff}(\mathcal{S})] - \varepsilon - \Pr[\sigma_j] - \Pr[\sigma_k] = \mathrm{E}[\mathrm{Huff}(\mathcal{S}')] - \varepsilon \qquad (6.21)$$

(this is always possible because the nodes for σ_j and σ_k are siblings in the optimal code tree, as explained before). However, this contradicts the assumption that the Huffman tree for $\mathcal{S}'$ is optimal. Hence, a prefix code for $\mathcal{S}$ with cost smaller than $\mathrm{E}[\mathrm{Huff}(\mathcal{S})]$ cannot exist. The Huffman tree for $\mathcal{S}$ must be optimal.

Complexity

The second phase of Huffman's algorithm, assigning codewords to symbols by traversing the tree built in the first phase, can trivially be done in time $\Theta(n)$, since there are $2n - 1$ nodes

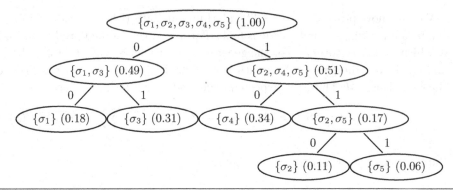

Figure 6.3   Canonical version of the Huffman code from Figure 6.2. All symbols at the same level in the tree are sorted in lexicographical order.

in the tree. The first phase, building the tree, is slightly more complicated. It requires us to continually keep track of the two trees $T_j, T_k \in \mathcal{T}$ with minimum probability mass. This can be realized by maintaining a priority queue (e.g., a min-heap; see page 141) that always holds the minimum-probability tree at the beginning of the queue. Such a data structure supports INSERT and EXTRACT-MIN operations in time $\Theta(\log(n))$. Because, in total, Huffman's algorithm needs to perform $2(n-1)$ EXTRACT-MIN operations and $n-1$ INSERT operations, the running time of the first phase of the algorithm is $\Theta(n \log(n))$. Hence, the total running time of the algorithm is also $\Theta(n \log(n))$.

Canonical Huffman codes

When using Huffman coding for data compression, a description of the actual code needs to be prepended to the compressed symbol sequence so that the decoder can transform the encoded bit sequence back into the original symbol sequence. This description is known as the *preamble*. It usually contains a list of all symbols along with their codewords. For the Huffman code from Figure 6.2, the preamble could look as follows:

$$\langle (\sigma_1, \overline{10}), (\sigma_2, \overline{110}), (\sigma_3, \overline{01}), (\sigma_4, \overline{00}), (\sigma_5, \overline{111}) \rangle. \tag{6.22}$$

Describing the Huffman code in such a way can be quite costly in terms of storage space, especially if the actual message that is being compressed is relatively short.

Fortunately, it is not necessary to include an exact description of the actual code; a description of certain aspects of it suffices. Consider again the Huffman tree constructed in Figure 6.2. An equivalent Huffman tree is shown in Figure 6.3. The length of the codeword for each symbol σ_i is the same in the original tree as in the new tree. Thus, there is no reason why the code from Figure 6.2 should be preferred over the one from Figure 6.3.

Reading the symbols σ_i from left to right in Figure 6.3 corresponds to ordering them by the length of their respective codewords (short codewords first); ties are broken according to the natural ordering of the symbols (e.g., σ_1 before σ_3). A code with this property is called a *canonical Huffman code*. For every possible Huffman code $\mathcal{C}$, there is always an equivalent canonical Huffman code $\mathcal{C}_{can}$.

When describing a canonical Huffman code, it is sufficient to list the bit lengths of the codewords for all symbols, not the actual codewords. For example, the tree in Figure 6.3 can be described by

$$\langle\, (\sigma_1, 2), (\sigma_2, 3), (\sigma_3, 2), (\sigma_4, 2), (\sigma_5, 3) \,\rangle. \tag{6.23}$$

Similarly, the canonicalized version of the Huffman code in Figure 6.1 is

$$\langle\, (\text{``a''}, \overline{0}), (\text{``b''}, \overline{10}), (\text{``c''}, \overline{110}), (\text{``d''}, \overline{111}) \,\rangle. \tag{6.24}$$

It can be described by

$$\langle\, (\text{``a''}, 1), (\text{``b''}, 2), (\text{``c''}, 3), (\text{``d''}, 3) \,\rangle. \tag{6.25}$$

If the symbol set $\mathcal{S}$ is known by the decoder a priori, then the canonical Huffman code can be described as $\langle 1, 2, 3, 3\rangle$, which is about twice as compact as the description of an arbitrary Huffman code.

Length-limited Huffman codes

Sometimes it can be useful to impose an upper bound on the length of the codewords in a given Huffman code. This is mainly for performance reasons, because the decoder can operate more efficiently if codewords are not too long (we will discuss this in more detail in Section 6.3.6).

We know that, for an alphabet of n symbols, we can always find a prefix code in which no codeword consumes more than $\lceil\log_2(n)\rceil$ bits. There are algorithms that, given an upper bound L on the bit lengths of the codewords ($L \geq \lceil\log_2(n)\rceil$), produce a prefix code $\mathcal{C}_L$ that is optimal among all prefix codes that do not contain any codewords longer than L. Most of those algorithms first construct an ordinary Huffman code $\mathcal{C}$ and then compute $\mathcal{C}_L$ by performing some transformations on the binary tree representing $\mathcal{C}$. Technically, such a code is not a Huffman code anymore because it lost its universal optimality (it is optimal only among all length-limited codes). However, in practice the extra redundancy in the resulting code is negligible.

One of the most popular methods for constructing length-limited prefix codes is Larmore and Hirschberg's (1990) PACKAGE-MERGE algorithm. It produces an optimal length-limited prefix code in time $O(nL)$, where n is the number of symbols in the alphabet. Since L is usually small (after all, this is the purpose of the whole procedure), PACKAGE-MERGE does not add an unreasonable complexity to the encoding part of a Huffman-based compression algorithm. Moreover, just as in the case of ordinary Huffman codes, we can always find an equivalent canonical code for any given length-limited code, thus allowing the same optimizations as before.

6.2.3 Arithmetic Coding

The main limitation of Huffman coding is its inability to properly deal with symbol distributions in which one symbol occurs with a probability that is close to 1. For example, consider the following probability distribution for a two-symbol alphabet $\mathcal{S} = \{\,\text{"a"}, \text{"b"}\,\}$:

$$\Pr[\text{"a"}] = 0.8, \ \Pr[\text{"b"}] = 0.2. \tag{6.26}$$

Shannon's theorem states that symbol sequences generated according to this distribution cannot be encoded using less than

$$-\Pr[\text{"a"}] \cdot \log_2(\Pr[\text{"a"}]) - \Pr[\text{"b"}] \cdot \log_2(\Pr[\text{"b"}]) \ \approx \ 0.2575 + 0.4644 \ = \ 0.7219 \tag{6.27}$$

bits per symbol on average. With Huffman coding, however, the best that can be achieved is 1 bit per symbol, because each codeword has to consume an integral number of bits. Thus, we increase the storage requirements by 39% compared to the lower bound inferred from Shannon's theorem.

In order to improve upon the performance of Huffman's method, we need to move away from the idea that each symbol is associated with a separate codeword. This could, for instance, be done by combining symbols into m-tuples and assigning a codeword to each unique m-tuple (this technique is commonly known as *blocking*). For the example above, choosing $m = 2$ would result in the probability distribution

$$\Pr[\text{"aa"}] = 0.64, \ \Pr[\text{"ab"}] = \Pr[\text{"ba"}] = 0.16, \ \Pr[\text{"bb"}] = 0.04. \tag{6.28}$$

A Huffman code for this distribution would require 1.56 bits per 2-tuple, or 0.78 bits per symbol on average (see Exercise 6.1). However, grouping symbols into blocks is somewhat cumbersome and inflates the size of the preamble (i.e., the description of the Huffman code) that also needs to be transmitted from the encoder to the decoder.

Arithmetic coding is a method that solves the problem in a more elegant way. Consider a sequence of k symbols from the set $\mathcal{S} = \{\sigma_1, \ldots, \sigma_n\}$:

$$\langle s_1, s_2, \ldots, s_k \rangle \ \in \ \mathcal{S}^k. \tag{6.29}$$

Each such sequence has a certain probability associated with it. For example, if we consider k to be fixed, then the above sequence will occur with probability

$$\Pr[\langle s_1, s_2, \ldots, s_k \rangle] = \prod_{i=1}^{k} \Pr[s_i]. \tag{6.30}$$

Obviously, the sum of the probabilities of all sequences of the same length k is 1. Hence, we may think of each such sequence x as an interval $[x_1, x_2)$, with $0 \le x_1 < x_2 \le 1$ and $x_2 - x_1 = \Pr[x]$.

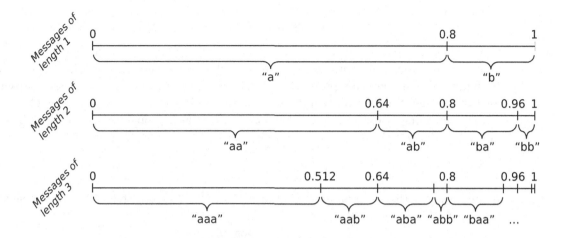

Figure 6.4 Arithmetic coding: transforming symbol sequences into subintervals of the interval $[0, 1)$. A message M (sequence of symbols) is encoded as a binary subinterval of the interval corresponding to M. Probability distribution assumed for the example: $\Pr[\text{``a''}] = 0.8$, $\Pr[\text{``b''}] = 0.2$.

These intervals are arranged as subintervals of the interval $[0, 1)$, in lexicographical order of the respective symbol sequences, and form a partitioning of $[0, 1)$.

Consider again the distribution from Equation 6.26. Under the interval representation, the symbol sequence "aa" would be associated with the interval $[0, 0.64)$; the sequence "ab" with the interval $[0.64, 0.80)$; the sequence "ba" with $[0.80, 0.96)$; and, finally, "bb" with $[0.96, 1.0)$. This method can be generalized to symbol sequences of arbitrary length, as shown in Figure 6.4.

With this mapping between messages and intervals, a given message can be encoded by encoding the associated interval $\mathcal{I}$ instead of the message itself. As it might be difficult to encode $\mathcal{I}$ directly, however, arithmetic coding instead encodes a smaller interval $\mathcal{I}'$ that is contained in the interval $\mathcal{I}$ (i.e., $\mathcal{I}' \subseteq \mathcal{I}$) and that is of the special form

$$\mathcal{I}' = [x, x + 2^{-q}), \quad \text{with } x = \sum_{i=1}^{q} a_i \cdot 2^{-i} \quad (a_i \in \{0, 1\}). \tag{6.31}$$

We call this a *binary interval*. A binary interval can be encoded in a straightforward fashion, as a bit sequence $\langle a_1, a_2, \ldots, a_q \rangle$. For instance, the bit sequence $\overline{0}$ represents the interval $[0, 0.5)$; the bit sequence $\overline{01}$ represents the interval $[0.25, 5)$; and the bit sequence $\overline{010}$ represents the interval $[0.25, 0.375)$.

The combination of these two steps — (1) transforming a message into an equivalent interval $\mathcal{I}$ and (2) encoding a binary interval within $\mathcal{I}$ as a simple bit sequence — is called *arithmetic coding*. When presented the message "aab", an arithmetic coder would find the corresponding interval $\mathcal{I} = [0.512, 0.64)$ (see Figure 6.4). Within this interval it would identify the binary subinterval

$$\mathcal{I}' \; = \; [0.5625, 0.625) \; = \; [x, x + 2^{-4}), \tag{6.32}$$

with $x = 1 \cdot 2^{-1} + 0 \cdot 2^{-2} + 0 \cdot 2^{-3} + 1 \cdot 2^{-4}$. Thus, the message "aab" would be encoded as $\overline{1001}$.

It turns out that $\overline{1001}$ with its 4 bits is actually 1 bit longer than the 3-bit sequence of a Huffman code for the same probability distribution. On the other hand, the code sequence for the message "aaa" would require 3 bits with a Huffman code but only a single bit ($\overline{0}$) if arithmetic coding is used. In general, for a message with probability p corresponding to an interval $\mathcal{I} = [y, y + p)$, we need to find a binary interval $[x, x + 2^{-q})$ with

$$y \le x < x + 2^{-q} \le y + p. \tag{6.33}$$

It can be shown that such an interval always exists for every q with $2^{-q} \le p/2$. The smallest q that meets this requirement is

$$q = \lceil -\log_2(p) \rceil + 1. \tag{6.34}$$

Thus, in order to encode a message

$$M = \langle s_1, s_2, \dots, s_k \rangle \tag{6.35}$$

with associated probability $p = \prod_{i=1}^{k} \Pr[s_i]$, we need no more than $\lceil -\log_2(p) \rceil + 1$ bits. For messages that contain only a few symbols, the "+1" term may sometimes make arithmetic coding less space-efficient than Huffman coding. For $k \to \infty$, however, the average number of bits per symbol approaches the theoretical optimum, as given by Shannon's source coding theorem (see Section 6.2.2). Thus, under the assumption that the compression model $\mathcal{M}$ perfectly describes the statistical properties of the symbol sequence to be compressed, arithmetic coding is asymptotically optimal.

Two convenient properties of arithmetic coding are:

- A different model may be used for each position in the input sequence (subject to the constraint that it may depend only on information already accessible to the decoder), thus making arithmetic coding the method of choice for adaptive compression methods.

- The length of the message need not be known to the decoder ahead of time. Instead, it is possible to add an artificial end-of-message symbol to the alphabet and treat it like any other symbol in the alphabet (in particular, to continually update its probability in the compression model so that it consumes less and less probability mass as the message gets longer).

For the purpose of this chapter, we may safely ignore these rather specific aspects of arithmetic coding. If you are interested in the details, you can find them in any standard textbook on data compression (see Section 6.6).

Implementation

It might seem from our description of arithmetic coding that the encoding and decoding procedures require floating-point operations and are susceptible to rounding errors and other problems that would arise from such an implementation. However, this is not the case. Witten et al. (1987), for instance, show how arithmetic coding can be implemented using integer arithmetic, at the cost of a tiny redundancy increase (less than 10^{-4} bits per symbol).

Huffman coding versus arithmetic coding

The advantage, in terms of bits per symbol, that arithmetic coding has over Huffman codes depends on the probability distribution $\mathcal{M}$. Obviously, if all symbol probabilities are inverse powers of 2, then Huffman is optimal and arithmetic coding has no advantage. For an arbitrary model $\mathcal{M}$, on the other hand, it is easy to see that the redundancy of a Huffman code (i.e., the number of bits wasted per encoded symbol), compared with the optimal arithmetic code, is at most 1 bit. This is true because we can trivially construct a prefix code with codeword lengths $|\mathcal{C}(\sigma_i)| = \lceil -\log_2(p_i) \rceil$. Such a code has a redundancy of less than 1 bit per symbol, and because it is a prefix code, it cannot be better than $\mathcal{M}$'s Huffman code.

In general, the redundancy of the Huffman code depends on the characteristics of the symbol set's probability distribution. Gallager (1978), for instance, showed that, for a given compression model $\mathcal{M}$, the redundancy of a Huffman code is always less than $\mathcal{M}(\sigma_{max}) + 0.0861$, where σ_{max} is the most likely symbol. Horibe (1977) showed that the redundancy is at most $1 - 2 \cdot \mathcal{M}(\sigma_{min})$, where σ_{min} is the least likely symbol.

Because the compression rates achieved by Huffman coding are usually quite close to the theoretical optimum and because decoding operations for Huffman codes can be realized more efficiently than for arithmetic codes, Huffman coding is often preferred over arithmetic coding. This is especially true in the context of index compression, where query processing performance, and not the size of the inverted index, is typically the main criterion when developing a search engine. Length-limited canonical Huffman codes can be decoded very efficiently, much faster than arithmetic codes.

6.2.4 Symbolwise Text Compression

What you have just learned about general-purpose symbolwise data compression can be applied directly to the problem of compressing text. For example, if you want to decrease the storage requirements of a given text collection, you can write a semi-static, Huffman-based compression algorithm that compresses the text in a two-pass process. In the first pass it collects frequency information about all characters appearing in the collection, resulting in a zero-order compression model. It then constructs a Huffman code $\mathcal{C}$ from this model, and in a second pass replaces each character σ in the text collection with its codeword $\mathcal{C}(\sigma)$.

If you implement this algorithm and run it on an arbitrary piece of English text, you will find that the compressed version of the text requires slightly more than 5 bits per character. This

Table 6.2 Text compression rates (in bits per character) for the three example collections. For Huffman and arithmetic coding, numbers do not include the size of the compression model (e.g., Huffman tree) that also needs to be transmitted to the decoder.

Collection	Huffman			Arithmetic Coding			Other	
	0-order	1-order	2-order	0-order	1-order	2-order	gzip	bzip2
Shakespeare	5.220	2.852	2.270	5.190	2.686	1.937	2.155	1.493
TREC45	5.138	3.725	2.933	5.105	3.676	2.813	2.448	1.812
GOV2	5.413	3.948	2.832	5.381	3.901	2.681	1.502	1.107

is in line with the conventional wisdom that the zero-order entropy of English text is around 5 bits per character. The exact numbers for our three example collections are shown in Table 6.2.

You can refine this algorithm and make it use a first-order compression model instead of a zero-order one. This requires you to construct and store/transmit up to 256 Huffman trees, one for each possible context (where the context is the previous byte in the uncompressed text), but it pays off in terms of compression effectiveness, by reducing the space requirements to less than 4 bits per character. This method may be extended to second-order, third-order, ... models, resulting in better and better compression rates. This shows that there is a strong interdependency between consecutive characters in English text (for example, every "q" in the Shakespeare collection is followed by a "u"). By exploiting this interdependency we can achieve compression rates that are much better than 5 bits per character.

Regarding the relative performance of Huffman coding and arithmetic coding, the table shows that the advantage of arithmetic coding over Huffman is very small. For the zero-order model the difference is less than 0.04 bits per character for all three collections. For the higher-order models this difference becomes larger (e.g., 0.12–0.33 bits for the second-order model) because the individual probability distributions in those models become more and more skewed, thus favoring arithmetic coding.

Note, however, that the numbers in Table 6.2 are slightly misleading because they do not include the space required by the compression model (the Huffman trees) itself. For example, with a third-order compression model we may need to transmit $256^3 = 16.8$ million Huffman trees before we can start encoding the actual text data. For a large collection like GOV2 this may be worthwhile. But for a smaller collection like Shakespeare this is clearly not the case. Practical compression algorithms, therefore, use adaptive methods when working with finite-context models and large alphabets. Examples are PPM (prediction by partial matching; Cleary and Witten, 1984) and DMC (dynamic Markov compression; Cormack and Horspool, 1987).

Starting with an initial model (maybe a zero-order one), adaptive methods gradually refine their compression model $\mathcal{M}$ based on the statistical information found in the data seen so far. In practice, such methods lead to very good results, close to those of semi-static methods, but with the advantage that no compression model needs to be transmitted to the decoder (making them effectively better than semi-static approaches).

Finally, the table compares the relatively simple compression techniques based on Huffman coding or arithmetic coding with more sophisticated techniques such as Ziv-Lempel (Ziv and Lempel, 1977; `gzip`[3]) and Burrows-Wheeler (Burrows and Wheeler, 1994; `bzip2`[4]). At heart, these methods also rely on Huffman or arithmetic coding, but they do some extra work before they enter the coding phase. It can be seen from the table that this extra work leads to greatly increased compression effectiveness. For example, `bzip2` (with parameter `--best`) can compress the text in the three collections to between 1.1 and 1.8 bits per character, an 80% improvement over the original encoding with 8 bits per character. This is consistent with the general assumption that the entropy of English text is between 1 and 1.5 bits per character — bounds that were established more than half a century ago (Shannon, 1951).

6.3 Compressing Postings Lists

Having discussed some principles of general-purpose data compression, we can apply these principles to the problem of compressing an inverted index, so as to reduce its potentially enormous storage requirements. As mentioned in Chapter 4 (Table 4.1 on page 106), the vast majority of all data in an inverted index are postings data. Thus, if we want to reduce the total size of the index, we should focus on ways to compress the postings lists before dealing with other index components, such as the dictionary.

The exact method that should be employed to compress the postings found in a given index index depends on the type of the index (docid, frequency, positional, or schema-independent), but there is some commonality among the different index types that allows us to use the same general approach for all of them.

Consider the following sequence of integers that could be the beginning of a term's postings list in a docid index:

$$L = \langle 3, 7, 11, 23, 29, 37, 41, \ldots \rangle.$$

Compressing L directly, using a standard compression method such as Huffman coding, is not feasible; the number of elements in the list can be very large and each element of the list occurs only a single time. However, because the elements in L form a monotonically increasing sequence, the list can be transformed into an equivalent sequence of differences between consecutive elements, called Δ-*values*:

$$\Delta(L) = \langle 3, 4, 4, 12, 6, 8, 4, \ldots \rangle.$$

---

[3] gzip (`www.gzip.org`) is actually not based on the Ziv-Lempel compression method but on the slightly different DEFLATE algorithm, since the use of the Ziv-Lempel method was restricted by patents during gzip's initial development.

[4] bzip2 (`www.bzip.org`) is a freely available, patent-free data compression software based on the Burrows-Wheeler transform.

The new list $\Delta(L)$ has two advantages over the original list L. First, the elements of $\Delta(L)$ are smaller than those of L, meaning that they can be encoded using fewer bits. Second, some elements occur multiple times in $\Delta(L)$, implying that further savings might be possible by assigning codewords to Δ-values based on their frequency in the list.

The above transformation obviously works for docid indices and schema-independent indices, but it can also be applied to lists from a document-centric positional index with postings of the form $(d, f_{t,d}, \langle p_1, \ldots, p_{f_{t,d}} \rangle)$. For example, the list

$$L = \langle\, (3, 2, \langle 157, 311 \rangle), (7, 1, \langle 212 \rangle), (11, 3, \langle 17, 38, 133 \rangle), \ldots \rangle$$

would be transformed into the equivalent Δ-list

$$\Delta(L) = \langle\, (3, 2, \langle 157, 154 \rangle), (4, 1, \langle 212 \rangle), (4, 3, \langle 17, 21, 95 \rangle), \ldots \rangle\,.$$

That is, each docid is represented as a difference from the previous docid; each within-document position is represented as a difference from the previous within-document position; and the frequency values remain unchanged.

Because the values in the three resulting lists typically follow very different probability distributions (e.g., frequency values are usually much smaller than within-document positions), it is not uncommon to apply three different compression methods, one to each of the three sublists of the Δ-transformed postings list.

Compression methods for postings in an inverted index can generally be divided into two categories: *parametric* and *nonparametric* codes. A nonparametric code does not take into account the actual Δ-gap distribution in a given list when encoding postings from that list. Instead, it assumes that all postings lists look more or less the same and share some common properties — for example, that smaller gaps are more common than longer ones. Conversely, prior to compression, parametric codes conduct an analysis of some statistical properties of the list to be compressed. A parameter value is selected based on the outcome of this analysis, and the codewords in the encoded postings sequence depend on the parameter.

Following the terminology from Section 6.2.1, we can say that nonparametric codes correspond to static compression methods, whereas parametric codes correspond to semi-static methods. Adaptive methods, due to the complexity associated with updating the compression model, are usually not used for index compression.

6.3.1   Nonparametric Gap Compression

The simplest nonparametric code for positive integers is the *unary code*. In this code a positive integer k is represented as a sequence of $k - 1$ $\overline{0}$ bits followed by a single $\overline{1}$ bit. The unary code is optimal if the Δ-values in a postings list follow a geometric distribution of the form

$$\Pr[\Delta = k] = \left(\frac{1}{2}\right)^k, \tag{6.36}$$

that is, if a gap of length $k + 1$ is half as likely as a gap of length k (see Section 6.2.1 for the relationship between codes and probability distributions). For postings in an inverted index this is normally not the case, except for the most frequent terms, such as "the" and "and", that tend to appear in almost every document. Nonetheless, unary encoding plays an important role in index compression because other techniques (such as the γ code described next) rely on it.

Elias's γ code

One of the earliest nontrivial nonparametric codes for positive integers is the γ code, first described by Elias (1975). The γ codeword for a positive integer k consists of two components. The second component, the *body*, contains k in binary representation. The first component, the *selector*, contains the length of the body, in unary representation. For example, the codewords of the integers 1, 5, 7, and 16 are:

k	selector(k)	body(k)
1	1	1
5	001	101
7	001	111
16	00001	10000

You may have noticed that the body of each codeword in the above table begins with a $\overline{1}$ bit. This is not a coincidence. If the selector for an integer k has a value selector$(k) = j$, then we know that $2^{j-1} \leq k < 2^j$. Therefore, the j-th least significant bit in the number's binary representation, which happens to be the first bit in the codeword's body, must be $\overline{1}$. Of course, this means that the first bit in the body is in fact redundant, and we can save one bit per posting by omitting it. The γ codewords for the four integers above then become $\overline{1}$ (1), $\overline{001\ 01}$ (5), $\overline{001\ 11}$ (7), and $\overline{00001\ 0000}$ (16).

The binary representation of a positive integer k consists of $\lfloor \log_2(k) \rfloor + 1$ bits. Thus, the length of k's codeword in the γ code is

$$|\gamma(k)| \;=\; 2 \cdot \lfloor \log_2(k) \rfloor + 1 \text{ bits.} \qquad (6.37)$$

Translated back into terms of gap distribution, this means that the γ code is optimal for integer sequences that follow the probability distribution

$$\Pr[\Delta = k] \;\approx\; 2^{-2 \cdot \log_2(k) - 1} \;=\; \frac{1}{2 \cdot k^2}. \qquad (6.38)$$

δ and ω codes

γ coding is appropriate when compressing lists with predominantly small gaps (say, smaller than 32) but can be quite wasteful if applied to lists with large gaps. For such lists the δ code, a variant of γ, may be the better choice. δ coding is very similar to γ coding. However, instead of storing the selector component of a given integer in unary representation, δ encodes the selector using γ. Thus, the δ codewords of the integers 1, 5, 7, and 16 are:

k	selector(k)	body(k)
1	1	
5	01 1	01
7	01 1	11
16	001 01	0000

(omitting the redundant $\overline{1}$ bit in all cases). The selector for the integer 16 is $\overline{001\ 01}$ because the number's binary representation requires 5 bits, and the γ codeword for 5 is $\overline{001\ 01}$.

Compared with γ coding, where the length of the codeword for an integer k is approximately $2 \cdot \log_2(k)$, the δ code for the same integer consumes only

$$|\delta(k)| = \lfloor \log_2(k) \rfloor + 2 \cdot \lfloor \log_2(\lfloor \log_2(k) \rfloor + 1) \rfloor + 1 \text{ bits}, \tag{6.39}$$

where the first component stems from the codeword's body, while the second component is the length of the γ code for the selector. δ coding is optimal if the gaps in a postings list are distributed according to the following probability distribution:

$$\Pr[\Delta = k] \approx 2^{-\log_2(k) - 2 \cdot \log_2(\log_2(k)) - 1} = \frac{1}{2k \cdot (\log_2(k))^2}. \tag{6.40}$$

For lists with very large gaps, δ coding can be up to twice as efficient as γ coding. However, such large gaps rarely appear in any realistic index. Instead, the savings compared to γ are typically somewhere between 15% and 35%. For example, the γ codewords for the integers 2^{10}, 2^{20}, and 2^{30} are 21, 41, and 61 bits long, respectively. The corresponding δ codewords consume 17, 29, and 39 bits (-19%, -29%, -36%).

The idea to use γ coding to encode the selector of a given codeword, as done in δ coding, can be applied recursively, leading to a technique known as ω coding. The ω code for a positive integer k is constructed as follows:

1. Output $\overline{0}$.
2. If $k = 1$, then stop.
3. Otherwise, encode k as a binary number (including the leading $\overline{1}$) and prepend this to the bits already written.
4. $k \leftarrow \lfloor \log_2(k) \rfloor$.
5. Go back to step 2.

For example, the ω code for $k = 16$ is

$$\overline{10\ 100\ 10000\ 0} \tag{6.41}$$

Table 6.3 Encoding positive integers using various nonparametric codes.

Integer	γ Code	δ Code	ω Code
1	1	1	0
2	01 0	01 0 0	10 0
3	01 1	01 0 1	11 0
4	001 00	01 1 00	10 100 0
5	001 01	01 1 01	10 101 0
6	001 10	01 1 10	10 110 0
7	001 11	01 1 11	10 111 0
8	0001 000	001 00 000	11 1000 0
16	00001 0000	001 01 0000	10 100 10000 0
32	000001 00000	001 10 00000	10 101 100000 0
64	0000001 000000	001 11 000000	10 110 1000000 0
127	0000001 111111	001 11 111111	10 110 1111111 0
128	00000001 0000000	0001 000 0000000	10 111 10000000 0

because $\overline{10000}$ is the binary representation of 16, $\overline{100}$ is the binary representation of 4 ($= \lfloor \log_2(16) \rfloor$), and $\overline{10}$ is the binary representation of 2 ($= \lfloor \log_2(\lfloor \log_2(16) \rfloor) \rfloor$). The length of the ω codeword for an integer k is approximately

$$|\omega(k)| = 2 + \log_2(k) + \log_2(\log_2(k)) + \log_2(\log_2(\log_2(k))) + \cdots \qquad (6.42)$$

Table 6.3 lists some integers along with their γ, δ, and ω codewords. The δ code is more space-efficient than γ for all integers $n \geq 32$. The ω code is more efficient than γ for all integers $n \geq 128$.

6.3.2 Parametric Gap Compression

Nonparametric codes have the disadvantage that they do not take into account the specific characteristics of the list to be compressed. If the gaps in the given list follow the distribution implicitly assumed by the code, then all is well. However, if the actual gap distribution is different from the implied one, then a nonparametric code can be quite wasteful and a parametric method should be used instead.

Parametric compression methods can be divided into two classes: *global* methods and *local* methods. A global method chooses a single parameter value that is used for all inverted lists in the index. A local method chooses a different value for each list in the index, or even for each small chunk of postings in a given list, where a chunk typically comprises a few hundred or a few thousand postings. You may recall from Section 4.3 that each postings list contains a list of synchronization points that help us carry out random access operations on the list. Synchronization points fit naturally with chunkwise list compression (in fact, this is the application from which they initially got their name); each synchronization point corresponds to the beginning of a new chunk. For heterogeneous postings lists, in which different parts of the list have different statistical characteristics, chunkwise compression can improve the overall effectiveness considerably.

Under most circumstances local methods lead to better results than global ones. However, for very short lists it is possible that the overhead associated with storing the parameter value outweighs the savings achieved by choosing a local method, especially if the parameter is something as complex as an entire Huffman tree. In that case it can be beneficial to choose a global method or to employ a *batched* method that uses the same parameter value for all lists that share a certain property (e.g., similar average gap size).

Because the chosen parameter can be thought of as a brief description of a compression model, the relationship between local and global compression methods is a special instance of a problem that we saw in Section 6.1 when discussing the relationship between modeling and coding in general-purpose data compression: When to stop modeling and when to start coding? Choosing a local method leads to a more precise model that accurately describes the gap distribution in the given list. Choosing a global method (or a batched method), on the other hand, makes the model less accurate but also reduces its (amortized) size because the same model is shared by a large number of lists.

Golomb/Rice codes

Suppose we want to compress a list whose Δ-values follow a *geometric distribution*, that is, the probability of seeing a gap of size k is

$$\Pr[\Delta = k] \;=\; (1-p)^{k-1} \cdot p, \tag{6.43}$$

for some constant p between 0 and 1. In the context of inverted indices this is not an unrealistic assumption. Consider a text collection comprising N documents and a term T that appears in N_T of them. The probability of finding an occurrence of T by randomly picking one of the documents in the collection is N_T/N. Therefore, under the assumption that all documents are independent of each other, the probability of seeing a gap of size k between two subsequent occurrences is

$$\Pr[\Delta = k] \;=\; \left(1 - \frac{N_T}{N}\right)^{k-1} \cdot \frac{N_T}{N}. \tag{6.44}$$

That is, after encountering an occurrence of T, we will first see $k-1$ documents in which the term does not appear (each with probability $1 - \frac{N_T}{N}$), followed by a document in which it does appear (probability $\frac{N_T}{N}$). This gives us a geometric distribution with $p = \frac{N_T}{N}$.

Figure 6.5 shows the (geometric) gap distribution for a hypothetical term with $p = 0.01$. It also shows the distribution that emerges if we group Δ-values into buckets according to their bit

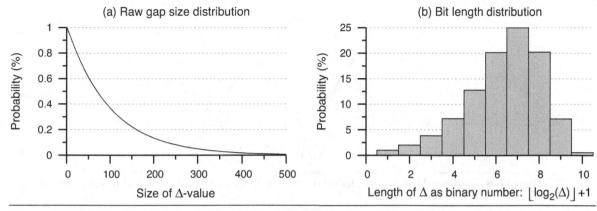

Figure 6.5   Distribution of Δ-gaps in a hypothetical postings list with $N_T/N = 0.01$ (i.e., term T appears in 1% of all documents). (a) distribution of raw gap sizes; (b) distribution of bit lengths (i.e., number of bits needed to encode each gap as a binary number).

length $\text{len}(k) = \lfloor \log_2(k) \rfloor + 1$, and compute the probability of each bucket. In the figure, 65% of all Δ-values fall into the range $6 \leq \text{len}(k) \leq 8$. This motivates the following encoding:

1. Choose an integer M, the *modulus*.

2. Split each Δ-value k into two components, the quotient $q(k)$ and the remainder $r(k)$:

$$q(k) = \lfloor (k-1)/M \rfloor, \quad r(k) = (k-1) \bmod M.$$

3. Encode k by writing $q(k)+1$ in unary representation, followed by $r(k)$ as a $\lfloor \log_2(M) \rfloor$-bit or $\lceil \log_2(M) \rceil$-bit binary number.

For the distribution shown in Figure 6.5 we might choose $M = 2^7$. Few Δ-values are larger than 2^8, so the vast majority of the postings require less than 3 bits for the quotient $q(k)$. Conversely, few Δ-values are smaller than 2^5, which implies that only a small portion of the 7 bits allocated for each remainder $r(k)$ is wasted.

The general version of the encoding described above, with an arbitrary modulus M, is known as *Golomb coding*, after its inventor, Solomon Golomb (1966). The version in which M is a power of 2 is called *Rice coding*, also after its inventor, Robert Rice (1971).[5]

---

[5] Strictly speaking, Rice did not invent Rice codes — they are a subset of Golomb codes, and Golomb's research was published half a decade before Rice's. However, Rice's work made Golomb codes attractive for practical applications, which is why Rice is often co-credited for this family of codes.

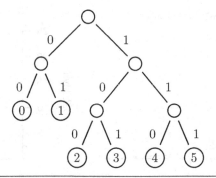

Figure 6.6   Codewords of the remainders $0 \le r(k) < 6$, for the Golomb code with parameter $M = 6$.

Let us look at a concrete example. Suppose we have chosen the modulus $M = 2^7$, and we want to encode a gap of size $k = 345$. Then the resulting Rice codeword is

$$\text{Rice}_{M=2^7}(345) \;=\; \overline{001\ 1011000},$$

since $q(345) = \lfloor (345 - 1)/2^7 \rfloor = 2$, and $r(345) = (345 - 1) \bmod 2^7 = 88$.

Decoding a given codeword is straightforward. For each posting in the original list, we look for the first $\overline{1}$ bit in the code sequence. This gives us the value of $q(k)$. We then remove the first $q(k) + 1$ bits from the bit sequence, extract the next λ bits (for $\lambda = \lceil \log_2(M) \rceil$), thus obtaining $r(k)$, and compute k as

$$k \;=\; q(k) \cdot 2^\lambda + r(k) + 1. \tag{6.45}$$

For efficiency, the multiplication with 2^λ is usually implemented as a bit shift.

Unfortunately, the simple encoding/decoding procedure described above works only for Rice codes and cannot be applied to general Golomb codes where M is not a power of 2. Since we allocate $\lceil \log_2(M) \rceil$ bits to each remainder $r(k)$, but there are only $M < 2^{\lceil \log_2(M) \rceil}$ possible remainders, some parts of the code space would be left unused, leading to a suboptimal code. In fact, if we used $\lceil \log_2(M) \rceil$ bits for each remainder regardless of the value of M, the resulting Golomb code would always be inferior to the corresponding Rice code with parameter $M' = 2^{\lceil \log_2(M) \rceil}$.

The solution is to reclaim the unused part of the code space by encoding some of the remainders using $\lfloor \log_2(M) \rfloor$ bits and others using $\lceil \log_2(M) \rceil$ bits. Which remainders should receive the shorter codewords, and which the longer ones? Since Golomb coding is based on the assumption that the Δ-values follow a geometric distribution (Equation 6.44), we expect that smaller gaps have a higher probability of occurrence than larger ones. The codewords for the remainders $r(k)$ are therefore assigned in the following way:

- Values from the interval $[0, 2^{\lceil \log_2(M) \rceil} - M - 1]$ receive $\lfloor \log_2(M) \rfloor$-bit codewords.
- Values from the interval $[2^{\lceil \log_2(M) \rceil} - M, M - 1]$ receive $\lceil \log_2(M) \rceil$-bit codewords.

Table 6.4 Encoding positive integers (e.g., Δ-gaps) using parameterized Golomb/Rice codes. The first part of each codeword corresponds to the quotient $q(k)$. The second part corresponds to the remainder $r(k)$.

Integer	Golomb Codes			Rice Codes	
	$M = 3$	$M = 6$	$M = 7$	$M = 4$	$M = 8$
1	1 0	1 00	1 00	1 00	1 000
2	1 10	1 01	1 010	1 01	1 001
3	1 11	1 100	1 011	1 10	1 010
4	01 0	1 101	1 100	1 11	1 011
5	01 10	1 110	1 101	01 00	1 100
6	01 11	1 111	1 110	01 01	1 101
7	001 0	01 00	1 111	01 10	1 110
8	001 10	01 01	01 00	01 11	1 111
9	001 11	01 100	01 010	001 00	01 000
31	00000000001 0	000001 00	00001 011	00000001 10	0001 110

Figure 6.6 visualizes this mechanism for the Golomb code with modulus $M = 6$. The remainders $0 \leq r(k) < 2$ are assigned codewords of length $\lfloor \log_2(6) \rfloor = 2$; the rest are assigned codewords of length $\lceil \log_2(6) \rceil = 3$. Looking at this approach from a slightly different perspective, we may say that the codewords for the M different remainders are assigned according to a canonical Huffman code (see Figure 6.3 on page 184). Table 6.4 shows Golomb/Rice codewords for various positive integers k and various parameter values M.

Compared with the relatively simple Rice codes, Golomb coding achieves slightly better compression rates but is a bit more complicated. While the $r(k)$-codewords encountered by a Rice decoder are all of the same length and can be decoded using simple bit shifts, a Golomb decoder needs to distinguish between $r(k)$-codewords of different lengths (leading to branch mispredictions) and needs to perform relatively costly integer multiplication operations, since M is not a power of 2. As a consequence, Rice decoders are typically between 20% and 40% faster than Golomb decoders.

Finding the optimal Golomb/Rice parameter value

One question that we have not yet addressed is how we should choose the modulus M so as to minimize the average codeword length. Recall from Section 6.2.1 that a code $\mathcal{C}$ is optimal with respect to a given probability distribution $\mathcal{M}$ if the relationship

$$|\mathcal{C}(\sigma_1)| = |\mathcal{C}(\sigma_2)| + 1, \tag{6.46}$$

for two symbols σ_1 and σ_2, implies

$$\mathcal{M}(\sigma_1) = \frac{1}{2} \cdot \mathcal{M}(\sigma_2). \tag{6.47}$$

We know that the Golomb codeword for the integer $k + M$ is 1 bit longer than the codeword for the integer k (because $q(k + M) = q(k) + 1$). Therefore, the optimal parameter value M^* should satisfy the following equation:

$$\Pr[\Delta = k + M^*] = \frac{1}{2} \cdot \Pr[\Delta = k] \quad \Leftrightarrow \quad (1 - N_T/N)^{k+M^*-1} = \frac{1}{2} \cdot (1 - N_T/N)^{k-1}$$

$$\Leftrightarrow \quad M^* = \frac{-\log(2)}{\log(1 - N_T/N)}. \tag{6.48}$$

Unfortunately, M^* is usually not an integer. For Rice coding, we will have to choose between $M = 2^{\lfloor \log_2(M^*) \rfloor}$ and $M = 2^{\lceil \log_2(M^*) \rceil}$. For Golomb coding, we may choose between $M = \lfloor M^* \rfloor$ and $M = \lceil M^* \rceil$. In general, it is not clear, which one is the better choice. Sometimes one produces the better code, sometimes the other does. Gallager and van Voorhis (1975) proved that

$$M_{opt} = \left\lceil \frac{\log(2 - N_T/N)}{-\log(1 - N_T/N)} \right\rceil \tag{6.49}$$

always leads to the optimal code.

As an example, consider a term T that appears in 50% of all documents. We have $N_T/N = 0.5$, and thus

$$M_{opt} = \lceil -\log(1.5)/\log(0.5) \rceil \approx \lceil 0.585/1.0 \rceil = 1. \tag{6.50}$$

The optimal Golomb/Rice code in this case, perhaps as expected, turns out to be the unary code.

Huffman codes: LLRUN

If the gaps in a given list do not follow a geometric distribution — for example, because the document independence assumption does not hold or because the list is not a simple docid list — then Golomb codes may not lead to very good results.

We already know a compression method that can be used for lists with arbitrary distribution and that yields optimal compression rates: Huffman coding (see Section 6.2.2). Unfortunately, it is difficult to apply Huffman's method directly to a given sequence of Δ-values. The difficulty stems from the fact that the set of distinct gaps in a typical postings list has about the same size as the list itself. For example, the term "aquarium" appears in 149 documents in the TREC45 collection. Its docid list consists of 147 different Δ-values. Encoding this list with Huffman is unlikely to decrease the size of the list very much, because the 147 different Δ-values still need to be stored in the preamble (i.e., the Huffman tree) for the decoder to know which Δ-value a particular codeword in the Huffman-encoded gap sequence corresponds to.

Instead of applying Huffman coding to the gap values directly, it is possible to group gaps of similar size into buckets and have all gaps in the same bucket share a codeword in the Huffman code. For example, under the assumption that all gaps from the interval $[2^j, 2^{j+1} - 1]$ have approximately the same probability, we could create buckets $B_0, B_1, \ldots$ with $B_j = [2^j, 2^{j+1} - 1]$. All Δ-values from the same bucket B_j then share the same Huffman codeword w_j. Their encoded representation is w_j, followed by the j-bit representation of the respective gap value as a binary number (omitting the leading $\overline{1}$ bit that is implicit from w_j).

The resulting compression method is called *LLRUN* and is due to Fraenkel and Klein (1985). It is quite similar to Elias's γ method, except that the selector value (the integer j that defines the bucket in which a given Δ-value lies) is not encoded in unary, but according to a minimum-redundancy Huffman code. LLRUN's advantage over a naïve application of Huffman's method is that the bucketing scheme dramatically decreases the size of the symbol set for which the Huffman tree is created. Δ-values, even in a schema-independent index, are rarely greater than 2^{40}. Thus, the corresponding Huffman tree will have at most 40 leaves. With a canonical, length-limited Huffman code and a limit of $L = 15$ bits per codeword (see Section 6.2.2 for details on length-limited Huffman codes), the code can then be described in $4 \times 40 = 160$ bits. Moreover, the assumption that gaps from the same bucket B_j appear with approximately the same probability is usually reflected by the data found in the index, except for very small values of j. Hence, compression effectiveness is not compromised much by grouping gaps of similar size into buckets and having them share the same Huffman codeword.

6.3.3 Context-Aware Compression Methods

The methods discussed so far all treat the gaps in a postings list independently of each other. In Section 6.1, we saw that the effectiveness of a compression method can sometimes be improved by taking into account the context of the symbol that is to be encoded. The same applies here. Sometimes consecutive occurrences of the same term form clusters (many occurrences of the same term within a small amount of text). The corresponding postings are very close to each other, and the Δ-values are small. A compression method that is able to properly react to this phenomenon can be expected to achieve better compression rates than a method that is not.

Huffman codes: Finite-context LLRUN

It is straightforward to adjust the LLRUN method from above so that it takes into account the previous Δ-value when encoding the current one. Instead of using a zero-order model, as done in the original version of LLRUN, we can use a first-order model and have the codeword w_j for the current gap's selector value depend on the value of the previous gap's selector, using perhaps 40 different Huffman trees (assuming that no Δ-value is bigger than 2^{40}), one for each possible predecessor value.

The drawback of this method is that it would require the encoder to transmit the description of 40 different Huffman trees instead of just a single one, thus increasing the storage requirements

encodeLLRUN-2 $(\langle L[1], \ldots, L[n]\rangle,\ \vartheta,\ output) \equiv$

1   let $\Delta(L)$ denote the list $\langle L[1], L[2] - L[1], \ldots, L[n] - L[n-1]\rangle$

2    $\Delta_{max} \leftarrow \max_i\{\Delta(L)[i]\}$

3   initialize the array $bucketFrequencies[0..1][0..\lfloor \log_2(\Delta_{max})\rfloor]$ to zero

4    $c \leftarrow 0$ // the context to be used for finite-context modeling

5   **for** i $\leftarrow$ 1 **to** n **do**   // collect context-specific statistics

6        $b \leftarrow \lfloor \log_2(\Delta(L)[i])\rfloor$ // the bucket of the current Δ-value

7        $bucketFrequencies[c][b] \leftarrow bucketFrequencies[c][b] + 1$

8   **if** $b < \vartheta$ **then** $c \leftarrow 0$ **else** $c \leftarrow 1$

9   **for** i $\leftarrow$ 0 **to** 1 **do**   // build two Huffman trees, one for each context

10        $T_i \leftarrow$ **buildHuffmanTree**$(bucketFrequencies[i])$

11    $c \leftarrow 0$ // reset the context

12   **for** i $\leftarrow$ 1 **to** n **do**   // compress the postings

13        $b \leftarrow \lfloor \log_2(\Delta(L)[i])\rfloor$

14   write b's Huffman codeword, according to the tree T_c, to *output*

15   write $\Delta(L)[i]$ to *output*, as a b-bit binary number (omitting the leading $\bar{1}$)

16   **if** $b < \vartheta$ **then** $c \leftarrow 0$ **else** $c \leftarrow 1$

17   **return**

Figure 6.7   Encoding algorithm for LLRUN-2, the finite-context variant of LLRUN with two different Huffman trees. The threshold parameter ϑ defines a binary partitioning of the possible contexts.

of the compressed list. In practice, however, using 40 different models has almost no advantage over using just a few, say two or three. We refer to this revised variant of the LLRUN method as LLRUN-k, where k is the number of different models (i.e., Huffman trees) employed by the encoder/decoder.

Figure 6.7 shows the encoding algorithm for LLRUN-2. The threshold parameter ϑ, provided explicitly in the figure, can be chosen automatically by the algorithm, by trying all possible values $0 < \vartheta < \log_2(\max_i\{\Delta(L)[i]\})$ and selecting the one that minimizes the compressed size of the list. Note that this does not require the encoder to actually compress the whole list $\Theta(\log(\max_i\{\Delta(L)[i]\}))$ times but can be done by analyzing the frequencies with which Δ-values from each bucket B_j follow Δ-values from each other bucket $B_{j'}$. The time complexity of this analysis is $\Theta(\log(\max_i\{\Delta(L)[i]\})^2)$.

Interpolative coding

Another context-aware compression technique is the *interpolative coding* method invented by Moffat and Stuiver (2000). Like all other list compression methods, interpolative coding uses the fact that all postings in a given inverted list are stored in increasing order, but it does so in a slightly different way.

Consider the beginning of the postings list L for the term "example" in a docid index for the TREC45 collection:

$$L = \langle 2, 9, 12, 14, 19, 21, 31, 32, 33\rangle.$$

encodeInterpolative $(\langle L[1], \ldots, L[n]\rangle,\ output) \equiv$
1   **encodeGamma** (n)
2   **encodeGamma** $(L[1],\ output)$
3   **encodeGamma** $(L[n] - L[1],\ output)$
4   **encodeInterpolativeRecursively** $(\langle L[1], \ldots, L[n]\rangle,\ output)$

encodeInterpolativeRecursively $(\langle L[1], \ldots, L[n]\rangle,\ output) \equiv$
5   **if** $n < 3$ **then**
6   **return**
7   $middle \leftarrow \lceil n/2 \rceil$
8   $firstPossible \leftarrow L[1] + (middle - 1)$
9   $lastPossible \leftarrow L[n] + (middle - n)$
10   $k \leftarrow \lceil \log_2(lastPossible - firstPossible + 1) \rceil$
11   write $(L[middle] - firstPossible)$ to $output$, as a k-bit binary number
12   **encodeInterpolativeRecursively** $(\langle L[1], \ldots, L[middle]\rangle,\ output)$
13   **encodeInterpolativeRecursively** $(\langle L[middle], \ldots, L[n]\rangle,\ output)$

Figure 6.8 Compressing a postings list $\langle L[1], \ldots, L[n]\rangle$ using interpolative coding. The resulting bit sequence is written to $output$.

The interpolative method compresses this list by encoding its first element $L[1] = 2$ and its last element $L[9] = 33$ using some other method, such as γ coding. It then proceeds to encode $L[5] = 19$. However, when encoding $L[5]$, it exploits the fact that, at this point, $L[1]$ and $L[9]$ are already known to the decoder. Because all postings are stored in strictly increasing order, it is guaranteed that

$$2 = L[1] < L[2] < \ldots < L[5] < \ldots < L[8] < L[9] = 33.$$

Therefore, based on the information that the list contains nine elements, and based on the values of $L[1]$ and $L[9]$, we know that $L[5]$ has to lie in the interval $[6, 29]$. Because this interval contains no more than $2^5 = 32$ elements, $L[5]$ can be encoded using 5 bits. The method then proceeds recursively, encoding $L[3]$ using 4 bits (because, based on the values of $L[1]$ and $L[5]$, it has to be in the interval $[4, 17]$), encoding $L[2]$ using 4 bits (because it has to be in $[3, 11]$), and so on.

Figure 6.8 gives a more formal definition of the encoding procedure of the interpolative method. The bit sequence that results from compressing the list L according to interpolative coding is shown in Table 6.5. It is worth pointing out that $L[8] = 32$ can be encoded using 0 bits because $L[7] = 31$ and $L[9] = 33$ leave only one possible value for $L[8]$.

As in the case of Golomb coding, the interval defined by $firstPossible$ and $lastPossible$ in Figure 6.8 is rarely a power of 2. Thus, by encoding each possible value in the interval using k bits, some code space is wasted. As before, this deficiency can be cured by encoding $2^k - (lastPossible - firstPossible + 1)$ of all possible values using $k - 1$ bits and the remaining

Table 6.5 The result of applying interpolative coding to the first nine elements of the docid list for the term "example" (data taken from TREC45).

Postings (orig. order)	Postings (visitation order)	Compressed Bit Sequence	
($n = 9$)	($n = 9$)	0001001	(γ codeword for $n = 9$)
2	2	010	(γ codeword for 2)
9	33	000011111	(γ codeword for $31 = 33 - 2$)
12	19	01101	($13 = 19 - 6$ as 5-bit binary number)
14	12	1000	($8 = 12 - 4$ as 4-bit binary number)
19	9	0110	($6 = 9 - 3$ as 4-bit binary number)
21	14	001	($1 = 14 - 13$ as 3-bit binary number)
31	31	1010	($10 = 31 - 21$ as 4-bit binary number)
32	21	0001	($1 = 21 - 20$ as 4-bit binary number)
33	32		($0 = 32 - 32$ as 0-bit binary number)

values using k bits. For simplicity, this mechanism is not shown in Figure 6.8. The details can be found in the material on Golomb coding in Section 6.3.2.

Unlike in the case of Golomb codes, however, we do not know for sure which of the ($lastPossible - firstPossible + 1$) possible values are more likely than the others. Hence, it is not clear which values should receive the k-bit codewords and which values should receive ($k-1$)-bit codewords. Moffat and Stuiver (2000) recommend giving the shorter codewords to the values in the middle of the interval [$firstPossible, lastPossible$], except when the interval contains only a single posting (corresponding to $n = 3$ in the function **encodeInterpolativeRecursively**), in which case they recommend assigning the shorter codewords to values on both ends of the interval so as to exploit potential clustering effects. In experiments this strategy has been shown to save around 0.5 bits per posting on average.

6.3.4   Index Compression for High Query Performance

The rationale behind storing postings lists in compressed form is twofold. First, it decreases the storage requirements of the search engine's index. Second, as a side effect, it decreases the disk I/O overhead at query time and thus potentially improves query performance. The compression methods discussed in the previous sections have in common that they are targeting the first aspect, mainly ignoring the complexity of the decoding operations that need to be carried out at query time.

When choosing between two different compression methods A and B, aiming for optimal query performance, a good rule of thumb is to compare the decoding overhead of each method with the read performance of the storage medium that contains the index (e.g., the computer's hard drive). For example, a hard drive might deliver postings at a rate of 50 million bytes

($= 400$ million bits) per second. If method A, compared to B, saves 1 bit per posting on average, and A's relative decoding overhead per posting, compared to that of method B, is less than 2.5 ns (i.e., the time needed to read a single bit from the hard disk), then A should be preferred over B. Conversely, if the relative overhead is more than 2.5 ns, then B should be preferred.

2.5 ns is not a lot of time, even for modern microprocessors. Depending on the clock frequency of the CPU, it is equivalent to 2–10 CPU cycles. Therefore, even if method A can save several bits per posting compared to method B, its decoding routine still needs to be extremely efficient in order to have an advantageous effect on query performance.

The above rule of thumb does not take into account the possibility that compressed postings can be decoded in parallel with ongoing disk I/O operations or that postings lists may be cached in memory, but it serves as a good starting point when comparing two compression methods in terms of their impact on the search engine's query performance. As we shall see in Section 6.3.6, the methods discussed so far do not necessarily lead to optimal query performance, as their decoding routines can be quite complex and time-consuming. Two methods that were specifically designed with high decoding throughput in mind are presented next.

Byte-aligned codes

Byte-aligned gap compression is one of the simplest compression methods available. Its popularity is in part due to its simplicity but mostly due to its high decoding performance. Consider the beginning of the postings list for the term "aligned", extracted from a docid index for the GOV2 collection:

$$L \;=\; \langle\, 1624, 1650, 1876, 1972, \ldots \,\rangle,$$
$$\Delta(L) \;=\; \langle\, 1624, 26, 226, 96, 384, \ldots \,\rangle. \tag{6.51}$$

In order to avoid expensive bit-fiddling operations, we want to encode each Δ-value using an integral number of bytes. The easiest way to do this is to split the binary representation of each Δ-value into 7-bit chunks and prepend to each such chunk a *continuation flag* — a single bit that indicates whether the current chunk is the last one or whether there are more to follow. The resulting method is called *vByte* (for *variable-byte* coding). It is used in many applications, not only search engines. The vByte-encoded representation of the above docid list is

   1 1011000 0 0001100 0 0011010 1 1100010 0 0000001 0 1100000 1 0000000 0 0000011 ...

(spaces inserted for better readability).

For example, the body of the first chunk ($\overline{1011000}$) is the representation of the integer 88 as a 7-bit binary number. The body of the second chunk ($\overline{0001100}$) is the integer 12 as a 7-bit binary number. The $\overline{0}$ at the beginning of the second chunk indicates that this is the end of the current codeword. The decoder, when it sees this, combines the two numbers into $88 + 12 \times 2^7 = 1624$, yielding the value of the first list element.

```
encodeVByte (⟨L[1], ..., L[n]⟩, outputBuffer) ≡
1      previous ← 0
2      for i ← 1 to n do
3          delta ← L[i] − previous
4          while delta ≥ 128 do
5              outputBuffer.writeByte(128 + (delta & 127))
6              delta ← delta ≫ 7
7          outputBuffer.writeByte(delta)
8          previous ← L[i]
9      return

decodeVByte (inputBuffer, ⟨L[1], ..., L[n]⟩) ≡
10     current ← 0
11     for i ← 1 to n do
12         shift ← 0
13         b ← inputBuffer.readByte()
14         while b ≥ 128 do
15             current ← current + ((b & 127) ≪ shift)
16             shift ← shift + 7
17             b ← inputBuffer.readByte()
18         current ← current + (b ≪ shift)
19         L[i] ← current
20     return
```

Figure 6.9   Encoding and decoding routine for vByte. Efficient multiplication and division operations are realized through bit-shift operations ("$\ll$": left-shift; "$\gg$": right-shift; "&": bit-wise AND).

The encoding and decoding routines of the vByte method are shown in Figure 6.9. When you look at the pseudo-code in the figure, you will notice that vByte is obviously not optimized for maximum compression. For example, it reserves the codeword $\overline{00000000}$ for a gap of size 0. Clearly, such a gap cannot exist, since the postings form a strictly monotonic sequence. Other compression methods (γ, LLRUN, ...) account for this fact by not assigning any codeword to a gap of size 0. With vByte, however, the situation is different, and it makes sense to leave the codeword unused. vByte's decoding routine is highly optimized and consumes only a few CPU cycles per posting. Increasing its complexity by adding more operations (even operations as simple as $+1/-1$) would jeopardize the speed advantage that vByte has over the other compression methods.

Word-aligned codes

Just as working with whole bytes is more efficient than operating on individual bits, accessing entire machine words is normally more efficient than fetching all its bytes separately when decoding a compressed postings list. Hence, we can expect to obtain faster decoding routines if we enforce that each posting in a given postings list is always stored using an integral number

Table 6.6 Word-aligned postings compression with Simple-9. After reserving 4 out of 32 bits for the selector value, there are 9 possible ways of dividing the remaining 28 bits into equal-size chunks.

Selector	0	1	2	3	4	5	6	7	9
Number of Δ's	1	2	3	4	5	7	9	14	28
Bits per Δ	28	14	9	7	5	4	3	2	1
Unused bits per word	0	0	1	0	3	0	1	0	0

of 16-bit, 32-bit, or 64-bit machine words. Unfortunately, doing so would defeat the purpose of index compression. If we encode each Δ-value as a 32-bit integer, we might as well choose an even simpler encoding and store each posting directly as an uncompressed 32-bit integer.

The following idea leads us out of this dilemma: Instead of storing each Δ-value in a separate 32-bit machine word, maybe we can store several consecutive values, say n of them, in a single word. For example, whenever the encoder sees three consecutive gaps $k_1 \ldots k_3$, such that $k_i \leq 2^9$ for $1 \leq i \leq 3$, then it may store all three of them in a single machine word, assigning 9 bits within the word to each k_i, thus consuming 27 bits in total and leaving 5 unused bits that can be used for other purposes.

Anh and Moffat (2005) discuss several word-aligned encoding methods that are based on ideas similar to those described above. Their simplest method is called *Simple-9*. It works by inspecting the next few Δ-values in a postings sequence, trying to squeeze as many of them into a 32-bit machine word as possible. Of course, the decoder, when it sees a 32-bit word, supposedly containing a sequence of Δ-values, does not know how many bits in this machine word were reserved for each Δ. Therefore, Simple-9 reserves the first 4 bits in each word for a selector: a 4-bit integer that informs the decoder about the split used within the current word. For the remaining 28 bits in the same word, there are nine different ways of dividing them into chunks of equal size (shown in Table 6.6). This is how the method received its name.

For the same Δ-sequence as before (docid list for the term "aligned" in the GOV2 collection), the corresponding code sequence now is

$$0001\ 00011001011000\ 00000000011001\ 0010\ 011100001\ 001011111\ 101111111\ \text{U}, \qquad (6.52)$$

where $\overline{0010}$ ($=2$) is the selector used for the second machine word and $\overline{011100001}$ is the integer 225 ($= 1876 - 1650 - 1$) as a 9-bit binary number. "U" represents an unused bit.

For the example sequence, Simple-9 does not allow a more compact representation than vByte. This is because the term "aligned" is relatively rare and its postings list has rather large gaps. For frequent terms with small gaps, however, Simple-9 has a clear advantage over vByte because it is able to encode a postings list using as little as 1 bit per gap (plus some overhead for the selectors). Its decoding performance, on the other hand, is almost as high as that of vByte, because the shift-mask operations necessary to extract the n $\lfloor \frac{28}{n} \rfloor$-bit integers from a given machine word can be executed very efficiently.

Efficiently decoding unaligned codes

Even though the unaligned methods from the previous sections, unlike vByte and Simple-9, were not designed with the specific target of achieving high decoding performance, most of them still allow rather efficient decoding. However, in order to attain this goal, it is imperative that expensive bit-by-bit decoding operations be avoided whenever possible.

We illustrate this through an example. Consider the γ code from Section 6.3.1. After transforming the postings list

$$L = \langle\, 7, 11, 24, 26, 33, 47 \,\rangle \tag{6.53}$$

into an equivalent sequence of Δ-values

$$\Delta(L) = \langle\, 7, 4, 13, 2, 7, 14 \,\rangle, \tag{6.54}$$

the bit sequence produced by the γ coder is

$$\gamma(L) = \overline{001\ 11\ 001\ 00\ 0001\ 101\ 01\ 0\ 001\ 11\ 0001\ 110}. \tag{6.55}$$

In order to determine the bit length of each codeword in this sequence, the decoder repeatedly needs to find the first occurrence of a $\overline{1}$ bit, indicating the end of the codeword's selector component. It could do this by processing $\gamma(L)$ in a bit-by-bit fashion, inspecting every bit individually and testing whether it is $\overline{0}$ or $\overline{1}$. However, such a decoding procedure would not be very efficient. Not only would each code bit require at least one CPU operation, but the conditional jumps associated with the decision *"Is the current bit a $\overline{0}$ bit?"* are likely to result in a large number of branch mispredictions, which will flush the CPU's execution pipeline and slow down the decoding process dramatically (see the appendix for a brief introduction to the concepts of high-performance computing; or see Patterson and Hennessy (2009) for more detailed coverage of the topic).

Suppose we know that no element of $\Delta(L)$ is larger than $2^4 - 1$ (as is the case in the above example). Then this implies that none of the selectors in the code sequence are longer than 4 bits. Hence, we may construct a table T containing $2^4 = 16$ elements that tells us the position of the first $\overline{1}$ bit in the sequence, given the next 4 bits:

$$
\begin{aligned}
T[\,\overline{0000}\,] &= 5, & T[\,\overline{0001}\,] &= 4, & T[\,\overline{0010}\,] &= 3, & T[\,\overline{0011}\,] &= 3, \\
T[\,\overline{0100}\,] &= 2, & T[\,\overline{0101}\,] &= 2, & T[\,\overline{0110}\,] &= 2, & T[\,\overline{0111}\,] &= 2, \\
T[\,\overline{1000}\,] &= 1, & T[\,\overline{1001}\,] &= 1, & T[\,\overline{1010}\,] &= 1, & T[\,\overline{1011}\,] &= 1, \\
T[\,\overline{1100}\,] &= 1, & T[\,\overline{1101}\,] &= 1, & T[\,\overline{1110}\,] &= 1, & T[\,\overline{1111}\,] &= 1
\end{aligned} \tag{6.56}
$$

(where "5" indicates "not among the first 4 bits").

We can use this table to implement an efficient decoding routine for the γ code, as shown in Figure 6.10. Instead of inspecting each bit individually, the algorithm shown in the figure loads them into a 64-bit *bit buffer*, 8 bits at a time, and uses the information stored in the lookup table T, processing up to 4 bits in a single operation. The general approach followed

decodeGamma $(inputBuffer, T[0..2^k - 1], \langle L[1], \ldots, L[n] \rangle) \equiv$
1    $current \leftarrow 0$
2    $bitBuffer \leftarrow 0$
3    $bitsInBuffer \leftarrow 0$
4   **for** $i \leftarrow 1$ **to** n **do**
5   **while** $bitsInBuffer + 8 \leq 64$ **do**
6            $bitBuffer \leftarrow bitBuffer + (inputBuffer.readByte() \ll bitsInBuffer)$
7            $bitsInBuffer \leftarrow bitsInBuffer + 8$
8        $codeLength \leftarrow T[bitBuffer \,\&\, (2^k - 1)]$
9        $bitBuffer \leftarrow bitBuffer \gg (codeLength - 1)$
10       $mask \leftarrow (1 \ll codeLength) - 1$
11       $current \leftarrow current + (bitBuffer \,\&\, mask)$
12       $bitBuffer \leftarrow bitBuffer \gg codeLength$
13       $bitsInBuffer \leftarrow bitsInBuffer - 2 \times codeLength - 1$
14       $L[i] \leftarrow current$
15   **return**

Figure 6.10 Table-driven γ decoder. Bit-by-bit decoding operations are avoided through the use of a bit buffer and a lookup table T of size 2^k that is used for determining the length of the current codeword. Efficient multiplication and division operations are realized through bit-shift operations ("$\ll$": left shift; "$\gg$": right shift; "$\&$": bitwise AND).

by the algorithm is referred to as *table-driven decoding*. It can be applied to γ, δ, Golomb, and Rice codes as well as the Huffman-based LLRUN method. In the case of LLRUN, however, the contents of the table T depend on the specific code chosen by the encoding procedure. Thus, the decoder needs to process the Huffman tree in order to initialize the lookup table before it can start its decoding operations.

Table-driven decoding is the reason why length-limited Huffman codes (see Section 6.2.2) are so important for high-performance query processing: If we know that no codeword is longer than k bits, then the decoding routine requires only a single table lookup (in a table of size 2^k) to figure out the next codeword in the given bit sequence. This is substantially faster than explicitly following paths in the Huffman tree in a bit-by-bit fashion.

6.3.5 Compression Effectiveness

Let us look at the compression rates achieved by the various methods discussed so far. Table 6.7 gives an overview of these rates, measured in bits per posting, on different types of lists (docids, TF values, within-document positions, and schema-independent) for the three example collections used in this book. For the Shakespeare collection, which does not contain any real *documents*, we decided to treat each `<SPEECH>`···`</SPEECH>` XML element as a document for the purpose of the compression experiments.

The methods referred to in the table are: γ and δ coding (Section 6.3.1); Golomb/Rice and the Huffman-based LLRUN (Section 6.3.2); interpolative coding (Section 6.3.3); and the two

Table 6.7   Compression effectiveness of various compression methods for postings lists, evaluated on three different text collections. All numbers represent compression effectiveness, measured in bits per posting. Bold numbers indicate the best result in each row.

	List Type	γ	δ	Golomb	Rice	LLRUN	Interp.	vByte	S-9
Shakesp.	Document IDs	8.02	7.44	6.48	6.50	6.18	**6.18**	9.96	7.58
	Term frequencies	1.95	2.08	2.14	2.14	1.98	**1.70**	8.40	3.09
	Within-doc pos.	8.71	8.68	6.53	6.53	**6.29**	6.77	8.75	7.52
	Schema-indep.	15.13	13.16	10.54	10.54	**10.17**	10.49	12.51	12.75
TREC45	Document IDs	7.23	6.78	5.97	6.04	5.65	**5.52**	9.45	7.09
	Term frequencies	2.07	2.27	1.99	2.00	1.95	**1.71**	8.14	2.77
	Within-doc pos.	12.69	11.51	8.84	8.89	**8.60**	8.83	11.42	10.89
	Schema-indep.	17.03	14.19	12.24	12.38	**11.31**	11.54	13.71	15.37
GOV2	Document IDs	8.02	7.47	5.98	6.07	5.98	**5.97**	9.54	7.46
	Term frequencies	2.74	2.99	2.78	2.81	2.56	**2.53**	8.12	3.67
	Within-doc pos.	11.47	10.45	9.00	9.13	**8.02**	8.34	10.66	10.10
	Schema-indep.	13.69	11.81	11.73	11.96	**9.45**	9.98	11.91	n/a

performance-oriented methods vByte and Simple-9 (Section 6.3.4). In all cases, postings lists were split into small chunks of about 16,000 postings each before applying compression. For the parametric methods (Golomb, Rice, and LLRUN), compression parameters were chosen separately for each such chunk (*local parameterization*), thus allowing these methods to take into account small distributional variations between different parts of the same postings list — an ability that will come in handy in Section 6.3.7.

As you can see from the table, interpolative coding consistently leads to the best results for docids and TF values on all three text collections, closely followed by LLRUN and Golomb/Rice. Its main advantage over the other methods is its ability to encode postings using less than 1 bit on average if the gaps are predominantly of size 1. This is the case for the docid lists of the most frequent terms (such as "the", which appears in 80% of the documents in GOV2 and 99% of the documents in TREC45), but also for lists of TF values: When picking a random document D and a random term T that appears in D, chances are that T appears only a single time.

For the other list types (*within-document positions* and *schema-independent*), the methods' roles are reversed, with LLRUN taking the lead, followed by interpolative coding and Golomb/Rice. The reason why Golomb/Rice codes perform so poorly on these two list types is that the basic assumption on which Golomb coding is based (i.e., that Δ-gaps follow a geometric distribution) does not hold for them.

Under the document independence assumption, we know that the gaps in a given docid list roughly follow a distribution of the form

$$\Pr[\Delta = k] \;=\; (1-p)^{k-1} \cdot p \tag{6.57}$$

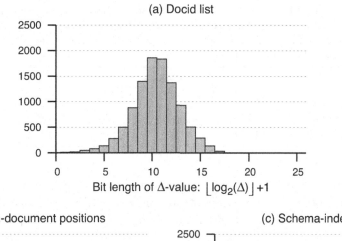

(a) Docid list

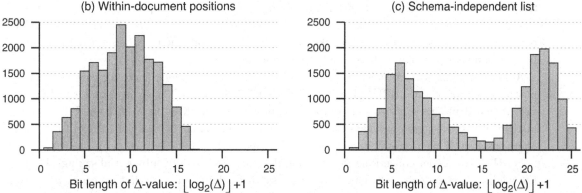

(b) Within-document positions

(c) Schema-independent list

Figure 6.11 Gap distributions in different postings lists for the term "huffman" in the GOV2 collection. Vertical axis: Number of Δ-values of the given size. Only the gaps in the docid list follow a geometric distribution.

(see Equation 6.43). For within-document positions and schema-independent lists, this assumption does not hold. If a random term T appears toward the beginning of a document, then it is more likely to appear again in the same document than if we first see it toward the end of the document. Therefore, the elements of these lists are not independent of each other, and the gaps do not follow a geometric distribution.

The occurrence pattern of the term "huffman" in the GOV2 collection is a good example of this phenomenon. Figure 6.11 shows the gap distribution exhibited by the term's docid list, its document-centric positional list, and its schema-independent list. After a logarithmic transformation, putting all Δ-gaps of the same length $\mathrm{len}(\Delta) = \lfloor \log_2(\Delta) \rfloor + 1$ into the same bucket, plot (a) shows the curve that is characteristic for a geometric distribution, with a clear peak around $\mathrm{len}(\Delta) \approx 10$. Plot (b), for the list of within-document positions, also has a peak, but it is not as clearly distinguished as in (a). Finally, the schema-independent list in plot (c) does not follow a geometric distribution at all. Instead, we can see two peaks: one corresponding to two

Table 6.8 Zero-order LLRUN versus first-order LLRUN. Noteworthy improvements are achieved only for the two positional indices (within-document positions and schema-independent) built from GOV2. All other indices either are too small to absorb the storage overhead due to the more complex model, or their list elements do not exhibit much interdependency.

List type	TREC45			GOV2		
	LLRUN	LLRUN-2	LLRUN-4	LLRUN	LLRUN-2	LLRUN-4
Within-doc positions	8.60	8.57	8.57	8.02	7.88	7.82
Schema-independent	11.31	11.28	11.28	9.45	9.29	9.23

or more occurrences of "huffman" in the same document ($\text{len}(\Delta) \approx 6$), the other corresponding to consecutive occurrences in different documents ($\text{len}(\Delta) \approx 22$). Obviously, if a method is tailored toward geometric distributions, it will not do very well on a postings list that follows a clearly nongeometric distribution, such as the one shown in Figure 6.11(c). This is why LLRUN's performance on positional postings lists (document-centric or schema-independent) is so much better than that of Golomb/Rice — up to 2.5 bits per posting.

A method that was specifically designed with the interdependencies between consecutive postings in mind is the LLRUN-k method (Section 6.3.3). LLRUN-k is very similar to LLRUN, except that it utilizes a first-order compression model, materialized in k different Huffman trees instead of just a single one. Table 6.8 shows the compression rates attained by LLRUN-k in comparison with the original, zero-order LLRUN method.

For the two smaller collections, the method does not achieve any substantial savings, because the slightly better coding efficiency is compensated for by the larger that precedes the actual codeword sequence. For the two positional indices built from GOV2, however, we do in fact see a small reduction of the storage requirements of the inverted lists. In the case of within-document positions, LLRUN-2/LLRUN-4 leads to a reduction of 0.14/0.20 bits per posting (-1.7%/-2.5%); for the schema-independent index, it saves 0.16/0.22 bits per posting (-1.7%/-2.3%). Whether these savings are worthwhile depends on the application. For search engines they are usually not worthwhile, because the 2% size reduction is likely to be outweighed by the more complex decoding procedure.

6.3.6 Decoding Performance

As pointed out in Section 6.3.4, when motivating byte- and word-aligned compression methods, reducing the space consumed by the inverted index is only one reason for applying compression techniques. Another, and probably more important, reason is that a smaller index may also lead to better query performance, at least if the postings lists are stored on disk. As a rule of thumb, an index compression method may be expected to improve query performance if the decoding overhead (measured in nanoseconds per posting) is lower than the disk I/O time saved by storing postings in compressed form.

Table 6.9 Cumulative disk I/O and list decompression overhead for a docid index built from GOV2. The cumulative overhead is calculated based on a sequential disk throughput of 87 MB/second ($\hat{=}$ 1.37 nanoseconds per bit).

Compression Method	Compression (bits per docid)	Decoding (ns per docid)	Cumulative Overhead (decoding + disk I/O)
γ	4.94	7.67	14.44 ns
Golomb	4.10	10.82	16.44 ns
Rice	4.13	6.45	12.11 ns
LLRUN	4.09	7.04	12.64 ns
Interpolative	4.19	27.21	32.95 ns
vByte	8.77	1.35	13.36 ns
Simple-9	5.32	2.76	10.05 ns
Uncompressed (32-bit)	32.00	0.00	43.84 ns
Uncompressed (64-bit)	64.00	0.00	87.68 ns

Table 6.9 shows compression effectiveness (for docid lists), decoding efficiency, and cumulative overhead for various compression methods. All values were obtained by running the 10,000 queries from the efficiency task of the TREC Terabyte Track 2006 and decompressing the postings lists for all query terms (ignoring stopwords). Note that the compression effectiveness numbers shown in the table ("bits per docid") are quite different from those in the previous tables, as they do not refer to the entire index but only to terms that appear in the queries. This difference is expected: Terms that are frequent in the collection tend to be frequent in the query stream, too. Since frequent terms, compared to infrequent ones, have postings lists with smaller Δ-gaps, the compression rates shown in Table 6.9 are better than those in Table 6.7.

To compute the cumulative decoding + disk I/O overhead of the search engine, we assume that the hard drive can deliver postings data at a rate of 87 MB per second ($\hat{=}$ 1.37 ns per bit; see the appendix). vByte, for instance, requires 8.77 bits (on average) per compressed docid, which translates into a disk I/O overhead of $8.77 \times 1.37 = 12.01$ ns per posting. In combination with the decoding overhead of 1.35 ns per posting, this results in a cumulative overhead of 13.36 ns per posting.

Most methods play in the same ballpark, exhibiting a cumulative overhead of 10–15 ns per posting. Interpolative coding with its rather complex recursive decoding routine is an outlier, requiring a total of more than 30 ns per posting. In comparison with the other techniques, the byte-aligned vByte proves to be surprisingly mediocre. It is outperformed by three other methods, including the relatively complex LLRUN algorithm. Simple-9, combining competitive compression rates with very low decoding overhead, performed best in the experiment.

Of course, the numbers shown in the table are only representative of docid indices. For a positional or a schema-independent index, for example, the results will look more favorable for vByte. Moreover, the validity of the simplistic performance model applied here (calculating the total overhead as a sum of disk I/O and decoding operations) may be questioned in the presence of caching and background I/O. Nonetheless, the general message is clear: Compared to an uncompressed index (with either 32-bit or 64-bit postings), every compression method leads to improved query performance.

6.3.7 Document Reordering

So far, when discussing various ways of compressing the information stored in the index's postings lists, we have always assumed that the actual information stored in the postings lists is fixed and may not be altered. Of course, this is an oversimplification. In reality, a document is not represented by a numerical identifier but by a file name, a URL, or some other textual description of its origin. In order to translate the search results back into their original context, which needs to be done before they can be presented to the user, each numerical document identifier must be transformed into a textual description of the document's location or context. This transformation is usually realized with the help of a data structure referred to as the *document map* (see Section 4.1).

This implies that the docids themselves are arbitrary and do not possess any inherent semantic value. We may therefore reassign numerical identifiers as we wish, as long as we make sure that all changes are properly reflected by the document map. We could, for instance, try to reassign document IDs in such a way that index compressibility is maximized. This process is usually referred to as *document reordering*. To see its potential, consider the hypothetical docid list

$$L = \langle 4, 21, 33, 40, 66, 90 \rangle \tag{6.58}$$

with γ-code representation

$$\overline{001\ 00\ 00001\ 0001\ 0001\ 100\ 001\ 11\ 00001\ 1010\ 000001\ 00010} \tag{6.59}$$

(46 bits). If we were able to reassign document identifiers in such a way that the list became

$$L = \langle 4, 6, 7, 45, 51, 120 \rangle \tag{6.60}$$

instead, then this would lead to the γ-code representation

$$\overline{001\ 00\ 01\ 0\ 1\ 000001\ 00110\ 001\ 10\ 0000001\ 000101} \tag{6.61}$$

(36 bits), reducing the list's storage requirements by 22%.

It is clear from the example that we don't care so much about the average magnitude of the gaps in a postings list (which is 17.2 in Equation 6.58 but 23.2 in Equation 6.60) but are instead interested in minimizing the average codeword length, which is a value closely related to the logarithm of the length of each gap. In the above case, the value of the sum

$$\sum_{i=1}^{5} \lceil \log_2(L[i+1] - L[i]) \rceil \qquad (6.62)$$

is reduced from 22 to 18 (−18%).

In reality, of course, things are not that easy. By reassigning document identifiers so as to reduce the storage requirements of one postings list, we may increase those of another list. Finding the optimal assignment of docids, the one that minimizes the total compressed size of the index, is believed to be computationally intractable (i.e., NP-complete). Fortunately, there are a number of document reordering heuristics that, despite computing a suboptimal docid assignment, typically lead to considerably improved compression effectiveness. Many of those heuristics are based on clustering algorithms that require substantial implementation effort and significant computational resources. Here, we focus on two particular approaches that are extremely easy to implement, require minimal computational resources, and still lead to pretty good results:

- The first method reorders the documents in a text collection based on the number of distinct terms contained in each document. The idea is that two documents that each contain a large number of distinct terms are more likely to share terms than are a document with many distinct terms and a document with few distinct terms. Therefore, by assigning docids so that documents with many terms are close together, we may expect a greater clustering effect than by assigning docids at random.

- The second method assumes that the documents have been crawled from the Web (or maybe a corporate Intranet). It reassigns docids in lexicographical order of URL. The idea here is that two documents from the same Web server (or maybe even from the same directory on that server) are more likely to share common terms than two random documents from unrelated locations on the Internet.

The impact that these two document reordering heuristics have on the effectiveness of various index compression methods is shown in Table 6.10. The row labeled "Original" refers to the official ordering of the documents in the GOV2 collections and represents the order in which the documents were crawled from the Web. The other rows represent random ordering, documents sorted by number of unique terms, and documents sorted by URL.

For the docid lists, we can see that document reordering improves the effectiveness of every compression method shown in the table. The magnitude of the effect varies between the methods, because some (e.g., interpolative coding) can more easily adapt to the new distribution than others (e.g., Golomb coding). However, the general trend is the same for all of them. In some cases the effect is quite dramatic. With interpolative coding, for example, the average space consumption can be reduced by more than 50%, from 5.97 to 2.84 bits per posting. This is mainly because of the method's ability to encode sequences of very small gaps using less than 1

Table 6.10   The effect of document reordering on compression effectiveness (in bits per list entry). All data are taken from GOV2.

	Doc. Ordering	γ	Golomb	Rice	LLRUN	Interp.	vByte	S-9
Doc. IDs	Original	8.02	6.04	6.07	5.98	5.97	9.54	7.46
	Random	8.80	6.26	6.28	6.35	6.45	9.86	8.08
	Term count	5.81	5.08	5.15	4.60	4.26	9.18	5.63
	URL	3.88	5.10	5.25	3.10	2.84	8.76	4.18
TF values	Original	2.74	2.78	2.81	2.56	2.53	8.12	3.67
	Random	2.74	2.86	2.90	2.60	2.61	8.12	3.87
	Term count	2.74	2.59	2.61	2.38	2.31	8.12	3.20
	URL	2.74	2.63	2.65	2.14	2.16	8.12	2.83

bit on average. The other methods need at least 1 bit for every posting (although, by means of blocking (see Section 6.2.3), LLRUN could easily be modified so that it requires less than 1 bit per posting for such sequences).

What might be a little surprising is that document reordering improves not only the compressibility of docids, but also that of TF values. The reason for this unexpected phenomenon is that, in the experiment, each inverted list was split into small chunks containing about 16,000 postings each, and compression was applied to each chunk individually instead of to the list as a whole. The initial motivation for splitting the inverted lists into smaller chunks was to allow efficient random access into each postings list, which would not be possible if the entire list had been compressed as one atomic unit (see Section 4.3). However, the welcome side effect of this procedure is that the compression method can choose different parameter values (i.e., apply different compression models) for different parts of the same list (except for nonparametric methods, such as γ coding and vByte). Because the basic idea behind document reordering is to assign numerically close docids to documents that are similar in content, different parts of the same inverted lists will have different properties, which leads to better overall compression rates. When using LLRUN, for example, the average number of bits per TF value decreases from 2.56 to 2.14 (-16%).

6.4   Compressing the Dictionary

In Chapter 4, we showed that the dictionary for a text collection can be rather large. Not quite as large as the postings lists, but potentially still too large to fit into main memory. In addition, even if the dictionary is small enough to fit into RAM, decreasing its size may be a good idea because it allows the search engine to make better use of its memory resources — for example, by caching frequently accessed postings lists or by caching search results for popular queries.

The goal here is to reduce the size of the dictionary as much as possible, while still providing low-latency access to dictionary entries and postings lists. Because dictionary lookups represent one of the main bottlenecks in index construction, and because the merge-based indexing algorithm presented in Section 4.5.3 is largely independent of the amount of main memory available to the indexing process, there is usually no reason to apply dictionary compression at indexing time. We therefore restrict ourselves to the discussion of compression techniques that can be used for the query-time dictionary, after the index has been built.

Recall from Figure 4.1 (page 107) that a sort-based in-memory dictionary is essentially an array of integers (the *primary* array) in which each integer is a pointer to a variable-size term descriptor (i.e., dictionary entry), an element of the *secondary* array. Each term descriptor contains the term itself and a file pointer indicating the location of the term's inverted list in the postings file. Dictionary entries in this data structure are accessed through binary search on the primary array, following the pointers into the secondary array to perform string comparisons. The pointers in the primary array usually consume 32 bits each (assuming that the secondary array is smaller than 2^{32} bytes).

A sort-based dictionary contains three sources of memory consumption: the pointers in the primary array, the file pointers in the term descriptors, and the terms themselves. We can take care of all three components at the same time by combining multiple consecutive term descriptors into groups and compressing the contents of each group, taking into account the fact that all data in the secondary array are sorted.

Dictionary groups

The fundamental insight is that it is not necessary (and in fact not beneficial) to have a pointer in the primary array for every term in the dictionary. Suppose we combine g consecutive terms into a group (g is called the *group size*) and keep a pointer only for the first term in each group (called the *group leader*). If $g = 1$, then lookups are realized in the way we are used to — by performing a binary search on the list of all $|\mathcal{V}|$ term descriptors. For $g > 1$, a lookup requires a binary search on the $\lceil |\mathcal{V}|/g \rceil$ group leaders, followed by a sequential scan of the remaining $g - 1$ members of the group identified through binary search.

The revised version of the sort-based dictionary data structure is shown in Figure 6.12 (for a group size of $g = 3$). When searching for the term "shakespeareanism" using the dictionary shown in the figure, the implementation would first identify the group led by "shakespeare" as potentially containing the term. It would then process all terms in that group in a linear fashion, in order to find the dictionary entry for "shakespeareanism". Conceptually, this lookup procedure is quite similar to the dictionary interleaving technique discussed in Section 4.4.

Let us calculate the number of string comparisons performed during a lookup for a single term T. For simplicity, we assume that T appears in the dictionary, that the dictionary contains a total of $|\mathcal{V}| = 2^n$ terms, and that the group size is $g = 2^m$, for some positive integers m and n (with $m < n$ and $n \gg 1$).

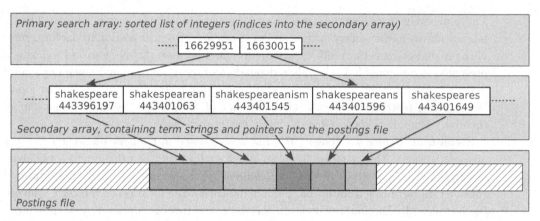

Figure 6.12   Sort-based dictionary with grouping: reducing the pointer overhead in the primary array by combining dictionary entries into groups.

- If $g = 1$, then a lookup requires approximately $n - 1$ string comparisons on average. The "-1" stems from the fact that we can terminate the binary search as soon as we encounter T. There is a 50% chance that this happens after n comparisons, a 25% chance that it happens after $n-1$ comparisons, a 12.5% chance that it happens after $n-2$ comparisons, and so forth. Thus, on average we need $n - 1$ string comparisons.

- For $g > 1$, we have to distinguish between two cases:

  1. The term is one of the $|\mathcal{V}|/g$ group leaders. The probability of this event is $1/g$, and it requires $n - m - 1$ string comparisons on average.

  2. The term is not a group leader. The probability of this happening is $(g-1)/g$. It requires $(n - m) + g/2$ string comparisons on average, where the first summand corresponds to a full binary search on the $|\mathcal{V}|/g$ group leaders (which cannot be terminated early because T is not a group leader), while the second summand corresponds to the linear scan of the $g-1$ non-leading members of the final group. The scan is terminated as soon as the matching term is found.

Combining 1 and 2, the expected number of comparison operations is

$$\frac{1}{g}(n - m - 1) + \frac{g - 1}{g}\left(n - m + \frac{g}{2}\right) \;=\; \log_2(|\mathcal{V}|) - \log_2(g) - \frac{1}{g} + \frac{g - 1}{2}.$$

Table 6.11 lists the average number of comparisons for a dictionary of size $|\mathcal{V}| = 2^{20}$, using various group sizes. It shows that choosing $g = 2$ does not increase the number of comparisons per lookup at all. Selecting $g = 8$ increases them by about 7%. At the same time, however, it substantially reduces the pointer overhead in the primary array and improves the dictionary's cache efficiency, because fewer memory pages have to be accessed.

Table 6.11   Average number of string comparisons for a single-term lookup on a sort-based dictionary containing $|\mathcal{V}| = 2^{20}$ terms.

Group size	1	2	4	8	16	32	64
String comparisons	19.0	19.0	19.3	20.4	23.4	30.5	45.5

Front coding

Once we have combined dictionary entries into groups, we can compress the term descriptors by using the set of group leaders as synchronization points. Because the term descriptors within a given group have to be traversed sequentially anyway, regardless of whether we store them compressed or uncompressed, we may as well compress them in order to reduce the storage requirements and the amount of data that needs to be accessed during a lookup.

Term strings in a sort-based dictionary are usually compressed by using a technique known as *front coding*. Because the terms are sorted in lexicographical order, consecutive terms almost always share a common prefix. This prefix can be quite long. For example, all five terms shown in Figure 6.12 share the prefix "shakespeare".

In front coding we omit the prefix that is implicitly given by the term's predecessor in the dictionary and store only the length of the prefix. Thus, the front-coded representation of a term is a triplet of the form

$$(prefixLength, \; suffixLength, \; suffix). \tag{6.63}$$

For ease of implementation, it is common to impose an upper limit of 15 characters on the length of both prefix and suffix, as this allows the dictionary implementation to store both *prefixLength* and *suffixLength* in a single byte (4 bits each). Cases in which the suffix is longer than 15 characters can be handled by storing an escape code $(prefix, suffix) = (*, 0)$ and encoding the string in some other way.

The front-coded representation of the terms shown in Figure 6.12 is

$$\langle \text{ "shakespeare", } (11, 2, \text{ "an"}), (13, 3, \text{ "ism"}) \rangle, \; \langle \text{ "shakespeareans", } (11, 1, \text{ "s"}), \dots \rangle.$$

As mentioned earlier, the first element of each group is stored in uncompressed form, serving as a synchronization point that can be used for binary search.

In a last step, after compressing the term strings, we can also reduce the file pointer overhead in the dictionary. Because the lists in the postings file are sorted in lexicographical order, in the same order as the terms in the dictionary, the file pointers form a monotonically increasing sequence of integers. Thus, we can reduce their storage requirements by applying any of the Δ-based list compression techniques described in Section 6.3. For example, using the byte-aligned

Table 6.12   The effect of dictionary compression on a sort-based dictionary for GOV2, containing 49.5 million entries. Dictionary size and average term lookup time are given for different group sizes and different compression methods.

Group Size	No Compression	Front Coding	Front Coding +vByte	Front Coding +vByte+LZ
1 term	1046 MB / 2.8 μs	n/a	n/a	n/a
2 terms	952 MB / 2.7 μs	807 MB / 2.6 μs	643 MB / 2.6 μs	831 MB / 3.1 μs
4 terms	904 MB / 2.6 μs	688 MB / 2.5 μs	441 MB / 2.4 μs	533 MB / 2.9 μs
16 terms	869 MB / 2.7 μs	598 MB / 2.2 μs	290 MB / 2.3 μs	293 MB / 4.4 μs
64 terms	860 MB / 3.9 μs	576 MB / 2.4 μs	252 MB / 3.2 μs	195 MB / 8.0 μs
256 terms	858 MB / 9.3 μs	570 MB / 4.8 μs	243 MB / 7.8 μs	157 MB / 29.2 μs

vByte method, the compressed representation of the dictionary group led by "shakespeare" is

$$\langle\,(\langle 101, 96, 54, 83, 1\rangle,\text{``shakespeare''}), (\langle 2, 38\rangle, 11, 2, \text{``an''}), (\langle 98, 3\rangle, 13, 3, \text{``ism''})\,\rangle$$

$$\equiv\quad \langle\,(443396197, \text{``shakespeare''}), (4866, 11, 2, \text{``an''}), (482, 13, 3, \text{``ism''})\,\rangle, \tag{6.64}$$

where the first element of each dictionary entry is the Δ-encoded file pointer (vByte in the first line, simple Δ-value in the second line). As in the case of front coding, the file pointer of each group leader is stored in uncompressed form.

The effect of the methods described above, on both dictionary size and average lookup time, is shown in Table 6.12. By arranging consecutive dictionary entries into groups but not applying any compression, the size of the dictionary can be decreased by about 18% (858 MB vs. 1046 MB). Combining the grouping technique with front coding cuts the dictionary's storage requirements approximately in half. If, in addition to grouping and front coding, file pointers are stored in vByte-encoded form, the dictionary can be shrunk to approximately 25% of its original size.

Regarding the lookup performance, there are two interesting observations. First, arranging term descriptors in groups improves the dictionary's lookup performance, despite the slightly increased number of string comparisons, because reducing the number of pointers in the primary array makes the binary search more cache-efficient. Second, front-coding the terms makes dictionary lookups faster, regardless of the group size g, because fewer bytes need to be shuffled around and compared with the term that is being looked up.

The last column in Table 6.12 represents a dictionary compression method that we have not described so far: combining grouping, front coding, and vByte with a general-purpose Ziv-Lempel compression algorithm (as implemented in the `zlib`[6] compression library) that is run on each group after applying front coding and vByte. Doing so is motivated by the fact that

---

[6] `www.zlib.net`

Table 6.13 Total size of in-memory dictionary when combining dictionary compression with the interleaved dictionary organization from Section 4.4. Compression method: FC+vByte+LZ. Underlying index data structure: frequency index (docids + TF values) for GOV2.

		Index Block Size (in bytes)						
		512	1,024	2,048	4,096	8,192	16,384	32,768
Group Size	1 term	117.0 MB	60.7 MB	32.0 MB	17.1 MB	9.3 MB	5.1 MB	9.9 MB
	4 terms	68.1 MB	35.9 MB	19.2 MB	10.4 MB	5.7 MB	3.2 MB	1.8 MB
	16 terms	43.8 MB	23.4 MB	12.7 MB	7.0 MB	3.9 MB	2.3 MB	1.3 MB
	64 terms	32.9 MB	17.8 MB	9.8 MB	5.4 MB	3.1 MB	1.8 MB	1.0 MB
	256 terms	28.6 MB	15.6 MB	8.6 MB	4.8 MB	2.7 MB	1.6 MB	0.9 MB

even a front-coded dictionary exhibits a remarkable degree of redundancy. For example, in a front-coded dictionary for the TREC collection (containing 1.2 million distinct terms) there are 171 occurrences of the suffix "ation", 7726 occurrences of the suffix "ing", and 722 occurrences of the suffix "ville". Front coding is oblivious to this redundancy because it focuses exclusively on the terms' prefixes. The same is true for the Δ-transformed file pointers. Because many postings lists (in particular, lists that contain only a single posting) are of the same size, we will end up with many file pointers that have the same Δ-value. We can eliminate this remaining redundancy by applying standard Ziv-Lempel data compression on top of front coding + vByte. Table 6.12 shows that this approach, although it does not work very well for small group sizes, can lead to considerable savings for $g \geq 64$ and can reduce the total size of the dictionary by up to 85% compared to the original, uncompressed index.

Combining dictionary compression and dictionary interleaving

In Section 4.4, we discussed a different way to reduce the memory requirements of the dictionary. By interleaving dictionary entries with the on-disk postings lists and keeping only one dictionary entry in memory for every 64 KB or so of index data, we were able to substantially reduce the dictionary's memory requirements: from a gigabyte down to a few megabytes. It seems natural to combine dictionary compression and dictionary interleaving to obtain an even more compact representation of the search engine's in-memory dictionary.

Table 6.13 summarizes the results that can be obtained by following this path. Depending on the index block size B (the maximum amount of on-disk index data between two subsequent in-memory dictionary entries — see Section 4.4 for details) and the in-memory dictionary group size g, it is possible to reduce the total storage requirements to under 1 MB (B=32,768; g=256). The query-time penalty resulting from this approach is essentially the I/O overhead caused by having to read an additional 32,768 bytes per query term: less than 0.5 ms for the hard drives used in our experiments.

Even more remarkable, however, is the dictionary size resulting from the configuration $B{=}512$, $g{=}256$: less than 30 MB. Choosing an index block size of $B{=}512$ does not lead to any measurable degradation in query performance, as 512 bytes ($=1$ sector) is the minimum transfer unit of most hard drives. Nevertheless, the memory requirements of the dictionary can be decreased by more than 97% compared to a data structure that does not use dictionary interleaving or dictionary compression.

6.5   Summary

The main points of this chapter are:

- Many compression methods treat the message to be compressed as a sequence of symbols and operate by finding a code that reflects the statistical properties of the symbols in the message by giving shorter codewords to symbols that appear more frequently.

- For any given probability distribution over a finite set of symbols, Huffman coding produces an optimal prefix code (i.e., one that minimizes the average codeword length).

- Arithmetic coding can attain better compression rates than Huffman coding because it does not assign an integral number of bits to each symbol's codeword. However, Huffman codes can usually be decoded much faster than arithmetic codes and are therefore given preference in many applications (e.g., search engines).

- Compression methods for inverted lists are invariably based on the fact that postings within the same list are stored in increasing order. Compression usually takes place after transforming the list into an equivalent sequence of Δ-values.

- Parametric methods usually produce smaller output than nonparametric methods. When using a parametric method, the parameter should be chosen on a per-list basis (*local parameterization*).

- If the Δ-gaps in a postings list follow a geometric distribution, then Golomb/Rice codes lead to good compression results.

- If the Δ-gaps are very small, then interpolative coding achieves very good compression rates, due to its ability to encode postings using less than 1 bit on average (arithmetic coding has the same ability but requires more complex decoding operations than interpolative coding).

- For a wide range of gap distributions, the Huffman-based LLRUN method leads to excellent results.

- Front coding has the ability to reduce the memory requirements of the search engine's dictionary data structure significantly. In combination with dictionary interleaving, it can reduce the size of the in-memory dictionary by more than 99% with virtually no degradation in query performance.

6.6   Further Reading

An excellent overview of general-purpose data compression (including text compression) is given by Bell et al. (1990) and, more recently, by Sayood (2005) and Salomon (2007). An overview of compression techniques for postings lists in inverted files is provided by Witten et al. (1999). Zobel and Moffat (2006) present a survey of research carried out in the context of inverted files, including an overview of existing approaches to inverted list compression.

Huffman codes were invented by David Huffman in 1951, while he was a student at MIT. One of his professors, Robert Fano, had asked his students to come up with a method that produces an optimal binary code for any given (finite) message source. Huffman succeeded and, as a reward, was exempted from the course's final exam. Huffman codes have been studied extensively over the past six decades, and important results have been obtained regarding their redundancy compared to the theoretically optimal (arithmetic) codes (Horibe, 1977; Gallager, 1978; Szpankowski, 2000).

Arithmetic codes can overcome the limitations of Huffman codes that are caused by the requirement that an integral number of bits be used for each symbol. Arithmetic coding was initially developed by Rissanen (1976) and Rissanen and Langdon (1979), and by Martin (1979) under the name *range encoding*, but did not experience widespread adoption until the mid-1980s, when Witten et al. (1987) published their implementation of an efficient arithmetic coder. Many modern text compression algorithms, such as DMC (Cormack and Horspool, 1987) and PPM (Cleary and Witten, 1984), are based upon variants of arithmetic coding.

γ, δ, and ω codes were introduced by Elias (1975), who also showed their *universality* (a set of codewords is called *universal* if, by assigning codewords C_i to symbols σ_i in such a way that higher-probability symbols receive shorter codewords, the expected number of bits per encoded symbol is within a constant factor of the symbol source's entropy). Golomb codes were proposed by Golomb (1966) in a very entertaining essay about "Secret Agent 00111" playing a game of roulette. Interpolative coding is due to Moffat and Stuiver (2000). In addition to the method's application in inverted-file compression, they also point out other applications, such as the efficient representation of the (i.e., description of the code used by the encoder) in Huffman coding or the encoding of move-to-front values used in compression algorithms based on the Burrows-Wheeler transform.

Byte-aligned compression methods such as vByte (Section 6.3.4) were first explored academically by Williams and Zobel (1999) but had been in use long before. Trotman (2003), in the context of on-disk indices, explores a number of compression effectiveness versus decoding performance trade-offs, showing that variable-byte encoding usually leads to higher query performance than bitwise methods. Scholer et al. (2002) come to the same conclusion but also show that a byte-aligned compression scheme can sometime even lead to improvements over an uncompressed *in-memory* index. In a recent study, Büttcher and Clarke (2007) show that this is true even if the search engine's index access pattern is completely random.

Reordering documents with the goal of achieving better compression rates was first studied by Blandford and Blelloch (2002), whose method is based on a clustering approach that tries to assign nearby docids to documents with similar content. In independent research, Shieh et al. (2003), present a similar method that reduces document reordering to the traveling salesperson problem (TSP). The idea to improve compressibility by sorting documents according to their URLs is due to Silvestri (2007).

6.7   Exercises

Exercise 6.1   Consider the symbol set $\mathcal{S} = \{\text{"a", "b"}\}$ with associated probability distribution $\Pr[\text{"a"}] = 0.8$, $\Pr[\text{"b"}] = 0.2$. Suppose we group symbols into blocks of $m = 2$ symbols when encoding messages over $\mathcal{S}$ (resulting in the new distribution $\Pr[\text{"aa"}] = 0.64$, $\Pr[\text{"ab"}] = 0.16$, etc.). Construct a Huffman tree for this new distribution.

Exercise 6.2   Show that the γ code is prefix-free (i.e., that there is no codeword that is a prefix of another codeword).

Exercise 6.3   Give an example of an unambiguous binary code that is not prefix-free. What is the probability distribution for which this code is optimal? Construct an optimal prefix-free code for the same distribution.

Exercise 6.4   Write down the decoding procedure for ω codes (see Section 6.3.1).

Exercise 6.5   Find the smallest integer n_0 such that the ω code for all integers $n \geq n_0$ is shorter than the respective δ code. Be prepared for n_0 to be very large ($> 2^{100}$).

Exercise 6.6   What is the expected number of bits per codeword when using a Rice code with parameter $M = 2^7$ to compress a geometrically distributed postings list for a term T with $N_T/N = 0.01$?

Exercise 6.7   Consider a postings list with geometrically distributed Δ-gaps and average gap size $N/N_T = 137$ (i.e., $p = 0.0073$). What is the optimal parameter M^* in the case of Golomb coding? What is the optimal Rice parameter M^*_{Rice}? How many bits on average are wasted if the optimal Rice code is used instead of the Golomb code? How many bits on average are wasted by using the optimal Golomb instead of arithmetic coding?

Exercise 6.8   In Section 6.2.2 we discussed how to construct a Huffman tree in time $\Theta(n \log(n))$, where $n = |\mathcal{S}|$ is the size of the input alphabet. Now suppose the symbols in $\mathcal{S}$ have already been sorted by their respective probability when they arrive at the encoder. Design an algorithm that builds a Huffman tree in time $\Theta(n)$.

Exercise 6.9 The Simple-9 compression method from Section 6.3.4 groups sequences of Δ-values into 32-bit machine words, reserving 4 bits for a selector value. Consider a similar method, Simple-14, that uses 64-bit machine words instead. Assuming that 4 bits per 64-bit word are reserved for the selector value, list all possible splits of the remaining 60 bits. Which of the two methods do you expect to yield better compression rates on a typical docid index? Characterization the type of docid lists on which Simple-9 will lead to better/worse results than Simple-14.

Exercise 6.10 One of the document reordering methods from Section 6.3.7 assigns numerical document identifiers according to the lexicographical ordering of the respective URLs. Is there another method, also based on the documents' URLs, that might achieve even better compression rates? Consider the individual components of a URL and how you could use them.

Exercise 6.11 (project exercise) Add index compression to your existing implementation of the inverted index data structure. Implement support for the byte-aligned vByte method from Section 6.3.4 as well as your choice of γ coding (Section 6.3.1) or Simple-9 (Section 6.3.4). Your new implementation should store all postings lists in compressed form.

6.8 Bibliography

Anh, V. N., and Moffat, A. (2005). Inverted index compression using word-aligned binary codes. *Information Retrieval*, 8(1):151–166.

Bell, T. C., Cleary, J. G., and Witten, I. H. (1990). *Text Compression*. Upper Saddle River, New Jersey: Prentice-Hall.

Blandford, D. K., and Blelloch, G. E. (2002). Index compression through document reordering. In *Data Compression Conference*, pages 342–351. Snowbird, Utah.

Burrows, M., and Wheeler, D. (1994). *A Block-Sorting Lossless Data Compression Algorithm*. Technical Report SRC-RR-124. Digital Systems Research Center, Palo Alto, California.

Büttcher, S., and Clarke, C. L. A. (2007). Index compression is good, especially for random access. In *Proceedings of the 16th ACM Conference on Information and Knowledge Management*, pages 761–770. Lisbon, Portugal.

Cleary, J. G., and Witten, I. H. (1984). Data compression using adaptive coding and partial string matching. *IEEE Transactions on Communications*, 32(4):396–402.

Cormack, G. V., and Horspool, R. N. S. (1987). Data compression using dynamic Markov modelling. *The Computer Journal*, 30(6):541–550.

Elias, P. (1975). Universal codeword sets and representations of the integers. *IEEE Transactions on Information Theory*, 21(2):194–203.

Fraenkel, A. S., and Klein, S. T. (1985). Novel compression of sparse bit-strings. In Apostolico, A., and Galil, Z., editors, *Combinatorial Algorithms on Words*, pages 169–183. New York: Springer.

Gallager, R. G. (1978). Variations on a theme by Huffman. *IEEE Transactions on Information Theory*, 24(6):668–674.

Gallager, R. G., and Voorhis, D. C. V. (1975). Optimal source codes for geometrically distributed integer alphabets. *IEEE Transactions on Information Theory*, 21(2):228–230.

Golomb, S. W. (1966). Run-length encodings. *IEEE Transactions on Information Theory*, 12:399–401.

Horibe, Y. (1977). An improved bound for weight-balanced tree. *Information and Control*, 34(2):148–151.

Larmore, L. L., and Hirschberg, D. S. (1990). A fast algorithm for optimal length-limited Huffman codes. *Journal of the ACM*, 37(3):464–473.

Martin, G. N. N. (1979). Range encoding: An algorithm for removing redundancy from a digitised message. In *Proceedings of the Conference on Video and Data Recording*. Southampton, England.

Moffat, A., and Stuiver, L. (2000). Binary interpolative coding for effective index compression. *Information Retrieval*, 3(1):25–47.

Patterson, D. A., and Hennessy, J. L. (2009). *Computer Organization and Design: The Hardware/Software Interface* (4th ed.). San Francisco, California: Morgan Kaufmann.

Rice, R. F., and Plaunt, J. R. (1971). Adaptive variable-length coding for efficient compression of spacecraft television data. *IEEE Transactions on Commununication Technology*, 19(6):889–897.

Rissanen, J. (1976). Generalized Kraft inequality and arithmetic coding. *IBM Journal of Research and Development*, 20(3):198–203.

Rissanen, J., and Langdon, G. G. (1979). Arithmetic coding. *IBM Journal of Research and Development*, 23(2):149–162.

Salomon, D. (2007). *Data Compression: The Complete Reference* (4th ed.). London, England: Springer.

Sayood, K. (2005). *Introduction to Data Compression* (3rd ed.). San Francisco, California: Morgan Kaufmann.

Scholer, F., Williams, H. E., Yiannis, J., and Zobel, J. (2002). Compression of inverted indexes for fast query evaluation. In *Proceedings of the 25th Annual International ACM SIGIR Conference on Research and Development in Information Retrieval*, pages 222–229. Tampere, Finland.

Shannon, C. E. (1948). A mathematical theory of communication. *Bell System Technical Journal*, 27:379–423, 623–656.

Shannon, C. E. (1951). Prediction and entropy of printed English. *Bell System Technical Journal*, 30:50–64.

Shieh, W. Y., Chen, T. F., Shann, J. J. J., and Chung, C. P. (2003). Inverted file compression through document identifier reassignment. *Information Processing & Management*, 39(1):117–131.

Silvestri, F. (2007). Sorting out the document identifier assignment problem. In *Proceedings of the 29th European Conference on IR Research*, pages 101–112. Rome, Italy.

Szpankowski, W. (2000). Asymptotic average redundancy of Huffman (and other) block codes. *IEEE Transactions on Information Theory*, 46(7):2434–2443.

Trotman, A. (2003). Compressing inverted files. *Information Retrieval*, 6(1):5–19.

Williams, H. E., and Zobel, J. (1999). Compressing integers for fast file access. *The Computer Journal*, 42(3):193–201.

Witten, I. H., Moffat, A., and Bell, T. C. (1999). *Managing Gigabytes: Compressing and Indexing Documents and Images* (2nd ed.). San Francisco, California: Morgan Kaufmann.

Witten, I. H., Neal, R. M., and Cleary, J. G. (1987). Arithmetic coding for data compression. *Commununications of the ACM*, 30(6):520–540.

Ziv, J., and Lempel, A. (1977). A universal algorithm for sequential data compression. *IEEE Transactions on Information Theory*, 23(3):337–343.

Zobel, J., and Moffat, A. (2006). Inverted files for text search engines. *ACM Computing Surveys*, 38(2):1–56.

7   Dynamic Inverted Indices

In Chapter 4, when we discussed how to construct an inverted index from a given text collection, many of our arguments were based on the assumption that the collection is *static* and does not change during the index construction process nor after the index has been built. Obviously, this assumption does not always hold. In many applications the collection may be expected to change over time. Examples of those *dynamic* text collections include file systems, digital libraries, and the Web.

Dynamic text collections typically allow three types of operations: document insertions, deletions, and modifications. When building an inverted index for a dynamic text collection, the volatile nature of the data needs to be taken into account and appropriate strategies need to be employed to keep the index consistent with the text in the collection. Such *index maintenance strategies* are the topic of this chapter.

In the first part of the chapter (Section 7.1) we discuss how to deal with semi-static document collections. A semi-static collection allows insertions and deletions (treating document modifications as deletions followed by insertions), but the updates do not have to be reflected by the index immediately. Instead, a small delay of perhaps a few hours or even a few days is tolerable. Web search engines typically treat large portions of the Web as a semi-static text collection; it may take several days or weeks for a new Web page to be included in the search engine's index (although popular pages, such as `www.whitehouse.gov`, are usually re-indexed more frequently).

The second part (Section 7.2) is concerned with *incremental* text collections. An incremental collection allows new documents to be added to the collection. Existing documents, however, may never be modified or removed. We examine several index update strategies for incremental text collections and show that splitting the index into a set of independent subindices ("index partitions") allows the search engine to update its index structures very efficiently, while not impacting query performance unreasonably. The method can be used to keep the index up to date even if documents are arriving at very high rates.

In the third and final part of this chapter, we discuss index update policies for *non-incremental* dynamic text collections that support the full range of update operations: insertions, deletions, and modifications. In Section 7.3 we show how to implement a lazy deletion procedure that does not remove obsolete postings from the index immediately but merely marks them as deleted; garbage collection is executed periodically to clean up the index and remove all garbage postings. Section 7.4 discusses how the search engine's index structures need to be modified if the engine has to support document modifications (e.g., append operations). We point out some of the difficulties that arise under such circumstances. Our discussion sheds some light on why search engines typically do not support document modifications directly but instead treat them as a combination of deletion and re-insertion — even though this approach can be rather inefficient when applied to very long documents.

As in Chapter 4, the basic assumption throughout this chapter is that memory resources are scarce compared to the total size of the index and that the majority of the index data needs to be kept on disk. In the context of large-scale search engines with plentiful memory resources, this may limit the applicability of the techniques discussed here, although the general set of problems encountered is usually quite similar in both cases (disk-based and in-memory).

7.1 Batch Updates

In some applications, it may be tolerable if changes to the text collection are not immediately reflected by the index. Instead, the indexing process may wait for a while, accumulating new documents, before it adds all new data to the index in a single *batch update* operation. This is the typical index update behavior in Web search, where days or even weeks may pass before a new Web page makes it into the index of one of the major Web search engines. Batch updates to an existing index can be realized in two different ways:

- A new index is built from scratch. When the indexing process is finished, the old index is deleted and replaced by the new one. This procedure is referred to as the REBUILD update strategy.
- An index is built from the text found in the newly inserted documents. After the index has been created, it is merged with the original index, resulting in a new index that supersedes the old one. This procedure is referred to as the REMERGE update strategy. The merge operations in the REMERGE strategy can be carried out in essentially the same way as the final merge operation in merge-based index construction (see Section 4.5.3).

Which strategy is the better choice, REBUILD or REMERGE? From a developer's point of view, REBUILD is more attractive because it is easier to implement. However, REBUILD needs to parse and re-index all documents in the collection, regardless of whether they have already been indexed. With REMERGE, we can reuse some of the existing index data, thus giving the method a potential performance advantage over REBUILD.

If the batch update consists exclusively of document insertions (no deletions), then it is obvious that the REMERGE policy leads to better performance than REBUILD. However, if the update is not strictly incremental but consists of both insertions and deletions, then the situation is not so clear. REMERGE, in this case, would spend some time reading and decoding postings that belong to deleted documents and will not be included in the new index. REBUILD, on the other hand, would never encounter those postings, which gives it a potential advantage over REMERGE.

Suppose the original index, I_{old}, contains postings for d_{old} documents and all these documents are about the same size. Suppose further that the batch update consists of d_{delete} deletions and d_{insert} insertions. Thus, after applying all updates in the batch, the new index, I_{new}, will contain postings for

$$d_{new} \;\; = \;\; d_{old} - d_{delete} + d_{insert} \tag{7.1}$$

documents. The time it takes REBUILD to construct I_{new} depends only on d_{new}. Employing the merge-based index construction method from Chapter 4, it can build I_{new} in

$$
\begin{aligned}
time_{rebuild}(d_{old}, d_{delete}, d_{insert}) \;\; &= \;\; c \cdot d_{new} \\
&= \;\; c \cdot (d_{old} - d_{delete} + d_{insert}),
\end{aligned}
\tag{7.2}
$$

for some system-specific constant c.

How long does it take to build I_{new} if the REMERGE strategy is used instead? The answer depends on the relative performance of indexing and merging operations in the search engine. From Table 4.7 (page 130), we know that the final merge operation in merge-based index construction takes about 25% of the total time required to build a full-text index for GOV2. The remaining 75% are spent on parsing documents and constructing subindices. Therefore, we may assume that the total time required to build a new index for the collection, using REMERGE, is approximately

$$time_{remerge}(d_{old}, d_{delete}, d_{insert}) \;\; = \;\; c \cdot d_{insert} + \frac{c}{4} \cdot (d_{old} + d_{insert}), \tag{7.3}$$

where the first summand corresponds to constructing an index I_{insert} for the d_{insert} incoming documents and the second summand corresponds to merging I_{old} with I_{insert}, resulting in the new index I_{new}.

Equation 7.3 does not take into account that the merge operation carried out here is slightly more time-consuming than the one from Section 4.5.3 because it also needs to garbage-collect postings that refer to deleted documents instead of just merging postings lists. For the sake of simplicity, however, let us assume that this overhead is negligible, and that merging is in fact about four times as fast as re-indexing (a proper discussion of the effect of deletions on update performance can be found in Section 7.3). Under this assumption, REBUILD and REMERGE exhibit the same performance if

$$time_{rebuild}(d_{old}, d_{delete}, d_{insert}) \;\; = \;\; time_{remerge}(d_{old}, d_{delete}, d_{insert}) \tag{7.4}$$

$$\Leftrightarrow \quad d_{old} - d_{delete} + d_{insert} \;\; = \;\; d_{insert} + \frac{1}{4} \cdot (d_{old} + d_{insert}) \tag{7.5}$$

$$\Leftrightarrow \quad d_{delete} \;\; = \;\; \frac{3}{4} \cdot d_{old} - \frac{1}{4} \cdot d_{insert}. \tag{7.6}$$

Suppose the collection, although changing over time, is in *steady state*, that is, the number of insertions equals the number of deletions ($d_{insert} = d_{delete}$). In practice this is often the case because many collections, even though they might experience a large number of updates, grow very slowly compared to their total size. Equation 7.6 then reduces to

$$d_{delete} = \frac{3}{5} \cdot d_{old}. \tag{7.7}$$

Hence, the REBUILD strategy is more efficient than REMERGE if at least 60% of all documents from the old index have been deleted and no longer appear in the new index. If the deletion rate is smaller than 60%, then REMERGE will be the better choice.

In most applications, the relative number of deletions between two consecutive batch updates is much smaller than 60%. This is not necessarily because text collections are changing so slowly, but because a search engine whose results predominantly refer to documents that don't exist anymore is not of great utility to its users. To ensure user satisfaction, a rapidly changing text collection requires more frequent index updates. Thus, in practice, REMERGE almost always leads to better results than REBUILD.

Given that every search engine with a merge-based indexing procedure (see Section 4.5.3) automatically has the ability to merge two inverted files, there is no real reason to choose REBUILD over REMERGE. Since REMERGE is so much faster than REBUILD, it allows for shorter index update cycles and thus a greater index freshness. Admittedly, the need to integrate support for document deletions into the merge operation makes a REMERGE update slightly more complex than the final merge operation in merge-based indexing. The necessary adjustments, however, are not overly complicated. A method that can be used to remove garbage postings from an existing index is discussed in Section 7.3.

7.2 Incremental Index Updates

While the batch update strategies discussed in the previous section may be appropriate for certain applications, in many search environments it is critical that the search engine's index always reflects the current contents of the text collection. Examples include Internet news search, file system search, and proprietary search systems used by Internet merchants such as Amazon[1] and eBay[2]. In all these cases the index needs to be updated immediately after a change to the text collection has been detected; batch update is no longer an appropriate strategy. In this section we show how this goal can be reached if the text collection is strictly incremental, that is, if new documents can be added but existing documents will never be modified or removed from the collection.

---

[1] www.amazon.com

[2] www.ebay.com

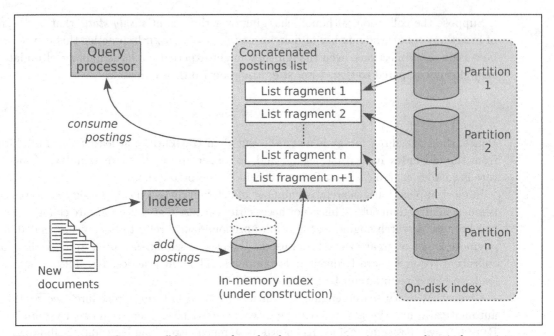

Figure 7.1 Transforming off-line merge-based index construction into an on-line index maintenance strategy (NO MERGE). The postings list for each query term is fetched from the in-memory index currently being built and from the on-disk index partitions created earlier. The final inverted list is constructed by concatenating the sublists.

Consider again the structure of the in-memory index constructed by the hash-based in-memory indexing procedure from Section 4.5.1. The backbone of this index is an in-memory hash table that maps from term strings to the memory addresses of the corresponding postings lists. Although this data structure was originally motivated by the specific requirements of the indexing process, it may just as well be used for query processing.

Suppose that, while the search engine is building an index, perhaps after creating n on-disk index partitions, we want it to process a keyword query composed of m query terms. This can easily be realized by repeating the following procedure for each of the m terms:

1. Fetch the term's postings list fragment from each of the n on-disk index partitions.

2. Use the in-memory hash table to fetch the term's in-memory list fragment.

3. Concatenate all $n + 1$ fragments to form the term's postings list.

This procedure is shown in Figure 7.1. It requires a total of $m \cdot n$ random disk accesses. We refer to it as the NO MERGE index update strategy, for reasons that will become clear very soon.

Although NO MERGE can be used to transform an off-line index construction method for static text collections into an on-line method that allows document insertions to be interleaved with search queries, it is often not a very attractive strategy, due to the large number of disk seeks required to process a search query (one seek for every query term and every index partition). If the number of partitions is large, then NO MERGE's query performance can be extremely low. Nonetheless, the method may serve as a baseline for other, more sophisticated strategies.

In the remainder of this section, we discuss several index update policies for incremental text collections. These policies are all based upon the same general idea that forms the foundation of the NO MERGE policy: to index incoming documents as if they were part of a static text collection, and to process queries by concatenating the query terms' postings lists found in the on-disk and in the in-memory index. Unlike NO MERGE, however, they aim to keep the amount of fragmentation in the on-disk index low, by rearranging small list fragments into larger lists.

7.2.1 Contiguous Inverted Lists

The most drastic way to guarantee a low degree of fragmentation in the on-disk postings lists is to not allow the creation of a new on-disk list fragment for a term for which a list fragment already exists in the index. This can be done in two fundamentally different ways: in-place update and remerge update.

Remerge update

Reconsider the REMERGE strategy from Section 7.1. REMERGE can be used not only for batch update operations arising in the context of semi-static document collections but also as an update policy for incremental collections. The search engine's indexing module processes incoming documents in the same way it would in the static case. In contrast to the static case, however, whenever the indexer runs out of memory, a fresh on-disk index is created by merging the existing on-disk index with the data accumulated in main memory. The general procedure is shown in Figure 7.2.

Merging the old index data with the in-memory data requires the engine to read the existing on-disk index and write the new index at the same time. By reading/writing all data in larger chunks, perhaps several megabytes at a time, the number of nonsequential disk operations (switching between the old index and the new one) can be kept very low and the whole update operation can be carried out very efficiently.

In the context of real-time (non-batch) updates, REMERGE is sometimes referred to as IMMEDIATE MERGE to distinguish it from other merge-based update strategies that do not always perform a merge operation when the indexing process runs out of main memory.

In order to quantify the performance difference between IMMEDIATE MERGE and NO MERGE, and to show how important it is to store on-disk postings lists in a contiguous fashion, we had our search engine index the 25.2 million documents in the GOV2 collection with a memory budget of roughly 800 MB (enough to build an in-memory index for 250,000 documents). Whenever the system ran out of memory, an on-disk index update was carried out, merging the in-memory index with the existing on-disk index, followed by a sequence of 1,000 search queries.

buildIndex_ImmediateMerge $(M) \equiv$

1    $I_{mem} \leftarrow \emptyset$ // initialize in-memory index
2    $currentPosting \leftarrow 1$
3   **while** there are more tokens to index **do**
4        $T \leftarrow$ next token
5        $I_{mem}.addPosting(T, currentPosting)$
6        $currentPosting \leftarrow currentPosting + 1$
7   **if** I_{mem} contains more than $M - 1$ tokens **then**
8   **if** I_{disk} exists **then**
9                $I_{disk} \leftarrow$ **mergeIndices**($\{I_{mem}, I_{disk}\}$)
10   **else**
11               $I_{disk} \leftarrow I_{mem}$
12           $I_{mem} \leftarrow \emptyset$ // reset in-memory index
13   **return**

Figure 7.2   On-line index construction with IMMEDIATE MERGE. The procedure **mergeIndices** appears in Figure 4.13 (page 129).

Figure 7.3 shows the average time per query for the two index update strategies. As expected, IMMEDIATE MERGE, due to its strictly contiguous on-disk postings lists, exhibits better query performance than NO MERGE. What might be somewhat surprising, however, is the large margin by which it beats its competitor. After the whole collection had been indexed, NO MERGE was more than seven times slower than IMMEDIATE MERGE (690 ms for IMMEDIATE MERGE vs. 5,100 ms for NO MERGE).

What is the reason for this enormous difference? With a memory budget sufficient to index 250,000 documents, NO MERGE accumulates a total of 100 on-disk index partitions for GOV2, resulting in approximately 100 random disk seeks per query term. With a random access cost of approximately 12 ms (disk seek plus rotational latency) and an average of 3.5 terms per query, we expect a total overhead of

$$12 \text{ ms} \cdot 100 \cdot 3.5 = 4{,}200 \text{ ms} \tag{7.8}$$

per query — a factor-of-7 slowdown compared to the 690 ms per query achieved by IMMEDIATE MERGE. This calculation shows that there are some fundamental limitations to the usefulness of NO MERGE. Even if we increased the search engine's memory budget by a factor of 5, we would still end up with 20 index partitions and a random access overhead of around 800 ms per query. Conversely, if the indexing process's memory budget is decreased, query performance becomes truly unbearable, as shown in Figure 7.3 for $M = 100{,}000$ documents.

Unfortunately, despite its clear advantage over the NO MERGE policy, IMMEDIATE MERGE is not the final answer to the index update problem. Whenever the indexing process runs out of memory, it reads the entire index from disk, merges it with the in-memory data, and writes the

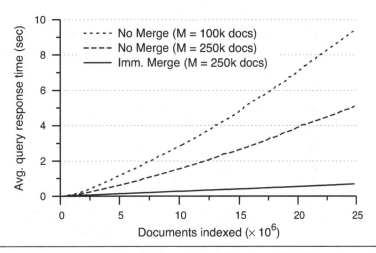

Figure 7.3 Average query performance for IMMEDIATE MERGE and NO MERGE as a function of index size. Document collection: GOV2 (25.2 million documents). Query set: Random queries from TREC Terabyte 2006, evaluated using proximity ranking (Section 2.2.2).

new index back to disk. Over time, this strategy leads to a number of disk read/write operations that is quadratic in the size of the collection.

Suppose the indexing process may buffer M postings in memory and is building an index for a collection containing N tokens. When it runs out of memory for the first time, M postings are transferred to disk. When it runs out of memory the second time, those M postings are loaded into memory, merged with the in-memory index, and $2M$ postings are written back to disk. Thus, for the N tokens in the collection, the total number of postings transferred from/to disk is

$$\sum_{k=1}^{\lfloor N/M \rfloor} (k-1)M + kM \;\; = \;\; M \cdot \sum_{k=1}^{\lfloor N/M \rfloor} (2k-1) \tag{7.9}$$

$$= \;\; M \cdot \left(\left\lfloor \frac{N}{M} \right\rfloor \right)^2 \;\; \in \;\; \Theta\left(\frac{N^2}{M} \right). \tag{7.10}$$

If the available amount of main memory is small compared to the total size of the collection, then this quadratic complexity renders IMMEDIATE MERGE impractical, as shown by Figure 7.4, which depicts the cumulative index update cost for both NO MERGE and IMMEDIATE MERGE as the index grows. Even with a moderately generous memory budget of 800 MB ($\cong$ 250,000 documents), IMMEDIATE MERGE is roughly six times slower than NO MERGE.

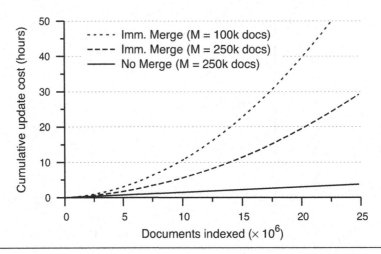

Figure 7.4   Cumulative index update cost for IMMEDIATE MERGE and NO MERGE as a function of index size. Data set: GOV2 (25.2 million documents).

In-place update

In-place index update strategies try to overcome IMMEDIATE MERGE's limitations by not requiring the search engine to read the entire index from disk every time it runs out of memory. Instead, whenever a postings list is written to disk during an on-disk index update, some free room is left at the end of the list. When additional postings for the same term have to be transferred to disk at a later point in time, they can simply be appended to the existing list. If the amount of free space available at the end of a list is insufficient for the incoming postings, the entire list is relocated to a new position in the on-disk index, where there is enough space for old and new postings. An example of this general procedure is shown in Figure 7.5.

Individual in-place update strategies differ mainly in the way they pre-allocate space at the end of a given list. The most common allocation scheme (with which you may already be familiar from Section 4.5.1) is called *proportional pre-allocation*. Suppose a postings list L of size b bytes is transferred to disk (or relocated to a new position). Then the total space the search engine reserves for L is $k \cdot b$ bytes. That is, $(k - 1) \cdot b$ bytes at the end of the list will be available for future postings. Common pre-allocation factors are $k = 1.5$ and $k = 2$. Compared with other pre-allocation policies, such as reserving a constant number of bytes at the end of each list, proportional pre-allocation has the advantage that the total number of bytes read/written from/to disk during relocation operations is linear in the final size of the list (Exercise 7.2). In the remainder of this section, we refer to the in-place update policy with proportional pre-allocation simply as INPLACE.

Because the total number of bytes that INPLACE transfers from/to disk for a given list is linear in the size of the list, we may conclude that the total number of bytes transferred from/to disk for the entire inverted index is linear in the size of the index. This seems to imply that

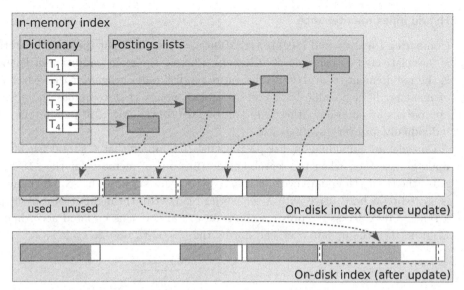

Figure 7.5   In-place index update with pre-allocation. At the end of the on-disk list for term T_3, there is not enough room for the new postings. The list has to be relocated.

INPLACE achieves a better update performance than IMMEDIATE MERGE with its quadratic disk complexity. However, this is not so. In-place update strategies exhibit a highly nonsequential disk access pattern that involves costly random-access disk operations. Thus, the raw amount of data transferred to/from disk is not indicative of the overall update performance.

Consider again the example shown in Figure 7.5. The postings list for term T_3 needs to be relocated because there is insufficient space for the new postings from the in-memory index. Relocating the list requires two random disk accesses: one to read the original list from its old location and one to write the augmented list (including the postings from the in-memory index) to the new location. With the hard drives used in our experiments (see Appendix A), performing a single random disk access carries approximately the same cost as reading or writing 1 MB of data sequentially.

Because most postings lists are very short (Zipf's law), INPLACE's nonsequential index access pattern has disastrous effects on its update performance. For instance, updating a set of 100,000 very short postings lists in-place takes about 20 minutes (assuming one disk seek per list). Updating them in a sequential read/write operation (as part of a merge update) can be done in a few seconds.

The index maintenance literature is rich in optimizations to the basic INPLACE strategy; see, for instance, Shieh and Chung (2005) or Lester et al. (2006). We leave the discussion of those efforts to the existing literature and instead focus our attention on a more principled way of reducing the overall update overhead: by combining INPLACE and IMMEDIATE MERGE into a single, *hybrid* update strategy.

Hybrid index maintenance

Comparing INPLACE and IMMEDIATE MERGE, we can say that the main limitation of INPLACE is the relatively large number of disk seeks, whereas the main limitation of IMMEDIATE MERGE is the requirement to read/write the entire on-disk index whenever the search engine runs out of memory. It is possible to devise an update policy that combines the advantages of both approaches by choosing either INPLACE or IMMEDIATE MERGE, not for the entire index but individually for every postings list.

Consider an individual on-disk postings list L. Suppose that L's total size after the i-th index update cycle (i.e., when the search engine runs out of memory for the i-th time) is s_i bytes. After the $(i+1)$-th update cycle, it is s_{i+1} bytes. Now suppose the search engine's on-disk index is stored on a hard drive with a sequential read/write throughput of b bytes per second and a random disk access requires r seconds on average. If L is updated according to IMMEDIATE MERGE, then the update overhead during the $(i+1)$-th update cycle is

$$D_{i+1} = \frac{s_i + s_{i+1}}{b}, \qquad (7.11)$$

where the two summands stem from the necessity to read the old list and write the new one. If an in-place update policy is employed instead, the update overhead is

$$D_{i+1} = 2r + \frac{s_{i+1} - s_i}{b}, \qquad (7.12)$$

assuming that two disk seeks are necessary to update the list (in a hybrid index maintenance policy, each in-place update requires two disk seeks instead of one because it interrupts a sequential merge operation). Equating 7.11 and 7.12 yields:

$$s_i = r \cdot b. \qquad (7.13)$$

That is, as soon as an on-disk postings list is bigger than $r \cdot b$ bytes, it is more efficient to update it in-place than to use REMERGE. For a typical consumer hard drive, this corresponds roughly to $s_i = 0.5$ MB. For shorter lists IMMEDIATE MERGE is more efficient. For longer lists INPLACE is the more appropriate strategy.

The idea is formalized by the algorithm shown in Figure 7.6. The algorithm maintains two on-disk indices: I_{merge} and $I_{inplace}$. Initially all postings lists are stored in I_{merge}. Whenever a list reaches the predefined threshold ϑ (the hardware-specific REMERGE versus INPLACE break-even point), it is transferred from I_{merge} to $I_{inplace}$. The algorithm uses the variable $\mathcal{L}$ to keep track of all *long* lists stored in the in-place index section.

Because this update strategy combines the advantages of REMERGE and INPLACE, it is usually referred to as *hybrid index maintenance*. The specific method shown in the figure is called HYBRID IMMEDIATE MERGE *with contiguous postings lists* (HIM$_C$). It is analyzed by Büttcher and Clarke (2008), who show that its theoretical complexity depends on the term distribution

buildIndex_HybridImmediateMerge $(M) \equiv$

1   let I_{merge} denote the primary on-disk index (merge-maintained, initially empty)
2   let $I_{inplace}$ denote the secondary on-disk index (updated in-place, initially empty)
3    $I_{mem} \leftarrow \emptyset$ // initialize in-memory index
4    $currentPosting \leftarrow 1$
5    $\mathcal{L} \leftarrow \emptyset$ // the set of long lists is empty initially
6   **while** there are more tokens to index **do**
7        $T \leftarrow$ next token
8        $I_{mem}.addPosting(T,\ currentPosting)$
9        $currentPosting \leftarrow currentPosting + 1$
10   **if** I_{mem} contains more than $M - 1$ postings **then**
11   // merge I_{mem} and I_{merge} by traversing their lists in lexicographical order
12           $I'_{merge} \leftarrow \emptyset$ // create new on-disk index
13   **for each** term $T \in I_{mem} \cup I_{merge}$ **do**
14   **if** $(T \in \mathcal{L}) \vee (I_{mem}.getPostings(T).size + I_{merge}.getPostings(T).size > \vartheta)$ **then**
15                   $I_{inplace}.addPostings(T,\ I_{merge}.getPostings(T))$
16                   $I_{inplace}.addPostings(T,\ I_{mem}.getPostings(T))$
17                   $\mathcal{L} \leftarrow \mathcal{L} \cup \{T\}$
18   **else**
19                   $I'_{merge}.addPostings(T,\ I_{merge}.getPostings(T))$
20                   $I'_{merge}.addPostings(T,\ I_{mem}.getPostings(T))$
21           $I_{merge} \leftarrow I'_{merge}$ // replace the old on-disk index with the new one
22           $I_{mem} \leftarrow \emptyset$ // re-initialize the in-memory index

Figure 7.6   On-line index construction according to HYBRID IMMEDIATE MERGE with contiguous postings lists (HIM$_C$). Input parameter: long-list threshold ϑ.

in the text collection and is

$$\Theta\left(\frac{N^{1+1/\alpha}}{M}\right), \tag{7.14}$$

where N is the size of the collection, M is the indexing process's memory budget, and α is the Zipf parameter of the collection being indexed. For text collections around the size of GOV2, HIM$_C$'s index update overhead is about 50% lower than that of IMMEDIATE MERGE. Their query performance, on the other hand, is almost exactly the same, since both methods maintain strictly contiguous on-disk postings lists.

7.2.2   Noncontiguous Inverted Lists

Hybrid index maintenance is a significant improvement over the basic IMMEDIATE MERGE strategy. However, if memory resources are scarce, its update performance is still somewhat unsatisfactory and can easily become the main bottleneck of the search engine. Unfortunately, if we insist that all on-disk postings lists be stored contiguously, then this is the best that can be achieved. In order to obtain better update performance, we need to move away from the idea that all postings lists are stored in a contiguous fashion.

```
        buildIndex_LogarithmicMerge (M) ≡
1       I₀ ← ∅   // initialize in-memory index
2       currentPosting ← 1
3       while there are more tokens to index do
4           T ← next token
5           I₀.addPosting(T, currentPosting)
6           currentPosting ← currentPosting + 1
7           if I₀ contains more than M − 1 tokens then
8               // construct I, the set of index partitions to be merged
9               I ← {I₀}
10              g ← 1
11              while I_g exists do    // anticipate collisions
12                  I ← I ∪ {I_g}
13                  g ← g + 1
14              I_g ← mergeIndices(I)
15              delete every I ∈ I
16              I₀ ← ∅   // reset in-memory index
17      return
```

Figure 7.7 On-line index construction with LOGARITHMIC MERGE (anticipatory version). The procedure **mergeIndices** appears in Figure 4.13 (page 129).

Index partitioning

Index update strategies that maintain multiple on-disk inverted files, where each inverted file contains a small part of any given inverted list, are called *index-partitioning schemes*. Dividing the on-disk index into a set of independent index partitions can greatly improve the search engine's update performance. On the downside, however, because each postings list is no longer stored in a contiguous region of the hard drive, query performance may be a bit lower. By ensuring that the number of index partitions remains small, it is often possible to keep the degradation at an acceptable level.

Logarithmic merging

One of the most common index-partitioning algorithms is LOGARITHMIC MERGE. It is the standard index maintenance policy in several open-source text retrieval systems, including Lucene and Wumpus. LOGARITHMIC MERGE maintains a set of index partitions. Each partition carries a label g, the *generation number* of that partition. Whenever the search engine's indexing process runs out of memory, it creates a new on-disk index partition from the data found in the in-memory index. This new inverted file receives the provisional label "1". The search engine then inspects all index partitions created so far and checks whether there are two with the same label g'. If that is the case, it merges these two partitions into a new one with the label $g' + 1$. This procedure is repeated until there are no more such collisions (i.e., until there is at most one index partition for any given label g).

Table 7.1   Sequence of nonempty index partitions maintained by LOGARITH-
MIC MERGE. The variable M denotes the number of postings that may be
buffered in main memory. The column labeled "Postings Written" shows the
cumulative number of postings written to disk after each merge operation.

Tokens Read	Index Partitions						Postings Written
	1	2	3	4	5	#	
$0 \times M$	·	·	·	·	·	0	0
$1 \times M$	⋆	·	·	·	·	1	$1 \times M$
$2 \times M$	·	⋆	·	·	·	1	$3 \times M$
$3 \times M$	⋆	⋆	·	·	·	2	$4 \times M$
$4 \times M$	·	·	⋆	·	·	1	$8 \times M$
$5 \times M$	⋆	·	⋆	·	·	2	$9 \times M$
$6 \times M$	·	⋆	⋆	·	·	2	$11 \times M$
$7 \times M$	⋆	⋆	⋆	·	·	3	$12 \times M$
$8 \times M$	·	·	·	⋆	·	1	$20 \times M$

The basic strategy outlined above can be improved slightly by *anticipating* collisions. For example, when merging two partitions of generation g', and there already exists a partition of generation $g' + 1$, we can simply include it in the first merge operation so that there is no need for a second merge that results from the collision caused by the first one. Instead of merging two partitions of generation g' and then merging two partitions of generation $g' + 1$, we perform a single three-way merge operation, merging two partitions of generation g' and one of generation $g' + 1$, resulting in a new partition of generation $g' + 2$.

This procedure is formalized in Figure 7.7, which shows the anticipatory version of LOGA-RITHMIC MERGE. In the algorithm, I_g refers to the on-disk index partition of generation g. I_0 refers to the in-memory index.

Before we analyze the update complexity of LOGARITHMIC MERGE, let us look at a concrete example. Suppose the search engine may buffer up to M postings in main memory. It starts indexing a given text collection. After it has accumulated M postings, it builds an inverted file from the in-memory index data. This newly created index partition receives the label "1". The search engine continues to index documents. When it runs out of memory the second time (after $2M$ postings), it creates another partition. The new partition cannot receive the label "1" because there is already a partition with that label. Therefore, it is merged with the existing partition, yielding a new partition, with label "2". When the search engine runs out of memory the third time (after $3M$ postings), it creates a new index partition with label "1". Because at that point no other partition with label "1" exists, there is no need to perform a merge operation and the system may continue indexing documents. The continuation of this process is shown in Table 7.1.

What is the total number of postings written to disk by the index maintenance operations carried out by the basic (i.e., non-anticipatory) LOGARITHMIC MERGE policy? Suppose we are building an index for a text collection containing $N = 2^k M$ tokens, for some positive integer k. When the indexing process is done, there will be a single index partition I_{k+1} of generation $k + 1$. I_{k+1} was created by merging two index partitions of generation k. Each partition of generation k, in turn, was created by merging two partitions of generation $k - 1$, and so forth.

Every merge operation resulting in a partition of generation i requires the search engine to write $2^{i-1}M$ postings to disk. Therefore, the total number of postings written to disk by LOGARITHMIC MERGE is

$$2^k M + 2 \cdot (2^{k-1}M + 2 \cdot (2^{k-2}M + \cdots)) \tag{7.15}$$

$$= \sum_{i=1}^{k+1} 2^{k+1-i}\, 2^{i-1}\, M \tag{7.16}$$

$$= (k+1) \cdot 2^k M \tag{7.17}$$

$$= \left(\log_2\left(\frac{N}{M}\right) + 1\right) \cdot N \tag{7.18}$$

because $k = \log_2(N/M)$.

The number of postings *read* from disk is upper-bounded by the number of postings *written* (nothing is read twice). Hence, the total disk complexity of the basic LOGARITHMIC MERGE strategy, measured by the number of postings transferred from/to disk, is

$$D_{\text{LogMerge}}(N) \in \Theta\left(N \cdot \log\left(\frac{N}{M}\right)\right). \tag{7.19}$$

The anticipatory version of LOGARITHMIC MERGE leads only to a constant-factor improvement over the basic version and thus has the same asymptotic complexity (see Exercise 7.3).

Figure 7.8 shows the update and query performance of LOGARITHMIC MERGE and its competitors for an update buffer size of approximately 250,000 documents. LOGARITHMIC MERGE performs well in both aspects. Its cumulative indexing overhead is only about 40% higher than that of NO MERGE. Its average query response time, on the other hand, stays close to that of IMMEDIATE MERGE throughout the experiment.

The sudden "jumps" in both plots in Figure 7.8 are due to merge operations. Since the buffer load in the experiment is 250,000 documents, LOGARITHMIC MERGE performs a complete remerge whenever $2^k \cdot 250{,}000$ documents have been added to the index (e.g., after 4 million, 8 million, 16 million documents). This remerge results in an on-disk index composed of only a single partition. In terms of query performance, then, for a short period of time there is no difference between LOGARITHMIC MERGE and IMMEDIATE MERGE, as both methods have a fragmentation-free index.

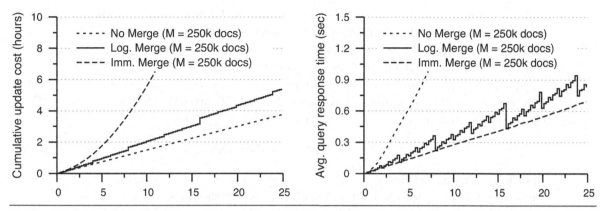

Figure 7.8   Overall performance of Logarithmic Merge, compared to No Merge and Immediate Merge. Data set: GOV2 (25.2 million documents). Horizontal axis: Number of documents indexed ($\times 10^6$).

7.3   Document Deletions

Although support for incremental updates might be sufficient for some applications, in many realistic environments the search engine also needs to be able to deal with deletions. On the Internet, for example, it is quite common that existing Web pages disappear after a while. Such documents should no longer show up in the result list produced by the search engine. If the rate at which deletions occur is relatively small, and if it is tolerable that a small fraction of the search results refers to documents that are no longer available, then the Rebuild strategy from Section 7.1 can be an appropriate index maintenance policy. However, even then it might be advisable to exclude deleted documents from the search results shown to the user. If a search engine keeps referring its users to nonexistent documents, the users may quickly become frustrated and stop using that search engine.

7.3.1   Invalidation List

One possible way to ensure that deleted documents do not appear in the search results is to remove all corresponding postings from the index. Unfortunately, this would require reading each postings list, decompressing it, removing the obsolete postings, recompressing the list, and writing it back to disk. As in the case of incremental updates, it is not feasible to perform such an operation after every deletion. Instead, information about deleted documents can be accumulated in the search engine and maintained as an *invalidation list* used to filter out obsolete postings during the search process, or to filter out deleted documents before presenting the final search results to the user.

If the search engine is based on a document-oriented index, such as a docid index or a frequency index, then the invalidation list is simply a list of docids. If a schema-independent index is used instead, then the invalidation list is a sequence of (*start*, *end*) tuples indicating the start and end offsets of the deleted documents in the index address space.

Suppose an index has been created for five documents $D_1, \ldots, D_5$, containing 100, 200, 150, 100, and 200 tokens, respectively. Now D_2 and D_5 are deleted from the index. Then the invalidation list, in a schema-independent index representation, is

$$I = \langle (101, 300), (551, 750) \rangle . \tag{7.20}$$

Applying I to a postings list or to a set of search results is not very complicated. If the structural query operators from Section 5.2 have been implemented, then it is as simple as replacing each postings list P in the query tree with its filtered version $P^{(I)} = (P \not\subset I)$, where "$\not\subset$" denotes a *not-contained-in* relationship (see Table 5.2 on page 162 for the exact definition).

In practice, this approach works reasonably well, especially if the "$\not\subset$" operator is designed for *lazy evaluation* and allows efficient random access operations on the filtered list $P^{(I)}$. If, however, the search engine always eagerly computes the entire list $P^{(I)}$, regardless of whether it is actually needed for query processing, advanced operators such as the **next** method from Figure 2.5 (page 42) are likely to lose their advantage over simple linear index access strategies.

Although the general idea behind the invalidation list approach is rather simple, details of the implementation can have a great impact on the actual performance of the method — as is often the case. For example, even though we have claimed above that the invalidation list I should be applied to each individual postings list P, it is sometimes beneficial to reorder the query tree and apply I only after combining the postings lists P_i for all query terms T_i. Consider the query "to be or not to be", run against the Shakespeare collection. The phrase occurs only a single time in the collection (act 3, scene 1), whereas the individual terms appear between 2,425 times ("or") and 19,898 times ("to"). Thus, instead of finding the above phrase by intersecting the filtered postings lists $P_i^{(I)}$, filtering against I over and over again, it might be more efficient to intersect the unfiltered lists P_i and perform only a single application of "$(\ldots \not\subset I)$" at the very end of the computation.

The question of how to apply the invalidation list to a given query is closely tied to optimization problems in traditional (i.e., relational) database systems, in which the optimal query execution plan, among other factors, depends on the selectivity on each predicate in the query (see García-Molina et al. (2002) for an introduction to relational database systems). Translated back into the context of text retrieval, this means that, if a term tends to appear a lot in deleted documents, the invalidation list I should be applied directly to the term's postings list.

If queries are processed according to a Boolean AND of the query terms, then it may be sufficient to apply I to only one of the query terms because the application to the other terms is implicit from the semantics of the AND operator. For Boolean-OR queries, Büttcher and Clarke (2005b) suggest, as a rule of thumb, that it is usually advisable to apply the restriction as high in the query tree as possible. However, the optimal choice may very well be different from application to application and even from query to query.

collectGarbage $(P, I) \equiv$
1   ($startDeleted, endDeleted$) $\leftarrow$ **nextInterval**($I, -\infty$)
2   **for** $i \leftarrow 1$ **to** $|P|$ **do**
3   **if** $P[i] > endDeleted$ **then**
4   // find the next interval that may potentially contain $P[i]$
5   ($startDeleted, endDeleted$) $\leftarrow$ **nextInterval**($I, P[i] - 1$)
6   **if** $P[i] < startDeleted$ **then**
7   output $P[i]$
8   **else**
9   // garbage-collect the current posting

nextInterval $(I, current) \equiv$
10   $intervalEnd \leftarrow$ **next**($I.end, current$)
11   // $c_{I.end}$ now contains the cached position in the postings list $I.end$
12   // (see Figure 2.5 for details)
13   **if** $intervalEnd = \infty$ **then**
14      $intervalStart \leftarrow \infty$
15   **else**
16      $intervalStart \leftarrow I.start[c_{I.end}]$)
17   **return** ($intervalStart, intervalEnd$)

Figure 7.9   Garbage-collecting obsolete postings from a schema-independent postings list. The function **collectGarbage** takes two arguments: a postings list P and an invalidation list $I = (I.start[], I.end[])$ corresponding to deleted index ranges. It outputs the list of postings that are not covered by I. The helper function **nextInterval** returns the first interval in I ending after the index position *current*. It uses the function **next** shown in Figure 2.5 (page 42).

7.3.2   Garbage Collection

The invalidation list approach outlined above is viable only if the number of obsolete postings (i.e., postings referring to deleted documents) is small compared to the total number of postings in the index. Since inverted lists are usually organized in blocks of postings, with compression applied to each block as a whole (see Sections 4.3 and 6.3.2), it is likely that many obsolete postings have to be loaded into memory and decompressed during query processing, simply because they are in the same postings block as the non-obsolete postings needed to process the query. If the number of deleted documents keeps growing over time, the performance impact due to obsolete postings will become larger and larger, up to a point where the resulting degradation in query performance is no longer tolerable. Therefore, at some point all obsolete postings will have to be removed from the index, leading to a fresh index that contains only postings for documents that still exist. This process is referred to as *garbage collection*.

Garbage collection is usually performed in a list-by-list fashion. From an abstract point of view, it is not much different from query processing: We may simply apply the invalidation list I to each postings list P in the original index, which gives us a filtered list P' that is then added to the new, garbage-free index. However, there is a slight difference. Because we know that the new index created by the garbage collection process will contain all postings from the original index (except for the deleted ones, of course), there is no need for a lazy evaluation of the "$\mathcal{A}$" operator. Instead, each postings list P in the old index may be filtered eagerly against the invalidation list I, one posting at a time. Figure 7.9 shows a possible implementation of the per-list garbage collection procedure, utilizing the galloping-search-based implementation of the **next** index access method from Chapter 2 for fast intersection of the postings list P with the invalidation list I.

How often should the garbage collector be invoked? That depends primarily on how much of a query slowdown is tolerable by the application. For example, if a 10% drop in query performance is acceptable, then there is no good reason for running the garbage collector on an index that contains only 5% garbage postings. In general, it is advisable not to invoke the garbage collector too often. Garbage collection is very costly, even more so than an ordinary remerge operation. In addition to just reading the old index into memory and writing the new one back to disk, the system has to decompress postings and compute list intersections, which can easily add 30–40% to the already rather high cost of a normal remerge update. Hence, in order to keep the overall cost low, all garbage collection activity should be integrated into regular index merge operations, so that merger and garbage collector can share the cost of transferring the index from disk into memory and back to disk.

In practical implementations the garbage collection strategy is usually defined through a threshold parameter ρ. Whenever a merge operation needs to be carried out and the relative amount of garbage postings in the input indices exceeds the threshold ρ, that is, if

$$\frac{\#\text{garbage postings in the input indices}}{\#\text{postings in the input indices}} > \rho,$$

then the garbage collector is included in the merge operation.

Apart from its impact on query performance, the threshold ρ also affects the performance of the search engine's index update operations. If ρ is too small, the garbage collector is invoked too often and update performance suffers. Conversely, if ρ is too large, merge operations might entail too many garbage postings, which may reduce the system's update performance as well.

Figure 7.10 shows the outcome of an experiment in which we had the search engine index 50% (= 12.6 million documents) of the GOV2 collection. After the index had been built, interleaved insert/delete commands were sent to the engine, gradually increasing the size of the indexed collection, at a ratio of 9 deletions for every 10 insertions. The system's merge strategy was set to IMMEDIATE MERGE, with in-memory buffers large enough to accumulate postings for 250,000 documents. The total index update overhead was measured for different threshold values ρ.

The experimental results confirm our expectation that eagerly collecting all garbage postings in every single remerge operation yields suboptimal update performance. In fact, setting $\rho = 0$ in the experiment led to an index update overhead that was almost 20% higher than that achieved by $\rho = 0.1$. The third value tested, $\rho = 0.25$, led to an update performance somewhere in between, having the advantage of less frequent invocations of the garbage collector but shuffling around an excessive amount of obsolete postings during the remerge operations.

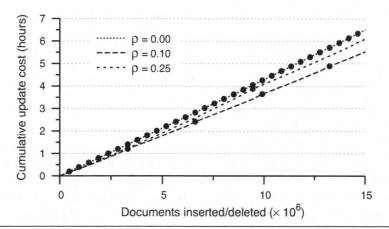

Figure 7.10   Non-incremental index updates with a delete/insert ratio of 0.9 (i.e., 9 deletions for every 10 insertions). Data set: GOV2. Memory limit: $M = 250,000$ documents. Remerge operations that include the garbage collector are indicated by a "•" symbol.

How can we find the threshold value that minimizes the overall update cost? We know that the cost of an ordinary merge operation without garbage collection is approximately linear in the number of postings in the input index and the output index:

$$C_{merge}(I_{in}, I_{out}) \ = \ c \cdot (\#postings(I_{in}) + \#postings(I_{out})), \tag{7.21}$$

for some system-specific constant c. Including the garbage collector increases the merge cost by 30–40%, as mentioned above. However, the main complexity of the garbage collection procedure stems from filtering the input lists against the invalidation list and thus is largely independent of the size of the output index I_{out}. We may therefore assume that the cost of a merge operation with integrated garbage collection is approximately

$$C_{merge+gc}(I_{in}, I_{out}) \ = \ c \cdot (1.6 \cdot \#postings(I_{in}) + \#postings(I_{out})), \tag{7.22}$$

for the same constant c as before.

Let us ignore the update cost caused by legitimate postings not corresponding to deleted documents and focus solely on the effect of garbage postings in the index. For a regular merge operation, the overhead caused by garbage postings is directly proportional to their quantity in the index:

$$O_{merge}(I_{in}, I_{out}) \ = \ c \cdot (\#garbage(I_{in}) + \#garbage(I_{out})). \tag{7.23}$$

Since, without garbage collection, we have $\#garbage(I_{in}) = \#garbage(I_{out})$, it follows:

$$O_{merge}(I_{in}, I_{out}) \ = \ 2c \cdot \#garbage(I_{in}). \tag{7.24}$$

For a merge operation with garbage collection, the overhead is

$$O_{merge+gc}(I_{in}, I_{out}) \;=\; c \cdot (\#garbage(I_{in}) + 0.6 \cdot \#postings(I_{in})) \tag{7.25}$$

because the system first needs to read the garbage postings (in addition to all legitimate postings) and then filter all postings, legitimate and garbage, against the invalidation list. This causes a 60% overhead.

Now suppose the garbage threshold ρ is chosen in such a way that the garbage collector is integrated in every n-th merge operation. Further suppose that we start with a fresh index containing P postings and no garbage, that the search engine accumulates M postings between each two subsequent remerge operations, and that the rate of document deletions, relative to the number of insertions, is g (e.g., $g = 0$ means no deletions at all; $g = 1$ means the system is in *steady state*, where the total number of documents in the index remains constant over time). Then the number of garbage postings participating in the k-th merge operation ($k \leq n$) is $k \cdot g \cdot M$. Hence, the total garbage-related update overhead of a sequence of n merge operations, the first $n - 1$ without garbage collection and the last one with garbage collection, is

$$O_{total}(n) \;=\; \sum_{k=1}^{n-1}(2kgM) + ngM + 0.6 \cdot (P + nM) \tag{7.26}$$

$$=\; (n-1)ngM + ngM + 0.6 \cdot (P + nM) \tag{7.27}$$

$$=\; n^2 gM + 0.6 \cdot nM + 0.6 \cdot P \tag{7.28}$$

(omitting the constant c, which is the same for all terms in the equation). The average overhead for each of the n merge operations is

$$O_{avg}(n) \;=\; \frac{O_{total}(n)}{n} \;=\; ngM + 0.6 \cdot M + 0.6 \cdot \frac{P}{n}. \tag{7.29}$$

Finding the optimal value n that minimizes $O_{avg}(n)$ is equivalent to finding the one that makes the derivative $\frac{d}{dn}(O_{avg}(n))$ become zero:

$$\frac{d}{dn}(O_{avg}(n)) = 0 \quad \Leftrightarrow \quad gM - 0.6 \cdot \frac{P}{n^2} = 0 \quad \Leftrightarrow \quad n = \sqrt{\frac{0.6 \cdot P}{gM}}. \tag{7.30}$$

We can now compute the optimal threshold value ρ_{opt} according to the inequality

$$\frac{(n_{opt} - 1) \cdot gM}{P + (n_{opt} - 1) \cdot M} \;<\; \rho_{opt} \;<\; \frac{n_{opt} \cdot gM}{P + n_{opt} \cdot M}. \tag{7.31}$$

For example, if nothing is ever deleted ($g = 0$), we obtain $n_{opt} = \infty$ and $\rho_{opt} = undefined$, that is, the garbage collector should never be invoked. If we have $P = 50 \cdot M$ and $g = 0.9$, as in the experiment shown in Figure 7.10, then the optimal values are $n_{opt} = \sqrt{33.3} \approx 6$ and

$0.082 < \rho_{opt} < 0.096$. The value $\rho = 0.1$, which performed best in the experiment, triggered the garbage collector for every seventh remerge operation, which was close to optimal.

It is worth pointing out that ρ_{opt}, since n_{opt} grows only as fast as $\sqrt{P}$, gets smaller as the index gets larger and P becomes the dominant term in Equation 7.31. Therefore, a constant garbage threshold ρ is advisable only if the size of the index is expected to stay approximately constant over time.

A two-tiered garbage collection policy

So far, we have discussed garbage collection only in the context of IMMEDIATE MERGE as the main update policy. Of course, garbage collection can also be integrated into update schemes that maintain more than one index partition, such as LOGARITHMIC MERGE, but doing so is slightly more complicated.

If the index is maintained according to IMMEDIATE MERGE, then we can be confident that every now and then a remerge operation will take place that involves all postings in the index. Before that operation starts, the search engine may compute the ratio of garbage postings versus all postings in the index, based on its internal deletion log. If the ratio exceeds the garbage collection threshold ρ, then the garbage collector is included in the merge operation.

Suppose the system is in steady state and the rate at which documents are deleted is approximately the same as the rate at which new documents are inserted. Then we know that the engine will accumulate about M garbage postings between two consecutive merge operations (where M is the system's memory capacity, measured in postings). If M is small compared to the total size of the index N, say $N > 10M$, then we know that the index's garbage ratio cannot grow by more than 10% between two remerge events. This allows us to keep the total amount of garbage well under control.

If an index-partitioning scheme is used, individual merge operations no longer necessarily involve the whole index. Hence, it is possible that garbage postings keep piling up in one of the older partitions that are rarely included in a merge. Let us assume that LOGARITHMIC MERGE is used as the update strategy and that the engine has just finished a merge operation, creating a new index partition I_g of generation g that contains $2^{g-1}M$ postings. The engine will index $2^{g-1}M$ tokens before the postings in I_g participate in their next merge event. Because the index is in steady state, $2^{g-1}M$ postings will have become obsolete by that point. Under the assumption that the obsolete postings are uniformly distributed across the whole index, $2^{g-2}M$ of them will be in I_g. Hence, the relative amount of garbage in I_g is 50%, and the relative amount of garbage in the whole index is somewhere between 33% and 50%, depending on how eagerly garbage postings are removed from the younger index partitions $I_1, \ldots, I_{g-1}$. For many applications this is too much.

The above problem can be addressed by defining two threshold values ρ and ρ' ($0 \le \rho < \rho'$). Whenever the system merges a set $\mathcal{S}$ of index partitions, it may take one of three possible actions:

1. If the relative amount of garbage in $\mathcal{S}$ exceeds ρ, then the garbage collector is included in the merge operation.

2. If the relative amount of garbage in the entire index exceeds ρ', then instead of merging only $\mathcal{S}$, the system merges all partitions in the index, collects all the garbage it can find, and produces a fresh index without any fragmentation or garbage.

3. If neither of the above conditions is met, then the engine performs an ordinary merge operation on the index partitions in $\mathcal{S}$, without removing any garbage.

This two-tiered garbage collection policy ensures that no excessive amounts of garbage pile up in the older index partitions. On the downside, it eliminates some of the performance advantages of index partitioning schemes such as LOGARITHMIC MERGE because full remerge operations now have to be carried out more often than before.

As a final note, it needs to be pointed out that the naïve version of LOGARITHMIC MERGE described in Section 7.2.2, even with a two-tiered garbage collection policy, will not work very well in the presence of deletions. The whole concept of *index generations* breaks down if the output partition of a merge operation can be smaller than the input partitions, which may happen when there are many garbage postings in the index. The algorithm in Figure 7.7 (page 240) needs to be modified so that it considers the size of the individual partitions (as opposed to their generation number) when deciding which partitions to include in the next merge operation.

7.4   Document Modifications

The third type of update operation is document modification. Most search engines do not employ any special strategies to deal with this type of update but instead treat each modification as a deletion followed by the re-insertion of the new version of the document. If each document is small compared to the total size of the collection, this approach usually leads to acceptable performance. However, it breaks down when applied to relatively small modifications to relatively large documents.

As an illustrative example, consider the log files maintained by a UNIX-like operating system (e.g., `/var/log/messages` in Linux). When searching over these log files, it is often useful to perform search operations that can match multiple log entries at the same time — for instance, to identify recurring patterns such as unauthorized intrusion attempts. Although the log file as a whole can be very large, potentially tens or hundreds of megabytes, each update involves only a single line, typically a few dozen or maybe a few hundred bytes. Re-indexing the entire file after every update is clearly not feasible. Treating each line in the log file as a separate document, on the other hand, is not a good solution, either; it prevents us from specifying search constraints that involve multiple consecutive lines. It would be convenient to have an index update mechanism that reflects the nature of the update operation applied to the file.

Unfortunately, this is extremely difficult to accomplish using the established index maintenance framework outlined in the previous sections of this chapter. For instance, suppose that we are dealing with a positional index containing postings of the form

$$(d, \; f_{t,d}, \; \langle p_1, \ldots, p_{f_{t,d}} \rangle) \tag{7.32}$$

and that the search engine employs the LOGARITHMIC MERGE update strategy from Section 7.2.2. If the search engine's reaction to a file append operation is simply to index the new tokens and write the corresponding postings to disk when it runs out of memory, then we will end up with multiple postings for the same (*term, document*) pair, each in a different index partition. This causes complications for query processing and index updates:

- If the search engine maintains n independent index partitions, then a call to the **next** method (see page 33) requires n random access operations instead of just one because each of the n partitions may contain a fragment of the result posting.
- The garbage collection mechanism from Section 7.3.2 can no longer be carried out on a single index partition, as the postings that correspond to the deleted documents may be scattered across the entire index. This implies that each invocation of the garbage collector must trigger a remerge of the entire index.

Büttcher (2007, ch. 6) presents an update method based on a schema-independent index with dynamic address space translation that can partially address the above problems. However, it comes at the cost of an increased memory consumption and a reduced query processing performance and is therefore not always desirable.

Because it is not clear how to deal with the problem of arbitrary document modifications (or even simple append operations of the type described above) in a satisfactory way, it is often simply ignored. Most desktop search systems, for example, index only the first few kilobytes of each file/document and ignore the rest. This allows them to treat each file modification as a combination of a deletion and an insertion without having to re-index many megabytes of text.

7.5 Discussion and Further Reading

The first comparative evaluation of in-place and remerge index maintenance found in the literature is given by Cutting and Pedersen (1990), who find that remerge update usually performs better. Their implementation of in-place update, however, based on an on-disk B-tree with in-memory caching for recently accessed tree nodes, is quite different from in-place update schemes used today. Lester et al. (2004, 2006), more than a decade later and using more up-to-date implementations of the various update schemes, conduct a performance comparison of INPLACE, REBUILD, and REMERGE. Their experiments confirm Cutting and Pedersen's finding that in-place update is competitive only if memory resources are extremely scarce and on-disk index updates have to be carried out often.

Zobel et al. (1993) discuss a storage management scheme for variable-length records and its application to in-place index maintenance. Shieh and Chung (2005) describe a variant of INPLACE in which the pre-allocation factor is term-dependent and is computed based on historical data on inverted INPLACE implementation with constant pre-allocation factor.

The hybrid index maintenance strategy from Section 7.2.1, dividing the index into an in-place-updated section and a merge-maintained section, is due to Büttcher and Clarke (2006, 2008). It is similar in spirit to the *pulsing* method described by Cutting and Pedersen (1990). Related dual-structure index organizations are explored by Shoens et al. (1994) and Tomasic et al. (1994).

Logarithmic merging is studied by Büttcher and Clarke (2005a) and, in its more general form, known as *geometric partitioning*, by Lester et al. (2005). Both studies find that the method can reduce the search engine's index maintenance overhead dramatically, at the cost of a minor query slowdown, usually less than 20%. They conclude that logarithmic merging is often an appropriate choice in the wide indexing-time-versus-query-time performance trade-off spectrum. A hybridization of LOGARITHMIC MERGE is discussed by Büttcher et al. (2006).

Despite their great potential, index-partitioning schemes such as logarithmic merging can play out their full advantage only if the index is a pure inverted index. In some applications, such as Web search, the index will also contain some auxiliary information that is used for ranking purposes: anchor text, PageRank scores, and so on (see Chapter 15). In that case, adding a document D_1 may affect the index data for a document D_2 because D_1 may contain a link to D_2. A document insertion then is no longer a local event affecting only a single document but must be assumed to have global consequences, leaving INPLACE/REBUILD/REMERGE as the only feasible solutions. Alternatively, one might decide to ignore the application-specific components of the index for the sake of improved performance and update anchor information and PageRank scores only once in a while. However, the effect that such an approach would have on the search engine's effectiveness and on the happiness of its users has not been studied.

Ways to deal with document deletions are discussed by Chiueh and Huang (1998) and by Büttcher and Clarke (2005a). Chiueh and Huang's approach is especially interesting; they propose to integrate the garbage collector not only into the search engine's merge operations but also into the query processing logic: Whenever a query term's postings list is fetched from the index, it is filtered against the current invalidation list and the garbage-free list is put back into the index.

Lim et al. (2003) discuss a method that can be used to speed up index maintenance in the presence of content-preserving changes to the document collection (i.e., document modifications). They show that their *landmark-diff* method can reduce the index maintenance overhead by about 50% compared to a REBUILD baseline. However, given that a large portion of the total index construction cost stems from reading and tokenizing the input data (see Section 4.5.3), and given that the performance numbers in their paper do not include the time needed to produce the `diff` between the old and the new version of each document, it is unclear how the method would perform in practice.

In our discussion of index maintenance strategies, we have ignored the implications of blocking index updates. For example, the IMMEDIATE MERGE algorithm in Figure 7.2 performs a merge operation whenever it runs out of memory. While this merge operation is going on, no postings can be added to the index. In the case of GOV2, merging the in-memory index with the existing on-disk index can take up to one hour — hardly fast enough to qualify as *real-time*. Strohman (2005) describes a set of techniques (e.g., background disk I/O) that can be used to support true real-time update and query operations.

As a final note, it is worth pointing out that the performance of all index maintenance mechanisms described in this chapter is tightly coupled with the index compression techniques applied to the index. Merge operations, for instance, can easily take twice as long when carried out on an uncompressed or poorly compressed index, due to the increased disk I/O. Better compression rates translate directly into better update performance. For garbage collection, on the other hand, where a good portion of the complexity stems from decompressing and recompressing postings lists, it is important to choose a compression method that allows very efficient encoding and decoding; compression rates are not as important. In particular, nonparametric codes such as vByte (Section 6.3.4) should usually be preferred over parametric ones such as LLRUN (Section 6.3.2) because the former require only a single pass over the input data when encoding a given list.

7.6 Exercises

Exercise 7.1 Suppose the search engine employs an in-place update strategy to maintain its on-disk index. The in-memory buffers are large enough to hold 10 million postings and the search engine is indexing a text collection with Zipf parameter $\alpha = 1.33$ (GOV2). How many on-disk inverted lists need to be created or updated when the search engine runs out of memory? If each list update requires one disk seek, and each disk seek takes 10 ms, how long does it take to perform the disk seeks necessary to update all those lists?

Exercise 7.2 Suppose the search engine employs the INPLACE strategy with proportional pre-allocation (pre-allocation factor: $k = 2$). Prove that, for any given list, the total number of bytes transferred from/to disk is less than $5 \times s$, where s is the list's size in bytes. You may assume that all postings have constant size (e.g., 4 bytes).

Exercise 7.3 Section 7.2.2 states the index construction complexity of the basic LOGARITHMIC MERGE policy as $\Theta(N \cdot \log(N/M))$. Prove that the anticipatory version of LOGARITHMIC MERGE, performing multiway merge operations to avoid collisions, is also $\Theta(N \cdot \log(N/M))$.

Exercise 7.4 (project exercise) Implement the IMMEDIATE MERGE index maintenance strategy from Section 7.2.1. After finishing the implementation, your search engine should be able to process search queries over a newly added document immediately after the document has been added to the index, without having to wait for the next remerge operation.

7.7   Bibliography

Büttcher, S. (2007). *Multi-User File System Search*. Ph.D. thesis, University of Waterloo, Waterloo, Canada.

Büttcher, S., and Clarke, C. L. A. (2005a). *Indexing Time vs. Query Time Trade-offs in Dynamic Information Retrieval Systems*. Technical Report CS-2005-31. University of Waterloo, Waterloo, Canada.

Büttcher, S., and Clarke, C. L. A. (2005b). A security model for full-text file system search in multi-user environments. In *Proceedings of the 4th USENIX Conference on File and Storage Technologies*, pages 169–182. San Francisco, California.

Büttcher, S., and Clarke, C. L. A. (2006). A hybrid approach to index maintenance in dynamic text retrieval systems. In *Proceedings of the 28th European Conference on Information Retrieval*, pages 229–240. London, England.

Büttcher, S., and Clarke, C. L. A. (2008). Hybrid index maintenance for contiguous inverted lists. *Information Retrieval*, 11(3):175–207.

Büttcher, S., Clarke, C. L. A., and Lushman, B. (2006). Hybrid index maintenance for growing text collections. In *Proceedings of the 29th Annual International ACM SIGIR Conference on Research and Development in Information Retrieval*, pages 356–363. Seattle, Washington.

Chiueh, T., and Huang, L. (1998). *Efficient Real-Time Index Updates in Text Retrieval Systems*. Technical report. SUNY at Stony Brook, Stony Brook, New York.

Cutting, D. R., and Pedersen, J. O. (1990). Optimization for dynamic inverted index maintenance. In *Proceedings of the 13th Annual International ACM SIGIR Conference on Research and Development in Information Retrieval*, pages 405–411. Brussels, Belgium.

García-Molina, H., Ullman, J., and Widom, J. (2002). *Database Systems: The Complete Book*. Upper Saddle River, New Jersey: Prentice Hall.

Lester, N., Moffat, A., and Zobel, J. (2005). Fast on-line index construction by geometric partitioning. In *Proceedings of the 14th ACM Conference on Information and Knowledge Management*, pages 776–783. Bremen, Germany.

Lester, N., Zobel, J., and Williams, H. E. (2004). In-place versus re-build versus re-merge: Index maintenance strategies for text retrieval systems. In *Proceedings of the 27th Conference on Australasian Computer Science*, pages 15–22. Dunedin, New Zealand.

Lester, N., Zobel, J., and Williams, H. E. (2006). Efficient online index maintenance for contiguous inverted lists. *Information Processing & Management*, 42(4):916–933.

Lim, L., Wang, M., Padmanabhan, S., Vitter, J. S., and Agarwal, R. (2003). Dynamic maintenance of web indexes using landmarks. In *Proceedings of the 12th International Conference on World Wide Web*, pages 102–111. Budapest, Hungary.

Shieh, W. Y., and Chung, C. P. (2005). A statistics-based approach to incrementally update inverted files. *Information Processing & Management*, 41(2):275–288.

Shoens, K. A., Tomasic, A., and García-Molina, H. (1994). Synthetic workload performance analysis of incremental updates. In *Proceedings of the 17th Annual International ACM SIGIR Conference on Research and Development in Information Retrieval*, pages 329–338. Dublin, Ireland.

Strohman, T. (2005). *Dynamic Collections in Indri*. Technical Report IR-426. University of Massachusetts Amherst, Amherst, Massachusetts.

Tomasic, A., García-Molina, H., and Shoens, K. (1994). Incremental updates of inverted lists for text document retrieval. In *Proceedings of the 1994 ACM SIGMOD International Conference on Management of Data*, pages 289–300. Minneapolis, Minnesota.

Zobel, J., Moffat, A., and Sacks-Davis, R. (1993). Storage management for files of dynamic records. In *Proceedings of the 4th Australian Database Conference*, pages 26–38. Brisbane, Australia.

III   Retrieval and Ranking

8 Probabilistic Retrieval

In this chapter and the next we examine a number of IR models that have had substantial influence on both research and practice. In this chapter we present what is known as the *probabilistic model*. In Chapter 9 we cover what is known as the *language modeling* approach and related approaches. In the context of information retrieval, the word "model" has at least two distinct and important meanings (Ponte and Croft, 1998). In one sense it means "an abstraction of the retrieval task itself" (e.g., the vector space model). As we shall see, it may also be used in the sense of "statistical model", in reference to models of relevance or models of document content.

Although many IR models might be described as probabilistic, the term is usually associated with the methods arising from the work of Stephen Robertson, Karen Spärck Jones, and their colleagues at the City University London, at the University of Cambridge, and at Microsoft Research, Cambridge, beginning in the early 1970s. Over that period they developed the probabilistic retrieval model through a series of innovations that have led to its current status as one of the most successful IR models. The model has been adopted by other research groups who have incorporated its retrieval formulae into their experimental IR systems and have often proposed and evaluated extensions of their own.

The organization of this chapter closely follows the historical development of the model, highlighting each significant extension and innovation in turn. A substantial portion of the chapter builds toward Equation 8.48, the BM25 formula, which currently represents one of the best performing (and best-known) retrieval formulae within the field. Although the BM25 formula may be used without understanding the details of its development, we cover this development in considerable detail not only for its own sake but also as a worked example of the reasoning processes underlying much of IR theory.

The chapter concludes with an overview of relevance feedback, a query expansion technique closely associated with the probabilistic and vector space models. We also introduce an important extension to the BM25 formula, known as BM25F, which applies differential weights to terms appearing in different document elements, thus recognizing that the presence of a query term in a document's title may be a stronger indicator of relevance than that term's presence in the document's body.

8.1   Modeling Relevance

The probabilistic model takes as its starting point the Probability Ranking Principle introduced in Section 1.2.3:

> If an IR system's response to each query is a ranking of the documents in the collection in order of decreasing probability of relevance, the overall effectiveness of the system to its user will be maximized.

As we indicated in Section 1.2.3, this principle oversimplifies the retrieval problem in a number of important ways by ignoring issues such as novelty, specificity and exhaustivity. Nonetheless, it directly supplies us with the outline of a retrieval algorithm: Given a query, determine the probability of relevance for each document in the collection and sort the documents accordingly. Implementing this algorithm immediately leads us to what Spärck Jones et al. (2000a) call the "Basic Question", which we state in a slightly modified form:

> What is the probability that a user will judge *this* document relevant to *this* query?

We now turn to the problem of estimating this probability.

Following the approach taken by Lafferty and Zhai (2003) in their discussion of the probabilistic model, we translate the Basic Question into statistical notation by introducing three random variables: D for documents, Q for queries, and the binary random variable R for the user's judgment of relevance. For the random variable D you might view its sample space, or set of outcomes, as a collection of documents indexed by a search engine. You might then imagine a group of users typing queries into the same search engine, with the sample space for Q being any query that the search engine allows a user to express. The engine might require these queries to be term vectors, but for now we do not assume this limitation. Finally, the binary random variable R takes on the value either 1 or 0, relevant or not relevant. Using this notation, we translate the Basic Question into the problem of estimating the probability of a positive relevance judgment, which we express as follows:

$$p(R = 1 \mid D = d, Q = q). \tag{8.1}$$

This formula may be viewed as a probability mass function over documents and queries. As a notational convenience consistent with the practice in the research literature, we often simply write "D" to stand for "$D = d$" and "Q" to stand for "$Q = q$"; this gives

$$p(R = 1 \mid D, Q). \tag{8.2}$$

Similarly, we write "r" to mean "$R = 1$" and "$\bar{r}$" to mean "$R = 0$". Thus, we have

$$p(r \mid D, Q) \;=\; 1 - p(\bar{r} \mid D, Q). \tag{8.3}$$

Bayes' Theorem, a fundamental theorem in probability theory, states that

$$p(A \mid B) = \frac{p(B \mid A) \; p(A)}{p(B)}.$$

(8.4)

Applying Bayes' Theorem to Equation 8.3 gives

$$p(r \mid D, Q) = \frac{p(D, Q \mid r) \; p(r)}{p(D, Q)}, \quad \text{and}$$

(8.5)

$$p(\bar{r} \mid D, Q) = \frac{p(D, Q \mid \bar{r}) \; p(\bar{r})}{p(D, Q)}.$$

(8.6)

Now, rather than continue to work directly with probabilities, we switch to a *log-odds*, or *logit*, formulation that will simplify the presentation and manipulation of equations. Given a probability p, the logit of p is defined as

$$\text{logit}(p) = \log\left(\frac{p}{1-p}\right),$$

(8.7)

where the base of the logarithm may be chosen arbitrarily. Continuing the practice we follow throughout the book when choosing a specific base for an example or experiment, we choose a base of 2.

Log-odds has a number of useful properties. As p varies from 0 to 1, $\text{logit}(p)$ varies from $-\infty$ to ∞. If the odds are even (i.e., $p = 0.5$), then $\text{logit}(p) = 0$. Given two probabilities p and q, $\text{logit}(p) > \text{logit}(q)$ if and only if $p > q$. Thus log-odds and probability are *rank-equivalent* — ranking by one produces the same ordering as ranking by the other. Rank-equivalent transformations such as this one (also called *rank-preserving* or *order-preserving* transformations) represent a valuable tool for simplifying the development of IR models.

Taking the log-odds of Equation 8.2 and applying Bayes' Theorem (Equations 8.5 and 8.6) gives the following:

$$\log \frac{p(r \mid D, Q)}{1 - p(r \mid D, Q)} = \log \frac{p(r \mid D, Q)}{p(\bar{r} \mid D, Q)}$$

(8.8)

$$= \log \frac{p(D, Q \mid r) \; p(r)}{p(D, Q \mid \bar{r}) \; p(\bar{r})}.$$

(8.9)

An immediate benefit of switching to log-odds is that the term $p(D, Q)$ cancels out, and does not need to be estimated.

We may expand the joint probabilities in Equation 8.8 into conditional probabilities using the equality $p(D, Q \mid R) = p(D \mid Q, R) \cdot p(Q \mid R)$. Expanding the joint probabilities in this way and applying Bayes' Theorem a second time gives

$$\log \frac{p(D,Q\,|\,r)\;p(r)}{p(D,Q\,|\,\bar{r})\;p(\bar{r})} \;\; = \;\; \log \frac{p(D\,|\,Q,r)\;p(Q\,|\,r)\;p(r)}{p(D\,|\,Q,\bar{r})\;p(Q\,|\,\bar{r})\;p(\bar{r})} \tag{8.10}$$

$$= \;\; \log \frac{p(D\,|\,Q,r)\;p(r\,|\,Q)}{p(D\,|\,Q,\bar{r})\;p(\bar{r}\,|\,Q)} \tag{8.11}$$

$$= \;\; \log \frac{p(D\,|\,Q,r)}{p(D\,|\,Q,\bar{r})} + \log \frac{p(r\,|\,Q)}{p(\bar{r}\,|\,Q)}\,. \tag{8.12}$$

The term "$\log\left(p(r\,|\,Q)/p(\bar{r}\,|\,Q)\right)$" is independent of D. You might consider it an indicator of query difficulty. In any case it may be safely ignored for ranking purposes — another order-preserving transform — leaving us with the ranking formula

$$\log \frac{p(D\,|\,Q,r)}{p(D\,|\,Q,\bar{r})}\,. \tag{8.13}$$

This formula sits at the heart of the probabilistic retrieval model, and we will return to it several times as we examine various methods for estimating its value.

8.2   The Binary Independence Model

For our first attempt to estimate a value for Equation 8.13, we consider only the presence and absence of terms in documents and queries. We re-define the random variable D, representing documents, into a vector of binary random variables $D = \langle D_1, D_2, ...\rangle$ with one dimension for each term in the vocabulary $\mathcal{V}$ and with $D_i = 1$ indicating term presence and $D_i = 0$ indicating term absence. Similarly, we refine the random variable Q, representing queries, into a vector of binary random variables $Q = \langle Q_1, Q_2, ...\rangle$ with $Q_i = 1$ indicating term presence and $Q_i = 0$ indicating term absence.

We now make two strong assumptions. The first is an independence assumption:

Assumption T: Given relevance, terms are statistically independent.

In other words, given a positive relevance judgment, the presence or absence of one term does not depend on the presence or absence of any other terms. Similarly, given a negative relevance judgment, the presence or absence of one term does not depend on the presence or absence of any other terms. Naturally, if we do not condition on relevance, terms are not independent because there are usually multiple terms for which the probability of presence depends on relevance.

This assumption does not accurately reflect reality. For example, the presence of the term "shakespeare" in a document increases the probability that the terms "william", "hamlet", "stratford" and so on will also occur in the document. Nonetheless, the assumption does greatly simplify the problem of estimating a value for Equation 8.13. Independence assumptions such as this one are common in information retrieval. Methods developed under these assumptions often provide good performance despite their unrealistic nature.

As a result of this assumption we may rewrite the probabilities appearing in Equation 8.13 as the product of probabilities for the individual random variables associated with the dimensions of D:

$$p(D\,|\,Q,r) \;=\; \prod_{i=1}^{|\mathcal{V}|} p(D_i\,|\,Q,r) \quad \text{and} \tag{8.14}$$

$$p(D\,|\,Q,\bar{r}) \;=\; \prod_{i=1}^{|\mathcal{V}|} p(D_i\,|\,Q,\bar{r}). \tag{8.15}$$

Equation 8.13 then becomes

$$\log \frac{p(D\,|\,Q,r)}{p(D\,|\,Q,\bar{r})} \;=\; \sum_{i=1}^{|\mathcal{V}|} \log \frac{p(D_i\,|\,Q,r)}{p(D_i\,|\,Q,\bar{r})}. \tag{8.16}$$

Our second strong assumption links the appearance of a term in the query to the probability of its appearance in a relevant document, thus clarifying the role of the query as a bridge between a user's need and a document's relevance.

Assumption Q: The presence of a term in a document depends on relevance only when that term is present in the query.

To formalize this assumption we need to fix the query, giving $Q = q = \langle q_1, q_2, ...\rangle$, where each q_i is either 0 or 1. As a result of Assumption Q, if $q_i = 0$ then

$$p(D_i\,|\,Q,r) \;=\; p(D_i\,|\,Q,\bar{r}),$$

and therefore

$$\log \frac{p(D_i\,|\,Q,r)}{p(D_i\,|\,Q,\bar{r})} \;=\; 0.$$

The effect of this assumption is to change the summation in Equation 8.16 from a summation over all terms in the vocabulary to a summation over all terms in the query. Because conditioning on the query is now redundant, we can drop it and our ranking formula then becomes

$$\sum_{t\in q} \log \frac{p(D_t\,|\,r)}{p(D_t\,|\,\bar{r})}, \tag{8.17}$$

where D_t is the random variable corresponding to term t in the vector $\langle d_1, d_2, ...\rangle$.

Like Assumption T, Assumption Q does not accurately reflect reality. If we are interested in the marriage of William Shakespeare and enter the query

$$\langle \text{ "william", "shakespeare", "marriage" } \rangle,$$

a relevant document is much more likely to contain the term "hathaway" than one that is nonrelevant, even though this term does not appear in the query. Nonetheless, from a practical standpoint a summation over query terms appears more tractable than a summation over all terms in the vocabulary, and we greet this development with a certain amount of relief.

We now fix $D = d = \langle d_1, d_2, ... \rangle$, where each d_i is either 0 or 1, thus making explicit the values of the random variables. Extending our earlier notation, we then write $D_t = d_t$ to represent the value of the random variable from $\langle d_1, d_2, ... \rangle$ corresponding to the term t:

$$\sum_{t \in q} \log \frac{p(D_t = d_t \,|\, r)}{p(D_t = d_t \,|\, \bar{r})} \tag{8.18}$$

We then subtract from Equation 8.18 its own value when no query terms appear in the document and all D_t are 0:

$$\sum_{t \in q} \log \frac{p(D_t = d_t \,|\, r)}{p(D_t = d_t \,|\, \bar{r})} \; - \; \sum_{t \in q} \log \frac{p(D_t = 0 \,|\, r)}{p(D_t = 0 \,|\, \bar{r})} \tag{8.19}$$

Because the value of Equation 8.18 when all query terms are absent is a constant, and because the subtraction of a constant value has no impact on ranking, the subtraction of this value represents another order-preserving transform. A little rearranging then gives:

$$\sum_{t \in (q \cap d)} \log \frac{p(D_t = 1 \,|\, r)\, p(D_t = 0 \,|\, \bar{r})}{p(D_t = 1 \,|\, \bar{r})\, p(D_t = 0 \,|\, r)} \; - \; \sum_{t \in (q \backslash d)} \log \frac{p(D_t = 0 \,|\, r)\, p(D_t = 0 \,|\, \bar{r})}{p(D_t = 0 \,|\, \bar{r})\, p(D_t = 0 \,|\, r)}, \tag{8.20}$$

where the summation on the left is over all terms appearing in both the query and the document, and the summation on the right is over terms appearing in the query but not in the document. Because the term on the right is 0, the equation becomes

$$\sum_{t \in (q \cap d)} \log \frac{p(D_t = 1 \,|\, r)\, p(D_t = 0 \,|\, \bar{r})}{p(D_t = 1 \,|\, \bar{r})\, p(D_t = 0 \,|\, r)}. \tag{8.21}$$

This refinement of Equation 8.13 under assumptions T and Q, and considering only the presence and absence of terms, is known as the *Binary Independence Model*.

8.3   The Robertson/Spärck Jones Weighting Formula

For simplicity we now make a substantial shift in notation, clearing away the clutter of Equation 8.21 and rewriting it as

$$\sum_{t\in(q\cap d)} w_t, \qquad (8.22)$$

where w_t is a weight associated with each term. If we let $p_t = p(D_t = 1\,|\,r)$ and $\bar{p}_t = p(D_t = 1\,|\,\bar{r})$, then w_t becomes

$$w_t = \log \frac{p_t\,(1-\bar{p}_t)}{\bar{p}_t\,(1-p_t)} \qquad (8.23)$$

because $p(D_t = 0\,|\,r) = 1 - p(D_t = 1\,|\,r) = 1 - p_t$ and $p(D_t = 0\,|\,\bar{r}) = 1 - p(D_t = 1\,|\,\bar{r}) = 1 - \bar{p}_t$.

Estimates for p_t and $\bar{p}_t$ may be determined if we have estimates for the expected number of relevant documents in the collection and the expected number of relevant documents containing t. These estimates might be obtained, for example, by sampling the collection and making a relevance judgment for each document in the sample. Although such an effort would be impossibly onerous to undertake for every query, it might not be unreasonable when we plan to execute a query many times, perhaps because the collection changes on a regular basis.

For a given query let N_r be the expected number of relevant documents in the collection and let $N_{t,r}$ be the expected number of relevant documents containing the term t. We may then estimate p_t and $\bar{p}_t$ as

$$p_t = \frac{N_{t,r}}{N_r} \quad\text{and}\quad \bar{p}_t = \frac{N_t - N_{t,r}}{N - N_r}, \qquad (8.24)$$

where N is the number of documents in the collection and N_t is the number of documents containing t. Substituting into Equation 8.23 gives the weight

$$w_t = \log \frac{N_{t,r}\,(N - N_t - N_r + N_{t,r})}{(N_r - N_{t,r})\,(N_t - N_{t,r})}. \qquad (8.25)$$

When we have actual counts of relevant and nonrelevant documents available, this formula is often written

$$w_t = \log \frac{(n_{t,r}+0.5)\,(N - N_t - n_r + n_{t,r}+0.5)}{(n_r - n_{t,r}+0.5)\,(N_t - n_{t,r}+0.5)}, \qquad (8.26)$$

where n_r represents the count of relevant documents and $n_{t,r}$ represents the count of relevant documents containing t. The value 0.5, which appears throughout the equation, *smooths* the counts so that, for example, counts of 0 do not lead to an unreasonable (i.e., infinite) weight. As mentioned in Chapter 1, this type of simple smoothing is common in information retrieval, as well as in other statistical natural language processing applications.

You may find Equations 8.25 and 8.26 reminiscent of the inverse document frequency (IDF) formula introduced in Chapter 2 (Equation 2.13) because the number of documents N appears in the numerator and the number of documents containing the term N_t appears the denominator.

To push this observation a little further, we rewrite Equation 8.23 into a form with two terms, one related to relevance and one related to nonrelevance:

$$w_t = \log \frac{p_t}{1-p_t} + \log \frac{1-\bar{p}_t}{\bar{p}_t} \tag{8.27}$$

$$= \log \frac{N_{t,r}}{N_r - N_{t,r}} + \log \frac{N - N_r - N_t + N_{t,r}}{N_t - N_{t,r}}. \tag{8.28}$$

The term on the left is the log-odds of a relevant document containing the term t. If we assume that both N_r and $N_{t,r}$ are small relative to both N and N_t, which may not be unreasonable for relatively common terms over a large collection, we can approximate the term on the right by setting $N_r = N_{t,r} = 0$, giving

$$w_t = \text{logit}(p_t) + \log \frac{N - N_t}{N_t}. \tag{8.29}$$

The resemblance to IDF becomes stronger. Croft and Harper (1979), who derived this formula, note that if $p_t = 0.5$ and N_t is small relative to N, then the standard IDF formula approximates this formula. Robertson and Walker (1997) note that if we set $p_t = 1/(1 + ((N - N_t)/N))$ then the formula becomes

$$w_t = \log \frac{N}{N_t}, \tag{8.30}$$

the standard IDF formula.

Equation 8.23 is called the *Robertson/Spärck Jones weighting formula*. Depending on available relevance information, we may use any of Equations 8.25, 8.26, or 8.30 to estimate its value. Robertson and Walker (1997) suggest additional blended variants for use when minimal relevance information is available. Throughout the remainder of the chapter, the appearance of w_t implies any or all of these variants.

When no relevance information is available, it is generally acceptable to assume that w_t represents the standard IDF formula. It is also acceptable to use Equation 8.26 by setting $n_r = n_{t,r} = 0$, but care must be taken to make certain that the weight is not negative (see Exercise 8.2). If the weight would be negative, a weight of 0 should be used instead.

When relevance information is available, it is normal practice to use Equation 8.26 even when we do not have accurate estimates for $N_{t,r}$ and N_r. For example, after executing a query a search engine might ask the user to identify a small number of relevant documents. If the user identifies three relevant documents, two of which contain the term t, we would set $n_r = 3$ and $n_{t,r} = 2$. Once again, care should be taken to avoid negative weights.

Thus we come full circle back to IDF, a formulation that in Chapter 2 we justified only through intuition and experimentation. Although we traced a rocky path littered with unrealistic independence assumptions and crude approximations, we have now reached IDF through a theoretical route that has its starting point at the Probability Ranking Principle. This experience is typical of IR research. Successful retrieval approaches are often created and validated through a combination of theory and experiment with one supporting the other.

Unfortunately, in terms of the development of an effective ranking formula we have made little progress. Direct application of Equation 8.22 with no available relevance information amounts to nothing more than the vector space model of Chapter 2, with the TF factor set to a constant value of 1 and no document length normalization.

However, as a simple example we return to the document collection of Table 2.1 (page 50). We apply Equation 8.22, using the IDF estimate for w_t, to rank the collection with respect to the query $\langle$ "quarrel", "sir"$\rangle$. The collection contains $N = 5$ documents. Of these documents two contain the term "quarrel" and four contain the term "sir", giving IDF values as follows:

$$w_{\text{quarrel}} = \log(5/2) \approx 1.32, \quad w_{\text{sir}} = \log(5/4) \approx 0.32. \tag{8.31}$$

Using these weights, we assign a score of 1.64 to both document 1 and document 2, a score of 0.32 to both document 3 and document 5, and a score of zero to document 4. Because these scores reflect only term presence, documents 1 and 2 are tied, even though document 2 contains more occurrences of "sir".

8.4   Term Frequency

In Chapter 2 we list a number of simple document features used by basic ranking methods to compare documents and determine an appropriate ranking. These features include term frequency, term proximity, and document length. Thus far, our development of the probabilistic model has considered only term presence, essentially a weakened form of term frequency. In order to extend the model to fully accommodate term frequency, we must return to Equation 8.13 and reconsider our representation of documents by the random variable D.

At the start of Section 8.2 we refined our definition of the random variable D into a vector of binary random variables $D = \langle D_1, D_2, ...\rangle$, where each random variable D_i represents the presence or absence of a specific term. Returning to this point, we can retrace our steps with a revised definition for D as a vector of random variables $D = \langle F_1, F_2, ...\rangle$, where each F_i represents the within-document term frequency for the corresponding term. As we did in that section, we also define F_t as notation for the random variable from this vector corresponding to the term t.

Following a path similar to that taken through Section 8.2, leaving Assumptions T and Q unchanged, and making minor adjustments to the argument in order to accommodate our switch from term presence to term frequency, brings us to the following analogue of Equation 8.21:

$$\sum_{t \in q} \log \frac{p(F_t = f_t \mid r) \; p(F_i = 0 \mid \bar{r})}{p(F_t = f_t \mid \bar{r}) \; p(F_i = 0 \mid r)}, \tag{8.32}$$

where f_t represents the number of times t appears in the document (see Exercise 8.3). For this equation to be usable we must estimate values for $p(F_t = f_t \mid r)$ and $p(F_t = f_t \mid \bar{r})$, the term frequency probabilities given relevance and nonrelevance. In order to estimate these values, we must in turn consider the relationship between term frequency and relevance.

When writing a document about a particular topic, an author will generally choose terms related to that topic. As a result, when a term is associated with a particular topic, we might expect that term to appear more frequently in a document about the topic than in a document not about the topic. On the other hand that term will still occasionally appear in documents not related to the topic.

Bookstein and Swanson (1974) attempt to capture this relationship between topics and terms with a notion that Robertson et al. (1981) and Robertson and Walker (1994) call *eliteness*. A document is said to be *elite* in term t when it is somehow "about" the topic associated with the term. By turning this relationship around it may thus be possible for us to infer a probability of eliteness from term frequency — the greater the term frequency, the more likely that the term is elite in the document. Thus, the relationship between relevance and term frequency flows through this notion of eliteness. Roughly, documents about a topic are more likely to be elite in the terms related to that topic and therefore these terms are more likely to appear in these documents.

For each term we define a binary random variable E_t corresponding to each F_t and representing eliteness of the term t. $E_t = 1$ indicates that a document is elite in t, and $E_t = 0$ indicates that the document is not elite in t. Much as we did for relevance, we define e as shorthand for $E_t = 1$ and $\bar{e}$ as shorthand for $E_t = 0$. We omit the subscript t in this shorthand notation because the term being referenced is usually obvious. The relationship between relevance and term frequency may then be formalized as follows:

$$
\begin{aligned}
p(F_t = f_t \mid r) &= p(F_t = f_t \mid e) \cdot p(e \mid r) + p(F_t = f_t \mid \bar{e}) \cdot p(\bar{e} \mid r) \quad \text{and} \\
p(F_t = f_t \mid \bar{r}) &= p(F_t = f_t \mid e) \cdot p(e \mid \bar{r}) + p(F_t = f_t \mid \bar{e}) \cdot p(\bar{e} \mid \bar{r}).
\end{aligned}
\tag{8.33}
$$

Substituting these expansions into the term of Equation 8.32 gives

$$
\sum_{t \in q} \log \frac{(p(F_t = f_t \mid e)p(e \mid r) + p(F_t = f_t \mid \bar{e})p(\bar{e} \mid r))(p(F_t = 0 \mid e)p(e \mid \bar{r}) + p(F_t = 0 \mid \bar{e})p(\bar{e} \mid \bar{r}))}{(p(F_t = f_t \mid e)p(e \mid \bar{r}) + p(F_t = f_t \mid \bar{e})p(\bar{e} \mid \bar{r}))(p(F_t = 0 \mid e)p(e \mid r) + p(F_t = 0 \mid \bar{e})p(\bar{e} \mid r))}.
$$

We now turn to the problem of estimating the individual probabilities in this equation.

8.4.1 Bookstein's Two-Poisson Model

We can make our somewhat vague notion of eliteness more concrete by positing a specific distribution for terms in documents as a mixture of two *Poisson distributions*, with one Poisson distribution corresponding to documents that are elite in the term and the other corresponding to documents that are not elite in the term. This two-Poisson distribution was suggested by

Bookstein (see Harter, 1975, page 199) and was subsequently developed and validated by Harter (1975), Bookstein and Swanson (1974), Bookstein and Kraft (1977), and Robertson et al. (1981).

The Poisson distribution, invented by the French mathematician Siméon Denis Poisson in 1838, is often used to model the number of events or arrivals of some defined type that occur within a given time period. For example, a Poisson distribution might be used to model the number of car accidents per year at a particular intersection, the number of times a Web server is accessed each minute, or the number of alpha particles emitted by a gram of uranium-238 in one second. Events occurring in one time period are assumed to be *stochastically independent* of events occurring in another nonoverlapping time period. That is to say, the number of events in one time period has no influence on the number of events occurring in a separate time period. In our case we use the Poisson distribution to model the number of occurrences of a given term in a document, with the occurrence of a term representing an "event" and the document as a whole taking on the role of a "time period".

Given a random variable X over the nonnegative integers and a real valued parameter μ representing the mean number events in a given period, the Poisson distribution is defined as

$$g(x, \mu) \;=\; \frac{e^{-\mu}\mu^{x}}{x!}\,. \tag{8.34}$$

In order to use this distribution to model term distribution, we need to assume that all documents are of equal length. Because a collection may contain both books and e-mail messages that differ in length by a factor of 1,000 or more, this assumption is not at all realistic. Nonetheless, we accept the assumption for now and revisit it later in the chapter.

To construct the two-Poisson distribution, we assume different means for elite and nonelite documents — μ_e and $\mu_{\bar{e}}$ — with the notion of eliteness requiring that $\mu_e > \mu_{\bar{e}}$. If we let $q = p(e\,|\,r)$ and $\bar{q} = p(e\,|\,\bar{r})$ and substitute into Equation 8.33, we get the following equations, which constitute our two models for relevant and nonrelevant documents:

$$p(F_t = f_t\,|\,r) \;=\; g(f_t, \mu_e) \cdot q + g(f_t, \mu_{\bar{e}}) \cdot (1 - q), \tag{8.35}$$

$$p(F_t = f_t\,|\,\bar{r}) \;=\; g(f_t, \mu_e) \cdot \bar{q} + g(f_t, \mu_{\bar{e}}) \cdot (1 - \bar{q}). \tag{8.36}$$

Substituting into Equation 8.32 gives

$$\sum_{t \in q} \log \frac{(g(f_t, \mu_e)\, q + g(f_t, \mu_{\bar{e}})\,(1 - q)) \cdot (g(0, \mu_e)\, \bar{q} + g(0, \mu_{\bar{e}})\,(1 - \bar{q}))}{(g(f_t, \mu_e)\, \bar{q} + g(f_t, \mu_{\bar{e}})\,(1 - \bar{q})) \cdot (g(0, \mu_e)\, q + g(0, \mu_{\bar{e}})\,(1 - q))}\,. \tag{8.37}$$

Although the term weight in this equation may appear complex at first glance, its structure is actually fairly simple. Each factor appearing in the numerator and the denominator is a mixture of the same two Poisson distributions representing eliteness and noneliteness. For a given term there are four parameters to be determined: μ_e, $\mu_{\bar{e}}$, q, and $\bar{q}$. It is conceivable that these parameters could be estimated from term statistics by determining the set of parameters that provides the best fit between this term weight and the actual distribution of terms in the collection.

Unfortunately, although various researchers have made attempts along these lines, little success has been reported. In particular, eliteness is a hidden variable that we cannot directly observe, which greatly complicates the estimation process. Nonetheless, we can make several valuable observations from this term weight.

First, when a term is absent ($f_t = 0$) the term weight assigns a value of 0, as we might expect. Second, as f_t increases, the assigned weight also increases. Again, this behavior is consistent with our expectations.

Finally, we consider the behavior of the weight as the number of terms goes to infinity ($f_t \to \infty$). With some rearrangement, Equation 8.37 becomes

$$\sum_{t \in q} \log \frac{\left(q + \frac{g(f_t, \mu_{\bar{e}})}{g(f_t, \mu_e)} (1 - q) \right) \left(\frac{g(0, \mu_e)}{g(0, \mu_{\bar{e}})} \bar{q} + (1 - \bar{q}) \right)}{\left(\bar{q} + \frac{g(f_t, \mu_{\bar{e}})}{g(f_t, \mu_e)} (1 - \bar{q}) \right) \left(\frac{g(0, \mu_e)}{g(0, \mu_{\bar{e}})} q + (1 - q) \right)}. \tag{8.38}$$

Now

$$\frac{g(f_t, \mu_{\bar{e}})}{g(f_t, \mu_e)} = \frac{e^{-\mu_{\bar{e}}} \mu_{\bar{e}}^{f_t}}{e^{-\mu_e} \mu_e^{f_t}} = e^{\mu_e - \mu_{\bar{e}}} \cdot \left(\frac{\mu_{\bar{e}}}{\mu_e} \right)^{f_t},$$

which goes to 0 as f_t goes to infinity because $\mu_{\bar{e}} < \mu_e$, and

$$\frac{g(0, \mu_e)}{g(0, \mu_{\bar{e}})} = e^{\mu_{\bar{e}} - \mu_e}.$$

Thus, as $f_t \to \infty$, the term weight in Equation 8.38 goes to

$$\log \frac{q \left(\bar{q} e^{\mu_{\bar{e}} - \mu_e} + (1 - \bar{q}) \right)}{\bar{q} \left(q e^{\mu_{\bar{e}} - \mu_e} + (1 - q) \right)}, \tag{8.39}$$

a constant for any given term. Thus, as the number of terms increases, the weight *saturates*, reaching an asymptotic maximum given by Equation 8.39. In other words, there is a limit to how much the repetition of a term can contribute to a document's score. Moreover, if we assume that $e^{\mu_{\bar{e}} - \mu_e}$ is small, contributing little to the weight, we may approximate it with 0. The weight then becomes

$$\log \frac{q (1 - \bar{q})}{\bar{q} (1 - q)}. \tag{8.40}$$

The resemblance between this weight and the Robertson/Spärck Jones weight given in Equation 8.23 is more than coincidental. This equation is the analogue of Equation 8.23 when term presence is replaced by the notion of eliteness. We might even view Equation 8.23 as an approximation to Equation 8.40.

8.4.2   Approximating the Two-Poisson Model

Based on the observations we listed regarding Equation 8.37, Robertson and Walker (1994) suggest a simple approximation to the two-Poisson term weight, which we write as

$$\sum_{t \in q} \frac{f_{t,d}\,(k_1 + 1)}{k_1 + f_{t,d}} \cdot w_t \,, \tag{8.41}$$

where $f_{t,d}$ represents the frequency of term t in document d, w_t represents any variant of the Robertson/Spärck Jones weight, and $k_1 > 0$.

Consistent with our observations the term weight is 0 when $f_{t,d} = 0$ and grows with increasing $f_{t,d}$. When $f_{t,d} = 1$, the weight is equal to w_t. As $f_{t,d} \to \infty$ the weight goes to $(k_1 + 1)w_t$. Thus, the weight saturates to a constant factor of the Robertson/Spärck Jones weight, consistent with Equation 8.38.

Typically, $1 \le k_1 < 2$, with the same value used for all terms in all queries. We use $k_1 = 1.2$ as our default value for examples and experiments because this value is often accepted as the default value in the research literature. In practice, since k_1 is the same for all terms in all queries, we may treat it as a system parameter and tune its value to optimize effectiveness over the collection and application environment. Chapter 11 covers methods for parameter tuning in this and other retrieval formulae.

Returning again to the example document collection in Table 2.1 (page 50), we apply Equation 8.41 to rank the collection with respect to the query $\langle$"quarrel","sir"$\rangle$. We compute a score for document 1 of

$$\frac{f_{\text{quarrel},1}\,(k_1 + 1)}{k_1 + f_{\text{quarrel},1}} \cdot w_{\text{quarrel}} + \frac{f_{\text{sir},1}\,(k_1 + 1)}{k_1 + f_{\text{sir},1}} \cdot w_{\text{sir}} \approx \frac{k_1 + 1}{k_1 + 1} \cdot 1.32 + \frac{k_1 + 1}{k_1 + 1} \cdot 0.32 \approx 1.64$$

and a score for document 2 of

$$\frac{f_{\text{quarrel},2}\,(k_1 + 1)}{k_1 + f_{\text{quarrel},2}} \cdot w_{\text{quarrel}} + \frac{f_{\text{sir},2}\,(k_1 + 1)}{k_1 + f_{\text{sir},2}} \cdot w_{\text{sir}} \approx \frac{k_1 + 1}{k_1 + 1} \cdot 1.32 + \frac{2(k_1 + 1)}{k_1 + 2} \cdot 0.32 \approx 1.76.$$

The additional occurrence of "sir" in document 2 leads to a higher score. Note, however, that even a document containing an infinite number of occurrences of "sir" but no occurrences of "quarrel" could receive a score lower than a document containing a single occurrence of "quarrel". Documents 3 and 5 both receive a score of 0.32, even though the difference in length might suggest that one should be ranked above the other. Document 4 receives a score of zero because it contains none of the query terms.

Note that the term weight in Equation 8.41 belongs to the TF-IDF family. However, the saturation property represents a critical difference between this weight and other weights introduced in the research literature, such as Equation 2.14. As the example demonstrates, the saturation property places a limit on the impact that a term can have on a document's score, regardless of the number of times it occurs.

8.4.3   Query Term Frequency

Equation 8.41 may be extended to encompass query term frequency q_t — the number of times term t appears in the query — by drawing a parallel with document term frequency. Repetition of query terms in short queries may be relatively unusual. However, as we mention in Chapter 2 an entire document might be used as a query in some circumstances, perhaps to implement a "More Like This" feature. Similarly, a user might easily generate a longer query by copying a passage from a document and pasting it into a search engine.

If we view a document as a potential query, a symmetry between queries and documents becomes apparent, suggesting a query term frequency factor of the form

$$\frac{q_t\,(k_3 + 1)}{k_3 + q_t}\,, \tag{8.42}$$

where $k_3 > 0$ is a system parameter similar to k_1. (Use of k_3 is standard for this parameter because the symbol k_2 was used for other purposes in some of the research literature related to the probabilistic model.) Incorporating this factor into Equation 8.41 gives

$$\sum_{t \in q} \frac{q_t\,(k_3 + 1)}{k_3 + q_t} \cdot \frac{f_{t,d}\,(k_1 + 1)}{k_1 + f_{t,d}} \cdot w_t\,. \tag{8.43}$$

However, notwithstanding those occasions when the query is very long, the repetition of a term in a query can be a much stronger indicator of the term's significance than repetition in a document. As a result typical values for k_3 are often much larger than the corresponding values for k_1. Indeed, it is not uncommon to set $k_3 = \infty$, thus reducing Equation 8.42 to q_t, its limit as $k_3 \to \infty$, and resulting in the ranking formula

$$\sum q_t \cdot \frac{f_{t,d}\,(k_1 + 1)}{k_1 + f_{t,d}} \cdot w_t\,. \tag{8.44}$$

If we wish, we may again view the summation as being over the entire vocabulary because terms not appearing in both the query and the document automatically receive a term weight of 0. As a result, and in keeping with a common practice in the research literature, we omit the range of the summation in the remainder of the chapter.

8.5   Document Length: BM25

Implicit in the two-Poisson model is the unrealistic assumption that all documents are the same length. One simple technique to account for varying document length is to normalize the actual term frequency $f_{t,d}$, scaling it according to the document length:

$$f'_{t,d} \;=\; f_{t,d} \cdot (l_{avg}/l_d)\,, \tag{8.45}$$

where l_d is the length of document d and l_{avg} is the average document length across the entire collection. This normalized term frequency may then be used in place of the actual term frequency in Equation 8.44:

$$\sum q_t \cdot \frac{f'_{t,d}\,(k_1+1)}{k_1 + f'_{t,d}} \cdot w_t \,. \tag{8.46}$$

Expanding and rearranging this equation gives

$$\sum q_t \cdot \frac{f_{t,d}\,(l_{avg}/l_d)\,(k_1+1)}{k_1 + f_{t,d}\,(l_{avg}/l_d)} \cdot w_t \;=\; \sum q_t \cdot \frac{f_{t,d}\,(k_1+1)}{k_1\,(l_d/l_{avg}) + f_{t,d}} \cdot w_t \,. \tag{8.47}$$

Although this adjustment is consistent with the two-Poisson model, the formula still may not be consistent with reality. Consider two documents, one twice as long as the other, with the longer containing twice as many occurrences of each query term as the shorter. Equation 8.47 assigns both documents the same score. Although these equal scores would be reasonable if the longer document consisted of the shorter document concatenated to itself, in reality we might expect the longer document to contain more information and perhaps be worthy of a higher score.

Robertson et al. (1994) suggest a blending of Equations 8.47 and 8.44 with a parameter b controlling the level of normalization for document length

$$\sum q_t \cdot \frac{f_{t,d}\,(k_1+1)}{k_1\,((1-b) + b\,(l_d/l_{avg})) + f_{t,d}} \cdot w_t \,, \tag{8.48}$$

where $0 \le b \le 1$. When $b = 0$ the equation is equivalent to Equation 8.44; when $b = 1$ the equation is equivalent to Equation 8.47. Like the parameter k_1 the parameter b is the same for all queries, and may be tuned to the collection and the environment of the IR system. In examples and experiments we use a default value of $b = 0.75$.

We have now reached a major milestone in the development of the probabilistic model. When only the basic features listed in Chapter 2 are available, Equation 8.48 represents one of the best-known methods for ranked retrieval. Although it debuted at TREC-3 in 1993, contemporaneous with the use of the vector space model of Chapter 2, it remains competitive with the more modern language modeling techniques presented in the next chapter. It often forms a baseline that newer methods may be judged against. Substantial performance improvements beyond what it can achieve generally require extensions that depend upon additional information, such as automatic query expansion, document structure, link structure, and machine learning techniques trained over large volumes of relevance information. We present one form of automatic query expansion, known as pseudo-relevance feedback, in the next section of this chapter. Considerations of document structure in the context of the probabilistic model are covered in Section 8.7. We will also return to the probabilistic model when we discuss machine learning and link structure in later chapters.

Equation 8.48 is widely known as "Okapi BM25", or just "BM25". Okapi is the name of the retrieval system, created by Robertson and co-workers at City University London, in which the equation was first implemented. The "BM" stands for "Best Match". BM25 is just one of a family of BM formulae implemented by versions of the Okapi system. Equation 8.22 is essentially BM1, Equation 8.47 is essentially BM11, and Equation 8.44 is essentially BM15. However, none of these methods matches the fame of BM25. In part this fame is due to it relative simplicity and effectiveness. Participants in TREC evaluations since TREC-5 have achieved reliable and respectable performance in many TREC tasks by creating and building upon their own implementations of BM25.

Consider the application of BM25 to rank the collection in Table 2.1 (page 50) with respect to the query $\langle$"quarrel", "sir"$\rangle$. The average document length is $l_{avg} = (4 + 4 + 16 + 2 + 2)/5 = 28/5 = 5.6$. Document 1 receives a score of

$$\frac{f_{\text{quarrel},1}\,(k_1 + 1)}{k_1\,((1 - b) + b\,(l_d/l_{avg})) + f_{\text{quarrel},1}} \cdot w_{\text{quarrel}} + \frac{f_{\text{sir},1}\,(k_1 + 1)}{k_1\,((1 - b) + b\,(l_d/l_{avg})) + f_{\text{sir},1}} \cdot w_{\text{sir}}$$

$$\approx \frac{k_1 + 1}{k_1\,((1 - b) + b\,(5/5.6)) + 1} \cdot 1.32 + \frac{k_1 + 1}{k_1\,((1 - b) + b\,(5/5.6)) + 1} \cdot 0.32 \approx 1.72$$

Similarly, document 2 receives a score of 1.98, document 3 receives a score of 0.18, document 4 receives a score of 0, and document 5 receives a score of 0.44. Although both document 3 and document 5 contain a single occurrence of the term "sir" and no occurrences of the term "quarrel", document 5 receives a higher score due to the difference in length between these documents.

8.6 Relevance Feedback

As Section 8.3 suggests, the availability of relevance information may improve our ability to estimate a value for w_t and consequently may improve retrieval performance. In one scenario for obtaining this information, the IR system conducts an initial search, presents the results to the user, and allows her to identify a number of relevant documents from these results. Even if these relevance judgments are few in number, they may be used to set values for n_r and $n_{t,r}$ in Equation 8.26. A final search is then conducted using these refined weights.

Perhaps more significantly, the system may also use these relevance judgments to obtain additional information on the nature of relevant documents. For example, we might select appropriate terms from the identified documents and add them to the query. This expanded query would then be used for the second and final search. *Query expansion* techniques such as this one implicitly recognize the limitations of Assumption Q: that the presence of a term in a document can depend on relevance even when that term does not appear in the query.

Leaving aside for the moment the question of term selection and assuming only that we have some method for scoring terms, the basic *relevance feedback* process proceeds as follows:

1. Execute the user's initial query.

2. Present the retrieval results to the user, allowing her to browse the results and indicate relevant documents.

3. Score the terms appearing in the relevant documents and select the top m expansion terms, ignoring terms in the initial query.

4. Add the new terms to the initial query, adjust weights w_t, and execute the expanded query.

5. Present the final retrieval results to the user.

The adjusted weight for term t in the fourth step is determined from Equation 8.26 with n_r equal to the number of relevant documents identified by the user and $n_{t,r}$ equal to the number of these documents containing t. In addition it is not unusual to accord special status to the terms appearing in the initial query, recognizing that these may best reflect the user's information need. This additional adjustment may be effected by multiplying the weight of the expansion terms by a constant factor γ, where $\gamma = 1/3$ is typical.

Relevance feedback has been the subject of a substantial body of research, and the basic feedback process may be extended and modified in a number of ways. For example the user might be allowed to identify nonrelevant documents, to interactively adjust the list of selected terms, or to repeat the feedback process multiple times, adding and removing terms as she sees fit. In addition, various methods have been proposed for scoring terms. We present one such method next.

8.6.1   Term Selection

Robertson (1990) proposes a simple term selection method based on the expected change in the scores of relevant and nonrelevant documents if a term is added to a query. Suppose we are considering adding the term t to the query. In Section 8.3 we defined p_t as the probability that a relevant document contains t and $\bar{p}_t$ as the probability that a nonrelevant document contains t. Consider Equation 8.22. If we add t to the query, the score of a relevant document will increase by an average of $p_t w_t$. The score of a nonrelevant document will increase by an average of $\bar{p}_t w_t$.

The greater the difference between these expected increases — between $p_t w_t$ and $\bar{p}_t w_t$ — the better the term helps to differentiate between relevant and nonrelevant documents. For relevance feedback we therefore score terms using the *term selection value*

$$w_t \cdot (p_t - \bar{p}_t). \tag{8.49}$$

In the context of relevance feedback, if the user identifies n_r relevant documents, of which $n_{t,r}$ contain t, we may estimate p_t as $(n_{t,r}/n_r)$. A value for $\bar{p}_t$ is harder to estimate. However, we might assume that the value is small relative to p_t and treat it as 0. Thus, our term selection value becomes

$$\frac{n_{t,r}}{n_r} \cdot w_t \, . \tag{8.50}$$

We can also drop n_r from the denominator because it is the same for all terms and multiplication by a constant factor is order-preserving, giving

$$n_{t,r} \cdot w_t \, . \tag{8.51}$$

For relevance feedback we rank each query term according to Equation 8.51, select the top m, and add them to the initial query, reweighting as necessary.

Unfortunately, this method provides us with no guidance regarding the number of terms m to select. A value of $m = 10$ is known to provide reasonable improvement over TREC collections, and we will take this value as our default in experiments. Robertson and Walker (1999) present a method for estimating a cutoff threshold for term selection based on the probability of accepting a noise term.

8.6.2   Pseudo-Relevance Feedback

Pseudo-relevance feedback (PRF), also known as *blind feedback*, is a variant of relevance feedback in which the interaction step is eliminated. Instead of requiring the user to identify relevant documents, *the retrieval system simply assumes that all of the top-k documents retrieved by the initial query are relevant*. A value of $k = 20$ is known to provide reasonable improvement over TREC collections, and we will take this value as our default in experiments. The remainder of the process proceeds as before: Terms are selected from these documents, added to the original query, and the expanded query is used to generate the final retrieval results.

Because it depends on positive feedback, PRF has the potential to seriously harm performance, particularly when few or none of the top-k documents is actually relevant. Nonetheless, PRF often produces significant effectiveness gains when averaged over many queries, such as by mean average precision and similar effectiveness measures. Moreover, it is an entirely automatic process placing no burden of interaction on the user, and thus can be performed invisibly for every query.

As an example we return to TREC topic 426 on law enforcement dogs (Figure 1.8 on page 25). The results of pseudo-relevance feedback over the $N = 528,155$ documents in the TREC45 collection are shown in Table 8.1. We assume the top $k = n_r = 20$ documents are relevant.

The first three rows of the table give statistics for the three original query terms. Because these terms appear in most or all of the top-20 documents, their adjusted term weights nearly double after feedback. The bottom rows of the table list the top-10 expansion terms, ordered by the term selection value of Equation 8.51 ($n_{t,r} \cdot w_t$). The final column of the table lists the adjusted values of w_t used in the execution of the expanded query, with $\gamma = 1/3$. The original query gives a precision@10 of 0.300 and a MAP of 0.043. The expanded query gives a precision@10 of 0.500 and a MAP of 0.089, a substantial improvement.

Table 8.1 Pseudo-relevance feedback applied to TREC topic 426, with a weight adjustment factor of $\gamma = 1/3$.

Query Term (t)	N_t	$n_{t,r}$	Original w_t	$n_{t,r} \cdot w_t$	Adjusted w_t	
dogs	2163	20	7.93178		13.29648	
law	49792	19	3.40698		6.96509	
enforcement	10635	19	5.63407		9.30767	
dog	3126	12	7.40050	88.80600	2.64856	$= 7.95363\gamma$
sniffing	194	6	11.41069	68.46414	3.42793	$= 10.29407\gamma$
canine	150	5	11.78178	58.90890	3.44006	$= 10.33051\gamma$
pooper	20	4	14.68867	58.75468	4.35952	$= 13.09164\gamma$
officers	15006	11	5.13735	56.51085	1.78900	$= 5.37239\gamma$
metro	39887	15	3.72697	55.90455	1.70128	$= 5.10896\gamma$
canines	34	4	13.92314	55.69256	4.06435	$= 12.20526\gamma$
police	30589	13	4.10988	53.42844	1.62250	$= 4.87237\gamma$
animal	5304	8	6.63774	53.10192	2.02091	$= 6.06879\gamma$
narcotics	3989	7	7.04879	49.34153	2.06199	$= 6.19217\gamma$

The inclusion of the term "pooper" as an expansion term hints at the possible problems that pseudo-relevance feedback can cause. The query ⟨ "law", "enforcement", "dogs"⟩ might relate to the enforcement of laws regarding dogs as easily as to the use of dogs in law enforcement. Although the latter interpretation is clearly indicated by the topic's description and narrative, the IR system is not privy to this information. Under the first interpretation "pooper" would be an excellent expansion term because laws often require owners to clean up after their dogs, possibly using "pooper scoopers".

Because pseudo-relevance feedback can produce such substantial improvements, you may wonder why we stop at a single iteration of the feedback process. You might hope that additional iterations would produce additional improvements. However, if we execute additional iterations for our example topic, we get following sequence of expansions shown below.

Iteration	Expansion Terms
1	dog, sniffing, canine, pooper, officers, metro, canines, police, animal, narcotics
2	dog, canine, pooper, sniffing, leash, metro, canines, animal, officers, narcotics
3	dog, canine, pooper, sniffing, leash, metro, canines, animal, owners, pets
4	dog, leash, animal, metro, canine, pooper, sniffing, canines, owners, pets
5	dog, leash, metro, canine, pooper, sniffing, canines, owners, animal, pets
6	dog, leash, metro, pooper, canines, owners, pets, animals, canine, scooper
7	dog, leash, metro, pooper, canines, owners, pets, animals, canine, scooper

After seven iterations the query has drifted solidly toward one interpretation. Additional iterations do not produce further changes.

The *query drift* seen in this example illustrates the major risk of indiscriminate pseudo-relevance feedback. Even a single iteration can sometimes seriously harm effectiveness. Perhaps for this reason most commercial IR systems do not incorporate pseudo-relevance feedback. The potential benefits of an average-case improvement may not outweigh the negative user experience engendered by a failure. Moreover, pseudo-relevance feedback can be costly from an efficiency standpoint because it requires the analysis of multiple documents and the execution of a second query. Again,the potential benefits may not outweigh the increased response time.

8.7   Field Weights: BM25F

In Chapter 2, along with a list of basic features for ranking such as term frequency and term proximity, we listed a number of additional features usable for ranking, including document structure. For example, terms appearing in certain fields, such as a document's title, may be given more weight than terms appearing in the document's body. In this section we present an important extension to BM25, known as BM25F that takes this document structure into account.

Exploiting document structure is particularly important in the context of Web search. Figure 8.1 illustrates some of the rich structure available to a Web search engine. This figure is a greatly simplified version of the Web page `en.wikipedia.org/wiki/Shakespeare` as it appeared in the English-language Wikipedia in mid-2007.

The HTML is split into two parts: (1) the *header*, delimited by `<head>` ...`</head>` tags, which provide a title and other *metadata* describing the document; and (2) the *body*, which provides the content of the article for display. The metadata includes important dates related to Shakespeare and annotations related to the organization of Wikipedia. For example, the keyword `Persondata` indicates that the page contains a standardized table of biographical information. The body of the document includes a section title, which is indicated by `<h1>` tags, as well as text to be displayed in a **bold font**, which is indicated by `<b>` tags.

The body also contains hypertext links to the Wikipedia pages for "poet" and "playwright". The *anchor text* between the start tag `<a>` and the end tag `</a>` of these links can be interpreted as indicating something about the content of the referenced pages, in this case simply restating their titles. Anchor text is an important feature in Web search, which we return to again in Chapter 15.

Although HTML is particularly rich in structure, many documents contain similar fields. For example, the "Subject", "To", and "From" fields in e-mail messages may be exploited for similar purposes. The goal of BM25F is to appropriately reflect the emphasis implied by this structure.

```
<html>
  <head>
    <title>William Shakespeare - Wikipedia, the free encyclopedia</title>
    <meta
      name="keywords"
      content="William Shakespeare,Persondata,Sister projects, Earlybard,
              1582,1583,1585,1616"/>
  </head>
  <body>
    <h1>William Shakespeare</h1>
    <b>William Shakespeare</b> (baptised 26 April 1564 - died 23 April 1616)
    was an English <a href="http://en.wikipedia.org/wiki/Poet">poet</a> and
    <a href="http://en.wikipedia.org/wiki/Playwright"> playwright</a>.
    He is widely regarded as the greatest writer of the English language
    and the world's pre-eminent dramatist.  He wrote approximately 38 plays
    and 154 sonnets, as well as a variety of other poems...
  </body>
</html>
```

Figure 8.1   A simple HTML page showing typical structure on the Web.

The intuition underlying BM25F is similar to the intuition underlying the document length normalization of Equation 8.45. That equation specifies an adjusted term frequency, scaled to account for document length, that replaces the actual term frequency in the retrieval formula. We may extend this idea to field weights by computing an adjusted term frequency that depends on the field in which a term occurs. For example, we might consider the occurrence of a query term in the title of a document to be equivalent to ten occurrences in the document and scale the term frequency accordingly.

To formalize this notion we define $f_{t,d,s}$ to be the number of occurrences of term t in field s of document d. We then apply field-specific document length normalization similar to the BM25 normalization but applied at the field level, reflecting the differences in average length between different field types. For example, the title of a document is usually very short relative to its body.

$$f'_{t,d,s} = \frac{f_{t,d,s}}{(1 - b_s) + b_s \left(l_{d,s}/l_s\right)}, \tag{8.52}$$

where $l_{d,s}$ is the length of field s in document d, l_s is the average length of field s across all documents, and b_s is a field-specific parameter similar to the b parameter in BM25. Like the b parameter the b_s parameters can range from 0 to 1, producing no normalization at one extreme and complete normalization at the other.

Table 8.2 Effectiveness measures for selected retrieval methods discussed in this chapter.

| | TREC45 | | | | GOV2 | | | |
| | 1998 | | 1999 | | 2005 | | 2006 | |
Method	P@10	MAP	P@10	MAP	P@10	MAP	P@10	MAP
Equation 8.22	0.256	0.141	0.224	0.148	0.069	0.050	0.106	0.083
Equation 8.44	0.402	0.177	0.406	0.207	0.418	0.171	0.538	0.207
BM25	0.424	0.178	0.440	0.205	0.471	0.243	0.534	0.277
BM25 + PRF	0.452	0.239	0.454	0.249	0.567	0.277	0.588	0.314
BM25F					0.482	0.242	0.544	0.277

These field-specific adjusted term frequencies, or *pseudo-frequencies*, may then be combined into an adjusted term frequency for the document as a whole.

$$f'_{t,d} = \sum_s v_s \cdot f'_{t,d,s} \tag{8.53}$$

where v_s is the weight for field s. For example we might define $v_{\text{title}} = 10$ and $v_{\text{body}} = 1$.

We may then replace the actual term frequency with this adjusted term frequency in Equation 8.44 to give the BM25F formula:

$$\sum q_t \cdot \frac{f'_{t,d}(k_1 + 1)}{k_1 + f'_{t,d}} \cdot w_t . \tag{8.54}$$

Because length normalization is applied as part of computing the adjusted term frequency, no explicit normalization is required in this formula. We continue to compute w_t, the Robertson/Spärck Jones weight, at the document level. The use of BM25F requires that we tune two parameters for each field, b_s and v_s, as well as the overall parameter k_1.

Implementing BM25F requires documents to contain appropriate tagging and requires the computation of term frequency with respect to each field. The query processing techniques for lightweight structure presented in Chapter 5 may help with the implementation.

8.8 Experimental Comparison

Table 8.2 charts the progress of the probabilistic model through each major innovation, using the test collections described in Section 1.4. The results in this table may be compared directly with those in Table 2.5. The BM25 row appears in both.

For BM25 the experiments use parameter values of $k_1 = 1.2$ and $b = 0.75$. Equation 8.30 is used to calculate w_t. For pseudo-relevance feedback (PRF) we retrieve the top $k = 20$ documents and add the top $m = 10$ terms to the query, reweighting the original and new query terms as described in Section 8.6 with $\gamma = 1/3$. For BM25F we consider only two fields — title and body — where anything not in the title is considered to be in the body. The experiments for BM25F use parameter values $k_1 = 1.2$, $v_{\text{title}} = 10$, $v_{\text{body}} = 1$, and $b_{\text{title}} = b_{\text{body}} = 0.75$.

As we see in the table, a substantial performance improvement comes from the introduction of the term frequency component. The impact of pseudo-relevance feedback varies considerably from collection to collection, with precision@10 improving 3–20% and MAP improving 13–34%. Field weights (BM25F) have little impact on these GOV2 topics. In Chapter 15, where we apply these same retrieval methods to a Web-oriented retrieval task, the impact of field weights will be more apparent (see Table 15.6 on page 539).

8.9   Further Reading

The earliest probabilistic model for IR is perhaps the one described by Maron and Kuhns (1960). Fuhr (1992) provides a comparison of the Maron/Kuhns model with the Robertson/Spärck Jones probabilistic model. The inference network model builds on the probabilistic model, providing a rich set of probabilistic operators (Turtle and Croft, 1991; Greiff et al., 1999). Lafferty and Zhai (2003) explore at a fundamental level the relationship between the probabilistic model and the language modeling approach we introduce in the next chapter. Our exposition of both methods is based on their analysis. Roelleke and Wang (2006) extend this analysis, carefully detailing the correspondence between the elements of each model.

The development of the Robertson/Spärck Jones probabilistic model can be traced through a series of papers, most notably Spärck Jones (1972), Robertson and Spärck Jones (1976), Robertson (1977), Croft and Harper (1979), Robertson and Walker (1994), Robertson et al. (1994), and Robertson and Walker (1997). Spärck Jones et al. (2000a,b) provide a detailed summary of developments up to 1999 including a substantial discussion of enhancements and extensions.

Robertson (2004) provides addition insight into the theoretical principles underlying inverse document frequency and its relationship to the probabilistic model. This relationship is further explored by de Vries and Roelleke (2005). They view the provision of relevance information as a loss of entropy and provide a curious explanation for the 0.5 smoothing applied in Equation 8.26 through the addition of "virtual documents". Church and Gale (1995) model IDF as a mixture of Poisson distributions and highlighting important differences between document frequency and within-collection term frequency. Roelleke and Wang (2008) provide a careful review of the theoretical underpinnings of TF-IDF, and its interpretation under various retrieval models.

One of the first algorithms for query expansion through relevance feedback was invented by Joseph J. Rocchio in the context of the SMART system (see Rocchio (1971) or Baeza-Yates and Ribeiro-Neto (1999) for details). Ruthven and Lalmas (2003) provide a thorough survey of both interactive relevance feedback and pseudo-relevance feedback. Wang et al. (2008) discuss relevance feedback when only negative (nonrelevant) examples are available.

Experiments by many groups at TREC between 1992 and 1998 established pseudo-relevance feedback as a technique for reliably improving mean average precision. However, the benefit of pseudo-relevance feedback in production environments has never been clearly demonstrated. Lynam et al. (2004) provide an experimental comparison of the pseudo-relevance feedback techniques used by a number of leading research groups for TREC-style experiments circa 2003. Building on a language modeling approach, Lee et al. (2008) apply clustering methods to select better documents for feedback. Also building on a language modeling approach, Cao et al. (2008) apply classification methods to select better expansion terms from feedback documents. Collins-Thompson (2009) presents a framework for minimizing the risk associated with query expansion techniques such as pseudo-relevance feedback.

The theory underlying BM25F was first presented by Robertson et al. (2004), well after BM25 had been established as a top-tier ranking formula. Okapi BM25F in the form presented here was described and evaluated as part of the Microsoft Cambridge experiments for TREC-13 (Zaragoza et al., 2004) and TREC-14 (Craswell et al., 2005b). Other extensions to BM25 include proposals to incorporate proximity (Rasolofo and Savoy, 2003; Büttcher et al., 2006) and the position of query terms within the document (Troy and Zhang, 2007), as well as proposals to account for anchor text and other Web-related features (Hawking et al., 2004; Craswell et al., 2005a). Robertson and Zaragoza (2010) provide a recent survey of probabilistic retrieval as embodied in BM25F.

8.10 Exercises

Exercise 8.1 Show that $\text{logit}(p) = -\text{logit}(1 - p)$ for $0 \leq p \leq 1$.

Exercise 8.2 Under what circumstances would Equation 8.26 give a negative value? Are these circumstances likely to occur in practice?

Exercise 8.3 Apply Assumptions Q and T (pages 261–262) to derive Equation 8.32 from Equation 8.13.

Exercise 8.4 Our description of BM25F implicitly assumes that a field s appears at most once in each document. However, a document might have many occurrences of section headers, bolded text, and similar structural elements. Suggest an extension to BM25F to handle multiple fields of the same type.

Exercise 8.5 (project exercise) Implement the BM25 ranking formula (Equation 8.48). Test your implementation using the test collection developed in Exercise 2.13 or with any other available collection, such as a TREC collection.

Exercise 8.6 (project exercise) Implement the term selection step of the pseudo-relevance feedback method described in Section 8.6. Given a query q, execute it over any text collection, using any retrieval method, and return the top 20 documents. Using Equation 8.51, extract the top ten terms from these documents. Test your implementation with the following queries:

(a) ⟨ "law", "enforcement", "dogs" ⟩

(b) ⟨ "marine", "vegetation" ⟩

(c) ⟨ "black", "bear", "attacks" ⟩

(d) ⟨ "journalist", "risks" ⟩

(e) ⟨ "family", "leave", "law" ⟩

These queries are taken from the TREC 2005 Robust track[1], which had the goal of improving "the consistency of retrieval technology by focusing on poorly performing topics". Pseudo-relevance feedback often has a detrimental impact on such topics.

8.11   Bibliography

Baeza-Yates, R. A., and Ribeiro-Neto, B. (1999). *Modern Information Retrieval*. Reading, Massachusetts: Addison-Wesley.

Bookstein, A., and Kraft, D. (1977). Operations research applied to document indexing and retrieval decisions. *Journal of the ACM*, 24(3):418–427.

Bookstein, A., and Swanson, D. R. (1974). Probabilistic models for automatic indexing. *Journal of the American Society for Information Science*, 25(5):312–319.

Büttcher, S., Clarke, C. L. A., and Lushman, B. (2006). Term proximity scoring for ad-hoc retrieval on very large text collections. In *Proceedings of the 29th Annual International ACM SIGIR Conference on Research and Development in Information Retrieval*, pages 621–622. Seattle, Washington.

Cao, G., Nie, J. Y., Gao, J., and Robertson, S. (2008). Selecting good expansion terms for pseudo-relevance feedback. In *Proceedings of the 31st Annual International ACM SIGIR Conference on Research and Development in Information Retrieval*, pages 243–250. Singapore.

Church, K. W., and Gale, W. A. (1995). Inverse document frequency (IDF): A measure of deviation from poisson. In *Proceedings of the 3rd Workshop on Very Large Corpora*, pages 121–130. Cambridge, Massachusetts.

Collins-Thompson, K. (2009). Reducing the risk of query expansion via robust constrained optimization. In *Proceedings of the 18th ACM Conference on Information and Knowledge Management*, pages 837–846. Hong Kong, China.

---

[1] `trec.nist.gov/data/robust.html`

Craswell, N., Robertson, S., Zaragoza, H., and Taylor, M. (2005a). Relevance weighting for query independent evidence. In *Proceedings of the 28th Annual International ACM SIGIR Conference on Research and Development in Information Retrieval*, pages 416–423. Salvador, Brazil.

Craswell, N., Zaragoza, H., and Robertson, S. (2005b). Microsoft Cambridge at TREC 14: Enterprise track. In *Proceedings of the 14th Text REtrieval Conference*. Gaithersburg, Maryland.

Croft, W. B., and Harper, D. J. (1979). Using probabilistic models of document retrieval without relevance information. *Journal of Documentation*, 35:285–295.

de Vries, A. P., and Roelleke, T. (2005). Relevance information: A loss of entropy but a gain for IDF? In *Proceedings of the 28th Annual International ACM SIGIR Conference on Research and Development in Information Retrieval*, pages 282–289. Salvador, Brazil.

Fuhr, N. (1992). Probabilistic models in information retrieval. *The Computer Journal*, 35(3):243–255.

Greiff, W. R., Croft, W. B., and Turtle, H. (1999). PIC matrices: A computationally tractable class of probabilistic query operators. *ACM Transactions on Information Systems*, 17(4):367–405.

Harter, S. P. (1975). A probabilistic approach to automatic keyword indexing: Part I. On the distribution of specialty words in a technical literature. *Journal of the American Society for Information Science*, 26:197–206.

Hawking, D., Upstill, T., and Craswell, N. (2004). Toward better weighting of anchors. In *Proceedings of the 27th Annual International ACM SIGIR Conference on Research and Development in Information Retrieval*, pages 512–513. Sheffield, England.

Lafferty, J., and Zhai, C. (2003). Probabilistic relevance models based on document and query generation. In Croft, W. B., and Lafferty, J., editors, *Language Modeling for Information Retrieval*, chapter 1, pages 1–10. Dordrecht, The Netherlands: Kluwer Academic Publishers.

Lee, K. S., Croft, W. B., and Allan, J. (2008). A cluster-based resampling method for pseudo-relevance feedback. In *Proceedings of the 31st Annual International ACM SIGIR Conference on Research and Development in Information Retrieval*, pages 235–242. Singapore.

Lynam, T. R., Buckley, C., Clarke, C. L. A., and Cormack, G. V. (2004). A multi-system analysis of document and term selection for blind feedback. In *Proceedings of the 13th ACM International Conference on Information and Knowledge Management*, pages 261–269. Washington, D.C.

Maron, M. E., and Kuhns, J. L. (1960). On relevance, probabilistic indexing and information retrieval. *Journal of the ACM*, 7(3):216–244.

Ponte, J. M., and Croft, W. B. (1998). A language modeling approach to information retrieval. In *Proceedings of the 21st Annual International ACM SIGIR Conference on Research and Development in Information Retrieval*, pages 275–281. Melbourne, Australia.

Rasolofo, Y., and Savoy, J. (2003). Term proximity scoring for keyword-based retrieval systems. In *Proceedings of the 25th European Conference on Information Retrieval Research*, pages 207–218. Pisa, Italy.

Robertson, S. (1977). The probability ranking principle in IR. *Journal of Documentation*, 33:294–304.

Robertson, S. (2004). Understanding inverse document frequency: On theoretical arguments for IDF. *Journal of Documentation*, 60(5):503–520.

Robertson, S., and Spärck Jones, K. (1976). Relevance weighting of search terms. *Journal of the American Society for Information Science*, 27(3):129–146.

Robertson, S., and Zaragoza, H. (2010). The probabilistic relevance framework: Bm25 and beyond. *Foundations and Trends in Information Retrieval*, 4.

Robertson, S., Zaragoza, H., and Taylor, M. (2004). Simple BM25 extension to multiple weighted fields. In *Proceedings of the 13th ACM International Conference on Information and Knowledge Management*, pages 42–49. Washington, D.C.

Robertson, S. E. (1990). On term selection for query expansion. *Journal of Documentation*, 46(4):359–364.

Robertson, S. E., van Rijsbergen, C. J., and Porter, M. F. (1981). Probabilistic models of indexing and searching. In Oddy, R. N., Robertson, S. E., van Rijsbergen, C. J., and Williams, P. W., editors, *Information Retrieval Research*, chapter 4, pages 35–56. London, England: Butterworths.

Robertson, S. E., and Walker, S. (1994). Some simple effective approximations to the 2-Poisson model for probabilistic weighted retrieval. In *Proceedings of the 17th Annual International ACM SIGIR Conference on Research and Development in Information Retrieval*, pages 232–241. Dublin, Ireland.

Robertson, S. E., and Walker, S. (1997). On relevance weights with little relevance information. In *Proceedings of the 20th Annual International ACM SIGIR Conference on Research and Development in Information Retrieval*, pages 16–24. Philadelphia, Pennsylvania.

Robertson, S. E., and Walker, S. (1999). Okapi/keenbow at TREC-8. In *Proceedings of the 8th Text REtrieval Conference*. Gaithersburg, Maryland.

Robertson, S. E., Walker, S., Jones, S., Hancock-Beaulieu, M. M., and Gatford, M. (1994). Okapi at TREC-3. In *Proceedings of the 3rd Text REtrieval Conference*. Gaithersburg, Maryland.

Rocchio, J. J. (1971). Relevance feedback in information retrieval. In Salton, G., editor, *The SMART Retrieval System: Experiments in Automatic Document Processing*, chapter 14, pages 313–323: Prentice-Hall.

Roelleke, T., and Wang, J. (2006). A parallel derivation of probabilistic information retrieval models. In *Proceedings of the 29th Annual International ACM SIGIR Conference on Research and Development in Information Retrieval*, pages 107–114. Seattle, Washington.

Roelleke, T., and Wang, J. (2008). TF-IDF uncovered: A study of theories and probabilities. In *Proceedings of the 31st Annual International ACM SIGIR Conference on Research and Development in Information Retrieval*, pages 435–442. Singapore, Singapore.

Ruthven, I., and Lalmas, M. (2003). A survey on the use of relevance feedback for information access systems. *Knowledge Engineering Review*, 18(2):95–145.

Spärck Jones, K. (1972). A statistical interpretation of term specificity and its application in retrieval. *Journal of Documentation*, 28(1):11–21.

Spärck Jones, K., Walker, S., and Robertson, S. E. (2000a). A probabilistic model of information retrieval: Development and comparative experiments – Part 1. *Information Processing & Management*, 36(6):779–808.

Spärck Jones, K., Walker, S., and Robertson, S. E. (2000b). A probabilistic model of information retrieval: Development and comparative experiments – Part 2. *Information Processing & Management*, 36(6):809–840.

Troy, A. D., and Zhang, G. Q. (2007). Enhancing relevance scoring with chronological term rank. In *Proceedings of the 30th Annual International ACM SIGIR Conference on Research and Development in Information Retrieval*, pages 599–606. Amsterdam, The Netherlands.

Turtle, H., and Croft, W. B. (1991). Evaluation of an inference network-based retrieval model. *ACM Transactions on Information Systems*, 9(3):187–222.

Wang, X., Fang, H., and Zhai, C. (2008). A study of methods for negative relevance feedback. In *Proceedings of the 31st Annual International ACM SIGIR Conference on Research and Development in Information Retrieval*, pages 219–226. Singapore.

Zaragoza, H., Craswell, N., Taylor, M., Saria, S., and Robertson, S. (2004). Microsoft Cambridge at TREC 13: Web and Hard tracks. In *Proceedings of the 13th Text REtrieval Conference*. Gaithersburg, Maryland.

9 Language Modeling and Related Methods

This chapter presents alternative views of the ranking problem that are different from the probabilistic model introduced in Chapter 8. The retrieval methods presented in this chapter, although they have differing theoretical underpinnings, share several important characteristics. All may be viewed as ranking documents through some form of *language modeling*, in the sense that the actual occurrences of terms in a document are compared with the expected occurrences predicted from the characteristics of the collection and the document. The methods are also distinguished from the probabilistic model by their reduced emphasis on relevance, which may not be explicitly considered.

Although the methods presented in this chapter may be viewed as language modeling approaches in a broad sense, Sections 9.1 to 9.4 focus on the foundations of what is generally termed the "language modeling approach" in a narrower sense. This approach — established through the work of Berger, Croft, Hiemstra, Lafferty, Ponte, Zhai, and others — is characterized by its use of a document to construct a *generative model* for queries (Ponte and Croft, 1998; Hiemstra, 2001; Song and Croft, 1999; Miller et al., 1999; Berger and Lafferty, 1999; Lafferty and Zhai, 2001; Zhai and Lafferty, 2001, 2004). Over a short span of time, approximately 1998 to 2001, this language modeling approach grew from its roots in a SIGIR paper by Ponte and Croft (1998) into a leading framework for new IR research (Croft and Lafferty, 2003). Whenever references are made to "the language modeling approach" in the research literature, this narrower meaning is often intended.

Section 9.1 takes the Probability Ranking Principle as its starting point to derive and justify this generative query model. Given a document that is assumed to be relevant, we develop a language model from the document to estimate $p(q \mid d)$, the probability that query q would be entered to retrieve document d, and rank documents accordingly. We introduced the idea of language modeling in Chapter 1 when we examined term frequencies and developed the idea further in the context of data compression in Chapter 6. In the present chapter our language models are based on the simplest of those introduced in Chapter 1 — we work only with zero-order models derived from document and collection statistics.

Section 9.2 discusses the details of constructing a language model from a document, with particular emphasis on the smoothing process through which we assign nonzero probabilities to terms that do not appear within the document. It is important to assign positive probabilities to these terms because a relevant document may not contain every query term. In Section 9.3 we apply our smoothed language models to the ranking problem and develop specific ranking formulae by combining results from Sections 9.1 and 9.2. Section 9.4 considers an alternative theoretical foundation for the language modeling approach based on *Kullback-Leibler divergence*, a method for determining the difference between two probability distributions. Building on this alternative foundation, we outline a method for query expansion under the language modeling approach.

Later sections consider a broader interpretation of language modeling. In Section 9.5 we introduce a retrieval method known as *divergence from randomness* (DFR), which explicitly compares a model for distributing terms at random with the actual distribution of these terms within documents to be ranked. Section 9.6 presents an approach to passage retrieval, the foundations of which are closely related to DFR and other language modeling approaches. Section 9.7 provides a comparative evaluation of several of the retrieval methods presented in the chapter and in previous chapters. Section 9.8 lists a number of emerging retrieval methods derived from or related to language modeling.

9.1   Generating Queries from Documents

As we did in Chapter 8, we take as our starting point the Probability Ranking Principle, as embodied in Equation 8.8:

$$\log \frac{p(r\,|\,D,Q)}{1 - p(r\,|\,D,Q)} \;=\; \log \frac{p(r\,|\,D,Q)}{p(\bar{r}\,|\,D,Q)} \tag{9.1}$$

$$\;=\; \log \frac{p(D,Q\,|\,r)\;p(r)}{p(D,Q\,|\,\bar{r})\;p(\bar{r})}. \tag{9.2}$$

In Equation 8.10 we expanded the joint probabilities appearing in this equation using the equality $p(D,Q\,|\,R) = p(D\,|\,Q,R) \cdot p(Q\,|\,R)$. In this section we develop the equation in the opposite direction, expanding the joint probabilities using the equality $p(D,Q\,|\,R) = p(Q\,|\,D,R) \cdot p(D\,|\,R)$.

$$\log \frac{p(r\,|\,D,Q)}{p(\bar{r}\,|\,D,Q)} \;=\; \log \frac{p(D,Q\,|\,r)\;p(r)}{p(D,Q\,|\,\bar{r})\;p(\bar{r})} \tag{9.3}$$

$$\;=\; \log \frac{p(Q\,|\,D,r)\;p(D\,|\,r)\;p(r)}{p(Q\,|\,D,\bar{r})\;p(D\,|\,\bar{r})\;p(\bar{r})} \tag{9.4}$$

$$\;=\; \log \frac{p(Q\,|\,D,r)\;p(r\,|\,D)}{p(Q\,|\,D,\bar{r})\;p(\bar{r}\,|\,D)} \tag{9.5}$$

$$\;=\; \log p(Q\,|\,D,r) - \log p(Q\,|\,D,\bar{r}) + \log \frac{p(r\,|\,D)}{p(\bar{r}\,|\,D)} \tag{9.6}$$

$$\;=\; \log p(Q\,|\,D,r) - \log p(Q\,|\,D,\bar{r}) + \mathrm{logit}(p(r\,|\,D)) \tag{9.7}$$

We examine each of the probabilities in this last formula in detail.

For a given query q and a relevant document d, the value $p(Q = q \mid D = d, r)$ represents the probability that the user would enter the query q in order to retrieve d. In essence, conditioning on d provides us with an example of a relevant document. From this example we may then estimate the probability of a user entering q if a document such as d is desired. In particular, if a term appears in d with much greater frequency than random chance suggests, we might expect it to have a higher probability of appearing in the query.

On the other hand, consider the role of d in the probability $p(Q = q \mid D = d, \bar{r})$ in Equation 9.7. Here conditioning on d provides us with a weaker picture of the user's requirements. We have an example of what is not relevant but still can only guess about what is relevant. As a result it may be reasonable to assume that this probability is independent of d, that is $p(Q = q \mid D = d, \bar{r})$ is a constant. If we accept this assumption, we can drop the constant, leaving us with the rank-equivalent formula

$$\log p(Q \mid D, r) + \operatorname{logit}(p(r \mid D)). \tag{9.8}$$

The probability $p(r \mid D)$ in the second term is independent of q and is the same for all queries. This prior probability of relevance might be interpreted as indicating something about the quality or importance of the document. In the context of Web search, for example, the home page of a university might be assigned a higher prior probability than the personal home page of a student attending the university (see Section 15.3). In the context of file system search, e-mail addressed to you personally might be assigned a higher value than e-mail you receive from a mailing list.

Nonetheless, in the absence of information suggested by the context of the application, the prior probability of relevance $p(r \mid D)$ is often assumed to be the same for all documents. Again, if we accept this assumption, we may drop this constant as an order-preserving transformation. Moreover, because exponentiation is also order-preserving, we may remove the logarithm, which leaves us with the ranking formula

$$p(Q \mid D, r). \tag{9.9}$$

If we wish, conditioning on relevance can be made implicit, thus reducing the equation to

$$p(Q = q \mid D = d). \tag{9.10}$$

This very simple formula plays the same role in relation to the language modeling approach as Equation 8.13 does in relation to the probabilistic retrieval model of Chapter 8. Given a document d and a query q, we score d for ranking purposes by estimating the probability $p(q \mid d)$.

In order to estimate this probability, the document is often considered to provide a *model* for generating the query q. Imagine a user formulating a query to retrieve relevant documents. She might attempt to think of some terms that should appear often in these relevant documents but rarely in nonrelevant documents. In making this attempt the user forms an image in her mind of what a relevant document looks like — what terms might distinguish it from other documents in the collection. She then selects a few of these terms and enters them into a search engine. These terms become the query q.

To score d we assume it matches the image in the user's mind and estimate the probability that the user would select q to retrieve it. It is because of this assumed link between the user's information need — the image in her mind — and the document d that we can view d as providing a *generative model* for q.

Some IR researchers justify Equation 9.10 more directly through a different reasoning process. They simply state that we are interested in $p(Q, D)$, the joint distribution of queries and documents. The issue of relevance is ignored. Documents are ranked by

$$p(Q, D) = p(Q \mid D) \cdot p(D),$$

or equivalently by

$$\log p(Q \mid D) + \log p(D). \tag{9.11}$$

Similarly to how we handled the second term in Equation 9.8, we may interpret $\log p(D)$ as indicating the quality or importance of the document and treat it as a constant in the absence of other information. Note, however, the difference in this second term between Equations 9.11 and 9.8.

9.2 Language Models and Smoothing

In Chapter 1 we examined term distributions in the Shakespeare and other collections and introduced basic language modeling approaches. In addition, in the context of text compression in Chapter 6, we further explored the idea of finite-context models over a set of symbols. For predictive purposes we can imagine reading the unseen text of a document from left to right, using the language models to guess what will come next and assigning a probability to each possible symbol. If we do a good job of guessing, we are able to encode the document in fewer bits.

For retrieval our goal is slightly different. We must imagine that we have an example of a relevant document and ask: *What is the probability that term t would be entered by a user in order to retrieve a document such as this one?*

To answer this question we use the document to create a language model for the queries that may be entered to retrieve it. Our goal is to construct a document language model $\mathcal{M}_d(t)$ from document d. The simplest document language model is the maximum likelihood model $\mathcal{M}_d^{\mathrm{ml}}(t)$ based on the counts of the terms appearing in the document:

$$\mathcal{M}_d^{\mathrm{ml}}(t) \;=\; \frac{f_{t,d}}{l_d} \,. \tag{9.12}$$

Here, as usual, $f_{t,d}$ is the number of times t appears in d and l_d is the length of the document. Thus, for terms not appearing in the document $\mathcal{M}_d^{ml}(t) = 0$. Because $\mathcal{M}_d^{ml}(t)$ is a probability we have, as required,

$$\sum_{t \in \mathcal{V}} \mathcal{M}_d^{ml}(t) = \sum_{t \in d} \mathcal{M}_d^{ml}(t) = \sum_{t \in d} f_{t,d}/l_d = l_d/l_d = 1. \tag{9.13}$$

For example, the term "lord" appears 624 times in *Hamlet*, which has length 43,314, but only 78 times in *Macbeth*, which has length 26,807. Thus, a language model based on *Hamlet* predicts a much higher probability for that term than one based on *Macbeth*.

$$\mathcal{M}_{\text{Hamlet}}^{ml}(\text{"lord"}) = \frac{f_{\text{lord,Hamlet}}}{l_{\text{Hamlet}}} = \frac{624}{43,314} \approx 1.441\%$$

$$\mathcal{M}_{\text{Macbeth}}^{ml}(\text{"lord"}) = \frac{f_{\text{lord,Macbeth}}}{l_{\text{Macbeth}}} = \frac{78}{26,807} \approx 0.291\%$$

On the other hand, *Hamlet* predicts a lower probability for the term "lady" because it appears 30 times in *Hamlet* but 196 times in *Macbeth*.

$$\mathcal{M}_{\text{Hamlet}}^{ml}(\text{"lady"}) = \frac{f_{\text{lady,Hamlet}}}{l_{\text{Hamlet}}} = \frac{30}{43,314} \approx 0.069\%$$

$$\mathcal{M}_{\text{Macbeth}}^{ml}(\text{"lady"}) = \frac{f_{\text{lady,Macbeth}}}{l_{\text{Macbeth}}} = \frac{196}{26,807} \approx 0.731\%$$

Because $\mathcal{M}_d^{ml}(t)$ is nothing more than term frequency scaled by document length, we might suspect that by itself it may not be sufficient to compute estimates of $p(q \mid d)$ that will provide a satisfactory document ranking. In particular, given that d is just a single example of a relevant document and that d may consist of only a few hundred words, the estimates it provides have the potential to be wildly inaccurate. Moreover, the model assigns a probability of 0 to all terms not appearing in the document, implying that it is impossible for these terms to appear in the query.

To address these problems when using language models based on documents or examples of similar size, it is common in information retrieval, as well as in other areas such as speech recognition, to *smooth* these models using a *background language model* in the hope of improving accuracy. In information retrieval the collection as a whole provides a convenient basis for this background model.

We define $\mathcal{M}_{\mathcal{C}}(t)$ as the maximum likelihood language model based on term frequencies in the collection as a whole:

$$\mathcal{M}_{\mathcal{C}}(t) = l_t/l_{\mathcal{C}}, \tag{9.14}$$

where l_t is the number of times t occurs in the collection $\mathcal{C}$ and $l_\mathcal{C}$ is the total number of tokens in the collection.

$$\mathcal{M}_\mathcal{C}(\text{``lord''}) = \frac{l_{\text{lord}}}{l_\mathcal{C}} = \frac{3,346}{1,271,504} \approx 0.263\%$$

$$\mathcal{M}_\mathcal{C}(\text{``lady''}) = \frac{l_{\text{lady}}}{l_\mathcal{C}} = \frac{1,031}{1,271,504} \approx 0.081\%$$

Unlike the examples in Chapter 1, in this example $l_\mathcal{C}$ includes all tokens, tags as well as words.

We now consider two well-known smoothing methods. The first method, known as *Jelinek-Mercer smoothing* (Jelinek and Mercer, 1980; Chen and Goodman, 1998), is a simple linear combination of the document language model and the collection language model,

$$\mathcal{M}_d^\lambda(t) = (1-\lambda) \cdot \mathcal{M}_d^{\text{ml}}(t) + \lambda \cdot \mathcal{M}_\mathcal{C}(t), \tag{9.15}$$

where λ is a parameter with a value between 0 and 1 that controls the relative weight given to the document and collection language models. For example, if $\lambda = 0.5$,

$$\mathcal{M}_{\text{Hamlet}}^\lambda(\text{``lord''}) = (1-\lambda) \cdot \mathcal{M}_{\text{Hamlet}}^{\text{ml}}(\text{``lord''}) + \lambda \cdot \mathcal{M}_\mathcal{C}(\text{``lord''})$$

$$= 0.5 \cdot \frac{78}{26,807} + 0.5 \cdot \frac{3,346}{1,271,504} \approx 0.277\%.$$

Because $\mathcal{M}_d^\lambda(t)$ represents a probability, we have, as required,

$$\sum_{t \in \mathcal{V}} (1-\lambda) \cdot \mathcal{M}_d^{\text{ml}}(t) + \lambda \cdot \mathcal{M}_\mathcal{C}(t) = (1-\lambda) \cdot \sum_{t \in \mathcal{V}} \mathcal{M}_d^{\text{ml}}(t) + \lambda \cdot \sum_{t \in \mathcal{V}} \mathcal{M}_\mathcal{C}(t) = 1. \tag{9.16}$$

The intuition underlying our second smoothing method is to pretend we have added an extra $\mu > 0$ tokens to each document in the collection and have distributed them according to the collection language model $\mathcal{M}_\mathcal{C}(t)$. For example, if $\mu = 1,000$, we would conceptually add $\mu \cdot \mathcal{M}_\mathcal{C}(\text{``lord''}) = 2.6315$ occurrences of the term "lord" to every document. Obviously, in reality it is not possible to add a fractional number of terms to a document, but it works as a mathematical trick. The maximum likelihood language model based on these new documents would then be

$$\mathcal{M}_d^\mu(t) = \frac{f_{t,d} + \mu \mathcal{M}_\mathcal{C}(t)}{l_d + \mu},$$

where $f_{t,d}$ is the number of times t appears in the original document and l_d is the original length. The impact of the additional terms depends on the length of the document. The longer the document, the lower the impact, with values approaching $\mathcal{M}_d(t)$ in the limit. This smoothing method is known as *Dirichlet smoothing* (Chen and Goodman, 1998) because it can be derived from a Dirichlet distribution with appropriate parameters.

If a term t does not appear in a document d, then $\mathcal{M}_d^{\lambda}(t) = \lambda \cdot \mathcal{M}_{\mathcal{C}}(t)$ and $\mathcal{M}_d^{\mu}(t) = (\mu/(l_d + \mu)) \cdot \mathcal{M}_{\mathcal{C}}(t)$. In both cases the smoothed models assign a probability that is a constant factor of the collection probability, and thus the relative probability assigned to terms not appearing in the document remains the same.

9.3   Ranking with Language Models

Equation 9.10 suggests that we are ranking documents according to the probability that q will be entered as a query, given that d is an example of a relevant document. We are now ready to apply the smoothed language models of Section 9.2 to the problem of estimating this probability. We start by applying independence assumptions similar to Assumption Q on page 262, thereby reducing the problem to that of estimating probabilities for individual terms in the query. Given a query vector $q = \langle t_1, t_2, ..., t_n \rangle$ and a document d, we may estimate $p(q \mid d)$ as

$$p(q \mid d) \;=\; p(|q| = n) \cdot \prod_{i=1}^{n} p(t_i \mid d), \qquad (9.17)$$

where $p(|q| = n)$ represents the probability that the user would enter a query of length n. In order to estimate the probability that the user will enter q, we must estimate this probability for the query length — assuming that this length is independent of the document and query terms — as well as a probability for each individual term — assuming that the selection of one term is independent of the selection of the others.

Fortunately, it is safe to ignore the query length. Because the query is fixed, it is sufficient to consider the probability that the user would enter q out of all possible queries of length n rather than out of all possible queries of any length. In Section 9.4, where we briefly consider query expansion under the language modeling approach, the need to estimate query length will reappear. For now, however, we estimate $p(q \mid d)$ as

$$p(q \mid d) \;=\; \prod_{i=1}^{n} p(t_i \mid d). \qquad (9.18)$$

Because the order of terms in the query vector is of no significance in this equation, we may treat q as a set and make the query-term frequency explicit in the equation:

$$p(q \mid d) \;=\; \prod_{t \in q} p(t \mid d)^{q_t}. \qquad (9.19)$$

A document language model may then be used to estimate a value for each $p(t \mid d)$, and thus we would rank documents according to

$$p(q \mid d) \; = \; \prod_{t \in q} \mathcal{M}_d(t)^{q_t}, \tag{9.20}$$

where $\mathcal{M}_d(t)$ may be $\mathcal{M}_d^\lambda(t)$, $\mathcal{M}_d^\mu(t)$, or another document language model. If we substitute $\mathcal{M}_d^\lambda(t)$ for $\mathcal{M}_d(t)$, we get

$$p(q \mid d) \; = \; \prod_{t \in q} \left((1 - \lambda) \cdot \mathcal{M}_d^{\mathrm{ml}}(t) + \lambda \cdot \mathcal{M}_\mathcal{C}(t) \right)^{q_t}. \tag{9.21}$$

If we substitute $\mathcal{M}_d^\mu(t)$ for $\mathcal{M}_d(t)$, we get

$$p(q \mid d) \; = \; \prod_{t \in q} \left(\frac{f_{t,d} + \mu \mathcal{M}_\mathcal{C}(t)}{l_d + \mu} \right)^{q_t}. \tag{9.22}$$

We could stop at this point and use either Equation 9.21 or Equation 9.22 for ranking. However, it is valuable to expend a little extra effort over the next few pages in order to achieve some additional insight into the language modeling approach and its relationship to other methods. You may have noticed that many of the characteristics saw in the ranking formulae of Chapters 2 and 8 are absent from these equations. Unlike the previous formulae, these equations do not take a TF-IDF form. Moreover, the number of documents in the collection (N) and the number of documents containing the term (N_t) do not appear in the equations at all. Nonetheless, with a little work we can find something close to TF-IDF hidden in these equations while simplifying them at the same time.

For convenience as well as consistency with the other approaches, we work with logarithms from this point forward rather than directly with the probabilities. First, we consider the terms contained in the document separately from the terms not contained in the document.

$$\log p(q \mid d) \; = \; \sum_{t \in q} q_t \cdot \log p(t \mid d) \tag{9.23}$$

$$= \; \sum_{t \in q \cap d} q_t \cdot \log p(t \mid d) + \sum_{t \in q \setminus d} q_t \cdot \log p(t \mid d) \tag{9.24}$$

When t is contained in the document, we use $\mathcal{M}_d(t)$ to estimate $p(t \mid d)$, where $\mathcal{M}_d(t)$ may be either $\mathcal{M}_d^\lambda(t)$ or $\mathcal{M}_d^\mu(t)$. When t is not contained in the document, $\mathcal{M}_d(t)$ takes the form $\alpha_d \mathcal{M}_\mathcal{C}(t)$, where α_d is a factor depending only on characteristics of d (and not on q). As indicated at the end of Section 9.2, $\alpha_d = \lambda$ for $\mathcal{M}_d^\lambda(t)$ and $\alpha_d = \mu/(l_d + \mu)$ for $\mathcal{M}_d^\mu(t)$.

We may now substitute $\mathcal{M}_d(t)$ and $\alpha_d \cdot \mathcal{M}_{\mathcal{C}}(t)$ into Equation 9.24, and with a little rearrangement, we eliminate summation over the query terms not appearing in the document:

$$\log p(q\,|\,d) \;=\; \sum_{t\in q\cap d} q_t \cdot \log \mathcal{M}_d(t) + \sum_{t\in q\backslash d} q_t \cdot \log(\alpha_d \cdot \mathcal{M}_{\mathcal{C}}(t)) \tag{9.25}$$

$$=\; \sum_{t\in q\cap d} q_t \cdot \log \mathcal{M}_d(t) - \sum_{t\in q\cap d} q_t \cdot \log(\alpha_d \cdot \mathcal{M}_{\mathcal{C}}(t)) \tag{9.26}$$

$$+\; \sum_{t\in q\cap d} q_t \cdot \log(\alpha_d \cdot \mathcal{M}_{\mathcal{C}}(t)) + \sum_{t\in q\backslash d} q_t \cdot \log(\alpha_d \cdot \mathcal{M}_{\mathcal{C}}(t)) \tag{9.27}$$

$$=\; \sum_{t\in q\cap d} q_t \cdot \log \frac{\mathcal{M}_d(t)}{\alpha_d\,\mathcal{M}_{\mathcal{C}}(t)} + \sum_{t\in q} q_t \cdot \log(\alpha_d \cdot \mathcal{M}_{\mathcal{C}}(t)) \tag{9.28}$$

$$=\; \sum_{t\in q\cap d} q_t \cdot \log \frac{\mathcal{M}_d(t)}{\alpha_d\,\mathcal{M}_{\mathcal{C}}(t)} + n \cdot \log \alpha_d + \sum_{t\in q} q_t \cdot \log \mathcal{M}_{\mathcal{C}}(t). \tag{9.29}$$

Here $n = \sum_{t\in q} q_t$ represents the number of tokens in the query. The last term, $\sum_{t\in q} q_t \cdot \log \mathcal{M}_{\mathcal{C}}(t)$, is constant for all documents and may be dropped to give the rank-equivalent formula

$$\sum_{t\in q\cap d} q_t \cdot \log \frac{\mathcal{M}_d(t)}{\alpha_d\,\mathcal{M}_{\mathcal{C}}(t)} + n \cdot \log \alpha_d. \tag{9.30}$$

This formula has two parts. The part on the left is a sum over weights associated with the query terms appearing in the document and is reminiscent of the ranking formulae presented in previous chapters. The part on the right may be viewed as a document-specific adjustment or normalization that is independent of the specific query terms but not of query or document length.

We now specialize Equation 9.30 by replacing $\mathcal{M}_d(t)$ with each of our two smoothed language models, $\mathcal{M}_d^\lambda(t)$ and $\mathcal{M}_d^\mu(t)$. Substituting $\mathcal{M}_d^\lambda(t)$ gives

$$\sum_{t\in q\cap d} q_t \cdot \log \frac{\mathcal{M}_d^\lambda(t)}{\alpha_d\,\mathcal{M}_{\mathcal{C}}(t)} + n \cdot \log \alpha_d \;=\; \sum_{t\in q\cap d} q_t \cdot \log \frac{(1-\lambda)\,\mathcal{M}_d^{\mathrm{ml}}(t) + \lambda \mathcal{M}_{\mathcal{C}}(t)}{\lambda \mathcal{M}_{\mathcal{C}}(t)} + n \cdot \log \lambda$$

$$=\; \sum_{t\in q\cap d} q_t \cdot \log \frac{(1-\lambda)\,f_{t,d}/l_d + \lambda l_t/l_{\mathcal{C}}}{\lambda l_t/l_{\mathcal{C}}} + n \cdot \log \lambda.$$

The term $n \cdot \log \lambda$ is a constant and may be dropped. A little re-arranging gives the final form of the ranking formula:

$$\sum_{t\in q} q_t \cdot \log \left(1 + \frac{1-\lambda}{\lambda} \cdot \frac{f_{t,d}}{l_d} \cdot \frac{l_{\mathcal{C}}}{l_t} \right). \tag{9.31}$$

In the remainder of the book we refer to this formula as *language modeling with Jelinek-Mercer smoothing* (LMJM). In general the optimal value for λ appears to be related to query length, with larger values being more appropriate for longer queries. In the absence of training data or other information, experience has shown $\lambda = 0.5$ to be an acceptable value. Unless otherwise indicated, we use $\lambda = 0.5$ for examples and experiments.

We return to consider the document collection in Table 2.1. Given the query $\langle$ "quarrel", "sir" $\rangle$, we would compute the LMJM score for document 1 as follows:

$$\log \left(1 + \frac{1-\lambda}{\lambda} \cdot \frac{f_{\text{quarrel},1}}{l_1} \cdot \frac{l_{\mathcal{C}}}{l_{\text{quarrel}}} \right) + \log \left(1 + \frac{1-\lambda}{\lambda} \cdot \frac{f_{\text{sir},1}}{l_1} \cdot \frac{l_{\mathcal{C}}}{l_{\text{sir}}} \right)$$

$$= \log \left(1 + \frac{0.5}{0.5} \cdot \frac{1}{4} \cdot \frac{28}{2} \right) + \log \left(1 + \frac{0.5}{0.5} \cdot \frac{1}{4} \cdot \frac{28}{5} \right) \approx 3.43.$$

Before proceeding, it is worthwhile to examine briefly the structure of Equation 9.31. Document-oriented collection statistics, such as N and N_t, are nowhere to be seen. However, the presence of the collection language model, $l_{\mathcal{C}}/l_t$, inside the logarithm is suggestive of IDF and its close association with $f_{t,d}$ is suggestive of TF-IDF, so something of the equations of Chapters 2 and 8 can be seen here.

The document length plays an interesting role. The fraction $f_{t,d}/l_d$ is the average number of occurrences of t per document token. When it is multiplied by $l_{\mathcal{C}}/l_t$, the result may be interpreted as the ratio of the actual number of occurrences per token to the expected number of occurrences based on the collection language model.

We now consider Dirichlet smoothing. Substituting $\mathcal{M}_d^\mu(t)$ for $\mathcal{M}_d(t)$ in Equation 9.30 and simplifying gives the ranking formula for $\mu > 0$,

$$\sum_{t \in q \cap d} q_t \cdot \log \frac{\mathcal{M}_d^\mu(t)}{\alpha_d \mathcal{M}_{\mathcal{C}}(t)} + n \cdot \log \alpha_d = \sum_{t \in q} q_t \cdot \log \left(1 + \frac{f_{t,d}}{\mu} \cdot \frac{l_{\mathcal{C}}}{l_t} \right) - n \cdot \log \left(1 + \frac{l_d}{\mu} \right), \quad (9.32)$$

which we refer to as *language modeling with Dirichlet smoothing* (LMD). In this formula the document length normalization is separated out into the term on the right. As in Equation 9.31, you may detect a hint of TF-IDF in the relationship between term frequency and the collection language model. Unless otherwise indicated we use this formula for experiments and examples with $\mu = 1000$. We emphasize, however, that in practice the value of μ should be tuned using appropriate training data (see Chapter 11).

If all documents in the collection have the same length, the two smoothing methods can be made equivalent by setting $\mu = l_d \cdot \frac{\lambda}{1-\lambda}$. This observation suggests that we might pick an acceptable value for μ, based on an existing value for λ, by replacing l_d with the average document length l_{avg}, resulting in the value $\mu = l_{avg} \cdot \frac{\lambda}{1-\lambda}$. If we treat 0.5 as the default value for λ, the corresponding default value for μ is then simply the average document length. By substituting l_{avg} for μ in Equation 9.32 and by noting that $l_{avg} = l_{\mathcal{C}}/N$, the LMD ranking formula reduces to

$$\sum_{t \in q} q_t \cdot \log \left(1 + f_{t,d} \cdot \frac{N}{l_t} \right) - n \cdot \log \left(1 + \frac{l_d}{l_{avg}} \right). \quad (9.33)$$

The presence of N in this formula strengthens the relationship with IDF that we noted earlier. The equation also contains hints of the document length normalization seen in Okapi BM25.

If we use LMD to rank the collection in Table 2.1 with respect to the query $\langle$"quarrel","sir"$\rangle$, we would compute a score for document 1 as follows:

$$\log\left(1 + f_{\text{quarrel},1} \cdot \frac{N}{l_{\text{quarrel}}}\right) + \log\left(1 + f_{\text{sir},1} \cdot \frac{N}{l_{\text{sir}}}\right) - n \cdot \log\left(1 + \frac{l_1}{l_{\text{avg}}}\right)$$
$$= \log\left(1 + 1 \cdot \tfrac{5}{2}\right) + \log\left(1 + 1 \cdot \tfrac{5}{5}\right) - 2 \cdot \log\left(1 + \tfrac{4}{5.6}\right) \approx 1.25.$$

9.4   Kullback-Leibler Divergence

An alternative theoretical framework for understanding and working with the language modeling approach is provided by a concept known as *Kullback-Leibler divergence*. KL divergence, also known as *relative entropy*, is a method for comparing two probability distributions.

Given continuous probability distributions $f(x)$ and $g(x)$ the KL divergence between them is defined as

$$\int_{-\infty}^{\infty} f(x) \cdot \log \frac{f(x)}{g(x)} \, dx . \tag{9.34}$$

In information retrieval, we normally work with discrete distributions, for which KL divergence takes the form

$$\sum_x f(x) \cdot \log \frac{f(x)}{g(x)} . \tag{9.35}$$

Larger values indicate greater divergence. When f and g represent the same distribution, their KL divergence is zero, since $\log\left(f(x)/g(x)\right) = \log 1 = 0$.

For example, the flip of a "fair" coin will produce heads or tails with equal probability. If an "unfair" coin produces heads with a 40% probability and tails with a 60% probability, the KL divergence between the fair and unfair coin may be computed as

$$0.5 \cdot \log \frac{0.5}{0.4} + 0.5 \cdot \log \frac{0.5}{0.6} \approx 0.02945.$$

In this example, we choose 2 for the base of the logarithm because the choice is arbitrary.

KL divergence is not symmetric in the sense that reversing the roles of $f(x)$ and $g(x)$ may produce a different value. For example, if we reverse the roles of the fair and unfair coins, the KL divergence becomes

$$0.4 \cdot \log \frac{0.4}{0.5} + 0.6 \cdot \log \frac{0.6}{0.5} = 0.02905.$$

Due to this asymmetry KL divergence is sometimes viewed as comparing a "true" distribution with another distribution in which $f(x)$ in Equation 9.35 represents this true distribution. From an information-theoretic standpoint, KL divergence indicates the average number of extra bits per symbol needed to transmit or compress a message if we assume its symbols are distributed according to g instead of the true distribution f.

In order to apply KL divergence to ranking, we construct a language model from the query $\mathcal{M}_q(t)$ in much the same way that we constructed a language model from the document. The simplest language model is the maximum likelihood model: the ratio of the number of times t appears in the query to the length of the query:

$$\mathcal{M}_q^{\mathrm{ml}}(t) \;=\; \frac{q_t}{n}\,. \tag{9.36}$$

It is also possible to create more complex query language models through smoothing or other processes, just as we did for the document language models.

We then apply KL divergence to rank documents by computing the divergence between the query language model and the document language model:

$$\sum_{t\in\mathcal{V}} \mathcal{M}_q(t) \cdot \log \frac{\mathcal{M}_q(t)}{\mathcal{M}_d(t)} \;=\; \sum_{t\in\mathcal{V}} \mathcal{M}_q(t) \cdot \log \mathcal{M}_q(t) - \sum_{t\in\mathcal{V}} \mathcal{M}_q(t) \cdot \log \mathcal{M}_d(t)\,. \tag{9.37}$$

The summation on the left is the same for all documents and may be dropped as an order-preserving transform. The summation on the right, without the negative sign, increases with decreasing divergence and is therefore suitable as a ranking formula:

$$\sum_{t\in\mathcal{V}} \mathcal{M}_q(t) \cdot \log \mathcal{M}_d(t)\,. \tag{9.38}$$

Now, if we replace $\mathcal{M}_q(t)$ with the maximum likelihood language model $\mathcal{M}_q^{\mathrm{ml}}(t)$, the formula becomes

$$\sum_{t\in\mathcal{V}} \mathcal{M}_q^{\mathrm{ml}}(t) \cdot \log \mathcal{M}_d(t) \;=\; \frac{1}{n} \cdot \sum_{t\in q} q_t \cdot \log \mathcal{M}_d(t)\,. \tag{9.39}$$

The constant $\frac{1}{n}$ may be dropped to give the rank-equivalent formula

$$\sum_{t\in q} q_t \cdot \log \mathcal{M}_d(t)\,, \tag{9.40}$$

which is exactly Equation 9.20 (in log-space).

Instead of using a maximum likelihood model for $\mathcal{M}_q(t)$ in Equation 9.38, we may instead view the presence of a query language model as an opportunity for query expansion, extending the query language model to estimate nonzero probabilities for terms not appearing in the original query. In this way we can assign positive scores to documents that may not contain any of the query terms. For example, given the query ⟨"law", "enforcement", "dogs"⟩ in Figure 1.8 (page 25), a document discussing the use of police canine (or K-9) units for drug searches would certainly be relevant. As a result, performance might be improved by adding the terms "police", "canine", "K-9", "drug", and "searches" to the query, perhaps with appropriate weighting to reflect their secondary status as expansion terms. The language model $\mathcal{M}_q(t)$ represents a bridge between the original query terms and potential expansion terms, thereby providing a theoretically sound route for their identification and weighting.

Lafferty and Zhai (2001) suggest an approach for expanding the query language model based on a random "walk" through the collection, starting at a document containing a query term. At the first step of the walk a random document containing a query term is selected in which the selection is weighted by term frequency and perhaps other factors. A random term is then selected from the new document according to $\mathcal{M}_d(t)$. With probability p_{stop} the walk stops. With probability $1 - p_{stop}$ it continues. We then randomly select a document containing the new term, then a new term from that document, and so on. The query language model $\mathcal{M}_q(t)$ is then based on the probability of stopping at term t during this walk.

Lafferty and Zhai present a matrix formalization of this informal idea, thus effectively allowing the walk to be performed for all terms simultaneously. For efficiency they stop the walk after a small number of steps in order to avoid assigning a tiny probability to a prohibitively large number of terms. They report significant effectiveness improvements over several collections, including TREC45.

9.5   Divergence from Randomness

The *divergence from randomness* (DFR) approach to information retrieval explicitly assumes a random process for the distribution of terms in documents, and then ranks documents by considering the probability that the actual term distribution found in a document would occur by chance. Similar considerations appear implicitly in the language modeling approach through its incorporation of a collection language model into the smoothing process. For example, we noted on page 295 that Equation 9.31 includes the ratio of the actual number of occurrences in a document to the expected number of occurrences based on the collection language model.

An important property of DFR is the absence of the seemingly arbitrary parameters that appear in other methods and require tuning over a training set. Parameters such as μ in LMD, λ in LMJM, and k_1 in BM25 often appear unintuitive, defying an easy explanation for their presence. DFR offers retrieval effectiveness comparable with these methods in a non-parametric form.

In this section we also revisit the notion of eliteness that we introduced in Section 8.4. Having determined the probability that a random document d would contain $f_{t,d}$ occurrences of term t where $f_{t,d} > 0$, we exploit the notion of eliteness to estimate the probability that the document is actually "about" the concept embodied in the term. In Section 8.4 this notion was modeled by a two-Poisson distribution. In this section we present an approach based on Laplace's *law of succession*.

At its most generic the core of the DFR approach may be summarized by the formula

$$(1 - P_2) \cdot (- \log P_1), \tag{9.41}$$

In this formula P_1 represents the probability that a random document d contains exactly $f_{t,d}$ occurrences of t. The value $-\log P_1$ may be viewed as the number of bits of information, called the *self-information*, associated with d containing exactly $f_{t,d}$ occurrences of t (see Section 6.1). Our random process for distributing occurrences of the term t across the document collection is unlikely to assign a large proportion of these terms to the specific document d. Thus P_1 may decrease rapidly as $f_{t,d}$ increases.

P_2 provides an adjustment that reflects eliteness, thus correcting for this rapid decrease. If d is elite in the t, we might assume that the occurrences of t that appear within it are not accidental. Suppose we begin reading d, which is elite in t, in order to count the number of occurrences of t it contains. Well before we reach its end, we discover $f_{t,d} - 1$ occurrences of t. This discovery suggests that we should expect to find more occurrences and P_2 is the probability of finding at least one. P_2 increases as $f_{t,d}$ increases. Thus, $(1 - P_2)$ in Equation 9.41 decreases as $f_{t,d}$ increases.

Thus far we have considered only a single term. To rank documents with respect to a multi-term query, we make the usual independence assumption, giving the ranking formula

$$\sum_{t \in q} q_t \cdot (1 - P_2) \cdot (-\log P_1). \tag{9.42}$$

In the remainder of the presentation we focus on estimating P_1 and P_2 for a given term t with the understanding that these estimates will be used in this formula for ranking.

The theory underlying the DFR was first developed by Amati and van Rijsbergen (2002), and was validated through experimentation at TREC conferences (Plachouras et al., 2002; Amati et al., 2003). In addition to providing substantial theoretical justification for Equation 9.41, Amati and van Rijsbergen (2002) present and evaluate seven methods for estimating P_1 and two methods for estimating P_2. In this chapter we examine in detail only one of each, chosen for their ability to illustrate the reasoning underlying the approach as well as their retrieval effectiveness.

In addition Amati and van Rijsbergen present two methods for incorporating document length normalization into the DFR approach. For the time being we will ignore this complicating issue by assuming that all documents are of the same length. Toward the end of our presentation we will return to the issue by handling document length normalization in the spirit of Equation 8.45, computing an adjusted term frequency for documents of nonaverage length and using it to replace the actual term frequency.

9.5.1 A Model of Randomness

Suppose we randomly distribute terms into documents. If we have l_t occurrences of term t distributed across N documents, then

$$f_{t,1} + f_{t,2} + \ldots + f_{t,N} = l_t, \tag{9.43}$$

where $f_{t,i}$ is the number of occurrences of term t in the ith document. How many different ways can l_t occurrences be distributed across N documents, assuming that the documents are indistinguishable? For example, four occurrences can be distributed across three documents in four different ways: (1) all occurrences into one document, (2) three occurrences into one document and one into another, (3) two occurrences in one document and one in each of the other documents, or (4) two occurrences in two documents. In other words, how many different arrangements of terms will satisfy Equation 9.43?

To answer this question, Amati and van Rijsbergen recognize that this problem is identical to the problem addressed by *Bose-Einstein statistics*, which computes the number of ways indistinguishable particles may be assigned to energy states in thermal equilibrium. The solution may be expressed as a binomial coefficient:

$$\binom{N + l_t - 1}{l_t} = \frac{(N + l_t - 1)!}{(N - 1)!\, l_t!}. \tag{9.44}$$

Alternatively, the problem may be viewed as equivalent to the problem of determining the number of ways in which m balls can be distributed across n indistinguishable bins, a version of the *occupancy problem* from combinatorics.

In order to compute an estimate of P_1 for term t, we assume that a given document d is found to contain $f_{t,d}$ occurrences of t. A random distribution of the remaining $l_t - f_{t,d}$ occurrences into the remaining documents must satisfy the equation

$$f_{t,1} + \cdots + f_{t,d-1} + f_{t,d+1} + \cdots + f_{t,N} = l_t - f_{t,d}. \tag{9.45}$$

The number of ways to satisfy this equation follows from Equation 9.44:

$$\binom{(N - 1) + (l_t - f_{t,d}) - 1}{l_t - f_{t,d}} = \frac{((N - 1) + (l_t - f_{t,d}) - 1)!}{(N - 2)!\, (l_t - f_{t,d})!}. \tag{9.46}$$

This equation assumes that a selected document contains $f_{t,d}$ occurrences and represents the number of ways the remaining terms can be distributed. Equation 9.44 represents the number of ways l_t occurrences may be distributed across N documents. Thus, the ratio of these equations represents P_1, the probability that a selected document contains $f_{t,d}$ occurrences:

$$P_1 = \frac{\binom{(N - 1) + (l_t - f_{t,d}) - 1}{l_t - f_{t,d}}}{\binom{N + l_t - 1}{l_t}} = \frac{((N - 1) + (l_t - f_{t,d}) - 1)!\, (N - 1)!\, l_t!}{(N - 2)!(l_t - f_{t,d})!\, (N + l_t - 1)!}. \tag{9.47}$$

Unfortunately, the presence of factorials in Equation 9.47 makes it difficult to work with it directly. Instead, Amati and van Rijsbergen provide two methods for estimating its value and demonstrate that both methods provide similar performance in terms of effectiveness. The simpler of these methods provides an estimate for P_1 of

$$P_1 = \left(\frac{1}{1+l_t/N}\right)\left(\frac{l_t/N}{1+l_t/N}\right)^{f_{t,d}},$$
(9.48)

and therefore

$$-\log P_1 = \log(1+l_t/N) + f_{t,d} \cdot \log(1+N/l_t).$$
(9.49)

The term on the right has a form reminiscent of TF-IDF, but with l_t taking the role of N_t.

9.5.2   Eliteness

Amati and van Rijsbergen obtain one estimate for P_2 by way of Laplace's law of succession, which can best be explained by an example. Suppose we have seen the sun rise on each of $m-1$ successive mornings. In the absence of other information, such as a physical model of the Earth orbiting the sun, what probability should we assign to the event that the sun will rise tomorrow? Even though we are fairly certain this event will happen, it is not appropriate to assign it a value of 1, absolute certainty. After all, the sun may not rise tomorrow. Instead (without getting into the mathematical details) the law of succession suggests the value $m/(m+1)$.

Amati and van Rijsbergen apply the law of succession to estimate

$$P_2 = \frac{f_{t,d}}{f_{t,d}+1}.$$
(9.50)

They explain this equation as the "conditional probability of having one more token of the term in the document [...], assuming that the length of a relevant document is very large". Substituting this estimate along with Equation 9.49 into 9.41 gives

$$(1-P_2)(-\log P_1) = \frac{\log(1+l_t/N) + f_{t,d}\log(1+N/l_t)}{f_{t,d}+1}.$$
(9.51)

The term-frequency component in this formula resembles the term-frequency component of the Okapi BM25 ranking formula (Equation 8.48 on page 272), and possesses a similar saturation property. Regardless of the value of $f_{t,d}$, the value of Equation 9.51 is bounded by $\log(1+l_t/N) + \log(1+N/l_t)$.

9.5.3   Document Length Normalization

Equation 9.51 assumes that all documents have the same length. When documents vary in length, Amati and van Rijsbergen suggest a normalization in which an adjusted term frequency $f'_{t,d}$ replaces $f_{t,d}$ in the equation. They derive and evaluate two methods for computing this adjustment. The better-performing of these methods is

$$f'_{t,d} \;=\; f_{t,d} \cdot \log\left(1 + l_{avg}/l_d\right). \tag{9.52}$$

They call the combination of Equation 9.49 and 9.50, as adjusted by Equation 9.52, the GL2 variant of the DFR approach. We use this variant for the experiments reported in this book.

9.6   Passage Retrieval and Ranking

Most of the ranking methods we examine in this book rank documents. Depending on the application environment, these documents may correspond to Web pages, news articles, e-mail messages, or a combination of these and other document types. In some environments it may be appropriate to rank elements within documents, such as the pages in a book or the sections in a news article. In other circumstances *arbitrary passage retrieval* may be desirable so that any fragment of text within a document may be returned as a ranked result.

William **Shakespeare** — Wikipedia, the free encyclopedia

At the age of 18, **Shakespeare** married the 26-year-old Anne Hathaway. The consistory court of the Diocese of Worcester issued a **marriage** licence on 27 November 1582. Two of Hathaway's neighbours posted bonds the next day ...

en.wikipedia.org/wiki/William_**Shakespeare**

Figure 9.1   A typical search engine result for the query ⟨"shakespeare", "marriage"⟩, evaluated against Wikipedia. The result provides a brief snippet from the document that shows the query terms in context.

One such circumstance is generation of snippets to provide a simple summary of the contents of a retrieved document for presentation to the user. Figure 9.1 provides an example of the result a search engine might return from Wikipedia given the query ⟨"shakespeare", "marriage"⟩. Along with the title of the Web page and its URL, the search engine provides a snippet extracted from the body of the document to illustrate the context in which the search terms appear.

Question answering is another application in which arbitrary passage retrieval may be valuable (Tellex et al., 2003). Given a question such as "What is the population of India?", a question answering system attempts to provide an exact answer ("1.12 billion") rather than a document that may contain the answer. Passage retrieval is often an early step in question answering. Keywords are extracted from the question and formed into a query for processing by an IR system (⟨"population", "india"⟩). Passages containing these terms are then retrieved from the corpus and analyzed to extract and validate possible answers. An interval containing the query terms in close proximity ("...population of India, ...") is likely to be part of a slightly longer but still short passage containing the answer ("...The population of India is..."). The interval represents a "hot spot" within the collection near which the answer may be found.

In Section 2.2.2 we presented a simple ranking method based solely on term proximity. That method locates *covers* for a query vector $q = \langle t_1, t_2, ..., t_n \rangle$, where a cover is defined as an interval of text $[u, v]$ that contains at least one occurrence of each term in the query and does not contain a smaller interval that also contains all the terms.

We now extend the notion of a cover to subsets of the query terms. We define an *m-cover* for $m \leq n$ terms as an interval $[u, v]$ in the collection that contains an occurrence of at least m distinct terms in the query and does not contain a smaller interval that also contains m distinct terms. For simplicity we assume that terms are not repeated in q because the passage ranking method in this section does not take repeated query terms into account. For example, the set of 2-covers for the query vector $\langle$"you", "quarrel", "sir"$\rangle$ over the collection in Table 2.1 (page 50) consists of the intervals $[2, 3]$, $[3, 4]$, $[4, 5]$, $[5, 6]$, $[8, 10]$, $[10, 12]$, $[12, 16]$, $[24, 28]$. Note that the interval $[12, 24]$ is not included in the set because it contains $[12, 16]$. Note also that $[24, 28]$ is included even though it cuts across the last three documents. In most applications *m*-covers such as this one would be filtered from the set before use. However, for simplicity we define *m*-covers without consideration for document boundaries and other structures and apply a postprocessing pass as appropriate.

The notion of an *m*-cover may be used to support snippet generation and arbitrary passage retrieval for question answering. Suppose we are looking for a snippet to display within an indexed Web page. Ideally we would display a snippet containing all the query terms in close proximity, but this goal is not always possible. Some of the query terms may appear only far apart, at the start and the end of the document. Some of the query terms may appear only in the title of the document and not in the body. Some of the query terms may not appear in the document at all. Instead, the snippet might be composed of text fragments corresponding to one or more *m*-covers that together contain as many of the terms as possible. Once an appropriate set of *m*-covers is determined, each could be extended to include the nearest sentence boundaries and then trimmed to fit into the required space.

In the context of question answering, a passage containing a strict subset of the query terms in close proximity may be more likely to yield an answer than a much longer passage containing all the query terms. For example, suppose we are answering the question "Who starred in the film *Shakespeare in Love*?" We might execute the query vector $\langle$"starred", "film", "shakespeare", "love"$\rangle$ and analyze the result for possible answers. A short 3-cover containing the terms "shakespeare" and "love" along with just one of the terms "starred" or "film" may be a better indicator of an answer than a longer passage containing all the terms, in which the answer may be mixed with other names and details. More generally, for applications such as snippet generation and question answering, we must select intervals by trading off length against the combination of query terms they contain.

9.6.1   Passage Scoring

Assume we have an interval $[u, v]$ that we wish to score with respect to a query $q = \langle t_1, t_2, ..., t_n \rangle$. Further assume that the interval contains a subset of the query terms $q' \subseteq q$, where $q' = \langle t_1', t_2', ..., t_m' \rangle$ and $m \leq n$. We assign a score to $[u, v]$, with length $l = v - u + 1$, by estimating the probability that a randomly selected interval of this length would contain at least one occurrence of these query terms. Like the method described in Section 9.5, the passage scoring method relates the actual distribution of terms to a random distribution.

For this purpose we model the collection as a sequence of independently generated terms and assume that there is a fixed probability p_t of a term $t \in q'$ matching at any given document location. Note that this assumption allows multiple terms to match at a particular location. Although unrealistic, this assumption is tolerable when p_t is small, as it is for most terms, and helps to simplify the derivation of a passage scoring formula.

Given the interval $[u, v]$ with length $l = v - u + 1$, the probability $p(t, l)$ that the interval contains one or more occurrences of t is

$$p(t, l) \quad = \quad 1 - (1 - p_t)^l \tag{9.53}$$

$$= \quad 1 - (1 - lp_t + O(p_t{}^2)) \tag{9.54}$$

$$\approx \quad l \cdot p_t . \tag{9.55}$$

The probability that $[u, v]$ contains all the terms from q' is then

$$p(q', l) \quad = \quad \prod_{t \in q'} p(t, l) \quad \approx \quad \prod_{t \in q'} l \cdot p_t \quad = \quad l^m \cdot \prod_{t \in q'} p_t . \tag{9.56}$$

Finally, we estimate p_t as the collection frequency of the term t:

$$p_t \quad = \quad l_t / l_{\mathcal{C}} , \tag{9.57}$$

where l_t is the total number of times t appears in the collection and $l_{\mathcal{C}}$ is the total length of the collection. Substituting and taking a negative logarithm (i.e., the self-information) gives

$$\sum_{t \in q'} (\log(l_{\mathcal{C}} / l_t)) - m \cdot \log(l) . \tag{9.58}$$

The relationship between length and collection frequency in this equation resembles the relationship in Equation 9.32.

9.6.2   Implementation

Perhaps not surprisingly, the algorithm to locate m-covers is a simple extension of the adaptive algorithm appearing in Figure 2.10 (page 61). The details of the extended algorithm are given in Figure 9.2. For a given value of m the algorithm locates the next m-cover after a given position.

nextCover $(\langle t_1, ..., t_n \rangle,\ position,\ m) \equiv$
1   **for** $i \leftarrow 1$ **to** n **do**
2        $V[i] \leftarrow$ **next**$(t_i,\ position)$
3    $v \leftarrow m$th largest element of V
4   **if** $v = \infty$ **then**
5   **return** $[\infty, \infty]$
6    $u \leftarrow v$
7   **for** $i \leftarrow 1$ **to** n **do**
8   **if** $V[i] < v$ and **prev**$(t_i,\ v + 1) < u$ **then**
9            $u \leftarrow$ **prev**$(t_i,\ v + 1)$
10   **return** $[u, v]$

Figure 9.2   Function to locate the next occurrence of an m-cover for the term vector $\langle t_1, ..., t_n \rangle$ after a given position. The integer array V is used to store intermediate calculations.

Lines 1–2 find the next occurrence of each individual term after this position. The m-th largest term becomes the end point (v) for the m-cover (line 3). For each term occurring before v we locate its last occurrence before v (lines 7–9). The smallest of these values becomes the start point (u) for the m-cover.

To generate all m-covers we repeatedly call this extended version of **nextCover** across the collection for all values of $m > 1$.

for $m \leftarrow n$ **down to** 2 **do**
    $u \leftarrow -\infty$
    while $u < \infty$ **do**
        $[u, v] \leftarrow$ **nextCover**$(\langle t_1, t_2, ..., t_n \rangle, u, m)$
        if $u \neq \infty$ **then**
            report the m-cover $[u, v]$

It is not necessary to explicitly generate 1-covers because these can be taken directly from the postings lists for the terms.

Depending on the application, it is not usually necessary to generate all m-covers across the entire collection. For snippet generation we are interested only in the m-covers contained in top ranking documents. For question answering we are interested only in a single best m-cover from a fixed number of documents. Clarke et al. (2006) discuss optimizations for fast m-cover generation in this second case.

9.7   Experimental Comparison

Table 9.1   Effectiveness measures for selected retrieval methods discussed in this chapter.

| | TREC45 | | | | GOV2 | | | |
| | 1998 | | 1999 | | 2005 | | 2006 | |
Method	P@10	MAP	P@10	MAP	P@10	MAP	P@10	MAP
LMJM (Eq. 9.31)	0.390	0.179	0.432	0.209	0.416	0.211	0.494	0.257
LMD (Eq. 9.32)	0.450	0.193	0.428	0.226	0.484	0.244	0.580	0.293
DFR (Eq. 9.51/9.52)	0.426	0.183	0.446	0.216	0.465	0.248	0.550	0.269

Table 9.1 shows the effectiveness of the retrieval methods presented in this chapter. The numbers in this table may be compared with those in Tables 2.5 (page 72) and 8.2 (page 279). Results for the passage retrieval algorithm of Section 9.6 are not shown in the table because the method ranks passages, not documents. Although in principle it could be used for document ranking purposes, by assigning each document the score of its highest-scoring passage, this approach breaks down for one-word queries.

9.8   Further Reading

The seminal work on the language modeling approach to information retrieval, as presented in this chapter, includes that of Ponte and Croft (1998), Berger and Lafferty (1999), Zhai and Lafferty (2004), and the Ph.D. thesis of Hiemstra (2001). A volume edited by Croft and Lafferty consolidates much of the work up to 2003 (Croft and Lafferty, 2003). Lavrenko and Croft (2001) explore the role of relevance in the language modeling approach. Other early work includes that of Miller et al. (1999), who derive Equation 9.21 by assuming that queries are generated from documents using a hidden Markov model (HMM), where λ selects between a document state and a general language state, as represented by the collection. They then extend this HMM framework to incorporate pseudo-relevance feedback, proximity, and document priors.

Smoothing plays an important part in language modeling techniques across the full range of human language technologies. Chapter 6 of Manning and Schütze (1999) includes a general introduction to language modeling. Chen and Goodman (1998) provide a tutorial comparison of smoothing techniques.

The language modeling approach forms the foundation for a noticeable segment of current IR research. Most IR conference proceedings from the past several years contain papers that build upon or depend upon the insights of the language modeling approach. Although a complete bibliography is outside the scope of this book, we provide a few examples of recent research: Metzler and Croft (2004) combine the language modeling approach with the probabilistic inference model (Turtle and Croft, 1991; Greiff et al., 1999); Cao et al. (2005) integrate term dependence into the language modeling approach; Tao and Zhai (2007) and Zhao and Yun (2009) integrate proximity measures into the language modeling approach; Cao et al. (2008) consider pseudo-relevance feedback within a language modeling framework. Lv and Zhai (2009) consider the integration of term positional information. Zhai (2008b) provides a recent survey of language modeling for information retrieval.

9.9 Exercises

Exercise 9.1 You have discovered that documents in a certain collection have a "half-life" of 30 days. After any 30-day period a document's prior probability of relevance $p(r\,|\,D)$ is half of what it was at the start of the period. Incorporate this information into Equation 9.8. Simplify the equation into a rank-equivalent form, making any assumptions you believe are reasonable.

Exercise 9.2 Show that models resulting from Dirichlet smoothing can be treated as probability distributions. That is, show $\sum_{t \in \mathcal{V}} \mathcal{M}_d^\mu(t) = 1$.

Exercise 9.3 (project exercise) Implement the LMD ranking formula (Equation 9.33). Test your implementation using the test collection developed in Exercise 2.13 or any other available collection, such as a TREC collection.

Exercise 9.4 (project exercise) Implement DFR ranking as described in Section 9.5. Test your implementation using the test collection developed in Exercise 2.13 or with any other available collection, such as a TREC collection.

Exercise 9.5 (project exercise) Implement the passage retrieval and scoring method described in Section 9.6. Use your implementation to provide result snippets for one of the document retrieval methods described in this book.

9.10 Bibliography

Amati, G., Carpineto, C., and Romano, G. (2003). Fondazione Ugo Bordoni at TREC 2003: Robust and Web Track. In *Proceedings of the 12th Text REtrieval Conference*. Gaithersburg, Maryland.

Amati, G., and van Rijsbergen, C. J. (2002). Probabilistic models of information retrieval based on measuring the divergence from randomness. 20(4):357–389.

Berger, A., and Lafferty, J. (1999). Information retrieval as statistical translation. In *Proceedings of the 22nd Annual International ACM SIGIR Conference on Research and Development in Information Retrieval*, pages 222–229. Berkeley, California.

Cao, G., Nie, J. Y., and Bai, J. (2005). Integrating word relationships into language models. In *Proceedings of the 28th Annual International ACM SIGIR Conference on Research and Development in Information Retrieval*, pages 298–305. Salvador, Brazil.

Cao, G., Nie, J. Y., Gao, J., and Robertson, S. (2008). Selecting good expansion terms for pseudo-relevance feedback. In *Proceedings of the 31st Annual International ACM SIGIR Conference on Research and Development in Information Retrieval*, pages 243–250. Singapore.

Chen, S. F., and Goodman, J. (1998). *An Empirical Study of Smoothing Techniques for Language Modeling*. Technical Report TR-10-98. Aiken Computer Laboratory, Harvard University.

Clarke, C. L. A., Cormack, G. V., Lynam, T. R., and Terra, E. L. (2006). Question answering by passage selection. In Strzalkowski, T., and Harabagiu, S., editors, *Advances in Open Domain Question Answering*. Berlin, Germany: Springer.

Croft, W. B., and Lafferty, J., editors (2003). *Language Modeling for Information Retrieval*. Dordrecht, The Netherlands: Kluwer Academic Publishers.

Greiff, W. R., Croft, W. B., and Turtle, H. (1999). PIC matrices: A computationally tractable class of probabilistic query operators. *ACM Transactions on Information Systems*, 17(4):367–405.

Hiemstra, D. (2001). *Using language models for information retrieval*. Ph.D. thesis, University of Twente, The Netherlands.

Jelinek, F., and Mercer, R. L. (1980). Interpolated estimation of Markov source parameters from sparse data. In *Proceedings of the Workshop on Pattern Recognition in Practice*. Amsterdam, The Netherlands.

Lafferty, J., and Zhai, C. (2001). Document language models, query models, and risk minimization for information retrieval. In *Proceedings of the 24th Annual International ACM SIGIR Conference on Research and Development in Information Retrieval*, pages 111–119. New Orleans, Louisiana.

Lavrenko, V., and Croft, W. B. (2001). Relevance based language models. In *Proceedings of the 24th Annual International ACM SIGIR Conference on Research and Development in Information Retrieval*, pages 120–127. New Orleans, Louisiana.

Lv, Y., and Zhai, C. (2009). Positional language models for information retrieval. In *Proceedings of the 32nd International ACM SIGIR Conference on Research and Development in Information Retrieval*, pages 299–306. Boston, Massachusetts.

Manning, C. D., and Schütze, H. (1999). *Foundations of Statistical Natural Language Processing*. Cambridge, Massachusetts: MIT Press.

Metzler, D., and Croft, W. B. (2004). Combining the language model and inference network approaches to retrieval. *Information Processing & Management*, 40(5):735–750.

Miller, D. R. H., Leek, T., and Schwartz, R. M. (1999). A hidden Markov model information retrieval system. In *Proceedings of the 22nd Annual International ACM SIGIR Conference on Research and Development in Information Retrieval*, pages 214–221. Berkeley, California.

Plachouras, V., Ounis, I., Amati, G., and Rijsbergen, C. V. (2002). University of Glasgow at the Web Track of TREC 2002. In *Proceedings of the 11th Text REtrieval Conference*. Gaithersburg, Maryland.

Ponte, J. M., and Croft, W. B. (1998). A language modeling approach to information retrieval. In *Proceedings of the 21st Annual International ACM SIGIR Conference on Research and Development in Information Retrieval*, pages 275–281. Melbourne, Australia.

Song, F., and Croft, W. B. (1999). A general language model for information retrieval. In *Proceedings of the 8th International Conference on Information and Knowledge Management*, pages 316–321. Kansas City, Missouri.

Tao, T., and Zhai, C. (2007). An exploration of proximity measures in information retrieval. In *Proceedings of the 30th Annual International ACM SIGIR Conference on Research and Development in Information Retrieval*, pages 295–302. Amsterdam, The Netherlands.

Tellex, S., Katz, B., Lin, J., Fernandes, A., and Marton, G. (2003). Quantitative evaluation of passage retrieval algorithms for question answering. In *Proceedings of the 26th Annual International ACM SIGIR Conference on Research and Development in Informaion Retrieval*. Toronto, Canada.

Turtle, H., and Croft, W. B. (1991). Evaluation of an inference network-based retrieval model. *ACM Transactions on Information Systems*, 9(3):187–222.

Zhai, C. (2008a). *Statistical Language Models for Information Retrieval*. Synthesis Lectures on Human Language Technologies: Morgan & Claypool.

Zhai, C. (2008b). Statistical language models for information retrieval: A critical review. *Foundations and Trends in Information Retrieval*, 2.

Zhai, C., and Lafferty, J. (2001). A study of smoothing methods for language models applied to ad hoc information retrieval. In *Proceedings of the 24th Annual International ACM SIGIR Conference on Research and Development in Information Retrieval*, pages 334–342. New Orleans, Louisiana.

Zhai, C., and Lafferty, J. (2004). A study of smoothing methods for language models applied to information retrieval. *ACM Transactions on Information Systems*, 22(2):179–214.

Zhao, J., and Yun, Y. (2009). A proximity language model for information retrieval. In *Proceedings of the 32nd International ACM SIGIR Conference on Research and Development in Information Retrieval*, pages 291–298. Boston, Massachusetts.

10 Categorization and Filtering

In this chapter we consider information needs that are longstanding, recurring, or common for a large population of users. Table 10.1 shows short excerpts from 60 Wikipedia articles. Can you identify the language of each excerpt? Figure 10.1 shows an e-mail in-box with 18 messages. Can you identify the 10 spam messages?

In both of these examples the essential information need — to identify the language or to identify spam — is commonly understood and likely to arise in many circumstances. A search engine might need to identify the language of a query so as to provide a relevant response; or a searcher might wish to explicitly specify the language of documents to be retrieved (which may be different from that of the query). An e-mail spam filter must identify spam in order to prevent its delivery. A customer-support "help desk" might need to route incoming e-mail to personnel capable of reading and responding to it.

As a third and final example consider a search-oriented information need statement such as topic 383 from the TREC Filtering Track (shown in Figure 10.2), which concerns medical treatments for mental illness. A search engine, as described in the previous chapters, may be used to find historical documents in a corpus. But the user, perhaps a health-care professional, may wish to remain abreast of developments by being informed on an ongoing basis of any new articles relevant to the query. The essential information need is the same, but in the first case it is transitory, whereas in the second, it is longstanding.

Categorization is the process of labeling documents to satisfy some information need; in our examples the documents might be labeled with a tag indicating language, spam or ham (i.e., not spam), relevance or nonrelevance. *Filtering* is the process of evaluating documents on an ongoing basis according to some standing information need. Generally the outcome of filtering is to deliver the document to zero or more destinations, depending on the information need. A spam filter, for example, will either delete spam or deliver it to a junk folder but deliver ham to the user's in-box. A news filter might deliver articles on mental health to our health-care professional. *Routing* is a synonym for filtering with the connotation that documents are delivered to distinct locations, according to their category. *Selective dissemination of information* (SDI) is another synonym.

The problems of categorization and filtering are similar to those of search. In a sense they are dual formulations of the same problem: Classification and filtering find the categories to which a given document belongs; that is, the longstanding information needs that are met by the document. Search, on the other hand, finds the documents that satisfy a given information need; that is, documents belonging to a particular category, whether relevant or not.

Table 10.1 Snippets from 60 language-specific editions of Wikipedia. Each snippet is the first 50 bytes of the text of an article retrieved via the "random article" link.

18ος αιώνας | 19ος αιώνας |	8052 Novalis is a Main belt asteroid found on Sep
A távolsági jelzőmozzanatok a látás során t	Artikulu hau ez dator formatu hitzarmenekin bat.
Auzainvilliers é uma comuna francesa na região	Brgudac je selo na sjeveru Istre , u općini Lani
Burung Pacat ekor Biru adalah salah satu daripada	Byrteåi er ei elv i Tokke kommune i Telemark . H
Básendar (Bátsandar) voru fyrrum kaupstaður og	Cet article est une ébauche concernant une
Ciklobutan je bezbojni gas koji pripada grupi cik	Coordinates: 53°23′40″N 14°23′30″E
Danang (Da Nang , Đà Nẵng , fransk navn Tour	De Audi S4 is een sportieve versie van de Audi A4
Den Henri Grethen (* 16. Juli 1950 zu Esch-Uelzec	Flavius Constantius (mati 2 September 421) atau
George Thomas Moore (* 23 de febrero 1871 ,	Gijang-gun là một hạt (gun) trực thuộc
Gold Medal är den högsta utmärkelsen från Roy	Guido (-onis) [1] est nomen masculinum originis G
Her Majesty je píseň britské hudební skupiny	Hirdskjald hos Harald Hårfager , kendt fra digte
Jelizaveta Petrovna. Portree autor Charles-Amédé	Komz a raer eus filistenerezh evit ober anv en un
Koordinatės : 42°04′N 19°30′E	La strashimirita és un mineral de la classe dels
Maria Theresia Opladen (* 6. April 1948 in Engels	Ministerul Integrării Europene a fost un organ d
NGC 782 je galaxia v súhvezdí Eridanus , ktorú	Ofersǣwisc rind is plante and pyrt, þe hātte
Pedr III (21 Chwefror , 1728 – 17 Gorffennaf ,	Piec martenowski – dokładnie piec Siemensa-Mar
Püstəqasım , Azərbaycan ın Quba rayonunda bi	Questa voce di asteroidi è solo
Rënia heroike e dëshmorëve Isa Kastrati, Sokol	Sun Wukong (geleneksel Çince : 孫悟空 , basi
Suster-vaihe eli Susterian oli luultavasti ylämi	USS Gato je ime več plovil Vojne mornarice ZDA :
Èdè ni ìlànà kan pàtàkì tó jé gbòóg	Ĥarkiva Nacia Universitato nome de Vasil Karazin
Більче-Золотецький ландша	Война между родами Токугав
За филма от 1994 вижте Гарван	Курија е село во Општина Не
Уколико сте тражили расу п	מורוני הינה העיר הגדולה בי
مبارک آباد ، روستایی است از	هذه المقالة وسمت عن طريق بو
अनुबंधालु छगु तेल	कृपया या लेखाचा/वि
यह शब्द हिंदी में क	কানুডোস মিউনিসিপি
জয়গাঁ (ইংরেজি :Jaygaon)	੧੯੬੪ (1964) ২০ਮੀ ਸਦੀ ਦਾ
ஓமான் சுல்த்தானகம	หน้านี้เป็น ชื่อบ
პატარა გუფთა – სოფ	リューディガー・ゲルシュト (Rüdiger
袁武 , GBS , JP (1941年 11月 一), 又	아일랜드 국민당 (Irish Nationalist Party)

Categorization and filtering differ from search in a number of ways. Categories are typically (but not always) specified quite differently from the information need statements or queries associated with search. One would hardly expect the search methods presented in the preceding chapters to give a meaningful response to an information need statement such as "find documents written in Dutch" or "find spam". Even given an amenable information need, such as that of our health-care professional, the longstanding nature of information needs makes it worthwhile to spend more effort communicating the need to the system. One way to do so is to have an expert

Subject		Sender	Recipient
Washington Mutual Urgent Credit/Debit card update		service@wamu.com	emclaug@enron.com
Urgent Humanitarian Relief required for Tsunamis Indonesia		SEHAT CHARITIES	SKean@enron.com
worthy Christian		Khushab	joydish@bareed.alburaq.net
FW: Bin Laden Shoot em up		Dernehl, Ginger	"Shapiro, Richard"
REVISION!		Fresquez, Rick	"Adams, Jacqueline P.", "Bump...
Start Date: 10/25/01; HourAhead hour: 3; <CODESITE>		Schedule Crawler	pete.davis@enron.com
Gift shipment ready KAM.KEISER@enron.com need address		DVDPlayer	KAM.KEISER@enron.com
ERV Notification: (Enron Americas Position Report - 11/21/2001)		Wallace, Cassi	"Abel, Chris", "Allison, John", "...
Rate and Currency Counterparty Exposure as of 12/12/2001		Carrington, Clara	"Moran, Tom", "Shackleton, Sa...
The Internets #1 IRS tax solution.	[omzl2]	3myjd9@msn.com	nqeb5e6@msn.com
The Internets #1 IRS tax solution.	[omzl2]	3myjd9@msn.com	nqeb5e6@msn.com
The TechNews - Bulletin, April 2005		The TechNews	skean@enron.com
Start Date: 1/31/02; HourAhead hour: 13;		Schedule Crawler	pete.davis@enron.com
Pharrmacy for you		Faith Hightower	kholst
Re:		Quigley, Dutch	"Scott, Susan M."
Windows XP Pro $49.95, Office 2003 $69.95 Win XP		Lynda Hyatt	mmotley@enron.com
3 Days left to Respond		Anthony	kholst@enron.com
佡侂偤儊偱12000媩偺亀忾偐傑偣侂佡		iouityy	keith.holst@enron.com

Figure 10.1 Ten of these 18 e-mail messages are spam. Can you identify them?

manually specify a number of rules: the vocabulary, grammar, and identifying characteristics of the various languages, spam messages, or mental health treatments. These rules are in effect complex Boolean search queries. With sufficient effort it is possible to define rules to distinguish languages, or spam from ham, or reports on treatments for depression from other articles. But, as just as they are for search, automatic methods for categorization and filtering are more efficient and typically more effective. The automatic approaches we shall consider are *machine learning* methods known as *classifiers*. A classifier learns from examples how to distinguish documents belonging to different categories.

In a sense any search method is a classifier because it aims to distinguish relevant from non-relevant documents. In the same way that a search engine may return either a set of documents or a ranked list, a classifier may be *hard* or *soft*. A hard classifier returns a Boolean result indicating whether or not a document belongs to a category, whereas a soft classifier returns a confidence score. Soft classification is often called *ranking*, and the study of soft classifiers is called *learning to rank*.

Although it is not traditionally considered machine learning, the BM25 ranking method from Chapter 8 meets our definition of a soft classifier, and may be applied with reasonable effectiveness to the filtering and categorization problems introduced in this chapter. In Section 10.1 we develop the example problems outlined previously, showing the role of classification and ranking in their solution. To illustrate this role we use BM25 because it is familiar and yields results that are good enough to serve as baselines for comparison with other methods presented in this chapter and the next. Along the way we develop evaluation measures specific to this purpose.

```
<top>
<num> Number: 383
<title> mental illness drugs
<desc> Description:
Identify drugs used in the treatment of mental illness.
<narr> Narrative:
A relevant document will include the name of a specific
or generic type of drug. Generalities are not relevant.
</top>
```

Figure 10.2 TREC 7 Adhoc and TREC 8 Filtering Topic 383.

In Section 10.2 we treat classification more formally, and in Sections 10.3 through 10.7 we describe a wide variety of learning methods that are useful for categorization and filtering. In Section 10.8, we compare the results from these methods with the BM25 baselines of Section 10.1.

10.1 Detailed Examples

Through a series of graduated examples we illustrate typical filtering and categorization problems, solutions, and evaluation methods. The problems are variants of those posed above: topic-oriented filtering, language categorization, and spam filtering. The solutions illustrated in this section employ the BM25 ranking and relevance feedback methods from Chapter 8. Although BM25 is not typically used for filtering and classification, it provides a convenient starting point for understanding the area as well as a solid baseline for comparison. Evaluation measures are developed in conjunction with the problems and solutions to which they apply. We begin with an example that is similar to the ranked retrieval task for which BM25 was designed, then progress through several variants that highlight differences in the task, approach, and evaluation measures.

10.1.1 Topic-Oriented Batch Filtering

Consider the needs of our health-care professional. The topic format is suitable as input to a search engine, but at the outset of a filtering task the documents to be searched do not yet exist! So there is nothing to do but wait for documents to arrive. If we can afford to wait for a large number of documents to arrive, we can accumulate them into a corpus, index them, and apply a search method such as BM25 to yield a ranked list of the most likely relevant documents, which is then presented to the user. We can then wait for more documents to arrive and repeat the process for each new batch of documents in turn. This approach is known as *batch filtering*. From the user's perspective batch filtering yields a viable solution if enough

Table 10.2   Topic-oriented batch filtering results. Undefined results are represented by a dash.

# Batches	n	First Batch			Second Batch			Avg. (all batches)		
		|Rel|	AP	P@10	|Rel|	AP	P@10	|Rel|	AP	P@10
1000	141	1	1.00	0.1	0	–	0.0	0.07	–	0.01
500	281	1	0.50	0.1	0	–	0.0	0.13	–	0.01
100	1407	3	0.33	0.2	0	–	0.0	0.67	–	0.04
50	2814	3	0.15	0.1	1	0.33	0.1	1.34	–	0.05
10	14070	6	0.06	0.0	8	0.17	0.1	6.70	0.10	0.07
5	28140	14	0.08	0.1	14	0.09	0.1	13.00	0.07	0.10
1	140651	67	0.05	0.1				67.00	0.05	0.10

documents arrive within a suitable time interval. Our health-care professional may be satisfied to see new articles once a week or once a month. Indeed, this may be the preferred mode of delivery. In other circumstances, such as e-mail filtering, the delay associated with batching is probably not acceptable.

To illustrate the batch filtering approach, we assume that topic 383 represents the user's information need, and process a chronological subsequence of the TREC45 corpus using BM25. In particular:

- We use the title field as a query: ⟨ "mental", "illness", "drugs" ⟩.

- Guided by our experience with multilingual search and spam filtering, we use byte 4-grams as tokens (see Section 3.3). For topic 383 stemmed and unstemmed words yield similar results, which we do not report.

- We use the BM25 parameter settings $k_1 = 1.1$ and $b = 0$, effectively ignoring document length. We retain these settings for the subsequent experiments reported in this chapter.

- For this experiment we do not use relevance feedback or pseudo-relevance feedback (Section 8.6).

- We use the *Financial Times* (FT) documents, dated 1993 and later from the TREC45 collection. These documents are chronologically ordered over a period of about two years. There are $N = 140{,}651$ documents, of which 67 are relevant to topic 383. This sequence of documents was used as the evaluation set for the *routing* and *batch filtering* tasks of the TREC 8 Filtering Track.

- To simulate batch filtering with various batch sizes, we group the documents into equal-sized batches of consecutive documents ranging from 141 documents (1000 batches; each the better part of a day's messages) to 140,651 documents (one batch; the full two years' messages). Each batch is indexed as a separate and independent document collection. The batches are presented to the BM25 filter, one batch at a time, in chronological order.

The problem of evaluating filter effectiveness is somewhat different from that of evaluating ranked retrieval. We introduce notions as necessary to evaluate our examples and relate them to the more general evaluation framework.

For the single batch of 140,651 documents, batch filtering is equivalent to ranked retrieval. We could use any of the measures introduced in Section 2.3 and expanded upon in Chapter 12. On the single batch BM25 yields P@10=0.1, P@1000=0.04, and AP=0.053.

When more than one batch is considered, an obvious but unsatisfactory approach is to compute the evaluation measure separately for each batch, then average these results to yield a summary measure. This approach is unsatisfactory for the following reasons:

- When we divide the documents into more batches, the number of documents per batch (n) and the number of relevant documents per batch ($|Rel|$) decrease. When the number of batches is large, many batches will have no relevant documents (i.e., $|Rel| = 0$). Average precision (AP) is undefined if any batch has $|Rel| = 0$. In general any measure that depends on $|Rel|$ will not work for small batches.

- Measures such as precision at k (P@k) are heavily influenced by n, thus rendering it impossible to compare results using different batch sizes.

Table 10.2 illustrates these issues. For batch sizes varying between $n = 141$ (1000 batches) and $n =$ 28,140 (5 batches), we show AP and P@10 for the first two batches and the average over all $\lceil N/n \rceil$ batches. For $n = 1$ there is only one batch.

AP is undefined for most batch sizes because many batches contain no relevant documents. Both P@10 and AP (where it is defined) vary with batch size and convey little information about the effectiveness of the method for its intended purpose.

P@k is not a suitable measure for comparing results using different batch sizes because for any given k the number of retrieved documents is proportional to the number of batches. Consider the two extreme cases of 1000 batches and a single batch. If 1000 batches are used, P@10 is the precision achieved when the user is presented 10,000 documents in total, 10 per batch. If a single batch is used, P@10 is the precision achieved when she is presented only 10 documents. A more reasonable approach is to hold the total number of documents presented to the user constant over all batches. This is achieved by evaluating P@$\lfloor \rho n \rfloor$, where $\frac{1}{n} \leq \rho \ll 1$; that is, we assume that the user is presented the top-ranked fraction ρ of each batch of documents and hence this same fraction ρ of all documents in the corpus. For our purposes we choose $\rho = \frac{k}{N}$ where N is the corpus size and k is the total number of documents presented to the user. So regardless of the batch size n, the average of P@$\lfloor \frac{kn}{N} \rfloor$ over all batches is comparable with P@k for the single batch. Table 10.3 shows P@$\lfloor \rho n \rfloor$, which corresponds to k between 10 and 2000. The numbers in each column pertain to the same overall number of retrieved documents. From this table we see that for this example, the average is largely unaffected by batch size so long as the batch size is large enough that $\lfloor \rho n \rfloor > 0$.

The measure P@$\lfloor \rho n \rfloor$ assumes that an equal proportion of documents from each batch is presented to the user. This assumption may be unrealistic because some batches will contain

Table 10.3 Size-specific P@k results for topic-oriented batch filtering.

# Batches	n	$\rho = \frac{10}{N}$	$\rho = \frac{20}{N}$	$\rho = \frac{100}{N}$	$\rho = \frac{200}{N}$	$\rho = \frac{1000}{N}$	$\rho = \frac{2000}{N}$
				P@$\lfloor \rho n \rfloor$			
1000	141	–	–	–	–	0.03	0.02
500	281	–	–	–	–	0.04	0.01
100	1407	–	–	0.05	0.04	0.04	0.02
50	2814	–	–	0.07	0.05	0.04	0.01
10	14070	0.1	0.10	0.07	0.06	0.04	0.03
5	28140	0.2	0.10	0.06	0.06	0.04	0.01
1	140651	0.1	0.15	0.07	0.06	0.04	0.03

Table 10.4 Aggregate results for topic-oriented batch filtering.

# Batches	n	P@10	P@20	P@100	P@200	P@1000	P@2000	AP
1000	141	0.2	0.10	0.07	0.08	0.04	0.02	0.058
500	281	0.1	0.15	0.08	0.08	0.04	0.03	0.056
100	1407	0.1	0.15	0.06	0.07	0.04	0.03	0.053
50	2814	0.1	0.15	0.07	0.06	0.04	0.03	0.053
10	14070	0.1	0.15	0.07	0.06	0.04	0.03	0.053
5	28140	0.1	0.15	0.07	0.06	0.04	0.03	0.053
1	140651	0.1	0.15	0.07	0.06	0.04	0.03	0.053

more relevant documents than others. This situation may arise entirely due to chance, or because the documents are chronologically ordered and their makeup will naturally be be influenced by current events. A filtering system that reflects this variable proportion may better meet the user's information needs. Suppose that the user is prepared to examine documents at an average rate of ρ; that is, over time to examine ρN of the N documents processed by the filter. Precision over these ρN documents is not optimized by presenting exactly ρn documents per batch to the user. Precision may be improved if the filter presents to the user more documents from the batches that it deems to contain a larger number of relevant documents.

Because BM25 orders documents ranked by a relevance score s, we may select, rather than the top-ranked $\lfloor \rho n \rfloor$ documents from every batch, those documents with $s > t$ for some fixed threshold t. Overall, a larger value of t will result in fewer documents being returned with higher precision, and vice versa. Therefore, for any particular k there exists a value of t such that about $k = \rho N$ documents have a score $s > t$. For the moment we assume that it is possible to determine in advance the appropriate value of t for any k. Under this assumption we coin the term *aggregate* P@k to characterize the effectiveness of the system under the choice of t that yields k documents in total (see Table 10.4). *Aggregate* AP, also shown, is derived from

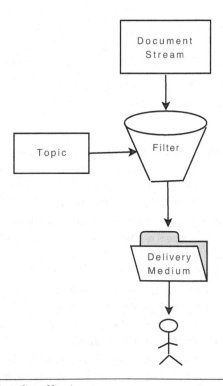

Figure 10.3   Topic-oriented on-line filtering.

aggregate P@k in the normal way. As we would expect, the numbers in each column are nearly identical. The variations are due to slight differences in IDF values from batch to batch.

Aggregate P@k and aggregate AP aptly model the real-world scenario in which the filter may be tuned to a particular user's requirement by setting t as described above. They also model the real-world scenario in which the results of each batch are entered successively into a common priority queue that the user may peruse at will. Aggregate P@k is the precision of the top k elements of the queue once all batches are processed, whereas aggregate AP measures the effectiveness of the final ranking.

10.1.2   On-Line Filtering

On-line filtering is analogous to batch filtering with batch size $n = 1$. As depicted in Figure 10.3, an on-line filter acts immediately on each message in sequence rather than on batches of messages. Messages deemed likely to be relevant are delivered to the user; those deemed unlikely to be relevant are discarded. The delivery medium may be a text message system or an e-mail system, or a result archive that the user consults when convenient. The possible media form a continuum largely characterized by immediacy, storage capacity, and access capability.

Table 10.5   Aggregate results for topic-oriented batch versus on-line filtering. The first row is repeated from Table 10.4.

Method	P@10	P@20	P@100	P@200	P@1000	P@2000	AP
Single batch	0.1	0.15	0.07	0.06	0.04	0.03	0.053
On-line	0.2	0.15	0.05	0.05	0.03	0.02	0.041

Like batch filtering, on-line filtering requires a trade-off between precision and recall. In general it is possible to increase recall at the expense of precision by delivering more messages to the user. Nowadays even the most immediate media (e.g., text messaging) have large storage capacity and sophisticated access capabilities, so the user's capacity to deal with the messages is more likely to be a constraint than that of the medium. To that end it is advantageous, where possible, to *prioritize* messages delivered to the medium, which in effect acts as a *priority queue*. As with ranked retrieval, the user tacitly determines the trade-off by examining some number of the highest-priority documents.

In the event that prioritization is impossible, it is necessary to determine a threshold t such that an appropriate number of documents is delivered. We may set t so that the rate of delivery is ρ (as described in the previous section) or to optimize some function (e.g., F_β; page 68) that captures the trade-off between precision and recall.

The relevance score of a ranked retrieval method like BM25 is a suitable indicator of priority, provided the score can be computed on a per-document basis. In this regard BM25 is not entirely amenable, because it depends on the term count N_t, whose computation assumes a large collection of documents. That said, we may apply BM25 to the near-vacuous collection consisting of only the document to be filtered, and come up with aggregate results that are not dramatically inferior to those for batch filtering, as shown in Table 10.5. In any event both batch and on-line filtering are improved substantially by the use of historical examples, as detailed in the following section.

10.1.3   Learning from Historical Examples

Generally, when a filter is deployed, we have available historical examples of documents from the same source or a similar source. Recall that the filter in our running example is to be deployed on *Financial Times* documents dated 1993 or later. The TREC45 collection also contains 69,508 *Financial Times* documents dated 1992 or earlier that can serve as historical examples.

We know from previous TREC evaluation efforts that 22 of these historical documents are relevant to topic 383. But this information would not necessarily be known at the time of filter deployment. We first consider using the historical documents without this relevance information, and then how this information, if available, may be harnessed to dramatically improve effectiveness.

Table 10.6 The effect of historical collection statistics on aggregate results for topic-oriented on-line filtering. The first two rows are repeated from Table 10.5. The third row represents a filter that uses historical collection statistics to compute IDF values. The last row shows the effect of augmenting the query with 20 terms extracted from labeled training examples through BM25 relevance feedback prior to filter deployment.

Method	P@10	P@20	P@100	P@200	P@1000	P@2000	AP
Single batch	0.1	0.15	0.07	0.06	0.04	0.03	0.053
On-line no history	0.2	0.15	0.05	0.05	0.03	0.02	0.041
On-line historical IDF	0.1	0.15	0.07	0.06	0.04	0.03	0.054
On-line historical IDF + training	1.0	0.95	0.39	0.24	0.06	0.03	0.555

Historical collection statistics

Perhaps the simplest way to use historical documents is to increase the effective batch size for batch filtering. For any given batch the historical documents are combined with those of the batch and the entire collection is ranked. Then the historical documents are removed from the ranked list, thus yielding a rank and a score for each document in the batch to be filtered. The principal effect of this approach is to yield better collection statistics (IDF in particular) and hence a more accurate relevance score. A secondary effect is that rather than returning a fixed number k of documents per batch, we can return only those that appear among the top $k' > k$ in the combined ranked list. If the batch contains more high scoring documents, more documents will be returned. For a suitable choice of k' the system will return the same number of documents overall while achieving better precision.

The use of historical documents effectively transforms the on-line filtering problem into a batch problem in which the only work to be done is to compute the score of each filtered document and, perhaps, its relative rank within the historical collection. For this purpose the index structures detailed in previous chapters are overkill. All we need to compute BM25 and similar scores is a dictionary indicating the document count N_t for each term and, if a rank score is desired, an ordered list of the historical documents' scores. To compute the relevance score we simply fetch the relevant N_t values and apply the formula; to compute rank we apply a binary search to the list of historical scores.

The third row in Table 10.6 shows the effect of using historical collection statistics on the aggregate effectiveness of our on-line filter. The aggregate result is nearly identical to that achieved by our batch filter.

Historical training examples

Because the information need associated with a filter is ongoing, it is likely that examples of relevant documents are already known or can be found without too much effort. These examples are known as *training examples* or *labeled data*. In machine learning using labeled data to build a classifier is known as *supervised learning*. In this book we have already described one simple method of supervised learning: the BM25 relevance feedback approach (Section 8.6).

As we mentioned previously, there are 22 relevant documents in our historical *Financial Times* data. We used BM25 relevance feedback to select the best $m = 20$ terms from these documents, which were used to augment the 3 terms from the topic. Using these terms, the BM25 scoring formula was applied to each document in turn as an on-line filter.

The aggregate results of this method of supervised learning are shown in the bottom row of Table 10.6. The first and last columns of results are not misprints: For this specific task the use of historical training examples yields roughly a tenfold improvement in both P@10 and AP.

10.1.4 Language Categorization

From the 60 language-specific editions of Wikipedia in Table 10.7, we fetched 8012 articles using the "random article" link and extracted from each the first 50 bytes of the main text (shown in Table 10.1 on page 311). We consider the dual problems of categorization and filtering:

- *Categorization*: Given a document d and a set of possible categories, identify the category (or categories) to which d belongs. Categorization may be reduced to *category ranking*, which ranks the categories according to how likely they are to contain the document.

- *Filtering*: Given a particular category c, identify documents that belong to c. Filtering may be reduced to *document ranking*, which ranks documents according to how likely they are to belong to the category.

For the purposes of our example the documents are snippets from Wikipedia articles and the categories are languages. By definition each document in our example belongs to exactly one category, determined by the Wikipedia edition from which it was extracted. In other situations it may make sense to consider a document as belonging to several categories; for example, a document might contain several languages or a language might have several overlapping dialects. When working with full documents, language identification is relatively straightforward (McNamee, 2005), but we deliberately limit ourselves to short snippets for the purposes of this example.

Our language categorization problem may arise when we wish to identify the language of a message for routing purposes or to organize documents into language-specific collections. Neither of these problems is readily expressed as a query that can be processed by a search engine. Instead, we rely exclusively on training examples to communicate the information need. To this end we arbitrarily consider 4000 of the snippets to be historical, and the remaining 4012 snippets as the ones to be categorized or filtered. In machine-learning terms, the historical examples form a *training set* and the others form a *test set*. The overall objective is to categorize or filter a set of examples much larger than the test set, which should be viewed as a *sample* for the purpose of estimating classifier effectiveness on the larger set.

Filtering and document ranking can be done with the methods we have introduced for topic-oriented filtering with historical examples. We consider each language to be a separate topic and apply BM25 ranking with relevance feedback (Section 8.6). For this example we treat each

Table 10.7 Tags identifying 60 language-specific Wikipedia editions.

Tag	Language	Tag	Language	Tag	Language
ang	Anglo-Saxon	fi	Finnish	nn	Nynorsk
ar	Arabic	fr	French	no	Bokmål
az	Azeri	he	Hebrew	pa	Punjabi
bg	Bulgarian	hi	Hindi	pl	Polish
bn	Bengali	hr	Croatian	pt	Portuguese
bpy	Bishnupriya	hu	Hungarian	ro	Romanian
br	Breton	id	Indonesian	ru	Russian
bs	Bosnian	is	Icelandic	simple	Simple English
ca	Catalan	it	Italian	sk	Slovak
cs	Czech	ja	Japanese	sl	Slovenian
cy	Welsh	ka	Georgian	sq	Albanian
da	Danish	ko	Korean	sr	Serbian
de	German	la	Latin	sv	Swedish
el	Greek	lb	Luxembourgish	ta	Tamil
en	English	lt	Lithuanian	th	Thai
eo	Esperanto	mk	Macedonian	tr	Turkish
es	Spanish	mr	Marathi	uk	Ukrainian
et	Estonian	ms	Malay	vi	Vietnamese
eu	Basque	new	Nepal Bhasa	yo	Yoruba
fa	Persian	nl	Dutch	zh	Chinese

of the training snippets in a topic language as a "relevant document". For a given language we create a query from the training snippets by treating each byte 4-gram as a query term.

Table 10.8 shows the per-language AP results that are achieved by applying BM25 to each of the 60 filtering problems, as well as the overall MAP. By usual search standards MAP=0.78 would indicate extremely high effectiveness, but it tells us little about how effectively (or indeed how) BM25 addresses the categorization problem.

To address the categorization problem we must rank languages instead of documents, and we must compute this ranking for every document. To do so we use the relevance scores from the document ranking. Given a document d and a language l, let $s(d,l)$ be the relevance score for d in the document ranking for language l. Now consider two languages l_1 and l_2. We assume that $s(d,l_1) > s(d,l_2)$ indicates that d is more likely to be written in language l_1 than in l_2. Under this assumption $s(d,l)$ is also the relevance score for l in the category ranking for document d.

It is infeasible to show all 4012 category rankings. Table 10.9 shows one example: the complete ranking of languages for a snippet drawn from the German Wikipedia. We see that the correct category ($l_1 = \text{de}$) is ranked first and other categories that are apparently similar — the Germanic languages — are ranked ahead of those that are dissimilar, such as Asian languages.

Table 10.8   AP results for 60 language-specific filtering problems, using BM25 with terms selected from 4000 training examples.

Tag	AP	Tag	AP	Tag	AP
ang	0.91	ar	0.99	az	0.53
bg	0.67	bn	0.84	bpy	0.81
br	0.94	bs	0.48	ca	0.70
cs	0.67	cy	0.95	da	0.40
de	0.76	el	1.00	en	0.59
eo	0.72	es	0.67	et	0.45
eu	0.82	fa	0.95	fi	0.85
fr	0.79	he	1.00	hi	0.72
hr	0.47	hu	0.75	id	0.67
is	0.93	it	0.79	ja	0.94
ka	0.99	ko	1.00	la	0.79
lb	0.97	lt	0.82	mk	0.81
mr	0.86	ms	0.68	new	0.91
nl	0.84	nn	0.63	no	0.45
pa	0.96	pl	0.83	pt	0.83
ro	0.92	ru	0.75	simple	0.54
sk	0.75	sl	0.59	sq	0.60
sr	0.68	sv	0.76	ta	0.97
th	1.00	tr	0.82	uk	0.84
vi	0.96	yo	0.63	zh	0.87

MAP: 0.78

Strictly applying our problem definition, there is exactly one relevant result: the correct category. All others are nonrelevant.

Table 10.10 lists overall summary measures for the 4012 language rankings. In this table P@1 is more commonly called *accuracy*: the proportion of documents for which the correct category was ranked first. MAP is equal to the measure known as *mean reciprocal rank* (MRR) because there is exactly one relevant result per ranking (see page 409). For a single topic, reciprocal rank is defined as $RR = \frac{1}{r}$, where r is the rank of the first (and only) relevant result. Because $AP = P@r = \frac{1}{r}$, in this case $RR = AP$ and $MRR = MAP$.

The summaries shown in the table are expressed as *micro-averages* and as *macro-averages*, defined as follows:

- *Micro-average*: A summary measure over all documents, without regard to category.
- *Macro-average*: The average of summary measures computed for each category.

Table 10.9 Language ranking for the German snippet shown at the top of the table (correct tag: **de**). $s(d,l)$ denotes the BM25 score for the given language.

Werner Haase (* 2. August 1900 in Köthen (Anhalt					
Tag	$s(d,l)$	**Tag**	$s(d,l)$	**Tag**	$s(d,l)$
de	58.2	lb	35.2	da	33.6
no	29.1	en	28.4	tr	19.4
sk	18.5	hu	17.5	bs	16.4
la	14.7	cs	14.5	et	13.2
fi	13.0	es	12.7	cy	12.0
is	11.8	sl	10.6	simple	10.4
nl	9.3	pl	7.3	yo	7.1
sv	6.0	sq	5.9	ru	5.0
ro	4.6	ang	4.5	lt	3.9
el	3.4	eo	3.3	az	2.4
sr	2.4	nn	2.4	ms	1.7
fr	1.4	zh	0.0	vi	0.0
uk	0.0	th	0.0	ta	0.0
pt	0.0	pa	0.0	new	0.0
mr	0.0	mk	0.0	ko	0.0
ka	0.0	ja	0.0	it	0.0
id	0.0	hr	0.0	hi	0.0
he	0.0	fa	0.0	eu	0.0
ca	0.0	br	0.0	bpy	0.0
bn	0.0	bg	0.0	ar	0.0
AP (RR): 1.00					

For this example the difference between micro-average and macro-average is small because there are roughly the same number of examples of each language in the test. The difference may be profound when the number of examples differs or when the effectiveness of the ranking varies from category to category. To illustrate the difference, we extrapolate the summary measures from our test set to the entire Wikipedia.

Table 10.11 shows, for each Wikipedia edition, the fraction of all articles in the edition and the MRR summary for those articles. The editions vary substantially in size, and the largest edition (English) contains vastly more articles than any other but achieves a mediocre MRR score of 0.71. The net result is that for the test set, micro-averaged MRR is lower than macro-averaged MRR (0.82 versus 0.86). In other applications, such as spam filtering, the difference is even more important. Overall, a macro-average is independent of the proportion of documents

Table 10.10 Summary measures for language ranking over 4012 snippets. P@1 is equivalent to accuracy: the total fraction of correctly classified snippets. MAP is equivalent to MRR, since the problem statement defines exactly one "relevant" language for each snippet.

	Accuracy (P@1)	Error (1-accuracy)	MRR (MAP)
Micro-average	0.79	0.21	0.860
Macro-average	0.79	0.21	0.857

Table 10.11 Language categorization results extrapolated over the contents of 60 Wikipedia editions. The columns labeled "%" contain the fraction of all Wikipedia articles that belong to the given edition. Some editions (e.g., English) contain far more articles than others (e.g., Icelandic).

Tag	%	MRR	Tag	%	MRR	Tag	%	MRR
ang	0.01	0.90	ar	0.81	0.99	az	0.19	0.91
bg	0.60	0.87	bn	0.16	0.89	bpy	0.20	0.84
br	0.21	0.89	bs	0.22	0.69	ca	1.45	0.80
cs	1.05	0.77	cy	0.19	0.95	da	0.90	0.65
de	7.52	0.88	el	0.35	1.00	en	23.95	0.71
eo	0.95	0.80	es	3.91	0.78	et	0.52	0.73
eu	0.32	0.87	fa	0.50	0.97	fi	1.69	0.88
fr	6.66	0.88	he	0.77	1.00	hi	0.25	0.93
hr	0.49	0.58	hu	1.04	0.87	id	0.86	0.68
is	0.21	0.94	it	4.71	0.81	ja	4.88	0.94
ka	0.25	0.99	ko	0.80	1.00	la	0.23	0.80
lb	0.22	0.99	lt	0.72	0.91	mk	0.24	0.88
mr	0.19	0.81	ms	0.32	0.83	new	0.42	0.85
nl	4.47	0.89	nn	0.40	0.71	no	1.81	0.57
pa	0.01	0.96	pl	5.03	0.89	pt	3.98	0.90
ro	1.04	0.93	ru	3.20	0.81	simple	0.49	0.79
sk	0.90	0.79	sl	0.63	0.78	sq	0.19	0.88
sr	0.62	0.70	sv	2.63	0.85	ta	0.15	0.97
th	0.38	1.00	tr	1.07	0.85	uk	1.21	0.88
vi	0.68	0.96	yo	0.05	0.93	zh	2.10	0.91

MRR: 0.82/0.86 (micro-average/macro-average)

in each category, whereas a micro-average is weighted by that proportion. To extrapolate micro-average from one collection to another, it is necessary to know both the proportions and the class-specific summary scores. The distinction between micro-averaging and macro-averaging is specific to categorization: MAP and other summary measures, when applied to search results, are invariably macro-averages.

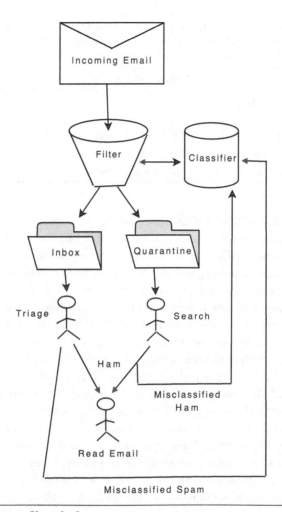

Figure 10.4   On-line spam filter deployment.

10.1.5   On-Line Adaptive Spam Filtering

Figure 10.4 shows the context of the spam filtering problem that we address in our third and final example. The filter receives a stream of e-mail messages and must deliver each, in turn, to the user's in-box or to a quarantine file. The messages in the in-box are read by the user in chronological order, whereas the quarantine file is occasionally searched to find ham (i.e., non-spam) messages that may have been placed there incorrectly by the filter. When, through either of these processes, the user notices spam in the in-box or ham in the quarantine, feedback is given to the filter. For this application it is useful to consider the in-box to be a simple queue and the quarantine a priority queue (that is, a dynamically updated ranked list).

Table 10.12   Command-line interface for the TREC Spam Filter Evaluation Toolkit. For evaluation within the toolkits framework a filter must implement these five operations, which are invoked in sequence by the toolkit.

Command	Filter Action
initialize	Create a filter to process a new stream of messages.
classify *file*	Return a category and priority score for the message in *file*.
train spam *file*	Use *file* as a historical example of spam.
train ham *file*	Use *file* as a historical example of ham.
finalize	Shut down the filter.

We use the TREC 2005 Public Spam Corpus[1], a sequence of 92,180 messages, of which 39,399 are spam and 78,798 are ham. Rather than splitting the sequence into training and test sets, we employ *on-line feedback* in which an *ideal* user is assumed to detect and report all errors. Under this assumption every message may be used as a historical training example immediately after it is delivered: Those reported as errors are assumed to belong to the category indicated by the user, and those not reported as errors are assumed to have been correctly categorized by the filter. Although the assumption of an ideal user is unrealistic, evaluation results based on it serve as a well-defined basis for comparison.

The on-line adaptive filtering scenario is implemented by the TREC Spam Filter Evaluation Toolkit, a test harness that, along with test corpora and sample filters, may be downloaded from the Web.[2] Although the toolkit uses categories that happen to be named spam and ham, it works equally well for any *on-line binary categorization* task. All of the examples presented in this chapter were prepared using the toolkit. For evaluation using the toolkit the filter must implement the five command-line operations detailed in Table 10.12.

As an illustrative example we again use BM25, applying it to build an on-line adaptive spam filter. Again we emphasize that this is not a typical application of BM25, but it does provide a solid baseline for the techniques we discuss later in the chapter. Spam filtering is an example of *binary categorization*, for which there are exactly two exclusive categories: each document, by definition, belongs to one category or the other. In contrast to our previous examples, in this one there are neither topic statements nor historical examples. The training examples are derived exclusively from on-line feedback. At the outset the filter has no information on which to base its decision, but as more messages are processed, it learns the characteristics of messages that distinguish the categories. The rate and manner in which the filter improves with training is known as the *learning curve*.

Our baseline approach is the same as for language categorization. We apply BM25 with relevance feedback separately to each of the document ranking problems: identifying spam

---

[1] trec.nist.gov/data

[2] plg.uwaterloo.ca/~gvcormac/jig

Table 10.13   Effectiveness measures for the document ranking problem associated with spam filtering. The three rows show the effectiveness of document ranking using separate spam and ham relevance scores, and their difference.

Relevance Score	P@10	P@20	P@100	P@200	P@1000	P@2000	AP
$s(d, \texttt{spam})$	1	1	1	1	1	1	0.9918
$s(d, \texttt{ham})$	1	1	1	1	1	1	0.9906
$s(d, \texttt{spam}) - s(d, \texttt{ham})$	1	1	1	1	1	1	0.9927

Table 10.14   IR-oriented effectiveness measures for the primary categorization problem in an on-line spam filter.

Class	Accuracy (P@1)	Error (%)	Precision	Recall	F_1
Spam	0.99989	0.011	0.80308	0.99989	0.89074
Ham	0.67149	32.860	0.99977	0.67149	0.80339
Micro-average	0.85954	14.055	0.85945	0.85954	0.85954
Macro-average	0.83569	16.431	–	–	0.84707
Logit average	0.99260	0.740	–	–	0.85233

and identifying ham, yielding two scores for each document d: $s(d, \texttt{spam})$ and $s(d, \texttt{ham})$. The category ranking for d is determined by the difference $s(d) = s(d, \texttt{spam}) - s(d, \texttt{ham})$. If $s(d) > 0$, the message is deemed to be spam; otherwise it is ham.

As before, query terms are byte 4-grams taken from messages labeled as spam or ham. As the filtering progresses, we create and maintain separate queries for ham and spam. As feedback is provided, new terms are added to the appropriate queries and IDF values are updated. Initially both queries are empty, yielding scores of 0, but they quickly grow as messages are seen. In contrast to the previous experiments we do not restrict the number of feedback terms added to each query, but allow both queries to grow without limits.

The score $s(d)$ also serves as a priority for the purpose of on-line ranking. Evaluation measures for the the document ranking problem, shown in Table 10.13, fail to shed much light on the intended purpose of our method: spam filtering. Broadly speaking, this is because the purpose of search is to identify documents of interest and effectiveness measures such as P@k and AP reward systems that find the documents that are easiest to categorize. Such measures tell us little about how well the filter works for difficult-to-categorize documents, the crux of spam filter effectiveness.

Evaluation measures for the primary categorization problem in an online spam filter are shown in Table 10.14. Because there are only two categories, reciprocal rank is redundant and not reported. For computing the filter's F_1 score we assumed that spam constitutes the relevant class. This is a common assumption in the literature. Whenever you encounter recall or precision numbers for which it is not obvious whether they refer to ham or spam, you should assume that the author treats spam as the relevant class.

As you see from Table 10.14, the accuracy (P@1) for spam messages is so high that it is difficult to interpret due to the large number of leading nines. Error (1-P@1) expressed as a percentage is more convenient and intuitive. In assessing filter effectiveness it is quite easy to observe that an error rate of, say, 0.1% is ten times better than an error rate of 1%. The observation that an accuracy of 0.999 is ten times better than an accuracy of 0.990 requires mental arithmetic and counting nines. Returning to our example, the spam error rate is 0.01%, meaning that about 1 in 10,000 spam messages is delivered to the user's in-box. On the other hand, the ham error rate is 32.9%, meaning that about a third of the user's good messages are delivered to quarantine. The user is unlikely to find this behavior acceptable; but if the situation were reversed, she might. If the ham error rate were 0.01% and the spam error rate were 32.9%, the filter would deliver the overwhelming majority of ham to the in-box while eliminating two-thirds of the spam.

Summary statistics, whether micro-averages or macro-averages, fail to consider the category-specific consequences of errors. In addition, micro-averages are highly sensitive to the overall proportion of spam. Suppose, for example, that the amount of spam were to double while the amount of ham — and the filter's spam and ham error rates – remained constant. The micro-averaged error rate would fall from 14% to 8.9%. Did the filter improve? Of course not. Micro-averaging measures the *prevalence* of spam as much as any property of the filter.

The logit average (LAM) is a macro-average under the logit transformation (see Equation 10.38):

$$lam(x, y) \ = \ \text{logit}^{-1} \left(\frac{\text{logit}(x) + \text{logit}(y)}{2} \right) . \tag{10.1}$$

Intuitively, this average interprets the scores as probabilities and combines them according to the weight of evidence they afford. Under the logit average the difference between scores of 0.1 and 0.01 has the same impact as the difference between scores of 0.9 and 0.99. In a sense each of these pairs represents an order of magnitude difference in effectiveness. On the other hand, the difference between 0.5 and 0.51 has little impact. Cormack (2008) gives a more formal derivation of LAM based on *odds ratios* (Section 10.2.1).

Precision and recall, along with other summary measures based on them, are difficult to interpret for filtering tasks and also are strongly influenced by prevalence. For spam filtering we must arbitrarily deem either spam or ham to be "relevant" in order to compute precision and recall. The results in Table 10.14 show precision and recall under the common assumption that spam is "relevant". Note that micro-averaged precision and recall are redundant; both are equal to accuracy. It can easily be shown that this equality will hold whenever the categories are exclusive — as is the case for our spam filtering and language categorization examples. Macro-averaging precision and recall separately makes no sense, but it is possible to compute the macro-average of a summary recall/precision measure such as F_1, also shown in Table 10.14. We have difficulty offering a sensible interpretation for precision, recall, or F_1 in this context, and suggest they be avoided as evaluation measures for filtering tasks.

Table 10.15 The trade-off between spam and ham error rates as a function of the threshold setting.

Threshold t	Spam Error	Ham Error	Macro-Avg. Error	Logit Avg. Error	Macro-Avg. F_1
2156	56.8%	0.0%	28.4%	1.1%	0.66
1708	36.2%	0.1%	18.2%	2.3%	0.79
1295	10.0%	0.4%	5.2%	2.0%	0.94
1045	2.2%	1.0%	1.6%	1.5%	0.98
931	1.0%	2.8%	1.9%	1.7%	0.98
713	0.1%	10.0%	5.1%	1.0%	0.95
-180	0.0%	34.9%	17.4%	0.7%	0.84

10.1.6 Threshold Choice for Binary Categorization

When a ranking method such as BM25 is used for binary categorization, the choice of the threshold t involves a direct trade-off between the two category-specific error rates. In our spam filtering example we somewhat arbitrarily chose to label messages with $s(d) > 0$ as spam and the others as ham. We could have used any t instead of 0 and labeled messages with $s(d) > t$ as spam and the rest as ham. The error rates for several values of t are shown in Table 10.15.

As we can see, the threshold values in themselves are quite meaningless, but larger values of t yield lower ham error rates at the expense of higher spam error rates, and vice versa. A *receiver operating characteristic* (ROC) *curve* consists of all points (x, y) where x is the spam error and $1 - y$ is the ham error (that is, y is the ham accuracy) for some threshold t. The ROC curve thus provides a geometric characterization of filter effectiveness, independent of any particular threshold setting, in the same way that a recall-precision curve characterizes ranked retrieval effectiveness, independent of any particular cutoff.

Plotted on a linear scale (Figure 10.5), the ROC curve isn't much use as a visual indication of filter performance: It follows the x and y axes too closely. For this purpose the logit-transformed representation shown in Figure 10.6 is preferred. From this curve one can readily determine what spam error would result if were t adjusted to achieve some particular ham error or vice versa. One can also use the curve to compare filters. If one curve is superior to another, it indicates better effectiveness across the board. If the curves cross, which one is better depends on the relative importance of spam and ham errors. For comparison we juxtapose our BM25 results with those achieved by the popular SpamAssassin[3] filter on the same messages (version 3.02 with default parameters). We see that BM25 is superior to SpamAssassin for much of the range, but at very low ham error rates the curves cross and SpamAssassin is slightly better.

The *area under the ROC curve* (AUC or ROCA) is a number between 0 and 1 that may be used as a threshold-independent indicator of filter performance. A filter with a superior ROC

---

[3] spamassassin.apache.org

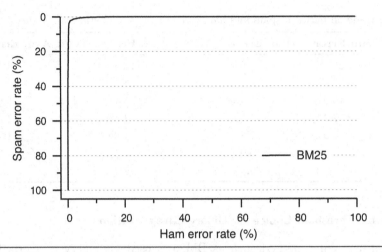

Figure 10.5   Linear-scale ROC curve for our BM25-based spam filter.

curve will tend to have a larger AUC. In addition to this geometric interpretation AUC has a probabilistic interpretation. It is the probability that a random spam message will have a higher score than a random ham message:

$$\text{AUC} = \Pr[s(d_1) > s(d_2) \mid d_1 \in \texttt{spam},\ d_2 \in \texttt{ham}]. \tag{10.2}$$

Our BM25 filter has AUC = 0.9981. For ease of interpretation, it is convenient to state the area *above* the ROC curve, 1 − AUC, as a percentage: 1 − AUC = 0.1896%. SpamAssassin has 1 − AUC = 0.5163%.

In the event that the threshold is fixed prior to evaluation, the ROC curve consists of exactly one point (x, y), so AUC is undefined. In this event the logistic average LAM offers a summary measure that is much less sensitive to threshold setting than others, as shown in Table 10.15. Micro- or macro-averaged error and F_1 are much more strongly influenced by threshold setting — to the extent that they measure little else.

If the filter is trained on historical data, it is a reasonably straightforward process to try several values of t to determine the one that achieves the desired trade-off between spam error and ham error. In an on-line setting with feedback, t may be adjusted dynamically by incrementing it by a small amount if the ham error is too high and decrementing it otherwise. But it is not easy to formalize "desired trade-off", and in many circumstances the choice of threshold is best determined by the user, either explicitly or implicitly. The user interface may solicit threshold adjustment (e.g., a slider from "show fewer" to "show more" or a set of buttons labeled "strict filtering", "moderate filtering", "none"). Or it may require the user to specify an acceptable error rate for one of the categories, or to specify some number of documents per unit time, or some fraction of the incoming documents that should be delivered. These quantities are easily estimated; t can be adjusted automatically to maintain them over time at the specified level.

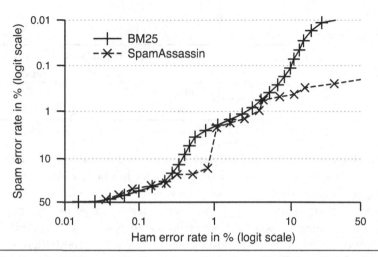

Figure 10.6   Logit-scale ROC curve for SpamAssassin and our BM25-based spam filter.

10.2   Classification

Having used BM25 to illustrate the nature of classification and filtering through detailed examples, we now examine other methods for solving the same types of problems. At the core of filtering and categorization is *classification*. The most fundamental classification problem is that of *binary classification*, the process of determining whether or not an object has some particular property P. A *binary classifier* is an automated procedure for binary classification. Throughout our development of binary classification methods we shall rely heavily on the example of spam filtering, in which the objects are e-mail messages, the property P is "being spam", and the classifier is the spam filter. Later we consider the application of the methods to our other examples, where the objects are documents and the property is relevance, or a particular language such as "Ukrainian".

The problem of classification long predates computer science. Much of the early work in classical statistics concerned binary classification problems such as identifying bad batches of beer for quality control at a brewery. From these efforts arose some arcane terminology that remains in common use. Then, as now, any real classifier will necessarily be imperfect. A *type 1 error* occurs when the classifier determines the object to have the property when it does not (identifies a good batch of beer as bad). A *type 2 error* occurs when the classifier fails to determine that the object has the property when it does (fails to detect a bad batch). The consequences of these errors depend on the intended purpose of classification. For beer the purpose of classification is presumably to avoid shipping bad beer to customers. If type 1 errors are frequent, profits are lost due to waste; if type 2 errors are frequent, the consequences are less tangible but potentially more severe, including lost goodwill and compromised public health.

Table 10.16 Contingency table for diagnostic test results.

| | | Property or Condition | |
		absent	present
Test result	negative	tn	fn
	positive	fp	tp

The study of classification was further advanced through *signal detection theory*, invented in conjunction with radar. Signal detection theory has been widely adopted in medical diagnostic testing and other fields. Practically everyone is familiar with the use of diagnostic tests in this context. For example, a positive pregnancy test is taken as evidence (but not proof) that a person is pregnant. A *positive* test result is evidence for some condition; a *negative* test result is evidence against it. A *true positive* (tp) is a positive result that is correct, whereas a *false positive* (fp) is a positive result that is incorrect. Similarly, a *true negative* (tn) is a negative test result that is correct, and a *false negative* is a negative result that is incorrect. That is, false positives and false negatives are exactly type 1 and type 2 errors, respectively. Table 10.16 illustrates the four possibilities. It is known as the *contingency table* for diagnostic test results.

The effectiveness of a diagnostic test is typically characterized by its *sensitivity* and *specificity*, also known as *true positive rate* (tpr) and *true negative rate* (tnr). If we take the elements of Table 10.16 to represent the frequencies of the four possibilities for a particular test, we have

$$sensitivity = tpr = \frac{tp}{tp + fn}, \quad specificity = tnr = \frac{tn}{tn + fp}. \tag{10.3}$$

Because sensitivity and specificity approach 1 for good tests, it is more convenient to work with the complementary error rates, *false negative rate* (fnr) and *false positive rate* (fpr):

$$fnr = 1 - sensitivity = \frac{fn}{tp + fn}, \quad fpr = 1 - specificity = \frac{fp}{tn + fp}. \tag{10.4}$$

In pregnancy testing, the condition of interest is pregnancy. The false negative rate is the fraction of pregnant individuals for which the test is negative; the false positive rate is the fraction of nonpregnant individuals for which the test is positive.

False negative rates and false positive rates are very commonly misinterpreted through specious reasoning known as the *prosecutor's fallacy*. Suppose we administer a pregnancy test that has *fpr* = 1% and *fnr* = 10% to an individual getting a positive result. The prosecutor's fallacy asserts that the probability that the individual is pregnant is $1 - fpr = 99\%$. The absurdity of this conclusion is obvious when we consider the case of administering the test to a man. The probability of a man being pregnant is vanishingly small, regardless of what the test says. By far the most likely explanation is that the test result is a false positive. On the other hand, if the individual is a fertile woman displaying symptoms of pregnancy, the most likely explanation is that the test result is a true positive, with probability much higher than 99%. In order to quantify the consideration of such prior probabilities, we introduce the notions of odds, odds ratios, and likelihood ratios.

10.2.1   Odds and Odds Ratios

The manipulation of probabilities and conditional probabilities may be simplified considerably by recasting them as *odds* and *odds ratios* (OR), respectively. Given an event e conditioned on x, we define

$$\text{Odds}[e] \;=\; \frac{\Pr[e]}{\Pr[\bar{e}]}, \tag{10.5}$$

$$\text{OR}(e, x) \;=\; \frac{\text{Odds}[e\,|\,x]}{\text{Odds}[e]}. \tag{10.6}$$

From the definition it follows directly that

$$\text{Odds}[e\,|\,x] \;=\; \text{Odds}[e] \cdot \text{OR}(e, x). \tag{10.7}$$

By applying Bayes' rule to $\Pr[e\,|\,x]$ and to $\Pr[\bar{e}\,|\,x]$ in Equation 10.7, we arrive at

$$\text{OR}(e, x) \;=\; \frac{\frac{\Pr[e|x]}{\Pr[\bar{e}|x]}}{\frac{\Pr[e]}{\Pr[\bar{e}]}} \;=\; \frac{\frac{\Pr[x|e]\cdot\Pr[e]\cdot\Pr[x]}{\Pr[x|\bar{e}]\cdot\Pr[\bar{e}]\cdot\Pr[x]}}{\frac{\Pr[e]}{\Pr[\bar{e}]}} \;=\; \frac{\Pr[x\,|\,e]}{\Pr[x\,|\,\bar{e}]}. \tag{10.8}$$

In this form the odds ratio is commonly known the *likelihood ratio* (LR) for x given e:

$$\text{LR}(e, x) \;=\; \frac{\Pr[x\,|\,e]}{\Pr[x\,|\,\bar{e}]}, \tag{10.9}$$

where $\Pr[x\,|\,e]$ is the likelihood of x given e, and $\Pr[x\,|\,\bar{e}]$ is the likelihood of x given $\bar{e}$.

Odds are easily interpreted and easily estimated by counting "wins" and "losses". If a sports team wins 50 games and loses 30, we estimate its odds of winning to be $\frac{50}{30} \approx 1.67$. An odds ratio may be interpreted as how much the odds would change if x were true. For example, if acquiring a new player, Mika, would improve our team's odds of winning to $\frac{51}{29} \approx 1.76$, we say that the odds ratio is

$$\text{OR}(\text{winning, Mika}) \;=\; \frac{\frac{51}{29}}{\frac{50}{30}} \approx 1.06. \tag{10.10}$$

In general, if $\text{OR}(e, x) > 1$, we say that x improves the odds of e; if $\text{OR}(e, x) < 1$, then x diminishes the odds. Now consider the effect of adding a different player, Jenson, where $\text{OR}(\text{winning, Jenson}) \approx 1.12$. This evidence indicates that Jenson would be the better acquisition. But what if it were possible to acquire both players? What would the value of

OR(winning, Mika *and* Jenson) be? The *naïve Bayes* assumption asserts that

$$OR(e, x \text{ } and \text{ } y) = OR(e, x) \cdot OR(e, y). \tag{10.11}$$

Under this assumption

$$OR(\text{winning, Mika } and \text{ Jenson}) \approx 1.18. \tag{10.12}$$

But in many circumstances this assumption is unrealistic. If Mika and Jenson play the same position on the team, for example, goalkeeper, there may be little cumulative benefit in hiring both. And if there were a personality conflict between Mika and Jenson, the overall effect might even be to diminish the odds of winning.

Now consider pregnancy testing. We wish to compute the odds of pregnancy, given a positive test result:

$$\text{Odds[pregnant} \mid \text{positive]} = \text{Odds[pregnant]} \cdot OR(\text{pregnant, positive}). \tag{10.13}$$

From Equation 10.8 we have

$$OR(\text{pregnant, positive}) = LR(\text{pregnant, positive}) = \frac{tpr}{fpr} = \frac{90\%}{1\%} = 90. \tag{10.14}$$

The *prior odds*, Odds[pregnant], depend entirely on evidence other than the test. If about 80% of women requesting a pregnancy test are in fact pregnant, we have

$$\text{Odds[pregnant} \mid \text{positive]} = \frac{80\%}{20\%} \cdot \frac{90\%}{1\%} = 360 \tag{10.15}$$

and thus

$$\text{Pr[pregnant} \mid \text{positive]} = \frac{360}{1 + 360} \approx 99.7\%. \tag{10.16}$$

On the other hand, if the test were negative,

$$\text{Odds[pregnant} \mid \text{negative]} = \frac{80\%}{20\%} \cdot \frac{fnr}{tnr} = \frac{80\%}{20\%} \cdot \frac{10\%}{99\%} \approx 0.404 \tag{10.17}$$

and thus

$$\text{Pr[pregnant} \mid \text{negative]} \approx \frac{0.404}{1 + 0.404} = 28.8\%. \tag{10.18}$$

In such a situation a second test would be in order.

10.2.2 Building Classifiers

For categorization and filtering applications, we wish to build binary classifiers automatically from examples of documents that do and do not belong to specific categories. When there are two exclusive categories (e.g., ham and spam), a binary classifier is constructed to identify membership in one of the categories. A positive result indicates membership in that category, and a negative result indicates membership in the other. When the categories are nonexclusive, we may construct a separate binary classifier to identify each. For $n > 2$ categories it is necessary either to combine several binary classifiers or to build an n-way classifier (see Section 11.6). In this section we consider the problem of constructing a binary classifier, taking into account its role in categorization and filtering.

Classification may be formalized as a learner L that builds a classifier c, where c renders either a positive/negative result or a continuous score. Given a collection of documents D, we denote by $P \subset D$ the subset of documents having some property of interest. For convenience we denote by $\overline{P} = D \backslash P$ the complementary subset from which the property is absent. The key challenge is to build a classifier — a concrete function that for any document d accurately answers the question "Given d, is $d \in P$?" An ideal classifier would be a total function

$$isp : \; D \to \{pos, neg\} \tag{10.19}$$

such that $isp(d) = pos$ if and only if $d \in P$. No such ideal classifier exists; instead, we build an approximation $c \approx isp$. Hard and soft classifiers employ different notions of approximation. A hard classifier

$$c : \; D \to \{pos, neg\} \tag{10.20}$$

approximates isp to the extent that $c(d) = isp(d)$ for most $d \in D$. A soft classifier

$$c : \; D \to \mathbb{R} \tag{10.21}$$

approximates isp to the extent that $c(d) > c(d')$ for most $(d, d') \in P \times \overline{P}$. A hard classifier c_h may be defined in terms of a soft classifier c_s and a fixed threshold t:

$$c_h(d) = \begin{cases} pos & (c_s(d) > t) \\ neg & (c_s(d) \le t) \end{cases} . \tag{10.22}$$

A naïve utility measure for the effectiveness of a hard classifier is

$$accuracy = 1 - error = \frac{|\{d \,|\, c_h(d) = isp(d)\}|}{|D|} . \tag{10.23}$$

Accuracy and *error* are commonly reported and commonly optimized in filter construction, notwithstanding their dependence on prevalence. As a pair we use the error measures

$$fpr = \frac{|\overline{P} \cap \{d \,|\, c(d) = pos\}|}{|\overline{P}|} , \quad fnr = \frac{|P \cap \{d \,|\, c(d) = neg\}|}{|P|} . \tag{10.24}$$

For a soft classifier, we use the cost measure

$$1 - \text{AUC} = \frac{\left|P \times \overline{P} \cap \{(d,d') \,|\, c(d) < c(d')\}\right| + \frac{1}{2}\left|P \times \overline{P} \cap \{(d,d') \,|\, c(d) = c(d')\}\right|}{|P| \cdot |\overline{P}|}. \quad (10.25)$$

For filtering it is useful to regard c as a fixed formula with a hidden parameter specifying a learned *profile*; that is, $c(d)$ is shorthand for $c(profile, d)$ where *profile* is created by a learner L.

10.2.3 Learning Modes

The learner L constructs the *profile* from evidence presented to it. The manner in which the evidence is presented depends on the *learning mode*.

- **Supervised learning** is a common mode for machine-learning classifiers. The learner's input $(T, label)$ consists of a set $T \subseteq D$ of training examples and a function $label : T \to \{pos, neg\}$ that approximates isp over the subdomain T. The function *label* is typically handcrafted by human adjudicators. Under the assumption that T is an independent and identically distributed (i.i.d.) sample of D and that $label(d) = isp(d)$ for all $d \in T$, the learner induces a *profile* that optimizes c for some utility function, typically *accuracy*. Supervised learning, along with its associated assumptions, is so common that it is often assumed without question. But it can be exceedingly difficult to obtain a sample — especially an i.i.d. sample — of documents to be classified. Indeed, many members of D (the ones we are interested in classifying) exist only in the future and are therefore simply impossible to sample. Constructing *label* is sufficiently onerous and error-prone that the assumption of its existence may be questionable. One should not assume that optimizing accuracy yields the classifier most suitable for its intended purpose.

- **Semi-supervised learning** assumes input $(T, S, label)$ where $T \subseteq D$, $S \subset T$, and $label : S \to \{pos, neg\}$; that is, *label* is defined for only a subset of the training examples. Semi-supervised learning accommodates the fact that obtaining sample documents may be considerably easier than labeling them. Like supervised learning, it assumes that T is an *i.i.d.* sample of D. This assumption may allow the learner to learn more about the distribution of D from the unlabeled examples in $T \backslash S$. A vacuous semi-supervised learner is simply the supervised learner with input $(S, S, label)$; this special case provides a convenient baseline with which semi-supervised learners may be compared.

- **Transductive learning**, like semi-supervised learning, uses labeled and unlabeled examples $(T, S, label)$ as before. The difference is that the unlabeled examples include all of the test examples; that is, $T = D$. So the classifier $c : T \to \{true, false\}$ or $c : T \to \mathbb{R}$ applies only to the elements of T. Classical information retrieval is an example of transductive learning, as the entire corpus is used for document statistics, and the set of documents classified as relevant is a subset of the corpus.

- **Unsupervised learning** assumes no *label* function at all; that is, the input is simply a set $T \subseteq D$ and is rarely used directly to construct a classifier. Unsupervised learning methods may nevertheless be used in conjunction with others; for example, *clustering* methods may be used to find groups of similar messages under the assumption that each member of a group belongs to the same class.

- In **on-line learning** there is no a priori division between training and test examples. The examples to be classified form a sequence $S = d_1, d_2, \ldots, d_n$. When each document d_k is classified, all previous documents $\{d_{i<k}\}$ are available as training examples. Every example is first used to test the classifier and subsequently used for training. An on-line classifier, but not necessarily an efficient or effective one, may be implemented by constructing a new batch classifier for each d_k, using $T_k = \{d_i \,|\, i < k\}$ as the training set. If every document is labeled, we have supervised on-line learning; otherwise it is semisupervised or unsupervised. This approach has two principal shortcomings:

  1. The nature of the examples may change considerably over time, a phenomenon known as *concept drift*. The proposed method is unable to model this phenomenon because it ignores the temporal cues inherent in the sequencing of the training examples.

  2. If we use every available training example to construct a new classifier c_k from scratch to classify each d_k, the overall running time over S will be quadratic or worse. When building c_k there are $k - 1$ training examples, and examining each takes time proportional to k. A lower bound on the time to create all c_k is therefore

  $$\sum_{i=k}^{n} k - 1 \;\in\; \Omega(n^2). \tag{10.26}$$

- **Incremental learning** may be used to reduce the overall cost of classifying a sequence. An incremental learner efficiently constructs c_{k+1} from the hidden *profile$_k$* underlying the classifier c_k constructed for d_k, without necessarily examining all of the examples in T_k. The amenability of the learner to efficient incremental construction is an important criterion in the choice of a method for on-line filtering. Incremental learning may be approximated by using a non-incremental learner that uses batches and a sliding window.

- **Active learning** allows the classifier to request labels for a limited number of the unlabeled training examples. A filter may, for example, solicit the user to label particular messages and classify the rest based on these examples. The prototypical method for active learning is *uncertainty sampling* (Lewis and Catlett, 1994), in which a soft classifier is applied to each unlabeled example and labels are requested for those examples whose classifier result is closest to the threshold t.

10.2.4   Feature Engineering

Although we have characterized the classifier's domain D as a set of documents, few classifiers operate directly on the textual representation. Instead, each document is typically represented as a collection of *features* derived from the text or from extrinsic information related to it, such as the time of arrival of an e-mail message. The process of defining and extracting features likely to be useful to the classifier — called *feature engineering* — has a profound impact on overall filter effectiveness. The reader should be skeptical of published results (good or bad) for any particular learning method that fail to note the method of feature representation.

A document d is typically represented as a vector of n features $x^{[d]} = \langle x_1^{[d]}, x_2^{[d]}, \ldots, x_n^{[d]} \rangle$, where each $x_i^{[d]}$ is a real or discrete value quantifying some evidence pertaining to the message that might be useful to the classifier. Each message is thus represented as a point in an n-dimensional *feature space*. The most obvious features are simple statistics computed from the tokens and terms detailed in Chapter 3.

The issues involved in tokenization are generally the same for classification as for search, with a few differences in emphasis. In filtering and categorization applications, documents are processed in sequence rather than fetched from a large corpus, so index construction is unnecessary. It is possible to use far more features for classification than might be appropriate for a search engine, which would have to retrieve a postings list for each. Features such as character and word n-grams (see Section 3.3) are practical and have been found useful in a number of applications. *Sparse bigrams* — pairs of tokens separated by k or fewer tokens — increase the dimension of the feature space but have been used to good effect in filtering (Siefkes et al., 2004).

Some learners nevertheless perform poorly, either in terms of efficiency or of classification performance, for large n. Consider the problem of learning a classifier from training set T where $|T| \ll n$. In such a case it is almost certainly possible to solve a set of simultaneous equations so as to build a perfect classifier for T. But that classifier would have poor performance over D as a whole, a flaw known as *overfitting*. All classifiers exhibit some *generalization error* in that they perform worse on D than on T. One of the primary differences among methods is their ability to minimize such error.

Feature selection is commonly used to reduce n, and hence the dimensionality of the feature space X. More generally, *dimensionality reduction* techniques may be used to project or transform X to a space of smaller dimension. There are two principal purposes for dimensionality reduction: It may be required to achieve reasonable time or space efficiency and it may be required to reduce generalization error.

Historically, feature selection or dimensionality reduction has been considered a separate preprocessing step done prior to building the classifier. In light of modern advances in classifier construction, this view is no longer appropriate. There is a strong interaction between feature selection and the classifier, so the two should be considered together. There is nothing in our definition of c that prevents it from projecting its input onto a smaller space as part of its internal working. Some classifiers, such as the naïve Bayes and decision tree methods we shall consider, do this quite aggressively. Some of the best classifiers, such as logistic regression and support vector machines, do no explicit dimensionality reduction, handling the issues of efficiency and generalization error by other means. We are not saying that feature selection and dimensionality reduction have no use; rather we are saying that they must be considered in the context of a particular application and classification method, and in many circumstances are unnecessary.

Feature selection is the most direct method of dimensionality reduction; stopping (Section 3.1.3) is a trivial example. Many statistical techniques have been proposed and used to identify the most *important* features; the rest are eliminated. Stemming (Section 3.1.2) is a simple example of dimensionality reduction in which multiple features are conflated into one. Hashing has also been used successfully to reduce very large spaces by arbitrarily combining dimensions whose tokens hash to the same value. More sophisticated methods, such as principal component analysis, use linear algebra to transform the entire space to one of smaller dimension.

Some feature engineering choices may be difficult to reconcile with incremental classifier construction, and hence with efficient on-line adaptive filtering. Previously unseen features may be encountered at any point, thus expanding the dimensionality of the space. The set of known values for a particular feature may grow as new examples are learned. Global statistics such as IDF must be recomputed when used because the addition of a single document changes the IDF for every term it contains. This change may dramatically alter the effective scores of previously filtered documents. Statistical feature selection and dimensionality reduction are problematic in an on-line environment because the statistics are ever-changing.

A common error in evaluating classifiers is to perform feature selection or dimensionality reduction based on the training and test documents. This approach is simply wrong; it effectively communicates information about the test examples to the classifier's profile.

10.3   Probabilistic Classifiers

A probabilistic classifier computes an estimate $p^{[d]} \approx \Pr[d \in P \mid x^{[d]}]$ of the probability that a given document d, represented by $x^{[d]} = \langle x_1^{[d]}, x_2^{[d]}, \dots, x_n^{[d]} \rangle$, has property P or equivalently, is contained in the set P of documents with that property. This estimate may be used directly as a soft classifier

$$c(d) = p^{[d]} \tag{10.27}$$

or, in combination with some threshold $0 < t < 1$, as a hard classifier

$$c(d) = \begin{cases} pos & (p^{[d]} > t) \\ neg & (p^{[d]} \le t) \end{cases}. \tag{10.28}$$

Probabilistic classification involves two steps:

1. Estimating $p_i^{[x]} \approx \Pr[d \in P \mid x_i^{[d]}]$ for each $x_i^{[d]}$ in $x^{[d]}$.
2. Combining the estimates to yield $p^{[d]} \approx \Pr[d \in P \mid x^{[d]}]$.

10.3.1   Probability Estimates

Features may be either discrete or continuous. A discrete feature (also called a *categorical feature*) can assume one of a finite number of possible values. For a continuous feature the set of possible values is infinite. Different methods are used to estimate probabilities for categorical and for continuous features.

Probability estimates from categorical features

We first consider the special case of a *binary* feature that has exactly two possible values, 0 and 1. Although the values of a binary feature $x_i^{[d]} : \{0, 1\}$ have no intrinsic meaning, $x_i^{[d]} = 1$ often represents the presence of some token in d, whereas $x_i^{[d]} = 0$ indicates its absence. The odds that d is in P given $x_i^{[d]} = k$ may be estimated as the ratio of positive to negative examples in the training set T:

$$\text{Odds}[d \in P \,|\, x_i^{[d]} = k] \;\approx\; \frac{\left| \left\{ d \in T \,|\, x_i^{[d]} = k \right\} \cap P \right|}{\left| \left\{ d \in T \,|\, x_i^{[d]} = k \right\} \cap \overline{P} \right|}. \tag{10.29}$$

For example, consider the hypothetical situation in which the word "money" occurs in 100 spam messages and 5 ham messages. The odds that a particular message d containing "money" is spam may be estimated as $\text{Odds}[d \in P \,|\, x_i^{[d]} = 1] \approx \frac{100}{5} = \frac{20}{1}$. The same estimate, expressed as a probability, is $\text{Pr}[d \in P \,|\, x_i^{[d]} = 1] \approx \frac{20}{1+20} = 0.952$. The value $k = 1$ is not particularly special; assuming that T consists of, say, 1000 spam and 1000 ham messages, we may deduce that 900 spam messages and 995 ham messages have $x_i = 0$, so the odds of a message not containing "money" being spam are $\text{Odds}[d \in P \,|\, x_i^{[d]} = 0] = \frac{900}{995} \approx 0.9$, that is, nearly even odds. Intuitively, the nonoccurrence of "money" contributes little to solving the filtering problem; for this reason filters usually ignore the information obtainable from the absence of a token.

The ratio $\frac{a}{b}$ of the number of positive to negative training examples is a good odds estimate if these numbers, a and b, are sufficiently large. If they are small, the estimates will be unreliable due to chance, and if either or both are 0, the resulting estimates are $\frac{0}{1}$, $\frac{1}{0}$, or $\frac{0}{0}$, none of which is a sensible estimate. A simple way to mitigate this problem is smoothing: We add small positive constants γ and ϵ to the numerator and denominator, respectively; that is, we use $\frac{a+\gamma}{b+\epsilon}$ as the odds estimate. In the case of $a = b = 0$ this yields an estimate of $\frac{\gamma}{\epsilon}$, whereas for large a and b the estimate is indistinguishable from $\frac{a}{b}$. Typically $\gamma = \epsilon = 1$.

We note that this derivation may be extended to non-binary categorical features, where k may take on values other than 0 or 1. Odds are then estimated separately for each k.

Probability estimates from continuous features

If $x_i^{[d]}$ is a real-valued feature, a direct way to estimate a probability is to transform its value to a binary value $b_i^{[d]} : \{0, 1\}$ by comparing it against a threshold t

$$b_i^{[d]} = \begin{cases} 1 & x_i^{[d]} > t \\ 0 & x_i^{[d]} \le t \end{cases} \tag{10.30}$$

and to estimate $\text{Odds}[d \in P \,|\, b_i^{[d]} = k]$ as described in the previous section. Although a real value, like a discrete value, has no intrinsic meaning, features may be engineered so that a larger value of $x_i^{[d]}$ indicates higher odds that $d \in P$. In other words, $x_i^{[d]}$ is itself a soft classifier and $b_i^{[d]}$ is the corresponding hard classifier. An n-ary categorical value $b_i^{[d]} \in \{0, 1, \ldots, n-1\}$ may be computed using n *bins* delimited by $n-1$ threshold values:

$$b_i^{[d]} = \begin{cases} n-1 & t_{n-1} < x_i^{[d]} \\ \cdots & \cdots \\ 1 & t_1 < x_i^{[d]} \le t_2 \\ 0 & x_i^{[d]} \le t_1 \end{cases}, \tag{10.31}$$

thus effecting a piecewise approximation of the odds implied by the continuous value $x_i^{[d]}$.

The principal drawback of this approach is that as n increases, the number of documents with $b_i^{[d]} = k$ for any particular k decreases, and the odds estimates become less reliable. An alternative approach is to define a transformation $f : \mathbb{R} \to \mathbb{R}$ such that

$$f(k) \approx \text{Odds}[d \in P \,|\, x_i^{[d]} = k]. \tag{10.32}$$

Parametric models may be used instead of simple counting to estimate the distributions of $x_i^{[d \in P]}$ and $x_i^{[d \in \overline{P}]}$. For example, if a Gaussian[4] (normal) distribution is assumed, the four parameters $\mu_{(i,P)}, \sigma_{(i,P)}, \mu_{(i,\overline{P})}, \sigma_{(i,\overline{P})}$ — the means and standard deviations for $x_i^{[d \in P]}$ and $x_i^{[d \in \overline{P}]}$ — fully characterize the distributions. Given these parameters, we may compute the likelihood ratio

$$\text{LR}(d \in P, \ x_i^{[d]} = k) \approx \frac{g(\mu_{(i,P)}, \sigma_{(i,P)}, k)}{g(\mu_{(i,\overline{P})}, \sigma_{(i,\overline{P})}, k)}, \tag{10.33}$$

where g is the probability density function of the Gaussian distribution. By equations 10.7 and 10.8, we have

$$\text{Odds}[d \in P \,|\, x_i^{[d]} = k] \approx \frac{N_P}{N_{\overline{P}}} \cdot \frac{g(\mu_{(i,P)}, \sigma_{(i,P)}, k)}{g(\mu_{(i,\overline{P})}, \sigma_{(i,\overline{P})}, k)}, \tag{10.34}$$

where N_P and $N_{\overline{P}}$ are the number of positive and negative examples in T.

---

[4] See Section 12.3.2 for a discussion of the Gaussian distribution: $g(\mu, \sigma^2, x) = \varphi_{\mu, \sigma^2}(x)$.

Table 10.17   Example from the TREC 2005 Public Spam Corpus.

Message tag	True Class	head:enron	body:enron
016/201	spam	12	0
033/101	spam	11	0
050/001	spam	10	0
066/186	ham	7	24
083/101	ham	21	0
083/101	ham	21	0
100/001	ham	27	4
133/101	spam	12	17
148/013	ham	22	5
166/201	ham	13	23
183/101	spam	11	0
200/001	spam	14	4
216/201	ham	25	2
233/101	spam	13	20
250/001	ham	5	0
266/201	spam	12	0
283/101	spam	13	0
300/001	spam	11	22

An example

We illustrate the methods described above by using two features derived from the TREC 2005 Public Spam Corpus (Cormack and Lynam, 2005). Our features are chosen to harness the knowledge that all messages in the corpus were delivered to individuals at one particular organization and that the organization's name (Enron in this instance) might have different prevalence in spam and ham messages. Our two features simply count the number of occurrences of the character sequence "enron" in the header and in the body of each message after conversion to lowercase. The notation **head : enron** indicates the number of instances of "enron" in the header, and **body : enron** indicates the number in the body. Table 10.17 presents these attributes for 18 messages selected from the corpus, 10 of which are spam and 8 of which are ham.

As a binary feature indicating the presence of "enron" in the respective message components, this information is of limited use. The token "enron" occurs in *every* header, and therefore its presence yields no information beyond the ratio of spam to ham in the sample (i.e., a likelihood ratio of 1). The token occurs in the bodies of 4 spam and 5 ham messages, yielding a 4:5 estimate of the odds that a message whose body contains "enron" is spam. It does not occur in the bodies of 6 spam and 3 ham message, yielding a 2:1 odds estimate for such messages.

Table 10.18 Sample versus gold standard estimates for the example shown in Table 10.17.

Feature f	Training Data		Gold Standard	
	Frequency	Pr[spam|f]	Frequency	Pr[spam|f]
head : enron $\neq 0$	1.0	0.56	0.9999	0.57
head : enron $= 0$	0.0	0.50	0.0001	0.00
body : enron $\neq 0$	0.5	0.44	0.62	0.45
body : enron $= 0$	0.5	0.67	0.38	0.77
Overall	1.0	0.56	1.00	0.57

Table 10.19 Discrete range feature estimates for the example shown in Table 10.17.

Feature f	Training Data			Gold Standard	
	Frequency	$\gamma = \epsilon = 0$	$\gamma = \epsilon = 1$	Frequency	Pr[spam|f]
$0 \leq$ head : enron < 10	0.11	0.00	0.25	0.18	0.05
$10 \leq$ head : enron < 20	0.61	0.91	0.85	0.74	0.75
$20 \leq$ head : enron < 30	0.28	0.00	0.14	0.05	0.19

Table 10.18 compares these estimates (recast as probabilities) with our "gold standard" best estimate of the *true* probability — computed over the entire corpus.

Table 10.19 shows the result of splitting the values of head:enron into three discrete ranges: $[0, 9]$, $[10, 19]$, and $[20, 30]$. Probability estimates derived from the training data are shown for two choices of smoothing parameters: $\gamma = \epsilon = 0$ and $\gamma = \epsilon = 1$ (see page 340 for a reminder of how this kind of smoothing works). Values in the center range ($10 \leq$ head : enron < 20) clearly predict spam, whereas extreme values indicate ham.

Table 10.20 shows the predictions made for each possible value of head:enron assuming a Gaussian distribution with parameters computed from the sample: $\mu_P = 11.9$, $\sigma_P = 1.2$, $\mu_{\overline{P}} = 17.6$, $\sigma_{\overline{P}} = 8.3$. The model aptly estimates $\Pr[d \in P \,|\, \text{head} : \text{enron} = k]$ for small values of k but dramatically underestimates it for larger values. These larger values are fairly rare, thus mitigating the effect of the underestimate; and even the underestimates will yield a correct classification more often than not. Nevertheless, there is plenty of room to improve the model.

10.3.2   Combining Probability Estimates

We wish to estimate

$$p^{[d]} \approx \Pr[d \in P \,|\, x^{[d]}], \tag{10.35}$$

given separate estimates for the individual features of d:

$$p_i^{[d]} \approx \Pr[d \in P \,|\, x_i^{[d]}] \quad (\text{for } 1 \leq i \leq n). \tag{10.36}$$

Table 10.20 Sample versus gold standard spam estimates under the Gaussian model for the example shown in Table 10.17.

	Training Data		Gold Standard	
k	Frequency	$\Pr[\text{spam} \mid \text{head} : \text{enron} = k]$	Frequency	$\Pr[\text{spam} \mid \text{head} : \text{enron} = k]$
5	0.06	0.0000	0.00	0.0000
6	0.00	0.0000	0.01	0.0705
7	0.06	0.0017	0.08	0.0000
8	0.00	0.0311	0.05	0.0409
9	0.00	0.2315	0.03	0.1767
10	0.06	0.5880	0.07	0.6191
11	0.17	0.7735	0.28	0.8366
12	0.17	0.8049	0.19	0.7343
13	0.17	0.7158	0.09	0.7838
14	0.06	0.4371	0.04	0.7269
15	0.00	0.1079	0.02	0.6321
16	0.00	0.0094	0.01	0.4687
17	0.00	0.0004	0.01	0.4162
18	0.00	0.0000	0.01	0.4838
19	0.00	0.0000	0.01	0.3539
20	0.00	0.0000	0.01	0.5745
21	0.11	0.0000	0.01	0.4236
22	0.06	0.0000	0.01	0.4008
23	0.00	0.0000	0.00	0.5281
24	0.00	0.0000	0.00	0.1026
25	0.06	0.0000	0.02	0.0114
26	0.00	0.0000	0.00	0.0629
27	0.06	0.0000	0.00	0.0026

For convenience, we compute instead the corresponding log-odds estimate

$$l^{[d]} \approx \text{logOdds}[d \in P \mid x^{[d]}], \tag{10.37}$$

where

$$l^{[d]} = \text{logit}(p^{[d]}) = \log \frac{p^{[d]}}{1 - p^{[d]}}, \quad p^{[d]} = \text{logit}^{-1}(l^{[d]}) = \frac{1}{1 + e^{-l^{[d]}}}. \tag{10.38}$$

We also define

$$l_i^{[d]} \approx \text{logOdds}[d \in P \mid x_i^{[d]}] \quad (\text{for } 1 \leq i \leq n). \tag{10.39}$$

We consider the special cases $n = 0 \ldots 2$, as well as their generalization to $n > 2$:

- $n = 0$ denotes the empty vector, so the estimate, which we denote l_0, reduces to

$$l^{[d]} \;=\; l_0^{[d]} \;=\; \frac{|P \cap T| + \gamma}{|\overline{P} \cap T| + \epsilon} \;\approx\; \mathrm{logOdds}[d \in P] \tag{10.40}$$

(where γ and ϵ are smoothing parameters, as before).

- $n = 1$ is also trivial; we have

$$l^{[d]} \;=\; l_1^{[d]} \;\approx\; \mathrm{logOdds}[d \in P \,|\, x_1^{[d]}] . \tag{10.41}$$

- $n = 2$ is more problematic; there is no general method of combining $l_1^{[d]}$ and $l_2^{[d]}$ into a common estimate without considering the conditional dependence of $x_1^{[d]}$ and $x_2^{[d]}$. From Equations 10.7 and 10.40 we have

$$\log \mathrm{OR}(d \in P, x_1^{[d]}) \;\approx\; l_1^{[d]} - l_0^{[d]} , \tag{10.42}$$

$$\log \mathrm{OR}(d \in P, x_2^{[d]}) \;\approx\; l_2^{[d]} - l_0^{[d]} . \tag{10.43}$$

Under the naïve Bayes assumption (Equation 10.11) we have

$$\log \mathrm{OR}(d \in P, x^{[d]}) \;=\; \log \mathrm{OR}(d \in P, x_1^{[d]} \, and \, x_2^{[d]}) \;\approx\; l_1^{[d]} - l_0^{[d]} + l_2^{[d]} - l_0^{[d]} \tag{10.44}$$

and therefore

$$l^{[d]} \;=\; -l_0^{[d]} + l_1^{[d]} + l_2^{[d]} \;\approx\; \mathrm{logOdds}[d \in P \,|\, x^{[d]}] . \tag{10.45}$$

The naïve Bayes assumption seldom holds in practice; the word "sildenafil", for example, is far more likely to be found in e-mail messages — spam and ham alike — that also contain the word "Viagra". Invalid assumptions aside, naïve Bayes classifiers are commonly used because they are simple and perform adequately as hard classifiers with a probability threshold $t = 0.5$, even if their probability estimates are far from accurate (Domingos and Pazzani, 1997).

A contrasting assumption is that x_1 and x_2 are dependent; for example, that the presence of both "sildenafil" and "Viagra" is an indicator of spam; but whether one, or the other, or both occur in a particular message is of no consequence. In short, a message containing "sildenafil" *and* "Viagra" is no more and no less likely to be spam than a message containing either term alone. Under this assumption l_1 and l_2 may be averaged because they are both estimates of the same quantity and differ only in estimation error:

$$l^{[d]} \;=\; \frac{l_1^{[d]} + l_2^{[d]}}{2} . \tag{10.46}$$

Table 10.21   Combining probability estimates using log-odds averaging and Naïve Bayes.

		$\Pr[\text{spam} \mid f_1, f_2]$		
Feature f_1	Feature f_2	Log-Odds Avg.	Naïve Bayes	Gold Standard
$0 \leq \text{head : enron} < 10$	$\text{body : enron} = 0$	0.45	0.36	0.14
$0 \leq \text{head : enron} < 10$	$\text{body : enron} > 0$	0.33	0.16	0.03
$10 \leq \text{head : enron} < 20$	$\text{body : enron} = 0$	0.77	0.90	0.86
$10 \leq \text{head : enron} < 20$	$\text{body : enron} > 0$	0.66	0.76	0.65
$20 \leq \text{head : enron} < 30$	$\text{body : enron} = 0$	0.36	0.21	0.40
$20 \leq \text{head : enron} < 30$	$\text{body : enron} > 0$	0.25	0.08	0.12

For both naïve Bayes and log-odds averaging the general solution for $n \geq 2$ computes $l^{[d]}$ as a linear combination of the individual $l_i^{[d]}$:

$$l^{[d]} = \sum_{i=0}^{n} \beta_i \cdot l_i^{[d]}.$$

(10.47)

For naïve Bayes,

$$\beta_i = \begin{cases} 1 - n & (i = 0) \\ 1 & (i > 0) \end{cases},$$

(10.48)

for log-odds averaging,

$$\beta_i = \begin{cases} 0 & (i = 0) \\ \frac{1}{n} & (i > 0) \end{cases}.$$

(10.49)

Table 10.21 compares the two methods, using all combinations of values for the two discrete features in our running example. We see that averaging tends to yield conservative results closer to $p_0 = 0.55$, whereas those due to naïve Bayes are more extreme. For some examples, averaging appears to yield the better estimate; for others, naïve Bayes does.

Many other choices of β_i are possible. One might, for example, average the naïve Bayes and log-odds averaging estimates, which would yield a different linear combination that reflects partial conditional dependence among the various $x_i^{[d]}$. Or one might choose weights other than $\frac{1}{n}$ for specific β_i, depending on the accuracy of the corresponding $l_i^{[d]}$.

Logistic regression is a method that computes β_i so as to maximize *likelihood*, given a set of labeled training examples. Likelihood is simply the combined probability of the examples under the assumption that the estimate $p^{[d]} = \frac{1}{1+e^{-l^{[d]}}} = \Pr[d \in P \mid x^{[d]}]$; that is,

$$likelihood = \prod_{d \in T \cap P} p^{[d]} \cdot \prod_{d \in T \cap \overline{P}} 1 - p^{[d]}.$$

(10.50)

Inputs:
> Set $T \subset D$ of training examples $d \in T$, represented by $x^{[d]} = \langle 1, x_1^{[d]}, x_2^{[d]}, \ldots, x_n^{[d]} \rangle$
> Labeling $label : T \rightarrow \{0, 1\}$
> Smoothing parameters γ, ϵ

Output:
> $\beta \cdot x^{[d]}$ is the naïve Bayes estimate of $\mathrm{logOdds}[label(d) = 1]$, where $\beta = \langle \beta_0, \ldots, \beta_n \rangle$

1    $p \leftarrow a \leftarrow \langle 0, \ldots 0 \rangle$
2   **for** $d \in T$ **do**
3   **for** $i \in [0..n]$ **do**
4   **if** $x_i^{[d]} = 1$ **then**
5   **if** $label(i) = 1$ **then** $p_i \leftarrow p_i + 1$ **else** $a_i \leftarrow a_i + 1$
6    $\beta_0 \leftarrow \mathrm{logit}(\frac{p_0 + \gamma}{a_0 + \epsilon})$
7   **for** $i \leftarrow 1$ **to** n **do**
8      $\beta_i \leftarrow \mathrm{logit}(\frac{p_i + \gamma}{a_i + \epsilon}) - \beta_0$

Figure 10.7 Naïve Bayes classifier construction.

Because logistic regression solves for β_i, it is not essential that the separate $l_i^{[d]}$ be calibrated as log-odds estimates. In particular it is unnecessary to transform categorical features for the purpose of logistic regression. Instead, a feature $x_i^{[d]} : \{k_1, k_2, \ldots, k_m\}$ may be interpreted as m distinct binary features $x_{i1}^{[d]}, x_{i2}^{[d]}, \ldots, x_{im}^{[d]}$ where

$$ x_{ij}^{[d]} = \begin{cases} 1 & (x_i^{[d]} = k_j) \\ 0 & (x_i^{[d]} \neq k_j) \end{cases} . $$

Commonly $x_i^{[d]}$ is binary-valued and $x_{i0}^{[d]}$ is discarded for the reasons stated in Section 10.3.1, so $x_i^{[d]}$ is effectively replaced by $x_{i1}^{[d]}$. It is also unnecessary to transform continuous features, so long as they are proportional (or nearly proportional) to log-odds.

10.3.3 Practical Considerations

The choice of feature representation and combining method may have a dramatic effect on the simplicity and efficiency of the resulting classifier, particularly for on-line deployment. We have previously mentioned that feature transformations such as TF-IDF and statistical feature selection are difficult to reconcile with adaptive classifiers. Probability-based interpretations that model global distributions entail similar difficulties. For this purpose discrete features that may be derived from individual messages, independent of others in the training set, are more amenable to on-line settings. Even for batch filtering, these simple feature representations usually work as well as or better than more complex and less adaptive ones based on global statistics.

Inputs:
> Set $T \subset D$ of training examples $d \in T$, represented by $x^{[d]} = \langle 1, x_1^{[d]}, x_2^{[d]}, \ldots, x_n^{[d]} \rangle$
> Labeling $label : T \to \{0, 1\}$
> Rate parameter δ

Output:
> $\beta \cdot x^{[d]}$ is the maximum likelihood estimate of $\Pr[label(d) = 1]$ over $d \in T$

1    $\beta \leftarrow \langle 0, \ldots, 0 \rangle$
2   **loop** until convergence:
3   **for** $d \in T$ **do**
4           $p \leftarrow \frac{1}{1 + e^{-\beta \cdot x^{[d]}}}$
5           $\beta \leftarrow \beta + (label(d) - p) \cdot \delta \cdot x^{[d]}$

Figure 10.8   Logistic regression using the gradient descent method.

Provided amenable features are used, a naïve Bayes classifier is very easy to implement and there is little difference between batch and on-line versions. The batch version is shown in Figure 10.7. It simply counts the number of occurrences of each feature in $T \cap P$ and $T \cap \overline{P}$ and then computes the log-odds coefficients from them. An equivalent on-line adaptive version (not shown) simply combines the counting and coefficient calculations. Incremental discovery of new features is easily accomplished by setting the initial count of each new feature to 0 when it first occurs in a document.

Although the naïve Bayes method makes an adequate hard classifier, it is a horrible soft classifier because it overestimates the combined effect of the individual features. The more features considered, the larger the overestimate. To mitigate this effect we may select a fixed number of terms per document. For some fixed value m only the m largest and m smallest values of $x_i^{[d]}$ are used in computing $x^{[d]}$. This selection process tends to normalize the magnitude of the overestimate among documents, and among positive and negative features.

Logistic regression is traditionally viewed as a batch algorithm, but a simple *gradient descent* method yields an implementation that is simpler and more effective than naïve Bayes and that may be used in on-line or batch scenarios. Gradient descent methods find the local minimum of a function by taking a step along the direction of the negative gradient at each iteration. The batch version is presented in Figure 10.8. The simplest incremental version, instead of iterating until convergence, performs exactly one gradient step for each incoming document. It is also possible to maintain an incremental history of training examples seen so far and to train on them. For example, when training a new positive example, one could also train a negative example selected at random, and so on. The net effect is to balance the number of positive and negative examples, which may yield better classification.

In many circumstances the space efficiency of gradient descent makes it attractive for very large problems. However, if the number of training examples is large, more time-efficient algorithms are available.

The relatively slow convergence of the gradient descent method may be an advantage in combating overfitting. Logistic regression, after all, can solve a system of simultaneous equations, and hence overfit, when the number of features exceeds the number of examples. Through a suitable choice of the learning rate δ, the gradient descent method avoids this pitfall. Batch methods, on the other hand, use a technique known as *regularization* to avoid overfitting. Regularization involves not only maximizing the likelihood with respect to the training examples but also minimizing the magnitude of β because large coefficients tend to indicate overfitting. The trade-off between maximizing likelihood and minimizing $|\beta|$ is specified by a regularization parameter, often denoted as C.

All major statistical and mathematical software packages implement batch logistic regression, which is a standard tool for scientific research. For classification notable implementations include Weka (Witten and Frank, 2005), LR-TRIRLS (Komarek and Moore, 2003), and LibLinear.[5]

10.4   Linear Classifiers

A linear classifier views the feature vector $x^{[d]}$ for a message d as a point in an n-dimensional space, where n is the number of features. The classifier consists of a vector of coefficients $\beta = \langle \beta_1, \beta_2, \dots, \beta_n \rangle$ and a threshold t. The equation $\beta \cdot x = t$ defines a hyperplane that divides the space into half-spaces. All points on one side of the hyperplane $(\beta \cdot x^{[d]} > t)$ are classified as positive and the ones on the other side $(\beta \cdot x^{[d]} \leq t)$ are classified as negative. $\beta \cdot x = t$ is a *separating hyperplane* if $\forall_{d \in P}$: $\beta \cdot x^{[d]} > t$ and $\forall_{d \in \overline{P}}$: $\beta \cdot x^{[d]} \leq t$. A set of messages is said to be *linearly separable* if there exists a separating hyperplane for the set. The log-odds formulation of the probabilistic classifier developed in the previous section is an example of a linear classifier. In this section we describe a geometric interpretation and several construction methods.

For convenience we limit our illustrations to the case of $n = 2$; it should be kept in mind that typical filtering applications involve more features and hence more dimensions. Figure 10.9 shows the vector space representation for the 18 messages in our running example (Table 10.17). The x-axis corresponds to the `head:enron` feature transformed using the Gaussian model (Table 10.20). The y-axis corresponds to the `body:enron` feature represented as a simple count. The diagonal line is a separating hyperplane because all positive examples fall on one side and all negative examples on the other. Thus it is a perfect classifier — at least for the sample data.

Figure 10.10 shows that the same line is not a separating hyperplane for a larger sample from the same source; indeed, none exists. Still, most positive examples lie on the *spam* side of the line and most negative ones lie on the other side. Thus the line is a reasonable classifier. But is it the *best* linear classifier within this vector space? And how may it be chosen using only the training data? The answer depends on the definition of *best*.

---

[5] `www.csie.ntu.edu.tw/~cjlin/liblinear`

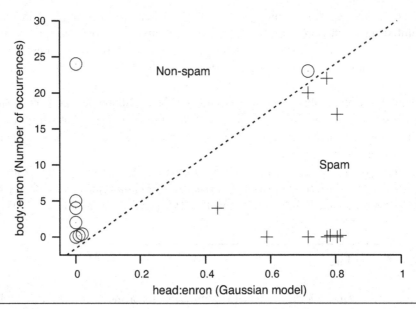

Figure 10.9 A linearly separable sample along with one possible separating hyperplane.

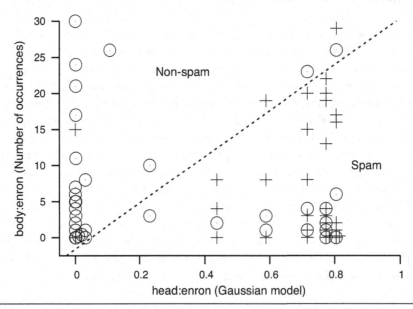

Figure 10.10 A larger linearly inseparable sample.

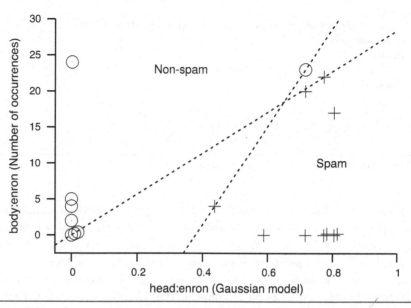

Figure 10.11   A linearly separable sample with two separating hyperplanes. Which one is "better"?

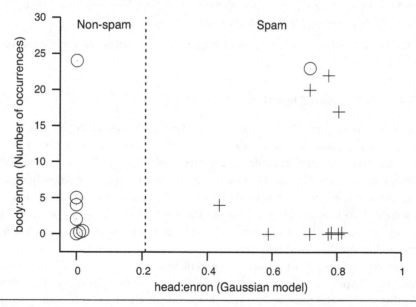

Figure 10.12   Ignoring one point.

Inputs:

Set $T \subset D$ of training examples $d \in T$, represented by $x^{[d]} = \langle 1, x_1^{[d]}, x_2^{[d]}, \ldots, x_n^{[d]} \rangle$

Labeling $label : T \to \{-1, 1\}$

Output:

if linearly separable, β such that $\beta \cdot x^{[d]} > 0$ if and only if $label(d) = 1$

else fails to terminate

```
1    β ← ⟨0, . . . , 0⟩
2    while ∃_{d∈T} :  β · x^{[d]} · label(d) < 0 do
3        β ← β + x^{[d]} · label(d)
```

Figure 10.13 The perceptron learning algorithm.

If the points are linearly separable, there are in general an infinite number of separating hyperplanes. Any positive linear combination of the extreme curves shown in Figure 10.11 will itself separate positive from negative. It is not apparent that the best classifier is a separating hyperplane, even if one exists. If one were to assume that the ham $\langle 0.72, 23 \rangle$ were an outlier — perhaps a mistake in the training data — one might reasonably choose the vertical separator in Figure 10.12, which reflects the assumption that the second feature has no real effect. Hindsight (i.e., Figure 10.10) tells us intuitively that our original separator was more appropriate. However, we are concerned here with justifying the choice based on the training data alone. Figures 10.9 and 10.12 represent two competing views of what constitutes the best classifier:

- One that correctly classifies all training examples while maximizing the distance from the nearest example to the hyperplane (Figure 10.9)

- One that allows one or more examples to be misclassified while increasing the distance to the rest (Figure 10.12).

10.4.1 Perceptron Algorithm

The perceptron algorithm (Figure 10.13) iteratively finds a separating hyperplane — any separating hyperplane, if one exists — starting with a weight vector β that is incremented or decremented for every example on the wrong side of the hyperplane specified by β. The algorithm ignores correctly classified examples. If the examples are linearly separable, the algorithm converges in a finite number of steps; otherwise it fails to terminate. For practical purposes it is sufficient to stop training after some time, under the assumption that a good, if not optimal in any sense, classifier has been found. The perceptron is attractive for filtering because it is simple, incremental, and adaptive.

The *margin perceptron* algorithm increments β for examples that are near but on the correct side of the hyperplane, and also for examples that are on the wrong side. *Margin* is defined to be the distance to the nearest example in Euclidean space. The margin perceptron (Figure 10.14; see Sculley et al. (2006) for details) adds a margin parameter τ so as to bias the method to prefer higher margin separators. Where the standard perceptron would stop, the margin perceptron

Inputs:
  Set $T \subset D$ of training examples $d \in T$, represented by $x^{[d]} = \langle 1, x_1^{[d]}, x_2^{[d]}, \ldots, x_n^{[d]} \rangle$
  Labeling $label : T \rightarrow \{-1, 1\}$
  Margin parameter τ
Output:
  if linearly separable, β such that $\beta \cdot x^{[d]} \geq \tau$ if $label(d) = 1$, $\beta \cdot x^{[d]} \leq -\tau$ if $label(d) = -1$
  else fails to terminate

1 $\beta \leftarrow \langle 0, \ldots, 0 \rangle$
2 **while** $\exists_{d \in T} :\ \beta \cdot x^{[d]} \cdot label(d) < \tau$ **do**
3    $\beta \leftarrow \beta + x^{[d]} \cdot label(d)$

Figure 10.14 Margin perceptron.

continues to adjust the hyperplane until a margin of $\frac{\tau}{|\beta|}$ is achieved. Note that $|\beta|$ grows with each step, effectively reducing the margin until a suitable hyperplane is found. There is no guarantee that the largest possible margin (i.e., the smallest possible $|\beta|$) is found, but for sufficiently large τ the margin perceptron usually finds a reasonable approximation.

10.4.2 Support Vector Machines

A support vector machine (SVM) directly computes the separating hyperplane that maximizes the margin or distance to the nearest example points. Several points will be at the same distance; these points are known as the *support vectors* and the resulting classifier is a linear combination of these vectors — all other points may be ignored. Thus the SVM would prefer the solution in Figure 10.9 over the ones in Figure 10.11 with support vectors of $\langle 0, 0 \rangle$, $\langle 0.72, 23 \rangle$ on the ham side and $\langle 0.72, 20 \rangle$ on the spam side.

 In the case of nonseparable data or of separable data in which a few points dramatically affect the solution (e.g., Figure 10.12 or point $\langle 0.72, 23 \rangle$ in our training data), it may be desirable to relax the requirement that all training data be correctly classified. Contemporary SVM formulations implement a trade-off between maximizing the margin and minimizing the magnitude of training errors. The trade-off parameter C determines the relative weight of the second objective to the first. $C = 0$ specifies the pure SVM detailed in the previous paragraph; $C = 1$ gives the objectives balanced weight and is a typical default value; $C = 100$ gives the second objective substantial weight and has been found to be appropriate for spam filtering (see Drucker et al. (1999) or Sculley et al. (2006)).

 A number of software packages implementing SVMs are available, including Weka,[6] SVM-light,[7] and LibSVM[8]. Sculley and Wachman (2007) describe a gradient method for efficient incremental on-line filtering using SVMs.

---

[6] www.cs.waikato.ac.nz/ml/weka

[7] svmlight.joachims.org

[8] www.csie.ntu.edu.tw/~cjlin/libsvm

10.5   Similarity-Based Classifiers

In this section we consider similarity-based classifiers, which harness the assumption that similar documents are more likely to belong to the same category than dissimilar ones. For classification it is necessary to formalize the notion of similarity as a function $sim : D \times D \to \mathbb{R}$, where $sim(d_1, d_2) > sim(d_3, d_4)$ means that in some sense d_1 and d_2 are more similar to one another than are d_3 and d_4. Perhaps the most familiar example is the vector space model for information retrieval from Chapter 2, where sim is the cosine formula (Equation 2.12):

$$sim(d_1, d_2) \; = \; \frac{|x^{[d_1]} \cdot x^{[d_2]}|}{|x^{[d_1]}| \cdot |x^{[d_2]}|} . \qquad (10.51)$$

For topic-oriented filtering without historical examples, documents may be prioritized by similarity to the query q, exactly as for ranked retrieval, yielding a soft classifier:

$$c(d) = sim(d, q) . \qquad (10.52)$$

If historical examples are available, we may compute the similarity of d to any or all of them, and combine the resulting evidence to classify d. We formalize this approach by defining a new similarity function $Sim : D \times 2^D \to \mathbb{R}$, where $Sim(d, D')$ indicates the similarity of d to the documents in a set $D' \subset D$. Various similarity-based classifiers are distinguished by how they define sim and by how Sim is derived from sim.

10.5.1   Rocchio's Method

Rocchio's method (Rocchio, 1971) defines

$$Sim(d, D') = sim(d, d'), \quad \text{where } x^{[d']} = \frac{1}{|D'|} \sum_{d \in D'} x^{[d]} . \qquad (10.53)$$

That is, D' is represented by a hypothetical surrogate document d' whose feature vector is the centroid of all members of D'. In its simplest form the Rocchio classifier uses only positive training examples:

$$c(d) \; = \; Sim(d, T \cap P) . \qquad (10.54)$$

For categorization, where positive and negative examples are available, a better classifier is derived from the difference

$$c(d) \; = \; Sim(d, T \cap P) - Sim(d, T \cap \overline{P}) . \qquad (10.55)$$

Rocchio's method has been used extensively for relevance feedback in the vector space model. Like the cosine measure on which it is based, Rocchio's method is essentially obsolete for this purpose; methods like BM25 relevance feedback work better. It is not difficult to see that

Rocchio's method is in fact a linear classifier, but it is not as effective as the other classifiers presented here.

Our application of BM25 to language categorization and spam filtering (Section 10.1) may be considered a variant of Rocchio's method in which *Sim* is defined in terms of the BM25 relevance feedback formula instead of the cosine measure.

10.5.2 Memory-Based Methods

Memory-based methods, also known as *case-based* methods, use the training examples themselves as the classifier profile. These examples are searched as necessary to classify a document or set of documents. Perhaps the simplest memory-based method is *nearest neighbor* (NN), which is traditionally taken to be a hard classifier:

$$c_h(d) \;=\; label\left(\arg\max_{d' \in T} sim(d, d')\right).$$ (10.56)

If *sim* happens to be one of the ranking methods we have considered for standard search tasks, the nearest neighbor classifier may be implemented efficiently by indexing the training examples and using a search engine to retrieve the most similar document. Otherwise it may be necessary to enumerate $sim(d, d')$ for every $d' \in T$.

More generally, we may compute a soft nearest neighbor classifier and derive the hard classifier from it:

$$Sim(d, D') \;=\; \max_{d' \in D'} sim(d, d')$$ (10.57)

$$c_s(d) \;=\; Sim(d, T \cap P) - Sim(d, T \cap \overline{P})$$ (10.58)

$$c_h(d) \;=\; \begin{cases} pos & (c_s(d) > 0) \\ neg & (c_s(d) \leq 0) \end{cases}.$$ (10.59)

An efficient implementation of c_s involves the construction of separate search indices for T_{pos} and T_{neg}.

A simple variant is *k-nearest neighbor* (kNN), in which the k documents most similar to d are considered, for some fixed k. Most commonly a hard classifier is then defined as the majority vote among the most similar k documents.

10.6 Generalized Linear Models

As we have noted previously, there is no firm distinction between feature engineering and classifier construction. Through a suitable choice of the feature representation $x^{[d]}$ one can

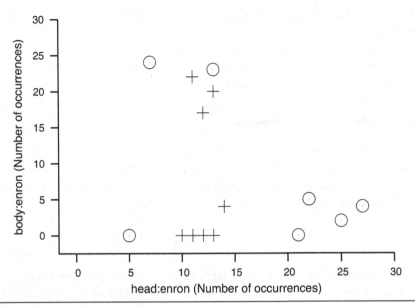

Figure 10.15   Untransformed features.

transform essentially any classification problem into one that may be solved by a linear classifier. The examples we have presented so far rely on such feature engineering:

- For probabilistic classifiers we applied the logit transformation, known as a *link function* or *transfer function*, to make the problem amenable to linear classification.

- For our linear classification example we applied a Gaussian transformation to one of the dimensions.

Figure 10.15 shows the linear classification example without transformation. The feature representation is the raw term frequency for both dimensions. In this exposition we distinguish raw and transformed representations using the following notation:

- $x^{[d]}$ is the *raw* representation of d. For this example $x^{[d]}$ is the vector of the frequencies of the two terms. In general, $x^{[d]}$ is a representation that is in some sense a straightforward representation of d.

- $X^{[d]} = \varphi(x^{[d]})$ is the *transformed* representation of d, where φ is a mapping function. X is a vector space whose dimensionality need not be the same as x. It may be smaller, in which case the transformation is an example of *dimensionality reduction*. Or it may be considerably larger, even infinite. In this second situation *kernel methods* may be used to construct linear classifiers over X without having to calculate $X^{[d]}$. Perceptrons and SVMs are readily implemented as kernel methods.

Using Equation 10.34, the mapping for our example is

$$X^{[d]} \ = \ \varphi(x^{[d]}) \ = \ \left\langle \frac{N_P}{N_{\overline{P}}} \cdot \frac{g(\mu_{(1,P)}, \sigma_{(1,P)}, x_1^{[d]})}{g(\mu_{(1,\overline{P})}, \sigma_{(1,\overline{P})}, x_1^{[d]})}, \ x_2^{[d]} \right\rangle . \tag{10.60}$$

Note that the four parameters $\mu_{(1,P)}, \sigma_{(1,P)}, \mu_{(1,\overline{P})}, \sigma_{(1,\overline{P})}$ are estimated from the training examples as part of the feature engineering process. An alternative is to guess several values for these parameters and to see which one works best, a process known as *parameter selection* or, more colloquially, *tuning*. One may guess φ as well; the overall process of guessing φ and its parameters is known as *model selection*. In evaluating classifiers whose construction involves parameter or model selection, it is essential that the evaluation (i.e., test) data not be consulted. A common approach is to subdivide the training examples into separate training and *validation* sets (as detailed in Chapter 11). For our immediate purpose we assume that φ (including any implicit parameters on which it depends) is fixed.

For expository purposes we consider a second mapping φ^+ on the same data that augments the dimensionality of x, to form a three-dimensional space:

$$\varphi^+(x^{[d]}) \ = \ \left\langle x_1^{[d]}, \ x_2^{[d]}, \ \frac{N_P}{N_{\overline{P}}} \cdot \frac{g(\mu_{(1,P)}, \sigma_{(1,P)}, x_1^{[d]})}{g(\mu_{(1,\overline{P})}, \sigma_{(1,\overline{P})}, x_1^{[d]})} \right\rangle . \tag{10.61}$$

This mapping may be visualized as lifting the positive examples from the plane, along the new third dimension, while depressing the negative examples. In this new three-dimensional space the examples are linearly separable. Furthermore, the first dimension is unnecessary because the examples are still linearly separable when we reduce the space to two dimensions by eliminating it:

$$\varphi^-(X^{[d]}) = \left\langle X_3^{[d]}, \ X_2^{[d]} \right\rangle \tag{10.62}$$

Our original mapping φ is simply the composition of φ^+ and φ^-:

$$\varphi(x^{[d]}) = \varphi^-(\varphi^+(x^{[d]})) . \tag{10.63}$$

10.6.1   Kernel Methods

A linear classifier may be reformulated as a similarity-based classifier where

$$sim(d_1, d_2) \ = \ X^{[d_1]} \cdot X^{[d_2]} . \tag{10.64}$$

Consider the case in which the feature space x is linearly separable. The perceptron algorithm may be used to compute a weight vector β such that

$$c(d) = \beta \cdot X^{[d]} \qquad c(d \in P) > 0 \qquad c(d \in \overline{P}) < 0 . \tag{10.65}$$

Inputs:

  Set $T \subset D$ of training examples $d \in T$, represented arbitrarily

  Labeling $label : T \rightarrow \{-1, 1\}$

  Similarity (kernel) function $sim : D \times D \rightarrow \mathbb{R}$,

    where $sim(d_1, d_2) = X^{[d_1]} \cdot X^{[d_2]}$ in virtual feature space X

Output:

  if linearly separable,

    α such that $c(d) > 0$ if and only if $label(d) = 1$, where $c(d) = \sum_{d' \in T} \alpha_{d'} \, sim(d', d)$

  else fails to terminate

1    $\alpha \leftarrow \langle 0, \ldots, 0 \rangle$

2   **while** $\exists_{d \in T} : \ c(d) \cdot label(d) < 0$ **do**

3       $\alpha_d \leftarrow \alpha_d + label(d)$

Figure 10.16   Kernel perceptron learning algorithm.

From Figure 10.13 we see that β must be a linear combination of positive and negative training examples in which the positive and negative examples have nonnegative and nonpositive coefficients, respectively:

$$\beta = \sum_{d \in T} \alpha_i X^{[d]} \qquad \alpha_{d \in P} \geq 0 \qquad \alpha_{d \in \overline{P}} \leq 0 \,. \tag{10.66}$$

Here α is a vector of weights, one for each document in T. Combining Equations 10.64, 10.65, and 10.66, we have the *dual formulation* of the classifier:

$$c(d) \; = \; \Big(\sum_{d' \in T} \alpha_{d'} \cdot x^{[d']} \Big) \cdot x^{[d]} \; = \; \sum_{d' \in T} \alpha_{d'} \cdot (x^{[d']} \cdot x^{[d]}) \; = \; \sum_{d' \in T} \alpha_{d'} \cdot sim(d, d') \,. \tag{10.67}$$

This dual formulation does not reference $X^{[d]}$ except within the definition of sim. The *kernel perceptron* algorithm (figure 10.16) uses this representation and computes α instead of β, replacing the update rule

$$\beta \leftarrow \beta + X^{[d]} \cdot label(d) \quad \text{with} \quad \alpha_d \leftarrow \alpha_d + label(d) \,. \tag{10.68}$$

Thus the kernel perceptron manipulates sim and α, but never $X^{[d]}$ or β. Other methods, including the margin perceptron and SVM, may be formulated as kernel methods.

The so-called *kernel trick* is to implement $sim(d_1, d_2)$ without reference to X, thus avoiding its computation altogether. So long as Equation 10.64 holds, any implementation will do. Such an implementation is called a *kernel function*. The kernel trick enables us to use a vast or unlimited number of virtual features, which would not otherwise be possible.

Consider, for example, a set of documents $d \in D$ whose raw feature representation $x^{[d]}$ consists of n term frequencies. Rather than using the traditional cosine rule that directly yields a linear classifier, let us define similarity to be the number of terms that two documents share with identical frequencies:

$$sim(d_1, d_2) = |\{i \in [1, n] \,|\, x_i^{[d_1]} = x_i^{[d_2]}\}| \,. \tag{10.69}$$

In general there is an unbounded number of possible values for $f = x_i^{[d]}$, but we may enumerate them by defining a mapping π from combinations of (f, i) to $\mathbb{N}$:

$$\pi(f, i) = i + n \cdot f \,. \tag{10.70}$$

Given π, the virtual feature representation $X^{[d]}$ is defined by

$$X_{\pi(f,i)}^{[d]} = \begin{cases} 1 & (x_i^{[d]} = f) \\ 0 & (x_i^{[d]} \neq f) \end{cases} \,. \tag{10.71}$$

In this space we have $sim(d_1, d_2) = X^{[d_1]} \cdot X^{[d_2]}$, as required. But sim is implemented by enumerating $x^{[d_1]}$ and $x^{[d_2]}$, not $X^{[d_1]}$ and $X^{[d_2]}$.

The design of feature spaces and kernel functions is limited only by the imagination. Standard examples include string kernels, polynomial kernels, and radial basis function (Gaussian) kernels. SVM packages commonly support a variety of kernels, including user-defined kernels in which sim is specified in a programming language.

10.7 Information-Theoretic Models

A *model* is an estimate of the probability of some event derived from available evidence. A meteorologist might use evidence such as humidity and barometric pressure to predict an 80% chance of rain tomorrow. In this example the event is rain and the meteorologist's model estimates $\Pr[\text{rain}] \approx 0.8$ and $\Pr[\text{not rain}] \approx 0.2$.

In Chapter 6 we considered several models for data compression under the simplifying assumption that the model $\mathcal{M}$ predicting each symbol s from some alphabet $\mathcal{S}$ was exact:

$$\forall_{s \in \mathcal{S}} \; \Pr[s_i] = \mathcal{M}(s_i) \,. \tag{10.72}$$

Here we make the opposite assumption: that any real model $\mathcal{M}$ is necessarily inexact and that $\mathcal{M}$ is better than some other model $\mathcal{M}'$ if it is closer to the true probability. The task of determining which of $\mathcal{M}$ or $\mathcal{M}'$ is better presents two challenges:

- The *true probability* is intangible, and cannot be used as a gold standard for comparison.

- The notion of "closer to" has many possible interpretations.

Assuming these challenges are met and we have a method to determine which is the better model, we can construct a classifier in one of two ways:

- Construct separate *data compression models* from positive and negative training examples, and use them to estimate the likelihood ratio for an unknown document:

$$\mathcal{M}_P(d) \approx \Pr[d \,|\, d \in P] \qquad \mathcal{M}_{\overline{P}}(d) \approx \Pr[d \,|\, d \in \overline{P}] \qquad (10.73)$$

$$c_s(d) = \frac{\mathcal{M}_P(d)}{\mathcal{M}_{\overline{P}}(d)} \approx LR(d \in P, d). \qquad (10.74)$$

- From among many candidate models, choose $\mathcal{M}$ that best models the labels of the training examples, and use $\mathcal{M}$ itself for classification:

$$c_s(d) = \mathcal{M}(label(d) = pos \,|\, d) \approx \Pr[d \in P \,|\, d]. \qquad (10.75)$$

This approach is commonly used in constructing *decision tree classifiers*. More generally, the approach is known as *model selection*.

10.7.1 Comparing Models

We define $\mathcal{P}(x)$ to be the hypothetical true probability of an event x, and $\mathcal{M}$ to be a model for that probability:

$$\mathcal{M}(x) \approx \mathcal{P}(x) = \Pr[x]. \qquad (10.76)$$

$I_{\mathcal{P}}(x)$ is the *information content* of x given $\mathcal{P}$, measured in bits:

$$I_{\mathcal{P}}(x) = -\log_2 \mathcal{P}(x). \qquad (10.77)$$

$\mathcal{H}(\mathcal{P})$ is the *entropy*, or expected information content, of a random variable X with distribution $\mathcal{P}$ (also measured in bits):

$$\mathcal{H}(\mathcal{P}) = \mathrm{E}[I_{\mathcal{P}}(X)] = \sum_x \mathcal{P}(x) \cdot I_{\mathcal{P}}(x). \qquad (10.78)$$

$\mathcal{H}(\mathcal{P})$ is an information-theoretic lower bound on the expected number of bits that are needed to encode X. This lower bound is achieved if and only if every x is encoded with $I_{\mathcal{P}}(x)$ bits.

Real data compression methods, such as those considered in Chapter 6, fail to achieve this lower bound for two reasons:

- Under the assumption that $\mathcal{M}(x) = \mathcal{P}(x)$, they encode each x using about $I_{\mathcal{M}}(x)$ bits, thus optimizing $\mathcal{H}(\mathcal{M})$ instead of $\mathcal{H}(\mathcal{P})$.

- In general, $I_{\mathcal{M}}(x)$ is not an integer, so fractions of bits are wasted.

For our purposes only the first consideration is of any consequence: How far from the lower bound is a code that uses exactly $I_{\mathcal{M}}(x)$ bits to encode x? The expected length of such a code for a random variable X with distribution $\mathcal{P}$ is given by the *cross-entropy* between $\mathcal{P}$ and $\mathcal{M}$:

$$\mathcal{H}(\mathcal{P}; \mathcal{M}) \;=\; \mathrm{E}[I_\mathcal{M}(X)] \;=\; \sum_x \mathcal{P}(x) \cdot I_\mathcal{M}(x) \tag{10.79}$$

The difference between cross-entropy (the code length) and entropy (the lower bound) is KL divergence (see Section 9.4):

$$D_{KL}(\mathcal{P} \parallel \mathcal{M}) \;=\; \mathcal{H}(\mathcal{P}; \mathcal{M}) - \mathcal{H}(\mathcal{P}). \tag{10.80}$$

We say that model $\mathcal{M}_1$ is a better model than $\mathcal{M}_2$ if it yields a shorter expected code length; that is, if

$$\mathcal{H}(\mathcal{P}; \mathcal{M}_1) < \mathcal{H}(\mathcal{P}; \mathcal{M}_2) \;\;\Leftrightarrow\;\; D_{KL}(\mathcal{P} \parallel \mathcal{M}_1) < D_{KL}(\mathcal{P} \parallel \mathcal{M}_2) \tag{10.81}$$

$$\Leftrightarrow\;\; \sum_x \mathcal{P}(x) \cdot (I_{\mathcal{M}_1}(x) - I_{\mathcal{M}_2}(x)) < 0. \tag{10.82}$$

10.7.2   Sequential Compression Models

Sequential compression models such as prediction by partial matching (PPM; Cleary and Witten, 1984), dynamic Markov compression (DMC; Cormack and Horspool, 1987), and context-tree weighting (CTW; Willems et al., 1995), treat a message m as a sequence $s_1 s_2 \ldots s_n$ of symbols from a finite alphabet. The symbols are processed sequentially, and a separate model $\mathcal{M}_k$ is constructed for each prefix $s_1 s_2 \ldots s_k$ in turn, for $0 \leq k < n$. Each $\mathcal{M}_k$ is used to compress s_{k+1} and then discarded. The model $\mathcal{M}$ for the whole message is

$$\mathcal{M}(m) \;=\; \prod_{k=0}^{n-1} \mathcal{M}_k(s_{k+1}). \tag{10.83}$$

Under this model the optimal code length for m is

$$I_\mathcal{M}(m) \;=\; \sum_{k=0}^{n-1} I_{\mathcal{M}_k}(s_{k+1}). \tag{10.84}$$

For classification (Bratko et al., 2006) we represent each document d by some sequence of symbols $m^{[d]}$ and form a supersequence m^P by concatenating all $m^{[d \in T \cap P]}$ (the positive training examples), and $m^{\overline{P}}$ by concatenating all $m^{[d \in T \cap \overline{P}]}$ (the negative training examples). Two sequential models $\mathcal{M}_P$ and $\mathcal{M}_{\overline{P}}$ are constructed for these sequences. A new message $m^{[d]}$ to be classified is concatenated to m^P and to $m^{\overline{P}}$, yielding new models $\mathcal{M}_{Pd}$ and $\mathcal{M}_{\overline{P}d}$, respectively. The soft classifier is constructed as follows:

$$c(d) \;\approx\; \log \frac{\Pr[m^P m^{[d]} \,|\, d \in P]}{\Pr[m^{\overline{P}} m^{[d]} \,|\, d \in \overline{P}]} - \log \frac{\Pr[m^P \,|\, d \in P]}{\Pr[m^{\overline{P}} \,|\, d \in \overline{P}]} \;=\; \log \mathrm{LR}(d \in P, m^{[d]}) \tag{10.85}$$

$$c(d) \;=\; I_{\overline{P}d}(m^{\overline{P}}m^{[d]}) - I_{\overline{P}}(m^{\overline{P}}) - I_{Pd}(m^{P}m^{[d]}) + I_P(m^{P})\,. \qquad (10.86)$$

That is, the classifier is the difference between the increase in information content from adding d to the negative examples, and the increase from adding d to the positive examples.

In practice it is unnecessary to compute $\mathcal{M}_{Pd}$ and $\mathcal{M}_{\overline{P}d}$ from scratch. Sequential compression methods efficiently construct $\mathcal{M}_{Pd}$ and $\mathcal{M}_{\overline{P}d}$ from stored representations of $\mathcal{M}_P$ and $\mathcal{M}_{\overline{P}}$, along with $m^{[d]}$. Incremental training is easily effected by replacing $\mathcal{M}_P$ with $\mathcal{M}_{Pd}$ when it is discovered that $d \in P$, and $M_{\overline{P}}$ with $M_{\overline{P}d}$ when it is discovered that $d \in \overline{P}$.

For illustration we use Dynamic Markov Compression (DMC), arguably the simplest method that performs well. DMC treats each message as a sequence of bits, typically the obvious ASCII or Unicode representation of the text. Thus the message representation is a sequence of symbols from the alphabet $\{0,1\}$. Figure 10.17 illustrates how DMC works. It starts with an initial Markov model (Section 1.3.4) with very few states, as illustrated by the left panel (a). The message is processed as a sequence of binary bits, so there are transitions from each state labeled 0 and 1. Each transition is also labeled with a frequency indicating the number of times it has been followed. From this information we may deduce that panel (a) has been trained on a sequence of 22 bits, of which 16 were 1 and 6 were 0. Intuitively, the state A represents a sequence whose last bit is 0 while B represents a sequence whose last bit is 1. The odds of the next transition from these states may be estimated from the frequencies

$$\text{Odds}[1\,|\,A] \;\approx\; \frac{4}{2} \;=\; 2 \;\; \text{and} \;\; \text{Odds}[1\,|\,B] \;\approx\; \frac{12}{4} \;=\; 3\,. \qquad (10.87)$$

The method operates as an on-line classifier: Each bit is first predicted using the odds estimate, then the correct transition is taken and the corresponding frequency is incremented.

When a state is visited frequently through one transition, and also through other transitions, it is *cloned* to yield two similar states. This situation is illustrated by the right panel (b), in which the transition from A to B is about to be taken, raising its frequency to 5. B is cloned to create B', and the high-frequency transition is redirected to B'. The outgoing frequencies of B and B' are divided in proportion to the incoming frequencies, so that $\text{Odds}[1|B'] = \text{Odds}[1|B] = 3$. Finally, the transition to B' is taken, and its frequency is incremented. Through cloning, the Markov model grows, progressively modeling longer substrings of the training example. For this example B' models sequences ending in 01, and B models sequences ending in 11. The state A, as before cloning, models sequences ending in 0.

An implementation of DMC is available for download at no cost.[9] Table 10.22 illustrates the result of applying two DMC models (one for ham and one for spam) to the To: fields of the 18 messages in our running example, in order (see Table 10.17). The first column of Table 10.22 shows the true class of the message; the second, the overall log-likelihood ratio $c(d)$;

---

[9] plg.uwaterloo.ca/~ftp/dmc/dmc.c

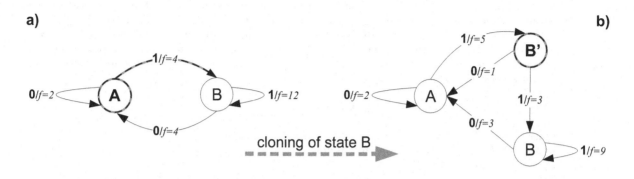

Figure 10.17   Example of DMC's Markov model cloning operation.

and the third, the `To:` field of the message. Each character x_i is darkened to indicate the log-likelihood ratio associated with it (that is, the sum of the log-likelihoods for the individual bits in the character): Black indicates spam ($\log LR(d \in spam, x_i) \gg 0$); light gray indicates ham ($\log LR(d \in spam, x_i) \ll 0$); and medium gray indicates neither ($\log LR(d \in spam, x_i) \approx 0$).

The first message is gray and has a log-likelihood ratio of 0 because there are no previous messages; thus the spam and ham models are identical. The next two messages are classified (correctly) as spam, which is perhaps not surprising as there are no ham examples with which to compare. Indeed the fourth message — the first ham — is incorrectly classified as spam with a positive log-likelihood ratio. As more examples are learned, the models are better able to distinguish spam from ham. The last seven messages are correctly classified. The shadings of individual characters reveal that some key indicators of ham are the following:

- quotation marks
- the token "ENRON", in upper case
- specific names like `Adams` and `pete.davis`.

Indicators of spam are the following:

- the token "enron", in lowercase
- variants of the name `kholst`.

The data compression models used for filtering harness the correlation between adjacent symbols in the message. DMC uses a bitwise dynamic Markov model that incrementally adapts to model longer sequences that occur frequently. PPM, in contrast, tacitly uses an n-gram character model ($4 \le n \le 8$ is typical) for which a suffix-tree representation is more amenable than a feature vector because it consumes linear space. Context-tree weighting is asymptotically optimal under certain theoretical assumptions, but is more complex and does not appear to yield better results than DMC or PPM.

Table 10.22 DMC results, when applied to the *To:* field extracted from each message, with on-line learning in the order shown. The first column gives the true category. The second column gives the log-likelihood ratio computed by DMC. Positive indicates spam and negative indicates ham. The third column shows the text itself, with dark print indicating high spam likelihood and light print indicating low spam likelihood. The *To:* field is used for brevity of exposition; superior results are achieved when the entire message text is used.

Class	Score	Message Snippet
spam	0.0	To: emclaug@enron.com
spam	3.9	To: SKean@enron.com
spam	0.1	To: <joydish@bareed.alburaq.net>
ham	1.1	To: "Shapiro, Richard" <Richard.Shapiro@ENRON.com>
ham	-0.8	To: "Adams, Jacqueline P." <Jacqueline.P.Adams@ENRON.com>,
ham	-4.4	To: "Adams, Jacqueline P." <Jacqueline.P.Adams@ENRON.com>,
ham	1.5	To: pete.davis@enron.com
spam	1.0	To: KAM.KEISER@enron.com
ham	-2.1	To: "Abel, Chris" <Chris.Abel@ENRON.com>,
ham	-1.8	To: "Moran, Tom" <Tom.Moran@ENRON.com>,
spam	-0.1	To: nqeb5e6@msn.com
spam	1.6	To: skean@enron.com
ham	-1.4	To: pete.davis@enron.com
spam	0.1	To: kholst <kholst@enron.com>
ham	-1.1	To: "Scott, Susan M." <Susan.M.Scott@ENRON.com>
spam	0.8	To: mmotley@enron.com
spam	3.2	To: kholst@enron.com
spam	3.1	To: keith.holst@enron.com

10.7.3 Decision Trees and Stumps

A *decision tree classifier* successively partitions D into subsets, each of which has a higher proportion of either positive or negative examples than D itself. The tree is constructed from the examples in T, under the assumption that the same tree will suitably partition D.

We consider binary decision trees in which the partitioning is expressed as a set of Boolean formulae, each specifying a binary partition on one of the subsets. Each formula is typically quite simple, based on a single binary feature or on comparing a continuous feature against a threshold value.

The simplest decision tree is a *binary decision stump,* which uses a binary formula b to partition D into two subsets:

$$D^b = \{d \in D | b\}, \qquad D^{\bar{b}} = \{d \in D | \bar{b}\}. \tag{10.88}$$

A decision tree is formed by repeatedly partitioning subsets of D. After $n-1$ steps we arrive at n disjoint subsets:

$$D = D_1 \cup D_2 \cup \ldots \cup D_n. \tag{10.89}$$

At each step $k = 1$ through $k = n - 1$, two decisions are taken:

1. Identify a particular D_i ($1 \le i \le k$) to be partitioned.
2. Identify b_{ik} to partition D_i into D_i and D_k.

The challenge is to make decisions that lead to a good classifier. For any reasonable definition of "good", the problem is intractable and the decisions are made one at a time in a "greedy" fashion using some heuristic. *Information gain* (IG) is commonly used for this purpose.

Consider the problem of finding a model $\mathcal{M}$ for a binary classification in which the possible events are *pos* and *neg*:

$$\mathcal{M}(pos) = 1 - \mathcal{M}(neg) \approx \Pr[d \in P]. \tag{10.90}$$

Given a set T of labeled training examples, we may derive a simple model from the proportion of positive examples

$$\mathcal{M}(pos) = \frac{|T \cap P|}{|T|}. \tag{10.91}$$

The information content of the set of training labels $label(T) = \{label(d) \,|\, d \in T\}$ is then

$$I_{\mathcal{M}}(label(T)) = \sum_{d \in T} I_{\mathcal{M}}(label(d)) = |T \cap P| \cdot I_{\mathcal{M}}(pos) + |T \cap \overline{P}| \cdot I_{\mathcal{M}}(neg). \tag{10.92}$$

Now consider the situation in which separate models are constructed for $T^b = T \cap D^b$ and $T^{\overline{b}} = T \cap D^{\overline{b}}$:

$$\mathcal{M}_b(pos) = \frac{|T^b \cap P|}{|T^b|} \tag{10.93}$$

$$\mathcal{M}_{\overline{b}}(pos) = \frac{|T^{\overline{b}} \cap P|}{|T^{\overline{b}}|} \approx \Pr[d \in P | \overline{b}]. \tag{10.94}$$

Assuming $B \in \{b, \overline{b}\}$ is known for the document that is to be classified, a combined model is

$$\mathcal{M}_B = \begin{cases} \mathcal{M}_b & (B = b) \\ \mathcal{M}_{\overline{b}} & (B = \overline{b}) \end{cases} \approx \Pr[d \in P | B]. \tag{10.95}$$

The information content of the training labels, given B, is

$$I_{\mathcal{M}_B}(label(T)) = I_{\mathcal{M}_b}(label(T^b)) + I_{\mathcal{M}_{\overline{b}}}(label(T^{\overline{b}})). \tag{10.96}$$

The *information gain* due to B is the amount by which the information content of the labels is reduced when B is known:

$$IG(B) \;=\; I_{\mathcal{M}}(label(T)) - I_{\mathcal{M}_B}(label(T)). \tag{10.97}$$

Among the 18 training examples in Table 10.17, we have 10 positive and 8 negative. Our simple model $\mathcal{M}$ uses the proportion of positive examples as a probability estimate:

$$\mathcal{M}(pos) \;=\; \frac{10}{18} \approx 0.556 \tag{10.98}$$

$$I_{\mathcal{M}}(label(T)) \approx -10 \cdot \log_2(0.556) - 8 \cdot \log_2(0.444) \approx 17.84 \text{ bits.} \tag{10.99}$$

Now we partition T using the formula "$b \Leftrightarrow$ the body of d contains `enron`":

$$\mathcal{M}_b(pos) \;=\; \frac{4}{9} \approx 0.444 \tag{10.100}$$

$$\mathcal{M}_{\bar{b}}(pos) \;=\; \frac{6}{9} \approx 0.667 \tag{10.101}$$

$$I_{\mathcal{M}_b}(label(T^b)) \approx -4 \cdot \log(0.444) - 5 \cdot \log(0.556) \approx 8.92 \text{ (bits)} \tag{10.102}$$

$$I_{\mathcal{M}_{\bar{b}}}(label(T^{\bar{b}})) \approx -6 \cdot \log(0.667) - 3 \cdot \log(0.333) \approx 8.26 \text{ (bits)} \tag{10.103}$$

$$I_{\mathcal{M}_B}(label(T)) \approx 8.92 + 8.26 = 17.18 \text{ (bits)} \tag{10.104}$$

$$IG(B) \;=\; I_{\mathcal{M}} - I_{\mathcal{M}_B} \approx 0.66 \text{ (bits).} \tag{10.105}$$

To build a decision tree, some set of possible formulae is searched at each step, and the one yielding the greatest information gain is selected. It is important not to search too many possible formulae, or to construct complex formulae, or to partition D into too many sets. Each choice will tend to overfit the model to the training data. This caveat is well-founded in information theory: In computing information gain, we should consider the information content of the formula itself in addition to the information content of the training labels. If the formula is selected from a fixed set of n candidates, its information content is $\log_2(n)$ bits. If the formula is more complex, its information content may be much larger. When the combined information content of the formula and the training labels shows a negative information gain, further partitioning is likely to be counterproductive.

10.8   Experimental Comparison

In this section we apply representative examples of the methods we have described to the three concrete examples introduced in Section 10.1. For ease of comparison, we repeat the BM25 baseline results. The results presented here may be used to form a general impression of the effectiveness of various approaches. They also serve as input and a baseline for comparison with the combination and fusion methods described in Chapter 11.

10.8.1   Topic-Oriented On-Line Filtering

In Table 10.23 the columns labeled "Historical Training" show the result of applying various methods to the topic-oriented filtering problem detailed in Section 10.1.2. The columns labeled "Adaptive Training" show the effect of adaptive training when supported by the method. Adaptive training processes the historical and test examples as one common sequence, classifying and then training on each document in turn. That is, the approach is exactly the same as the one described for spam filtering in Section 10.1.5. For comparison the summary measures consider only the classification results for the test examples (i.e., the *Financial Times* documents from 1993 and later).

The first row shows the result for BM25, as described in Section 10.1.2. For historical training examples the results are reproduced from the bottom row of Table 10.6 (page 319). The results in the row labeled NB are those of a naïve Bayes classifier, configured as follows:

- Byte 4-grams were used as binary features.

- Smoothing parameters $\gamma = \epsilon = 1$ were used.

- The 30 features with the largest score, and the 30 features with the smallest score, were selected for each document.

The results in the row labeled LR (gradient descent) employ on-line gradient descent logistic regression, detailed in Section 10.3.3, in the following configuration:

- Character 4-grams are used as binary features.

- Each feature vector $x^{[d]}$ is mapped to a length-normalized form $X^{[d]} = \frac{x^{[d]}}{\sqrt{|x^{[d]}|}}$.

- The rate parameter was $\delta = 0.004$.

- Adaptive training was used. For each new training example exactly one gradient step was taken. Following this step, a historical example of the complementary class was selected at random and used as a training example. The overall effect is that an equal number of training steps was taken for relevant and nonrelevant examples.

The results in the row labeled DMC applied the DMC compression method to the textual representation of the document. The remaining methods use batch training methods, so results are presented for historical training only. LR (batch) is logistic regression:

- The LibLinear package, version 1.33, was used with flag $-$s 0 (L2 regularized logistic regression) and default parameters.

- Binary 4-gram features were used.

Table 10.23   Classifier results for TREC topic 383 (Figure 10.2 on page 313).

Method	Historical Training		Adaptive Training	
	P@10	AP	P@10	AP
BM25	1.0	0.56	0.8	0.30
NB	0.0	0.00	0.4	0.06
LR (gradient descent)	0.7	0.39	1.0	0.55
DMC	0.0	0.01	0.1	0.06
LR (batch)	0.8	0.48		
SVM (batch)	0.8	0.49		
DT ($n=2$)	0.1	0.03		
DT ($n=8$)	0.9	0.53		
DT ($n=256$)	0.8	0.53		

For SVM:

- The SVM^{light} package, version 6.02, was used with no flags (linear kernel, default parameters).

- Binary 4-gram features were used.

For DT:

- The FEST[10] (Fast Ensembles of Sparse Trees) package was used. The flag -d 1 (depth 1, decision stump) was used for the results labeled $n = 2$; -d 3 was used for $n = 8$; -d 8 was used for $n = 256$.

It is perhaps unremarkable that BM25 performs better than the others with historical training because it is engineered specifically for this purpose. Its performance, on the other hand, is worsened by adaptive training. This effect is most likely due to the fact that our configuration uses the 20 highest-scoring features as feedback terms, and this set of features may change as more training examples are encountered. In contrast, the other adaptive methods show improved results with adaptive training.

Naïve Bayes, DMC, and decision stumps fare poorly. However, the other learning methods do quite well. Although it would be inappropriate to conclude which is best from this single example, these methods are certainly worthy of consideration.

Table 10.24 shows the result of applying essentially the same methods to language categorization. All methods were applied as described in Section 10.1.4. The documents were ranked according to each of the 60 languages, and the resulting scores were used to rank the categories

---

[10] www.cs.cornell.edu/~nk/fest/

Table 10.24 Classifier results for language categorization.

Method	Document Ranking MAP	Categorization Micro-Avg. Error (%)	MRR
BM25	0.78	20.6	0.86
NB	0.44	27.0	0.80
LR (gradient descent)	0.76	22.9	0.84
LR (batch)	0.82	20.0	0.86
SVM (batch)	0.83	20.0	0.80
DMC	0.74	20.0	0.86
DT ($n=2$)	0.33	64.1	0.44
DT ($n=8$)	0.54	43.7	0.63
DT ($n=256$)	0.63	34.8	0.70

Table 10.25 Classifier results for on-line spam filtering.

Method	Classification Error (%) fpr	fnr	Macro-Avg.	Logistic Avg.	1-AUC	CPU Time
BM25	32.85	0.01	16.43	0.77	0.190	8m
NB	1.21	1.21	1.21	1.21	0.062	24s
LR (gradient descent)	0.41	0.47	0.44	0.44	0.012	12s
ROSVM	0.32	0.42	0.37	0.37	0.013	4d
DMC	0.31	0.54	0.42	0.37	0.013	6m

for each document. For the document ranking we report MAP over the 60 rankings, and for categorization we report the error rate as well as MRR over the 4012 test documents. For document ranking, SVM appears to work best, but this advantage does not translate to category ranking. All in all, there is little to choose among DMC, LR, SVM, and BM25 for categorization performance. NB and DT (for all n) yield substantially poorer results for both document ranking and categorization.

10.8.2 On-Line Adaptive Spam Filtering

Table 10.25 shows the results achieved by adaptive methods when applied to on-line spam filtering, as outlined in Section 10.1.5. Figure 10.18 summarizes the results as an ROC curve. BM25, NB, LR, and DMC are as described previously, except for the following differences:

- Following practice that has been shown at TREC to work well, only the first 2500 bytes of each message are used.

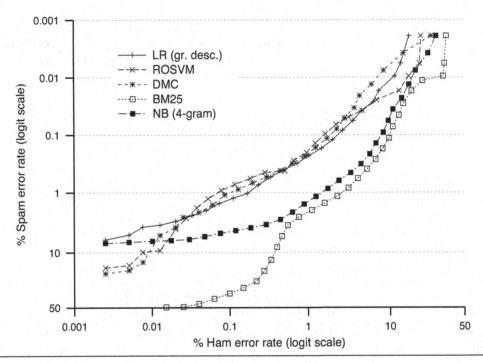

Figure 10.18   ROC curves for on-line spam filters.

- For BM25 the number of feedback terms was unlimited, rather than restricted to 20, as in topic-oriented filtering. Also, separate scores were computed considering spam and ham to be relevant, and the difference was used as the overall score.

ROSVM is the relaxed online SVM (Sculley and Wachman, 2007), which was among the two best-performing filters at the TREC 2007 Spam Track (Cormack, 2007). ROSVM is specifically engineered for efficient adaptive filtering, an application to which classical SVM methods are not inherently well suited. Even so, Sculley's ROSVM implementation for the TREC toolkit is about 25,000 times slower than gradient descent LR. An open-source version may be downloaded from the Web.[11]

By all measures, DMC, LR, and ROSVM show about the same effectiveness. The ROC curve suggests that NB is better than BM25, but both are substantially inferior to the other methods.

---

[11] www.eecs.tufts.edu/~dsculley/onlineSMO

10.9   Further Reading

Information retrieval and statistical learning methods evolved within largely separate research communities. A good but somewhat dated introduction to machine learning is provided by Mitchell (1997). A comprehensive theoretical treatment is given by Hastie et al. (2009). Support vector machines in particular are the subject of Joachims (2002). Logistic regression is a well-established method for general data analysis (Hosmer and Lemeshow, 2000), and has been shown to work well for text classification (Komarek and Moore, 2003), but has not attracted as much attention as other learning methods.

Within the IR community the primary focus has been on search, with categorization and filtering often an afterthought. Belkin and Croft (1992) discuss the relationship between search and filtering. Within the machine learning community, text categorization has typically been regarded as an application of supervised learning for classification, in which the features happen to represent documents. Sebastiani (2002) surveys learning methods for text categorization, covering aspects that we have mentioned only in passing. Among them are methods for dimensionality reduction by term selection and comparative results from the literature using F_1 and the RCV1 standard benchmark collection derived from Reuters news articles (Lewis et al., 2004).

The F_β measure is introduced as a measure for set-based retrieval by van Rijsbergen (1979), and justified on the basis of its mathematical properties, as opposed to a measure of user satisfaction. Lewis (1991) introduces the notion of micro-averaging, observing that when each document may belong to several categories, hard classification may be viewed as the problem of retrieving all pairs (d, q) from the collection $D \times Q$ in which document d is in category q. Micro-averaged set-based measures such as precision, recall, and F_β compare the retrieved set $Ret \subseteq D \times Q$ against the relevant set $Rel \subseteq D \times Q$.

Swets (1963, 1969) proposed the use of signal detection theory for IR evaluation. However, these methods were not widely adopted for ranked retrieval. True positive rate and false positive rate are equivalent to the IR measures recall and fallout, so recall-fallout and ROC curves are equivalent. Recently, ROC analysis has become standard in machine learning (Fawcett, 2006), and was used in the TREC Spam Track (Cormack and Lynam, 2005). LAM was introduced with the Spam Track, and was subsequently shown to be equivalent to the diagnostic odds ratio (Glas et al., 2003; Cormack, 2008), which is a measure used in epidemiology and medicine. The Spam Track also introduced the aggregate summary measure, which is the soft classification equivalent of micro-averaging.

TREC 1 through TREC 11 (1992–2002) included various routing and filtering tasks (Robertson and Callan, 2005). TREC 14 through TREC 16 (2005–2007) included the Spam Track. At TREC, the routing task is batch filtering, in which the collection from the previous year's adhoc task (including documents, topics, and qrels) are the historical examples, and systems are required to rank a new collection of documents by relevance. Standard ranked retrieval evaluation measures are applied to the results. Filtering, according to TREC, requires systems to return an unordered set that is evaluated according to several set-based measures, including linear utility and F_β. Ranked retrieval alone will not optimize these measures; a method of threshold setting is also required. Batch filtering uses the same historical examples and new documents as routing. Adaptive filtering is on-line filtering in which only those documents labeled relevant are available for use as training examples after they are classified. The problem of optimal threshold setting for adaptive filtering is particularly challenging because few training examples are available for calibration (Callan, 1998; Robertson, 2002). Sculley (2007) addresses a similar problem within the context of on-line spam filtering. The Spam Track evaluated filters using the methods detailed in this chapter. Several variants of the task explored the impact of incomplete and delayed feedback, interuser feedback, and active learning. A survey of Spam Track and related methods and results is given by Cormack (2008).

10.10   Exercises

Exercise 10.1 Download the TREC Spam Filter Evaluation Toolkit, and run several of the sample filters on the sample corpus.

Exercise 10.2 Identify the *Financial Times* documents in the TREC45 collection. Fetch the updated qrels for these documents.[12] Create a test corpus suitable for evaluation with the spam filter toolkit.

Exercise 10.3 Download one or more batch-oriented classifiers. Perform feature engineering on one of your corpora to prepare training and test input files for your classifiers. Evaluate the results. Note that SVMlight, Liblinear, LibSVM and FEST use a common file format. Systems like Weka and R each implement many methods.

Exercise 10.4 Fetch random pages from at least two different editions of Wikipedia and use them to prepare a corpus to evaluate categorization methods.

Exercise 10.5 Use a search engine to find one or more of the classical corpora for text categorization and filtering. Examples are Reuters, 20 Newsgroups, Spambase, Ling Spam, and the TREC collections used over the years for the routing, filtering, and spam tasks. Find the results of studies using these corpora. From these results can you determine which methods work best? Can you reproduce the results? How do the same methods compare when you test them on your corpora?

Exercise 10.6 Implement your own filter, and evaluate it. Your filter need not be complicated: methods such as naïve Bayes, logistic regression and perceptron are very simple if you use binary features. Practically any data compression method may be used as a filter: Simply measure the

---

[12] trec.nist.gov/data/qrels_eng/qrels.trec8.adhoc.parts1-5.tar.gz

output length as an estimate of cross-entropy. Implementations of DMC and other sequential methods may be downloaded from the Web. The model building code may be extracted from these implementations, and the coding part discarded. Sculley's on-line SVM is available on the Web.

Exercise 10.7 On a major highway 70% of the traffic exceeds the speed limit, and 80% of all two-car accidents on the same highway involve at least one car that is exceeding the speed limit. What is the odds ratio of having an accident when speeding?

Exercise 10.8 Of these two-car accidents 50% involve one vehicle that is stopped. What additional information do you need to calculate the odds ratio of having an accident when speeding, relative to driving at the speed limit?

Exercise 10.9 Suppose you had a complete log of the speed and plate number for each vehicle passing a certain point and also the plate number of each vehicle involved in an accident within the next hour. How would you estimate the probability that a particular vehicle will be involved in an accident in the next hour?

Exercise 10.10 The Highway Patrol identified but failed to catch a red car whose plate number begins with Q. In court the prosecution expert testified that $\frac{1}{36}$ of all plate numbers begin with Q, $\frac{1}{20}$ of all cars are red, and $\frac{1}{1400}$ are fast enough to outrun police. A search of the registration database reveals that Mr. X owns a red Ferrari. Mr. X is charged with evading police, and the prosecutor argues that the odds of Mr. X being innocent were a million to one, because $\frac{1}{20} \cdot \frac{1}{36} \cdot \frac{1}{1400} = \frac{1}{1008000}$. You have been hired as an expert witness for the defense. Can you earn your fee?

10.11 Bibliography

Belkin, N. J., and Croft, W. B. (1992). Information filtering and information retrieval: Two sides of the same coin? *Communications of the ACM*, 35(12):29–38.

Bratko, A., Cormack, G. V., Filipič, B., Lynam, T. R., and Zupan, B. (2006). Spam filtering using statistical data compression models. *Journal of Machine Learning Research*, 7:2673–2698.

Callan, J. (1998). Learning while filtering documents. In *Proceedings of the 21st Annual International ACM SIGIR Conference on Research and Development in Information Retrieval*, pages 224–231. Melbourne, Australia.

Cleary, J. G., and Witten, I. H. (1984). Data compression using adaptive coding and partial string matching. *IEEE Transactions on Communications*, 32(4):396–402.

Cormack, G. V. (2007). TREC 2007 Spam Track overview. In *Proceedings of the 16th Text REtrieval Conference*. Gaithersburg, Maryland.

Cormack, G. V. (2008). Email spam filtering: A systematic review. *Foundations and Trends in Information Retrieval*, 1(4):335–455.

Cormack, G. V., and Horspool, R. N. S. (1987). Data compression using dynamic Markov modelling. *The Computer Journal*, 30(6):541–550.

Cormack, G. V., and Lynam, T. R. (2005). TREC 2005 Spam Track overview. In *Proceedings of the 14th Text REtrieval Conference.* Gaithersburg, Maryland.

Domingos, P., and Pazzani, M. J. (1997). On the optimality of the simple bayesian classifier under zero-one loss. *Machine Learning*, 29(2-3):103–130.

Drucker, H., Wu, D., and Vapnik, V. N. (1999). Support vector machines for spam categorization. *IEEE Transactions on Neural Networks*, 10(5):1048–1054.

Fawcett, T. (2006). An introduction to ROC analysis. *Pattern Recognition Letters*, 27(8):861–874.

Glas, A. S., Lijmer, J. G., Prins, M. H., Bonsel, G. J., and Bossuyt, P. M. M. (2003). The diagnostic odds ratio: A single indicator of test performance. *Journal of Clinical Epidemiology*, 56(11):1129–1135.

Hastie, T., Tibshirani, R., and Friedman, J. H. (2009). *The Elements of Statistical Learning* (2nd ed.). Berlin, Germany: Springer.

Hosmer, D. W., and Lemeshow, S. (2000). *Applied Logistic Regression* (2nd ed.). New York: Wiley-Interscience.

Joachims, T. (2002). *Learning to Classify Text Using Support Vector Machines*. Norwell, Massachusetts: Kluwer Academic.

Komarek, P., and Moore, A. (2003). Fast robust logistic regression for large sparse datasets with binary outputs. In *Proceedings of the 9th International Workshop on Artificial Intelligence and Statistics.* Key West, Florida.

Lewis, D. D. (1991). Evaluating text categorization. In *Human Language Technologies Conference: Proceedings of the Workshop on Speech and Natural Language*, pages 312–318. Pacific Grove, California.

Lewis, D. D., and Catlett, J. (1994). Heterogeneous uncertainty sampling for supervised learning. In *Proceedings of the 11th International Conference on Machine Learning*, pages 148–156.

Lewis, D. D., Yang, Y., Rose, T. G., and Li, F. (2004). RCV1: A new benchmark collection for text categorization research. *Journal of Machine Learning Research*, 5:361–397.

McNamee, P. (2005). Language identification: A solved problem suitable for undergraduate instruction. *Journal of Computing Sciences in Colleges*, 20(3):94–101.

Mitchell, T. M. (1997). *Machine Learning*. Boston, Massachusetts: WCB/McGraw-Hill.

Robertson, S. (2002). Threshold setting and performance optimization in adaptive filtering. *Information Retrieval*, 5(2-3):239–256.

Robertson, S., and Callan, J. (2005). Routing and filtering. In Voorhees, E. M., and Harman, D. K., editors, *TREC — Experiment and Evaluation in Information Retrieval*, chapter 5, pages 99–122. Cambridge, Massachusetts: MIT Press.

Rocchio, J. J. (1971). Relevance feedback in information retrieval. In Salton, G., editor, *The SMART Retrieval System: Experiments in Automatic Document Processing*, chapter 14, pages 313–323: Prentice-Hall.

Sculley, D. (2007). Practical learning from one-sided feedback. In *Proceedings of the 13th ACM SIGKDD International Conference on Knowledge Discovery and Data Mining*, pages 609–618. San Jose, California.

Sculley, D., and Wachman, G. M. (2007). Relaxed online support vector machines for spam filtering. In *Proceedings of the 30th ACM SIGIR Conference on Research and Development on Information Retrieval*, pages 415–422. Amsterdam, The Netherlands.

Sculley, D., Wachman, G. M., and Brodley, C. E. (2006). Spam classification with on-line linear classifiers and inexact string matching features. In *Proceedings of the 15th Text REtrieval Conference*. Gaithersburg, Maryland.

Sebastiani, F. (2002). Machine learning in automated text categorization. *ACM Computing Surveys*, 34(1):1–47.

Siefkes, C., Assis, F., Chhabra, S., and Yerazunis, W. S. (2004). Combining winnow and orthogonal sparse bigrams for incremental spam filtering. In *Proceedings of the 8th European Conference on Principles and Practice of Knowledge Discovery in Databases*, pages 410–421. Pisa, Italy.

Swets, J. A. (1963). Information retrieval systems. *Science*, 141(357):245–250.

Swets, J. A. (1969). Effectiveness of information retrieval systems. *American Documentation*, 20:72–89.

van Rijsbergen, C. J. (1979). *Information Retrieval* (2nd ed.). London, England: Butterworths.

Willems, F. M. J., Shtarkov, Y. M., and Tjalkens, T. J. (1995). The context-tree weighting method: Basic properties. *IEEE Transactions on Information Theory*, 41:653–664.

Witten, I. H., and Frank, E. (2005). *Data Mining: Practical Machine Learning Tools and Techniques* (2nd ed.). San Francisco, California: Morgan Kaufmann.

11   Fusion and Metalearning

In the preceding chapters we have considered a number of core methods for search, categorization, and filtering. Many of these methods have parameters — such as BM25's k_1, v_{title}, v_{body}, b_{title}, and b_{body} — that alter their effectiveness. When one considers all the possible parameter settings of the core methods, along with other design choices such as tokenization and feature selection, one is left with a near-infinite space of methods from which to choose.

This vast space gives rise to an obvious question: Which combination of choices works best? Surely, if we knew the answer to this question, we could fix those choices to come up with the best method, and dispense with the rest. Perhaps surprisingly, it is often possible to improve on the best single method by combining the results of several, without necessarily identifying which is best.

The specific approaches we shall examine are the following:

- *Fusion* or *aggregation*, in which the results returned by several IR methods are combined into one (Section 11.1).

- *Stacking*, in which the best combination of several classifiers is learned, forming a meta-classifier. Section 11.2 considers stacking for adaptive filtering, and Section 11.3 considers stacking for nonadaptive filtering and categorization.

- *Bagging*, or *bootstrap aggregation*, in which the training examples are randomly resampled to generate a set of classifiers whose results are averaged (Section 11.4).

- *Boosting*, in which the training examples are progressively weighted to emphasize misclassified examples thus generating a set of classifiers whose results are combined as a weighted average (Section 11.5).

- *Multicategory ranking* and *categorization*, in which the results of many binary classifiers are combined (Section 11.6).

- *Learning to rank*, in which a ranking function is learned from distinct example rankings (Section 11.7).

Before considering specific illustrative examples, we offer a few general comments. All of the methods considered here aggregate evidence from separate methods into stronger evidence pertinent to the user's information need. Although some items of evidence may be more compelling than others, an appropriate combination of all available evidence, taken as a whole, is in general more compelling than any individual item. This phenomenon is not unique to information retrieval; it is commonly known as the *wisdom of crowds* (Surowiecki, 2004).

The evidence we shall consider takes one of three general forms:

1. *Categorical.* A discrete result indicating that a document or set of documents is relevant or belongs to a particular category. The problem of determining a categorical result is commonly known as *classification.*

2. *Ordinal.* A ranking or score that orders documents by the weight of evidence that they are relevant or belong to some category. The problem of determining an ordinal result is commonly known as *ranking.*

3. *Quantitative.* A calibrated score, typically a probability, indicating the weight of evidence that a document is relevant or belongs to some category. The problem of estimating a calibrated score is commonly known as *regression.*

Regression may be reduced to ranking through the use of a sort, and ranking to classification through the use of a cutoff rank or threshold. Each of these steps loses information. Sometimes the reduction is inherent in the method and therefore unavoidable. The more these losses are avoided, the more compelling the overall weight of evidence.

To illustrate the various methods of combining evidence, we consider the problems that have been addressed in previous chapters: ranked retrieval, topic-oriented filtering, language categorization, and on-line spam filtering. For each problem we take as input the results of the individual methods that we have evaluated for each purpose, and compare the aggregate result against the best individual method. In addition we illustrate learning-to-rank methods using the LETOR 3 data set,[1] a standard benchmark derived from several TREC corpora.

11.1 Search-Result Fusion

The simplest approach to combining evidence that we shall consider is *search-result fusion*, in which the lists of documents returned by several search engines are combined into one. No information other than the lists, and perhaps the ranks or scores of documents within the lists, is used. We investigate three variants of this approach: (1) fixed-cutoff retrieval, in which a fixed number of documents from each list is considered without regard to rank; (2) rank aggregation, in which the rank of each document within each list is considered; (3) score aggregation, in which the rank and score of each document within each list is considered.

To describe search-result fusion, we introduce the following notation. Consider a set of n systems returning document lists $Res_1, Res_2, \ldots, Res_n$ from collection D in response to some query q. We wish to construct a better list Res that aggregates the evidence of the n lists. For each Res_i we define the ranking function $r_i(d)$ to be the position of d in Res_i, or some large number c if d is not in Res_i:

---

[1] research.microsoft.com/en-us/um/beijing/projects/letor

Table 11.1 29 separate runs used for the fusion and learning-to-rank examples in this chapter. Bold numbers indicate the best run(s) in each column.

| | | | TREC45 | | | | GOV2 | | | |
| | | | 1998 | | 1999 | | 2004 | | 2005 | |
Method	Stop	Stem	P@10	MAP	P@10	MAP	P@10	MAP	P@10	MAP
bm25	No	No	0.424	0.178	0.440	0.205	0.471	0.242	0.534	0.277
bm25	No	Yes	0.440	0.199	**0.464**	0.247	**0.500**	0.266	0.600	0.334
bm25	Yes	No	0.424	0.178	0.438	0.205	0.467	0.243	0.538	0.276
bm25	Yes	Yes	0.440	0.199	**0.464**	0.247	**0.500**	0.266	0.592	0.333
bm25_b=0	No	No	0.402	0.177	0.406	0.207	0.418	0.171	0.538	0.207
bm25_notf_b=0	No	No	0.256	0.141	0.224	0.147	0.069	0.050	0.106	0.083
dfr-gb2	No	No	0.426	0.183	0.446	0.216	0.465	0.248	0.550	0.269
dfr-gb2	No	Yes	0.448	**0.204**	0.458	0.253	0.471	0.252	0.584	0.319
dfr-gb2	Yes	No	0.426	0.183	0.446	0.216	0.465	0.248	0.550	0.269
dfr-gb2	Yes	Yes	0.448	**0.204**	0.458	0.253	0.471	0.252	0.584	0.319
lm-dirichlet-1000	No	No	0.450	0.193	0.428	0.226	0.484	0.244	0.580	0.293
lm-dirichlet-1000	No	Yes	**0.464**	**0.204**	0.434	0.262	0.492	0.270	0.600	**0.343**
lm-dirichlet-1000	Yes	No	0.448	0.193	0.430	0.226	0.494	0.247	0.568	0.291
lm-dirichlet-1000	Yes	Yes	0.462	**0.204**	0.436	**0.262**	0.488	**0.272**	**0.602**	0.341
lm-jelinek-0.5	No	No	0.390	0.179	0.432	0.208	0.416	0.211	0.494	0.257
lm-jelinek-0.5	No	Yes	0.406	0.192	0.434	0.248	0.437	0.225	0.522	0.302
lm-jelinek-0.5	Yes	No	0.390	0.179	0.432	0.209	0.414	0.212	0.482	0.253
lm-jelinek-0.5	Yes	Yes	0.406	0.192	0.436	0.249	0.445	0.225	0.508	0.298
lm-unsmoothed	No	No	0.354	0.114	0.396	0.141	0.402	0.171	0.492	0.231
lm-unsmoothed	No	Yes	0.384	0.134	0.416	0.180	0.433	0.196	0.538	0.285
lm-unsmoothed	Yes	No	0.352	0.114	0.394	0.141	0.400	0.172	0.484	0.230
lm-unsmoothed	Yes	Yes	0.384	0.134	0.416	0.180	0.439	0.196	0.518	0.283
prox	No	No	0.396	0.124	0.370	0.146	0.424	0.173	0.560	0.230
prox	No	Yes	0.418	0.139	0.430	0.184	0.453	0.207	0.576	0.283
prox	Yes	No	0.396	0.123	0.370	0.146	0.422	0.173	0.546	0.232
prox	Yes	Yes	0.416	0.139	0.430	0.184	0.447	0.204	0.556	0.282
vsm-lintf-logidf	No	No	0.266	0.106	0.240	0.120	0.298	0.092	0.282	0.097
vsm-logtf-logidf	No	No	0.264	0.126	0.252	0.135	0.120	0.060	0.194	0.092
vsm-logtf-noidf-raw	No	No	0.342	0.132	0.328	0.154	0.400	0.144	0.466	0.151

$$r_i(d) = \begin{cases} k & (Res_i[k] = d) \\ c & (d \notin Res_i) \end{cases}. \tag{11.1}$$

The choice of c is arbitrary, so long as $c > |Res_i|$. Reasonable choices are $c = \infty$, $c = |D|$, $c = \frac{|D|}{2}$ and $c = |Res_i| + 1$. For our examples we use $c = \infty$.

For score aggregation we assume that each system returns a nonincreasing list $Score_i$, where $Score_i[k]$ is the relevance score associated with $Res_i[k]$. For each $Score_i$, we define the scoring function $s_i(d)$ to be the score of d in Rel_i, or the smallest score if d is not in Rel_i:

$$s_i(d) = \begin{cases} Score_i[k] & (Res_i[k] = d) \\ Score_i[|Score_i|] & (d \notin Res_i) \end{cases}. \tag{11.2}$$

Typically, we assume that $Score_i$ is normalized so that

$$Score_i[|Score_i|] = \min_d\{s_i(d)\} = 0, \qquad Score_i[1] = \max_d\{s_i(d)\} = 1. \tag{11.3}$$

We illustrate result fusion by applying three methods to the results of $n = 29$ variants of the search methods we have considered in previous chapters, as listed in Table 11.1. For each method the table shows P@10 and MAP results over each of the four TREC collections, with the best result indicated in bold font.

11.1.1 Fixed-Cutoff Aggregation

Consider the problem of combining the results in Table 11.1 so as to optimize P@10. For now we shall consider each of the results to be categorical, consisting of a set of 10 documents per topic in no particular order. For our set of 29 example methods, the union of these 29 sets contains somewhere between 10 and 290 documents per topic, from which we wish to identify the 10 most likely to be relevant; that is, to maximize P@10.

An obvious, if hypothetical, approach is to identify exactly those ten documents returned by the "best" system. But which is the best? Perhaps, based on previous evaluation, we are able to guess that BM25 or LMD is the most effective. There is no single method or set of parameter settings that is best for all four corpora. The reader has the luxury of consulting the table as an oracle, so as to come up with an idealized result for comparison: the best individual result. It is important to note that the "best individual result" is an upper bound on the effectiveness that can be achieved by selecting one result; it is an upper bound that cannot reliably be achieved in practice.

A simple and practical approach is to use an "election" strategy to select ten documents from among those "nominated" by the various methods. The study of election strategies is remarkably nuanced, but for now we will simply select the 10 documents that occur most frequently among the 29 results, breaking ties arbitrarily. In effect we are combining several categorical results

Table 11.2 P@10 categorical fusion results for retrieval methods and TREC collections discussed in this book.

| | TREC45 | | GOV2 | |
| | 1998 | 1999 | 2004 | 2005 |
Method	P@10	P@10	P@10	P@10
Best	0.464	0.464	0.500	0.602
Median	0.406	0.430	0.445	0.538
Election	0.452	0.460	0.492	0.554

into a ranked result, and then applying a cutoff (10 documents) to arrive at a new categorical result. The result of our effort is shown as "election" in Table 11.2. For each corpus our simple voting strategy approaches, but does not equal or exceed, the idealized best result.

11.1.2   Rank and Score Aggregation

Consider now the problem of optimizing MAP over the same four collections. Each of the results Res_i is a list from which a ranking r_i is derived. These rankings are combined to yield an aggregate ranking r. The approach is known as *rank aggregation, fusion,* or *metasearch.*

Perhaps the simplest and most effective rank-aggregation strategy is *reciprocal rank fusion* (RRF; Cormack et al., 2009). RRF simply sorts the documents according to a naïve scoring formula

$$RRFscore(d) \;=\; \sum_i \frac{1}{k + r_i(d)}\,, \tag{11.4}$$

where $k = 60$ has been found to work well for typical search results. The intuition in choosing this formula is that although highly ranked documents are more important, the importance of lower-ranked documents does not vanish. The harmonic series has these properties. The constant k mitigates the impact of high rankings by rogue methods.

More considered (but not necessarily more effective) methods are based on the theory of elections in which voters express preferences instead of categorical choices. Condorcet fusion (Montague and Aslam, 2002) combines rankings by sorting the documents according to the pairwise relation $r(d_1) < r(d_2)$, which is determined for each (d_1, d_2) by majority vote among the input rankings.

Some other approaches are not pure rank-aggregation methods in that they use score (which is quantitative, albeit arbitrarily calibrated, evidence) in addition to rank. CombMNZ (Lee, 1997), for example, sorts the documents according to the scoring formula

$$CMNZscore(d) \;=\; |\{i \mid d \in Res_i\}| \cdot \sum_i s_i(d)\,. \tag{11.5}$$

Table 11.3 Rank-based fusion results for retrieval methods and TREC collections discussed in this book.

Method	TREC45				GOV2			
	1998		1999		2004		2005	
	P@10	MAP	P@10	MAP	P@10	MAP	P@10	MAP
Best (by MAP)	0.462	0.204	0.434	0.262	0.500	0.272	0.602	0.341
Best (by P@10)	0.464	0.204	0.464	0.247	0.500	0.266	0.602	0.341
RRF ($k=60$)	0.462	0.215	0.464	0.252	0.543	0.297	0.570	0.352
Condorcet	0.446	0.207	0.462	0.234	0.525	0.281	0.574	0.325
CombMNZ	0.448	0.201	0.448	0.245	0.561	0.270	0.570	0.318

That is, *CMNZscore* multiplies the number of results in which the document occurs by the sum score, which yields a combined score that determines the ranking. Table 11.3 shows the results of these three methods when used to fuse the results of 29 IR methods. For three of the four corpora, RRF improves on the best MAP score. Condorcet also improves, but not by as large a margin. CombMNZ, although competitive with the best MAP scores, does not substantially better them. For comparison with our previous results, we also report P@10, computed by applying a cutoff of 10 to our combined ranking. The P@10 score derived from RRF in all cases exceeds that derived from voting, and is comparable to the best P@10.

Overall, rank and score aggregation methods are valuable because they match and often improve on the best ranking without any knowledge of the relative quality of the individual results. They may be used in conjunction with other approaches described in this chapter, such as *bootstrap aggregation* (Section 11.4).

11.2 Stacking Adaptive Filters

Consider again the problems of combining the categorical or quantitative results of on-line spam filters presented in Table 10.25 (page 369). The categorical result is simply an indication of whether each message, in turn, is spam or ham. We may use a simple majority vote to combine the results; because there is an odd number of filters, we need not concern ourselves with ties. In effect, the vote yields a ranking that is converted to a categorical result by comparing it against a threshold t. We can consider t of the five results to be necessary to label the message as spam. Majority vote performs about as well as the best individual filter (see Table 11.4). In practical terms, $t = 4$ or $t = 5$ might yield more satisfactory results for the intended purpose — filtering spam.

Rank aggregation is not applicable per se to an on-line filter because it requires that we sort the scores. Instead we calibrate the score s_i of document d_i, using past examples to approximate

Table 11.4 Combining on-line spam filters through voting.

| Method | Classification Error (%) | | |
	False Positive Rate	False Negative Rate	Logistic Average
Best	0.32	0.42	0.37
Majority vote	0.42	0.34	0.37
1 of 5	32.88	0.00	0.61
2 of 5	1.54	0.02	0.54
3 of 5	0.42	0.34	0.37
4 of 5	0.19	0.61	0.34
5 of 5	0.08	1.50	0.36

Table 11.5 Combining on-line spam filters through log-odds averaging and regression.

| Method | Classification Error (%) | | | |
	False Positive Rate	False Negative Rate	Logistic Average	1-AUC
Best (by AUC)	0.41	0.47	0.44	0.012
Majority vote	0.42	0.34	0.37	0.095
NB stacking	0.37	0.34	0.36	0.008
LR stacking	0.39	0.27	0.33	0.006

the log-odds that d_i is spam:

$$\text{logOdds}[d_i \in spam] \approx \log \frac{|\{d_{j<i} \in spam \mid s(d_j) \le s(d_i)\}|}{|\{d_{j<i} \notin spam \mid s(d_j) \ge s(d_i)\}|}. \tag{11.6}$$

These scores may be averaged in the same way as the features of a probabilistic classifier. The use of a (meta-)learning method to combine the results is known as *stacking*. For log-odds averaging, the metalearning method is equivalent to naïve Bayes (Section 10.3.2). Other adaptive metalearning methods, such as gradient descent logistic regression, may be used instead.

Table 11.5 shows spam filtering results for stacking using naïve Bayes and logistic regression metaclassifiers applied to log-odds transformed results. Both naïve Bayes and logistic regression lead to a considerable improvement over the best individual filter.

Now consider the results for topic-oriented filtering from Table 10.23 (page 368). Adaptive stacking methods may be applied directly to the four methods for which adaptive training results are shown. These methods were in fact trained sequentially on the entire data set, but the results are reported only for the test examples. We apply the same methodology as for spam filter stacking: Over the entire data set the scores are converted incrementally to log-odds and either averaged or combined using adaptive logistic regression. The results are reported only for the test examples. Table 11.6 shows that the effect of stacking is consistent

Table 11.6 Stacking results for TREC topic
383, adaptive training. The numbers shown in
this table may be compared with the "Adaptive
Training" part of Table 10.23 (page 368).

Method	Historical + Online	
	P@10	**AP**
Best individual	1.0	0.55
NB stacking	1.0	0.59
LR stacking	1.0	0.60

with that for spam filtering: Both methods show substantial improvement over the best, with
logistic regression somewhat better. All but one of the methods whose results are combined are
substantially inferior to the best. Nonetheless, they offer evidence that, when harnessed using
stacking, improves on the best.

11.3 Stacking Batch Classifiers

Stacking the results of batch-trained filters is problematic because it is difficult to calibrate the
scores returned by these filters in terms of log-odds or any other meaningful quantity. Even
methods such as logistic regression that directly estimate log-odds, do so only for the training
set T. Due to overfitting, it is not at all obvious that these estimates generalize to the test set.
Methods such as SVM and decision trees are in even worse shape: It is not at all uncommon for
these methods to achieve perfect scores on the training examples; these scores may bear little
resemblance to scores on the test examples.

Subject to these caveats, we adapt Equation 11.6 to calibrate the score s_i of document $d_i \in D$
based on the scores of training documents $d_j \in T$:

$$\text{logOdds}[d_i \in spam] \approx \log \frac{|\{d_j \in (T \cap spam) \mid s(d_j) \leq s(d_i)\}|}{|\{d_j \in (T \backslash spam) \mid s(d_j) \geq s(d_i)\}|} . \tag{11.7}$$

Table 11.7 shows the result of stacking the batch training results for all nine methods from
Table 10.23. The overall effect is similar to that in our previous examples: Naïve Bayes stacking
affords substantial improvement; (batch) logistic regression yields further improvement.

11.3.1 Holdout Validation

Our estimation of log-odds from training results is an example of regression — estimation of a
quantitative result from available data. In particular we are estimating the performance of each

Table 11.7 Stacking results for TREC topic 383, batch training. The numbers shown in this table may be compared with the "Historical Training" part of Table 10.23 (page 368).

Method	Historical Training	
	P@10	AP
Best individual	1.0	0.56
NB stacking	1.0	0.62
LR stacking	1.0	0.65

method in terms of its classification effectiveness as a function of the score $s(d)$. These estimates allow us to construct a better combined ranking method (or classifier).

However, the technique used in the previous section estimates log-odds from $s(d)$, where $d \in T$, and is therefore subject to generalization error. This source of error may be avoided by calculating log-odds (or any other regression quantity) using $s(d)$ from a separate validation set $V \subset D$, where $T \cap V = \emptyset$. That is, the method is trained on T and then used to score (or classify or rank) V.

The most obvious way to construct V is the *holdout* approach: We partition some larger set L of labeled examples, sampled from D, such that $L = T + V$. Assuming that L is an independent and identically distributed (i.i.d.) sample of D, and T is a random subset of L, both T and V may be considered i.i.d. samples of D. Thus our log-odds calculation uses an independent sample of D and is not influenced by the classifier overfitting to T. (However, our regression may overfit to V, but that is a separate matter.) V is known as a *validation set* and, in this particular circumstance, a *holdout set*. The overall method is known as *holdout validation*.

The main limitation of holdout validation derives from the scarcity of labeled examples. In general the size of L is limited by the cost and availability of labels, so there is a direct trade-off between the sizes of T and V. In general a larger T will yield a better base method, whereas a larger V will yield better validation. Each comes at the expense of the other.

A second limitation derives from the fact that the prevalence of positive examples may be different in T and V. Some methods, particularly classification methods that depend on a threshold setting, are very sensitive to prevalence. This limitation is mitigated through the use of *stratified sampling* to create T (and hence V) from L. In stratified sampling, the examples of each category in L are sampled separately so that T (and hence V) has roughly the same proportion of each category as L.

11.3.2   Cross-Validation

Cross-validation is a regression method in which the set of labeled examples L is partitioned into k *splits* (T_1, V_1), (T_2, V_2), ..., (T_k, V_k). The learning method is trained separately on each of the T_i and is used to score each $d \in V_i$. Regression is performed on the combined results, which

Table 11.8 Stacking results for TREC topic 383, using 22-fold stratified cross-validation.

Method	Historical Training	
	P@10	AP
Best individual	1.0	0.56
NB stacking	1.0	0.64
LR stacking	1.0	0.69

are regarded as one big validation set $V = \bigcup_{i=1}^{k} V_k$. The commonest approach is *k-fold cross-validation*, in which the validation sets are of equal size and pairwise disjoint: $\forall_{i \neq j} V_i \cap V_j = \emptyset$. Each training set consists of the examples not in the validation set: $T_i = L \backslash V_i$. For large k, $T_i \approx L$ and $V = L$. Thus, V is a reasonable approximation of an independent holdout set of the same size. The extreme case of $k = |L|$ is called *leave-one-out* validation.

If stratified sampling is to be used, k is limited by the least prevalent category. In our topic-based filtering example, T contains exactly 22 relevant documents, so we use 22-fold cross-validation with each V_i containing a single relevant document. When not limited by stratification, k may be limited by efficiency considerations because the training effort is proportional to k. Five-fold cross-validation ($k = 5$) and ten-fold cross-validation ($k = 10$) are common. The results in Table 11.8 show that 22-fold cross-validation substantially improves both the average and the stacked fusion results for topic 383.

An important role of cross-validation is in *selection* or *tuning* of learning methods. In this role cross-validation is used to estimate some overall effectiveness measure, and the space of methods and parameter settings is searched to optimize this measure. As we mentioned at the outset of this chapter, and have demonstrated through examples, selecting the single best method or parameter setting does not necessarily yield the best overall result.

11.4 Bagging

When a learning method is trained on the examples from a particular training set T and applied to documents from D, the resulting categorization, ranking, or regression is subject to two kinds of error: *training error* and *generalization error*. Both would be reduced if instead of a single training set T, we were to average the results achieved from training the same method separately on N training sets $T_1, T_2, \ldots, T_N$, where each T_i is an independent sample of D and the same size as T.

The reason is quite straightforward. Let $ideal(d)$ be the score returned by an ideal classifier for a document $d \in D$. A particular method trained on T_i will compute $c_i(d) \approx ideal(d)$. More specifically, $c_i(d) = ideal(d) + E_i$, where E_i is a random variable modeling the error associated

Table 11.9 Bootstrap aggregation (bagging) for decision trees on TREC topic 383. The numbers in this table represent AP values and may be compared with those in Table 10.23 (page 368).

Method	Number of Bootstrap Samples (N)												
	2	**4**	**8**	**16**	**32**	**64**	**128**	**256**	**512**	**1024**	**2048**	**4096**	**8192**
DT (n=2)	0.38	0.22	0.56	0.37	0.52	0.50	0.51	0.51	0.51	0.52	0.52	0.53	0.52
DT (n=8)	0.21	0.33	0.47	0.55	0.59	0.58	0.57	0.58	0.57	0.59	0.58	0.59	0.58
DT (n=256)	0.13	0.44	0.45	0.47	0.55	0.54	0.56	0.55	0.55	0.55	0.55	0.55	0.54

with training on T_i. Now suppose we average the results to form a combined result

$$c(d) \;=\; \frac{1}{N} \cdot \sum_{i=1}^{N} (ideal(d) + E_i) \;=\; ideal(d) + E, \tag{11.8}$$

where

$$E \;=\; \sum_{i=1}^{N} \frac{E_i}{N}. \tag{11.9}$$

If the E_i are pairwise independent, the variance of E is generally smaller than the variance of any particular E_i. In the particular situation where the $\sigma_{E_i}^2$ are all equal, σ_E^2 is a factor of N smaller:

$$\sigma_E^2 \;\approx\; \frac{\sigma_{E_i}^2}{N}. \tag{11.10}$$

If the T_i are in fact i.i.d. samples of D, then the E_i are independent and have equal variance, so the standard error σ_E is reduced by a factor of $\sqrt{N}$ compared with training on a single T_i.

In general, little is gained from splitting the set of labeled examples L into independent training sets, because training on one large set $T = L$ works just as well, if not better. Instead, a technique known as *the bootstrap* may be used to simulate $T_1, T_2, \ldots, T_N$, each of the same size as L (see Section 12.3.2). The bootstrap uses L as a proxy for D, selecting each member of T_i independently and at random from L. Because elements are selected independently, the same element may be repeated in T_i, and some elements may not appear at all. For any reasonable sample size ($N > 20$) of T_i, the probability that a given element $d \in L$ will occur k times is well approximated by the Poisson formula:

$$\Pr[|\{d \in T_i\}| = k] \;\approx\; \frac{1}{k! \cdot e}. \tag{11.11}$$

That is, about $\frac{1}{e} \approx 36.8\%$ of the documents will not appear in any given T_i, $\frac{1}{e} \approx 36.8\%$ will occur once, $\frac{1}{2e} \approx 18.4\%$ twice, and so on. These *bootstrap samples* have sufficient independence that the error variance is reduced. Provided L is large enough to contain a good representation of the sorts of documents in D, and provided the learning method treats duplicate examples as

Table 11.10 Boosting (AdaBoost) results for decision trees on TREC topic 383. The numbers in this table represent AP values and may be compared with those in Tables 10.23 (page 368) and 11.9.

Method	Number of Boosting Iterations (N)												
	2	4	8	16	32	64	128	256	512	1024	2048	4096	8192
DT ($n{=}2$)	0.19	0.31	0.38	0.52	0.48	0.50	0.49	0.53	0.54	0.59	0.60	0.61	0.59
DT ($n{=}8$)	0.21	0.22	0.27	0.41	0.54	0.59	0.60	0.63	0.61	0.62	0.64	0.64	0.63
DT ($n{=}256$)	0.60	0.51	0.54	0.54	0.53	0.49	0.55	0.57	0.56	0.56	0.57	0.57	0.57

separate individuals that happen to have the same properties, bootstrap training sets closely resemble training sets drawn from D instead of L (Efron and Tibshirani, 1993).

The technique of *bootstrap aggregation* or *bagging* averages the results from using bootstrap samples as training sets. Although bagging may be applied to any learning technique, it is most effective and most commonly used for *unstable* learning methods whose result is highly dependent on the particular training examples. Table 11.9 shows the results of bootstrap aggregation for decision tree methods and TREC topic 383. The improvement for decision stumps ($n = 2$) is the most dramatic. Larger trees with $n = 8$ and $n = 256$ leaves show reduced effectiveness for small N but very good effectiveness for $N \geq 32$. Little is gained for $N \geq 128$ because the results appear to approach their asymptote.

11.5 Boosting

Boosting, like bagging, is a method of perturbing the training examples so as to produce an *ensemble* of methods whose results are combined. Boosting systematically manipulates the training data to minimize training error, unlike bagging, which manipulates the training data randomly to minimize generalization error. In both cases the net effect is a better classifier, although the underlying assumptions are quite different.

In boosting, the overall training set T is a random sample of D, as for any supervised learning method. But T is not used directly for training; instead, each $d \in T$ is given a weight $w_d \in \mathbb{R}$ such that $1 = \sum_d w_d$. The base learning method assumes that the prevalence ρ_d of documents like d in D is $\rho_d = w_d$, as opposed to that suggested by the proportion in T (i.e., $\rho_d \approx \frac{1}{|T|}$). For base methods such as decision trees, the assumption is easily accommodated by multiplying the contribution of each d by w_d during classifier construction.

Boosting proceeds by computing a series of k weight vectors $w^{[1]}, w^{[2]}, \ldots w^{[k]}$ and associated classifiers $c^{[1]}, c^{[2]}, \ldots c^{[k]}$ learned using T and the corresponding weights. Initially, $w_d^{[1]} = \frac{1}{|T|}$ for all $d \in T$. In subsequent steps the weight $w_d^{[i+1]}$ is increased (relative to $w_d^{[i]}$) for examples that are incorrectly classified by $c^{[i]}(d)$, normalized so that $1 = \sum_d w_d^{[i+1]}$. The overall classifier is itself the weighted sum of the first k classifier results:

$$c(d) = \sum_{i=1}^{k} \alpha_i c^{[i]}(d),$$
(11.12)

where the weights α_i are chosen to minimize the overall error. Various methods of computing w and α give rise to a family of boosting methods. Perhaps the best known is AdaBoost, which is applied to decision trees; its results for TREC topic 383 are shown in Table 11.10. It has been shown that boosting bears a strong resemblance to logistic regression and other optimization-based methods (Schapire, 2003).

11.6   Multicategory Ranking and Classification

For multicategory ranking and classification problems, we require a score $s(d,q)$ that acts as a surrogate for the probability that document $d \in D$ belongs to category $q \in Q$ (i.e., $\Pr[d \in q]$). For our language categorization example (Section 10.1.4), the categories are the 60 possible languages, so each $q_j \equiv l_j$. For topic-oriented search or filtering, the categories are the separate topics, so each $q_j \equiv t_j$. We shall use language categorization as our principal motivating example, and return later to topic-oriented problems. By "acts as a surrogate for probability" we mean:

- If $s(d,q)$ is categorical, it is correct more often than chance.
- If $s(d,q)$ is ordinal, the rankings implied by it are positively correlated with probability.
- If $s(d,q)$ is quantitative, then for some known function f

$$f(s(d,q)) \approx \Pr[d \in q].$$
(11.13)

Using score as a surrogate for probability is not unique to multicategory ranking. It is the crux of relevance ranking and the fusion methods we have discussed so far. The difference here is the assumption that $s(d,q_j)$ and $s(d,q_k)$ are comparable even when $q_j \neq q_k$:

$$s(d,q_j) < s(d,q_k) \iff \Pr[d \in q_j] < \Pr[d \in q_k].$$
(11.14)

That is, $s(d,q)$ aptly ranks categories within documents, not just documents within categories.

In this section we consider several different ways to compute, and to combine, families of score functions $\{s^{[f]}: D \times Q \to \mathbb{R}\}$ for the purpose of multicategory ranking and classification.

11.6.1 Document Versus Category Scores

In our language categorization example (Section 10.1.4), for each language l we computed a scoring function $s_l(d_i)$ that is a surrogate for $\Pr[d_i \in l]$. To rank the languages that a particular document d may contain, we require $s_d(l_j)$, a surrogate for $\Pr[d \in l_j]$. The method we have used so far simply sets $s_{d_i}(l_j) = s_{l_j}(d_i)$. The assumption underlying this choice is that $s(d_i, l_j) = s_{l_j}(d_i)$ fulfills our previously stated criterion for s: that it is an apt surrogate for $\Pr[d_i \in l_j]$ over all d_i and l_j, not just for some specific language l. Under this assumption the most likely language for a document d is

$$\arg\max_{l_j} \left\{ s(d, l_j) \right\}. \tag{11.15}$$

Furthermore, the possible languages l_j that d may have are ranked by $s(d, l_j)$.

For logistic regression this assumption is reasonably well justified, because the method estimates probability (as log-odds) directly. For other linear and generalized linear classifiers, the signed distance from the separating hyperplane often yields an amenable, if uncalibrated, score. Nonlinear methods such as nearest neighbor typically use some sort of internal score that may be amenable, such as the proximity to the nearest neighbor or the prevalence of l_j among the k nearest neighbors. Decision trees partition D into discrete sets: A score may be derived from the prevalence of l_j among the partition to which d belongs. A hard classifier yields an extremely coarse estimate; the average of many such estimates using bagging, boosting, or stacking is itself a quantitative estimate.

If $s(d, l)$ is not a good surrogate, it may yield a good document ranking but poor categorization accuracy. This effect may be observed by the many inversions in Table 10.24 (page 369) between the document ranking effectiveness (MAP) and categorization effectiveness ($1 -$ error or MRR). In particular, NB yields a MAP result of 0.44 and an MRR of 0.8, whereas DT (n=8) yields superior MAP (0.54) but inferior MRR (0.64). Also, DMC achieves both the best MRR (0.86) and error (20.0%) results (tied with LR), but mediocre MAP (0.74). It is perhaps not surprising, given the assumptions behind the method, that logistic regression shows superior effectiveness for both document and category ranking.

When categorical or ordinal values of $s(d, l)$ are considered, a category ranking may not be uniquely defined. That is, $\arg\max$ may be ill-defined and as there may be ties in the ranking according to $s(d, l_j)$. In this event a tie breaking strategy is required. If ties are rare, random tie breaking might be acceptable. Or ties might be resolved in favor of the category known to have highest prevalence, a technique that optimizes micro-averaged (but not macro-averaged) error rate. More generally, ties may be resolved by deferring to a secondary surrogate measure $s^{[2]}(d, l)$. For the specific case of resolving by prevalence, $s^{[2]}(d, l) = prev(l)$.

The use of a secondary surrogate measure is a special case of a still more general approach: combining several $s^{[f]}$ to form an aggregate scoring function. Instances of this approach are the following:

Table 11.11 Document rank fusion results for language categorization. The numbers in this table may be compared with those in Table 10.24 (page 369).

Method	Dual Ranking MAP	Categorization Error (%)	MRR
Best (category ranking)	0.82	20.0	0.86
Best (document ranking)	0.83	20.0	0.80
RRF	0.83	18.9	0.87
NB stacking	0.84	19.2	0.87
LR stacking	0.82	18.6	0.87
Bagging (DT; n=8, N=1024)	0.77	25.9	0.82
Boosting (DT; n=8, N=1024)	0.75	35.7	0.69

- *Document rank fusion.* For each l, combine the results of k document scoring methods $s_l^{[1]}, s_l^{[2]}, \ldots, s_l^{[k]}$ to form an overall score $s_l(d)$; set the category scoring method $s_d(l) = s_l(d)$.

- *Category rank fusion.* For each d, combine the results of k category ranking methods $s_d^{[1]}, s_d^{[2]}, \ldots, s_d^{[k]}$ to form an overall score $s_d(l)$, which is used to rank the categories.

- *Multicategory methods.* Consider d and l in combination in order to compute $s(d, l)$.

11.6.2 Document Versus Category Rank Fusion

Table 11.11 shows the results of five methods of combining the nine language-specific document ranking methods whose results are listed in Table 10.24 (page 369). For comparison the results of the best individual methods are shown as well, as measured by categorization effectiveness and by document ranking effectiveness. RRF is applied exactly as for topic-oriented retrieval, in order to combine the nine separate document rankings into one. The score from RRF is then used to rank the languages for each document. Three of the base ranking methods (NB, DMC, and gradient descent LR) are on-line methods, so log-odds was estimated using Equation 11.6 (page 382). The other six are batch methods, so log-odds was estimated using Equation 11.7. The results were averaged to yield the result labeled "NB stacking" and combined using logistic regression on the training examples to yield the result labeled "LR stacking". Bagging and boosting were used to build ensembles of 1024 decision trees (n=8). The other document ranking methods played no role in the bagging and boosting results.

Table 11.12 shows the result of category rank fusion, which combines the various scores on a per-document basis. The fusion methods are a bit different because the languages to be ranked are not partitioned into training and test sets. Thus it is not immediately apparent how to convert the scores into probability estimates. Instead we directly apply the RRF and Condorcet rank aggregation methods, which require no estimate, as well as logistic regression to the scores

Table 11.12   Category rank fusion results for language categorization.

Method	Categorization	
	Error (%)	MRR
Reciprocal rank fusion (RRF)	27.0	0.80
Condorcet	19.5	0.87
Logistic regression (LR)	18.0	0.88

returned by the various methods. RRF performs relatively poorly, while Condorcet improves on the best base method. Logistic regression yields a further improvement. The logistic regression method is a special case of learning to rank, which is detailed in Section 11.7.

11.6.3   Multicategory Methods

A number of binary classification, ranking, or regression methods may be adapted to solve the category ranking problem directly; we call these methods *multicategory*. In the literature they are often characterized as *multinomial* or *polytomous*, as opposed to *binomial* or *dichotomous*.

One versus rest

The approach we have presented so far is first to solve the document ranking problem, then combine the results to solve the category ranking problem. This approach is generally known as *one versus rest* because it combines the results of n binary classification problems, each of which distinguishes one category from the rest. We have so far assumed that a soft classification result is an indication of confidence, and have chosen the category that is indicated with highest confidence among the n one versus rest results.

For hard binary classifiers the one versus rest strategy is problematic. It may be that exactly one of the classifiers yields a positive result, in which case the category is determined. But if no result is positive, or if many results are positive, some sort of tie breaking scheme is necessary.

One versus one

An alternative, *one versus one*, is to reduce the problem to $n(n-1)/2$ binary problems, one for each pair of categories. The $n(n-1)/2$ results are combined in an *election* to select the category for a particular document or to rank the categories. A wide variety of election strategies have been studied; a comprehensive discussion is beyond the scope of this book. Perhaps the simplest is to count the number of wins (i.e., positive results) for each category and to rank by this number. The possibility of a tie still exists, but only in the event that the binary results are inconsistent. Various *runoff* strategies can be used to resolve these ties. In many circumstances the tie may be resolved by repeating the election among only the tied categories. The confidence of soft classifiers may also be taken into account.

Multicategory logistic regression

Logistic regression is particularly easy to adapt to multicategory regression, and hence to ranking. Recall that (binomial) logistic regression estimates

$$\text{logOdds}[x] \;=\; \log\left(\frac{\Pr[x]}{\Pr[\bar{x}]}\right) \;=\; \log\left(\frac{\Pr[x]}{1-\Pr[x]}\right), \tag{11.16}$$

where x is some binary quantity of interest, and $\bar{x}$ is its complement.

In our language categorization example we used logistic regression for multicategory ranking in the following way. For each category $q_i (1 \le i \le n)$, let x_i denote the membership $d \in q_i$ of some document d in the category. Compute $l_i \approx \text{logOdds}[x_i]$ separately for each category using logistic regression. For the purpose of ranking, this method works reasonably well because l_i is a reasonable indication of the strength of the evidence that $d \in q_i$. It is also possible to derive a probability estimate:

$$p_i \;=\; \text{logit}^{-1}(l_i) \;=\; \frac{1}{1+e^{-l_i}} \;\approx\; \Pr[x_i], \tag{11.17}$$

but this estimate is unsatisfactory when the categories are exclusive (as they are in our language example). It fails to incorporate the constraint that the probabilities must sum to 1:

$$1 \;=\; \sum_{i=1}^{n} \Pr[x_i]. \tag{11.18}$$

Post-hoc attempts to fit this constraint yield poor estimates. We mention two solely to recommend that they be avoided. One is to normalize the p_i so that they sum to 1 as per Equation 11.18; the other is to estimate all but one of the p_i using logistic regression and then solve for the nth using Equation 11.18.

A better approach is to use logistic regression to estimate the *ratio* between pairs of probabilities

$$r_{ij} \;\approx\; \frac{\Pr[x_i]}{\Pr[x_j]} \tag{11.19}$$

and to compute p_i so as to satisfy both 11.18 and 11.19. This approach requires that we compute only $n-1$ of the $\frac{n(n-1)}{2}$ possible r_{ij} that might be estimated; the rest are redundant. The choice of which r_{ij} to compute is arbitrary, so long as they form a basis from which all r_{ij} may be derived.

A standard choice is the *baseline category logit model*. In this model we arbitrarily deem x_1 to be the baseline and compute r_{i1} for all i. For $i = 1$, by definition

$$r_{11} = 1. \tag{11.20}$$

Table 11.13 Results for one versus rest and multicategory language categorization.

Method	One versus rest		Multicategory	
	Error (%)	MRR	Error (%)	MRR
LR	20.0	0.86		
SVM (C=0.01)	20.1	0.85	29.9	0.79
SVM (C=1)	20.0	0.86	31.8	0.74
SVM (C=100)	20.0	0.86	22.8	0.84
SVM (C=10000)	20.0	0.86	19.7	0.86
Boosted stumps (N=1024)	46.4	0.63	32.2	0.76

For $i > 1$, we first note that it is possible to reformulate r_{ij} as the odds of x_i over x_j when all other categories are eliminated:

$$r_{ij} \approx \frac{\Pr[x_i]}{\Pr[x_j]} = \mathrm{Odds}[x_i \,|\, x_i \text{ or } x_j]. \qquad (11.21)$$

Therefore,

$$r_{1j} = e^{l_{i1}} \ (i > 1), \qquad (11.22)$$

where

$$l_{i1} \approx \mathrm{logOdds}[x_i \,|\, x_1 \text{ or } x_i]. \qquad (11.23)$$

That is, l_{i1} is calculated by applying logistic regression to training documents d with categories q_1 or q_j, but not the rest: $d \in (q_1 \cup q_j) \cap T$. For $i, j > 1$,

$$r_{ij} = \frac{r_{i1}}{r_{11}} \cdot \frac{r_{11}}{r_{j1}} = \frac{r_{i1}}{r_{j1}} \ (i, j > 1). \qquad (11.24)$$

Given $\{r_{i1}\}$, the computation of p_i is straightforward:

$$p_i = \frac{r_{i1}}{\sum_{i=1}^{n} r_{i1}}. \qquad (11.25)$$

For reasons beyond the scope of this exposition, the calculation of p_i yields the same result regardless of which category q_1 is chosen as the baseline (Agresti, 2007).

Multicategory SVM

Recall that a (binary) support vector machine finds a separating hyperplane between two classes, thus balancing a trade-off between the size of the margin and the number (and severity) of misclassified points. A multicategory SVM (Crammer and Singer, 2002) constructs n hyperplanes as for document ranking, but considers all margins and all misclassified points in a common optimization problem. That is, it trades off maximizing the size of the smallest of the n margins with the overall number (and severity) of misclassified points. Thus, it more directly addresses categorization error, in contrast to logistic regression, which is concerned with the probability distribution over all classes.

Multicategory boosting

A similar approach may be applied to boosting. Instead of computing w and α separately for each category, multicategory boosting optimizes the training error over all categories (Schapire and Singer, 2000).

Table 11.13 shows the results of one versus rest and multicategory methods for TREC topic 383. Overall, it is difficult to conclude from these results that any one of them yields a startling benefit. Multicategory SVM (SVM-Multiclass[2]) is worse except for the extreme setting of C=10,000, in which case it is marginally better. Multicategory boosting (Boostexter[3]) shows a definite improvement, but over a very weak baseline.

11.7   Learning to Rank

The term *learning to rank* refers to the problem of estimating the correct order

$$\prec:\ R \times R$$

among a set of objects R. In contrast, classification and regression estimate some ideal function on elements of R:

$$ideal:\ R \to \{true, false\} \quad \text{or} \quad ideal:\ R \to \mathbb{R}.$$

Under this broad characterization we have already considered many examples of learning to rank. For instance, when $R \subseteq D$, we have document ranking with respect to some assumed notion of relevance; for example, binary relevance to some particular query q:

$$d_1 \prec d_2 \ =_{def}\ (d_1 \notin rel_q \text{ and } d_2 \in rel_q). \tag{11.26}$$

For document ranking, the learner l takes as input a training set $T \subset D$ and a labeling function $label: T \to \{rel, non\}$, and produces a scoring function $s: D \to \mathbb{R}$. The result is recast in terms of learning to rank by defining its output to be $\precsim: D \times D$, which approximates the specified correct order $\prec$:

$$d_1 \precsim d_2 \ =_{def}\ s(d_1) < s(d_2). \tag{11.27}$$

---

[2] svmlight.joachims.org/svm_multiclass.html
[3] www.cs.princeton.edu/~schapire/boostexter.html

It is important to note that $\prec$ is typically a partial order. There may be pairs of documents $d_1 \neq d_2$ such that $d_1 \not\prec d_2$ and $d_2 \not\prec d_1$. For Equation 11.26 this situation arises whenever either $d_1, d_2 \in rel_q$ or $d_1, d_2 \notin rel_q$. The estimate $\precsim$ may also be a partial order. However, ranked IR evaluation measures such as MAP and P@k assume that it is total. If it is not, because $s(d_1) = s(d_2)$ for some $d_1 \neq d_2$, evaluation software such as `trec_eval` (Section 2.3.2) arbitrarily assumes either $d_1 \prec d_2$ or $d_2 \prec d_1$.

11.7.1 What Is Learning to Rank?

In the literature the phrase "learning to rank" suggests a more general learning problem than our introductory example, in which q and D are fixed and $\prec$ is binary relevance. Although there is no commonly accepted definition of what is or is not learning to rank, the term connotes several of the following aspects:

- Metalearning, where the feature representation $x^{[d]}$ of d is the result of applying many different feature engineering and ranking formulae to q and d.

- A more general characterization of $\prec$, as opposed to binary relevance (Equation 11.26). For example, *graded relevance* assumes an ordered set of k relevance categories $rel_q^{[1]}, \ldots, rel_q^{[k]}$, where $rel_q^{[1]}$ is the least relevant to q and $rel_q^{[k]}$ is the most relevant (see Section 12.5.1). Under graded relevance,

$$d_1 \prec d_2 \;\Leftrightarrow\; d_1 \in rel_q^{[i]} \text{ and } d_2 \in rel_q^{[j]} \, (i < j). \tag{11.28}$$

- The problem of learning a family of rankings, where $\prec_q$ and $\precsim_q$ are both parameterized by $q \in Q$.

- Query-limited training labels, where $d_1 \prec_q d_2$ is known only for $q \in Q_T$ and Q_T is a set of training queries, a very small subset of Q.

- Pairwise training, where $d_1 \prec_q d_2$ is known only for $(q, d_1, d_2) \subset Q_T \times D_T \times D_T$ and $D_T \subseteq D$ is a set of training documents.

- A standard example of learning to rank for IR, illustrated by the LETOR test data sets.[4] In LETOR the training set T consists of a number of triples $(q, x^{[d,q]}, r) \in Q_T \times \mathbb{R}^k \times \mathbb{Z}$, where $Q_T \subset Q$ is a set of training queries, $x^{[d,q]} = s_1(d, q), s_2(d, q), \ldots, s_k(d, q)$ is the feature representation derived by applying k different scoring functions to d with respect to q, and r represents $\prec$:

$$\forall_{q \in Q_T} : r_1 < r_2 \;\Leftrightarrow\; (q, d_1) \prec_q (q, d_2). \tag{11.29}$$

---

[4] `research.microsoft.com/en-us/um/beijing/projects/letor`

- A standard example of using *clickthrough data* (Joachims et al., 2005) to derive pairwise, uncertain training examples. Suppose that a search engine presents a ranked list *Res* to the user in response to query q. Suppose also that the user inspects the kth-ranked document $d_k = Res[k]$ but does not inspect a higher-ranked document $d_j = Res[j]$, where $j < k$. From this information we infer that, on balance of probability,

$$d_j \prec_q d_k \,. \tag{11.30}$$

This inference is uncertain in that it may be wrong, and incomplete in that $d_1 \prec_q d_2$ is defined for only a subset of $(d_1, d_2) \in D_T \times D_T$.

11.7.2   Learning-to-Rank Methods

Methods for learning to rank may be generally characterized as *pointwise*, *pairwise*, or *listwise*, depending on how they are trained (Cao et al., 2007). Pointwise methods reduce the problem to scoring each (d, q) according to the probability that document d is relevant to query q. Logistic regression directly estimates this probability (as log-odds) and maximizes the overall likelihood of the labeled examples. Other methods, such as linear regression, ranking perceptrons, and neural networks, generally give a higher score to (d, q) when d is labeled as relevant to q and a lower score when d is labeled as nonrelevant. A support vector machine seeks to find a hyperplane that separates relevant (d, q) examples from nonrelevant ones.

The pointwise SVM method illustrates a possible shortcoming in pointwise methods. Although by definition we have

$$(d_1, q_1) \not\prec (d_2, q_2) \quad (\text{for } q_1 \neq q_2)\,, \tag{11.31}$$

the SVM will attempt to separate all relevant (d_1, q_1) from nonrelevant (d_2, q_2) even when $q_1 \neq q_2$. A *ranking SVM* considers only the cases in which $q_1 = q_2$ in optimizing both margin and training error. In effect the ranking SVM builds $|Q_T|$ distinct separating hyperplanes, one for each $q \in Q_T$. Other pointwise methods may be adapted to pairwise training in a similar manner.

The listwise approach considers the ordering of the entire set $D_T \times \{q\}$ separately for each $q \in Q_T$. A possible advantage of this approach is that it is easy to place more weight on the highest-ranked documents in each D_T, to emphasize precision or any other aspect of retrieval effectiveness. On the other hand, there are $|D_T|!$ possible permutations of D_T, so finding a compact and generalizable representation of the best one presents a challenge.

11.7.3   What to Optimize?

Every learning method optimizes some objective function (minimizes some loss function) subject to a number of constraints. In learning to rank, perhaps the most obvious loss function is the number of inversions; pairs for which the learned and ideal orders are opposite:

$$inv = |\{(d_1, q_1), (d_2, q_2) \mid (d_1, q_1) \prec (d_2, q_2) \text{ and } s(d_2, q_2) < s(d_1, q_1)\}| . \tag{11.32}$$

When $\prec$ is binary relevance, minimizing inv is equivalent to minimizing AUC, the area under the ROC curve. When $\prec$ is a total order, minimizing inv is equivalent to maximizing Kendall's τ correlation:

$$\tau = 2 \cdot (1 - inv) . \tag{11.33}$$

Minimizing inv may not maximize retrieval effectiveness, which typically emphasizes precision over recall. Measures such as MAP, P@k, and nDCG are all improved when inversions among top-ranked documents are given higher weight than the rest. In general it is not feasible to optimize these measures directly, since they are discontinuous and nonconvex. A number of methods use continuous, convex surrogate loss functions that asymptotically bound these measures.

11.7.4 Learning to Rank for Categorization

The methods we employed for category rank fusion (Section 11.6) are examples of learning to rank, albeit with the senses of D and Q reversed from the presentation above. We wish to compute $\precsim: (D \times L) \times (D \times L)$ that nearly satisfies

$$(d, l') \prec (d, l) \iff d \text{ has language } l \neq l' . \tag{11.34}$$

Our two measures of "nearly" are accuracy ($1-$error) and MRR. The features representing each (d, l) comprise

$$x^{[d,l]} = (r, s_1(d, l), s_2(d, l), \ldots s_k(d, l)), \tag{11.35}$$

where

$$r = \begin{cases} 1 & (d \text{ has language } l) \\ 0 & (d \text{ has language } l' \neq l) \end{cases} \tag{11.36}$$

$$s_m(d, l) = \text{ the score for } d \text{ and } l \text{ from base method } m . \tag{11.37}$$

In Table 11.12 the results of RRF and Condorcet are fixed rules rather than learning methods, but they compute the same result as logistic regression, a pointwise learning method.

To employ a pairwise or listwise method, it is necessary to distinguish the particular document d in the feature representation of (d, l), so that the subsets with a common d are known:

$$x^{[d_i, l]} = (r, i, s_1(d_i, l), s_2(d_i, l), \ldots, s_k(d_i, l)) . \tag{11.38}$$

Table 11.14 repeats the LR pointwise result and shows the result of ranking SVM (SVM^{light}) applied to the language category ranking problem, for two values of the regularization parameter C. For both settings, ranking SVM yields slightly better categorization results than pointwise logistic regression.

Table 11.14 Ranking SVM results for language categorization.

Method	Error (%)	MRR
LR (pointwise)	18.0	0.88
Rank SVM (C=0.01)	17.3	0.88
Rank SVM (C=0.1)	17.6	0.88

Table 11.15 Logistic regression learning-to-rank results, trained on one year's runs and tested on the next year's topics.

Corpus	TREC45		GOV2	
Train	1998		2004	
Test	1999		2005	
Measure	P@10	MAP	P@10	MAP
RRF	0.464	0.252	0.570	0.352
LR	0.446	0.266	0.588	0.309
Rank SVM (C=0.02)	0.420	0.234	0.556	0.268

11.7.5 Learning for Ranked IR

Table 11.3 on page 381 shows that fixed-combination methods effectively combine the ranked results from various IR methods. Because exactly the same methods were employed for all four experiments, we explore the possibility of using learning-to-rank methods to come up with a better combination method. To this end we identify the TREC45 1998 and GOV2 2004 runs and qrels as training examples and labels, and the TREC45 1999 and GOV2 2005 runs as the corresponding test examples. Each example (d, q_j) was represented as a query vector

$$x^{[d,q_j]} = (r, j, s_1(d, q_j), s_2(d, q_j), \ldots, s_k(d, q_j)), \tag{11.39}$$

where $k = 29$ is the number of methods. We applied (pointwise) logistic regression and ranking SVM to the problem.

Table 11.15 shows the results of logistic regression and ranking SVM compared with the baseline of reciprocal rank fusion. It is difficult to argue that the LR result is substantively different from that of the baseline. Rank SVM (SVM-Rank[5]) appears to be inferior, and requires roughly four days of CPU time to process the GOV2 data set, as opposed to a few seconds for RRF and a few minutes for LR.

---

[5] `www.cs.cornell.edu/people/tj/svm_light/svm_rank.html`

Table 11.16 Learning-to-rank results for 583,850 document-query pairs in the LETOR 3 corpus. The P@10 and MAP scores are the averages of the scores for 680 topics over the seven LETOR 3 data sets. RRF, Condorcet, and CombMNZ fuse the results of the separate learning-to-rank methods.

Method	P@10	MAP
ListNet (Cao et al., 2007)	0.1853	0.5846
LR (gr. desc.)	0.1821	0.5837
AdaRank-MAP (Xu and Li, 2007)	0.1789	0.5778
RankSVM (Joachims, 2002)	0.1811	0.5737
LR (batch)	0.1780	0.5715
RankBoost (Freund et al., 2003)	0.1836	0.5622
RRF	0.1902	0.6051
Condorcet	**0.1907**	0.5917
CombMNZ	0.1893	**0.6107**

11.7.6 The LETOR Data Set

LETOR, a benchmark data set for learning to rank (Liu et al., 2007), is a test collection for evaluating learning-to-rank methods. At the time of writing, version 3 of the LETOR data set was current. LETOR 3 consists of seven data sets, each containing examples of the form shown in Equation 11.39. The examples are divided into five standard splits for the purpose of five-fold cross-validation. Six of the data sets use selected documents from the TREC GOV (not GOV2) collection and topics from the TREC 2003 and TREC 2004 Web Track tasks. One of the data sets uses selected documents and topics from the OHSUMED collection. For the TREC documents relevance is binary, and there are 64 features representing different features of the query and the document. For the OHSUMED documents relevance is ternary (not relevant, relevant, very relevant) and there are 45 content-based features. Standard evaluation tools are supplied with the corpus.

Included with the LETOR data set are raw results Res_i and $Score_i$ for several state-of-the-art learning-to-rank methods:

- ListNet (Cao et al., 2007) uses gradient descent to optimize a listwise objective function.

- AdaRank-MAP (Xu and Li, 2007) uses AdaBoost with a surrogate objective function specifically intended to optimize average precision.

- RankBoost (Freund et al., 2003) uses AdaBoost to minimize inversions between pairwise training examples and the resulting ranked list.

- RankSVM is the same SVM^{light} implementation we used for language categorization, which minimizes inversions between pairwise training examples.

For each of the 680 topics there are up to 1000 documents. Although the methods were trained separately on the seven data sets, we averaged the 680 per-topic P@10 and AP scores to yield the summary results shown in Table 11.16. We also included results from the LR (batch) pointwise method used in the previous examples. LR (gr. desc.) uses the gradient descent pairwise LR method with an objective function that gives increased weight to inversions involving highly ranked nonrelevant documents.

The fusion methods RRF, Condorcet, and CombMNZ combine the results of the six learning-to-rank methods, improving both P@10 and MAP effectiveness. At the time of writing, no learning-to-rank method surpasses these fusion results. Furthermore, statistical analysis fails to show any significant difference among the six individual methods (Cormack et al., 2009).

11.8   Further Reading

Belkin et al. (1995) report early efforts to combine search results generated by different queries, both manually and automatically derived from a TREC topic. A family of methods for score combination — of which CombMNZ is one — is presented. These methods are investigated in a number of subsequent studies and are found to be effective in combining a variety of retrieval results (e.g., Lee, 1997). Montague and Aslam (2002) survey and evaluate score combination and election methods, and propose Condorcet as the method of choice. Voorhees et al. (1995) consider test-collection fusion in which the same query is applied to disjoint collections of documents. The term *metasearch* is usually taken to mean the combination of results from autonomous search engines, as surveyed by Meng et al. (2002).

Vogt and Cottrell (1999) investigate the use of linear regression to combine search results based on training examples. Stacked generalization (stacking), proposed by Wolpert (1992), is a standard technique in machine learning. The particular method of log-odds transformation and gradient descent used in our examples is due to Lynam and Cormack (2006). Bootstrap aggregation (bagging; Breiman, 1996) and boosting (Schapire, 2003), like stacking, are staples of machine learning. Most machine learning textbooks (e.g., Hastie et al., 2009) treat *ensemble* methods such as stacking, bagging, and boosting as major topics.

Multicategory logistic regression, like logistic regression itself, is a standard technique for general data analysis (Hosmer and Lemeshow, 2000). Crammer and Singer (2002) describe practical algorithms for multiclass support vector machines. Schapire and Singer (2000) describe the application of boosting to multicategory problems.

Learning to rank has been the subject of workshops at NIPS 2005, SIGIR 2007, and SIGIR 2008. Even so, a precise definition of what is meant by the term remains elusive. Seminal papers by Burges et al. (2005) and Joachims et al. (2005) tacitly define the problem to be one of minimizing inversions between learned and target rankings: Burges et al. use gradient descent in a method known as Ranknet, whereas Joachims et al. use support vector machines.

Li et al. (2007) frame learning to rank as a multiple category classification problem in which each graded relevance level corresponds to a category. Herbrich et al. (2000) and Freund et al. (2003) describe pairwise methods. Xu and Li (2007) describe the AdaRank-MAP listwise method; Burges et al. (2006) descibe the LambdaRank listwise method. Svore and Burges (2009) demonstrate that LambdaRank can outperform BM25 using an equivalent feature set. Yilmaz and Robertson (2010) discuss the use of IR evaluation measures as optimization targets for learning to rank. The LETOR data set (Liu et al., 2007) provides a standard benchmark for evaluating learning-to-rank methods. Liu (2009) surveys current approaches for learning to rank. The sofia-ml package by D. Sculley provides a new suite of fast incremental algorithms for machine learning.[6]

11.9   Exercises

Exercise 11.1   Download a TREC test collection and one or more search engines. Run various configurations of the search engines on the topics, and combine their results using RRF, CombMNZ, and Condorcet. Compare the results.

Exercise 11.2   Download the TREC Spam Filter Evaluation Toolkit, and run several of the sample filters on the sample corpus. Combine the results using voting, naïve Bayes, and logistic regression. Evaluate the results.

Exercise 11.3   Use RRF, CombMNZ, and Condorcet to combine the results of your spam filter runs. Does this experiment aptly model the use of a spam filter? Do these methods improve on voting, naïve Bayes, and logistic regression?

Exercise 11.4   Download the LETOR 3 data set. Apply one or more learning-to-rank methods (e.g., SVM^{light}) to the data set and compare your results against the published baselines.

Exercise 11.5   Apply straightforward logistic regression (e.g., LibLinear) to the LETOR 3 data set, ignoring the `qid` field. Compare the results with those achieved by the learning-to-rank methods.

11.10   Bibliography

Agresti, A. (2007). *An Introduction to Categorical Data Analysis* (2nd ed.). New York: Wiley-Interscience.

---

[6] `code.google.com/p/sofia-ml`

Belkin, N., Kantor, P., Fox, E., and Shaw, J. (1995). Combining the evidence of multiple query representations for information retrieval. *Information Processing & Management*, 31(3):431–448.

Breiman, L. (1996). Bagging predictors. *Machine Learning*, 24(2):123–140.

Burges, C. J. C., Ragno, R., and Le, Q. V. (2006). Learning to rank with nonsmooth cost functions. In *Proceedings of the 20th Annual Conference on Neural Information Processing Systems*, pages 193–200. Vancouver, Canada.

Burges, C. J. C., Shaked, T., Renshaw, E., Lazier, A., Deeds, M., Hamilton, N., and Hullender, G. (2005). Learning to rank using gradient descent. In *Proceedings of the 22nd International Conference on Machine Learning*, pages 89–96. Bonn, Germany.

Cao, Z., Qin, T., Liu, T. Y., Tsai, M. F., and Li, H. (2007). Learning to rank: From pairwise approach to listwise approach. In *Proceedings of the 24th International Conference on Machine Learning*, pages 129–136. Corvalis, Oregon.

Cormack, G. V., Clarke, C. L. A., and Büttcher, S. (2009). Reciprocal rank fusion outperforms Condorcet and individual rank learning methods. In *Proceedings of the 32nd Annual International ACM SIGIR Conference on Research and Development in Information Retrieval*, pages 758–759. Boston, Massachusetts.

Crammer, K., and Singer, Y. (2002). On the algorithmic implementation of multiclass kernel-based vector machines. *Journal of Machine Learning Research*, 2:265–292.

Efron, B., and Tibshirani, R. J. (1993). *An Introduction to the Bootstrap*. Boca Raton, Florida: Chapman & Hall/CRC.

Freund, Y., Iyer, R., Schapire, R. E., and Singer, Y. (2003). An efficient boosting algorithm for combining preferences. *Journal of Machine Learning Research*, 4:933–969.

Hastie, T., Tibshirani, R., and Friedman, J. H. (2009). *The Elements of Statistical Learning* (2nd ed.). Berlin, Germany: Springer.

Herbrich, R., Graepel, T., and Obermayer, K. (2000). Large margin rank boundaries for ordinal regression. In Bartlett, P. J., Schölkopf, B., Schuurmans, D., and Smola, A. J., editors, *Advances in Large Margin Classifiers*, chapter 7, pages 115–132. Cambridge, Massachusetts: MIT Press.

Hosmer, D. W., and Lemeshow, S. (2000). *Applied Logistic Regression* (2nd ed.). New York: Wiley-Interscience.

Joachims, T. (2002). Optimizing search engines using clickthrough data. In *Proceedings of the 8th ACM SIGKDD International Conference on Knowledge Discovery and Data Mining*, pages 133–142. Edmonton, Canada.

Joachims, T., Granka, L., Pan, B., Hembrooke, H., and Gay, G. (2005). Accurately interpreting clickthrough data as implicit feedback. In *Proceedings of the 28th Annual International ACM SIGIR Conference on Research and Development in Information Retrieval*, pages 154–161. Salvador, Brazil.

Lee, J. H. (1997). Analyses of multiple evidence combination. In *Proceedings of the 20th Annual International ACM SIGIR Conference on Research and Development in Information Retrieval*, pages 267–276.

Li, P., Burges, C., and Wu, Q. (2007). McRank: Learning to rank using multiple classification and gradient boosting. In *Proceedings of the 21st Annual Conference on Neural Information Processing Systems*, pages 897–904. Vancouver, Canada.

Liu, T. Y. (2009). Learning to rank for information retrieval. *Foundations and Trends in Information Retrieval*, 3(3):225–331.

Liu, T. Y., Xu, J., Qin, T., Xiong, W., and Li, H. (2007). LETOR: Benchmark dataset for research on learning to rank for information retrieval. In *Proceedings of SIGIR 2007 Workshop on Learning to Rank for Information Retrieval*, pages 481–490. Amsterdam, The Netherlands.

Lynam, T. R., and Cormack, G. V. (2006). On-line spam filter fusion. In *Proceedings of the 29th Annual International ACM SIGIR Conference on Research and Development in Information Retrieval*, pages 123–130. Seattle, Washington.

Meng, W., Yu, C., and Liu, K. L. (2002). Building efficient and effective metasearch engines. *ACM Computing Surveys*, 34(1):48–89.

Montague, M., and Aslam, J. A. (2002). Condorcet fusion for improved retrieval. In *Proceedings of the 11th International Conference on Information and Knowledge Management*, pages 538–548. McLean, Virginia.

Schapire, R. (2003). The boosting approach to machine learning: An overview. In Denison, D. D., Hansen, M. H., Holmes, C. C., Mallick, B., and Yu, B., editors, *Nonlinear Estimation and Classification*, volume 171 of *Lecture Notes in Statistics*, pages 149–172. Berlin, Germany: Springer.

Schapire, R., and Singer, Y. (2000). BoosTexter: A boosting-based system for text categorization. *Machine learning*, 39(2):135–168.

Surowiecki, J. (2004). *The Wisdom of Crowds: Why the Many Are Smarter Than the Few and How Collective Wisdom Shapes Business, Economies, Societies and Nations*. New York: Doubleday.

Svore, K. M., and Burges, C. J. (2009). A machine learning approach for improved BM25 retrieval. In *Proceedings of the 18th ACM Conference on Information and Knowledge Management*, pages 1811–1814. Hong Kong, China.

Vogt, C., and Cottrell, G. (1999). Fusion via a linear combination of scores. *Information Retrieval*, 1(3):151–173.

Voorhees, E. M., Gupta, N. K., and Johnson-Laird, B. (1995). Learning collection fusion strategies. In *Proceedings of the 18th Annual International ACM SIGIR Conference on Research and Development in Information Retrieval*, pages 172–179. Seattle, Washington.

Wolpert, D. H. (1992). Stacked generalization. *Neural Networks*, 5:241–259.

Xu, J., and Li, H. (2007). Adarank: A boosting algorithm for information retrieval. In *Proceedings of the 30th Annual International ACM SIGIR Conference on Research and Development in Information Retrieval*, pages 391–398. Amsterdam, The Netherlands.

Yilmaz, E., and Robertson, S. (2010). On the choice of effectiveness measures for learning to rank. *Information Retrieval.*

IV Evaluation

12 Measuring Effectiveness

The purpose of evaluation is to measure how well IR methods achieve their intended purpose. Evaluation is essential to estimating the effectiveness of an IR method in a given situation, comparing it against the effectiveness of a different method in the same situation or predicting its effectiveness in a different situation. Without evaluation it is difficult to make informed deployment decisions or to discover better approaches. To be usable, an evaluation methodology must have the following:

- a characterization of the intended purpose of an IR method;
- a measure that quantifies the notion of how well this purpose is met;
- a precise, accurate, and economical measurement technique;
- an estimate of measurement error.

This chapter addresses the above aspects of IR evaluation. It builds directly upon the introductory material of Section 2.3, which focused on the evaluation of the basic adhoc retrieval task.

In Section 12.1 we revisit the main effectiveness measures used in traditional IR evaluation and discuss their corresponding retrieval tasks. Section 12.2 describes the evaluation methodology employed at the Text REtrieval Conference (TREC), which represents the de facto standard in IR evaluation and is followed by many researchers. The statistical analysis of evaluation results is the topic of Section 12.3. We discuss common analysis techniques, such as confidence intervals and significance tests as they apply to information retrieval, as well as less common methods, such as the meta-analysis of independent experiments. We also compare several statistical tests in terms of their *power* and *validity*, that is, how good they are at detecting differences between competing retrieval functions and how accurate their verdicts are. In Section 12.4 we explore ways to reduce the number of relevance judgments while maintaining the reliability of evaluation results. Finally, Section 12.5 covers effectiveness measures that extend — or address problems with — the traditional measures from Section 12.1. It includes measures for graded relevance assessments (going beyond the binary relevant/nonrelevant evaluation methodology) and incomplete judgments, as well as novelty and diversity.

Looking beyond the current chapter, other chapters discuss evaluation in other contexts. Chapter 10 covers evaluation for filtering and classification. Chapter 15 covers issues and measures specific to the Web. Chapter 16 provides an overview of effectiveness evaluation for XML information retrieval.

12.1   Traditional Effectiveness Measures

Traditional information retrieval evaluation is based on two fundamental assumptions:

1. Given a user's *information need*, represented by a search query, each document in a given text collection is either *relevant* or *nonrelevant* with respect to this information need.

2. The relevance of a document d depends only on the information need and d itself. It is independent of the search engine's ranking of the other documents in the collection.

Based on these two assumptions, various effectiveness measures can be defined. Some of them have already appeared in Section 2.3.

12.1.1   Recall and Precision

Recall and precision, perhaps the two oldest measures used in IR evaluation, apply to an unordered set of documents retrieved in response to a query. *Recall* is the fraction of relevant documents contained in the set. Let *Res* be the set of retrieved documents, and *Rel* the set of relevant documents. Then we have

$$\text{recall} \;=\; \frac{|Res \cap Rel|}{|Rel|}. \tag{12.1}$$

As an effectiveness measure, recall quantifies how exhaustively the search results satisfy the user's information need. It models a retrieval task in which the user wants to find all relevant documents, as in a literature review or legal search.

A search engine could trivially achieve a recall level of 1.0 simply by returning all documents in the collection. Of course, if it did that, most of the documents in the result list would be nonrelevant. *Precision* covers this second aspect of the result set — the fraction of relevant documents among the documents retrieved by the system:

$$\text{precision} \;=\; \frac{|Res \cap Rel|}{|Res|}. \tag{12.2}$$

The user model from which the precision measure is derived assumes that the user wishes to find a reasonable number of relevant documents, considering the effort needed to examine each document in the retrieved set. Precision is a measure of the number of relevant documents per unit of effort. Its reciprocal is equivalent to the expected number of documents from the retrieved set that the user needs to look at, in some arbitrary order, until she encounters a relevant one.

12.1.2   Precision at k Documents (P@k)

Although recall may have been an appropriate measure for the early information retrieval experiments conducted in the 1960s, its usefulness became more and more questionable as document collections grew larger over the years. For instance, TREC topic 426 ("law enforcement, dogs") has 202 known relevant documents in the TREC collections. Only the most inquisitive user would be interested in all of them. In Web search, recall is even less meaningful because it is not unusual for a topic to have tens of thousands of relevant documents (e.g., consider the TREC topics "drug abuse", "vietnam war", and "international space station").

Precision at k documents ("precision@k" or just "P@k") is meant to model the satisfaction of a user who is presented with a list of up to k highly ranked documents, for some small value of k (typically $k = 5$, 10, or 20). It is defined as

$$\text{P@}k = \frac{|Res[1..k] \cap Rel|}{k}, \tag{12.3}$$

where $Res[1..k]$ consists of the top k documents returned by the system. Like unconstrained precision, P@k assumes that the user inspects the results in arbitrary order, and that she inspects *all of them* even after she has found one or more relevant documents. It also assumes that if the search engine is unable to identify at least one relevant document in the top k results, it has failed, and the user's information need remains unfulfilled. Precision at k documents is sometimes referred to as an *early precision measure*. It does not have a recall component, thus acknowledging that no user would ever read all relevant documents about drug abuse or the Vietnam war.

12.1.3   Average Precision (AP)

In general it is not clear how the value of k in P@k should be chosen. The value $k = 10$ might suggest itself because many search engines, by default, show only the top 10 results to the user. But because we are concerned with the evaluation of result rankings, not with evaluating a user interface, $k = 10$ seems just as arbitrary as any other choice.

Average precision (AP) tries to address this problem by combining precision values at all possible recall levels:

$$\text{AP} = \frac{1}{|Rel|} \cdot \sum_{i=1}^{|Res|} \text{relevant}(i) \cdot \text{P@}i, \tag{12.4}$$

where relevant(i) is 1 if the i-th document in *Res* is relevant (i.e., $Res[i] \in Rel$); 0 otherwise. Thus, for every relevant document d, AP computes the precision of the result list up to and including d. If a document does not appear in *Res*, AP assumes the corresponding precision to be 0. Thus, we may say that AP contains an implicit recall component because it accounts for relevant documents that are not in the result list.

12.1.4 Reciprocal Rank (RR)

The measures discussed so far assume that there is a set of relevant documents, that all documents in this set are equally useful, and that the user is interested in seeing a number of relevant documents. Although this assumption is reasonable for adhoc retrieval tasks, there are situations in which a user wants a single relevant document, and this document should be ranked as high as possible. For instance, consider the query ⟨"white", "house", "official", "website"⟩. There is exactly one relevant result for this query (www.whitehouse.gov), and returning it in position 1 is clearly better than returning it in position 5 or 10.

Reciprocal rank is a measure that focuses on the top few results and that strongly favors rankings in which the relevant document is returned at the very top. It is defined as

$$\text{RR} = \frac{1}{\min\{k \mid Res[k] \in Rel\}}. \tag{12.5}$$

Note that Equation 12.5 allows the existence of more than one relevant document. If $|Rel| > 1$, then the assumption is that the user's task is completed as soon as she encounters the first relevant document. On the other hand, if there is exactly one relevant document, $|Rel| = 1$, reciprocal rank is equivalent to average precision.

12.1.5 Arithmetic Mean Versus Geometric Mean

Aggregate results are given by averaging over multiple topics (calculating the arithmetic mean). The corresponding measures are *mean average precision* (MAP), *mean reciprocal rank* (MRR), and so forth. Curiously, for some measures "mean" is not explicitly included in the name. For example, *mean precision at k* is usually referred to as just P@k, not as MP@k.

Recently it has been argued that computing the arithmetic mean may not be the best way to aggregate effectiveness measures over multiple topics (Robertson, 2006). As an illustrative example consider two topics T_1 and T_2, each of which has exactly one relevant document. Further consider the two result lists

$$Res(T_1) = \langle -,+,-,-,-,\ldots\rangle, \quad Res(T_2) = \langle -,+,-,-,-,\ldots\rangle, \tag{12.6}$$

where "+" denotes a relevant document and "−" denotes a nonrelevant document. The average precision for both lists is 0.5. Thus the MAP over both topics is 0.5 as well. Now consider an alternative scenario:

$$Res'(T_1) = \langle +,-,-,-,-,\ldots\rangle, \quad Res'(T_2) = \langle -,-,-,-,-,\ldots\rangle, \tag{12.7}$$

where AP for $Res'(T_1)$ is 1 and AP for $Res'(T_2)$ is 0. The MAP is the same in both cases (12.6 and 12.7), even though the overall utility for the user is likely to be considerably higher in 12.6 than in 12.7.

This observation leads to the definition of *geometric mean average precision* (GMAP) (Robertson, 2006):

$$\text{GMAP}(AP_1,\ldots,AP_n) \;=\; \sqrt[n]{\prod_{i=1}^{n}(AP_i + \varepsilon)} - \varepsilon, \tag{12.8}$$

where ε is a constant whose role is to eliminate pathologies due to one of the AP_i's being 0. Setting $\varepsilon = 0.01$, we obtain

$$\text{GMAP}(0.5, 0.5) = 0.5, \quad \text{GMAP}(1.0, 0.0) = \sqrt{1.01 \cdot 0.01} \approx 0.10 \tag{12.9}$$

for the examples in 12.6 and 12.7, which is consistent with our intuition that the overall utility of $Res(T_1)$ and $Res(T_2)$ is greater than that of $Res'(T_1)$ and $Res'(T_2)$.

Because the geometric mean of a set of AP values is equivalent to the arithmetic mean of logarithmic AP values, it may be argued that the problem is not caused by taking the arithmetic mean but by the AP measure itself.

12.1.6   User Satisfaction

Virtually all ranking functions devised in the last twenty years were evaluated using one or more of the effectiveness measures described above. Given their importance in IR evaluation, one might assume that the relationship between user satisfaction and, say, average precision has been thoroughly studied and is well understood. Unfortunately, this is not the case. User studies trying to find correlations between user satisfaction and various effectiveness measures are a relatively recent phenomenon. Initial results suggest that the correlation may in fact be quite low for AP (Turpin and Scholer, 2006) but reasonably high for early precision measures such as P@10 (Kelly et al., 2007). Nonetheless, AP still is, and will remain for the next while, the most widely used measure in IR evaluation.

12.2   The Text REtrieval Conference (TREC)

Section 2.3 provides a brief outline of the classic approach to measuring effectiveness, as codified by TREC and emulated by many other evaluation efforts. The TREC methodology provides a framework within which the evaluation measures from the previous section can be applied. It represents the de facto standard for IR evaluation; measurements taken using the TREC methodology dominate published results, especially for adhoc retrieval. Under this approach, the organizers of an evaluation experiment develop a set of topics and distribute them, along with a target document collection, to the groups participating in the experiment. Traditionally the document collection is relatively homogeneous, consisting of professionally written and edited material, such as newspaper or journal articles. Each group creates queries from the topics and executes them over the document collection. Usually these queries must be created automatically from the topics, without human intervention, but manual creation or modification of queries may also be permitted in some experiments.

A typical topic set comprises 50 or more topics. In many cases the organizers create topics in which one of the fields is explicitly intended to be used as a query with little or no modification. In the example topic shown in Figure 1.8 (page 25), the title field ("law enforcement, dogs") is intended for this purpose. The remainder of the topic provides additional details and resolves potential ambiguity caused by the brevity of the title. Ideally, the topic precisely and completely specifies the requirements for a relevant document. TREC topics rarely contain typographical or spelling errors, which are common in real-world queries.

After executing their queries over the collection, each group returns a ranked list of up to k document identifiers for each topic: $k=1000$ is a typical value for TREC experiments; $k=10,000$ was used for the experiments in this book. A set of ranked lists for an entire topic set is called a *run* in TREC jargon. Depending on the experiment, the organizers may permit each group to return several runs, allowing them to easily test different aspects of their system.

After receiving one or more runs from each group, the organizers create a *pool* of documents for evaluation. This pool is constructed as the union of the top documents from each run, where a per-run pool depth of 100 is typical. Human assessors judge each document on a binary scale: relevant or nonrelevant.[1] These judgments, called *qrels* in the TREC vernacular, are then used to compute recall, precision, average precision, and other measures, as described in the previous section. In computing these measures, documents that do not form part of the pool (because they were not returned in the top documents by any run) are considered to be nonrelevant.

The topics and judgments, together with the document collection, form a *test collection*. A central goal of TREC is to create test collections that may be re-used for later experiments. For instance, if a new IR technique or ranking formula is proposed, its inventor may use an established test collection to compare it against standard methods. Reusable test collections may also be employed to tune retrieval formulae, adjusting parameters to optimize performance. If a test collection is to be reusable, it is traditionally assumed that the judgments should be as exhaustive as possible. Ideally, all relevant documents would be located. Thus, many evaluation experiments actively encourage manual runs (involving human intervention) in order to increase the number of known relevant documents.

The pooling method can require substantial judging effort. With 50 topics, dozens of groups, and a pool of depth 100, assessors may need to make tens of thousands of judgments. For the TREC-8 adhoc task in 1999, 71 runs contributed to the pool (Voorhees and Harman, 1999). In theory the size of this pool could have been as large as $71 \cdot 50 \cdot 100 = 355,000$ if none of the runs had overlapped. Fortunately, the runs did overlap to a substantial extent, particularly at earlier ranks. Nonetheless, the total pool for all 50 topics included 86,830 documents. Assuming

---

[1] Some TREC experiments involve judgments on a ternary scale: nonrelevant, relevant, highly relevant. For the purpose of evaluating the individual runs, however, relevant and highly relevant documents are usually treated as equivalent.

we allow an assessor just 30 seconds to judge a single document, these 86,830 documents would correspond to a total of 724 hours of assessor time, enough to keep a team of ten assessors busy for two weeks.

12.3   Using Statistics in Evaluation

Given a test collection consisting of documents, topics, and qrels, we can use the measures from Section 12.1 to compute the effectiveness of some retrieval method A on the given test collection, and to compare it with the effectiveness of some other method B. However, the outcome of such an evaluation tells us only how the two methods compare with each other on the given test collection. Ideally, we would like to know which of the two methods is better in general, and by how much, for all possible collections of documents, topics, and relevance assessments.

Statistical analysis may be used to estimate how well an evaluation result predicts a system's performance beyond the particular test collection used to measure it. When we report AP for a particular topic or MAP over a set of topics, we are tacitly asserting that similar results would be achieved on other topics, because the intended purpose of the system surely extends well beyond these specific evaluation topics. Without statistical analysis, however, it is difficult to argue that the assertion holds or that measured results reflect how well the system fulfills its intended purpose.

Statistical analysis may be used to yield either an estimate of the precision of a quantitative measurement (e.g., "How good is method A?" or "How much better is A than B?") or an estimate of the force of evidence supporting a particular hypothesis (e.g., "Method A is better than method B!"). The traditional hypothesis test, which occupies many pages of experimental methodology books, declares a result to be statistically significant when the force of evidence exceeds an arbitrary threshold. Such a test yields strictly less information than a quantitative estimate of the force of evidence and is easily misinterpreted. Hypothesis tests have lost favor in fields such as medicine (Gardner and Altman, 1986). In the IR literature, statistical estimates and hypothesis tests are commonly absent or misapplied. We hope to influence this practice for the better.

This section is long, reviewing a range of foundational material and discussing its application to the evaluation of IR methods. Although you may be familiar with much of the foundational material, we take a viewpoint different from those traditionally taken by the mathematical or applied statistics literature. We consider the role of statistics in the scientific method, as opposed to statistics for its own sake or statistical tests that are applied as an afterthought, often for no reason other than to fulfill a condition of publication.

If statistics is a distant memory, and you wish to avoid digging through this material, you can skip or skim the remainder of this section (all the way to page 441). The "bottom line" of this material is essentially as follows: (1) establish an appropriate baseline for your IR experiment; (2) compare the effect of an alternative method or technique against this baseline; (3) report the magnitude of the difference, considering whether or not this magnitude will have any meaningful impact on users; and (4) report a measure of statistical confidence, such as a a p-value or confidence interval. For the last step a paired t-test is usually an acceptable choice.

12.3.1 Foundations and Terminology

In some sense, effectiveness measurements in IR evaluation are quite similar to physical measurements. Suppose that one of the authors of this book wants to determine his own height for the purpose of ordering a suit. He uses a ruler and measures it to be 5 feet 8 inches. Just to be sure he measures it again using a tape, obtaining the result 173cm. After making an exact conversion to a common unit, he gets values of 1727.2mm and 1730mm, respectively. Confused, he measures more precisely with the ruler and comes up with 5 feet $8\frac{3}{8}$ inches (exactly 1736.725mm). Is one of the measurements wrong? What is the author's true height? The answers are "No, the measurements agree as well as would be expected, given the technique of using a ruler or tape," and "It doesn't matter, because he'll get the same size suit regardless." Statistical methods help us answer questions like these.

If a more precise answer is required, he might average the measurements on a calculator to arrive at 1731.308333mm. If enough independent measurements are averaged, he can come up with a very precise estimate of his height but never one precise enough to justify reporting it to ten figures as shown, because our common understanding of a person's height breaks down under such close inspection. Should we measure the person's height in the morning or the evening, wearing heavy clothing or not? Does height include hair? It is utterly pointless to try to measure more precisely than our understood definition of height. Nevertheless, the notion of "true height" is a useful abstraction in characterizing the precision of our estimate; that is, to address the question "How close is the estimate to the true value?" For this purpose it is useful to define "true height" as the average of an infinite number of measurements that differ from each other only by chance. We may then think of the amount by which individual measurements differ from the true value as *random error*. Random error contrasts with *systematic error*, or *bias*, which might occur, for example, if the tape measure becomes stretched from overuse.

Precision of measurement[2] is the degree to which a measurement is free from random error. *Validity* is the degree to which the measure itself truly reflects what it is intended to measure (in our case, overall retrieval effectiveness). Our concern in this section is, in particular, the precision of measurement afforded by information retrieval experiments. If an experiment measuring an IR system's effectiveness were to be repeated using exactly the same technique but different topics, documents, or relevance assessments, how similar would the result be? Is it possible, without actually repeating the experiment, to predict this degree of similarity? Although these questions are largely amenable to statistical inference, they may be understood only in the

---

[2] Precision of measurement is known simply as *precision* in the statistics literature. When necessary for clarity, we use the longer name to distinguish it from the IR effectiveness measure.

context of a general investigative framework that includes questions of validity that are not necessarily statistical. Instead they are addressed by the tools of scientific inquiry — observation, induction, deduction, and experiment.

The notion of *population* is central to any discussion of statistical analysis and has been the subject of historical and current philosophical debate (Lenhard, 2006). We adopt the notion of an infinite hypothetical population, which is due to Ronald Fisher (Fisher, 1925):

> If, in a Mendelian experiment, we say that the probability is one half that a mouse born of a certain mating shall be white, we must conceive of our mouse as one of an infinite population of mice which might have been produced by that mating. The population must be infinite for in sampling from a finite population the fact of one mouse being white would affect the probability of others being white, and this is not the hypothesis which we wish to consider; moreover, the probability may not always be a rational number. Being infinite the population is clearly hypothetical, for not only must the actual number produced by any parents be finite, but we might wish to consider the possibility that the probability should depend on the age of the parents, or their nutritional conditions. We can, however, imagine an unlimited number of mice produced upon the conditions of our experiment, that is, by similar parents, in the same age, in the same environment. The proportion of white mice in this imaginary population appears to be the actual meaning to be assigned to our statement of probability. Briefly, the hypothetical population is the conceptual resultant of the conditions which we are studying. The probability, like other statistical parameters, is a numerical characteristic of that population.

With respect to the author's height, we are concerned with the outcome of using a ruler or tape to measure it. The population of immediate interest is the set of similar measurements (not, as one might casually think, the set of similar authors). With respect to IR evaluation, the outcome of interest is some effectiveness measure, such as MAP or P@k, applied to a system (or perhaps the difference in MAP or P@k between two systems), and the population is the set of similar measurements. We characterize the set of similar measurements as those resulting from experiments using exactly the same method but different documents, topics, or relevance assessments. The different documents, topics, and relevance assessments themselves represent hypothetical populations: the topics that might be presented to a system, the collections of documents from which the system may be expected to retrieve relevant documents, and the set of relevance assessments.

As with height we characterize "true effectiveness" as the average of all possible measurements. Also as with height the notion of effectiveness is necessarily inexact, as manifested by our inability to specify these populations exactly. Working definitions might be "all topics like those presented to an adhoc IR system, past, present, and future"; "all documents presented to a filter, past, present, and future"; "all assessments of the relevance of a particular document to a particular topic, past, present, and future." Because these populations, in part, have yet to exist, they certainly cannot be enumerated for the purpose of measurement.

Instead of trying to enumerate a hypothetical population, we use readily available data and observations (e.g., in the form of the topics, documents, and qrels in a TREC collection) and treat them as being drawn from the hypothetical population "all data like that which we collected". This hypothetical population is known as the *source population*, as opposed to the actual (but intangible) population of interest, which is known as the *target population*. The source population approximates the hypothetical target population. The better the approximation, the better a measurement using the source population will reflect a hypothetical measurement using the target population. The accuracy of the measurement may be thought of as having three separate aspects: the precision of the measurement; the validity of the measurement with respect to the true value as defined by the source population; and the validity of the measurement with respect to the target population. The two forms of validity are known as *internal validity* and *external validity*, respectively. External validity is also known as *transferability* or *generalizability*.

Statistical inference is concerned exclusively with precision and internal validity; that is, how good is the measurement with respect to the true value as defined by the source population? External validity is established not by statistical inference but by scientific inquiry in which (a) characteristics are identified that differ between the source population and the target population and may affect external validity; (b) a new source population is identified which differs in these characteristics; (c) effectiveness is measured with respect to the new source population; (d) the effect of the difference is assessed. For example, the original TREC collections consisted mostly of newswire and similar articles and the topics concerned current events. The TREC Web Track investigated the differences that might result from the use of Web pages and Web queries instead. The idea is not to find the ultimate source population that best represents the target population but to identify populations that illustrate possible differences. If the measured outcomes are similar, our confidence in the external validity of both increases. If the measured outcomes differ, the difference is worthy of further scientific investigation.

Any experimental technique has assumptions and limitations that affect its external validity. Such limitations are not cause for us to discard a particular technique. Instead they should be identified, and their impact assessed using the methods of scientific inquiry. The overall body of evidence afforded by these experiments serves to increase our understanding of IR effectiveness on an ongoing basis. This body of evidence may itself be treated as a population, and statistical inferences may be drawn from it using a technique known as *meta-analysis*. Current best practice in fields such as medicine involves meta-analysis, taking into account, for example, all known results concerning the effect of a particular treatment.[3]

In IR evaluation, as in many disciplines, assessment of external validity presents a challenge. For a laboratory experiment, which is our principal focus here, it may not be possible to obtain a realistic test collection. For instance, most of the collections used at TREC are free of spam (unwanted documents engineered by an adversary to appear relevant); the topics are usually

---

[3] www.gradeworkinggroup.org

Table 12.1 Effectiveness results and with 95% confidence intervals for selected retrieval methods discussed in this book. The intervals were computed under the assumption that the topics were sampled from a hypothetical population and that the measurement error followed a normal (i.e., Gaussian) distribution.

Method	TREC45 (1998)		GOV2 (2005)	
	P@10	**MAP**	**P@10**	**MAP**
Cosine (2.2.1)	0.264 *(0.19-0.34)*	0.126 *(0.09-0.16)*	0.194 *(0.13-0.26)*	0.092 *(0.06-0.12)*
Proximity (2.2.2)	0.396 *(0.30-0.49)*	0.124 *(0.08-0.17)*	0.560 *(0.48-0.64)*	0.230 *(0.18-0.28)*
Cosine (raw TF)	0.266 *(0.19-0.34)*	0.106 *(0.07-0.14)*	0.282 *(0.20-0.36)*	0.097 *(0.07-0.13)*
Cosine (TF docs)	0.342 *(0.27-0.42)*	0.132 *(0.10-0.17)*	0.466 *(0.37-0.56)*	0.151 *(0.11-0.19)*
BM25 (Ch. 8)	0.424 *(0.34-0.51)*	0.178 *(0.14-0.22)*	0.534 *(0.46-0.61)*	0.277 *(0.23-0.32)*
LMD (Ch. 9)	0.450 *(0.37-0.53)*	0.193 *(0.15-0.24)*	0.580 *(0.50-0.66)*	0.293 *(0.25-0.34)*
DFR (Ch. 9)	0.426 *(0.34-0.51)*	0.183 *(0.14-0.23)*	0.550 *(0.47-0.63)*	0.269 *(0.22-0.32)*

composed for evaluation rather than being examples of information needs arising in any real situation; the topics are often vetted using standard IR methods; and the topics' title fields, meant to be used as search queries, rarely contain misspellings. Moreover, even in cases in which realistic examples of queries can be obtained, the intent of a given query is not always obvious, and there is no guarantee that the relevance judgments are consistent with the user's information need. On the other hand, experiments with live systems and humans are logistically difficult due to a number of considerations, not the least of which include privacy, interactions between the experiment and user behavior, the difficulty of determining information need and relevance, and the difficulty of controlling differences for the purpose of repeatability and system comparison. The net effect is that live evaluations have their own limitations: They are very expensive and time consuming, and typically yield imprecise results. That said, the statistical precision estimation techniques described here may be used to estimate the precision of both laboratory and live measurements.

12.3.2 Confidence Intervals

A *confidence interval* $c = [l, u]$ is a range of values likely to contain the hypothetical "true value" of an experimentally measured quantity m (such as P@k or MAP computed using a particular test collection). "Likely" is quantified by the *confidence level* $1 - \alpha$, where α is known as the *significance level*. The "true value" $t = \mathrm{E}[M]$ is the expected value of M, a random variable characterizing the possible values of m over all materially similar experiments that differ only in their selection of examples from the subject population. Let C be a random variable characterizing the possible values of c resulting from similar measurements. A confidence interval with confidence level $1 - \alpha$ asserts that

$$\Pr[t \in C] \geq 1 - \alpha. \tag{12.10}$$

A confidence interval may be reported as a pair consisting of a *lower confidence limit* and an *upper confidence limit* $[l, u]$ that bound the interval or as a tolerance relative to the estimated value (e.g., $\pm \delta$). The confidence level associated with the interval, typically 95%, must be stated. Table 12.1 reproduces the results of the experiments reported in the first and the last columns of Table 2.5 (page 72), augmenting each estimate with a 95% confidence interval computed using the classical method detailed below. We see that for all results the confidence limits are about $\pm 20\%$ of the measured effectiveness.

Confidence intervals indicate the precision of the experimental technique used for measurement. When the same technique is used repeatedly, the resulting intervals may be expected to contain the true value with a frequency at least equal to the confidence level $1 - \alpha$. That is, no more than α of the confidence intervals would fail to contain the true value. Thus we expect about 5% of the 28 intervals in Table 12.1 (i.e., about 1 or 2) could miss the mark. Without additional information it is impossible to know which do miss the mark.

For a given confidence level $1 - \alpha$, a measurement that yields a smaller confidence interval is more precise. Precision of measurement depends on sample size, the measure that is estimated, and the method used. The design of an experiment to measure IR system effectiveness involves a trade-off among the size, cost, and practicality of measurement on the one hand, and precision and validity on the other.

Calculating confidence intervals

In describing how to compute a confidence interval, we return briefly to Fisher's mouse born of a certain mating. The color of the mouse is either white or black, so the outcome is completely characterized by

$$\Pr[\text{Color} = \text{white}] \;=\; 1 - \Pr[\text{Color} = \text{black}]. \tag{12.11}$$

If the outcome m of our experiment has many possible values, it is necessary to estimate $\Pr[M = m]$ for all possible m. Such an estimate is a *probability distribution*. When m is a continuous quantity, there is an infinite number of possible values. Such a distribution is characterized by a *probability density function*. For computing confidence intervals we are interested not in the distribution per se, but in the cumulative distribution characterized by the *cumulative density function*

$$\text{cdf}(x) \;=\; \Pr[M \leq x]. \tag{12.12}$$

The confidence interval is computed using an estimate of the distribution for M. The various methods for computing confidence intervals differ in how they characterize and estimate this distribution.

- Measurements of natural quantities are typically assumed to follow a **normal distribution** (also known as *Gaussian distribution*), with mean μ and variance σ^2. The

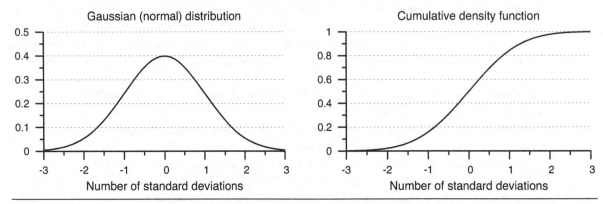

Figure 12.1   Probability density and cumulative probability density for the Gaussian distribution with mean $\mu = 0$ and variance $\sigma^2 = 1$.

probability density function for such a distribution is the Gaussian function

$$\varphi_{\mu,\sigma^2}(x) \;=\; \frac{1}{\sigma\sqrt{2\pi}} \cdot e^{-\frac{(x-\mu)^2}{2\sigma^2}}\,, \tag{12.13}$$

shown in Figure 12.1. The corresponding cumulative density function, also shown, is

$$\Phi_{\mu,\sigma^2}(y) \;=\; \int_{-\infty}^{y} \varphi_{\mu,\sigma^2}(x)\; dx\,. \tag{12.14}$$

The computation of Φ is complex and best left to mathematical software. Historically the value of Φ has been determined by consulting statistical tables. Some values of Φ are used so commonly, for reasons that will shortly become clear, that they are easily recognized and remembered:

$$\Phi_{\mu=0,\sigma=1}(-1.96) \;\approx\; 0.025\,, \qquad \Phi_{\mu=0,\sigma=1}(1.96) \;\approx\; 0.975\,. \tag{12.15}$$

- The **binomial distribution** arises from counting the number of positive results from a set of independent tests known as *Bernoulli trials*, where the probability q of a positive result is the same for every trial. For example, we observe the birth of $N = 100$ mice and count the number n that are white. The parameters N, the number of trials, and q, the fixed probability of a positive result, completely characterize the binomial distribution. Given N and q, the probability of any particular value of n is simply

$$\binom{N}{n} \cdot q^n \cdot (1-q)^{N-n}\,. \tag{12.16}$$

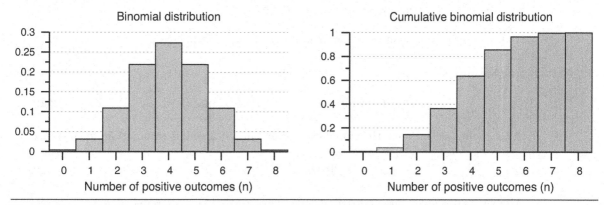

Figure 12.2   Binomial distribution and cumulative distribution for $N = 8$, $q = 0.5$.

Because the values of n are discrete, the cumulative probability is a summation:

$$\text{cdf}(y) \;=\; \sum_{n \leq y} \Pr[B = n]\,, \tag{12.17}$$

where B is a random variable with the specified distribution (characterizing, in our example, mouse births). The binomial and cumulative binomial distributions are illustrated in Figure 12.2.

When classical statistics was developed in the early 20th century, computation was performed by hand or with very simple calculators, and it was difficult to compute the cumulative probability for typical values of N. Simpler approximations were developed to mitigate computational effort. These methods remain in common use, although modern computers can compute the distribution exactly for almost any value of N that might arise in practice.

One such approximation is worthy of note and finds application beyond simply reducing computational effort. Given $0 \neq q \neq 1$, as $N \to \infty$ the binomial distribution approaches a normal distribution with $\mu = N \cdot q$ and $\sigma^2 = N \cdot q \cdot (1 - q)$. As a rule of thumb, if $\sigma^2 > 10$, the normal distribution may be considered a reasonable approximation of the binomial. That is, it is important to have a reasonable sample size and a reasonable number of positive *and* negative outcomes.

- The normal and binomial distributions are known as parametric distributions because any particular one is completely characterized by a few parameters. Thus the problem of estimating the distribution reduces to that of estimating the parameters. An **empirical distribution**, on the other hand, is simply a multiset of observed values; for example, our height measurements $H = \{1727.2, 1730, 1736.725\}$ or the colors of some newborn mice $B = \{\text{black, white, white, black, white}\}$. In an empirical distribution the probability of any value is its frequency, so for height we have

$$\Pr[H = 1727.2] \;=\; \Pr[H = 1730] \;=\; \Pr[H = 1736.725] \;=\; \frac{1}{3}, \qquad (12.18)$$

and for mice we have

$$\Pr[B = \text{white}] \;=\; \frac{3}{5}, \qquad \Pr[B = \text{black}] \;=\; \frac{2}{5}. \qquad (12.19)$$

If the values are ordered, the cumulative probability is a simple summation; for instance,

$$\Pr[H \leq 1735] \;=\; \frac{2}{3}. \qquad (12.20)$$

More formally, an empirical distribution is characterized by a discrete multiset, or *sample*, s of values, assuming that each element is equally probable. For a random variable X with this distribution, we have:

$$\Pr[X = x] \;=\; \frac{|\{i \in s \mid i = x\}|}{|s|}. \qquad (12.21)$$

The cumulative probability is

$$\Pr[X \leq x] \;=\; \frac{|\{i \in s \mid i \leq x\}|}{|s|}. \qquad (12.22)$$

The mean and variance of the empirical distribution are given by the familiar formulae

$$\mu_s \;=\; \frac{1}{|s|} \cdot \sum_{i \in s} i \qquad (12.23)$$

and

$$\sigma_s^2 \;=\; \frac{1}{|s|} \cdot \sum_{i \in S} (i - \mu_s)^2. \qquad (12.24)$$

The empirical distribution arising from measuring a natural phenomenon (such as the height of humans) often resembles a normal distribution with the same parameters.

From distribution to confidence interval

In the hypothetical situation in which the mean μ_M of the distribution is known with certainty, the problem of computing a confidence interval is moot: $t = \mu_M$, so $c = [\mu_M, \mu_M]$ with 100% confidence. More illuminating is the situation (also hypothetical) in which all aspects of the distribution except μ_M are known. Define E, a random variable characterizing measurement error, such that $M = t + E$. The distribution of E is identical to that of M except for its mean $\mu_E = 0$. We first consider how the confidence interval is constructed, assuming that the distribution is known except for t, and then how to estimate the distribution.

For any $a, b \geq 0$ such that

$$\Pr[E > a] + \Pr[E < -b] \leq \alpha, \tag{12.25}$$

$c = [m-a, m+b]$ is a confidence interval with confidence level $1-\alpha$. To see that this construction meets the definition, observe that the experimentally measured value m is an instance of M, so $C = [M - a, M + b]$. Rearranging the above inequality, we have

$$\Pr[t + E > t + a] + \Pr[t + E < t - b] \leq \alpha, \tag{12.26}$$

$$\Pr[M > t + a] + \Pr[M < t - b] \leq \alpha, \tag{12.27}$$

$$\Pr[t < M - a] + \Pr[t > M + b] \leq \alpha. \tag{12.28}$$

Typically a and b are chosen such that $a = b$, yielding a symmetric interval around m. In some circumstances a or b may be set to be a known limiting value such as 0 or ∞, yielding a *one-sided* or *single-tailed* interval.

Given an estimate of the distribution of E, calculating the confidence interval is straightforward. For a symmetric interval, which assumes the underlying distribution to be symmetric, we find $a = b$ such that

$$\Pr[E < -b] \leq \frac{\alpha}{2}. \tag{12.29}$$

For an asymmetric distribution the quasi-symmetric interval is yielded by finding a and b such that

$$\Pr[E < -b] \leq \frac{\alpha}{2}, \qquad \Pr[-E < -a] \leq \frac{\alpha}{2}. \tag{12.30}$$

For the normal distribution these values are given directly by the inverse cumulative density function Φ^{-1}. For binomial and empirical distributions, appropriate values may be found by using binary search.

Estimating the distribution

The overwhelming majority of reported IR results consider only that the topics vary from measurement to measurement, with the documents and relevance assessments fixed. This assumption — that the choice of topics represents the only source of chance — renders the problem amenable to classical estimates of precision. More sophisticated estimation methods are necessary to account for chance differences in documents or relevance assessments. Such methods have been proposed for IR (Savoy, 1997; Cormack and Lynam, 2006; Voorhees, 2000), but are not commonly used.

The estimation techniques we consider here assume that the individual documents, topics, or relevance assessments used in a particular measurement are selected independently and at random from a hypothetical infinite population of similar documents, topics, or relevance assessments. For exposition, we assume that only one class (documents, topics, or relevance assessments) differs from one measurement to the next, while the others are held constant. We refer to the elements that vary as individuals (denoted i), to the set of individuals used in a particular measurement as a sample s, and to the population of individuals simply as the population P.

Under the assumptions stated above, our measure m may be characterized as a function f applied to the sample s:

$$m = f(s). \tag{12.31}$$

A sample from the set of all possible samples may be viewed as a uniformly distributed random variable S, and $M = f(S)$ as a dependent variable. At this point we make no assumptions about f other than that it is a function in the mathematical sense: Its value depends on the sample and nothing else.

Classical estimation

The classical approach imposes the assumption that f is the mean of some elementary function g applied to each individual; that is,

$$f(s) = \frac{1}{|s|} \cdot \sum_{i \in s} g(i). \tag{12.32}$$

For example, if we consider the individuals to be topics, the assumption is met by $f = \text{MAP}$ and $g = \text{AP}$. When the classical assumption is not met, it may be possible to transform f into an amenable pair f' and g', using a bijective *transfer function* t:

$$f'(y) = \mathsf{t}(f(y)), \qquad g'(x) = \mathsf{t}(g(x)). \tag{12.33}$$

For example, GMAP is the geometric mean, rather than the arithmetic mean, of the sample AP values. The logarithm is a suitable transfer function, so $f' = \log(\text{MAP})$ and $g' = \log(\text{AP})$ meet the assumptions. Transfer functions such as *log* and *logit* find common use among values such as AP that fall within the range $[0, 1]$. An alternative is to use the binomial distribution (see Section 12.3.6).

If f conforms to this assumption, the population mean $\mathrm{E}[g(P)]$ is synonymous with the true value $t = \mathrm{E}[M] = \mathrm{E}[f(S)] = \mathrm{E}[g(P)]$. The population distribution $g(P)$ is assumed to be normal with population variance $\sigma_{g(P)}^2$. The population standard deviation $\sigma_{g(P)}$ is almost always referred to simply as "the standard deviation".

The sample s yields an empirical distribution $\{g(i) : i \in s\}$ from which the (population) standard deviation is estimated. This estimate is in turn used to compute the *standard error* σ_E, and hence the confidence interval. A naïve approach is to use the empirical sample variance as our estimate of the population variance $\sigma_s^2 \approx \sigma_{g(P)}^2$. The error variance is then $\sigma_E^2 = \sigma_M^2 = \frac{\sigma_{g(P)}^2}{|s|} \approx \frac{\sigma_s^2}{|s|}$. Given this estimate of variance, confidence intervals may be computed using the inverse normal distribution.

The naïve approach involves two approximation errors that manifest themselves for small sample sizes. First, the sample variance is not the best estimate of population variance, as is

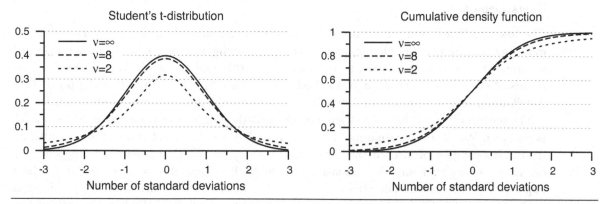

Figure 12.3   Probability density and cumulative density for Student's t-distribution with degrees of freedom $\nu = 2$, $\nu = 8$, and $\nu = \infty$ (the t-distribution with $\nu = \infty$ is equivalent to the Gaussian distribution).

illustrated by the extreme case of a sample size $|s| = 1$. The empirical distribution s has variance $\sigma^2 = 0$, which is surely not a good estimate. In the vernacular, "sample size of 1" is a synonym of "measurement of unknown precision". For small $|s| > 1$, there is still a problem, as illustrated by the case of $|s| = 2$. In this case, it is not hard to show that $\sigma_s \approx \frac{1}{2}\sigma_{g(P)}$. Generalizing, we arrive at the better estimate, familiar from introductory statistics texts:

$$\sigma_P^2 \approx \frac{\sum_{i \in s}(i - \mu_s)^2}{|s| - 1}. \tag{12.34}$$

Note that this formula differs from that for σ_s^2 only in that the denominator is $\nu = |s| - 1$ instead of $|s|$, where ν is the *degrees of freedom*.

A second approximation error derives from uncertainty in measuring σ_s^2. The formula above assumes that σ_s^2 is the "true" variance, in the sense of truth we have previously introduced. If we use any particular value and the associated normal distribution Φ_{0,σ^2}, the confidence interval will reflect the error in σ_s^2. For $N = |s| > 30$, the error is unlikely to be noticed, but for $N \leq 30$ it may be noticeable. The *t-distribution* developed by William Sealy Gosset, compensates for this effect. Gosset published under the pseudonym *The Student* because he worked for the Guinness brewing company, which considered his discoveries to be trade secrets. Student's t-distribution (Figure 12.3) is the average of all Φ_{0,σ_s^2} weighted by the probability distribution of σ_s^2 with ν degrees of freedom. That is, the t-score is an estimate of the "true" distribution in the same sense of truth. Recall that sample size $N = \nu + 1$.

The procedure for computing confidence intervals is identical to that of the naïve method, except that the cumulative t-distribution with $\nu = N - 1$ is used instead of Φ. Like Φ the computation of t is best deferred to mathematical software. Unless otherwise stated, reported results and statistics packages may be assumed to use this classical estimation method. For $N \leq 30$, the t-distribution should be used; for $N > 30$, Φ is fine.

Bootstrapping

The *bootstrap* (Efron and Tibshirani, 1993) is a method for simulating an empirical distribution modeling $f(S)$ by sampling the sample s. Because "sampling the sample" is somewhat awkward sounding, the process is referred to as *resampling*. Although the bootstrap can emulate the results of classical estimation, it is not bound by its assumptions about f or the population distribution, and is therefore applicable in situations in which the classical method is not.

The process of resampling is very simple: We treat the sample s as a surrogate for the source population. We then generate a multiset $R = \{r_j \mid 1 \le j \le k\}$ of independent and identically distributed samples of s, each the same size as s ($|r_j| = |s|$) is created. The independence condition implies that some individuals from s might be repeated in some r_j, whereas others might be absent. That is, individuals in r_j are drawn from s with replacement. The assumption is that repeated individuals act as surrogates for other members of the hypothetical infinite population that are indistinguishable in the computation of f. For example, in counting white and black mice it would make no difference whether we counted a particular black mouse ten times or ten different black mice once.

Once R is created, confidence intervals may be computed from the empirical distribution $f(R)$ in one of two ways:

1. By estimating $\sigma_M = \sigma_{f(S)} \approx \sigma_{f(R)}$ and using the cumulative normal distribution Φ as described above

2. By computing a very large number of auxiliary samples ($|R| \gg 100$) and using the cumulative empirical distribution directly (that is, $\Pr[f(S) < x] \approx \Pr[f(R) < x]$).

12.3.3 Comparative Evaluation

Let us return to our main goal of measuring the effectiveness of IR methods and generalize the results using statistical inference. In practice we are often interested not so much in measuring the effectiveness of a system in isolation as we are in comparing it with others. The results and confidence intervals shown in Table 12.1 (page 416) give us a general impression of the relative performances of the individual methods listed in the table. However, with the exception of Cosine with raw TF (Section 2.2.1), which is clearly outperformed by the three methods at the bottom of the table, these results do not allow us to infer with confidence that any particular method is better than any other.

Let m_A be the measured effectiveness of system A and m_B the measured effectiveness of system B. Provided m_A and m_B are measured under similar conditions, $m_A > m_B$ may be taken as evidence that A is more effective than B. But it gives no indication of the following:

- How much more effective is A than B?
- Is the difference substantive?
- How strong is the evidence that the difference is substantive?

Table 12.2 Pairwise comparisons of MAP results for various ranking functions, along with 95% confidence intervals and p-values indicating the significance levels of the individual differences.

Method A	Method B	MAP$_{A-B}$ (95% c.i.)	p-value
		TREC45 (1998)	
LMD	DFR	0.010 (-0.002 - 0.021)	0.09
DFR	BM25	0.005 (-0.004 - 0.013)	0.29
BM25	Cosine (TF docs)	0.046 (0.018 - 0.075)	0.002
Cosine (TF docs)	Cosine	0.006 (-0.021 - 0.033)	0.66
Cosine	Proximity	0.002 (-0.036 - 0.040)	0.92
Proximity	Cosine (raw TF)	0.018 (-0.021 - 0.056)	0.36

A measure of the difference, $m_{A-B} = m_A - m_B$, addresses the first question, whereas the second is addressed by considering how large a difference is necessary to distinguish A from B within the context of its intended purpose. For example, when comparing the height of two people, it is hard to imagine a situation in which a difference of less than 1mm would matter, so we would consider any such difference insubstantive. If we measured carefully enough, we could perhaps determine the difference between two people whose height differed by less than 1mm, but the conclusion that "A is taller than B" would be incorrect for most purposes. The third question — regarding the strength of the evidence — is addressed by a confidence interval for the measured difference. If the confidence interval contains only substantive differences, we may conclude with confidence $1 - \alpha$ that A is substantively better than B. If it contains only insubstantive differences, we may conclude with confidence $1 - \alpha$ that A is insubstantively different from B. If it contains both substantive and insubstantive differences, the proportion reflects the balance of probability.

Table 12.2 shows the results of comparing systems from Table 12.1, ranked by MAP for TREC topics 351–400. The differences between consecutively ranked systems are given, with confidence intervals and p-values estimated using the classical method discussed below.

Significance

The strength of the evidence is sometimes expressed as *statistical significance* or, more commonly, *significance*. "Significant difference" means that the $1 - \alpha$ confidence interval does not contain 0; that is, it indicates strong evidence that there is some difference, regardless of whether or not the difference is substantive. Without an estimate of the difference or substantiveness, significance alone conveys little useful information. Significance does not imply substantiveness: A "significant" measurement may be strong evidence of insubstantiality, or strong evidence of substantiality, or neither.

P-values

An alternative to reporting a confidence level with some fixed significance level α (typically 0.05) is to report a significance estimate or *p-value*. For a given measurement p is the smallest α such that the result is significant with significance level α. Put another way, it is the α value for the largest confidence interval that does not include 0. Coupled with a measure of the difference $m_A - m_B$, the p-value simply recasts the same precision estimate afforded by the confidence interval. The confidence interval holds α constant and computes the size of the interval; the p-value computes α for a specific interval that includes $m_A - m_B$ and is bounded by 0 on one side. Confidence intervals and p-values are computed using exactly the same cumulative probability estimate. There is no harm in reporting both, because they provide different views of the same precision estimate. A p-value should never be reported without a quantitative estimate of $m_A - m_B$ for the reasons illustrated above (and expanded upon in the next section).

Although p-values are commonly applied to differences, p may be computed for any measurement m. A two-sided p-value is the significance level α for the symmetric or quasi-symmetric confidence interval $c = (0, x]$ or $c = [x, 0)$, whichever contains m. For a symmetric interval we have $x = 2m$. The difference m_{A-B} necessarily yields a symmetric interval, provided A and B are selected independently from a common population.

A one-sided p-value presupposes that $t \geq 0$ (i.e., it assumes that the "true" value of the effect being measured is greater than 0) and chooses α such that $c = (0, \infty]$. In general (assuming the underlying distribution is symmetric or quasi-symmetric), the two-sided p-value is exactly double the one-sided p-value for the same experiment. It is important to note whether a p-value is one-sided or two-sided, and it is important that one-sided p-values be used only when the hypothesis that $t \geq 0$ is explicitly formulated prior to the measurement. Once m, the outcome of the measurement, is known, it is too late to form such a hypothesis. In particular, if A and B are selected at random from a common population, it is *never* appropriate to use a one-sided p-value to estimate the significance of m_{A-B}.

Despite these problems, one-sided p-values can be useful in assessing substantiveness. Consider the situation in which we wish to determine whether or not $t_{A-B} > \delta$, where δ is the minimum amount we consider substantive. The one-sided p-value for $t' = t_{A-B} - \delta$ allows us to assess whether the evidence that A is substantively better than B is significant.

The methodology presented here is well established in fields such as medicine. The measured difference is referred to as *effect size*, and substantiveness is known as *substantive significance* or *clinical significance*. In medicine, results are no longer publishable unless the hypothesis and predicted outcome, along with methods and measures to test the outcomes, are submitted to a public registry prior to conducting the experiment (De Angelis et al., 2004). This standard helps assure that hypotheses and the methods to test them are sound and subject to review. The collective body of evidence, materialized in the registry, grows more compelling with every experiment.

12.3.4   Hypothesis Tests Considered Harmful

As illustrated in the previous section, a measure of the difference between systems, coupled with an estimate of the precision of that measurement (e.g., in the form of a confidence interval), provides much more insight than an estimate of whether or not the difference is "significant with significance level α" for some arbitrarily chosen α. The use of such an estimate, known as a *hypothesis test*, should be avoided and is no longer accepted practice in fields such as medicine.

Hypothesis tests arise from the misinterpretation of a philosophical debate nearly a century ago between Ronald Fisher and Karl Pearson, pioneers of modern statistics. The basic idea is sound: Before performing any measurement, you should decide what you are looking for. Call your shot, so to speak. More formally, the scientific method, espoused by the influential philosopher of science Karl Popper, demands that you form a falsifiable *research hypothesis*, then use this research hypothesis to predict an event that is unlikely if the hypothesis is untrue. If the event occurs as predicted, confidence in the research hypothesis is increased. It is always possible that the event occurs for some reason other than the hypothesis being true; α is an estimated upper bound on the probability that the event occurs by chance.

The research hypothesis is often called the *alternative hypothesis*, denoted H_A. The alternative hypothesis stands in opposition to the *null hypothesis*, denoted H_0, which supposes that the predicted event e occurs by chance. A significant result asserts that

$$\Pr[e \,|\, H_0] \leq \alpha \,. \tag{12.35}$$

The all-too-common abuse of hypothesis tests derives from several factors:

1. Assumption of the vacuous hypothesis that $t_A \neq t_B$ (i.e., $t_{A-B} \neq 0$). The difference t_{A-B} is typically a real number with a continuous distribution, so $\Pr[t_A = t_B | A \neq B] \approx 0$. That is, H_0 is false by definition. All you need is an experiment with enough precision of measurement to show it.

2. A better alternative hypothesis is that $t_A > t_B$, which at least gives the null hypothesis $H_0 \equiv t_A \leq t_B$ a fighting chance. But it is all too common to measure m_A and m_B first, then to form the hypothesis based on observing $m_A > m_B$ and to claim significance based on a single-tailed test. Such a claim is deceptive, because it in fact tests the compound hypothesis $m_A > m_b \lor m_A < m_B$, which is equivalent to our vacuous hypothesis $m_A \neq m_B$, under-reporting α by a factor of 2. This is not to say that the inappropriate use of a single-tailed test is repaired by doubling α: Without the prior hypothesis $t_A > t_B$, the single-tailed test is fundamentally useless, just like the two-tailed test. The result of bad science cannot be repaired by any simple adjustment.

3. The verdict of "significant" or "not significant" relative to the fixed significance threshold α gives no indication of the weight of the evidence or, in the case of "not significant", even the polarity of the evidence. That is, whether it is evidence, albeit weak evidence, supporting or falsifying the alternative hypothesis.

4. Beyond the fact that a categorical verdict ("significant" or "not significant") fails to communicate information that is derivable from its underlying precision estimate, it is susceptible to many specious interpretations that are commonplace:

- It is *incorrect* to conclude that a significant result proves the alternative hypothesis.

- It is *incorrect* to conclude that a significant result shows that the alternative hypothesis is true with probability $\geq 1 - \alpha$.

- It is *incorrect* to conclude that a significant result shows that the null hypothesis is false with probability $\geq 1 - \alpha$.

- It is *incorrect* to conclude that a nonsignificant result is evidence against the alternative hypothesis.

- It is *incorrect* to conclude that a nonsignificant result yields no evidence in favor of the alternative hypothesis.

- It is *incorrect* to disregard nonsignificant results in forming an overall evaluation of an alternative hypothesis.

- It is *incorrect* to use significance as an estimate of the effect size.

- It is *incorrect* to use significance as an estimate of substantiveness of the result.

The correct use of hypothesis tests is to avoid categorical statements of significance altogether. A measure of the difference, coupled with a confidence interval or quantitative estimate of significance (p-value), provides strictly more information. Unfortunately, a large body of published IR research exists that reports the outcome of a hypothesis test, but no p-values or confidence intervals. When trying to interpret such results, some information may be salvaged:

- Look for an estimate of the magnitude of the difference, then determine whether this difference, if true, is substantive. If separate measurements are available, an estimate of the difference may be obtained by simple subtraction.

- Determine the number u of discarded nonsignificant results from the same study or experiment. Apply a *Bonferroni correction* to yield $p < (u + 1) \cdot \alpha$. This correction assumes the hypothesis H that any of the $u + 1$ results is true, so H_0 is that none of them are. Assuming H_0 to be true, each result may be deemed "significant" with probability α. The combined probability of some result being "significant" therefore may be as high as

$$1 - (1 - \alpha)^{u+1} \approx (u + 1) \cdot \alpha, \qquad (12.36)$$

for small α. Hence, the collective weight of evidence for H is $p < (u + 1) \cdot \alpha$. If many of the results are significant, or if the results are correlated (as in the case of related measures or the paired differences among ranked results), more sophisticated methods, such as the Bonferroni-Holm correction (Holm, 1979), may yield a tighter estimate.

12.3.5 Paired and Unpaired Differences

The naïve way to measure m_{A-B} is to compute m_A and m_B separately, and then to calculate $m_{A-B} = m_A - m_B$. The precision of m_{A-B} may be estimated from separate parametric estimates for m_A and m_B by summing the variances of their error distributions:

$$\sigma^2_{E_{A-B}} = \sigma^2_{E_A} + \sigma^2_{E_B}. \tag{12.37}$$

A rough estimate of the two-tailed p-value may be obtained from the measurements and their corresponding $1 - \alpha$ confidence intervals m_A, c_A, m_B, and c_B. If $m_A \in c_B$ or $m_B \in c_A$, we know that $p \gg \alpha$. If $c_A \cap c_B = \emptyset$, we know that $p \ll \alpha$. Given c_A and c_B, we may estimate the standard error σ_{E_A} and σ_{E_B} for each from their sizes, effectively reversing their computation. As a rule of thumb, if $|c_A \cap c_B| < \frac{1}{2\sqrt{2}}|m_A - m_B|$ (that is, the intervals overlap less than $\frac{1}{3}$ of the distance between m_A and m_B), we may assume that $p < \alpha$. More precisely, if the size of each interval is divided by $\sqrt{2}$, these smaller intervals touch but do not overlap when $p = \alpha$.

The paired-difference method takes advantage of the standard assumption (Section 12.3.2) that m_A and m_B are both means over the same sample s; that is,

$$m_A = f_A(s) = \frac{1}{|s|} \cdot \sum_{i \in s} g_A(i), \tag{12.38}$$

$$m_B = f_B(s) = \frac{1}{|s|} \cdot \sum_{i \in s} g_B(i). \tag{12.39}$$

Under this assumption the difference may be computed in two different ways, yielding estimates m_{A-B} and m'_{A-B}, which are identical for the sample s but which have error terms E and E' with different distributions.

$$m_{A-B} = f_A(s) - f_B(s) = \frac{1}{|s|} \cdot \sum_{i \in s} g_A(i) - \frac{1}{|s|} \cdot \sum_{i \in s} g_B(i) = \frac{1}{|s|} \cdot \sum_{i \in s} g_{A-B}(i), \tag{12.40}$$

$$m'_{A-B} = f(s) = \frac{1}{|s|} \cdot \sum_{i \in s} (g_A(i) - g_B(i)) = \frac{1}{|s|} \cdot \sum_{i \in s} g_{A-B}(i), \tag{12.41}$$

where $g_{A-B}(x) = g_A(x) - g_B(x)$.

In most situations $g_A(i)$ and $g_B(i)$ are strongly positively correlated, so although $m'_{A-B} = m_{A-B}$, the variance of the error is substantially smaller:

$$\sigma^2_{E'} \approx \frac{\sigma^2_{g_{A-B}(s)}}{|s| - 1} \ll \sigma^2_E \approx \frac{\sigma^2_{g_A(s)} + \sigma^2_{g_B(s)}}{|s| - 1}. \tag{12.42}$$

The paired-difference method yields much tighter confidence intervals for the same α, and a much smaller p-value for the same difference.

Table 12.3 Comparing BM25 and LMD on TREC topics 351–358. m_{BM25} and m_{LMD} denote the measured effectiveness (AP) of the respective method on each of the eight topics. $m_{BM25-LMD}$ denotes the per-topic difference, which underlies the t-test. The rows labeled w_{AB} and r_{AB} give the win rate and signed-rank surrogate measures underlying the sign test and the Wilcoxon test respectively.

Topic ID	351	352	353	354	355	356	357	358
m_{BM25}	0.343	0.040	0.223	0.114	0.078	0.012	0.294	0.134
m_{LMD}	0.409	0.045	0.311	0.105	0.149	0.019	0.311	0.105
$m_{BM25-LMD}$	-0.066	-0.005	-0.088	$+0.009$	-0.071	-0.007	-0.017	$+0.029$
w_{AB}	0	0	0	1	0	0	0	1
r_{AB}	-6	-1	-8	$+3$	-7	-2	-4	$+5$

12.3.6 Significance Tests

Table 12.3 shows an example measurement result that will guide us through three classical methods of computing p-values for paired differences: the t-test, the sign test, and the Wilcoxon signed-rank test. In general a p-value for a difference is computed in much the same way as a confidence interval for the difference: by estimating the cumulative error probability and using it to solve for p. For one-sided significance

$$p = \Pr[E_{A-B} \geq m_{A-B}] \qquad (12.43)$$

where, as before, E_{A-B} is the error of the measurement, and for two-sided significance

$$p = \Pr[|E_{A-B}| \geq |m_{A-B}|]. \qquad (12.44)$$

That is,

$$p = \Pr[E_{A-B} \geq |m_{A-B}|] + \Pr[E_{A-B} \leq -|m_{A-B}|]. \qquad (12.45)$$

From these formulations it is apparent that the one-sided p-value is the probability that chance accounts for a positive difference at least as large as the measured value m_{A-B}, and the two-sided p-value is the probability that chance accounts for any difference whose magnitude is at least as large as m_{A-B}. It is further apparent that the two-sided p-value is double the one-sided p-value for a symmetric distribution, as is common for the distribution of the difference between two similar measurements.

The t-test

The naïve method of computing the variance of E_{A-B} (Equation 12.37) may be used to compute p-values as described above. This method is useful for combining results when the raw data are not available or when the measure is not a sample mean. But if m_A and m_B are sample means, and if the empirical distributions over which they are means are available (as in Table 12.3),

Table 12.4   Summary statistics and test outcomes derived from the individual system comparisons in Table 12.3. The individual means and distribution estimates are given for reference. The naïve method, unpaired t-test, and paired t-test estimate the precision of the difference using the t distribution and different variance estimates. The sign test uses the win rate and the binomial distribution. The Wilcoxon test uses the signed-rank sum and the corresponding t-distribution. Precision estimates, where meaningful, are given as 95% confidence intervals and as p-values (two-sided).

Measure	Error distribution	Estimate	Test	p-value
m_{BM25}	t ($\nu = 7$, $\sigma = 0.12$)	0.155 (0.05, 0.26)		
m_{LMD}	t ($\nu = 7$, $\sigma = 0.14$)	0.182 (0.06, 0.30)		
$m_{BM25-LMD}$	t ($\nu = 7$, $\sigma = 0.18$)	−0.027 (−0.4, 0.33)	Eq. 12.37	0.9
$m_{BM25-LMD}$	t ($\nu = 14$, $\sigma = 0.07$)	−0.027 (−0.17, 0.11)	unpaired t	0.7
$m_{BM25-LMD}$	t ($\nu = 7$, $\sigma = 0.015$)	−0.027 (−0.06, 0.01)	paired t	0.1
$w_{BM25-LMD}$	binomial ($N = 8$, $q = 0.5$)	0.25 (0.03, 0.65)	sign	0.3
$r_{BM25-LMD}$	Wilcoxon T ($N = 8$)	−20	Wilcoxon	0.2

they may be combined to yield a better estimate of $\sigma^2_{E_{A-B}}$ and hence a smaller p-value. The (unpaired) t-test effectively computes the mean of the union of the two distributions, complementing the values corresponding to m_B. The resulting empirical distribution is doubled in size (assuming equal sample sizes), nearly halving the $\sigma^2_{E_{A-B}}$ and doubling the number of degrees of freedom $\nu_{E_{A-B}}$ over the naïve method. The resulting parameter estimates and p-values may be compared in Table 12.4. The net effect is that the naïve method's $p = 0.9$ is reduced to $p = 0.7$ by the t-test.

The paired t-test uses exactly the method of paired differences detailed in Section 12.3.5. If the conditions for its use are met, it almost certainly will yield a better estimate of precision than the unpaired t-test (for Table 12.4, $p = 0.1$). For this reason, the paired t-test is one of the commonest tests in IR.

The t-test and paired t-test rely on the assumption that the error E is normally distributed. When m is the mean of a large sample, this assumption is reasonable, because the *central limit theorem* states that the mean of N independent variables with the same (but not necessarily normal) distribution and variance $\sigma < \infty$ approaches a normal distribution with variance $\frac{\sigma}{N}$ as N approaches infinity.

The only reasons *not* to use the t-test are that m is not a sample mean or that N is too small to yield a good approximation of the normal distribution. In most of these circumstances the bootstrap provides a viable alternative. The reason that the bootstrap is absent from the the classical list of named tests is that although methods like it are ancient, its use as a formal statistical tool is relatively new; perhaps because it is too computationally intensive to have been considered practical when the classical tests were developed.

The sign test and the Wilcoxon signed-rank test

Instead of m_{A-B}, the sign test and the Wilcoxon test use a surrogate measure $\hat{m}_{A-B} \approx t_{A-B}$, where $\approx$ is interpreted quite loosely as

$$\Pr[\operatorname{sgn}(\hat{m}_{A-B}) = \operatorname{sgn}(t_{A-B})] \gg 0.5 \,. \tag{12.46}$$

For this reason these tests are more applicable to their historical role of hypothesis testing than to estimating the magnitude of the difference. They quantify the degree of evidence that a difference exists but yield marginal insight into the magnitude of the difference. Although the sign test and the Wilcoxon test measure the wrong quantity, so to speak, they may be applicable when the assumptions of the paired t-test are not met.

For a sign test, the underlying measure is in its own right a measure, albeit a different one, of the relative effectiveness of IR systems. It is the *win rate*

$$w_{AB} \;=\; \frac{|\{i \in s \mid g_{A-B}(i) > 0\}|}{|\{i \in s \mid g_{A-B}(i) \neq 0\}|}\,, \tag{12.47}$$

for g_{A-B} defined previously. The meaning of $w_{AB} > 0.5$ is that A is more effective than B in more than half of all measurements. A suitable surrogate measure is easily derived from w_{AB}:

$$\hat{m}_{A-B} \;=\; w_{AB} - 0.5 \,. \tag{12.48}$$

The random variable W_{AB}, of which w_{AB} is an instance, has a binomial distribution with parameters $N = |s|$ and $q = t_{AB} = \mathrm{E}[W_{AB}]$, the true win rate. The distribution of the error term $E_{AB} = W_{AB} - t_{AB}$ depends heavily on the unknown t_{AB}. To estimate a one-sided p-value, we assume the worst case and choose t_{AB} so as to maximize

$$p \;=\; \Pr[t_{AB} + E_{AB} \geq w_{AB}]\,. \tag{12.49}$$

It is not difficult to show that $t_{AB} = q = 0.5$ maximizes p, which is the result of the one-sided sign test. For a two-sided test we double the result.

We note that $w_{AB} = 0$ and $w_{AB} = 1$ are special cases for which a one-sided p-value is appropriate, even when two-sided values are used otherwise. This is because $w_{AB} < 0$ and $w_{AB} > 1$ are known in advance to be impossible. When confidence intervals are used, the one-sided interval should be calculated to yield the specified confidence level $1 - \alpha$.

For the eight topics in Table 12.3, there are two topics with $m_{\mathrm{BM25-LMD}} > 0$ and six topics with $m_{\mathrm{BM25-LMD}} < 0$, so $w_{AB} = 0.25$ and $\hat{m}_{A-B} = -0.25$. From the binomial distribution with $N = 8$ and $q = 0.5$, we have

$$p \;=\; \Pr[|E| \geq |-0.25|] \;=\; 2 \cdot \Pr[W_{AB} \leq 0.25] \;\approx\; 0.3 \,. \tag{12.50}$$

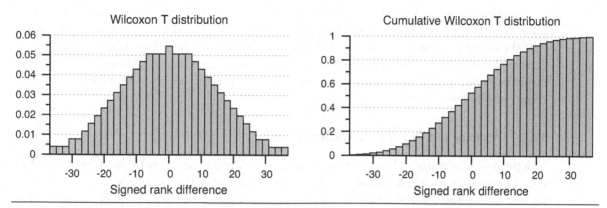

Figure 12.4 Wilcoxon T signed-rank sum distribution and cumulative distribution for $N = 8$.

The Wilcoxon test uses as a surrogate for m_{A-B} the signed-rank difference

$$r_{AB} = \sum_{i \in s} rnk(g_{A-B}(i)) \cdot \text{sgn}(g_{A-B}(i)), \qquad (12.51)$$

where $rnk(x) = |\{i \mid x \leq g_{A-B}(i)\}|$, under the simplifying assumption that $g_{A-B}(i) \neq g_{A-B}(j)$, if $i \neq j$. Relaxing this assumption introduces surprising complexity into the analysis, but for practical purposes it often makes sense to break ties at random or to assign the average rank:

$$rnk(x) = \frac{1}{2} + \frac{1}{2} \cdot |\{i \mid x = g_{A-B}(i)\}| + |\{i \mid x < g_{A-B}(i)\}|. \qquad (12.52)$$

The test models the assumption that the relative magnitude of the differences matters (although not their exact values) and that, for instance, $m_{\text{BM25}-\text{LMD}} = -0.066$ (topic 351) is more important than $m_{\text{BM25}-\text{LMD}} = +0.009$ (topic 354). It proceeds by sorting all differences in increasing order of absolute value and assigning integer weights to them according to their rank in the sorted list. For example, the difference for topic 352 receives weight 1 because it is the smallest difference among the eight topics in the table, whereas the difference for topic 353 receives weight 8. The test then computes the sum of the weights, counting weights as positive or negative, depending on the sign of the corresponding difference:

$$r_{AB} = -6 + 1 - 8 + 3 - 7 - 2 - 4 = -20. \qquad (12.53)$$

The distribution of possible signed-rank differences for a given N is called the *Wilcoxon T distribution* (shown in Figure 12.4). The cumulative probability may be computed by enumerating all 2^N possible outcomes. For this example, of the $2^8 = 256$ possible outcomes there are 50 of magnitude 20 or larger. The Wilcoxon test therefore reports a p-value of $50/256 \approx 0.2$.

A p-value based on a surrogate measure should be accompanied by an estimate of the true difference. The writer should make clear which test was used, and the reader should be aware that the actual difference estimate has unknown precision. In conjunction with a substantiveness threshold δ, surrogate tests are more informative. A surrogate test that determines with high confidence that $m_{A-B} > \delta$ is more useful than a surrogate test that determines with high confidence that $m_{A-B} > 0$.

12.3.7 Validity and Power of Statistical Tests

The purpose of a statistical test is to estimate the likelihood that a particular measurement m may be explained by chance. The test is valid if it estimates this likelihood as it is supposed to, and is powerful if the estimate is small when the measurement is not in fact due to chance. Together, validity and power characterize the test's suitability for its intended purpose. Validity is often simply assumed, and power is estimated using *power analysis* which itself assumes validity. We consider the design of a meta-experiment to determine the validity and power of statistical tests for the purpose of comparing IR systems.

Consider an IR experiment $x = \langle A_x, B_x, s \rangle$ that measures the difference in effectiveness between systems A_x and B_x, using topic set s. Let m_x be the measured difference according to an effectiveness measure such as MAP. Let p_x or c_x be the corresponding p-value or confidence interval computed using some statistical test.

Let $X_x = \langle A_x, B_x, S \rangle$ be an independent experiment comparing the same two systems using the same method and a different set of topics S, where $|S| = |s|$. Further, let M_x be the difference between A_x and B_x measured using S. The true value t_x of this difference is

$$t_x = \mathrm{E}[M_x]. \tag{12.54}$$

The computation of p_x uses an underlying model $\mathcal{M}_x$ that approximates the cumulative probability distribution of the error term $E_x = M_x - t_x$:

$$\mathcal{M}_x(e) \approx \Pr[E_x \le e]. \tag{12.55}$$

If Equation 12.55 holds within a reasonable tolerance for all x and for all e, the p-value or confidence interval derived from it is correct, and we say the statistical test is valid.

In general, t_x is unknown, so validity must be established indirectly. Suppose we have $X_x^{[1]}$ and $X_x^{[2]}$ which are independent copies of X_x. The corresponding measurements $M_x^{[1]}$ and $M_x^{[2]}$ are identically distributed, as are the error terms $E_x^{[1]}$ and $E_x^{[2]}$. Now consider the difference

$$D_x = E_x^{[1]} - E_x^{[2]} = (M_x^{[1]} - t_x) - (M_x^{[2]} - t_x) = M_x^{[1]} - M_x^{[2]}. \tag{12.56}$$

Given a model $\mathcal{M}_x^{[1]}$ derived from $X_x^{[1]}$, we may derive a model $\mathcal{D}_x^{[1]}$ for D_x, and validate $\mathcal{D}_x^{[1]}$ by comparing it with the empirical distribution yielded by a meta-experiment. If $\mathcal{D}_x^{[1]}(d) \approx \Pr[D_x \le d]$ for representative values of x and d, we may infer with high confidence that $\mathcal{D}_x$, and hence $\mathcal{M}_x$, are valid for all x.

Assuming the test to be valid, its power with respect to significance level α is

$$power_\alpha \;=\; \Pr[p_x \leq \alpha \,|\, \overline{H_0}]\,. \tag{12.57}$$

For a two-tailed test $H_0 \equiv t_x = 0$, so power may be estimated empirically with respect to a sample of experiments where $t_x \neq 0$. Such a sample is well approximated by one in which $m_x \neq 0$ because it is extremely unlikely that $t_x = 0$ when $m_x \neq 0$, and the possibility may be discounted. For a one-tailed test, either $H_0 \equiv t_x \leq 0$ or $H_0 \equiv t_x \geq 0$ must be chosen beforehand. Under the naïve assumption that $t_x \geq 0$ and $t_x \leq 0$ are equally probable, the one-tailed power for significance level α is the same as the two-tailed power for significance level 2α.

Empirical estimates of power are useful for comparing the relative effectiveness of statistical tests because a test that is more powerful than another over one population of experiments is also likely to be more powerful over a different population. To predict the power of a particular experiment, one must use power analysis to construct a model $\mathcal{M}_x$ from the assumed population distribution, considering the number of topics $|s|$, the estimated true difference t_x, and the estimated sample variance σ_s^2.

Measuring validity and power

As an example we used the results of the TREC 2004 Robust Track to represent a population of experiments, each comparing two of the 110 runs submitted to the track using a subset of the 249 topics to compute MAP. To compare the validity and power of the t-test, sign test, and Wilcoxon test, we constructed pairs of similar experiments $\langle x^{[1]}, x^{[2]} \rangle$ where $x^{[1]} = \langle A_x, B_x, s^{[1]} \rangle$ and $x_2 = \langle A_x, B_x, s^{[2]} \rangle$; $s^{[1]}$ and $s^{[2]}$ are nonintersecting sets of 124 topics each, selected at random without replacement from the 249 used in the track. The pairs were constructed so that each distinct pair of runs occurred 32 times, for a total of $191,840$ examples. From these, 32 were eliminated because $m_x^{[1]} = 0$, leaving a total of $191,808$ pairs of experiments.

For each pair we constructed $\mathcal{M}_x^{[1]}$ and from it derived $\mathcal{D}_x^{[1]}$, which was used to estimate without reference to x_2 the probability of *discordance* between $m_x^{[1]}$ and $m_x^{[2]}$:

$$d_x \;=\; \Pr[m_x^{[1]} \cdot M_x^{[2]} < 0] \;\approx\; \mathcal{D}_x^{[1]}(-|m_x^{[1]}|)\,. \tag{12.58}$$

Although it is not possible to validate any particular d_x, if the method of computing d_x is valid, it must be the case over a large set of examples $\mathbb{X}$ that the predicted and actual discordance rates are nearly equal:

$$\hat{d} \;=\; \sum_{x \in \mathbb{X}} d_x \;\approx\; d \;=\; \frac{\left\{ x \in \mathbb{X} \mid m_x^{[1]} \cdot m_x^{[2]} < 0 \right\}}{|\mathbb{X}|}\,. \tag{12.59}$$

Using $\mathcal{M}_x^{[1]}$, we computed the single-tailed p-value p_x and with it partitioned our $191,808$ examples into 6 bins. For the test to be valid, predicted and actual discordance must be nearly

Table 12.5   T-test predicted discordance, observed discordance, and power as a function of p. Error is the amount by which the ratio of the predicted and observed discordance differs from 1. RMS error summarizes the six error estimates.

Range	Pairs	Predicted Discordance	Actual Discordance	Error
$0.00 \le p < 0.01$	131567 (68.6%)	676.5	781	-13.4%
$0.01 \le p < 0.02$	7153 (3.7%)	427.6	458	-6.6%
$0.02 \le p < 0.05$	10775 (5.6%)	1025.7	981	4.6%
$0.05 \le p < 0.10$	9542 (5.0%)	1433.2	1397	2.6%
$0.10 \le p < 0.20$	11436 (6.0%)	2592.4	2455	5.6%
$0.20 \le p < 0.50$	21335 (11.1%)	8182.5	7837	4.4%
		RMS error: 7.1%		

Table 12.6   Sign test predicted discordance, observed discordance, and power as a function of p. Error is the amount by which the ratio of the predicted and observed discordance differs from 1. RMS error summarizes the six error estimates.

Range	Pairs	Predicted Discordance	Actual Discordance	Error
$0.00 \le p < 0.01$	125875 (65.6%)	675.0	822	-17.9%
$0.01 \le p < 0.02$	9318 (4.9%)	581.1	550	5.6%
$0.02 \le p < 0.05$	10068 (5.2%)	1009.9	965	4.6%
$0.05 \le p < 0.10$	9949 (5.2%)	1524.3	1402	8.7%
$0.10 \le p < 0.20$	10300 (5.4%)	2294.6	2107	8.9%
$0.20 \le p < 0.50$	26298 (13.7%)	10293.7	8063	27.7%
		RMS error: 14.7%		

equal for every bin. If they are not, the test is invalid. If they are, we may conclude with high confidence that the test is valid for the ranges of p-values represented by the bins.

Tables 12.5 through 12.7 show the validation results for the t-test, sign test, and Wilcoxon test. Each table shows the range of p, $\hat{d}_p$, and d_p for each bin, along with prediction error as a percentage:

$$error_p \;=\; \frac{\hat{d} - d}{d} \,. \tag{12.60}$$

RMS error summarizes prediction error over the six ranges:

$$RMS\,error \;=\; \sqrt{\sum_p error_p^2} \,. \tag{12.61}$$

Table 12.7   Wilcoxon signed-rank test predicted discordance, observed discordance, and power as a function of p. Error is the amount by which the ratio of the predicted and observed discordance differs from 1. RMS error summarizes the six error estimates.

Range	Pairs	Predicted Discordance	Actual Discordance	Error
$0.00 \leq p < 0.01$	137008 (71.4%)	655.2	981	-33.2%
$0.01 \leq p < 0.02$	6723 (3.5%)	402.1	466	-13.7%
$0.02 \leq p < 0.05$	10096 (5.3%)	956.6	1027	-6.9%
$0.05 \leq p < 0.10$	8737 (4.6%)	1311.7	1382	-5.1%
$0.10 \leq p < 0.20$	10267 (5.4%)	2320.1	2444	-5.1%
$0.20 \leq p < 0.50$	18977 (9.9%)	7287.5	7609	-4.2%

RMS error: 15.3%

Overall, the predicted and actual discordance rates for the t-test are reasonable, though it appears the test is optimistic for $p < 0.01$, yielding estimates 13.4% lower than the empirical outcome. The sign and Wilcoxon tests are dramatically worse for $p < 0.01$ and for the other ranges of p as well. Overall, the t-test gives the most consistently accurate predictions and the lowest RMS error rate.

Table 12.8 shows RMS error as well as one-tailed power for $\alpha = 0.01$ and $\alpha = 0.05$ for the three tests. The Wilcoxon test appears to have the highest power; however, this advantage is offset by the fact that it is consistently too optimistic and therefore the true power is is not as high as it appears: If the p-value were more accurate, the power would be lower. The sign test has lower power and also higher error than the t-test.

Concerns that have been raised regarding the validity of the t-test are not supported by these results; on the contrary, the lower error rate suggests that the t-test is the method of choice for comparing IR systems.

Different sample sizes

The results in the example above pertain to experiments that measure the difference in MAP scores over collections with $n = 124$ topics. To evaluate the effect of different choices of n on the validity and power of the t-test, we alter the experiment so that $X_x^{[1]} = \langle A_x, B_x, s \rangle$ and $X_x^{[2]} = \langle A_x, B_x, S \rangle$ where s and S contain different numbers of topics. We choose s to be a subset of the 249 TREC topics, and S to be the remainder, so $|s| = n$, $|S| = 249 - n$. In this situation the distributions of $E_x^{[1]}$ and $E_x^{[2]}$ are not identical. Under the t-test model we have $\mu_{E_x^{[1]}} = \mu_{E_x^{[2]}} = 0$, whereas

$$\frac{\sigma^2_{E_x^{[1]}}}{\sigma^2_{E_x^{[2]}}} \approx \frac{n-1}{249-n-1}. \tag{12.62}$$

Table 12.8 Validity versus one-tailed power of statistical tests for comparing pairs of runs from the TREC 2004 Robust Track, using difference in MAP over 124 topics. As shown in Table 12.7, Wilcoxon systematically underestimates p-values and thus overestimates power.

	RMS Error	Apparent Power	
		$\alpha = 0.1$	$\alpha = 0.05$
T-test	7.1%	0.69	0.78
Sign test	14.7%	0.66	0.76
Wilcoxon test	15.3%	0.71	0.80

Therefore, $\mu_{D_x} = 0$ and

$$\sigma_{D_x}^2 \approx (1 + \frac{249 - n - 1}{n - 1}) \cdot \sigma_{E_x^{[1]}}^2. \tag{12.63}$$

Table 12.9 shows RMS error and power for various n in increments of 25. Note that the t-test is generally valid for all values of n, with RMS error generally decreasing as n increases. It is not surprising that RMS error increases somewhat for small n because the predicted discordance is based on less information. It is similarly not surprising that RMS error increases for large $n = 225$, because the small number of topics in S causes uncertainty in the calculation of actual discordance. For $n = 249$, RMS error is undefined because $|S| = 0$. The RMS error results are consistent with the validity of the t-test being invariant for $25 \leq n \leq 249$. Although validity remains invariant, power increases substantially with n, as expected.

12.3.8   Reporting the Precision of Measurement

A statistical test makes a well-defined, but commonly misunderstood, quantitative estimate of the precision of measurement, expressed as a confidence limit or p-value. Thus, it augments but does not replace the quantitative estimate itself. We regard confidence intervals as much more appealing than p-values, because they include the same information but are more intuitive and put the measurement front and center.

Hypothesis testing is never absolute, and hiding the measurement and precision estimates behind a categorical declaration of "significant" or "not significant" is a mistake. The null hypothesis of "no difference" yields no information. A proper hypothesis should predict a nonzero difference that will be considered substantive; precision estimates quantify the force of evidence that a measurement does or does not reflect such a difference.

It appears that the paired t-test, where possible, is the method of choice. In situations where only win/loss results are available, the sign test works well enough. The Wilcoxon test is not particularly intuitive and, although more powerful than the sign test and apparently more powerful than the paired t-test, it can be spectacularly wrong for small p-values. The underlying distribution does not arise naturally, and its variance is unbounded as sample size increases, so

Table 12.9 Validity versus power for the t-test using a varying number of topics n.

n	RMS Error	Power	
		$\alpha = 0.1$	$\alpha = 0.05$
25	11.4%	0.39	0.56
50	10.0%	0.53	0.67
75	6.5%	0.61	0.72
100	7.7%	0.65	0.76
125	6.8%	0.69	0.78
150	6.0%	0.71	0.80
175	3.9%	0.73	0.81
200	3.4%	0.75	0.83
225	9.2%	0.77	0.84
249	–	0.78	0.85

there is no such thing as a true (population) value of the surrogate difference: The central limit theorem does not apply. Although the Wilcoxon test is often used in situations in which the paired t-test does not apply, the bootstrap may be a better choice.

12.3.9 Meta-Analysis

Meta-analysis is the technique of combining several estimates into one, yielding an overall estimate with greater confidence.[4] A naïve approach simply applies the sign test (Section 12.3.6) to a series of statistically independent experiments or measurements, each of which renders a binary yes/no judgment. For example, if we form the hypothesis that $A > B$ and conduct four independent measurements that all show $A - B > 0$, no matter by how much, we may use the one-tailed sign test to conclude that $A > B$ ($p < .06$). The standard caveat applies to the use of one-tailed tests. If we simply observe the same result four times out of four, without having formed the prior hypotheses, the two-tailed test is appropriate, yielding the same conclusion with lower confidence: $A > B$ ($p < .13$). In general the sign test may be used to combine the results of diverse experiments that compare the same things but for which effect sizes and precision estimates are unavailable. The general approach — combining the results of separate experiments to form a common result, with an associated precision estimate — is known as *meta-analysis*. In fields such as medicine, where lives and vast sums of money are at stake, systematic meta-analysis is de jure.

---

[4] `glass.ed.asu.edu/gene/papers/meta25.html`

Table 12.10 Meta-analysis of the MAP difference between LMD (Equation 9.32) and DFR (Equations 9.51 and 9.52): $\text{MAP}_{\text{LMD}-\text{DFR}}$. The combined significance level of all experiments (0.02) is lower than the significance level of each experiment alone.

Experiment	$\text{MAP}_{\text{LMD}-\text{DFR}}$	p (two-sided t-test)
TREC 1998	0.010 (-0.002 - 0.021)	0.09
TREC 1999	0.009 (-0.006 - 0.025)	0.24
GOV2 2005	-0.004 (-0.027 - 0.020)	0.75
GOV2 2006	0.023 (-0.000 - 0.047)	0.05
Sign test	> 0 -	0.13
Fixed-effect model	0.010 (0.002 - 0.018)	0.02

Fixed-effect model meta-analysis, as detailed below, is a much more powerful approach because it harnesses the effect size and precision estimates of the individual studies — information that is lost in the sign test — to yield a much more precise overall estimate. The first four rows of Table 12.10 show the results of comparing LMD and DFR. Three of the four results show LMD to be superior; the fourth shows the opposite. None of the results is significant ($\alpha = 0.05$). The reported p-value of 0.05 was rounded from 0.051. Hairsplitting aside, it would be inappropriate to cherry-pick this result in the face of contrary evidence (albeit weak). The sign test yields $p \approx 0.13$, less than compelling evidence. The fixed-effect model, on the other hand, gives an estimate of the difference along with a precision estimate indicating $p \approx 0.02$.

The fixed-effect model combines a set of results $R = \{(m_i, \pi_i)\}$ where each m_i is an independent measurement of a quantity with a common true value t and each π_i is its precision. In our example the quantity in question is $\text{MAP}_{LMD-DFR}$ over a perhaps more diverse hypothetical population. Precision, in the context of meta-analysis, is typically expressed as the reciprocal of the variance of the measurement:

$$\pi_i = \sigma_i^{-2} . \tag{12.64}$$

Reciprocal of variance is just another method of conveying the same information as a confidence interval or p-value; one can be recast as another provided the assumed distribution is valid. In meta-analysis contexts in which the term "precision" is used without qualification to refer to a number, the reader would be safe to assume that it means reciprocal of variance.

The first step in meta-analysis is to ensure that the individual measurements use the same measure and units, and in fact measure the same thing. The second step is to recast confidence intervals or p-values as reciprocal of variance by reversing the process used to calculate them. The common estimate and its precision are computed by averaging the individual measurements, weighted by precision:

$$m = \frac{\sum_i m_i \cdot \sigma_i^{-2}}{\sum_i \sigma_i^{-2}}, \qquad \sigma^{-2} = (\sum_i \sigma_i^{-2})^{-1}. \qquad (12.65)$$

A confidence interval or p-value for the combined result may computed in the normal way, using σ and the cumulative probability distribution.

The 2008 United States presidential election presents a case study of the use and misuse of statistics. Although polls consistently reported Obama to be in the lead, pundits repeatedly pronounced that the results were "within the margin of error" or "a statistical dead heat" or "too close to call". In contrast, meta-analysis of the paired differences arising from individual state-by-state polls showed that Obama had a significant and substantive lead, and in the end predicted the outcome to within one electoral vote.[5]

12.4 Minimizing Adjudication Effort

Substantial manual effort is required to adjudicate documents to produce a set of judgments for IR evaluation. To this point in the chapter, we have assumed that judgments are complete: that a binary relevance judgment is available for each document with respect to each query. The pooling method attempts to satisfy this assumption by requiring a judgment for each document in the pool and declaring documents outside the pool to be nonrelevant. In this section we weaken this assumption, first by modifying the pooling method to reduce the number of judgments, and second by modifying our method for estimating MAP to account for unjudged documents within the pool.

The judgments (in the form of qrels) are used as a gold standard of relevance for two distinct kinds of evaluation:

1. The evaluation of the systems whose results influenced the decision on what documents to judge (e.g., the systems that participated in a given TREC task)

2. The evaluation of systems whose results did not influence that decision.

Our concern here is the efficiency and effectiveness of adjudication strategies for these two purposes. Efficiency is measured in terms of human effort, and effectiveness is measured in terms of the validity and precision of the measurement, when using the qrels as a gold standard.

---

[5] `election.princeton.edu/history-of-electoral-votes-for-obama`

Throughout this section we assume MAP to be our primary effectiveness measure. That is, the various adjudication strategies covered are examined with respect to their ability to measure the systems' "true" AP.

Before we discuss the individual strategies, it is worthwhile to consider the properties of an ideal set of qrels that yield the most precise valid measurement possible, given a set of topics, documents, and systems to be used for measurement. The ideal set of qrels would represent the true relevance of every document with respect to every topic, independent of the systems to be measured. Thus there would be no distinction between the two purposes stated above.

Any real set of qrels will necessarily depart from the ideal for two reasons: imprecision in defining relevance, and the validity and precision of methods to estimate relevance, given a particular definition. The notion of true relevance is as intangible as any notion of truth. "Satisfying the user's information need" is perhaps a close approximation, but it is impossible to know with certainty what need the user was expressing or whether that need was met. Asking the user yields an approximation with unknown validity and precision. The need of an American searching for "cancer treatment" may or may not be well served by a report published by a Mexican laetrile clinic. Assuming the user meant "established cancer treatment", and if we agree that laetrile is not an established treatment in the United States, the user's need is not met. But the user may be uncertain whether or not laetrile is an established treatment, and therefore mistaken regarding relevance. A third-party adjudicator may be more informed about the efficacy of laetrile but not know with certainty whether the user meant "established cancer treatment" or "last-hope cancer treatment".

These issues notwithstanding, human adjudication constitutes best practice for assessing relevance. Whether the human is the user or a third party, the effort involved in adjudication is substantial and one of the principal factors limiting the scope of IR evaluation efforts. The obvious approach, *exhaustive adjudication*, is to have an assessor or a team of assessors label each document in the collection as relevant or nonrelevant for each topic. For modern collections the effort required for exhaustive adjudication is prohibitive. A small TREC corpus contains 50 topics and about 500,000 documents. Exhaustive judging would require 25 million separate judgments: about 20 person-years at 30 seconds per judgment. Even so, the qrels would be imprecise because the adjudicators would make mistakes or be uncertain in many situations. Better precision could be achieved, at the expense of 40 more person-years' effort, by having three independent adjudicators label each document and use the majority opinion as the qrel. In general, more human effort yields increased precision. However, there are far more efficient strategies than exhaustive adjudication to achieve similar or better measurements.

Regardless of the level of effort, a certain number of errors in the qrels is inevitable. The substantiveness of these errors is determined by observing their impact on the validity and precision of the IR effectiveness measurements that use them.

12.4.1 Selecting Documents for Adjudication

The TREC pooling method avoids the effort of exhaustive adjudication by forming for each topic a pool of the top-ranked k documents from each system under test. Only the documents in the pool are adjudicated; all others are assumed to be nonrelevant. The typical value of $k = 100$ appears to work well for test collections with 50 topics and 500,000 documents. However, the effort of conducting an evaluation is substantial even for a collection of this size (recall from Section 12.2 that the 86,830 relevance assessments for TREC-8 would correspond to about 724 hours of assessor time, even if we allow only 30 seconds per judgment). For larger collections with more documents, more topics, or both, the effort can be prohibitive. Yet, larger collections are desirable both to simulate large-scale information retrieval tasks and to improve the precision of measurement. We investigate the efficiency and effectiveness of alternative strategies to select documents for adjudication.

A true random sample of the documents in the collection could work, but unless the sample is quite large, it will contain very few relevant documents, thus compromising its utility for measuring IR effectiveness. Instead, a biased sampling technique is used, which is more likely to yield relevant documents. The pooling method is one example of such a technique: The highly ranked documents retrieved by systems under test (i.e., those in the pool) are much more likely to be relevant than randomly selected documents. Moreover, these documents are more likely to discriminate among systems than documents — even relevant ones — with lower rank.

With any biased sampling technique there is a risk that a measurement reflects not a system's effectiveness but the extent to which it agrees with the sample bias. In particular, the systems whose results determine the pool may receive higher scores than equally effective ones whose results do not. For TREC collections with 50 topics and 500,000 documents, the bias appears insubstantive; experiments have shown that the same system receives a similar score whether or not it contributes to the pool. The net effect is that TREC collections are useful as archival benchmarks: New systems and methods may be tested using the existing qrels, and the measurements compared with others conducted using the same collection. The TREC method sets the standard against which other methods are compared.

Interactive search and judging

Interactive search and judging (ISJ) is a straightforward but effective way of selecting and adjudicating documents. A skilled searcher simply uses a search engine to find and label as many relevant documents as possible. The particular search engine does not appear to matter much; useful features include relevance feedback, the ability to amend queries to explore different aspects of the topic, a mechanism to record the judgments, and a mechanism to suppress previously adjudicated documents from further consideration. Prior to TREC 6, Cormack et al. (1998) used ISJ to form a set of qrels for the adhoc task, using proximity ranking and a user interface supporting the features described above. The process took about two hours per topic, 100 hours in total — approximately one-seventh of the TREC adjudication effort. Studies by Cormack et al. (1998) and Voorhees (2000) showed that evaluation results using these qrels were similar to the official TREC results. Shorter ISJ efforts were simulated by considering only the qrels yielded by the (chronologically) first documents examined in the larger effort. Efforts requiring an order of magnitude less effort yielded evaluation results that were also quite similar to TREC efforts. The question of "How similar is similar enough?" is addressed later.

Move-to-front pooling

Move-to-front pooling (MTF) selects documents for adjudication incrementally, giving priority to highly ranked documents from well performing systems (Cormack et al., 1998). Conceptually, the documents returned by each system are considered in sequence. Each document in turn is adjudicated, if it has not been previously, and the qrel is recorded. Documents from the system continue to be examined in sequence until r consecutive ones are found to be nonrelevant, for some r. In practice we interleave the process for all systems, using a priority queue. Whenever a relevant document is selected, the system contributing it is moved to the front of the queue. MTF selects a much higher proportion of relevant documents than the pooling method; the resulting qrels yield similar evaluation results. How similar is addressed below.

Shallow pooling

A simple way to adjust the effort associated with pooling is to alter the pooling depth k. That is, exactly k documents from each system are selected without regard to the system's performance, whereas MTF selects more from the better systems. Depth-k pooling yields a lower density of relevant documents than MTF does but still finds common use, under the assumption that it yields lower bias. In particular it has been suggested that for small k, using P@k as a surrogate for MAP might yield lower bias (Sanderson and Zobel, 2005) than using MAP directly. The rationale behind this is that when measuring MAP, the result depends on the relevance of unadjudicated documents. On the other hand, when measuring P@k using pool depth k, we know that the relevance of every document on which P@k depends is known. Thus, measuring P@k as a surrogate for MAP might yield higher precision and lower bias. As shown in our example below, this rationale is not fully supported by experience.

More or fewer topics?

A less direct way to adjust the effort of pooling is to use a collection with more or fewer topics (Sanderson and Zobel, 2005). Overall adjudication effort is roughly proportional to $k \cdot n$, where k is the pool depth and n is the number of topics (although the result overlap between different systems is usually larger at higher ranks). There is a direct trade-off between the number of documents judged per topic and the number of topics. As shown in Table 12.9 (page 439), the validity and power of system comparisons increase with n. On the other hand, these same quantities also increase with pool depth. Larger k and larger n both increase precision of measurement. The question is: For a fixed adjudication effort, is it better to use more topics and a shallow pool, or fewer topics and a deep pool? The same question applies to other approaches, such as ISJ and MTF.

Evaluating pooling strategies

In evaluating strategies for selecting documents to adjudicate, one must consider the effect on measuring system effectiveness. If the true effectiveness is known, we can use it as the basis for comparison. The best gold standard we have is a set of results derived from the pooling method and some large k. Traditionally, pooling and adjudication strategies have been evaluated only on their ability to order systems by effectiveness, so that more effective systems are ranked before less effective ones. One ranking is compared with the other, and if they are similar, the difference is deemed to be insubstantive. The assumption — with which we do not entirely agree — is that the only purpose of measuring system effectiveness is to rank systems, and that the measurements themselves (e.g., the MAP values computed according to a given strategy) are irrelevant (Buckley and Voorhees, 2005). Whether or not one accepts this premise, good system ranking is evidence of the general validity of an approach.

Two different system rankings are traditionally compared using the Kendall τ rank correlation coefficient, named after its inventor, the British statistician Maurice Kendall. τ indicates the number of *inversions* between two rankings: An inversion is a pair (x, y) such that x comes before y in one ranking and after y in the other. If the two rankings are equal, $\tau = 1$; if they are opposite, $\tau = -1$; if they are uncorrelated, $\tau \approx 0$.

In the context of IR evaluation, consider the set of systems measured by a TREC experiment. Res_1 is the gold-standard ranking according to MAP, when evaluated using the traditional pooling method with $k = 100$. Res_2 is their ranking under some alternative adjudication strategy. Without formal justification, $\tau > 0.9$ (i.e., fewer than 5% inversions) has been taken to be *good agreement* with the gold standard (Voorhees, 2000).

A serious problem with using τ is that it does not take into account the precision of measurement. As we have seen in Table 12.9, the power of measuring MAP differences for $n = 50$, $k = 100$ (the pool depth for the TREC 2004 Robust Track) is about 67% (for $\alpha = 0.05$). That is, the t-test from Section 12.3.6 is able to distinguish only 67% of all system pairs under test with $p < 0.05$. Thus we expect at least 2.8% of the pairs of systems to be ranked incorrectly, even by the gold standard. An alternative method with the same 2.8% error rate might agree perfectly with the gold standard ($\tau = 1$), or have up to 5.6% inversions ($\tau = 0.89$). A method with a 5.6% error rate might yield as few as 2.8% inversions ($\tau = 0.94$) or as many as 8.4% ($\tau = 0.83$). Kendall's τ cannot reliably distinguish between these cases.

Instead of using Kendall's τ, we report ranking differences in terms of *significant inversion rate* for some significance level α (see Cormack and Lynam, 2007; Carterette, 2009b). A *significant pair* of systems is one for which the alternative pooling/adjudication method yields a significant difference in MAP compared with the gold standard ($p < \alpha$). A *significant inversion* is a significant pair whose order is transposed between the alternative and gold-standard rankings. The significant inversion rate is the fraction of all significant pairs that are significant inversions. A method with a significant inversion rate less than α is valid, because any error due to bias is less than random error. The precision of the alternative method is measured by its power.

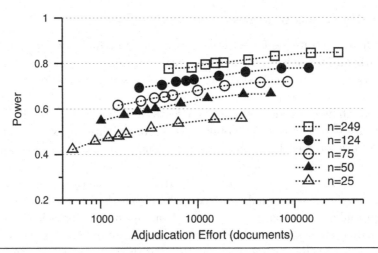

Figure 12.5   Power as a function of the number of documents judged for shallow pooling with various depths.

Overall, an alternative pooling method is good if it has high power and if its observed bias is insubstantial relative to random error.

Example experiment

We describe an example experiment to illustrate the trade-off between adjudication effort and the validity and precision of the resulting measurements (Cormack and Lynam, 2007). The alternatives compared were those mentioned above except ISJ, which cannot easily be simulated (but see Sanderson and Joho, 2004). As a function of the number of documents judged, and parameterized by the number of topics, the power and bias of alternative adjudication strategies were measured. The gold standard was the system ranking by MAP using pool depth $k = 100$. The alternative pooling methods were the following:

- shallow pooling with depth $k \leq 100$;
- using P@k as a surrogate for MAP, with pool depth $k \leq 100$;
- move-to-front pooling with a stopping condition of r consecutive nonrelevant documents.

All three methods were simulated using the runs submitted to the TREC 2004 Robust Retrieval Track (Voorhees, 2004), comprising 311,410 qrels for a total of 249 topics. To evaluate shallow pooling and move-to-front pooling, the selected qrels were used to rank the systems according to MAP and this ranking was then compared with the gold standard. To evaluate P@k as a surrogate measure, the systems were ranked by P@k instead of MAP, using pool depth k, and still compared with the gold standard ranked by MAP. For all pairs the one-tailed p-value was computed using the paired t-test. The fraction of significant results ($p \leq 0.05$) was taken as an

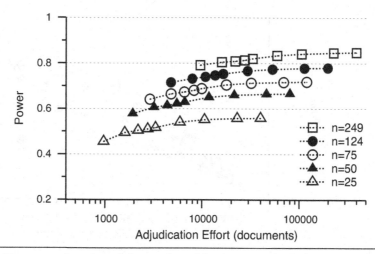

Figure 12.6   Power as a function of the number of documents judged, for move-to-front pooling with various depths.

estimate of power, and the proportion of all pairs that were significant inversions as an indication of bias. If this proportion is less than about $\alpha = 0.05$, bias is a negligible factor (compared with random error) in the validity of the estimate and may be considered insubstantive.

Figure 12.5 shows the effect of varying k (pool depth) and n (number of topics) on adjudication effort and power ($\alpha = 0.05$) for the standard and shallow TREC pooling methods. The y-axis is power and the x-axis is the number of relevance assessments necessary to achieve that power for a given n. Each point represents a different value of k. Figure 12.6 (in conjunction with Figure 12.5) shows that move-to-front pooling yields insubstantially different power for a given number of judgments, compared with the traditional top-k pooling strategy. Figure 12.7, on the other hand, shows that ranking by P@k is substantially less powerful than ranking by MAP with pool depth k. That is, P@k is not nearly as good at discriminating between systems for a given number of relevance assessments. Figure 12.8 shows the observed bias for each of the methods, measured by significant inversions compared with the gold standard, as a function of judging effort. We observe that move-to-front pooling exhibits substantially less bias than methods commonly perceived to be more *fair*. Perception is no substitute for measurement.

Taken together, the results shown in Figures 12.5–12.8 suggest that an experimental design using more topics and fewer judgments per topic (compared with the TREC standard of $n = 50$ and $k = 100$) is more efficient, as suggested by Sanderson and Zobel (2005). However, they do not support the claim that fixed-depth pools or a "fully judged" measure such as P@k yields either higher power or lower bias. We recommend that power and bias analysis be used instead of rank correlation in assessing new pooling strategies and evaluation measures (Buckley and Voorhees, 2004).

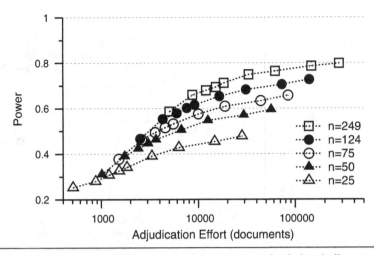

Figure 12.7 Power as a function of the number of documents judged, for shallow pooling with depth k and using P@k as a surrogate for MAP.

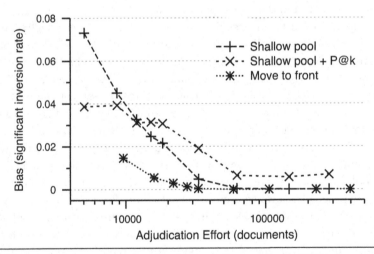

Figure 12.8 Bias of shallow pooling, move-to-front pooling, and use of P@k as a surrogate measure, as a function of adjudication effort. Bias is measured as the significant inversion rate for $\alpha = 0.05$ (see page 445).

12.4.2   Sampling the Pool

As an alternative to the selective judging methods described in the previous section (ISJ or move-to-front pooling), it is possible to leave the pool creation strategy untouched and judge only a random subset of the documents in the pool instead of the whole pool. Sampling the pool allows us to reduce the number of human relevance assessments while avoiding bias at the same time. If 10–20% of the pool is chosen, the judging effort is reduced by a factor of 5 to 10.

Of course, without judging the entire pool it is impossible to actually compute AP or any other effectiveness measure that is based on the assumption of exhaustive relevance assessments. However, we can *estimate* them, based on the random sample. For AP the resulting effectiveness measure is called *inferred average precision* or *infAP*. It provides an unbiased estimate of average precision (Yilmaz and Aslam, 2008).

Recall the formula for average precision (Equation 12.4 on page 408) repeated here for convenience:

$$\text{AP} = \frac{1}{|Rel|} \cdot \sum_{i=1}^{|Res|} \text{relevant}(i) \cdot \text{P@}i, \tag{12.66}$$

where $|Res|$ is the length of the ranked list returned by the system (usually 1000 or 10,000 for TREC experiments), and $\text{relevant}(i) = 1$ if the document at rank i is relevant; 0 if it is nonrelevant. In practice, $\text{relevant}(i) = 1$ if and only if the ith document is *judged* relevant. Similarly, Rel is the set of *judged* relevant documents.

To compute infAP, P@i is replaced by *expected* P@i:

$$\text{infAP} = \frac{1}{|Rel|} \cdot \sum_{i=1}^{|Res|} \text{relevant}(i) \cdot \text{E}[\text{P@}i]. \tag{12.67}$$

Expected P@i in this equation may be calculated as follows: To start, consider the document at rank i. We may assume that $\text{relevant}(i) = 1$, for otherwise there is no need to estimate P@i. Thus,

$$\text{E}[\text{P@}i] = \frac{1}{i} + \frac{i-1}{i} \cdot \text{E}[\text{P@}(i-1)]. \tag{12.68}$$

Now, to compute $\text{E}[\text{P@}(i-1)]$ consider each of the documents at ranks 1 to $i-1$. For the document at rank j, where $1 \leq j < i$, there are four possibilities:

1. If j is deep enough in the ranked list, it may not be part of the pool, in which case it is assumed to be nonrelevant.

2. It may be part of the pool but not be part of the sample chosen, in which case it is unjudged.

3. It may be part of the sample and be judged relevant.

4. It may be part of the sample and be judged nonrelevant.

Now, let *Jud* be the set of judged documents, and let *Pool* be the set of documents in the pool. The value $|Jud|/|Pool|$ represents the fraction of the pool included in our random sample. We estimate P@$(i-1)$ as

$$\text{E}[\text{P@}(i-1)] \;=\; \frac{|Pool \cap Res[1..i-1]|}{i-1} \cdot \frac{|Rel \cap Res[1..i-1]|}{|Jud \cap Res[1..i-1]|} , \tag{12.69}$$

where $Res[1..i-1]$ is the set of documents appearing as the top $i-1$ items in the ranked list. The right-hand side of this equation consists of two fractions. The first of these represents the fraction of the top $i-1$ documents that form part of the pool; the second one represents the fraction of the judged top $i-1$ documents that are relevant. This second fraction is an unbiased estimate of the precision of the top $i-1$ documents that are included in the pool. The first fraction adjusts this estimate to account for documents that are not in the pool (and thus are assumed to be nonrelevant).

One minor problem remains: It is possible for $Jud \cap Res[1..i]$ to be empty, with no judged documents appearing in the top $i-1$ documents. In this case, the fraction on the right will be $0/0$. To address this problem we apply a form of smoothing (see Section 1.3.4) to produce the equation

$$\text{E}[\text{P@}(i-1)] \;=\; \frac{|Pool \cap Res[1..i-1]|}{i-1} \cdot \frac{|Rel \cap Res[1..i-1]| + \varepsilon}{|Jud \cap Res[1..i-1]| + 2\varepsilon} , \tag{12.70}$$

where ε is a small constant value. Combining Equations 12.68 with 12.70 and canceling $i-1$ gives

$$\text{E}[\text{P@}i] \;=\; \frac{1}{i} + \frac{|Pool \cap Res[1..i-1]|}{i} \cdot \frac{|Rel \cap Res[1..i-1]| + \varepsilon}{|Jud \cap Res[1..i-1]| + 2\varepsilon} . \tag{12.71}$$

As an example consider a ranked list of documents represented by the vector

$$Res \;=\; \langle +, ?, -, +, -, \text{X}, \text{X}, ?, \text{X}, +, ... \rangle . \tag{12.72}$$

The vector encodes judgments for the top documents in the ranked list, where "+" represents a judged relevant document, "−" represents a judged nonrelevant document, "?" represents an unjudged document from the pool, and X represents a document not in the pool (which has depth 5). Assume that $\varepsilon = 0.00001$, the value used in NIST's `trec_eval`[6] program. For this example

$$\text{E}[\text{P@}10] \;=\; \frac{1}{10} + \frac{7}{10} \cdot \frac{2 + \varepsilon}{4 + 2\varepsilon} \;\approx\; 0.45 . \tag{12.73}$$

Of course, in more realistic cases the relative number of unjudged documents in such a list would be much higher. Under traditional assumptions, because only three judged relevant documents appear in the list, we would have P@10 = 0.3. The value E[P@10] is an estimate of what the precision would be if the remaining documents in the pool were judged.

---

[6] `trec.nist.gov/trec_eval`

12.5   Nontraditional Effectiveness Measures

The traditional evaluation methodology outlined in Sections 12.1 and 12.2 has consistently proved its worth over much of the history of information retrieval. Over the years it has served to demonstrate the effectiveness of many now-standard theories and techniques as each has been invented and refined. These techniques include the probabilistic model, the language modeling approach, divergence from randomness, and pseudo-relevance feedback (all described in Part III). As larger collections have been introduced, the methodology has held up surprisingly well, providing reasonable results over collections as large and diverse as GOV2. Nonetheless, it is proving inadequate in the face of recent demands. Such demands include the need for graded relevance assessments, the need to handle missing judgments, and the need to accommodate novelty and diversity. In this section we examine some of the many attempts to address these demands.

12.5.1   Graded Relevance

The scale of the Web far exceeds that of even the largest test collections. The Web includes many pages of marginal quality as well as many of extremely high quality. Some Web pages are actively harmful, advertising dubious or dangerous products, or attempting to infect the user's computer with malware or viruses. At the enterprise level a typical document-management platform or corporate intranet may be larger and more varied than most test collections. At the individual level many people (including the authors) maintain gigabytes of e-mail and other documents in their personal storage spaces, easily equaling the size of the smaller TREC test collections and exceeding them in the variety of their content.

To reflect the varying extent to which a given document may satisfy the needs of a particular user, and to address the varying quality of documents, graded relevance may be used instead of binary relevance. For example, assessors might judge documents on a six-point scale of "definitive", "excellent", "good", "fair", "bad", and "detrimental" (Najork et al., 2007). On this scale "bad" corresponds to "nonrelevant", the "detrimental" level indicates malicious or misleading content, and the remaining levels indicate varying degrees of relevance.

Graded relevance assessments are particularly useful in mixed navigational/information search tasks (see Section 15.2 for details on these types of tasks). For example, consider the search query "IBM". For this query IBM's Wikipedia page, which provides valuable information about the company, might be considered of "good" or "excellent" quality, whereas IBM's official Web site at www.ibm.com would have to be considered "definitive".

The Normalized Discounted Cumulative Gain (nDCG) measure takes direct advantage of graded relevance assessments (Järvelin and Kekäläinen, 2002). It operates by comparing the relevance values of a ranked result list with the "ideal" result that would be achieved by ranking all the most relevant documents first, followed by all the next-most-relevant documents, and so on. To compute nDCG, a *gain value* must be assigned to each relevance level. These gain values map relevance levels into a number that can be used to compute a score. Gain values should be chosen to reflect the relative differences between the levels. For example, suppose documents are evaluated on a four-point scale: "highly relevant", "relevant", "marginally relevant", and "nonrelevant". We might choose gain values such as

highly relevant $\rightarrow$	10
relevant $\rightarrow$	5
marginally relevant $\rightarrow$	1
nonrelevant $\rightarrow$	0

Given a ranked list of documents, the first step in the computation of nDCG is the construction of a *gain vector* G. For example, suppose the first six documents in a ranked list are judged: (1) relevant, (2) highly relevant, (3) nonrelevant, (4) relevant, (5) marginally relevant, and (6) highly relevant. The remaining documents are all nonrelevant. The gain vector corresponding to this list is

$$\mathrm{G} \ = \ \langle 5, 10, 0, 5, 1, 10, 0, 0, ... \rangle. \tag{12.74}$$

The second step in the computation of nDCG is the calculation of a *cumulative gain vector* CG. The value of the element k in CG is the sum from 1 to k of the elements in G

$$\mathrm{CG}[k] \ = \ \sum_{i=1}^{k} G[i]. \tag{12.75}$$

For our example

$$\mathrm{CG} \ = \ \langle 5, 15, 15, 20, 21, 31, 31, 31, ... \rangle. \tag{12.76}$$

Before computing the cumulative gain vector, a discount function may be applied at each rank to penalize documents lower in the ranking, thus reflecting the additional user effort required to reach them. This discount recognizes that users are less like to examine documents lower in the ranking because of the time and trouble required. A typical discount function is $\log_2(1+i)$, although other discount functions are possible and may better reflect user effort (Järvelin and Kekäläinen, 2002). This *discounted cumulative gain* is defined as

$$\mathrm{DCG}[k] \ = \ \sum_{i=1}^{k} \frac{G[i]}{\log_2(1+i)}. \tag{12.77}$$

For our example

$$\mathrm{DCG} \ = \ \langle 5.0, 11.3, 11.3, 13.5, 13.8, 17.4, 17.4, 17.4, ... \rangle. \tag{12.78}$$

The next step normalizes the discounted cumulative gain vector against an "ideal" gain vector. The ideal ranking is the ordering that maximizes cumulative gain at all levels. Suppose the collection contains two highly relevant documents, two relevant documents, and two marginally relevant documents. The remaining documents are all nonrelevant. Therefore, the ideal gain vector is

$$\mathbf{G}' \;=\; \langle 10, 10, 5, 5, 1, 1, 0, 0, ...\rangle, \tag{12.79}$$

the ideal cumulative gain vector is

$$\mathbf{CG}' \;=\; \langle 10, 20, 25, 30, 31, 32, 32, 32, ...\rangle, \tag{12.80}$$

and the ideal discounted cumulative gain vector is

$$\mathbf{DCG}' \;=\; \langle 10.0, 16.3, 18.8, 21.0, 21.3, 21.7, 21.7, 21.7, ...\rangle. \tag{12.81}$$

As the final step in the computation of nDCG, we normalize discounted cumulative gain by the ideal discounted cumulative gain vector:

$$\mathrm{nDCG}[k] \;=\; \frac{\mathrm{DCG}[k]}{\mathrm{DCG}'[k]}. \tag{12.82}$$

For our example

$$\mathrm{nDCG} \;=\; \langle 0.50, 0.69, 0.60, 0.64, 0.65, 0.80, 0.80, 0.80, ...\rangle. \tag{12.83}$$

As is typical for IR evaluation measures, nDCG is computed over a set of topics by taking the arithmetic mean of the nDCG values for the individual topics. nDCG is usually reported at various retrieval depths, similar to precision and recall. In our example nDCG@4 = 0.64 and nDCG@8 = 0.80.

The nDCG measure is popular for Web search, where pages may vary greatly in quality and a large number of more or less relevant pages may appear in the collection (Najork et al., 2007). It has also been employed for the evaluation of XML information retrieval (see Section 16.5). In addition to nDCG, both CG and DCG may be used directly as evaluation measures. In a study based on Web search results, Al-Maskari et al. (2007) provide evidence that CG and DCG may actually correlate better with user satisfaction than nDCG.

12.5.2 Incomplete and Biased Judgments

Unjudged documents pose a problem for most effectiveness measures. When large test collections are reused, either to test new methods or to tune existing ones, unjudged documents (i.e., documents that do not appear in the pool) may appear at high ranks. By convention these documents are considered nonrelevant (see Section 12.2). In truth, many of them might have been judged relevant if they had been seen by the assessor. Thus, the pooling method is inherently biased against runs that did not contribute to the pool. When test collections are reused, this bias may distort the results regarding the relative quality of runs, and may lead to incorrect conclusions.

Most methods for handling incomplete judgments assume an *unbiased* sample, in which no system or method has an advantage over any other. For example, inferred average precision (Section 12.4.2) allows us to measure effectiveness without judging the entire pool but requires an unbiased sample to obtain unbiased estimates of precision at various levels.

The ability to measure effectiveness in the face of incomplete and biased judgments has substantial practical importance. The ability to handle missing judgments is also a requirement for the ongoing evaluation of IR systems over dynamic collections. Experiments over large and dynamic collections often surface unjudged documents. In many cases time and expense preclude us from making on-demand judgments to repair holes in a test collection. For example, the operators of a Web search service might measure its performance by periodically running a fixed set of queries against it. Although a crawler constantly adds pages to the collection and judgments for these pages may not be immediately available, it should still be possible to meaningfully compare today's effectiveness with yesterday's effectiveness.

Despite the importance of the problems posed by incomplete and biased judgments, relatively little work has been done to address them. Of the work that has been done, several studies have shown that one particular measure, the *rank effectiveness* measure or *RankEff*, outperforms other proposed measures in terms of the stability of system ranking (Büttcher et al., 2007; Ahlgren and Grönqvist, 2008). This stability suggests that if one IR system outperforms another on RankEff, then the same relationship would hold under traditional measures with complete judgments. However, we caution you that this stability property is not absolute, and it becomes less certain as the number of missing judgments increases.

The formula for RankEff is reminiscent of the formula for average precision (Equation 12.4 on page 408), except that it ignores unjudged documents:

$$ \text{RankEff} \;=\; \frac{1}{|Rel|} \cdot \sum_{i=1}^{|Res|} \text{relevant}(i) \cdot \left(1 - \frac{|Res[1..i] \cap Non|}{|Non|} \right), \tag{12.84} $$

where $\text{relevant}(i) = 1$ if the document at rank i is judged relevant and 0 if it is not. In this formula *Rel* is the set of judged relevant documents, *Non* is the set of judged nonrelevant documents, and $Res[1..i]$ is the set of documents appearing as the top-i documents in the ranked list. The value

$$ \frac{|Res[1..i] \cap Non|}{|Non|} \tag{12.85} $$

is essentially recall@i of *judged nonrelevant* documents. For each judged relevant document in a ranked list, a penalty is applied for the fraction of judged nonrelevant documents that appear above it. The formula treats a judged relevant document that does not appear in *Res* as if it appeared below all judged nonrelevant documents, thus contributing nothing to the score.

As an example consider a ranked list of documents represented by the vector

$$Res = \langle +, ?, -, +, -, ?, ?, ?, ?, + \rangle. \tag{12.86}$$

The vector encodes judgments for the documents in a ranked list of length 10, where "+" represents a judged relevant document, "−" represents a judged nonrelevant document, and "?" represents an unjudged document. Suppose there are four judged relevant documents ($|Rel| = 4$) and six judged nonrelevant documents ($|Non| = 6$). Then RankEff may be computed as

$$\frac{1}{4} \cdot \left(\left(1 - \frac{0}{6}\right) + \left(1 - \frac{1}{6}\right) + \left(1 - \frac{2}{6}\right) \right) = \frac{5}{8} = 0.625. \tag{12.87}$$

For comparison, the AP value for the same vector would be

$$\frac{1}{4} \cdot \left(\frac{1}{1} + \frac{2}{4} + \frac{3}{10} \right) = \frac{9}{20} = 0.450. \tag{12.88}$$

12.5.3 Novelty and Diversity

Classic IR evaluation methodology assumes that the relevance of each document can be judged independently of other documents. Redundancy is rewarded. Suppose a test collection contains a number of nearly identical documents (and many do). If one of these documents is relevant, all are relevant. Returning them all in the top ranks may produce a high score on classic measures such as AP, but would certainly be viewed unfavorably by a real user. Collections crawled from the Web are especially prone to this problem. Bernstein and Zobel (2005) examined the presence of near duplicates in the GOV2 collection and found that more than 17% of its documents were essentially duplicates of other documents. The expedient solution of deleting duplicates from the collection merely sweeps the problem under the rug. Instead, the evaluation measure itself should directly accommodate the possibility of duplicates, rewarding documents that provide *novel* information instead of simply repeating information that is already known to the user from previous (i.e., more highly ranked) documents.

Another problematic assumption of classic IR evaluation is that relevance is judged with respect to a fully specified information need, as expressed through the topic. Consider TREC topic 426 in Figure 1.8 (page 25) in which the title ("law enforcement, dogs") is intended for use as a query. In the classic evaluation experiment for which it was created, this query had one interpretation: Only documents providing "information on the use of dogs worldwide for law enforcement purposes" are considered relevant. However, as illustrated by the example on page 277, this query has a second interpretation: as a request for information on the enforcement of laws regarding dogs (e.g., leash bylaws). Although this second interpretation is perfectly valid and may be desired by an actual user, documents reflecting this interpretation will be judged nonrelevant. Note that by simply changing the description and narrative, we can switch from one interpretation to another (turning a relatively easy query into a relatively hard one). At the time of writing, running this query on a commercial Web search engine returned a mixture of documents strongly favoring the first interpretation.

Table 12.11   Possible results for the Web query "UPS", covering different interpretations of the query.

Rank	Page Title	URL
1	UPS Global Home	`www.ups.com`
2	UPS: Tracking Information	`www.ups.com/tracking/tracking.html`
3	Uninterruptible power supply — Wikipedia,...	`en.wikipedia.org/wiki/Uninterruptible_power...`
4	The UPS Store: Retail packing, shipping,...	`www.theupsstore.com`
5	University of Puget Sound :: Home	`www.ups.edu`

Under either interpretation this query may be underspecified with respect to the information needs of a given user. For example, one user might be interested only in dogs for enforcing drug laws; another might be interested only in leash bylaws pertaining to their community. Ideally an IR system would return results reflecting the ambiguity inherent in the query and exhaustively covering all aspects. To address this requirement, effectiveness measures should appropriately reward *diversity* in retrieval results.

For a given query an IR system should respond with a ranked list that respects both the breadth of available information and any ambiguity inherent in the query. The query "jaguar" represents a standard example of an ambiguous query. In responding to this query an IR system might best return a mixture of documents discussing the cars, the cats, and the classic Fender guitar. Taken together, these documents should provide a complete picture of all interpretations. Ideally, the document ordering for this query would properly account for the interests of the overall user population. If cars were more popular than cats, it might be appropriate to devote the first few documents to them before switching topics. The earlier documents might cover key aspects of each topic. Later documents would supplement this basic information rather than redundantly repeating the same thing over and over again.

Before describing one proposed evaluation measure that accounts for both novelty and diversity, we present two examples as motivation that are derived from Clarke et al. (2008). The first is a Web search example. The second is based on an experimental question answering task conducted at TREC 2005 (Voorhees and Dang, 2005).

Web search example

Table 12.11 shows five of the top ten results for the Web query "UPS", as returned by a commercial search engine at the time of writing. We have retained the ordering specified by the search engine but have removed a few results to keep the example concise. The ambiguity is obvious. A user entering this query might be tracking a package sent via United Parcel Service, planning the purchase of an uninterruptible power supply, or searching for the home page of the University of Puget Sound. The correct expansion of the acronym depends on the user's intent.

It is difficult to argue that any one of these five pages is more relevant than any other. For all of them there is a group of users for which it is the best result. Under the classic evaluation

Table 12.12 TREC 2005 question answering topic 85. The topic consists of multiple questions, with each question aiming at a different aspect of the overall topic.

85: Norwegian Cruise Lines (NCL)
85.1: Name the ships of the NCL.
85.2: What cruise line attempted to take over NCL in 1999?
85.3: What is the name of the NCL's own private island?
85.4: How does NCL rank in size with other cruise lines?
85.5: Why did the Grand Cayman turn away a NCL ship?
85.6: Name so-called theme cruises promoted by NCL.

methodology, relevance judgments would depend on the details of the topic narrative, details that are hidden from the IR system. Depending on these hidden details, any of these documents might be judged relevant or nonrelevant. Naturally, because of the glaring ambiguity, a topic based on this query would not be accepted for inclusion at TREC, thus allowing the problem to be avoided. Unfortunately, the problem cannot be avoided in practice.

One possible guide for ranking these pages is the relative sizes of the groups for which they would be relevant. At a guess, the group of users intending the United Parcel Service is substantially larger than the group intending the University of Puget Sound, even within the state of Washington. The number of users interested in uninterruptible power supplies may fall somewhere in between. The ordering in Table 12.11 is consistent with this guess. But note that a page related to uninterruptible power supplies (#3) lies between two pages related to United Parcel Service. This arrangement may be justified by assuming that users interested in uninterruptible power supplies form a plurality of the users still scanning the result list at that point. By the fifth result users interested in the university may form a plurality. Thus, diversity in the results proceeds directly from the needs of the user population.

Assuming that Table 12.11 gives the best possible ranking (which it may not), it can be justified informally and intuitively. It should be possible for our evaluation measure to reflect this intuition by assigning the highest score to precisely this ranking.

Question answering example

Our second example is based on a topic taken from the TREC 2005 question answering task (Voorhees and Dang, 2005). In contrast to a traditional retrieval task, the goal of a question answering (QA) task is to return exact answers to specific questions, often by integrating information from multiple sources. In the TREC 2005 task, questions were grouped into series with a single target associated with each series. Participating systems were given the target and the questions, and were expected to return an answer to each. Table 12.12 gives the target and questions for topic 85: "Norwegian Cruise Lines (NCL)".

Table 12.13   Top ten documents returned by BM25 for the query "Norwegian Cruise Lines (NCL)" over the TREC 2005 QA task corpus. The questions answered by each document are indicated.

	Document Title	85.1	85.2	85.3	85.4	85.5	85.6	Total
a.	Carnival Re-Enters Norway Bidding		X		X			2
b.	NORWEGIAN CRUISE LINE SAYS...		X					1
c.	Carnival, Star Increase NCL Stake		X					1
d.	Carnival, Star Solidify Control							0
e.	HOUSTON CRUISE INDUSTRY GETS...	X					X	2
f.	TRAVELERS WIN IN CRUISE...	X						1
g.	ARMCHAIR QUARTERBACKS NEED...			X				1
h.	EUROPE, CHRISTMAS ON SALE	X						1
i.	TRAVEL DEALS AND DISCOUNTS							0
j.	HAVE IT YOUR WAY ON THIS SHIP							0

We might view this topic in a different light, treating the target as a query and the questions as representatives, or examples, of specific pieces of information a user may be seeking. Table 12.13 presents the results of executing the target as a query using the Wumpus implementation of the BM25 scoring formula. The corpus is the same collection of newspaper articles used for the TREC 2005 QA task. The titles of the top ten documents are shown. For each article the table indicates the questions answered by that article according to the official TREC judgments. For the purpose of this example we consider a document to answer question 85.1 if it lists the name of any NCL ship. The last column gives the total number of questions answered.

Although these questions certainly do not cover all aspects of the topic, we might view them as reasonable representatives. From this viewpoint we might base overall document relevance on these questions, treating the total number answered as a graded relevance value. Therefore, if we consider only the number of questions answered, one "ideal" ordering for the documents would be a-e-b-c-f-g-h-d-i-j-d, with those documents answering two questions placed before those answering one.

If we consider novelty, our ideal ordering would place document g third, ahead of other documents answering one question, because only document g answers question 85.3. Moreover, the ordering a-e-g covers all the questions with the exception of question 85.5, which is not answered by any document. The other documents might then be considered nonrelevant since they add nothing new. However, because these other documents likely contain aspects not covered by the questions, we should not stop at the third document. In addition the judgments may contain errors or the document may not fully answer an indicated question. Given the information available, we might complete our ranking by considering the number of times each question is answered. Document b (answering 85.2) might be ranked after document g, followed by document f (answering 85.1), and then by documents c and h (answering these questions for a third time). The final ordering would be a-e-g-b-f-c-h-i-j-d.

Measuring novelty and diversity

The development and validation of effectiveness measures for novelty and diversity remains an open research problem. Below, we present a measure proposed by Clarke et al. (2008). Other proposed measures are referenced as further reading.

To generalize from the examples above, we may consider an information need as being represented by a set of *nuggets*. Conceptually, a nugget might represent a specific fact related to the information need, or the answer to a specific question. It might even represent a structural or navigational requirement, indicating that a document belongs to a specific collection, was written in a specific time frame, or appears on a specific Web site. We then assign a graded relevance value to the document on the basis of the number of nuggets it contains: the more nuggets, the better. Furthermore, given a ranked list of documents, if a nugget appears in one document, its value in later documents may be reduced, thus favoring novelty over diversity. With graded relevance values available, a measure such as nDCG may be applied to measure effectiveness. The extension of nDCG to use these gain values is known as α-nDCG.

More formally, we model the user's information need as a set of nuggets $\{n_1, \ldots, n_m\}$. Given a ranked list of documents $\langle d_1, d_2, \ldots \rangle$, let $N(d_i, n_j) = 1$ if document d_i is judged to contain nugget n_j; otherwise, $N(d_i, n_j) = 0$. The number of nuggets contained in document d_i is thus

$$\sum_{j=1}^{m} N(d_i, n_j). \tag{12.89}$$

If redundancy were not an issue, this number could be used directly as a graded relevance value. However, as we go deeper in the result list, we may wish to adjust this number as nuggets are repeated, reflecting the decreased value of redundant information. To make this adjustment, we first define

$$r_{j,k-1} = \sum_{i=1}^{k-1} N(d_i, n_j), \tag{12.90}$$

the number of documents ranked up to position $k - 1$ that have been judged to contain nugget n_j. For convenience we define $r_{j,0} = 0$. We then define the kth element of the gain vector G as

$$G[k] = \sum_{j=1}^{m} N(d_k, n_j) \alpha^{r_{j,k-1}}, \tag{12.91}$$

where α is a constant, with $0 < \alpha \leq 1$. This constant represents the reduction in gain value from a repeated nugget. For example, if we set $\alpha = 1/2$, the document ordering listed in Table 12.13 would give the gain vector

$$G = \langle 2, \tfrac{1}{2}, \tfrac{1}{4}, 0, 2, \tfrac{1}{2}, 1, \tfrac{1}{4}, \ldots \rangle. \tag{12.92}$$

In this example the value of a nugget halves with each document containing it. When $\alpha = 1$, the gain value stays the same, no matter how many times the nugget appears. When $\alpha = 0$, the gain value drops to 0 after the nugget appears once.

Computation of nDCG can now proceed as described in Section 12.5.1. For normalization the ideal ordering is the ordering that maximizes cumulative gain at all levels. For our example the ideal ordering is a-e-g-b-f-c-h-i-j-d and the associated ideal gain vector is

$$G' = \langle 2, 2, 1, \tfrac{1}{2}, \tfrac{1}{2}, \tfrac{1}{4}, \tfrac{1}{4}, ... \rangle. \tag{12.93}$$

12.6 Further Reading

The first information retrieval test collections were created by Cyril Cleverdon and his co-workers in the 1960s, as part of a series of experiments known as the the Cranfield tests (Cleverdon, 1967). The basic approach of evaluating IR systems through the use of a fixed set of documents, queries, and manual judgments is still commonly known as the *Cranfield paradigm*. This approach was adopted by TREC in the early 1990s, and extended to larger collections (over a gigabyte in size). A history of TREC and its use of the Cranfield paradigm is provided by Voorhees and Harman (2005).

The appropriate use of statistical methods in IR evaluation is the subject of continued debate. Some of the statistical methods discussed in this chapter, which are standard in fields such as medicine, have not yet seen universal application within the field of information retrieval. Sanderson and Zobel (2005) examine the use of statistical tests in information retrieval and conclude that shallow judging of a larger number of topics is preferable to deep judging of a smaller number of topics. Webber et al. (2008b) measure experimentally the power of statistical tests for comparing pairs of IR systems, as a function of effect size, number of topics, and pooling depth. They extrapolate that using 617 topics and shallow pooling with a depth of $k=5$ would yield power of 80% for discriminating between pairs of systems at the TREC 2004 Robust Track, in agreement with Figure 12.5 (page 446). Smucker et al. (2007) evaluate the t-test, sign test, Wilcoxon test, and bootstrap methods, using the randomization test as a gold standard. They conclude that the randomization test, the t-test, and the bootstrap compute similar p-values, whereas the other tests differ substantially. Outside the field of information retrieval, Thomas (1997) discusses the controversial nature of retrospective power analysis and compares methods for computing retrospective power. The *British Medical Journal* maintains a summary page of articles related to meta-analysis.[7]

Many proposals have been made to reduce judging effort through selective judging. Cormack et al. (1998) explored the creation of test collections through a process of interactive searching, judging, and manual query reformulation. Their goal was to identify as many relevant documents as possible in a given period of time. Sanderson and Joho (2004) explored further in this direction, describing three methods for creating test collections without pooling. Both Zobel

---

[7] www.bmj.com/collections/ma.htm

(1998) and Cormack et al. (1998) propose the dynamic reordering of documents in the pool to increase the chance that a relevant document will be judged next. Carterette et al. (2006) describe an algorithm for selecting the next document for judging, which optimizes the impact of the judgment on the ability to differentiate between systems. Moffat et al. (2007) investigate adaptive judging in the context of a *rank-biased precision* measure that assigns exponentially decreasing weights to documents based on their rank in the result list. Sampling methods including infAP (Section 12.4.2), are described by Aslam et al. (2006) and by Yilmaz and Aslam (2008). This work was improved and extended to nDCG by Yilmaz et al. (2008). Soboroff et al. (2001) propose an interesting method for avoiding relevance assessments altogether.

Over the years dozens of IR evaluation measures have been invented. Other have been borrowed from other fields and pressed into the service of IR. The nDCG measure was first proposed and described by Järvelin and Kekäläinen (2002). It has since been applied in a number of areas, including Web search (Burges et al., 2005; Najork et al., 2007) and XML information retrieval (Al-Maskari et al., 2007). Buckley and Voorhees (2004) propose the *bpref* measure, which is similar to the RankEff in structure and intent. Shah and Croft (2004) apply the *reciprocal rank* measure (Equation 12.5 on page 409) to evaluate high-accuracy retrieval, where high precision in the top ranks is the governing concern. Aslam et al. (2005) propose a method for quantifying the quality of effectiveness measures. Moffat and Zobel (2008) describe and evaluate a rank-biased precision measure based on a simple model of user behavior. Chapelle et al. (2009) describe a reciprocal rank measure for graded relevance that incorporates a simple user model and is validated against user behavior, as extracted from the logs of a commercial search engine.

Both Amitay et al. (2004) and Büttcher et al. (2007) propose the creation of scalable test collections by characterizing relevant documents, so that the judging of new documents can be performed automatically. Carterette (2007) formally defines the notion of a reusable test collection. Custis and Al-Kofahi (2007) consider the evaluation of query expansion techniques. Webber et al. (2008a) address the problem of comparing scores across test collections. Sakai and Kando (2008) examine the impact of missing relevance judgments.

Novelty and diversity in IR evaluation has been explored by a number of researchers dating back to the 1960s (Goffman, 1964; Boyce, 1982). Carbonell and Goldstein (1998) describe the *maximal marginal relevance* method, which attempts to maximize relevance while minimizing similarity to higher-ranked documents. Zhai et al. (2003) develop and validate subtopic retrieval methods based on a risk-minimization framework and introduce corresponding measures for subtopic recall and precision. Chen and Karger (2006) describe a retrieval method incorporating negative feedback in which documents are assumed to be *not relevant* once they are included in the result list, with the goal of maximizing diversity. Agrawal et al. (2009) apply taxonomies to diversify search results and generalize several traditional effectiveness measures to account for diversity, including nDCG, MAP, and MRR. Spärck Jones et al. (2007) call for the creation of evaluation methodologies and test collections that incorporate diversity. Vee et al. (2008) consider diversity in the context of a shopping search application; van Zwol et al. (2008) consider diversity in the context of image search. Clarke et al. (2009) combine the rank-biased precision measure proposed by Moffat and Zobel (2008) with the novelty and diversity measures of Clarke et al. (2008) and Agrawal et al. (2009), extending them to account for underspecified queries through a simple model of user needs and behavior. Carterette (2009a) considers the problem of computing an ideal result for novelty and diversity measures.

12.7   Exercises

Exercise 12.1   In Equation 12.71 (page 450), assume $|Jud \cap Res[1..i-1]| = 0$. What is the value of $E[P@i]$ in this case?

Exercise 12.2   Consider a ranked list of documents represented by the vector

$$Res = \langle 0, -, +, 0, -, X, 0, X, X, +, ... \rangle, \qquad (12.94)$$

where "+" represents a judged relevant document, "−" represents a judged nonrelevant document, 0 represents an unjudged document from the pool, and X represents a document not in the pool. Compute $E[P@1]$ and $E[P@10]$. Assume that $\varepsilon = 0.00001$.

Exercise 12.3   Compute the nDCG vector given the gain vector

$$G = \langle 1, 3, 0, 2, 1, 3, 0, 0, ... \rangle \qquad (12.95)$$

and given the ideal gain vector

$$G' = \langle 3, 3, 2, 2, 2, 1, 1, 0, ... \rangle. \qquad (12.96)$$

Exercise 12.4   Consider a ranked list of documents represented by the vector

$$Res = \langle 0, -, +, 0, -, 0, 0, 0, 0, + \rangle. \qquad (12.97)$$

The vector encodes judgments for the documents in a ranked list of length $k = 10$, where "+" represents a judged relevant document, "−" represents a judged nonrelevant document, and 0 represents an unjudged document. Assume there are three judged relevant documents ($|Rel| = 3$) and four judged nonrelevant documents ($|Non| = 4$). Compute RankEff (Equation 12.84 on page 454) for this vector.

Exercise 12.5   Run the following ambiguous and under-specified queries on a commercial Web search engine: (a) "jaguar", (b) "windows", (c) "hello", and (d) "charles clarke". How many different interpretations appear in the top ten results?

Exercise 12.6   Suppose that you measure MAP for a particular system using a particular set s of n topics that results in an estimate of m with 95% confidence interval $c = [l, u]$. A second estimate m' is taken using n different topics with similar characteristics. No precision estimate for m' is available. What is the probability that c contains m'? Suppose we compute $\overline{m} = \frac{m+m'}{2}$. Without further information, determine the size of the smallest 95% confidence interval containing $\overline{m}$. How do your answers change if the size of the second topic set is $n' \neq n$?

12.8 Bibliography

Agrawal, R., Gollapudi, S., Halverson, A., and Ieong, S. (2009). Diversifying search results. In *Proceedings of the 2nd ACM International Conference on Web Search and Data Mining*, pages 5–14. Barcelona, Spain.

Ahlgren, P., and Grönqvist, L. (2008). Evaluation of retrieval effectiveness with incomplete relevance data: Theoretical and experimental comparison of three measures. *Information Processing & Management*, 44(1):212–225.

Al-Maskari, A., Sanderson, M., and Clough, P. (2007). The relationship between IR effectiveness measures and user satisfaction. In *Proceedings of the 30th Annual International ACM SIGIR Conference on Research and Development in Information Retrieval*, pages 773–774. Amsterdam, The Netherlands.

Amitay, E., Carmel, D., Lempel, R., and Soffer, A. (2004). Scaling IR-system evaluation using term relevance sets. In *Proceedings of the 27th Annual International ACM SIGIR Conference on Research and Development in Information Retrieval*, pages 10–17. Sheffield, England.

Aslam, J. A., Pavlu, V., and Yilmaz, E. (2006). A statistical method for system evaluation using incomplete judgments. In *Proceedings of the 29th Annual International ACM SIGIR Conference on Research and Development in Information Retrieval*, pages 541–548. Seattle, Washington.

Aslam, J. A., Yilmaz, E., and Pavlu, V. (2005). The maximum entropy method for analyzing retrieval measures. In *Proceedings of the 28th Annual International ACM SIGIR Conference on Research and Development in Information Retrieval*, pages 27–34. Salvador, Brazil.

Bernstein, Y., and Zobel, J. (2005). Redundant documents and search effectiveness. In *Proceedings of the 14th ACM International Conference on Information and Knowledge Management*, pages 736–743. Bremen, Germany.

Boyce, B. (1982). Beyond topicality: A two stage view of relevance and the retrieval process. *Information Processing & Management*, 18(3):105–109.

Buckley, C., and Voorhees, E. (2005). Retrieval system evaluation. In Voorhees, E. M., and Harman, D. K., editors, *TREC — Experiment and Evaluation in Information Retrieval*, chapter 3, pages 53–75. Cambridge, Massachusetts: MIT Press.

Buckley, C., and Voorhees, E. M. (2004). Retrieval evaluation with incomplete information. In *Proceedings of the 27th Annual International ACM SIGIR Conference on Research and Development in Information Retrieval*, pages 25–32. Sheffield, England.

Burges, C. J. C., Shaked, T., Renshaw, E., Lazier, A., Deeds, M., Hamilton, N., and Hullender, G. (2005). Learning to rank using gradient descent. In *Proceedings of the 22nd International Conference on Machine Learning*, pages 89–96. Bonn, Germany.

Büttcher, S., Clarke, C. L. A., Yeung, P. C. K., and Soboroff, I. (2007). Reliable information retrieval evaluation with incomplete and biased judgements. In *Proceedings of the 30th Annual International ACM SIGIR Conference on Research and Development in Information Retrieval*, pages 63–70. Amsterdam, The Netherlands.

Carbonell, J., and Goldstein, J. (1998). The use of MMR, diversity-based reranking for reordering documents and producing summaries. In *Proceedings of the 21st Annual International ACM SIGIR Conference on Research and Development in Information Retrieval*, pages 335–336. Melbourne, Australia.

Carterette, B. (2007). Robust test collections for retrieval evaluation. In *Proceedings of the 30th Annual International ACM SIGIR Conference on Research and Development in Information Retrieval*, pages 55–62. Amsterdam, The Netherlands.

Carterette, B. (2009a). An analysis of NP-completeness in novelty and diversity ranking. In *Proceedings of the 2nd International Conference on the Theory of Information Retrieval*, pages 200–211. Cambridge, England.

Carterette, B. (2009b). On rank correlation and the distance between rankings. In *Proceedings of the 29th Annual International ACM SIGIR Conference on Research and Development in Information Retrieval*, pages 436–443. Boston, Massachusetts.

Carterette, B., Allan, J., and Sitaraman, R. (2006). Minimal test collections for retrieval evaluation. In *Proceedings of the 29th Annual International ACM SIGIR Conference on Research and Development in Information Retrieval*, pages 268–275. Seattle, Washington.

Chapelle, O., Metzler, D., Zhang, Y., and Grinspan, P. (2009). Expected reciprocal rank for graded relevance. In *Proceedings of the 18th ACM Conference on Information and Knowledge Management*, pages 621–630. Hong Kong, China.

Chen, H., and Karger, D. R. (2006). Less is more: Probabilistic models for retrieving fewer relevant documents. In *Proceedings of the 29th Annual International ACM SIGIR Conference on Research and Development in Information Retrieval*, pages 429–436. Seattle, Washington.

Clarke, C. L., Kolla, M., Cormack, G. V., Vechtomova, O., Ashkann, A., Büttcher, S., and MacKinnon, I. (2008). Novelty and diversity in information retrieval evaluation. In *Proceedings of the 31st Annual International ACM SIGIR Conference on Research and Development in Information Retrieval*, pages 659–666. Singapore.

Clarke, C. L. A., Kolla, M., and Vechtomova, O. (2009). An effectiveness measure for ambiguous and underspecified queries. In *Proceedings of the 2nd International Conference on the Theory of Information Retrieval*, pages 188–199. Cambridge, England.

Cleverdon, C. W. (1967). The Cranfield tests on index language devices. *AsLib proceedings*, 19(6):173–193. Reprinted as Cleverdon (1997).

Cleverdon, C. W. (1997). The Cranfield tests on index language devices. In *Readings in Information Retrieval*, pages 47–59. San Francisco, California: Morgan Kaufmann.

Cormack, G. V., and Lynam, T. R. (2006). Statistical precision of information retrieval evaluation. In *Proceedings of the 29th Annual International ACM SIGIR Conference on Research and Development in Information Retrieval*, pages 533–540. Seattle, Washington.

Cormack, G. V., and Lynam, T. R. (2007). Power and bias of subset pooling strategies. In *Proceedings of the 30th Annual International ACM SIGIR Conference on Research and Development in Information Retrieval*, pages 837–838. Amsterdam, The Netherlands.

Cormack, G. V., Palmer, C. R., and Clarke, C. L. A. (1998). Efficient construction of large test collections. In *Proceedings of the 21st Annual International ACM SIGIR Conference on Research and Development in Information Retrieval*, pages 282–289. Melbourne, Australia.

Custis, T., and Al-Kofahi, K. (2007). A new approach for evaluating query expansion: Query-document term mismatch. In *Proceedings of the 30th Annual International ACM SIGIR Conference on Research and Development in Information Retrieval*, pages 575–582. Amsterdam, The Netherlands.

De Angelis, C., Drazen, J., Frizelle, F., Haug, C., Hoey, J., Horton, R., Kotzin, S., Laine, C., Marusic, A., Overbeke, A., et al. (2004). Clinical trial registration: A statement from the International Committee of Medical Journal Editors. *Journal of the American Medical Association*, 292(11):1363–1364.

Efron, B., and Tibshirani, R. J. (1993). *An Introduction to the Bootstrap*. Boca Raton, Florida: Chapman & Hall/CRC.

Fisher, R. A. (1925). Theory of statistical estimation. *Proceedings of the Cambridge Philosophical Society*, 22:700–725.

Gardner, M. J., and Altman, D. G. (1986). Confidence intervals rather than p values: Estimation rather than hypothesis testing. *British Medical Journal*, 292(6522):746–750.

Goffman, W. (1964). A searching procedure for information retrieval. *Information Storage and Retrieval*, 2:73–78.

Holm, S. (1979). A simple sequentially rejective multiple test procedure. *Scandinavian Journal of Statistics*, 6:65–70.

Järvelin, K., and Kekäläinen, J. (2002). Cumulated gain-based evaluation of IR techniques. *ACM Transactions on Information Systems*, 20(4):422–446.

Kelly, D., Fu, X., and Shah, C. (2007). *Effects of Rank and Precision of Search Results on Users' Evaluations of System Performance*. Technical Report 2007-02. University of North Carolina, Chapel Hill.

Lenhard, J. (2006). Models and statistical inference: The controversy between Fisher and Neyman-Pearson. *British Journal for the Philosophy of Science*, 57(1).

Moffat, A., Webber, W., and Zobel, J. (2007). Strategic system comparisons via targeted relevance judgments. In *Proceedings of the 30th Annual International ACM SIGIR Conference on Research and Development in Information Retrieval*, pages 375–382. Amsterdam, The Netherlands.

Moffat, A., and Zobel, J. (2008). Rank-biased precision for measurement of retrieval effectiveness. *ACM Transactions on Information Systems*, 27(1):1–27.

Najork, M. A., Zaragoza, H., and Taylor, M. J. (2007). HITS on the Web: How does it compare? In *Proceedings of the 30th Annual International ACM SIGIR Conference on Research and Development in Information Retrieval*, pages 471–478. Amsterdam, The Netherlands.

Robertson, S. (2006). On GMAP – and other transformations. In *Proceedings of the 15th ACM International Conference on Information and Knowledge Management*, pages 78–83. Arlington, Virginia.

Sakai, T., and Kando, N. (2008). On information retrieval metrics designed for evaluation with incomplete relevance assessments. *Information Retrieval*, 11(5):447–470.

Sanderson, M., and Joho, H. (2004). Forming test collections with no system pooling. In *Proceedings of the 27th Annual International ACM SIGIR Conference on Research and Development in Information Retrieval*, pages 33–40. Sheffield, England.

Sanderson, M., and Zobel, J. (2005). Information retrieval system evaluation: effort, sensitivity, and reliability. In *Proceedings of the 28th Annual International ACM SIGIR Conference on Research and Development in Information Retrieval*, pages 162–169. Salvador, Brazil.

Savoy, J. (1997). Statistical inference in retrieval effectiveness evaluation. *Information Processing & Management*, 33(4):495–512.

Shah, C., and Croft, W. B. (2004). Evaluating high accuracy retrieval techniques. In *Proceedings of the 27th Annual International ACM SIGIR Conference on Research and Development in Information Retrieval*, pages 2–9. Sheffield, England.

Smucker, M., Allan, J., and Carterette, B. (2007). A comparison of statistical significance tests for information retrieval evaluation. In *Proceedings of the 16th ACM conference on Conference on Information and Knowledge Management*, pages 623–632. Lisbon, Portugal.

Soboroff, I., Nicholas, C., and Cahan, P. (2001). Ranking retrieval systems without relevance judgments. In *Proceedings of the 24th Annual International ACM SIGIR Conference on Research and Development in Information Retrieval*, pages 66–73. New Orleans, Louisiana.

Spärck Jones, K., Robertson, S. E., and Sanderson, M. (2007). Ambiguous requests: Implications for retrieval tests. *ACM SIGIR Forum*, 41(2):8–17.

Thomas, L. (1997). Retrospective power analysis. *Conservation Biology*, 11(1):276–280.

Turpin, A., and Scholer, F. (2006). User performance versus precision measures for simple search tasks. In *Proceedings of the 29th Annual International ACM SIGIR Conference on Research and Development in Information Retrieval*, pages 11–18. Seattle, Washington.

van Zwol, R., Murdock, V., Garcia Pueyo, L., and Ramirez, G. (2008). Diversifying image search with user generated content. In *Proceedings of the 1st ACM International Conference on Multimedia Information Retrieval*, pages 67–74. Vancouver, Canada.

Vee, E., Srivastava, U., Shanmugasundaram, J., Bhat, P., and Amer-Yahia, A. (2008). Efficient computation of diverse query results. In *Proceedings of the 24th IEEE International Conference on Data Engineering*, pages 228–236. Cancun, Mexico.

Voorhees, E., and Harman, D. (1999). Overview of the eighth text retrieval conference. In *Proceedings of the 8th Text REtrieval Conference*, pages 1–24. Gaithersburg, Maryland.

Voorhees, E. M. (2000). Variations in relevance judgments and the measurement of retrieval effectiveness. *Information Processing & Management*, 36(5):697–716.

Voorhees, E. M. (2004). Overview of the TREC 2004 Robust Track. In *Proceedings of the 13th Text REtrieval Conference*. Gaithersburg, Maryland.

Voorhees, E. M., and Dang, H. T. (2005). Overview of the TREC 2005 Question Answering track. In *Proceedings of the 14th Text REtrieval Conference*. Gaithersburg, Maryland.

Voorhees, E. M., and Harman, D. K. (2005). The Text REtrieval Conference. In Voorhees, E. M., and Harman, D. K., editors, *TREC — Experiment and Evaluation in Information Retrieval*, chapter 1, pages 3–20. Cambridge, Massachusetts: MIT Press.

Webber, W., Moffat, A., and Zobel, J. (2008a). Score standardization for inter-collection comparison of retrieval systems. In *Proceedings of the 31st Annual International ACM SIGIR Conference on Research and Development in Information Retrieval*, pages 51–58. Singapore.

Webber, W., Moffat, A., and Zobel, J. (2008b). Statistical power in retrieval experimentation. In *Proceedings of the 17th ACM Conference on Information and Knowledge Management*, pages 571–580. Napa, California.

Yilmaz, E., and Aslam, J. A. (2008). Estimating average precision when judgments are incomplete. *International Journal of Knowledge and Information Systems*, 16(2):173–211.

Yilmaz, E., Kanoulas, E., and Aslam, J. A. (2008). A simple and efficient sampling method for estimating AP and NDCG. In *Proceedings of the 31st Annual International ACM SIGIR Conference on Research and Development in Information Retrieval*, pages 603–610. Singapore.

Zhai, C., Cohen, W. W., and Lafferty, J. (2003). Beyond independent relevance: Methods and evaluation metrics for subtopic retrieval. In *Proceedings of the 26th Annual International ACM SIGIR Conference on Research and Development in Information Retrieval*, pages 10–17. Toronto, Canada.

Zobel, J. (1998). How reliable are the results of large-scale information retrieval experiments? In *Proceedings of the 21st Annual International ACM SIGIR Conference on Research and Development in Information Retrieval*, pages 307–314. Melbourne, Australia.

13   Measuring Efficiency

Chapter 12 discusses methods for measuring the effectiveness of search engines, that is, the quality of the search results they produce. However, the quality of the results is only one criterion for the overall usefulness of a retrieval system. A second and equally important aspect is its efficiency. While *effectiveness* describes how well a system is doing the job it was designed for, *efficiency* refers to the system's resource consumption while doing that job.

In the context of search engines, *efficiency* can refer to one of three different aspects: time efficiency (How fast is it?), space efficiency (How much memory/disk does it need?), or cost efficiency (How much does it cost to set it up and keep it running?). All three aspects interact with each other closely. For instance, by spending more money one can increase the system's memory resources, which in turn may make it run faster because more data can be held in RAM; by applying more complicated index compression techniques, we may be able to decrease the memory requirements, which may reduce the overall cost but will probably also make query processing slower, due to the more complex decompression routines.

The discussion in this chapter is largely limited to time efficiency considerations, because time efficiency is the only efficiency aspect that is visible to the search engine's users and that may even be considered an aspect of its effectiveness: Faster is better (most of the time). Throughout the chapter we treat the terms *performance* and *time efficiency* as synonyms and use them to refer to query speed (e.g., seconds per query, queries per second).

The remainder of this chapter consists of three parts. The first part (Section 13.1) is concerned with performance measures: What does it mean for a search engine to be fast? We introduce *throughput* and *latency* as the two principal performance measures. In the second part (Section 13.2), we explore the relationship between those two measures, applying methods from queueing theory to analyze system behavior under high load. The last part (Sections 13.3 and 13.4) focuses on two particular types of performance optimizations: query scheduling and caching. Although neither of them is directly related to the measuring process, both can have a great impact on the outcome of the measurement, and it is important to understand their roles when designing a performance experiment.

13.1   Efficiency Criteria

Measuring the performance of a computer system is difficult. When personal computers became a commodity in the mid-1980s, most manufacturers used the MHz rating of the CPU as the main efficiency criterion when advertising their products. Over the years, the frequency of the processor became an increasingly unreliable indicator of the system's performance, as new generations of microprocessors were introduced that were faster than their predecessors, despite their similar — or even lower — clock frequency. With the recent shift of CPU manufacturer's focus away from CPU frequencies and instructions-per-clock-cycle execution rates, and toward a greater number of CPU cores per computer, it is now more difficult than ever to estimate the performance of a computer system based on its specifications.

People have tried to circumvent this problem by using actual performance measurements to tell how fast or slow a computer is. One of the first such initiatives was headed by the *Standard Performance Evaluation Corporation (SPEC)*, a nonprofit organization founded in 1988. SPEC has been involved in the development of a multitude of benchmarks that measure various performance aspects of computer systems. Their SPECfp benchmark, for instance, focuses on the computer's floating-point unit. The SPECfp score is an indicator of the computer's performance on tasks that require extensive numerical computations, such as physical simulations or 3D graphics. The SPECweb2005 benchmark, on the other hand, is designed to measure the computer's performance in tasks that a Web server might typically do: serving HTML pages, generating dynamic content using PHP, and so on. The full list of benchmarks can be found on SPEC's Web site[1].

For search engines, no standardized array of performance benchmarks exists. Even if one did, it is not clear how useful it would be, given that a deployment decision for a particular ranking algorithm always represents an efficiency-versus-effectiveness trade-off. As an example, consider the pseudo-relevance feedback mechanism from Section 8.6. The evaluation results in Table 8.2 (page 279) show that precision can be increased substantially by applying pseudo-relevance feedback. However, doing so requires a second pass over the data and thus makes the search engine slower. Without conducting a user study it is difficult, if not impossible, to tell whether pseudo-relevance feedback actually improves the overall quality of the search engine. In practice, because of the substantial time and cost overhead associated with a user study, such trade-offs are often subject to policy decisions that are not backed up by experimental data. Because there is no general solution to this problem, we will ignore it and assume that the search engine's ranking function is fixed, which allows us to focus exclusively on the system's efficiency.

13.1.1   Throughput and Latency

When fine-tuning the performance of a search engine, we often find ourselves in a situation in which there are two competing implementations (both producing the same search results), and we would like to know which one is better. The two most common performance measures that can help answer this question are *throughput* and *latency*.

---

[1] `www.spec.org`

- **Throughput** refers to the number of queries a search engine processes within a given period of time. It is usually given in *queries per second (qps)*. If a search engine processes 700 queries in 5 seconds, it achieves 140 qps.

  When we refer to throughput, we usually mean *theoretical throughput*, also known as *service rate*, which is the fastest possible rate at which the system can process queries. A closely related measure is *service time* — the amount of time per query that the processor(s) is/are actively working on the query. Service time is connected to service rate via the formula

  $$serviceRate = \frac{m}{serviceTime} \, , \tag{13.1}$$

  where m is the number of processors in the system.

- **Latency**, also known as *response time*, is the amount of time that elapses from the search engine's receipt of the query until the results are sent to the user. It is measured in *seconds per query*.

  Latency can be measured on the server side or on the client side. The latter is referred to as *end-to-end latency*; it is the time between the user issuing the query and her receiving the search results. It includes network latency and is more indicative of user satisfaction than the search engine's query processing latency alone. However, when conducting comparative performance evaluations, it is usually sufficient to focus on the actual search latency, because the extra latency caused by the network is a constant that is independent of the implementation.

Both latency and throughput are not very meaningful when reported for a single query. Instead, they are usually aggregated for a large number of queries, thousands or millions, and then reported as a mean: *mean throughput* or *mean latency*, similar to the way in which we report effectiveness measures such as mean average precision (see Section 12.1).

Getting back to the question of which of our two implementations is better, we can answer the question by using the same tools that we would apply for an effectiveness evaluation: by running the same set of queries $\mathcal{Q} = \{q_1, \ldots, q_n\}$ against both implementations, recording latency (or service time) for each query q_i, and computing a confidence interval for the difference between the two implementations (see Section 12.3.2 for a reminder of how to compute and interpret confidence intervals). If the confidence interval includes 0, we can treat this as evidence that there is no substantial difference between the two implementations. Otherwise, we may assume that one implementation is faster, and discard the other.

Compared with an effectiveness evaluation, a comparative performance evaluation has the advantage that it does not require any human judgments. We can easily measure the search engine's service time for tens of thousands of queries, which allows us to reliably detect relative performance differences well below 1%. Attaining a similar sensitivity level in an effectiveness evaluation would be prohibitively expensive.

Latency $\neq$ Service time

One might be tempted to think of latency and service time (or, equivalently, latency and throughput) as the same metric. However, the two are quite different. A system's latency is strictly greater than its service time, often considerably so. In addition to the time that is actually spent working on the query, latency includes periods of waiting, such as:

- Waiting for the hard disk to deliver postings data if the index is not stored in main memory. These periods of waiting do not count toward the system's service time, as it is possible to process other queries while waiting for postings to be read from disk.

- Waiting in the query queue until the CPU becomes available. Queueing effects can be a major source of latency if the system is under heavy load (see Section 13.2).

- In a distributed search engine with n independent index servers, waiting for the remaining $n - i$ servers to return their search results when the first i servers are already done.

In addition to this lower-bound relationship, throughput and latency are often also in an *adversarial* relationship in which improving the system's performance according to one measure decreases its performance according to the other. This becomes apparent if we widen our focus to include parallelism. Suppose we have a search engine that contains two index servers I_1 and I_2. Then there are at least two ways in which the query processing load can be split:

- **Index replication.** I_2 is an exact replica of I_1. Each maintains a copy of the full index. When a query arrives, it is sent either to I_1 or to I_2, each with a 50% chance.

- **Index partitioning.** I_1 and I_2 each have an index for 50% of the collection. When a query arrives, it is forwarded to both index servers. I_1 and I_2 each compute the top k search results for their part of the index. When they are both done, the two result sets are merged and the final results are sent to the user.

Let us compare both configurations with a single-server setup and analyze them with respect to throughput and latency. Index replication increases throughput by 100%, because each index server works on only 50% of the queries. It has no effect on latency, since each query is still processed by only one server. Index partitioning improves both throughput and latency to a similar degree, but the speedup is less than 100%, for multiple reasons:

- Some operations involved in processing a query have a cost that is independent of the size of the index. For instance, if the index is stored on disk, the system always needs to perform at least one disk seek per query term. This cost cannot be reduced by splitting the collection in half.

- The computational complexity of the search/ranking process is not quite linear in the size of the index. The MAXSCORE heuristic from Section 5.1.1 may be used to avoid scoring documents that we know cannot be among the top search results. With MAXSCORE enabled, the fraction of documents that need to be scored becomes smaller as the index gets larger.

Hence, if our focus is primarily on throughput and there is no need to improve latency, then index replication is the right choice.[2] Otherwise, index partitioning may be more appropriate. A large-scale search engine, facing latency and throughput issues at the same time, might employ a combination of the two.

13.1.2   Aggregate Statistics and User Satisfaction

As with effectiveness measures, aggregate statistics for efficiency measures (e.g., average throughput or average latency) are not always particularly meaningful. Consider two hypothetical search systems A and B. System A always needs exactly 500 ms to process a query. System B employs sophisticated caching strategies that allow it to process 90% of queries in 10 ms; for the remaining 10%, it requires 4.9 seconds per query. Both systems exhibit the same average latency, but A provides a far better user experience because 10% of B's users will be greatly irritated by the unexpectedly high response time.

Admittedly, the above example is contrived and such extreme differences are rarely encountered in practice. Nonetheless, it exemplifies the kind of trouble we may run into if we rely exclusively on average performance metrics. To overcome this problem, people often use percentiles instead of average values. For instance, a search engine company could have as one of its goals that 99% of all queries be processed in less than 1 second. From a user's perspective this metric is far more meaningful than the average latency metric. It also has the welcome side effect that it answers the latency-versus-throughput question alluded to in the previous section. Latency now is no longer a free variable. We may fine-tune the system for optimal throughput, subject to the condition that 99% of queries are processed in under 1 second.

13.2   Queueing Theory

Quite often the operators of a search engine are faced with determining the query capacity of their search engine, that is, estimating the maximum throughput that can be achieved while still meeting certain latency requirements, such as the 99% criterion from before. One way to do this is to conduct a performance experiment by sending queries to the search engine (for instance, by replaying a previously recorded query log) and gradually increasing the frequency with which queries arrive at the system, until the predefined latency limit is reached. Unfortunately, it is not always opportune or even feasible to run such an experiment. First, it consumes precious computing resources that would otherwise be available for processing real queries. Second, if the search engine is not yet in production, it might be difficult to obtain a query log that accurately reflects the temporal distribution of query arrivals.

---

[2] Aside from pure performance aspects, replication has an advantage over partitioning in that it provides fault tolerance: If I_1 or I_2 fails, the system can still process queries, albeit at a reduced rate. With index partitioning, if one of the index servers fails, the system will most likely be useless, as it will miss 50% of the search results. Fault tolerance in distributed search engines is discussed in Chapter 14.

An alternative to conducting an actual performance experiment is to use mathematical models to predict the outcome of the experiment, based on estimates of the search engine's query processing performance. Suppose we have an approximation of the mean service time per query. Then we can use methods from queueing theory to compute the system's average latency, given the average query arrival rate. By inverting the computation it is possible to calculate the maximum possible throughput, subject to predefined latency requirements.

The model that we employ to estimate latency, given average service time and query arrival rate, is based on three fundamental assumptions:

1. The time difference between two consecutive query arrivals (the *inter-arrival time*) is a random variable A that follows an exponential distribution, that is, with density function

$$f_A(x) = \lambda \cdot e^{-\lambda x} \quad \text{(for } x \geq 0\text{)}, \tag{13.2}$$

where λ is the *query arrival rate*. $E[A] = \int_0^\infty x \cdot f(x, \lambda) \ dx = 1/\lambda$ is the average time between two queries. This model is sometimes called a *Poisson process* because the number of queries arriving in a time interval of fixed length follows a *Poisson distribution* (Equation 8.34 on page 268).

2. The per-query service time is a random variable S that also follows an exponential distribution, with density function

$$f_S(x) = \mu \cdot e^{-\mu x} \quad \text{(for } x \geq 0\text{)}, \tag{13.3}$$

where μ is the system's service rate (i.e., its theoretical throughput). $E[S] = 1/\mu$ is the average service time per query. We assume $\mu > \lambda$, for otherwise the search engine will not be able to process all incoming queries.

3. Queries are processed in a *first-come-first-served* (*FCFS*) fashion. The system always works on one query at a time.

Assumption 1 is based on the insight that queries are largely independent of each other and are distributed uniformly in time. The assumption is usually valid, at least if we limit ourselves to short periods of time, such as a few minutes, perhaps half an hour. For longer time periods (days or weeks) it does not hold, because users tend to be more active during the day than at night, more active during the week than on weekends, and so forth.

Assumption 2 is not backed up by theoretical considerations but by service time distributions observed in practice. Figure 13.1, for instance, shows the service time distribution (CPU time only, not counting the time spent waiting for the hard drive) for proximity ranking (Figure 2.10 on page 61) and Okapi BM25 (Equation 8.48 on page 272), running the 10,000 queries from the TREC Terabyte 2006 efficiency task against a schema-independent index for the GOV2 collection. Although the two ranking algorithms are quite different, per-query service time for both algorithms can be modeled reasonably well by an exponential distribution with density function $f_S(x) = \mu \cdot e^{-\mu x}$, where $\mu = 4.37$ qps for proximity ranking and $\mu = 0.75$ qps for BM25.

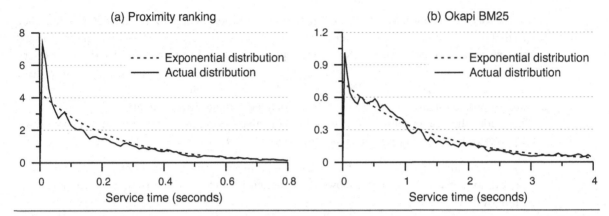

Figure 13.1 Modeling per-query service time (i.e., CPU time) as a random variable with exponential distribution. (a) Proximity ranking (Figure 2.10) with mean service time $E[S] = 0.23$ seconds ($\mu = 4.37$ qps). (b) Okapi BM25 (Equation 8.48) with mean service time $E[S] = 1.34$ seconds ($\mu = 0.75$ qps).

Assumption 3 is made for simplicity. Large-scale search engine installations usually employ more complicated scheduling algorithms. When the system is under high load, choosing the right scheduling algorithm may make a great difference in terms of latency. However, more complicated scheduling algorithms can be quite difficult to analyze, so we ignore them for now. We will revisit this topic in Section 13.3.

13.2.1 Kendall's Notation

The queueing model described above corresponds to the $M/M/c/\infty/\infty/F$ model in *Kendall's notation*, named after the British statistician David G. Kendall (not Maurice G. Kendall, another British statistician, who invented Kendall's τ):

- The first "M" denotes the query arrival process, which we assume to be *Markovian* (i.e., exponential).

- The second "M" denotes the service time distribution, which we also assume to be Markovian.

- The "c" denotes the number of *service channels* (i.e., servers) in the system. For the sake of simplicity, we limit ourselves to the case $c = 1$. However, note that this case also covers distributed systems with n parallel servers in which each server is responsible for $1/n$ of the index.

- The first "∞" denotes the number of slots in the queue, which we assume to be infinite.

- The second "∞" denotes the size of the query population, which we also assume to be infinite.

- The "F" denotes the *queue discipline*, that is, the order in which queries are processed by the system. As mentioned before, we assume FCFS.

Because the last three parameters in the full Kendall notation are often the same $(\infty/\infty/F)$, it is not uncommon to use the shorthand notation $M/M/c$ instead of the more cumbersome $M/M/c/\infty/\infty/F$.

13.2.2 The M/M/1 Queueing Model

We now describe how to calculate the latency distribution of a search engine according to the $M/M/1$ queueing model. Before we jump into the details of the calculation, however, let us restate a handy theorem that is often used in queueing analysis.

Little's Law (Little, 1961)
Let n be the average number of queries in the system (either being processed or waiting in the queue) at a random point in time. Further, let λ be the query arrival rate. Then the average query response time of the system, denoted as r, is

$$r = \frac{n}{\lambda} \tag{13.4}$$

The proof sketch for Equation 13.4 is straightforward (a formal proof can be found in Little's paper). Consider a sufficiently long time interval of length t with q query arrivals $(q = \lambda \cdot t)$. The total time spent in the system by these q queries, taken together, is $r_{total} = r \cdot q$. Since a query can count toward r_{total} only while it is in the system (either being processed or waiting in the queue), we have $r_{total} = n \cdot t$ and thus $r = n/\lambda$. Note that we do not make any assumptions about the distribution of service time or inter-arrival time. Thus, Little's law applies to any queueing model, not just to the $M/M/1$ model.

To compute the average latency of our search engine, we first calculate the expected number of queries in the system, at a random point in time. We view the search engine as a probabilistic state machine in which state Z_i represents "i queries in the system" (i.e., 1 query being processed and $i - 1$ queries waiting in the queue). Each state has an associated probability p_i: the probability that, at a random point in time, the system is in state Z_i. This type of state machine is called a *continuous Markov chain*. It is shown in Figure 13.2.

We are interested in the transitions between two adjacent states Z_i and Z_{i+1} and their relative frequencies. Let T^+ denote a transition from Z_i to Z_{i+1} and T^- a transition in the opposite direction. On average there are $\lambda \cdot p_i$ occurrences of T^+ per time unit and $\mu \cdot p_{i+1}$ occurrences of T^-. Because both the arrival process and the service process are assumed to be Markovian (i.e., memoryless), their relative number does not depend on the number of queries in the system. Thus, the fraction

$$\frac{\lambda \cdot p_i}{\mu \cdot p_{i+1}} \tag{13.5}$$

is the same for every $i \geq 0$. The essential observation now is that, on average, both types of transitions happen with exactly the same frequency. Obviously, T^- cannot be more frequent than T^+, as a query can be processed only after it has arrived. T^+, on the other hand, cannot

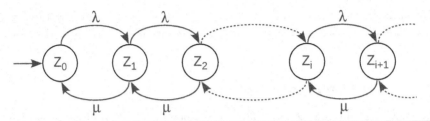

Figure 13.2   A continuous Markov chain, describing the system's query queue as a state machine with infinitely many states. State Z_i represents "i queries in the system". The relative frequency of $Z_i \rightarrow Z_{i+1}$ and $Z_{i+1} \rightarrow Z_i$ state transitions is given by the query arrival rate λ and the service rate μ, respectively.

be more frequent than T^-; if it were, then the average number of queries in the queue would be infinite (and we would have $\lambda \geq \mu$). Hence, the two terms must have the same value:

$$\lambda \cdot p_i = \mu \cdot p_{i+1}, \tag{13.6}$$

or equivalently,

$$p_{i+1} = \frac{\lambda}{\mu} \cdot p_i. \tag{13.7}$$

For convenience, let us define $\rho = \lambda/\mu$ (ρ is called the *traffic intensity*, or *utilization*). Then we have

$$p_i = p_0 \cdot \rho^i \quad \forall\, i \geq 0. \tag{13.8}$$

Since the p_i's form a probability distribution, their sum is 1. This allows us to compute p_0:

$$p_0 \cdot \sum_{i=0}^{\infty} \rho^i = 1 \quad \Leftrightarrow \quad p_0 \cdot \frac{1}{1-\rho} = 1 \quad \Leftrightarrow \quad p_0 = 1 - \rho = 1 - \lambda/\mu. \tag{13.9}$$

For N, the number of queries in the system, it then follows:

$$E[N] \; = \; \sum_{i=0}^{\infty} i \cdot p_i \; = \; \sum_{i=0}^{\infty} i \cdot (1-\rho) \cdot \rho^i \; = \; \frac{\rho}{1-\rho}. \tag{13.10}$$

Finally, by applying Little's law (Equation 13.4), we obtain:

$$E[R] \; = \; \frac{E[N]}{\lambda} \; = \; \frac{1}{\mu(1-\rho)} \; = \; \frac{1}{\mu - \lambda}, \tag{13.11}$$

where R is a random variable representing the per-query response time (i.e., latency). If the service time S and the inter-arrival time A both follow an exponential distribution, then so does

Table 13.1 Key equations for the M/M/1 queueing model (λ: arrival rate; μ: service rate).

Quantity	Equation
Average utilization	$\rho = \lambda/\mu$
Average number of queries in the system	$E[N] = \rho/(1 - \rho)$
Average response time	$E[R] = 1/(\mu - \lambda)$
Response time distribution	$f_R(x) = (\mu - \lambda) \cdot e^{-(\mu-\lambda)x}$

the response time R (Harrison, 1993):

$$f_R(x) = (\mu - \lambda) \cdot e^{-(\mu-\lambda)x}. \tag{13.12}$$

For convenience, Table 13.1 restates the essential equations derived from the M/M/1 model.

13.2.3 Latency Quantiles and Average Utilization

Let us return to the hypothetical goal stated in Section 13.1.2: that the search engine's latency be less than 1 second for 99% of all queries. Suppose the engine, on average, requires 100 ms per query (i.e., $\mu = 10$). Then the density function for the engine's response time is

$$f_R(x) = (10 - \lambda) \cdot e^{-(10-\lambda)x} \tag{13.13}$$

and the fraction of queries with a latency less than 1 second is

$$\int_0^1 f_R(x) \, dx \ = \ 1 - e^{\lambda-10}. \tag{13.14}$$

For the 99% quantile, we have $e^{\lambda-10} = 1 - 0.99$, implying $\lambda \approx 5.4$. That is, we can keep the search engine's average utilization at 54% and still achieve our stated goal of subsecond latency for 99% of all queries. If our goal were a bit more ambitious, and we wanted 99.9% of queries to have a latency below 1 second, then this would result in $\lambda \approx 3.1$, corresponding to an average utilization of 31%.

The above example illustrates the difference between the search engine's theoretical throughput (which is the same as its service rate) and the throughput it may realistically attain without causing unreasonably high latency. In practice, an average utilization of more than 50% may be considered exceptionally high and is rarely possible. Also, note that all our calculations are based on the assumption that the arrival rate λ is a constant. This assumption is usually valid only for short periods of time, perhaps a few minutes, but not for longer time intervals such as a whole day, because of periodic fluctuations in user activity (most people prefer to sleep at night). Due to changes in the arrival rate, long-term utilization levels of 20% or less are quite common. Thus, it may be necessary to spend 5 times more on hardware resources than predicted by a naïve throughput analysis that does not take latency into account.

13.3 Query Scheduling

Our derivation of the search engine's latency R in the previous section assumed that queries are always served in a first-come-first-served fashion. The rationale behind this queue discipline is the idea of fairness: We don't want Alice to receive her search results after Bob if she submits her query before Bob does. FCFS guarantees that the order in which search results are returned to the users is the same as the order in which the queries are received. However, if our primary goal is not fairness but minimizing latency, then FCFS may not be the optimal strategy.

Consider the situation in which there are two queries q_i and q_{i+1} waiting in the queue. Suppose we know their respective service times s_i and s_{i+1}, with $s_i = s_{i+1} + \delta$ ($\delta > 0$). Then we can swap the two queries, increasing q_i's latency by s_{i+1} and decreasing q_{i+1}'s latency by s_i, thus reducing their average latency by $\delta/2$.

A mechanism that changes the order in which queries are processed by the search engine is called a *scheduling algorithm*. For the sake of brevity, we limit our discussion to the following three algorithms:

- **FCFS** (first-come, first-served). This is the scheduling algorithm assumed in our discussion so far.

- **SJF** (shortest job first). Whenever the search engine is done processing a query and has to pick the next one from the queue, it selects the one with the smallest predicted service time.

- **DDS** (deadline-driven scheduling). For each query in the system we define its deadline to be 1 second after its arrival. Whenever the search engine is done with a query, it reorders the queries in the queue to minimize the number of queries that miss their deadline. In case of a tie (i.e., two orderings lead to the same number of missed deadlines), the engine selects the ordering that minimizes average latency.

Note that predicting the service time for a query q can be difficult. However, it is often sufficient to use a rough estimate, which can be obtained from the lengths of the query terms' postings lists and the number of terms in the query.

Figure 13.3 shows the outcome of an experiment in which we simulated a search engine with service rate $\mu = 10$ qps. We had it process queries for varying arrival rates between $\lambda = 1$ qps and $\lambda = 8$ qps (i.e., with average utilization between 10% and 80%). Each simulation lasted for several hours (simulated time) and involved a few hundred thousand queries. The figure depicts the engine's average latency and the fraction of queries with latency above 1 second for each of the three scheduling algorithms. You can see that, under high load, choosing the right scheduling algorithm can make a great difference. At $\rho = 0.7$, for instance, FCFS causes 5% of all queries to miss their deadline. With DDS, whose explicit goal is to minimize this number, only 1% miss their deadline.

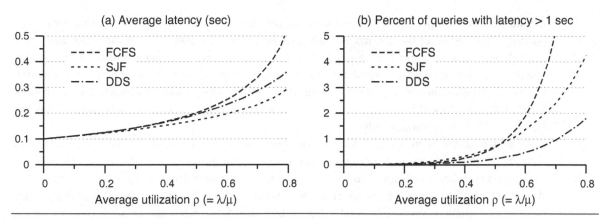

Figure 13.3 Simulated latency for different query scheduling algorithms, at various arrival rates λ. The service rate is fixed at $\mu = 10$ qps.

Latency cost functions

Despite their ability to reduce overall query latency, SJF and DDS share a significant shortcoming: *starvation*. If a query has a high predicted service time, it may have to wait a long time until it gets selected for processing. SJF, for instance, although reducing the fraction of queries with latency above 1 second from 5% to 2.5% (for $\rho = 0.7$), increases the fraction with latency above 2 seconds from 0.02% to 0.06%. With DDS this effect is slightly less pronounced, but it still causes latency to be above 2 seconds for 0.05% of the query stream.

In general, a single number, such as the fraction of queries below a certain latency threshold, can never fully describe the search engine's performance and its effects on user satisfaction. By decreasing latency for one class of queries we inevitably increase latency for another class. Thus, before choosing a concrete scheduling algorithm, we have to specify our overall goal, perhaps by defining a cost function that tells us how undesirable a given latency level is and then minimizing the average cost per query.

A linear cost function $c(x) = x$ represents the goal of minimizing average latency. A polynomial cost function $c(x) = x^q$ (for $q > 1$) takes into account that users tend to be irritated if the search engine's latency exhibits a high level of variance, with some queries taking considerably longer than others. An appropriate cost function can be found only through user studies. After one has been chosen, we can proceed to find a scheduling algorithm that is optimized for it.

13.4   Caching

In the previous section we explored ways to reduce the search engine's latency without changing the average service time. The query scheduling algorithms that we discussed do not require any modifications to the query processing logic; they achieve their goal simply by changing the order in which queries are processed by the search engine. In this section we focus on a complementary optimization: reducing the average service time by caching frequently used pieces of data.

Caching is a classic *time-versus-space trade-off*. If we give the system additional memory resources, it may use them to store the search results for previous queries. Whenever the search engine receives a query, it first checks its internal cache to see whether it already has the results for that query. Only if it does not find them in the cache does it need to actually process the query to obtain the search results.

At first it might seem that caching is unrelated to the problem of conducting reliable and meaningful performance measurements. However, it is important to understand the effect of caching on the characteristics of the query stream. For instance, the average query length in the AOL query log[3] is about 2.8 terms. If we assume a result cache with infinite capacity, so that each unique query is processed exactly once, then this figure increases to 3.5 terms per query, because longer queries are more likely to be unique. Thus, it can make a great difference whether we are measuring the pre-cache or the post-cache service rate of our search engine. Moreover, some caches attain their target hit rate only after some period of time (the *warmup period*), implying that, after a restart, the search engine's effective service rate can be be considerably lower than expected.

13.4.1 Three-Level Caching

When designing a caching system for a search engine, we first have to ask ourselves what kinds of data are worth caching. The most obvious answer is "search results". If user A types in a search query and a few minutes later user B types in the same query, there is no need to reprocess the whole query. Instead, the search engine should cache the final search results it produced for user A and send the cached version to user B.

Caching search results works well for popular queries, such as "elections" and "global warming", that are issued often. However, it has its limitations. Just like term frequencies in a text collection, query frequencies roughly follow a Zipfian distribution, where the frequency $f(i)$ of the i-th most common item is

$$f(i) = c \cdot i^{-\alpha}, \tag{13.15}$$

for some constant c and $\alpha > 1$ (see Section 1.3.3 for more details on Zipfian distributions). For query distributions, the parameter α is usually very close to 1, implying that the distribution has a "long tail" with a large number of singletons. Baeza-Yates et al. (2007) report in their analysis of a one-year query log from www.yahoo.co.uk that 44% of the total query volume was caused by singletons. On average, each query in the log was asked only about twice during the whole period. Thus, even with a cache of infinite capacity, the cache hit rate would not have

---

[3] The AOL query log contains approximately 20 million queries received by AOL's search engine between March and May 2006. It was released to the public in early August 2006 and, after a heated debate over privacy issues, was taken off-line a few days later. Copies of the data can still be found on the Internet, by typing "aol query log" into one's favorite search engine.

been higher than 50%. Needless to say, keeping a query in the cache for more than a few days is not acceptable in the context of an ever-changing text collection such as the Web. Cache hit rates lower than 50% are therefore not unusual.

Long and Suel (2005) address this limitation by proposing a *cache hierarchy* that interacts with the search engine on three different levels:

1. **Search results.** From a per-query point of view, this is the most effective caching strategy. When a query is found in the cache, the search engine can return the results almost instantaneously, reducing the service time from several hundred milliseconds to a few milliseconds. In a distributed search engine the cache is located either in the query broker or in a dedicated cache server. There is no need to even contact the index servers when the query is found in the cache.

   Unfortunately, as mentioned before, it is usually impossible to cache the search results for more than 50% of the query stream. Limiting the impact even further, the fraction of the query stream that can be cached tends to be dominated by short queries comprising 2 or 3 terms, because many of the longer queries are singletons. Thus, the total savings achieved by result caching are lower than what might be expected from the cache's hit rate. In the experiments conducted by Long and Suel, a hit rate of 50% could decrease the average cost per query by only 33%, because cached queries were shorter, and therefore cheaper to process, than uncached queries.

2. **List intersections.** Many search engines employ a conjunctive retrieval model (Boolean AND). In order to find the set of documents that contain all terms in the given query, they have to intersect the postings lists of all query terms. This may be done in a term-at-a-time fashion. In a first step, the postings lists for the first two query terms are intersected; in a second step, the third term's list is combined with the result of the first step; and so forth.

   By caching the intersection of common pairs of query terms, we can reduce the amount of work that needs to be done per query. For instance, when processing the query ⟨"global", "warming", "facts"⟩, we may cache the intersection of "global" and "warming". At a later time, when we see the query ⟨"global", "warming", "controversy"⟩, we can reduce its execution cost by reusing the cached intersection from the previous query. Long and Suel estimate that intersection caching can reduce the average service time by about 50% in a disk-based index configuration. If the index is kept in memory, the speedup is likely to be smaller.

3. **Postings lists.** In addition to the caching performed at the previous two levels, we may reduce the search engine's query processing cost by keeping frequently accessed postings lists in memory. The fruitfulness of this approach depends on whether intersection caching has been implemented or not. According to Long and Suel, if the engine caches search results but not intersections, then adding the list cache may reduce the average query cost by around 45%. However, if intersections are cached as well, the list cache saves only around 20%.

Turpin et al. (2007) add to this list a fourth item: documents. Caching documents, although it has no impact on the search process, can speed up the generation of the snippets displayed to the users — an aspect that is often ignored in (academic) information retrieval research.

13.4.2   Cache Policies

After we have decided what types of data we want to cache, we still have to address one final question: Which items should be kept in the cache? Since the cache is unlikely to be large enough to hold all possible search results, list intersections, and postings lists, we have to decide which items are worth keeping in the cache and which are not.

A *cache policy* (or *cache algorithm*) is an algorithm that, given a set of items and the cache's capacity, decides which items should be stored in the cache. Cache policies can be *static* or *dynamic*. When a static policy is used, the set of cached items is determined ahead of time and is kept fixed after the engine is started. It may be updated periodically, perhaps at the same time that an index refresh takes place. With a dynamic policy the set of cached items may change whenever the system encounters a new object (e.g., postings list) that it deems worth adding to the cache. Dynamic cache policies are also called *replacement algorithms*, because adding one item to the cache usually implies evicting another item.

General-purpose cache policies

Caching is a concept that is used in virtually all areas of computer science. We may therefore want to reuse existing cache policies that have proved to be successful in other areas. Two such policies are:

- **Least Recently Used (LRU).** Whenever a new item is added to a cache that has already reached its capacity, the item in the cache that has not been accessed for the longest time is evicted.

- **Least Frequently Used (LFU).** When a new item is added to a cache that has already reached its capacity, the item in the cache that has been accessed the least frequently (since it was loaded into the cache) is evicted.

LRU and LFU tend to work reasonably well when operating on a set of (approximately) fixed-size objects, such as the top-k search results for a set of queries, but they quickly reach their limits when confronted with objects of vastly different size. For example, if we naïvely applied LRU to the three-level cache hierarchy from the previous section, over 90% of the cache would be occupied by postings lists, simply because they are so much larger than intersections or search results. This might not be the most economical use of the cache.

Cost-aware cache policies

One way to address the problem described above is to split the cache into three buckets, one for each caching level. The size of each bucket might then be chosen based on past experience with the respective type of caching. If the bucket sizes are chosen well, this approach may yield acceptable performance. However, we can do better than that. The fundamental insight is that each cacheable item x may be represented by the following three attributes:

- c_x is the cost incurred by loading x into the cache. It is proportional to x's size in bytes.

- g_x is the gain we expect when using the cached version of x instead of its uncached version. Depending on x's type (i.e., its level in the cache hierarchy), this may be the service time of a query, the time required to compute a list intersection, or the time required to load a postings list into memory.

- p_x is the number of times we expect x to be used during a fixed period of time. You may think of p_x as a probability.

The expected net benefit we realize by loading x into the cache is

$$\text{ENB}(x) = \frac{p_x \cdot g_x}{c_x} . \tag{13.16}$$

Of course, this formula is not limited to search engines. Cost-aware caching is useful in many applications, including WWW proxies (Cao and Irani, 1997).

Equation 13.16 implicitly defines a caching policy: Sort all items x according to their ENB; store the top n items in the cache, where n is chosen such that the combined size of the top n items does not exceed the capacity of the cache. This cache policy has two convenient properties. First, it naturally covers all three item types discussed in Section 13.4.1. Second, the parameters c_x, g_x, and p_x can be estimated from past query logs. The second property is important because it allows us to turn ENB into a static policy in which we preload the top n items into the cache during initialization. Assuming that the distribution of queries and query terms changes only slowly over time, this static policy can achieve close-to-optimal performance.

It is sometimes argued that the policy described above is suboptimal because it may leave a small portion of the cache unused (*internal fragmentation*). However, this argument is only of theoretical interest. In practice, each cache item is small compared to the total size of the cache, and the space wasted due to fragmentation is negligible.

13.4.3 Prefetching Search Results

If we have access to an existing query log, we can use it to prefetch results for queries that we expect to be asked in the near future, even if they are not currently in the cache. As an example, suppose we are operating a search engine for news, blogs, or other time-sensitive information for which we cannot afford to reuse cached search results for more than an hour or two. At the end of each day, cache hit rates may be as high as 30–40%, but as our users go to sleep, traffic ebbs away, and in the morning the cache hit rate will be close to 0.

Under the assumption that tomorrow's queries will be similar to today's, we can proactively issue a set of popular queries so that their results are in the cache when the users wake up in the morning. Result prefetching does not reduce the overall load on the search engine, but it decreases its average latency by improving the cache hit rate for user-issued queries. In addition, it can help decrease the load difference between busy and quiet times of the day, which may be important if the search engine is operating near its theoretical throughput.

We may even take this idea a step further and continuously prefetch results for queries that we anticipate will be issued at a particular time of day. Beitzel et al. (2004) analyze a weeklong query log from a commercial Web search engine and find that "[p]ersonal finance, for example, becomes more popular from 7–10AM, while music queries become less popular." Of course, this strategy may only be expected to be beneficial if cache items expire or are evicted from the cache before the same query is reissued the next day.

13.5   Further Reading

An easy-to-read introduction to various aspects of measuring computer performance is provided by Lilja (2000). For an in-depth discussion of queueing analysis, including models that go beyond the simplistic $M/M/1$ model from Section 13.2, see Gross et al. (2008) or Kleinrock (1975).

The three-level cache hierarchy discussed in Section 13.4.1 was first proposed by Long and Suel (2005). It is based on a two-level cache hierarchy examined by Saraiva et al. (2001).

Baeza-Yates et al. (2007) investigate several algorithms for caching results and postings lists, including the QTFDF algorithm, an approximation of the ENB policy from Section 13.4.2. Garcia (2007) examines a large variety of cache policies, including cost-aware algorithms. Fagni et al. (2006) discuss ways to divide the search engine's cache into a static portion and a dynamic portion, using different algorithms for each part. They show that hybrid static/dynamic caching can outperform pure static and pure dynamic strategies, due to its ability to simultaneously make use of past query statistics and to adapt to changing query distributions. Zhang et al. (2008) study the interaction between list caching and index compression.

On several occasions, TREC organizers added efficiency-oriented tasks to the usual effectiveness-based evaluation conducted at TREC. Two such efforts were the VLC (very large corpus) and TB (terabyte) tracks. They are documented by Hawking and Thistlewaite (1997), Hawking et al. (1998), Clarke et al. (2005), and Büttcher et al. (2006).

13.6   Exercises

Exercise 13.1 Suppose a search engine can process queries at a rate of $\mu = 20$ qps. Queries arrive at a rate of $\lambda = 15$ qps. Assuming that service time and inter-arrival time follow an exponential distribution, what is the search engine's average latency? What fraction of the query stream has a latency above 1 second? What is the maximum throughput achievable by the search engine such that 99.9% of all queries have a latency below 1 second?

Exercise 13.2 For each of the two scheduling algorithms SJF and DDS (discussed in Section 13.3), give a latency cost function of the form

$$c : [0, \infty) \to [0, \infty),$$

mapping from latency to cost, such that the average cost per query is minimized by the respective algorithm.

Exercise 13.3 Consider an infinite query stream in which the query distribution follows a power law with

$$p(i) = \frac{c}{i^{1.05}},$$

where $p(i)$ is the probability of the i-th most frequent query and c is a constant such that $\sum_{i=1}^{\infty} p(i) = 1$. Using a static cache policy that selects the 1,000,000 most frequent queries, what fraction of the the query stream can be answered from the cache? You may find the following approximation helpful:

$$\sum_{i=1}^{\infty} i^{-\alpha} \approx 0.5772 + \int_{1}^{\infty} x^{-\alpha} dx .$$

Exercise 13.4 Consider the static cache policy QTFDF. The policy caches the postings lists of the n top-scoring terms, where the score of a term t is defined as follows:

$$score(t) = \frac{f_Q(t)}{N_t},$$

where $f_Q(t)$ is the number of times t appears in a query (according to an existing query log) and N_t is the number of documents that contain t. Under what conditions is QTFDF equivalent to the ENB policy from Section 13.4.2?

13.7 Bibliography

Baeza-Yates, R., Gionis, A., Junqueira, F., Murdock, V., Plachouras, V., and Silvestri, F. (2007). The impact of caching on search engines. In *Proceedings of the 30th Annual International ACM SIGIR Conference on Research and Development in Information Retrieval*, pages 183–190. Amsterdam, The Netherlands.

Beitzel, S. M., Jensen, E. C., Chowdhury, A., Grossman, D., and Frieder, O. (2004). Hourly analysis of a very large topically categorized Web query log. In *Proceedings of the 27th Annual International ACM SIGIR Conference on Research and Development in Information Retrieval*, pages 321–328. Sheffield, England.

Büttcher, S., Clarke, C. L. A., and Soboroff, I. (2006). The TREC 2006 terabyte track. In *Proceedings of the 15th Text REtrieval Conference (TREC 2006)*. Gaithersburg, Maryland.

Cao, P., and Irani, S. (1997). Cost-aware WWW proxy caching algorithms. In *Proceedings of the 1997 USENIX Symposium on Internet Technologies and Systems*, pages 193–206. Monterey, California.

Clarke, C. L. A., Scholer, F., and Soboroff, I. (2005). The TREC 2005 terabyte track. In *Proceedings of the 14th Text REtrieval Conference*. Gaithersburg, Maryland.

Fagni, T., Perego, R., Silvestri, F., and Orlando, S. (2006). Boosting the performance of web search engines: Caching and prefetching query results by exploiting historical usage data. *ACM Transactions on Information Systems*, 24(1):51–78.

Garcia, S. (2007). *Search Engine Optimisation Using Past Queries*. Ph.D. thesis, RMIT University, Melbourne, Australia.

Gross, D., Shortle, J., Thompson, J., and Harris, C. (2008). *Fundamentals of Queueing Theory* (4th ed.). New York: Wiley-Interscience.

Harrison, P. G. (1993). Response time distributions in queueing network models. In *Performance Evaluation of Computer and Communication Systems, Joint Tutorial Papers of Performance '93 and Sigmetrics '93*, pages 147–164. Santa Clara, California.

Hawking, D., Craswell, N., and Thistlewaite, P. (1998). Overview of TREC-7 very large collection track. In *Proceedings of the 7th Text REtrieval Conference*. Gaithersburg, Maryland.

Hawking, D., and Thistlewaite, P. (1997). Overview of TREC-6 very large collection track. In *Proceedings of the 6th Text REtrieval Conference*, pages 93–106. Gaithersburg, Maryland.

Kleinrock, L. (1975). *Queueing Systems. Volume 1: Theory*. New York: Wiley-Interscience.

Lilja, D. J. (2000). *Measuring Computer Performance: A Practitioner's Guide*. New York: Cambridge University Press.

Little, J. D. C. (1961). A proof for the queueing formula L=λW. *Operations Research*, 9(3):383–387.

Long, X., and Suel, T. (2005). Three-level caching for efficient query processing in large web search engines. In *Proceedings of the 14th International Conference on World Wide Web*, pages 257–266. Chiba, Japan.

Saraiva, P. C., de Moura, E. S., Ziviani, N., Meira, W., Fonseca, R., and Riberio-Neto, B. (2001). Rank-preserving two-level caching for scalable search engines. In *Proceedings of the 24th Annual International ACM SIGIR Conference on Research and Development in Information Retrieval*, pages 51–58. New Orleans, Louisiana.

Turpin, A., Tsegay, Y., Hawking, D., and Williams, H. E. (2007). Fast generation of result snippets in web search. In *Proceedings of the 30th Annual International ACM SIGIR Conference on Research and Development in Information Retrieval*, pages 127–134. Amsterdam, The Netherlands.

Zhang, J., Long, X., and Suel, T. (2008). Performance of compressed inverted list caching in search engines. In *Proceeding of the 17th International Conference on World Wide Web*, pages 387–396. Beijing, China.

V   Applications and Extensions

14 Parallel Information Retrieval

Information retrieval systems often have to deal with very large amounts of data. They must be able to process many gigabytes or even terabytes of text, and to build and maintain an index for millions of documents. To some extent the techniques discussed in Chapters 5–8 can help us satisfy these requirements, but it is clear that, at some point, sophisticated data structures and clever optimizations alone are not sufficient anymore. A single computer simply does not have the computational power or the storage capabilities required for indexing even a small fraction of the World Wide Web.[1]

In this chapter we examine various ways of making information retrieval systems scale to very large text collections such as the Web. The first part (Section 14.1) is concerned with parallel query processing, where the search engine's service rate is increased by having multiple index servers process incoming queries in parallel. It also discusses redundancy and fault tolerance issues in distributed search engines. In the second second part (Section 14.2), we shift our attention to the parallel execution of off-line tasks, such as index construction and statistical analysis of a corpus of text. We explain the basics of MapReduce, a framework designed for massively parallel computations carried out on large amounts of data.

14.1 Parallel Query Processing

There are many ways in which parallelism can help a search engine process queries faster. The two most popular approaches are *index partitioning* and *replication*. Suppose we have a total of n index servers. Following the standard terminology, we refer to these servers as *nodes*. By creating n replicas of the index and assigning each replica to a separate node, we can realize an n-fold increase of the search engine's service rate (its theoretical throughput) without affecting the time required to process a single query. This type of parallelism is referred to as *inter-query parallelism*, because multiple queries can be processed in parallel but each individual query is processed sequentially. Alternatively, we could split the index into n parts and have each node work only on its own small part of the index. This approach is referred to as *intra-query*

---

[1] While nobody knows the exact size of the indexable part of the Web, it is estimated to be at least 100 billion pages. In August 2005, when Yahoo! last disclosed the size of its index, it had reached a total size of 19.2 billion documents (http://www.ysearchblog.com/archives/000172.html).

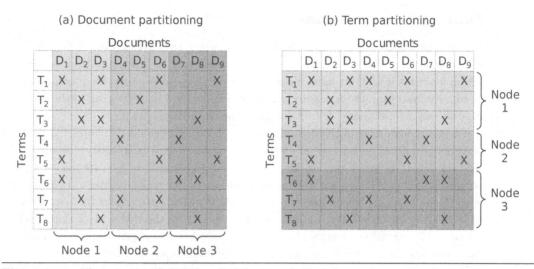

Figure 14.1 The two prevalent index partitioning schemes: document partitioning and term partitioning (shown for a hypothetical index containing 8 terms and 9 documents).

parallelism, because each query is processed by multiple servers in parallel. It improves the engine's service rate as well as the average time per query.

In this section we focus primarily on methods for intra-query parallelism. We study index partitioning schemes that divide the index into independent parts so that each node is responsible for a small piece of the overall index.

The two predominant index partitioning schemes are *document partitioning* and *term partitioning* (visualized in Figure 14.1). In a document-partitioned index, each node holds an index for a subset of the documents in the collection. For instance, the index maintained by node 2 in Figure 14.1(a) contains the following docid lists:

$$L_1 = \langle 4, 6 \rangle, \quad L_2 = \langle 5 \rangle, \quad L_4 = \langle 4 \rangle, \quad L_5 = \langle 6 \rangle, \quad L_7 = \langle 4, 6 \rangle.$$

In a term-partitioned index, each node is responsible for a subset of the terms in the collection. The index stored in node 1 in Figure 14.1(b) contains the following lists:

$$L_1 = \langle 1, 3, 4, 6, 9 \rangle, \quad L_2 = \langle 2, 5 \rangle, \quad L_3 = \langle 2, 3, 8 \rangle.$$

The two partitioning strategies differ greatly in the way queries are processed by the system. In a document-partitioned search engine, each of the n nodes is involved in processing all queries received by the engine. In a term-partitioned configuration, a query is seen by a given node only if the node's index contains at least one of the query terms.

14.1.1 Document Partitioning

In a document-partitioned index, each index server is responsible for a subset of the documents in the collection. Each incoming user query is received by a frontend server, the *receptionist*, which forwards it to all n index nodes, waits for them to process the query, merges the search results received from the index nodes, and sends the final list of results to the user. A schematic of a document-partitioned search engine is shown in Figure 14.2.

The main advantage of the document-partitioned approach is its simplicity. Because all index servers operate independently of each other, no additional complexity needs to be introduced into the low-level query processing routines. All that needs to be provided is the receptionist server that forwards the query to the backends and, after receiving the top k search results from each of the n nodes, selects the top m, which are then returned to the user (where the value of m is typically chosen by the user and k is chosen by the operator of the search engine). In addition to forwarding queries and search results, the receptionist may also maintain a cache that contains the results for recently/frequently issued queries.

If the search engine maintains a dynamic index that allows updates (e.g., document insertions/deletions), then it may even be possible to carry out the updates in a distributed fashion, in which each node takes care of the updates that pertain to its part of the overall index. This approach eliminates the need for a complicated centralized index construction/maintenance process that involves the whole index. However, it is applicable only if documents may be assumed to be independent of each other, not if inter-document information, such as hyperlinks and anchor text, is part of the index.

When deciding how to divide the collection across the n index nodes, one might be tempted to bias the document-node assignment in some way — for instance, by storing similar documents in the same node. In Section 6.3.7 we have seen that the index can be compressed better if the documents in the collection are reordered according to their URL, so that documents with similar URLs receive nearby docids. Obviously, this method is most effective if all pages from the same domain are assigned to the same node. The problem with this approach is that it may create an imbalance in the load distribution of the index servers. If a given node primarily contains documents associated with a certain topic, and this topic suddenly becomes very popular among users, then the query processing load for that node may become much higher than the load of the other nodes. In the end this will lead to a suboptimal utilization of the available resources. To avoid this problem, it is usually best to not try anything fancy but to simply split the collection into n completely random subsets.

Once the index has been partitioned and each subindex has been loaded into one of the nodes, we have to make a decision regarding the per-node result set size k. How should k be chosen with respect to m, the number of search results requested by the user? Suppose the user has asked for $m = 100$ results. If we want to be on the safe side, we can have each index node return $k = 100$ results, thus making sure that all of the top 100 results overall are received by the receptionist. However, this would be a poor decision, for two reasons:

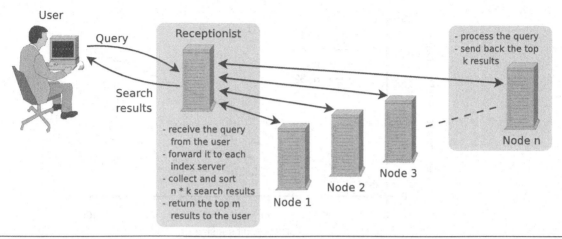

User

Query

Receptionist

- process the query
- send back the top
  k results

Search
results

Node n

- receive the query
  from the user
- forward it to each
  index server
- collect and sort
  n * k search results
- return the top m
  results to the user

Node 1

Node 2

Node 3

Figure 14.2 Document-partitioned query processing with one receptionist and several index servers. Each incoming query is forwarded to all index servers.

1. It is quite unlikely that all of the top 100 results come from the same node. By having each index server return 100 results to the receptionist, we put more load on the network than necessary.

2. The choice of k has a non-negligible effect on query processing performance, because of performance heuristics such as MaxScore (see Section 5.1.1). Table 5.1 on page 144 shows that decreasing the result set size from $k = 100$ to $k = 10$ can reduce the average CPU time per query by around 15%, when running queries against a frequency index for GOV2.

Clarke and Terra (2004) describe a method to compute the probability that the receptionist sees at least the top m results overall, given the number n of index servers and the per-node result set size k. Their approach is based on the assumption that each document was assigned to a random index node when the collection was split into n subsets, and thus that each node is equally likely to return the best, second-best, third-best, ... result overall.

Consider the set $\mathcal{R}_m = \{r_1, r_2, \ldots, r_m\}$ composed of the top m search results. For each document r_i the probability that it is found by a particular node is $1/n$. Hence, the probability that exactly l of the top m results are found by that node is given by the binomial distribution

$$b(n, m, l) = \binom{m}{l} \cdot \left(\frac{1}{n}\right)^l \cdot \left(1 - \frac{1}{n}\right)^{m-l}. \tag{14.1}$$

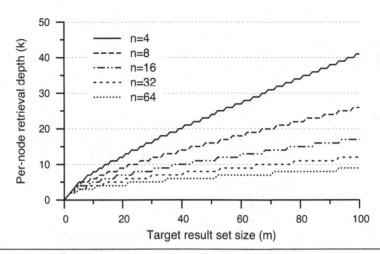

Figure 14.3   Choosing the minimum retrieval depth k that returns the top m results with probability $p(n, m, k) > 99.9\%$, where n is the number of nodes in the document-partitioned index.

The probability that all members of $\mathcal{R}_m$ are discovered by requesting the top k results from each of the n index nodes can be calculated according to the following recursive formula:

$$p(n, m, k) = \begin{cases} 1 & \text{if } m \leq k; \\ 0 & \text{if } m > k \text{ and } n = 1; \\ \sum_{l=0}^{k} b(n, m, l) \cdot p(n - 1, m - l, k) & \text{if } m > k \text{ and } n > 1. \end{cases} \tag{14.2}$$

The two base cases are obvious. In the recursive case, we consider the first node in the system and compute the probability that $l = 0, 1, 2, \ldots, k$ of the top m results overall are retrieved by that node (i.e., $b(n, m, l)$). For each possible value for l, this probability is multiplied by the probability $p(n - 1, m - l, k)$ that the remaining $m - l$ documents in $\mathcal{R}_m$ are found by the remaining $n - 1$ index nodes. Equation 14.2 does not appear to have a closed-form solution but can be solved through the application of dynamic programming in time $\Theta(n \cdot m \cdot k)$.

Figure 14.3 shows the per-node retrieval depth k required to find the top m results with probability at least 99.9%. For $m = 100$ and $n = 4$, a per-node retrieval depth of $k = 41$ achieves the desired probability level. If we decide to relax our correctness requirements from 99.9% to 95%, k can even be decreased a little further, from 41 to 35.

It can sometimes be beneficial to optimize the retrieval depth k for a different value m than the user has asked for. For example, if the receptionist maintains a cache for recently issued queries, it may be worthwhile to obtain the top 20 results for a given query even if the user has asked for only the top 10, so that a click on the "next page" link can be processed from the cache. Allowing the receptionist to inspect a result set $\mathcal{R}_{m'}$ for $m' > m$ is also useful because it facilitates the application of diversity-seeking reranking techniques, such as Carbonell and Goldstein's (1998) *maximal marginal relevance* or Google's *host crowding* heuristic.[2]

14.1.2   Term Partitioning

Although document partitioning is often the right choice and scales almost linearly with the number of nodes, it can unfold its true potential only if the index data found in the individual nodes are stored in main memory or any other low-latency random-access storage medium, such as flash memory, but not if it is stored on disk.

Consider a document-partitioned search engine in which all postings lists are stored on disk. Suppose each query contains 3 words on average, and we want the search engine to handle a peak query load of 100 queries per second. Recall from Section 13.2.3 that, due to queueing effects, we usually cannot sustain a utilization level above 50%, unless we are willing to accept occasional latency jumps. Thus, a query load of 100 qps translates into a required service rate of at least 200 qps or — equivalently — 600 random access operations per second (one for each query term). Assuming an average disk seek latency of 10 ms, a single hard disk drive cannot perform more than 100 random access operations per second, a factor of 6 less than what is required to achieve the desired throughput. We could try to circumvent this limitation by adding more disks to each index node, but equipping each server with six hard disks may not always be practical. Moreover, it is obvious that we will never be able to handle loads of more than a few hundred queries per second, regardless of how many nodes we add to the system.

Term partitioning addresses the disk seek problem by splitting the collection into sets of terms instead of sets of documents. Each index node v_i is responsible for a certain term set T_i and is involved in processing a given query only if one or more query terms are members of T_i. Our discussion of term-partitioned query processing is based upon the pipelined architecture proposed by Moffat et al. (2007). In this architecture, queries are processed in a term-at-a-time fashion (see Section 5.1.2 for details on term-at-a-time query processing strategies).

Suppose a query contains q terms $t_1, t_2, \ldots, t_q$. Then the receptionist will forward the query to the node $v(t_1)$ responsible for the term t_1. After creating a set of document score accumulators from t_1's postings list, $v(t_1)$ forwards the query, along with the accumulator set, to the node $v(t_2)$ responsible for t_2, which updates the accumulator set, sends it to $v(t_3)$, and so forth. When the last node in this pipeline, $v(t_q)$, is finished, it sends the final accumulator set to the receptionist. The receptionist then selects the top m search results and returns them to the user. A schematic of this approach is shown in Figure 14.4.

Many of the optimizations used for sequential term-at-a-time query processing also apply to term-partitioned query processing: infrequent query terms should be processed first; accumulator pruning strategies should be applied to keep the size of the accumulator set, and thus the

---

[2] www.mattcutts.com/blog/subdomains-and-subdirectories/

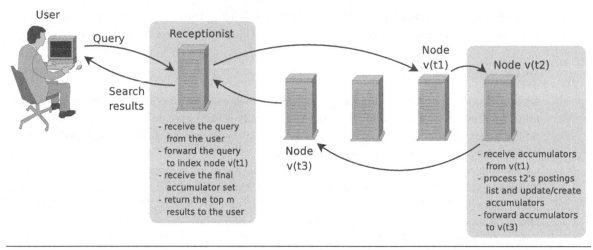

Figure 14.4 Term-partitioned query processing with one receptionist and four index servers. Each incoming query is passed from index server to index server, depending on the terms found in the query (shown for a query containing three terms).

overall network traffic, under control; impact ordering can be used to efficiently identify the most important postings for a given term.

Note that the pipelined query processing architecture outlined above does not use intra-query parallelism, as each query — at a given point in time — is processed by only a single node. Therefore, although it can help increase the system's theoretical throughput, term partitioning, in the simple form described here, does not necessarily decrease the search engine's response time. To some extent this limitation can be addressed by having the receptionist send prefetch instructions to the nodes $v(t_2), \ldots, v(t_q)$ at the same time it forwards the query to $v(t_1)$. This way, when a node $v(t_i)$ receives the accumulator set, some of t_i's postings may already have been loaded into memory and the query can be processed faster.

Despite its potential performance advantage over the document-partitioned approach, at least for on-disk indices, term partitioning has several shortcomings that make it difficult to use the method in practice:

- **Scalability.** As the collection becomes bigger, so do the individual postings lists. For a corpus composed of a billion documents, the postings list for a frequent term, such as "computer" or "internet", can easily occupy several hundred megabytes. Processing a query that contains one or more of these frequent terms will require at least a few seconds, far more than what most users are accustomed to. In order to solve this problem, large postings lists need to be cut into smaller chunks and divided among several nodes, with each node taking care of a small part of the postings list and all of them working in parallel. Unfortunately, this complicates the query processing logic quite a bit.

- **Load Imbalance.** Term partitioning suffers from an uneven load across the index nodes. The load corresponding to a single term is a function of the term's frequency in the collection as well as its frequency in users' queries. If a term has a long postings list and is also very popular in search queries, then the corresponding index node may experience a load that is much higher than the average load in the system. To address this problem, postings lists that are responsible for a high fraction of the overall load should be replicated and distributed across multiple nodes. This way, the computational load associated with a given term can be shared among several machines, albeit at the cost of increased storage requirements.

- **Term-at-a-Time.** Perhaps the most severe limitation of the term-partitioned approach is its inability to support efficient document-at-a-time query processing. In order to realize document-at-a-time scoring on top of a term-partitioned index, entire postings lists, as opposed to pruned accumulator sets, would need to be sent across the network. This is impractical, due to the size of the postings lists. Therefore, ranking methods that necessitate a document-at-a-time approach, such as the proximity ranking function from Section 2.2.2, are incompatible with a term-partitioned index.

Even with all these shortcomings, term partitioning can sometimes be the right choice. Recall, for instance, the three-level cache hierarchy from Section 13.4.1. The second level in this hierarchy caches list intersections (in search engines with Boolean-AND query semantics; see Section 2.2). Instead of following a document partitioning approach and equipping each index node with its own intersection cache, we may choose a term-partitioned index and treat the cached intersections just like ordinary postings lists. In the example shown in Figure 14.4, if we have already seen the query $\langle t_1, t_2 \rangle$ before, we may have cached the intersected list $(t_1 \wedge t_2)$ in index node $v(t_2)$ and may skip $v(t_1)$ when processing the new query $\langle t_1, t_2, t_3 \rangle$.

More generally, term partitioning suggests itself if postings lists are relatively short — either due to the nature of the information they represent (as in the case of list intersections) or because they are artificially shortened (for instance, by applying index pruning techniques; see Section 5.1.5 for details).

14.1.3 Hybrid Schemes

Consider a distributed index with n nodes, for a collection of size $|\mathcal{C}|$. Document partitioning becomes inefficient if $|\mathcal{C}|/n$ is too small and disk seeks dominate the overall query processing cost. Term partitioning, on the other hand, becomes impractical if $|\mathcal{C}|$ is too large, as the time required to process a single query is likely to exceed the users' patience.

Xi et al. (2002) propose a hybrid architecture in which the collection is divided into p subcollections according to a standard document partitioning scheme. The index for each subcollection is then term-partitioned across n/p nodes, so that each node in the system is responsible for all occurrences of a set of terms within one of the p subcollections. With the right load balancing policies in place, this can lead roughly to a factor-n increase in throughput and a factor-p latency reduction.

As an alternative to the hybrid term/document partitioning, we may also consider a hybrid of document partitioning and replication. Remember that the primary objective of term partitioning is to increase throughput, not to decrease latency. Thus, instead of term-partitioning each of the p subindices, we may achieve the same performance level by simply replicating each subindex n/p times and load-balancing the queries among n/p identical replicas. At a high level, this is the index layout that was used by Google around 2003 (Barroso et al., 2003). The overall impact on maximum throughput and average latency is approximately the same as in the case of the hybrid document/term partitioning. The storage requirements are likely to be a bit higher, due to the (n/p)-way replication. If the index is stored on disk, this is usually not a problem.

14.1.4   Redundancy and Fault Tolerance

When operating a large-scale search engine with thousands of users, reliability and fault tolerance tend to be of similar importance as response time and result quality. As we increase the number of machines in the search engine, so as to scale to higher query loads, it becomes more and more likely that one of them will fail at some point in time. If the system has been designed with fault tolerance in mind, then the failure of a single machine may cause a small reduction in throughput or search quality. If it has not been designed with fault tolerance in mind, a single failure may bring down the entire search engine.

Let us compare the simple, replication-free document partitioning and term partitioning schemes for a distributed search engine with 32 nodes. If one of the nodes in the term-partitioned index fails, the engine will no longer be able to process queries containing any of the terms managed by that node. Queries that do not contain any of those terms are unaffected. For a random query q containing three words (the average number of query terms for Web queries), the probability that q can be processed by the remaining 31 nodes is

$$\left(\frac{31}{32}\right)^3 \approx 90.9\%. \tag{14.3}$$

If one of the nodes in the document-partitioned index fails, on the other hand, the search engine will still be able to process all incoming queries. However, it will miss some search results. If the partitioning was performed bias-free, then the probability that j out of the top k results for a random query are missing is

$$\binom{k}{j} \cdot \left(\frac{1}{32}\right)^j \cdot \left(\frac{31}{32}\right)^{k-j}. \tag{14.4}$$

Thus, the probability that the top 10 results are unaffected by the failure is

$$\left(\frac{31}{32}\right)^{10} \approx 72.8\%. \tag{14.5}$$

It therefore might seem that the impact of the machine failure is lower for the term-partitioned than for the document-partitioned index. However, the comparison is somewhat unfair, because the inability to process a query is a more serious problem than losing one of the top 10 search results. If we look at the probability that at least 2 of the top 10 results are lost due to the missing index node, we obtain

$$1 - \left(\frac{31}{32}\right)^{10} - \binom{10}{1} \cdot \left(\frac{1}{32}\right) \cdot \left(\frac{31}{32}\right)^{9} \approx 3.7\%. \tag{14.6}$$

Thus, the probability that a query is impacted severely by a single node failure is in fact quite small, and most users are unlikely to notice the difference. Following this line of argument, we may say that a document-partitioned index degrades more gracefully than a term-partitioned one in the case of a single node failure.

For informational queries, where there are often multiple relevant results, this behavior might be good enough. For navigational queries, however, this is clearly not the case (see Section 15.2 for the difference between informational and navigational queries). As an example, consider the navigational query ⟨"white", "house", "website"⟩. This query has a single vital result (http://www.whitehouse.gov/) that *must* be present in the top search results. If 1 of the 32 nodes in the document-partitioned index fails, then for each navigational query there is a 3.2% chance that the query's vital result is lost (if there is a vital result for the query). There are many ways to address this problem. Three popular ones are the following:

- **Replication.** We can maintain multiple copies of the same index node, as described in the previous section on hybrid partitioning schemes, and have them process queries in parallel. If one of the r replicas for a given index node fails, the remaining $r-1$ will take over the load of the missing replica. The advantage of this approach is its simplicity (and its ability to improve throughput and fault tolerance at the same time). Its disadvantage is that, if the system is operating near its theoretical throughput and r is small, the remaining $r-1$ replicas may become overloaded.

- **Partial Replication.** Instead of replicating the entire index r times, we may choose to replicate index information only for important documents. The rationale behind this strategy is that most search results aren't vital and can easily be replaced by an equally relevant document. The downside of this approach is that it can be difficult to predict which documents may be targeted by navigational queries. Query-independent signals such as PageRank (Section 15.3.1) can provide some guidance.

- **Dormant Replication.** Suppose the search engine comprises a total of n nodes. We can divide the index found on each node v_i into $n-1$ fragments and distribute them evenly among the $n-1$ remaining nodes, but leave them dormant (on disk) and not use them for query processing. Only when v_i fails will the corresponding $n-1$ fragments be activated inside the remaining nodes and loaded into memory for query processing. It is important that the fragments are loaded into memory, for otherwise we will double the overall number of disk seeks per query. Dormant replication roughly causes a factor-2 storage overhead, because each of the n nodes has to store $n-1$ additional index fragments.

It is possible to combine the above strategies — for example, by employing dormant replication of partial indices. Instead of replicating the whole index found in a given node, we replicate only the part that corresponds to important documents. This reduces the storage overhead and limits the impact on the search engine's throughput in case of a node failure.

14.2   MapReduce

Apart from processing search queries, there are many other data-intensive tasks that need to be carried out by a large-scale search engine. Such tasks include building and updating the index; identifying duplicate documents in the corpus; and analyzing the link structure of the document collection (e.g., PageRank; see Section 15.3.1).

MapReduce is a framework developed at Google that is designed for massively parallel computations (thousands of machines) on very large amounts of data (many terabytes), and that can accomplish all of the tasks listed above. MapReduce was first presented by Dean and Ghemawat (2004). In addition to a high-level overview of the framework, their paper includes information about many interesting implementation details and performance optimizations.

14.2.1   The Basic Framework

MapReduce was inspired by the *map* and *reduce* functions found in functional programming languages, such as Lisp. The map function takes as its arguments a function f and a list of elements $l = \langle l_1, l_2, \ldots, l_n \rangle$. It returns a new list

$$map(f, l) \;=\; \langle\, f(l_1),\; f(l_2),\; \ldots,\; f(l_n)\,\rangle. \tag{14.7}$$

The reduce function (also known as *fold* or *accumulate*) takes a function g and a list of elements $l = \langle l_1, l_2, \ldots, l_n \rangle$. It returns a new element l', such that

$$l' \;=\; reduce(g, l) \;=\; g(l_1,\; g(l_2,\; g(l_3,\; \ldots))). \tag{14.8}$$

When people refer to the map function in the context of MapReduce, they usually mean the function f that gets passed to *map* (where *map* itself is provided by the framework). Similarly,

map $(k,\ v) \equiv$		**reduce** $(k,\ \langle v_1, v_2, \ldots, v_n \rangle) \equiv$
1	split v into tokens	5	$count \leftarrow 0$
2	**for each** token t **do**	6	**for** $i \leftarrow 1$ **to** n **do**
3	**output**$(t, 1)$	7	$count \leftarrow count + v_i$
4	**return**	8	**output**$(count)$
		9	**return**

Figure 14.5 A MapReduce that counts the number of occurrences of each term in a given corpus of text. The input values processed by the map function are documents or other pieces of text. The input keys are ignored. The outcome of the MapReduce is a sequence of (t, f_t) tuples, where t is a term, and f_t is the number of times t appeared in the input.

when they refer to the reduce function, they mean the function g that gets passed to *reduce*. We will follow this convention.

From a high-level point of view, a MapReduce program (often simply called "a MapReduce") reads a sequence of key/value pairs, performs some computations on them, and outputs another sequence of key/value pairs. Keys and values are often strings, but may in fact be any data type. A MapReduce consists of three distinct phases:

- In the *map phase*, key/value pairs are read from the input and the map function is applied to each of them individually. The function is of the general form

$$map: \ (k, v) \ \mapsto \ \langle (k_1, v_1),\ (k_2, v_2),\ \ldots \rangle. \tag{14.9}$$

  That is, for each key/value pair, map outputs a sequence of key/value pairs. This sequence may or may not be empty, and the output keys may or may not be identical to the input key (they usually aren't).

- In the *shuffle phase*, the pairs produced during the map phase are sorted by their key, and all values for the same key are grouped together.

- In the *reduce phase*, the reduce function is applied to each key and its values. The function is of the form

$$reduce: \ (k,\ \langle v_1, v_2, \ldots \rangle) \ \mapsto \ (k,\ \langle v_1', v_2', \ldots \rangle). \tag{14.10}$$

  That is, for each key the reduce function processes the list of associated values and outputs another list of values. The output values may or may not be the same as the input values. The output key usually has to be the same as the input key, although this depends on the implementation.

Figure 14.5 shows the map and reduce functions of a MapReduce that counts the number of occurrences of all terms in a given corpus of text. In the reduce function, the output key is omitted, as it is implicit from the input key.

MapReduces are highly parallelizable, because both map and reduce can be executed in parallel on many different machines. Suppose we have a total of $n = m + r$ machines, where m is the number of *map workers* and r is the number of *reduce workers*. The input of the MapReduce is broken into small pieces called *map shards*. Each shard typically holds between 16 and 64 MB of data. The shards are treated independently, and each shard is assigned to one of the m map workers. In a large MapReduce, it is common to have dozens or hundreds of map shards assigned to each map worker. A worker usually works on only 1 shard at a time, so all its shards have to be processed sequentially. However, if a worker has more than 1 CPU, it may improve performance to have it work on multiple shards in parallel.

In a similar fashion, the output is broken into separate *reduce shards*, where the number of reduce shards is often the same as r, the number of reduce workers. Each key/value pair generated by the map function is sent to one of the r reduce shards. Typically, the shard that a given key/value pair is sent to depends only on the key. For instance, if we have r reduce shards, the target shard for each pair could be chosen according to

$$shard(key, value) = hash(key) \bmod r, \tag{14.11}$$

where *hash* is an arbitrary hash function. Assigning the map output to different reduce shards in this manner guarantees that all values for the same key end up in the same reduce shard. Within each reduce shard, incoming key/value pairs are sorted by their key (this is the shuffle phase), and are eventually fed into the reduce function to produce the final output of the MapReduce.

Figure 14.6 shows the data flow for the MapReduce from Figure 14.5, for three small text fragments from the Shakespeare corpus. Each fragment represents a separate map shard. The key/value pairs emitted by the map workers are partitioned onto the three reduce shards based on the hash of the respective key. For the purpose of the example, we assume $hash(\text{"heart"}) \bmod 3 = 0$, $hash(\text{"soul"}) \bmod 3 = 1$, and so forth.

The map phase may overlap with the shuffle phase, and the shuffle phase may overlap with the reduce phase. However, the map phase may never overlap with the reduce phase. The reason for this is that the reduce function can only be called after all values for a given key are available. Since, in general, it is impossible to predict what keys the map workers will emit, the reduce phase cannot commence before the map phase is finished.

14.2.2 Combiners

In many MapReduce jobs, a single map shard may produce a large number of key/value pairs for the same key. For instance, if we apply the counting MapReduce from Figure 14.5 to a typical corpus of English text, 6–7% of the map outputs will be for the key "the". Forwarding all these tuples to the reduce worker responsible for the term "the" wastes network and storage resources. More important, however, it creates an unhealthy imbalance in the overall load distribution. Regardless of how many reduce workers we assign to the job, one of them will end up doing at least 7% of the overall reduce work.

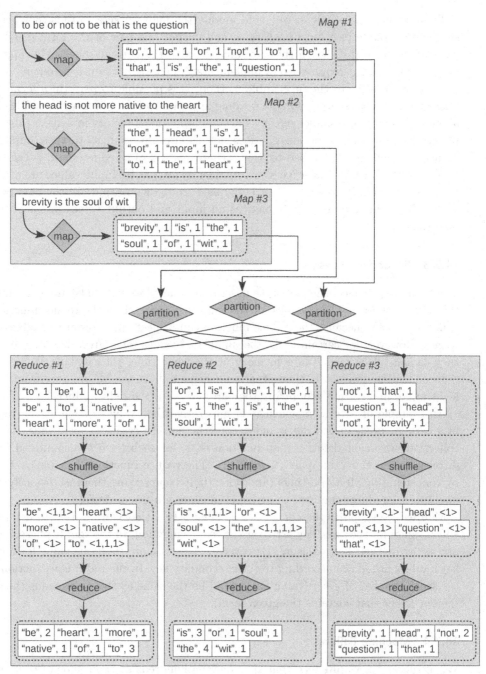

Figure 14.6 Data flow for the MapReduce definition shown in Figure 14.5, using 3 map shards and 3 reduce shards.

To overcome this problem, we could modify the map workers so that they accumulate per-shard term counts in a local hash table and output one pair of the form (t, f_t) instead of f_t pairs of the form $(t, 1)$ when they are finished with the current shard. This approach has the disadvantage that it requires extra implementation effort by the programmer.

As an alternative to the hash table method, it is possible to perform a local shuffle/reduce phase for each map shard before forwarding any data to the reduce workers. This approach has about the same performance effect as accumulating local counts in a hash table, but is often preferred by developers because it does not require any changes to their implementation. A reduce function that is applied to a map shard instead of a reduce shard is called a *combiner*. Every reduce function can serve as a combiner as long as its input values are of the same type as its output values, so that it can be applied to its own output. In the case of the counting MapReduce, this requirement is met, as all input and output values in the reduce phase are integers.

14.2.3   Secondary Keys

The basic MapReduce framework, as described so far, does not make any guarantees regarding the relative order in which values for the same key are fed into the reduce function. Often this is not a problem, because the reduce function can inspect and reorder the values in any way it wishes. However, for certain tasks the number of values for a given key may be so large that they cannot all be loaded into memory at the same time, thus making reordering inside the reduce function difficult. In that situation it helps to have the MapReduce framework sort each key's values in a certain way before they are passed to the reduce function.

An example of a task in which it is imperative that values arrive at the reduce function in a certain, predefined order is index construction. To create a docid index for a given text collection, we might define a map function that, for each term t encountered in a document d, outputs the key/value pair $(t, docid(d))$. The reduce function then builds t's postings list by concatenating all its postings (and potentially compressing them). Obviously, for this to be possible, the reduce input has to arrive in increasing order of $docid(d)$.

MapReduce supports the concept of *secondary keys* that can be used to define the order in which values for the same key arrive at the reduce function. In the shuffle phase, key/value pairs are sorted by their key, as usual. However, if there is more than one value for a given key, the key's values are sorted according to their secondary key. In the index construction MapReduce, the secondary key of a key/value pair would be the same as the pair's value (i.e., the docid of the document that contains the given term).

14.2.4   Machine Failures

When running a MapReduce that spans across hundreds or thousands of computers, some of the machines occasionally experience problems and have to be shut down. The MapReduce framework assumes that the map function behaves strictly deterministically, and that the map output for a given map shard depends only on that one shard (i.e., no information may be exchanged between two shards processed by the same map worker). If this assumption holds, then a map worker failure can be dealt with by assigning its shards to a different machine and reprocessing them.

Dealing with a reduce worker failure is slightly more complicated. Because the data in each reduce shard may depend on data in every map shard, assigning the reduce shard to a different worker may necessitate the re-execution of all map shards. In order to avoid this, the output of the map phase is usually not sent directly to the reduce workers but is temporarily stored in a reliable storage layer, such as a dedicated storage server or the Google file system (Ghemawat et al., 2003), from where it can be read by the new reduce worker in case of a worker failure. However, even if the map output is stored in a reliable fashion, a reduce worker failure will still require the re-execution of the shuffle phase for the failed shard. If we want to avoid this, too, then the reduce worker needs to send the output of the shuffle phase back to the storage server before it enters the reduce phase. Because, for a given shard, the shuffle phase and the reduce phase take place on the same machine, the additional network traffic is usually not worth the time savings unless machine failures occur frequently.

14.3 Further Reading

Compared with other topics covered by this book, the literature on parallel information retrieval is quite sparse. Existing publications are mostly limited to small or mid-size compute clusters comprising not more than a few dozen machines (the exception being occasional publications by some of the major search engine companies). In some cases it may therefore be difficult to assess the scalability of a proposed architecture. For instance, although the basic version of term partitioning discussed in Section 14.1.2 might work well on an 8-node cluster, it is quite obvious that it does not scale to a cluster containing hundreds or thousands of nodes. Despite this caveat, however, some of the results obtained in small-scale experiments may still be applicable to large-scale parallel search engines.

Load balancing issues for term-partitioned query evaluation are investigated by Moffat et al. (2006). Their study shows that, with the right load balancing policies in place, term partitioning can lead to almost the same query performance as document partitioning. Marín and Gil-Costa (2007) conduct a similar study and come to the conclusion that a term-partitioned index can sometimes outperform a document-partitioned one. Abusukhon et al. (2008) examine a variant of term partitioning in which terms with long postings lists are distributed across multiple index nodes.

Puppin et al. (2006) discuss a document partitioning scheme in which documents are not assigned to nodes at random but based on the queries for which they are ranked highly (according to an existing query log). Documents that rank highly for the same set of queries tend to be assigned to the same node. Each incoming query is forwarded only to those index nodes that are likely to return good results for the query. Xi et al. (2002) and Marín and Gil-Costa (2007) report on experiments conducted with hybrid partitioning schemes, combining term partitioning and document partitioning. A slightly different view of parallel query processing is presented by Marín and Navarro (2003), who discuss distributed query processing based on suffix arrays instead of inverted files.

Barroso et al. (2003) provide an overview of distributed query processing at Google. Other instruments for large-scale data processing at Google are described by Ghemawat et al. (2003), Dean and Ghemawat (2004, 2008), and Chang et al. (2008).

Hadoop[3] is an open-source framework for parallel computations that was inspired by Google's MapReduce and GFS technologies. Among other components, Hadoop includes HDFS (a distributed file system) and a MapReduce implementation. The Hadoop project was started by Doug Cutting, who also created the Lucene search engine. Yahoo is one of the main contributors to the project and is believed to be running the world's largest Hadoop installation, comprising several thousand machines.

Recently the use of graphics processing units (GPUs) for general-purpose, non-graphics-related computations has received some attention. Due to their highly parallel nature, GPUs can easily beat ordinary CPUs in applications in which long sequences of data have to be processed sequentially or cosequentially, such as sorting (Govindaraju et al., 2006; Sintorn and Assarsson, 2008) and disjunctive (i.e., Boolean-OR) query processing (Ding et al., 2009).

14.4 Exercises

Exercise 14.1 When replicating a distributed search engine, the replication may take place either at the node level (i.e., a single cluster with $2n$ index nodes, where two nodes share the query load for a given index shard), or at the cluster level (i.e., two identical clusters, but no replication within each cluster). Discuss the advantages and disadvantages of each approach.

Exercise 14.2 Describe possible scalability issues that may arise in the context of document-partitioned indices even if the index is held in main memory. (Hint: Consider query processing operations whose complexity is sublinear in the size of the index.)

Exercise 14.3 Given a document-partitioned index with $n = 200$ nodes and a target result set size of $m = 50$, what is the minimum per-node result set size k required to obtain the correct top m results with probability 99%?

Exercise 14.4 Generalize the dormant replication strategy from Section 14.1.4 so that it can deal with k simultaneous machine failures. How does this affect the overall storage requirements?

---

[3] `hadoop.apache.org`

Exercise 14.5 Describe how dormant replication for a term-partitioned index differs from dormant replication for a document-partitioned index.

Exercise 14.6 (a) Design a MapReduce (i.e., a map function and a reduce function) that computes the average document length (number of tokens per document) in a given corpus of text. (b) Revise your reduce function so that it can be used as a combiner.

Exercise 14.7 Design a MapReduce that computes the conditional probability $\Pr[t_1|t_2]$ of seeing the term t_1 in a document that contains the term t_2. You may find it useful to have your map function emit secondary keys to enforce a certain ordering among all values for a given key.

Exercise 14.8 (project exercise) Simulate a document-partitioned search engine using the BM25 ranking function you implemented for Exercise 5.9. Build an index for 100%, 50%, 25%, and 12.5% of the GOV2 collection. For each index size, measure the average time per query (for some standard query set). What do you observe? How does this affect the scalability of document partitioning?

14.5 Bibliography

Abusukhon, A., Talib, M., and Oakes, M. P. (2008). An investigation into improving the load balance for term-based partitioning. In *Proceedings of the 2nd International United Information Systems Conference*, pages 380–392. Klagenfurt, Austria.

Barroso, L. A., Dean, J., and Hölzle, U. (2003). Web search for a planet: The Google cluster architecture. *IEEE Micro*, 23(2):22–28.

Carbonell, J. G., and Goldstein, J. (1998). The use of MMR, diversity-based reranking for reordering documents and producing summaries. In *Proceedings of the 21st Annual International ACM SIGIR Conference on Research and Development in Information Retrieval*, pages 335–336. Melbourne, Australia.

Chang, F., Dean, J., Ghemawat, S., Hsieh, W. C., Wallach, D. A., Burrows, M., Chandra, T., Fikes, A., and Gruber, R. E. (2008). Bigtable: A distributed storage system for structured data. *ACM Transactions on Computer Systems*, 26(2):1–26.

Clarke, C. L. A., and Terra, E. L. (2004). Approximating the top-m passages in a parallel question answering system. In *Proceedings of the 13th ACM International Conference on Information and Knowledge Management*, pages 454–462. Washington, D.C.

Dean, J., and Ghemawat, S. (2004). MapReduce: Simplified data processing on large clusters. In *Proceedings of the 6th Symposium on Operating System Design and Implementation*, pages 137–150. San Francisco, California.

Dean, J., and Ghemawat, S. (2008). MapReduce: Simplified data processing on large clusters. *Communications of the ACM*, 51(1):107–113.

Ding, S., He, J., Yan, H., and Suel, T. (2009). Using graphics processors for high performance IR query processing. In *Proceedings of the 18th International Conference on World Wide Web*, pages 421–430. Madrid, Spain.

Ghemawat, S., Gobioff, H., and Leung, S. T. (2003). The Google file system. In *Proceedings of the 19th ACM Symposium on Operating Systems Principles*, pages 29–43. Bolton Landing, New York.

Govindaraju, N., Gray, J., Kumar, R., and Manocha, D. (2006). GPUTeraSort: High performance graphics co-processor sorting for large database management. In *Proceedings of the 2006 ACM SIGMOD International Conference on Management of Data*, pages 325–336. Chicago, Illinois.

Marín, M., and Gil-Costa, V. (2007). High-performance distributed inverted files. In *Proceedings of the 16th ACM Conference on Information and Knowledge Management*, pages 935–938. Lisbon, Portugal.

Marín, M., and Navarro, G. (2003). Distributed query processing using suffix arrays. In *Proceedings of the 10th International Symposium on String Processing and Information Retrieval*, pages 311–325. Manaus, Brazil.

Moffat, A., Webber, W., and Zobel, J. (2006). Load balancing for term-distributed parallel retrieval. In *Proceedings of the 29th Annual International ACM SIGIR Conference on Research and Development in Information Retrieval*, pages 348–355. Seattle, Washington.

Moffat, A., Webber, W., Zobel, J., and Baeza-Yates, R. (2007). A pipelined architecture for distributed text query evaluation. *Information Retrieval*, 10(3):205–231.

Puppin, D., Silvestri, F., and Laforenza, D. (2006). Query-driven document partitioning and collection selection. In *Proceedings of the 1st International Conference on Scalable Information Systems*. Hong Kong, China.

Sintorn, E., and Assarsson, U. (2008). Fast parallel GPU-sorting using a hybrid algorithm. *Journal of Parallel and Distributed Computing*, 68(10):1381–1388.

Xi, W., Sornil, O., Luo, M., and Fox, E. A. (2002). Hybrid partition inverted files: Experimental validation. In *Proceedings of the 6th European Conference on Research and Advanced Technology for Digital Libraries*, pages 422–431. Rome, Italy.

15 Web Search

Apart from an occasional example or exercise, the preceding chapters deal with information retrieval in a generic context. We assume the IR system contains a collection of documents, with each document represented by a sequence of tokens. Markup may indicate titles, authors, and other structural elements. We assume nothing further about the IR system's operating environment or the documents it contains.

In this chapter we consider IR in the specific context of Web search, the context in which it may be most familiar to you. Assuming this specific context provides us with the benefit of document features that cannot be assumed in the generic context. One of the most important of these features is the structure supplied by hyperlinks. These links from one page to another, often labeled by an image or anchor text, provide us with valuable information concerning both the individual pages and the relationship between them.

Along with these benefits come various problems, primarily associated with the relative "quality", "authority" or "popularity" of Web pages and sites, which can range from the carefully edited pages of a major international news agency to the personal pages of a high school student. In addition, many Web pages are actually *spam* — malicious pages deliberately posing as something that they are not in order to attract unwarranted attention of a commercial or other nature. Although the owners of most Web sites wish to enjoy a high ranking from the major commercial search engines, and may take whatever steps are available to maximize their ranking, the creators of spam pages are in an adversarial relationship with the search engine's operators. The creators of these pages may actively attempt to subvert the features used for ranking, by presenting a false impression of content and quality.

Other problems derive from the scale of the Web — billions of pages scattered among millions of hosts. In order to index these pages, they must be gathered from across the Web by a *crawler* and stored locally by the search engine for processing. Because many pages may change daily or hourly, this snapshot of the Web must be refreshed on a regular basis. While gathering data the crawler may detect duplicates and near-duplicates of pages, which must be dealt with appropriately. For example, the standard documentation for the Java programming language may be found on many Web sites, but in response to a query such as ⟨"java", "vector", "class"⟩ it might be best for a search engine to return only the official version on the java.sun.com site.

Another consideration is the volume and variety of queries commercial Web search engines receive, which directly reflect the volume and variety of information on the Web itself. Queries are often short — one or two terms — and the search engine may know little or nothing about the user entering a query or the context of the user's search. A user entering the query ⟨"UPS"⟩ may be interested in tracking a package sent by the courier service, purchasing a universal power supply, or attending night classes at the University of Puget Sound. Although such query ambiguity is a consideration in all IR applications, it reaches an extreme level in Web IR.

15.1   The Structure of the Web

Figure 15.1 provides an example of the most important features related to the structure of the Web. It shows Web pages on three sites: W, M, and H.[1] Site W provides a general encyclopedia including pages on Shakespeare (`w0.html`) and two of his plays, *Hamlet* (`w1.html`) and *Macbeth* (`w2.html`). Site H provides historical information including information on Shakespeare's wife (`h0.html`) and son (`h1.html`). Site M provides movie and TV information including a page on the 1971 movie version of *Macbeth* directed by Roman Polanski (`m0.html`).

The figure illustrates the link structure existing between these pages and sites. For example, the HTML *anchor* on page `w0.html`

```
<a href="http://H/h0.html">Anne Hathaway</a>
```

establishes a link between that page and `h0.html` on site H. The anchor text associated with this link ("Anne Hathaway") provides an indication of the content on the target page.

15.1.1   The Web Graph

The relationship between sites and pages indicated by these hyperlinks gives rise to what is called a *Web graph*. When it is viewed as a purely mathematical object, each page forms a node in this graph and each hyperlink forms a directed edge from one node to another. Figure 15.2 shows the Web graph corresponding to Figure 15.1. For convenience we have simplified the labels on the pages, with `http://W/w0.html` becoming w_0, for example.

From a practical standpoint it is important to remember that when we refer to a Web graph we are referring to more than just this mathematical abstraction — that pages are grouped into sites, and that anchor text and images may be associated with each link. Links may reference a labeled position within a page as well as the page as a whole. The highly dynamic and fluid nature of the Web must also be remembered. Pages and links are continuously added and removed at sites around the world; it is never possible to capture more than a rough approximation of the entire Web graph.

At times our interest may be restricted to a subset of the Web, perhaps to all the pages from a single site or organization. Under these circumstances, capturing an accurate snapshot of the Web graph for that site or organization is easier than for the entire Web. Nonetheless, most Web sites of any size grow and change on a continuous basis, and must be regularly recrawled for the snapshot to remain accurate.

---

[1] For simplicity we use single-letter site names and simplified page names rather than actual site and page names — for instance, `http://W/w0.html` instead of a full URL such as `http://en.wikipedia.org/wiki/William_Shakespeare`.

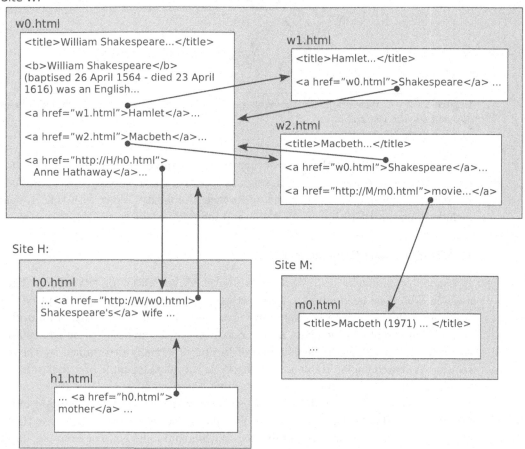

Figure 15.1   Structure on the Web. Pages can link to each other (`<a href=...>`) and can associate each link with anchor text (e.g., "mother").

We now introduce a formal notation for Web graphs that we use in later sections. Let Φ be the set of all pages in a Web graph, let $N = |\Phi|$ be the number of pages, and E the number of links (or edges) in the graph. Given a page $\alpha \in \Phi$, we define $out(\alpha)$ as the number of *out-links* from α to other pages (the *out-degree*). Similarly, we define $in(\alpha)$ as the number of *in-links* from other pages to α (the *in-degree*). In the Web graph of Figure 15.2, $out(w_0) = 3$ and $in(h_0) = 2$. If $in(\alpha) = 0$, then α is called a *source*; if $out(\alpha) = 0$, it is called a *sink*. We define Γ as the set of sinks. In the Web graph of Figure 15.2, page m_0 is a sink and page h_1 is a source.

The individual Web pages themselves may be highly complex and structured objects. They often include menus, images, and advertising. Scripts may be used to generate content when the page is first loaded and to update the content as the user interacts with it. A page may

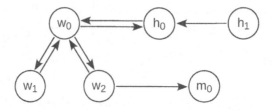

Figure 15.2 A Web graph for the Web pages shown in Figure 15.1. Each link corresponds to a directed edge in the graph.

serve as a frame to hold other pages or may simply redirect the browser to another page. These redirections may be implemented through scripts or through special HTTP responses, and may be repeated multiple times, thus adding further complexity. Along with HTML pages the Web includes pages in PDF, Microsoft Word, and many other formats.

15.1.2 Static and Dynamic Pages

It is not uncommon to hear Web pages described as "static" or "dynamic". The HTML for a static Web page is assumed to be generated in advance of any request, placed on disk, and transferred to the browser or Web crawler on demand. The home page of an organization is a typical example of a static page. A dynamic Web page is assumed to be generated at the time the request is made, with the contents of the page partially determined by the details of the request. A search engine result page (SERP) is a typical example of a dynamic Web page for which the user's query itself helps to determine the content.

There is often the implication in this dichotomy that static Web pages are more important for crawling and indexing than dynamic Web pages, and it is certainly the case that many types of dynamic Web pages are not suitable for crawling and indexing. For example, on-line calendar systems, which maintain appointments and schedules for people and events, will often serve up dynamically generated pages for dates far into the past and the future. You can reach the page for any date if you follow the links far enough. Although the flexibility to book appointments 25 years from now is appropriate for an online calendar; indexing an endless series of empty months is not appropriate for a general Web search engine.

Nonetheless, although many dynamic Web pages should not be crawled and indexed, many should. For example, catalog pages on retail sites are often generated dynamically by accessing current products and prices in a relational database. The result is then formatted into HTML and wrapped with menus and other fixed information for display in a browser. To meet the needs of a consumer searching for a product, a search engine must crawl and index these pages.

A dynamic page can sometimes be identified by features of its URL. For example, servers accessed through the Common Gateway Interface (CGI) may contain the path element `cgi-bin` in their URLs. Pages dynamically generated by Microsoft's Active Server Pages technology include the extension `.asp` or `.aspx` in their URLs. Unfortunately, these URL features are not always present. In principle any Web page can be static or dynamic, and there is no sure way to tell. For crawling and indexing, it is the content that is important, not the static or dynamic nature of the page.

15.1.3   The Hidden Web

Many pages are part of the so-called "hidden" or "invisible" or "deep" Web. This hidden Web includes pages that have no links referencing them, those that are protected by passwords, and those that are available only by querying a digital library or database. Although these pages can contain valuable content, they are difficult or impossible for a Web crawler to locate.

Pages in *intranets* represent a special case of the hidden Web. Pages in a given intranet are accessible only within a corporation or similar entity. An enterprise search engine that indexes an intranet may incorporate many of the same retrieval techniques that are found in general Web search engines, but may be tuned to exploit specific features of that intranet.

15.1.4   The Size of the Web

Even if we exclude the hidden Web, it is difficult to compute a meaningful estimate for the size of the Web. Adding or removing a single host can change the number of accessible pages by an arbitrary amount, depending on the contents of that host. Some hosts contain millions of pages with valuable content; others contain millions of pages with little or no useful content (see Exercise 15.14).

However, many Web pages would rarely, if ever, appear near the top of search results. Excluding those pages from a search engine would have little impact. Thus, we may informally define what is called the *indexable Web* as being those pages that should be considered for inclusion in a general-purpose Web search engine (Gulli and Signorini, 2005). This indexable Web would comprise all those pages that could have a substantial impact on search results.

If we may assume that any page included in the index of a major search engine forms part of the indexable Web, a lower bound for the size of the indexable Web may be determined from the combined coverage of the major search engines. More specifically, if the sets $A_1, A_2, \ldots$ represent the sets of pages indexed by each of these search engines, a lower bound on the size of the indexable Web is the size of the union of these sets $|\cup A_i|$.

Unfortunately, it is difficult to explicitly compute this union. Major search engines do not publish lists of the pages they index, or even provide a count of the number of pages, although it is usually possible to check if a given URL is included in the index. Even if we know the number of pages each engine contains, the size of the union will be smaller than the sum of the sizes because there is considerable overlap between engines.

Bharat and Broder (1998) and Lawrence and Giles (1998) describe a technique for estimating the combined coverage of major search engines. First, a test set of URLs is generated. This step may be achieved by issuing a series of random queries to the engines and selecting a random URL from the results returned by each. We assume that this test set represents a uniform

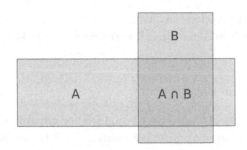

Figure 15.3 The collection overlap between search engines A and B can be used to estimate the size of the indexable Web.

sample of the pages indexed by the engines. Second, each URL from the test set is checked against each engine and the engines that contain it are recorded.

Given two engines, A and B, the relationship between their collections is illustrated by Figure 15.3. Sampling with our test set of URLs allows us to estimate $\Pr[A \cap B \,|\, A]$, the probability that a URL is contained in the intersection if it is contained in A:

$$\Pr[A \cap B \,|\, A] \;=\; \frac{\text{\# of test URLs contained in both } A \text{ and } B}{\text{\# of test URLs contained in } A}. \tag{15.1}$$

We may estimate $\Pr[A \cap B \,|\, B]$ in a similar fashion. If we know the size of A, we may then estimate the size of the intersection as

$$|A \cap B| \;=\; |A| \cdot \Pr[A \cap B \,|\, A]. \tag{15.2}$$

and the size of B as

$$|B| \;=\; \frac{|A \cap B|}{\Pr[A \cap B \,|\, B]}. \tag{15.3}$$

Thus, the size of the union may be estimated as

$$|A \cup B| \;=\; |A| + |B| - |A \cap B|. \tag{15.4}$$

If sizes for both A and B are available, the size of the intersection may be estimated from both sets, and the average of these estimates may be used to estimate the size of the union

$$|A \cup B| \;=\; |A| + |B| - \frac{1}{2}\left(|A| \cdot \Pr[A \cap B \,|\, A] + |B| \cdot \Pr[A \cap B \,|\, B] \right). \tag{15.5}$$

This technique may be extended to multiple engines. Using a variant of this method, Bharat and Broder (1998) estimated the size of the indexable Web in mid-1997 at 160 million pages. In a study conducted at roughly the same time, Lawrence and Giles (1998) estimated the size at 320 million pages. Approximately a year later the size had grown to 800 million pages (Lawrence and Giles, 1999). By mid-2005 it was 11.5 billion (Gulli and Signorini, 2005).

15.2   Queries and Users

Web queries are short. Several studies of query logs from major search engines are summarized by Spink and Jansen (2004). Although the exact numbers differ from study to study, these studies consistently reveal that many queries are just one or two terms long, with a mean query length between two and three terms. The topics of these queries range across the full breadth of human interests, with sex, health, commerce, and entertainment representing some of the major themes.

Perhaps it is not surprising that Web queries are short. Until quite recently, the query processing strategies of Web search engines actually discouraged longer queries. As we described in Section 2.3, these processing strategies filter the collection against a Boolean conjunction of the query terms prior to ranking. For a page to be included in the result set, all query terms must be associated with it in some way, either by appearing on the page itself or by appearing in the anchor text of links referencing it. As a result, increasing the length of the query by adding related terms could cause relevant pages to be excluded if they are missing one or more of the added terms. This strict filtering has been relaxed in recent years. For example, synonyms may be accepted in place of exact matches — the term "howto" might be accepted in place of the query term "FAQ". Nonetheless, for efficiency reasons filtering still plays a role in query processing, and Web search engines may still perform poorly on longer queries.

The distribution of Web queries follows Zipf's law (see Figure 15.4). In a representative log of 10 million queries, the single most frequent query may represent more than 1% of the total, but nearly half of the queries will occur only once. The tuning and evaluation of a search engine must consider this "long tail" of Zipf's law. In the aggregate, infrequent queries are at least as important as the frequent ones.

15.2.1   User Intent

Several researchers have examined collections of queries issued to Web search engines in an attempt to characterize the user intent underlying these queries. Broder (2002) surveyed users of the Altavista search engine and examined its query logs to develop a taxonomy of Web search. He classified Web queries into three categories reflecting users' apparent intent, as follows:

- The intent behind a *navigational* query is to locate a specific page or site on the Web. For example, a user intending to locate the home page of the CNN news network might enter the query ⟨"CNN"⟩. A navigational query usually has a single correct result. However, this correct result may vary from user to user. A Spanish-speaking user from the United States might want the CNN en Español home page (`www.cnn.com/espanol`); a user from Tunisia may want the Arabic edition (`arabic.cnn.com`).

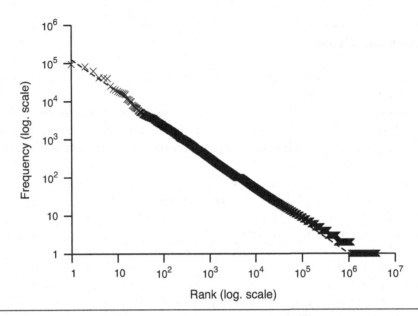

Figure 15.4 Frequency of queries by rank order, based on 10 million queries taken from the logs of a commercial search engine. The dashed line corresponds to Zipf's law with $\alpha = 0.85$.

- A user issuing an *informational* query is interested in learning something about a particular topic and has a lesser regard for the source of the information, provided it is reliable. The topics forming the test collections introduced in Chapter 1 and used for evaluation throughout the first four parts of the book reflect informational intent. A user entering the query ⟨"president", "obama"⟩ might find the information she is seeking on the CNN Web site, on Wikipedia, or elsewhere. Perhaps she will browse and read a combination of these before finding all the information she requires. The need behind an informational query such as this one may vary from user to user, and may be broad or narrow in scope. A user may be seeking a detailed description of government policy, a short biography, or just a birth date.

- A user issuing a *transactional* query intends to interact with a Web site once she finds it. This interaction may involve activities such as playing games, purchasing items, booking travel, or downloading images, music, and videos. This category may also include queries seeking services such as maps and weather, provided the user is not searching for a specific site providing that service.

Rose and Levinson (2004) extended the work of Broder by expanding his three categories into a hierarchy of user goals. They retained Broder's categories at the top level of their hierarchy but renamed the transactional category as the "resource" category. Under both the informational and the transactional categories they identified a number of subcategories. For example, the goal of a user issuing a *directed informational* query is the answer to a particular question ("When was President Obama born?"), whereas the goal of a user issuing an *undirected informational* query is simply to learn about the topic ("Tell me about President Obama."). In turn, directed informational queries may be classified as being *open* or *closed*, depending on whether the question is open-ended or has a specific answer.

The distinction between navigational and informational queries is relatively straightforward: Is the user seeking a specific site or not? The distinction between transactional queries and the other two categories is not always as clear. We can assume the query ⟨"mapquest"⟩ is navigational, seeking the site www.mapquest.com, but it is likely that the user will then interact with the site to obtain directions and maps. A user entering the query ⟨"travel", "washington"⟩ may be seeking both tourist information about Washington, D.C., and planning to book a hotel, making the intent both informational and transactional. In cases such as these, it may be reasonable to view such queries as falling under a combination of categories, as navigational/transactional and informational/transactional, respectively.

According to Broder (2002), navigational queries comprise 20–25% of all Web queries. Of the remainder, transactional queries comprise at least 22%, and the rest are informational queries. According to Rose and Levinson (2004), 12–15% of queries are navigational and 24–27% are transactional. A more recent study by Jansen et al. (2007) slightly contradicts these numbers. Their results indicate that more than 80% of queries are informational, with the remaining queries split roughly equally between the navigational and transactional categories. Nonetheless, these studies show that all three categories represent a substantial fraction of Web queries and suggest that Web search engines must be explicitly aware of the differences in user intent.

Referring to "navigational queries" and "informational queries" is common jargon. This usage is understandable when the goal underlying a query is the same, or similar, regardless of the user issuing it. But for some queries the category may differ from user to user. As a result we stress that these query categories fundamentally describe the goals and intentions of the users issuing the queries, and are not inherent properties of the queries themselves. For example, a user issuing our example query ⟨"UPS"⟩ may have

- Informational intent, wanting to know how universal power supplies work

- Transactional intent, wanting to purchase an inexpensive UPS for a personal computer

- Transactional/navigational intent, wanting to track a package or

- Navigational/informational intent, wanting information on programs offered by the University of Puget Sound.

Although this query is atypical, falling into so many possible categories, the assignment of any given query to a category (by anyone other than the user) may be little more than an educated guess.

15.2.2   Clickthrough Curves

The distinction between navigational and informational queries is visible in user behavior. Lee et al. (2005) examined *clickthroughs* as one feature that may be used to infer user intent. A clickthrough is the act of clicking on a search result on a search engine result page. Clickthroughs are often logged by commercial search engines as a method for measuring performance (see Section 15.5.2).

Although almost all clicks occur on the top ten results (Joachims et al., 2005; Agichtein et al., 2006b), the pattern of clicks varies from query to query. By examining clickthroughs from a large number of users issuing the same query, Lee et al. (2005) identified clickthrough distributions that are typical of informational and navigational queries. For navigational queries the clickthroughs are skewed toward a single result; for informational queries the clickthrough distribution is flatter.

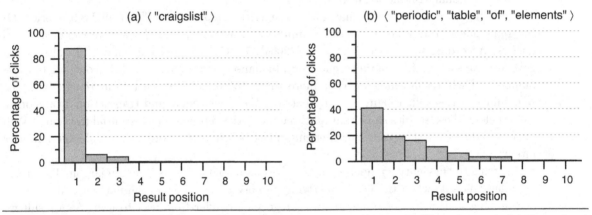

Figure 15.5   Clickthrough curve for a typical navigational query (⟨"craigslist"⟩) and a typical informational query (⟨"periodic", "table", "of", "elements"⟩).

Clarke et al. (2007) analyzed logs from a commercial search engine and provided further analysis and examples. The plots in Figure 15.5 are derived from examples in that paper. Both plots show the percentage of clickthroughs for results ranked 1 to 10. Each clickthrough represents the first result clicked by a different user entering the query. Figure 15.5(a) shows a clickthrough distribution for a stereotypical navigational query, exhibiting a spike at `www.craigslist.org`, a classified advertising site and the presumed target of the query. Figure 15.5(b) shows a clickthrough distribution for a typical informational query. For both queries the number of clickthroughs decreases with rank; the informational query receives proportionally more clicks at lower ranks.

15.3 Static Ranking

Web retrieval works in two phases. The first phase takes place during the indexing process, when each page is assigned a *static rank* (Richardson et al., 2006). Informally, this static rank may be viewed as reflecting the quality, authority, or popularity of the page. Ideally, static rank may correspond to a page's prior probability of relevance — the higher the probability, the higher the static rank.

Static rank is independent of any query. At query time the second phase of Web retrieval takes place. During this phase the static rank is combined with query-dependent features, such as term proximity and frequency, to produce a *dynamic rank*.

Assigning a static rank during indexing allows a Web search engine to consider features that would be impractical to consider at query time. The most important of these features are those derived from *link analysis* techniques. These techniques extract information encoded in the structure of the Web graph. Other features may also contribute to static rank, including features derived from the content of the pages and from user behavior (Section 15.3.5).

Our presentation of static ranking begins with the fundamentals of PageRank, easily the most famous of the link analysis techniques, in Section 15.3.1. Although this section presents the version of the algorithm generally known by the name PageRank, its practical value in Web search may be relatively limited because it depends on naïve assumptions regarding the structure of the Web. Sections 15.3.2 and 15.3.3 present and analyze an extended version of the algorithm, which accommodates a more sophisticated view of Web structure. Section 15.3.4 provides an overview of other link analysis techniques and Section 15.3.5 briefly discusses other features applicable to static ranking. Dynamic ranking is covered in Section 15.4.

15.3.1 Basic PageRank

PageRank was invented in the mid-1990s through the efforts of Larry Page and Sergey Brin, two Stanford computer science graduate students. The algorithm became a key element of their Backrub search engine, which quickly matured into Google.

The classic intuition behind the PageRank algorithm imagines a person surfing the Web at random. At any point a Web page is visible in her browser. As a next step she can either

1. Follow a link from the current page by clicking on it or

2. Select a page uniformly at random and jump to it, typing its URL into the address bar.

At any step the probability she will follow a link is fixed as δ. Thus, the probability of a jump is $1 - \delta$. Reasonable values for δ might range from 0.75 to 0.90, with 0.85 being the value quoted most often in the research literature. For simplicity we use $\delta = 3/4$ for our experiments and examples, unless otherwise stated.

Sinks in the Web graph force a jump: When our surfer reaches a sink, she always takes the second option. Assuming that our surfer could surf quickly and tirelessly for a long period of time, the value of PageRank $r(\alpha)$ for a page α would indicate the relative frequency at which the surfer visits that page.

The probability δ is sometimes referred to as the *restart probability* or *damping factor*, because it reduces the probability that the surfer will follow a link. The use of a damping factor to allow random jumps is known to improve the stability of PageRank, in a statistical sense, in comparison to an equivalent algorithm without jumps (Section 15.3.3). Informally, small changes to the Web graph will not generate large changes in PageRank.

The value of $r(\alpha)$ may be expressed in terms of the PageRank values of the pages that link to it and the PageRank values of the sinks in the graph, as follows:

$$r(\alpha) = \delta \cdot \left(\sum_{\beta \to \alpha} \frac{r(\beta)}{out(\beta)} + \sum_{\gamma \in \Gamma} \frac{r(\gamma)}{N} \right) + (1-\delta) \cdot \sum_{\alpha \in \Phi} \frac{r(\alpha)}{N} \tag{15.6}$$

For simplicity, and because the choice is arbitrary, we assume

$$\sum_{\alpha \in \Phi} r(\alpha) = N, \tag{15.7}$$

reducing the equation slightly to

$$r(\alpha) = \delta \cdot \left(\sum_{\beta \to \alpha} \frac{r(\beta)}{out(\beta)} + \sum_{\gamma \in \Gamma} \frac{r(\gamma)}{N} \right) + (1-\delta). \tag{15.8}$$

Because $\sum_{\alpha \in \Phi} r(\alpha)/N = 1$, the probability that the random surfer will be at page α at any given point is thus $r(\alpha)/N$.

Let us consider the composition of Equation 15.8 in detail. First, the value $(1-\delta)$ reflects the contribution from random jumps to α. The other contributions to the PageRank value of α — from links and sinks — are more complex. In the case of links, the page α may be reached by following a link from a page β. Because β may have links to multiple pages, its PageRank value is distributed according to its out-degree $out(\beta)$. Finally, jumps from sinks contribute in a small way to the PageRank value of α. Because a jump from sink γ may target any of the N pages in the graph — even itself — its contribution is $r(\gamma)/N$.

The application of Equation 15.8 to the Web graph of 15.2 gives the following set of equations:

$$r(w_0) = \delta \cdot \left(r(w_1) + \frac{r(w_2)}{2} + r(h_0) + \frac{r(m_0)}{6} \right) + (1-\delta)$$

$$r(w_1) = \delta \cdot \left(\frac{r(w_0)}{3} + \frac{r(m_0)}{6} \right) + (1-\delta)$$

$$r(w_2) = \delta \cdot \left(\frac{r(w_0)}{3} + \frac{r(m_0)}{6} \right) + (1 - \delta)$$

$$r(h_0) = \delta \cdot \left(\frac{r(w_0)}{3} + r(h_1) + \frac{r(m_0)}{6} \right) + (1 - \delta)$$

$$r(h_1) = \delta \cdot \left(\frac{r(m_0)}{6} \right) + (1 - \delta)$$

$$r(m_0) = \delta \cdot \left(\frac{r(w_2)}{2} + \frac{r(m_0)}{6} \right) + (1 - \delta)$$

Setting $\delta = 3/4$ and simplifying gives

$$r(w_0) = \frac{3\,r(w_1)}{4} + \frac{3\,r(w_2)}{8} + \frac{3\,r(h_0)}{4} + \frac{r(m_0)}{8} + \frac{1}{4}$$

$$r(w_1) = \frac{r(w_0)}{4} + \frac{r(m_0)}{8} + \frac{1}{4}$$

$$r(w_2) = \frac{r(w_0)}{4} + \frac{r(m_0)}{8} + \frac{1}{4}$$

$$r(h_0) = \frac{r(w_0)}{4} + \frac{3\,r(h_1)}{4} + \frac{r(m_0)}{8} + \frac{1}{4}$$

$$r(h_1) = \frac{r(m_0)}{8} + \frac{1}{4}$$

$$r(m_0) = \frac{3\,r(w_2)}{8} + \frac{r(m_0)}{8} + \frac{1}{4}$$

To compute PageRank, we solve for the six variables in the resulting system of linear equations $r(w_0)$, $r(w_1)$, $r(w_2)$, $r(h_0)$, $r(h_1)$, and $r(m_0)$. Many algorithms exist for the numerical solution of linear systems such as this one. The method particularly suited to PageRank is a form of *fixed-point iteration*.

Fixed point iteration is a general technique for solving systems of equations, linear and otherwise. To apply it, each variable must be expressed as a function of the other variables and itself. The PageRank equations are already expressed in this form, with the PageRank value for each page appearing alone on the left-hand side, and functions of these PageRank values appearing on the right-hand side.

The algorithm begins by making an initial guess for the value of each variable. These values are substituted into the right-hand equations, generating new approximations for the variables. We repeat this process, substituting the current values to generate new approximations. If the values converge, staying the same from iteration to iteration, we have solved the system of equations.

The method produces a series of approximations to $r(\alpha)$ for each page α: $r^{(0)}(\alpha)$, $r^{(1)}(\alpha)$, $r^{(2)}(\alpha),\ldots$ If we choose as our initial guess $r^{(0)}(\alpha) = 1$ for all pages, we have

$$\sum_{\alpha \in \Phi} r^{(0)}(\alpha) \; = \; N, \tag{15.9}$$

as required by Equation 15.7. From Equation 15.8 we then compute new approximations from existing approximations with the equation:

$$r^{(n+1)}(\alpha) \; = \; \delta \cdot \left(\sum_{\beta \to \alpha} \frac{r^{(n)}(\beta)}{\mathit{out}(\beta)} + \sum_{\gamma \in \Gamma} \frac{r^{(n)}(\gamma)}{N} \right) + (1 - \delta). \tag{15.10}$$

To compute PageRank for the Web graph of Figure 15.2, we iterate the following equations:

$$r^{(n+1)}(w_0) \; = \; \frac{3\,r^{(n)}(w_1)}{4} + \frac{3\,r^{(n)}(w_2)}{8} + \frac{3\,r^{(n)}(h_0)}{4} + \frac{r^{(n)}(m_0)}{8} + \frac{1}{4}$$

$$r^{(n+1)}(w_1) \; = \; \frac{r^{(n)}(w_0)}{4} + \frac{r^{(n)}(m_0)}{8} + \frac{1}{4}$$

$$r^{(n+1)}(w_2) \; = \; \frac{r^{(n)}(w_0)}{4} + \frac{r^{(n)}(m_0)}{8} + \frac{1}{4}$$

$$r^{(n+1)}(h_0) \; = \; \frac{r^{(n)}(w_0)}{4} + \frac{3\,r^{(n)}(h_1)}{4} + \frac{r^{(n)}(m_0)}{8} + \frac{1}{4}$$

$$r^{(n+1)}(h_1) \; = \; \frac{r^{(n)}(m_0)}{8} + \frac{1}{4}$$

$$r^{(n+1)}(m_0) \; = \; \frac{3\,r^{(n)}(w_2)}{8} + \frac{r^{(n)}(m_0)}{8} + \frac{1}{4}$$

Table 15.1 shows the successive approximations to PageRank for this system of equations. After 18 iterations the values have converged to within three decimal places.

Figure 15.6 presents a detailed algorithm for computing PageRank. The algorithm assumes that pages in the Web graph are numbered consecutively from 1 to N. The array *link*, of length E, stores the links in the Web graph, with *link*[i].*from* indicating the source of the link and *link*[i].*to* indicating the destination of the link. The array R stores the current approximation to PageRank; the array R' accumulates the new approximation.

The loop over lines 1–2 sets R to the initial approximation. At the end of each iteration of the main loop (lines 3–14) the array R contains the next approximation. As written, these lines form an infinite loop. In practice this loop would be terminated when the approximation converges or after a fixed number of iterations. We omit the exact termination condition because it depends on the accuracy desired and the precision of the computations. Over most Web graphs, acceptable values can be achieved after a few hundred iterations. Each iteration of the main loop takes $O(N + E)$ time; the time complexity of the overall algorithm depends on the number of iterations of the main loop.

Table 15.1 Iterative computation of PageRank for the Web graph of Figure 15.1.

n	$r^{(n)}(w_0)$	$r^{(n)}(w_1)$	$r^{(n)}(w_2)$	$r^{(n)}(h_0)$	$r^{(n)}(h_1)$	$r^{(n)}(m_0)$
0	1.000	1.000	1.000	1.000	1.000	1.000
1	2.250	0.625	0.625	1.375	0.375	0.750
2	2.078	0.906	0.906	1.188	0.344	0.578
3	2.232	0.842	0.842	1.100	0.322	0.662
4	2.104	0.891	0.891	1.133	0.333	0.648
5	2.183	0.857	0.857	1.107	0.331	0.665
6	2.128	0.879	0.879	1.127	0.333	0.655
7	2.166	0.864	0.864	1.114	0.332	0.661
8	2.140	0.874	0.874	1.123	0.333	0.657
9	2.158	0.867	0.867	1.116	0.332	0.660
10	2.145	0.872	0.872	1.121	0.332	0.658
11	2.154	0.868	0.868	1.118	0.332	0.659
12	2.148	0.871	0.871	1.120	0.332	0.658
13	2.152	0.869	0.869	1.119	0.332	0.659
14	2.149	0.870	0.870	1.120	0.332	0.658
15	2.151	0.870	0.870	1.119	0.332	0.659
16	2.150	0.870	0.870	1.119	0.332	0.658
17	2.151	0.870	0.870	1.119	0.332	0.659
18	2.150	0.870	0.870	1.119	0.332	0.658
19	2.150	0.870	0.870	1.119	0.332	0.659
20	2.150	0.870	0.870	1.119	0.332	0.658
...	...	...	...	...	...	...

Lines 4–5 initialize R' by storing the contribution from jumps. Lines 6–9 consider each link in turn, computing the contribution of the source page to the destination's PageRank value. Because $\sum_{\alpha \in \Phi} r(\alpha) = N$, the set of sinks need not be explicitly considered. Instead, after initializing R' and applying links we sum the elements of R'. The difference between the resulting sum and N represents $\sum_{\gamma \in \Gamma} r(\gamma)$, the contribution from sinks in the graph.

As an alternative to lines 6–9 we might consider iterating over all nodes. For each node we would then sum the PageRank contributions for the nodes linking to it, directly implementing Equation 15.8. Although this alternative is reasonable for small Web graphs, the current approach of iterating over links requires simpler data structures and saves memory, an important consideration for larger Web graphs.

Iterating over links also allows us to store the links in a file on disk, further reducing memory requirements. Instead of iterating over an array, the loop of lines 6–9 would sequentially read this file of links from end to end during each iteration of the main loop. If links are stored in a file, the algorithm requires only the $O(N)$ memory to store the arrays R and R'.

```
 1      for i ← 1 to N do
 2          R[i] ← 1
 3      loop
 4          for i ← 1 to N do
 5              R'[i] ← 1 − δ
 6          for k ← 1 to E do
 7              i ← link[k].from
 8              j ← link[k].to
 9              R'[j] ← R'[j] + δ·R[i]/out(i)
10          s ← N
11          for i ← 1 to N do
12              s ← s − R'[i]
13          for i ← 1 to N do
14              R[i] ← R'[i] + s/N
```

Figure 15.6   Basic PageRank algorithm. The array *link* contains the links in the Web graph. Lines 3-14 form an infinite loop. At the end of each interation of this loop, the array R contains a new estimate of PageRank for each page. In practice the loop would be terminated when the change in PageRank from iteration to iteration drops below a threshold or after a fixed number of iterations.

To demonstrate PageRank over a larger Web graph, we applied the algorithm to the English Wikipedia (see Exercise 1.9). The top 12 pages are listed in Table 15.2. Unsurprisingly, given that the collection includes only the English Wikipedia, major English-speaking countries figure prominently on the list. The remaining countries have large economies and close ties to the United States and to other English-speaking countries. Dates are often linked in Wikipedia, which explains the high ranks given to recent years. The high rank given to World War II, the pivotal event of the twentieth century, is also unsurprising. Overall, these results reflect the culture and times of Wikipedia's authors, an appropriate outcome.

15.3.2   Extended PageRank

The limitations of basic PageRank become evident if we revisit and reconsider its original motivation, the random surfer. No real user accesses the Web in the fashion of this random surfer. Even if we view the random surfer as an artificial construct — as a homunculus exhibiting the average behavior of Web users as a group — its selection of links and jumps uniformly at random remains unrealistic.

More realistically, our random surfer should have preferences for both links and jumps. For example, she might prefer navigational links over links to ads, prefer links at the top of the page to those at the bottom, and prefer links in readable fonts to those in tiny or invisible fonts. When the random surfer is jumping randomly, top-level pages may be preferred over deeply nested pages, longstanding pages may be preferred over newly minted pages, and pages with more text may be preferred over pages with less.

Table 15.2 The top 12 pages from a basic PageRank of Wikipedia.

Page: α	PageRank: $r(\alpha)$	Probability: $r(\alpha)/N$
United States	10509.50	0.004438
United Kingdom	3983.74	0.001682
2006	3781.65	0.001597
England	3421.03	0.001445
France	3340.53	0.001411
2007	3301.65	0.001394
2005	3290.57	0.001389
Germany	3218.33	0.001359
Canada	3090.20	0.001305
2004	2742.86	0.001158
Australia	2441.65	0.001031
World War II	2417.38	0.001021

Fortunately, we can easily extend PageRank to accommodate these preferences. To accommodate jump preferences, we define a *teleport vector* or *jump vector* J, of length N, where the element $J[i]$ indicates the probability that the random surfer will target page i when jumping. Because J is a vector of probabilities, we require $\sum_{i=1}^{N} J[i] = 1$. It is acceptable for some elements of J to be 0, but this may result in some pages having a zero PageRank value. If all elements of J are positive, $J[i] > 0$ for all $1 \leq i \leq N$, then all pages will have non-zero PageRank (Section 15.3.3).

To accommodate link preferences, we define an $N \times N$ *follow matrix* F, where element $F[i,j]$ indicates the probability that our random surfer will follow a link to page j from page i. Unless page i is a sink, the elements in its row of F must sum to 1, $\sum_{i=1}^{N} F[i,j] = 1$. If page i is a sink, all elements of the row are 0.

F is *sparse*. At most E of the N^2 elements are non-zero, with one element corresponding to each link. We exploit this property of F in our implementation of the extended PageRank algorithm. The algorithm is given in Figure 15.7. It is similar to the basic PageRank algorithm of Figure 15.6, with lines 5, 9, and 14 generalized to use the jump vector and follow matrix. This generalization has no impact on the algorithm's time complexity, with each iteration of the main loop requiring $O(N + E)$ time.

Because F is sparse, the elements of F may be stored with their corresponding links. More specifically, we may add a *follow* field to each element of the *link* array, defined so that

$$link[k].follow = F[link[k].from, link[k].to].$$

```
1     for i ← 1 to N do
2         R[i] ← J[i] · N
3     loop
4         for i ← 1 to N do
5             R'[i] ← (1 − δ) · J[i] · N
6         for k ← 1 to E do
7             i ← link[k].from
8             j ← link[k].to
9             R'[j] ← R'[j] + δ · R[i] · F[i, j]
10        s ← N
11        for i ← 1 to N do
12            s ← s − R'[i]
13        for i ← 1 to N do
14            R[i] ← R'[i] + s · J[i]
```

Figure 15.7 Extended PageRank algorithm. Each element $J[i]$ of the jump vector J indicates the probabilty of reaching page i when jumping randomly. Each element $F[i,j]$ of the follow matrix F indicates the probabilty of reaching page i from page j when following a link.

This extended link array could then be stored in a file on disk, with the loop of lines 6–9 changed to iterate over this file. With the links stored on disk, the algorithm requires only $O(N)$ RAM to store the arrays R and R' and the jump vector J.

To compute basic PageRank using this extended algorithm, we construct a jump vector with all elements equal to $1/N$. For the follow matrix we set its elements equal to $1/out(\alpha)$ for all pages to which a page α links, and to 0 otherwise. If we number the nodes in the graph of Figure 15.2 from 1 to 6 in the order w_0, w_1, w_2, h_0, h_1, and m_0, we obtain the corresponding follow matrix and jump vector for basic PageRank:

$$
F = \begin{pmatrix}
0 & \frac{1}{3} & \frac{1}{3} & \frac{1}{3} & 0 & 0 \\
1 & 0 & 0 & 0 & 0 & 0 \\
\frac{1}{2} & 0 & 0 & 0 & 0 & \frac{1}{2} \\
1 & 0 & 0 & 0 & 0 & 0 \\
0 & 0 & 0 & 1 & 0 & 0 \\
0 & 0 & 0 & 0 & 0 & 0
\end{pmatrix}, \qquad
J = \begin{pmatrix}
\frac{1}{6} \\
\frac{1}{6} \\
\frac{1}{6} \\
\frac{1}{6} \\
\frac{1}{6} \\
\frac{1}{6}
\end{pmatrix}. \tag{15.11}
$$

Now, suppose we know from external information that site W contains only high-quality and carefully edited information, and the relative quality of the information on the other sites remains unknown. We might adjust the follow matrix and jump vector to reflect this knowledge by assuming the random surfer is twice as likely to link or jump to site W than to any other site, as follows:

$$F = \begin{pmatrix} 0 & \frac{2}{5} & \frac{2}{5} & \frac{1}{5} & 0 & 0 \\ 1 & 0 & 0 & 0 & 0 & 0 \\ \frac{2}{3} & 0 & 0 & 0 & 0 & \frac{1}{3} \\ 1 & 0 & 0 & 0 & 0 & 0 \\ 0 & 0 & 0 & 1 & 0 & 0 \\ 0 & 0 & 0 & 0 & 0 & 0 \end{pmatrix}, \qquad J = \begin{pmatrix} \frac{2}{9} \\ \frac{2}{9} \\ \frac{2}{9} \\ \frac{1}{9} \\ \frac{1}{9} \\ \frac{1}{9} \end{pmatrix}. \qquad (15.12)$$

For general Web retrieval there are numerous adjustments we might make to the follow matrix and jump vector to reflect external knowledge. In general, however, we should not make adjustments to reflect properties of the Web graph itself. For example, if many pages link to a given page, we might view that page as having high "popularity" and be tempted to increase its probability in the jump vector. Avoid this temptation. Adjustments of this type are not required or recommended. Focus on external sources when adjusting the follow matrix and jump vector. It is the job of PageRank to account for the properties of the Web graph itself.

Many external sources can be enlisted when setting the follow matrix and jump vector. Although space does not allow us to describe and analyze all possibilities, we list a number of the possible sources below. This list is not exhaustive (see Exercise 15.6) nor is it the case that all (or any) of these suggestions are useful in practice.

- **Page content and structure.** During crawling and indexing, a search engine might analyze the structure and organization of a page as it would appear in a browser. This analysis might then be used to assign probabilities to links based on their layout and appearance. For example, users may be more likely to follow links near the top of the page or in menus. Various aspects of page content might also be interpreted as indicators of quality, thus influencing the jump vector by making the page a likelier target for a jump. Large blocks of readable text might be interpreted positively, while a low ratio of text to HTML tags might be interpreted negatively. Text in tiny and unreadable fonts may indicate an attempt to trick the search engine by misrepresenting what a user would actually see when the page is displayed.

- **Site content and structure.** Users may be more likely to jump to a site's top-level page than to a deeply nested page. Moreover, the longer the URL, the less likely a user will be to remember it or be willing to type it directly into a browser's address bar. The number of pages in a site may also be a factor when setting the jump vector: A site should not receive a high jump probability just because it contains a large number of pages. Depending on the site, users may be more likely to follow a link within a site, as they navigate about, than to follow a link off-site. On the other hand, a link between an educational site and a commercial site may represent a strong recommendation because these links are not usually motivated by commercial considerations. Older, more established, sites may be preferred over newer sites.

- **Explicit judgments.** Human editors might be recruited to manually identify (and classify) high-quality sites, which then receive higher jump probabilities. These editors could be professionals working for the search service itself or volunteers working for a Web directory such as the Open Directory Project (ODP—see Open Directory Project[2]). A major search engine might employ in-house editors to maintain their own Web directories as part of their overall service.

- **Implicit feedback.** A clickthrough on a Web search result might be interpreted as an implicit judgment regarding the quality of that page (see Section 15.5.2). Many of the major search services offer *toolbars*. These browser extensions provide additional features complementing the basic search service. With a user's explicit permission, a toolbar transmits information regarding the user's browsing behavior back to the search service. Pages and sites that the user visits might be recorded and then used to adjust probabilities in the follow matrix and jump vector. Many search services also provide free e-mail accounts. Links sent through these e-mail services might be accessible to these search services and may represent recommendations regarding site and page quality. Of course, any such use of implicit feedback must respect the privacy of users.

Adjustments in the jump vector may also be used to compute special variants of PageRank. To compute a *personalized PageRank* we assign high jump probabilities to pages of personal interest to an individual user (Page et al., 1999). These pages may be extracted from the user's browser bookmarks or her home page, or determined by monitoring her browsing behavior over a period of time. A *topic-oriented PageRank*, or *focused PageRank*, assigns high jump probabilities to pages known to be related to a specified topic, such as sports or business (Haveliwala, 2002). These topic-oriented pages may be taken from a Web directory such as the ODP.

For example, we can select a page from our Wikipedia corpus and generate a topic-specific PageRank focused just on that page. To generate the jump vector we assign a jump probability of 50% to the selected page and assign the remaining 50% uniformly to the other pages. We assign non-zero values to all elements of the jump vector in order to ensure that every page receives a non-zero PageRank value, but the outcome does not change substantially if we assign 100% probability to the selected page.

Table 15.3 shows the top 12 pages for a pair of topics: "William Shakespeare" and "Information Retrieval". The topic-specific PageRank for the topic "Information Retrieval" assigns high ranks to many pages related to that topic: The names Karen Spärck Jones and Gerard Salton should be familiar from Chapters 2 and 8; Rutgers University, City University London, and the University of Glasgow are home to prominent information retrieval research groups; the presence of Google and SIGIR is hardly unexpected. Surprisingly, however, the topic-specific PageRank for the topic "William Shakespeare" appears to be little different from the general

---

[2] www.dmoz.org

Table 15.3 The top 12 pages from a focused PageRank over Wikipedia for two topics.

William Shakespeare		Information Retrieval	
Article	PageRank	Article	PageRank
William Shakespeare	303078.44	Information retrieval	305677.03
United States	7200.15	United States	8831.25
England	5357.85	Association for Computing Machinery	6238.30
London	3637.60	Google	5510.16
United Kingdom	3320.49	GNU General Public License	4811.08
2007	3185.71	World Wide Web	4696.78
France	2965.52	SIGIR	4456.67
English language	2714.88	Rutgers University	4389.07
2006	2702.72	Karen Spärck Jones	4282.03
Germany	2490.50	City University, London	4274.76
2005	2377.21	University of Glasgow	4222.44
Canada	2058.84	Gerard Salton	4171.45

PageRank shown in Figure 15.2. Apart from a page on the "English language" and the Shakespeare page itself, all the pages appear in the top twelve of the general PageRank. Despite our topic-specific focus, the page for United States appears second in both lists.

A topic-specific PageRank and a general PageRank both represent probability distributions over the same set of pages. Continuing our example, we may obtain clearer results by comparing these distributions. In Section 9.4 (page 296) we defined the Kullback-Leibler divergence, or KL divergence, between two discrete probability distributions f and g as

$$\sum_x f(x) \cdot \log \frac{f(x)}{g(x)} \; . \tag{15.13}$$

Here we define f to be the topic-specific PageRank and g to be the general PageRank, normalized to represent probabilities. For each page α we rerank the page according to its *contribution* to the KL divergence (pointwise KL divergence) between f and g:

$$f(\alpha) \cdot \log \frac{f(\alpha)}{g(\alpha)} \; . \tag{15.14}$$

Recall that KL divergence indicates the average number of extra bits per symbol needed to compress a message if we assume its symbols are distributed according to g instead of the correct distribution f. Equation 15.14 indicates the extra bits due to α. Table 15.4 shows the impact of adjusting a focused PageRank using Equation 15.14.

All the top pages are now on-topic. Andrew Cecil Bradley, a Professor at Oxford University, was famous for his books on Shakespeare's plays and poetry. Ben Jonson and George Wilkins

Table 15.4   Reranking a focused PageRank according to each page's contribution to the KL divergence between the focused PageRank and the general PageRank.

William Shakespeare		Information Retrieval	
Article	KL divergence	Article	KL divergence
William Shakespeare	1.505587	Information retrieval	2.390223
First Folio	0.007246	SIGIR	0.027820
Andrew Cecil Bradley	0.007237	Karen Spärck Jones	0.026368
King's Men (playing company)	0.005955	C. J. van Rijsbergen	0.024170
Twelfth Night, or What You Will	0.005939	Gerard Salton	0.024026
Lord Chamberlain's Men	0.005224	Text Retrieval Conference	0.023260
Ben Jonson	0.005095	Cross-language information retrieval	0.022819
Stratford-upon-Avon	0.004927	Relevance (information retrieval)	0.022121
Richard Burbage	0.004794	Assoc. for Computing Machinery	0.022051
George Wilkins	0.004746	Sphinx (search engine)	0.021963
Henry Condell	0.004712	Question answering	0.021773
Shakespeare's reputation	0.004710	Divergence from randomness model	0.021620

were playwrights and contemporaries of Shakespeare. Richard Burbage and Henry Condell were actors and members of the King's Men playing company, for which Shakespeare wrote and acted. On the information retrieval side, Spärck Jones and Salton are joined by C. J. (Keith) van Rijsbergen, another great pioneer of the field. Sphinx is an open-source search engine targeted at relational database systems. The remaining topics should be familiar to readers of this book.

15.3.3   Properties of PageRank

In our presentation of PageRank we have been ignoring several important considerations: Will the fixed-point iteration procedure of Figure 15.7 always converge, or will the algorithm fail to work for some Web graphs? If it does converge, how quickly will it converge? Will it always convergence to the same PageRank vector, regardless of the initial estimate?

Fortunately the PageRank algorithm possesses properties that guarantee good behavior. To simplify our discussion of these properties, we combine the follow matrix and the jump vector into a single *transition matrix*. First we extend the follow matrix to handle sinks. Let F' be the $N \times N$ matrix

$$F'[i,j] = \begin{cases} J[j] & \text{if } i \text{ is a sink,} \\ F[i,j] & \text{otherwise.} \end{cases} \tag{15.15}$$

Next, let J' be the $N \times N$ matrix with each row equal to the jump vector. Finally, we define the transition matrix as

$$M = \delta \cdot F' + (1-\delta) \cdot J'. \tag{15.16}$$

For pages i and j, $M[i, j]$ represents the probability that a random surfer on page i will transition to page j without considering if this transition is made through a jump or by following a link. For example, the transition matrix corresponding to F and J in Equation 15.12 is

$$
M = \begin{pmatrix}
\frac{1}{18} & \frac{16}{45} & \frac{16}{45} & \frac{37}{180} & \frac{1}{18} & \frac{1}{18} \\
\frac{29}{36} & \frac{1}{18} & \frac{1}{18} & \frac{1}{18} & \frac{1}{18} & \frac{1}{18} \\
\frac{5}{9} & \frac{1}{18} & \frac{1}{18} & \frac{1}{18} & \frac{1}{18} & \frac{11}{36} \\
\frac{7}{9} & \frac{1}{36} & \frac{1}{36} & \frac{1}{36} & \frac{1}{36} & \frac{1}{36} \\
\frac{1}{36} & \frac{1}{36} & \frac{1}{36} & \frac{7}{9} & \frac{1}{36} & \frac{1}{36} \\
\frac{7}{36} & \frac{7}{36} & \frac{7}{36} & \frac{1}{9} & \frac{1}{9} & \frac{1}{9}
\end{pmatrix} .
\tag{15.17}
$$

You may recognize M as a stochastic matrix representing the transition matrix of a Markov chain, as introduced in Section 1.3.4. Each page corresponds to a state; the surfer's initial starting location corresponds to a starting state. Moreover, the PageRank vector R has the property that

$$
M^T R = R.
\tag{15.18}
$$

You may recognize R as being an eigenvector[3] of M^T, with a corresponding eigenvalue of 1. Given an $n \times n$ matrix A, recall that $\vec{x}$ is an *eigenvector* of A and λ is the corresponding *eigenvalue* of A, if $A\vec{x} = \lambda\vec{x}$.

A considerable amount is known about Markov chains and their eigenvectors, and we can turn to this knowledge to determine the properties of PageRank. For simplicity we temporarily assume that all elements of the jump vector are positive, but these properties also hold when elements are 0. We consider jump vectors with 0 elements later in the section.

Underlying PageRank is the idea that as our random surfer surfs for longer periods of time, the relative time spent on each page converges to a value that is independent of the surfer's starting location. This informal notion corresponds to an important property of Markov chains known as *ergodicity*. A Markov chain is *ergodic* if two properties hold, both of which trivially hold for M when J contains only positive values. The first property, *irreducibility*, captures the idea that the random surfer can get from any state to any other state after some finite number of steps. More specifically for any states i and j, if the surfer is currently in state i, there is a positive probability that she can reach state j after taking no more than k steps, where $k \leq N$. If the jump vector contains only positive elements, then $M[i, j] > 0$ for all states i and j, and there is a positive probability that the surfer will reach j from i after $k = 1$ step.

The second property, that the transition matrix be *aperiodic*, eliminates those Markov chains in which the probability of being in a given state cycles between multiple values. A state i is *periodic* with period k if it is possible to return to it only after a number of steps that is a multiple of k. For example, if the surfer can return to a state only after an even number of

---

[3] If linear algebra is a distant memory, you may safely skip to the start of Section 15.3.4.

steps, then the state is periodic with period 2. If all states in a matrix have period 1, then it is aperiodic. Because $M[i,j] > 0$ for all i, the surfer can reach any state from any other state. Thus, the period of all states is 1 and the property holds.

Let the eigenvectors of M^T be $\vec{x}_1$, $\vec{x}_2$,..., $\vec{x}_N$, with associated eigenvalues λ_1,..., λ_N. Following convention we order these eigenvectors so that $|\lambda_1| \geq |\lambda_2| > ... \geq |\lambda_N|$. Because all elements of M^T are positive and each row of M sums to 1, a theorem known as the *Perron-Frobenius theorem* tells us that $\lambda_1 = 1$, that all other eigenvectors satisfy $|\lambda_i| < 1$, and that all elements of $\vec{x}_1$ are positive. Thus, *the principal eigenvector of M^T is the PageRank vector.* Following convention, eigenvectors are scaled to unit length, with $\|\vec{x}_i\| = 1$ for all i, so that $\vec{x}_1 = R/N$.

We now re-express our algorithm for computing PageRank in matrix notation. Let $\vec{x}^{(0)}$ be our initial estimate of PageRank (normalized to have a length of 1). Each iteration of the main loop in Figure 15.7 multiplies M^T by our current estimate to produce a new estimate. The first iteration produces the estimate $\vec{x}^{(1)} = M^T \vec{x}^{(0)}$, the second iteration produces the estimate $\vec{x}^{(2)} = M^T \vec{x}^{(1)}$, and so on. After n iterations we have the estimate

$$\vec{x}^{(n)} = \left(M^T\right)^n \vec{x}^{(0)}. \tag{15.19}$$

Thus, the algorithm computes PageRank if

$$\lim_{n \to \infty} \vec{x}^{(n)} = \vec{x}_1. \tag{15.20}$$

The ergodicity of M guarantees this convergence. In the terminology of Markov chains, $\vec{x}_1$ is called the *stationary distribution* of M. This algorithm for computing the principal eigenvector of a matrix is called the *power method* (Golub and Van Loan, 1996).

To determine the rate of convergence, suppose the initial estimate $\vec{x}^{(0)}$ is expressed as a linear combination of the (unknown) eigenvectors.

$$\vec{x}^{(0)} = \vec{x}_1 + a_2 \vec{x}_2 + a_3 \vec{x}_3 + \cdots + a_N \vec{x}_N \tag{15.21}$$

After the first iteration we have

$$\begin{aligned}
\vec{x}^{(1)} &= M^T \vec{x}^{(0)} \\
&= M^T \left(\vec{x}_1 + a_2 \vec{x}_2 + \cdots + a_N \vec{x}_N\right) \\
&= M^T \vec{x}_1 + a_2 M^T \vec{x}_2 + \cdots + a_N M^T \vec{x}_N \\
&= \vec{x}_1 + a_2 \lambda_2 \vec{x}_2 + \cdots + a_N \lambda_N \vec{x}_N.
\end{aligned}$$

After n iterations, and recalling that λ_2 is the second-largest eigenvalue after λ_1, we have

$$
\begin{aligned}
\vec{x}^{(n)} &= \vec{x}_1 + a_2\,\lambda_2^n\,\vec{x}_2 + \cdots + a_N\,\lambda_N^n\,\vec{x}_N \\
&\leq \vec{x}_1 + \lambda_2^n\,(a_2\,\vec{x}_2 + \cdots + a_N\,\vec{x}_N) \\
&= \vec{x}_1 + O(\lambda_2^n).
\end{aligned}
$$

Thus, the rate of convergence depends on the value of the second eigenvalue of M^T. The smaller the value, the faster the convergence.

For PageRank, Haveliwala and Kamvar (2003) proved the remarkable result that the value of the second eigenvector is δ, the damping factor.[4] Provided that δ is not too close to 1, convergence should be acceptably fast. More important, the rate of convergence does not depend on characteristics of the Web graph. If convergence is acceptably fast for one Web graph, it should remain acceptably fast as the Web graph evolves over time.

Haveliwala and Kamvar note that the stability of PageRank is also associated with δ. With smaller values of δ, PageRank becomes less sensitive to small changes in the Web graph. Of course, if the value of δ is close to 0, PageRank may fail to capture any useful information regarding the Web graph because a random jump will happen at nearly every step. The traditional value of $\delta = 0.85$ appears to be a reasonable compromise, giving good stability and convergence properties while allowing PageRank to do its job.

Thus, it is the random jumps of the imaginary surfer that determines the convergence and stability of PageRank. The jump vector guarantees the ergodicity of M, and therefore the convergence of the PageRank algorithm. The damping factor determines stability and the rate of convergence. The structure of the Web graph itself does not play a major role.

The above discussion assumes that all elements of the jump vector are positive. If this assumption does not hold, and the jump vector contains a zero, M may not be irreducible. An element with value zero in the jump vector indicates a page to which the surfer will never jump at random. Suppose there is a page α that cannot be reached by following links from any of the pages with a non-zero jump probability. Once the surfer makes a random jump after leaving α, she can never return to it.

As the length of the surf goes to infinity, the probability that the surfer eventually makes a jump goes to one. After making a jump the probability of visiting α is zero. Thus, we can set the PageRank value for α to zero, without explicitly computing it.

Let Φ' be the set of pages reachable after a jump (Figure 15.8). The pages outside Φ' have a PageRank value of zero, and do not need to be involved in the PageRank computation for the pages in Φ'. Let M' be the transition matrix corresponding to Φ' and let J' be its jump vector. J' may still contain elements with value zero, but the pages associated with these elements will be reachable from pages with non-zero values. Because a jump is possible at any step, and any

---

[4] More accurately, $|\lambda_2| \leq \delta$, but $\lambda_2 = \delta$ for any realistic Web graph.

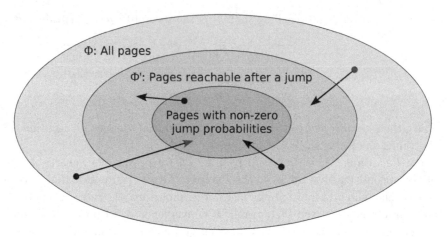

Figure 15.8   Pages reachable after a jump.

page in Φ' may be reached after a jump, M' is irreducible. The possibility of a jump at any step also helps to guarantee that M' is aperiodic (Exercise 15.5). Because M' is irreducible and aperiodic, it is ergodic and PageRank will converge. The other stability and convergence properties can also be shown to hold for M'.

15.3.4   Other Link Analysis Methods: HITS and SALSA

In addition to PageRank a number of other link analysis techniques have been proposed in the context of the Web. Two of these methods are Kleinberg's HITS algorithm (Kleinberg, 1998, 1999) and the related SALSA algorithm due to Lempel and Moran (2000). HITS was developed independently of PageRank during roughly the same time frame. SALSA was developed shortly after, in an attempt to combine features from both algorithms.

The intuition underlying HITS derives from a consideration of the roles a page may play on the Web with respect to a given topic. One role is that of an *authority*, a page that contains substantial and reliable information on the topic. A second role is that of a *hub*, a page that aggregates links to pages related to the topic. A good hub points to many authorities; a good authority is referenced by many hubs. We emphasize that these are idealized roles; a page may be both a hub and an authority to some extent.

In contrast to PageRank, which was envisioned as operating over the entire Web, Kleinberg envisioned HITS as operating over smaller Web graphs. These graphs may be generated by executing a query on a search engine to retrieve the contents of the top few hundred pages, along with pages in their immediate neighborhood. Based on the retrieved pages, HITS computes hubs and authorities with respect to the query. At the time HITS was invented, Web search engines were not known to incorporate link analysis techniques (Marchiori, 1997), and HITS provided a way of obtaining the benefit of these techniques without explicit support from the engine.

For a given page α, HITS computes two values: an authority value $a(\alpha)$ and a hub value $h(\alpha)$. The authority value of a page is derived from the hub values of the pages that link to it:

$$a(\alpha) \;=\; w_a \cdot \sum_{\beta \to \alpha} h(\beta). \tag{15.22}$$

The hub value of a page is derived from the authority values of the pages it references.

$$h(\alpha) \;=\; w_h \cdot \sum_{\alpha \to \beta} a(\beta). \tag{15.23}$$

The significance of the weights w_a and w_h is discussed shortly. Links from a page to itself (*self-loops*) and links within sites are ignored because these are assumed to represent navigational relationships rather than hub-authority relationships.

We may express Equations 15.22 and 15.23 in matrix/vector notation by defining $\vec{a}$ to be the authority values and $\vec{h}$ to be the hub values for the N pages in the Web graph.[5] Let W be the *adjacency matrix* of the Web graph, where $W[i,j] = 1$ if there is a link from the ith page to the jth page, and $W[i,j] = 0$ otherwise. For example, the adjacency matrix for the Web graph in Figure 15.2 (retaining links within sites) is

$$W \;=\; \begin{pmatrix} 0 & 1 & 1 & 1 & 0 & 0 \\ 1 & 0 & 0 & 0 & 0 & 0 \\ 1 & 0 & 0 & 0 & 0 & 1 \\ 1 & 0 & 0 & 0 & 0 & 0 \\ 0 & 0 & 0 & 1 & 0 & 0 \\ 0 & 0 & 0 & 0 & 0 & 0 \end{pmatrix}. \tag{15.24}$$

In matrix/vector notation, Equations 15.22 and 15.23 become

$$\vec{a} \;=\; w_a \cdot W^T \vec{h} \quad \text{and} \quad \vec{h} \;=\; w_h \cdot W \vec{a}. \tag{15.25}$$

Substituting gives

$$\vec{a} \;=\; w_a \cdot w_h \cdot W^T W \vec{a} \quad \text{and} \quad \vec{h} \;=\; w_a \cdot w_h \cdot W W^T \vec{h}. \tag{15.26}$$

If we define $A = W^T W$, $H = W W^T$, and $\lambda = 1/(w_a \cdot w_h)$, we have

$$\lambda \vec{a} \;=\; A \vec{a} \quad \text{and} \quad \lambda \vec{h} \;=\; H \vec{h}. \tag{15.27}$$

Thus, the authority vector $\vec{a}$ is an eigenvector of A and the hub vector $\vec{h}$ is an eigenvector of H.

---

[5] If you wish to avoid the details, you may safely skip to Section 15.3.5.

The matrices A and H have interesting interpretations taken from the field of bibliometrics (Lempel and Moran, 2000; Langville and Meyer, 2005): A is the *co-citation matrix* for the Web graph, where $A[i,j]$ is the number of pages that link to both i and j; H is the *co-reference* or *coupling matrix* for the Web graph, where $H[i,j]$ is the number of pages referenced by both i and j. Both A and H are symmetric, a property of importance for the computation of $\vec{a}$ and $\vec{h}$.

As we did for PageRank, we may apply fixed-point iteration — in the form of the power method — to compute $\vec{a}$ and $\vec{h}$. Let $\vec{a}^{(0)}$ and $\vec{h}^{(0)}$ be initial estimates for $\vec{a}$ and $\vec{h}$. The nth estimate, $\vec{a}^{(n)}$ and $\vec{h}^{(n)}$, may be computed from the previous estimate by the equations

$$\vec{a}^{(n)} \;=\; W^T \vec{h}^{(n-1)} / \|W^T \vec{h}^{(n-1)}\| \quad \text{and} \quad \vec{h}^{(n)} \;=\; W \vec{a}^{(n-1)} / \|W \vec{a}^{(n-1)}\|. \tag{15.28}$$

Normalization allows us to avoid explicit computation of the eigenvalue by ensuring that each estimate has unit length. Successive application of these equations will compute $\vec{a}$ and $\vec{h}$ if

$$\lim_{n \to \infty} \vec{a}^{(n)} = \vec{a} \quad \text{and} \quad \lim_{n \to \infty} \vec{h}^{(n)} = \vec{h}. \tag{15.29}$$

For PageRank the ergodicity of M guarantees convergence. For HITS the symmetric property of A and H provides this guarantee, as long as the initial estimates have a component in the direction of the principal eigenvector (Kleinberg, 1999; Golub and Van Loan, 1996). Any unit vector with all positive elements will suffice to satisfy this requirement, such as

$$\vec{a}^{(0)} \;=\; \vec{h}^{(0)} \;=\; \langle 1/\sqrt{N}, 1/\sqrt{N}, \ldots \rangle.$$

Unfortunately, convergence to a unique solution is not guaranteed (Langville and Meyer, 2005). Depending on the initial estimate, HITS may convergence to different solutions (see Exercise 15.9).

SALSA, the *stochastic approach for link-structure analysis*, introduces PageRank's random surfer into HITS (Lempel and Moran, 2000). The creation of SALSA was motivated by the observation that a small set of highly interconnected sites (or "tightly connected communities") can have a disproportionate influence on hub and authority values, by generating inappropriately high values for members of these communities.

SALSA imagines a random surfer following both links and *backlinks* (i.e., reversed links), alternating between them. On odd-numbered steps the surfer chooses an outgoing link from the current page uniformly at random and follows it. On even-numbered steps the surfer chooses an incoming link uniformly at random, from a page linking to the current page, and follows it backwards to its source. As the number of steps increases, the relative time spent on a page just before taking an odd-numbered step represents the page's hub score; the relative time spent on a page just before taking an even-numbered step represents the page's authority score.

Although we do not provide the details, SALSA may be formulated as an eigenvector problem. Lempel and Moran (2000) discuss properties that simplify the computation of SALSA. Rafiei and Mendelzon (2000) propose the introduction of random jumps into a SALSA-like algorithm, with the possibility for a random jump occurring after each odd-even pair of steps.

15.3.5 Other Static Ranking Methods

Static ranking provides a query-independent score for each Web page. Although link analysis is an essential component in the computation of static rank, other features may contribute.

As we mentioned with respect to link analysis in Section 15.3.2, some of the most important features are provided through *implicit user feedback*. By "implicit" we mean that the user provides this feedback while engaged in other activities, perhaps without being aware that she is providing feedback. For example, a click on a Web search result may indicate a preference for that site or page. If higher-ranked results were skipped, the click may also indicate a negative assessment of these skipped pages (Joachims et al., 2005). The toolbars provided by commercial search services track the sites visited by a user and return this information to the search service (with the user's permission). The popularity of a site may be measured through the number of users visiting it, and through the frequency and length of their visits (Richardson et al., 2006).

The content of the pages themselves may also contribute to their static rank. Ivory and Hearst (2002) describe how quantitative measures of page content and structure predict the quality scores assigned by expert assessors. These measures consider the quantity and complexity of text, the placement and formatting of graphical elements, and the choice of fonts and colors.

Finally, the content and structure of a URL may be considered. Short and simple URLs might be favored over long and complex ones, particularly for navigational queries (Upstill et al., 2003). Sites in the `com` domain might be more appropriate for commercial queries than sites in the `edu` domain; the opposite is true for academic queries.

Richardson et al. (2006) apply machine learning techniques, similar to those described in Section 11.7, to the computation of static rank. By combining popularity, page content, and URL features with basic PageRank, they demonstrate substantial improvements over basic PageRank alone. In Section 15.3.2 we discussed how these same features might be applied to adjust the follow and jump vectors in extended PageRank. The best methods for exploiting these features in the computation of static rank remains an area open for exploration.

15.4 Dynamic Ranking

At query time the search engine combines each page's static rank with query-dependent features — such as term frequency and proximity — to generate a dynamic ranking for that query. Although the dynamic ranking algorithms used in commercial search engines are grounded in the theory of Part III, the details of these algorithms vary greatly from one Web search engine to another. Moreover, these algorithms evolve continuously, reflecting the experience gained from the tremendous numbers of queries and users these search engines serve.

Although the scope of this book does not allow us to provide the details of the dynamic ranking algorithms used in specific Web search engines, two aspects of dynamic ranking deserve some attention. The first of these aspects — the availability of anchor text — represents a ranking feature of particular importance in Web search. Anchor text often provides a description of

Table 15.5 Anchor text for in-links to the Wikipedia page `en.wikipedia.org/wiki/William_Shakespeare`, ordered by number of appearances.

#	Anchor Text	#	Anchor Text
3123	Shakespeare	2	Will
3008	William Shakespeare	2	Shakesperean
343	Shakespeare's	2	Shakespere
210	Shakespearean	2	Shakespearean studies
58	William Shakespeare's	2	Shakepeare
52	Shakespearian	2	Bill Shakespeare...
10	W. Shakespeare	1	the Bard's
7	Shakespeare, William	1	lost play of Shakespeare
3	William Shakepeare	1	Shakespearesque
3	Shakesphere	1	Shakespearean theatre
3	Shakespeare's Theatre	1	Shakespearean plays
3	Bard		...
2	the Bard		...

the page referenced by its link, which may be exploited to improve retrieval effectiveness. The importance of the second aspect — novelty — derives from the scale and structure of the Web. Although many pages on a given site may be relevant to a query, it may be better to return one or two results from several sites rather than many pages from a single site, thereby providing more diverse information.

15.4.1 Anchor Text

Anchor text often provides a label or description for the target of its link. Table 15.5 lists the anchor text linking to the page `en.wikipedia.org/wiki/William_Shakespeare` from other pages within Wikipedia, ordered by the number of times each string appears. Pages outside of Wikipedia may also link to this page, but that anchor text can be discovered only through a crawl of the general Web. The table shows a mixture of text, including misspellings and nicknames ("the Bard"). In all, 71 different strings are used in 6889 anchors linking to the page. However, more than 45% of these anchors use the text "Shakespeare", and nearly as many use the text "William Shakespeare".

On the general Web the number of links to a page may vary from one to many millions. When a page is linked many times, the anchor text often repeats, and when it repeats, it usually represents an accurate description of the page (but see Exercise 15.12). Misspellings, nicknames, and similar anchor text can also prove valuable because these terms may not appear on the page, but may be entered by a user as part of a query.

For anchor text to be usable as a ranking feature, it must be associated with the target of the link. Before building a Web index, anchor text must be extracted from each page to create a set of tuples of the form

$$\langle \, target \ URL, anchor \ text \, \rangle \, .$$

These tuples are sorted by URL. The anchor text for each URL is then merged with the page contents for that URL to form a composite document for indexing purposes.

For retrieval, anchor text may be treated as a document field, much as we did for titles and other fields in Section 8.7. When computing term weights, anchor text may be weighted in the same way as other text, or term frequencies may be adjusted to dampen the influence of repeated terms (Hawking et al., 2004). The static rank of the page on which the anchor appears may also play a role in term weights (Robertson et al., 2004). Anchor text appearing on pages with high static rank may be given greater weight than text appearing on pages with low static rank.

15.4.2   Novelty

Given the variety and volume of information on the Web, it is important for a search engine to present a diverse set of results to the user. Given our example query $\langle$ "UPS"$\rangle$, a search engine might best return a mix of results related to the parcel service, to power supplies, and to the university. Simple ways to reduce redundancy include the identification of duplicate pages in the index and post-retrieval filtering to eliminate excessive results from a single Web site.

Although the Web contains many pages that are duplicates (or near-duplicates) of others, the result of a search should usually contain only a single copy. These duplicated pages occur on the Web for several reasons. Many sites return a default page when a URL path is invalid, and all invalid URLs from these sites appear to be duplicates of this default page. Certain types of content are frequently mirrored across multiple sites. For example, a newswire article might appear on the Web sites of multiple newspapers. These duplicates may be detected and flagged by the Web crawler during the crawl (Section 15.6.3), and static rank may be used to choose the best copy at query time.

In general, duplicated pages within a given site should be eliminated from the index. However, it may be reasonable to retain duplicates when they appear on different sites. Most commercial Web search engines allow searches to be restricted to a specified site or domain. For example, including the term `site:wikipedia.org` in a query would restrict a search to Wikipedia. Retaining pages duplicated on other sites allows these searches to be handled correctly.

Another method for improving diversity in search results is to apply post-retrieval filtering. After dynamic ranking, most commercial search engines filter the results to reduce redundancy.

For example, the documentation for the (now-deprecated) Google SOAP API[6] describes one simple post-retrieval filtering algorithm. After retrieval, results may be filtered in two ways:

1. If several results have identical titles and snippets, then only one is retained.

2. Only the two best results from a given Web site are retained.

The API calls this second filter "host crowding". Interestingly, the first filter may eliminate relevant results that are not in fact redundant in order to reduce the *appearance* of redundancy in the search results.

15.5   Evaluating Web Search

In principle it is possible to apply the traditional IR evaluation framework (e.g., P@10 and MAP) to Web search. However, the volume of material available on the Web introduces some problems. For example, an informational query could have hundreds or thousands of relevant documents. It is not uncommon that all of the top ten results returned for such a query are relevant. In that situation the binary relevance assessments ("relevant"/"not relevant") underlying the traditional methodology might not be a sufficient basis for a meaningful evaluation; graded relevance assessments may be more appropriate.

When graded relevance values are available, evaluation measures such as nDCG (Section 12.5.1) may be applied to take advantage of them (Richardson et al., 2006). For example, Najork (2007) uses nDCG in a Web search evaluation based on more than 28,000 queries taken from the Windows Live search engine. Nearly half a million manual judgments were obtained for these queries. These judgments were made on a six-point scale: definitive, excellent, good, fair, bad, and detrimental.

The nature of the Web introduces several novel aspects of evaluation. As we discussed in Section 15.2, many Web queries are navigational. For these queries only a single specific page may be relevant. In Section 15.5.1 we present an evaluation methodology addressing this query type. In addition, the volume of queries and users handled by commercial Web search services provides an opportunity to infer relevance judgments from user behavior, which may be used to augment or replace manual judgments. In Section 15.5.2 we provide an overview of techniques for interpreting clickthroughs and similar user actions for evaluation purposes.

15.5.1   Named Page Finding

A *named page finding* task is a Web evaluation task that imagines a user searching for a specific page, perhaps because she has seen it in the past or otherwise learned about it. The user enters a query describing the content of the page and expects to receive it as the first (or only) search

---

[6] `code.google.com/apis/soapsearch/reference.html` (accessed Dec 23, 2009)

Table 15.6   Named page finding results for selected retrieval methods from Part III. The best run from TREC 2006 (Metzler et al., 2006) is included for comparison.

Method	MRR	% Top 10	% Not Found
BM25 (Ch. 8)	0.348	50.8	16.0
BM25F (Ch. 8)	0.421	58.6	16.6
LMD (Ch. 9)	0.298	48.1	15.5
DFR (Ch. 9)	0.306	45.9	19.9
Metzler et al. (2006)	0.512	69.6	13.8

result. For example, the query $\langle$ "Apollo", "11", "mission" $\rangle$ might be used to describe NASA's history page on the first moon landing. Although other pages might be related to this topic, only that page would be considered correct. Named page finding tasks were included in TREC as part of the Web Track from 2002 to 2004 and in the Terabyte Track in 2005 and 2006 (Hawking and Craswell, 2001; Craswell and Hawking, 2004; Clarke et al., 2005; Büttcher et al., 2006).

The premise behind named page finding represents an important subset of navigational queries (see page 513). Nonetheless, many navigational queries (e.g., $\langle$ "UPS" $\rangle$) are seeking specific sites rather than specific content. To address this issue the scope of named page finding may be expanded to include "home page finding" queries (Craswell and Hawking, 2004).

For the 2006 Terabyte Track, 181 topics were created by track participants. For each topic the creator specified the answer page within the GOV2 collection. Each submitted run consisted of up to 1000 results. During the evaluation of the runs, near-duplicates of answer pages were detected using an implementation of Bernstein and Zobel's (2005) DECO algorithm, a variant of the near-duplicate detection algorithm from Section 15.6.3. All near-duplicates of a correct answer page were also considered correct. Three measures were used in the evaluation:

- **MRR**: The *mean reciprocal rank* of the first correct answer.

- **% Top 10**: The proportion of queries for which a correct answer was found in the top ten search results.

- **% Not Found**: The proportion of queries for which no correct answer was found in the top 1000 search results.

For a given topic, reciprocal rank is the inverse of the rank at which the answer first appears. If the answer is the top result, its reciprocal rank is 1; if the answer is the fifth result, its reciprocal rank is $1/5$. If the answer does not appear in the result list, it may be assigned a reciprocal rank of $1/\infty = 0$. Mean reciprocal rank is the average of reciprocal rank across all topics.

Full results for the track are provided by Büttcher et al. (2006). Table 15.6 shows the results of applying the retrieval methods from Part III to this task. For this task, BM25F improves upon BM25. For comparison we include the best result from the track itself (Metzler et al., 2006). This run incorporated a number of Web-specific techniques, such as link analysis (static ranking) and anchor text. The gap between the standard retrieval methods from Part III and Metzler's run illustrates the importance of these techniques for navigational search tasks.

15.5.2 Implicit User Feedback

Implicit feedback is provided by users as a side effect of their interaction with a search engine. Clickthroughs provide one important and readily available source of this implicit feedback. Whenever a user enters a query and clicks on the link to a result, a record of that clickthrough may be sent by the browser to the search engine, where it is logged for later analysis.

For a given query the clickthroughs from many users may be combined into a *clickthrough curve* showing the pattern of clicks for that query. The plots in Figure 15.5 provide examples of stereotypical clickthrough curves for navigational and informational queries. In both plots the number of clickthroughs decreases with rank. If we interpret a clickthrough as a positive preference on the part of the user, the shapes of these curves are just as we would expect: Higher-ranked results are more likely to be relevant and to receive more clicks. Even when successive results have the same relevance, we expect the higher ranked result to receive more clicks. If the user scans the results in order, higher-ranked results will be seen before lower-ranked ones. There is also a *trust bias* (Joachims et al., 2005) in user behavior: Users expect search engines to return the best results first, and therefore tend to click on highly ranked results even though they might not contain the information sought.

Figure 15.9 presents a third clickthrough curve, taken from the same paper as the previous two (Clarke et al., 2007). This figure plots clickthroughs for the informational/transactional query ⟨"kids", "online", "games"⟩. The plot includes a number of *clickthrough inversions*, in which a particular result received fewer clicks than the result ranked immediately below it (e.g., the result at rank 2 versus rank 3, or rank 7 versus rank 8).

Clickthrough inversions may indicate a suboptimal ranking, in which a less relevant document is ranked above a more relevant one. However, they may also arise for reasons unrelated to relevance. For example, the title and snippet of the higher-ranked result may not accurately describe the underlying page (Clarke et al., 2007; Dupret et al., 2007). If a user does not understand how or why a result is relevant after reading its title and snippet, she may be inclined to ignore it and to move on to other results. Nonetheless, when the titles and snippets provide accurate descriptions of results, a clickthrough inversion may be interpreted as a pairwise preference for the lower-ranked result (Joachims and Radlinski, 2007).

Query *abandonment* — issuing a query but not clicking on any result — suggests user dissatisfaction of a more substantial nature (Joachims and Radlinski, 2007). When many users abandon a given query, this behavior may indicate that none of the top results are relevant. In some cases an abandonment is followed by a query reformulation in which the user adds, removes, or corrects terms. A search service may capture these query reformulations by tracking search activity through browser cookies and similar mechanisms.[7]

By examining query reformulations from large numbers of users, it is possible to correct spelling errors, to suggest expansion terms, and to identify acronyms (Cucerzan and Brill, 2004; Jones et al., 2006). For example, a user entering the query ⟨"brittany", "spears"⟩ may correct

---

[7] www.w3.org/Protocols/rfc2109/rfc2109

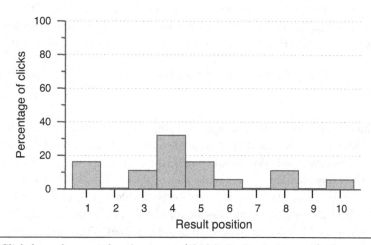

Figure 15.9   Clickthrough curve for the query ⟨"kids", "online", "games"⟩. Inversions (e.g., rank 2 versus rank 3) indicate a suboptimal ranking of search results.

it to ⟨"britney", "spears"⟩.[8] A click after a reformulation may indicate a page that is relevant to the original query. For example, Joachims and Radlinski (2007) report that users frequently reformulate ⟨"oed"⟩ to ⟨"oxford", "english", "dictionary"⟩ and then click on the first result.

Capturing other forms of implicit feedback requires the cooperation of the user, who must install a browser toolbar or similar application, and give explicit permission to capture this feedback (Kellar et al., 2007). Page *dwell time* provides one example of feedback that may be captured in this way. If a user clicks on a result and then immediately backtracks to the result page, this action may indicate that the result is not relevant.

Taken together, these and other sources of implicit feedback can lead to substantial improvements in the quality of Web search results, both by facilitating evaluation (Agichtein et al., 2006b) and by providing additional ranking features (Agichtein et al., 2006a).

15.6   Web Crawlers

The functioning of a Web crawler is similar to that of a user surfing the Web, but on a much larger scale. Just as a user follows links from page to page, a crawler successively downloads pages, extracts links from them, and then repeats with the new links. Many of the challenges associated with the development of a Web crawler relate to the scale and speed at which this process must take place.

---

[8] `labs.google.com/britney.html` (accessed Dec 23, 2009)

Suppose our goal is to download an 8-billion-page snapshot of the Web over the course of a week (a small snapshot by the standards of a commercial Web search engine). If we assume an average page is 64 KB in size, we must download data at a steady rate of

$$64 \text{ KB/page} \cdot 8 \text{ giga-pages/week} \; = \; 512 \text{ TB/week}$$
$$= \; 888 \text{ MB/second}$$

To achieve this tremendous download rate, the crawler must download pages from multiple sites concurrently because it may take an individual site several seconds to respond to a single download request. As it downloads pages, the crawler must track its progress, avoiding pages it has already downloaded and retrying pages when a download attempt fails.

The crawler must take care that its activities do not interfere with the normal operation of the sites it visits. Simultaneous downloads should be distributed across the Web, and visits to a single site must be carefully spaced to avoid overload. The crawler must also respect the wishes of the sites it visits by following established conventions that may exclude the crawler from certain pages and links.

Many Web pages are updated regularly. After a period of time the crawler must return to capture new versions of these pages, or the search engine's index will become stale. To avoid this problem we might recrawl the entire Web each week, but this schedule wastes resources and does not match the practical requirements of Web search. Some pages are updated regularly with "popular" or "important" information and should be recrawled more frequently, perhaps daily or hourly. Other pages rarely change or contain information of minimal value, and it may be sufficient to revisit these pages less frequently, perhaps biweekly or monthly.

To manage the order and frequency of crawling and recrawling, the crawler must maintain a priority queue of seen URLs. The ordering of URLs in the priority queue should reflect a combination of factors including their relative importance and update frequency.

15.6.1 Components of a Crawler

In this section we examine the individual steps and components of a crawler by tracing the journey of a single URL (`en.wikipedia.org/wiki/William_Shakespeare`) as it travels through the crawling process. Tracing a single URL allows us to simplify our presentation, but we emphasize that crawling at the rates necessary to support a Web search engine requires these steps to take place concurrently for large numbers of URLs.

Figure 15.10 provides an overview of these steps and components. The crawling process begins when a URL is removed from the front of the priority queue and ends when it is returned to the queue along with other URLs extracted from the visited page. Although specific implementation details vary from crawler to crawler, all crawlers will include these steps in one form or another. For example, a single thread may execute all steps for a single URL, with thousands of such threads executing concurrently. Alternatively, URLs may be grouped into large batches, with

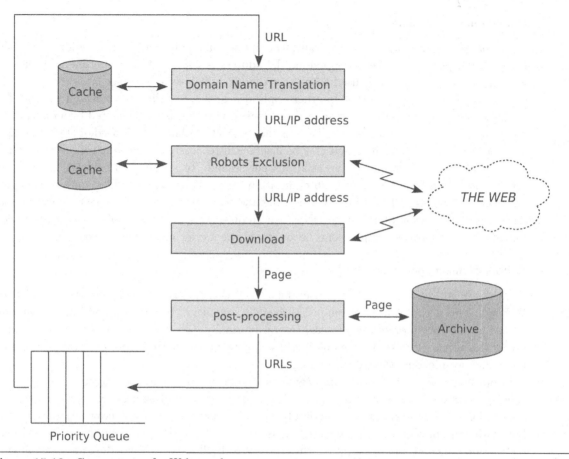

Figure 15.10   Components of a Web crawler.

each step executed for all URLs in the batch before the crawler moves on to execute the next step for the same batch.

Like the search engine it supports (Section 14.1), the activities of a large-scale Web crawler must be distributed across multiple machines in order to sustain the necessary download rates. This distribution may be achieved by assigning subsets of URLs to each machine, essentially giving each machine responsibility for a portion of the Web. The construction of these subsets may be based on host name, IP address, or other factors (Chung and Clarke, 2002). For example, we might assign each machine responsibility for certain hosts. The priority queue might be centralized at a single machine that would distribute URLs to other machines for crawling, or each machine might implement its own priority queue for its assigned subset.

Domain name translation

The processing of a URL begins by translating its host name into a 32-bit IP address. For the host `en.wikipedia.org` the corresponding IP address is `208.80.152.2` (at time and place of writing). This address will be used to contact the machine hosting the page.

As it is for browsers and other Internet applications, this translation is effected through the Domain Name System (DNS), a standard Internet service that is implemented by a distributed hierarchy of servers and caches spread across the Internet. Although the speed of DNS is acceptable for most applications, its speed may be insufficient to satisfy the demands of a Web crawler, which may require thousands of translations per second. To satisfy this translation rate, the crawler may need to maintain its own translation cache. This cache would maintain mappings between host names and IP addresses, expiring and refreshing these entries as they grow stale. Although the inclusion of a custom DNS cache represents a minor part of a crawler, the need for this cache illustrates the problems encountered when crawling at high speeds.

Robots exclusion protocol

With the IP address available the crawler must check that access to the page is permitted by the Web site. This permission is determined through an unofficial (but well-established) convention known as the *robots exclusion protocol* (more informally, the "`robots.txt` protocol"). For a given site, access permissions are obtained by appending the path `"/robots.txt"` to the host name and downloading the corresponding page.

In our example the URL is `http://en.wikipedia.org/robots.txt`. Figure 15.11 shows a small portion of the corresponding page. The page is structured as a series of comments and instructions. A "`User-agent`" instruction begins a list that applies to the crawler named on the line, with a "`*`" indicating that the instructions apply to all crawlers. For example, a "`Disallow`" instruction indicates a path prefix to which access is disallowed. Downloading any page having a path starting with a disallowed prefix is not permitted. The example in the figure denies all access to the `wget` program, and requests other crawlers to avoid the random article link and the search link, both of which generate content dynamically. Full details on the robots exclusion protocol may be found on the Web Robots site.[9]

A Web crawler will generally cache the `robots.txt` page for each host it encounters in order to avoid repeated downloads whenever a URL from that host is processed. This cached information should be expired on a regular basis, perhaps after a few hours or days.

When access by the crawler is not permitted, the URL may be returned to the priority queue and labeled to indicate that download was disallowed. The crawler may retry the URL at a future time, checking first that access has been permitted, or the URL may be permanently flagged as disallowed, never to be retried but maintained as a placeholder to prevent further attempts.

---

[9] `www.robotstxt.org`

```
#
# robots.txt for http://www.wikipedia.org/ and friends
#
...

#
# Sorry, wget in its recursive mode is a frequent problem.
#
User-agent: wget
Disallow: /
...

#
# Friendly, low-speed bots are welcome viewing article pages, but not
# dynamically-generated pages please.
#
User-agent: *
Disallow: /wiki/Special:Random
Disallow: /wiki/Special:Search
...
```

Figure 15.11   Extracts from a `robots.txt` file.

Download

After confirming that download is permitted, the crawler accesses the Web site via the HTTP protocol and downloads the page. The page may be formatted as HTML (e.g., Figure 8.1 on page 278) or in other formats, such as PDF. Associated pages may be identified and downloaded at the same time, or they may be left for a future crawling cycle. For example, if the page defines a frame set, all pages in the set might be downloaded together. Images may also be downloaded, perhaps in support of an image search service.

During download the crawler may be required to resolve redirections, which indicate that the actual content of the page is found elsewhere. These redirections can add considerable complexity to the download process, in part because redirections may be implemented in multiple ways. At the HTTP protocol level various responses generated by the Web server may indicate that a page has moved permanently or temporarily to a new location. Redirections may also be specified by tags appearing in HTML pages. Finally, JavaScript loaded with HTML pages may generate redirections during execution.

For example, Wikipedia uses an HTTP "301 Moved Permanently" response to redirect the URL `en.wikipedia.org/wiki/william_shakespeare` to `en.wikipedia.org/wiki/William_Shakespeare`. Redirections to correct spelling and capitalization are common in Wikipedia.

Other sites may use HTTP redirections when sites are redesigned or restructured, so that older URLs continue to work.

The use of JavaScript to generate redirections causes the most trouble for Web crawlers because correct determination of the redirection's target potentially requires the crawler to execute the JavaScript. Moreover, this JavaScript may redirect to different pages depending on factors such as the user's browser type. Covering all possibilities theoretically requires the crawler to repeatedly execute the JavaScript under different configurations until all possible redirection targets are determined.

Given resource limitations, it may not be feasible for a crawler to execute JavaScript for millions of downloaded pages. Instead the crawler may attempt partial evaluation or other heuristics, which may be sufficient to determine redirection targets in many cases. On the other hand, if the crawler ignores JavaScript redirections, it may be left with little useful content, perhaps no more than a message suggesting that JavaScript be enabled.

Post-processing

After download, the crawler stores the page in an archive for indexing by the search engine. Older copies of the page may be retained in this archive, thus allowing the crawler to estimate the frequency and types of changes the page undergoes. If the download fails, perhaps because the site is temporarily inaccessible, these older copies remain available for indexing. After a failed download the URL may be returned to the priority queue and retried at a later time. If several download attempts fail over a period of days, the older copies may be allowed to expire, thus removing the page from the index.

In addition to being stored in the archive, the page is analyzed, or *scraped*, to extract any URLs it contains. Much like a browser, the crawler parses the HTML to locate anchor tags and other elements containing links. Anchor text and other information required for indexing may be extracted at the same time, then stored in the archive for the convenience of the search engine. Pages that are duplicates (or near-duplicates) of the downloaded page may also be identified during this analysis (see Section 15.6.3).

During post-processing, the crawler must respect conventions requesting that it not index a page or follow certain links. If the tag

```
<meta name="robots" content="noindex">
```

appears in the header of page, it indicates that a search engine should not include the page in its index. The "`rel=nofollow`" attribute appearing in an anchor tag indicates that the crawler should essentially ignore the link. For example, the following external link appeared on the Wikipedia Shakespeare page at the time of writing:

```
<a href="http://www.opensourceshakespeare.org" rel="nofollow">
  Open Source Shakespeare
</a>
```

The crawler should crawl this page only if it finds a link elsewhere, and the link should not influence ranking in any way. Sites such as blogs and wikis, which allow their users to create external links, may automatically add "`rel=nofollow`" to all such links. This policy is intended to discourage the creation of inappropriate links solely for the purpose of increasing the PageRank value of the target page. With the addition of "`rel=nofollow`" users generating this link spam will garner no benefit from it.

As it did during download, JavaScript poses problems during post-processing. When it is executed, JavaScript is capable of completely rewriting a page with new content and links. If execution is not feasible, the crawler may apply heuristics to extract whatever URLs and other information it can, but without any guarantee of success.

Priority queue

URLs extracted during post-processing are inserted into the priority queue. If a URL already appears in the queue, information gathered during post-processing may alter its position.

Implementing the priority queue is a challenging problem. If we assume an average URL is 64 bytes in length, a priority queue for 8 billion pages requires half a terabyte just to store the URLs (ignoring compression). These storage requirements, coupled with the need to support millions of updates per second, may limit the sophistication of strategies used to manage the priority queue. In Section 15.6.2, where these strategies are discussed, we ignore implementation difficulties. However, when deploying an operational crawler, these difficulties cannot be ignored.

15.6.2   Crawl Order

Suppose we are crawling the Web for the first time, with the goal of capturing and maintaining a multibillion-page snapshot. We have no detailed knowledge of the sites and pages contained on the Web, which remain to be discovered. To begin, we might start with a small *seed set* of well-known URLs including major portals, retail sites, and news services. The pages linked from the ODP[10] or other Web directory could form one possible seed set. If we then proceed in a breadth-first manner, we should encounter many high-quality pages early in the crawl (Najork and Wiener, 2001).

As we conduct the crawl, our knowledge of the Web increases. At some point, especially if the crawler is feeding an operational search engine, it becomes important to revisit pages as well as to crawl new URLs. Otherwise, the index of the search service will become stale. From this point forward, crawling proceeds *incrementally*, with the crawler continuously expanding and updating its snapshot of the Web. As it visits and revisits pages, new URLs are discovered and deleted pages are dropped.

---

[10] `www.dmoz.org`

The activities of the crawler are then determined by its *refresh policy* (Olston and Pandey, 2008; Pandey and Olston, 2008; Cho and Garcia-Molina, 2000, 2003; Wolf et al., 2002; Edwards et al., 2001). Two factors feed into this policy: (1) the frequency and nature of changes to pages and (2) the impact that these changes have on search results, compared to the impact of crawling new URLs. The simplest refresh policy is to revisit all pages at a fixed rate, once every X weeks, while continuing to crawl new URLs in breadth-first order. However, although this policy is appropriate for pages that change infrequently, high-impact pages that undergo frequent alterations (e.g., `www.cnn.com`) should be revisited more often. Moreover, priority should be placed on crawling those new URLs that have the highest potential to affect search results. This potential may, for instance, be estimated by processing existing query logs and analyzing user behavior (e.g., clickthrough data). It is the role of the refresh policy to determine revisit rates for existing pages and the crawl order for new URLs.

The Web changes continuously. Ntoulas et al. (2004) tracked the changes to 154 Web sites over the course of a year and estimated that new pages were created at a rate of 8% per week and new links at a rate of 25% per week. The deletion rate was also high. After one year only 20% of the initial pages remained available. However, once created, most pages changed very little until they were deleted. Even after a year, less than half of the pages changed by more than 5% before deletion, as determined through a measure based on TF-IDF. When pages do change, Cho and Garcia-Molina (2003) demonstrate that the frequency of these changes may be modeled by the Poisson distribution (see page 268). Thus, if we know the history of a page, we can predict how often future changes will take place.

Even when a page does change frequently, the determination of the revisit rate depends on the nature of the changes. Olston and Pandey (2008) recognize that different parts of a Web page have different update characteristics, and these characteristics must be considered when establishing a refresh policy for that page. Some parts of a Web page may remain static, while other parts exhibit *churning behavior*. For example, the ads on a page may change each time it is accessed, or a page may update daily with a "quote of the day" while its other content remains the same. Blogs and forums may exhibit *scrolling behavior*, with new items pushing down older items that eventually fall away. Some pages, such as the home pages of news services, may have the bulk of their content revised several times an hour.

Both revisit rates and the ordering of unvisited URLs must be determined in light of the impact they have on search results. Pandey and Olston (2008) define impact in terms of the number of times a page appears, or would appear, in the top results for the queries received by the search engine. Their work suggests that when choosing a new URL to visit, priority should be given to URLs that are likely to improve the search results for one or more queries. Similarly, we may consider impact when determining revisit rates. It might be appropriate to revisit a news service every hour or more, because the top news services change constantly and have high impact. A user searching on the topic of a breaking story wants to know the latest news. On the other hand, a daily visit to a page featuring a "quote of the day" may be unnecessary if the rest of the page remains unchanged and the searches returning the page as a top result depend only on this static content.

Impact is related to static rank. Pages with high static rank may often be good candidates for frequent visits. However, impact is not equivalent to static rank (Pandey and Olston, 2008). For example, a page may have high static rank because it is linked by other pages on the same site with higher static rank. However, if it always appears well below other pages from the same site in search results, changes to that page will have little or no impact. On the other hand, a page may have a low static rank because its topic is relatively obscure, of interest only to a small subset of users. But for those users the absence of the page would have high impact on their search results.

15.6.3 Duplicates and Near-Duplicates

Roughly 30–40% of Web pages are exact duplicates of other pages and about 2% are near-duplicates (Henzinger, 2006). The volume of this data represents a major problem for search engines because retaining unnecessary duplicates increases storage and processing costs. More important, duplicates and near-duplicates can impact novelty and lead to less-than-desirable search results. Although host crowding or similar post-retrieval filtering methods might ameliorate the problem, the performance costs must still be paid and near-duplicates may still slip past the filter.

Detecting exact duplicates of pages is relatively straightforward. The entire page, including tags and scripts, may be passed to a hash function. The resulting integer hash value may then be compared with the hash value for other pages. One possible hash function for detecting duplicates is provided by the MD5 algorithm (Rivest, 1992). Given a string, MD5 computes a 128-bit "message digest" corresponding to that string. MD5 is often used to validate the integrity of files after a data transfer, providing a simple way of checking that the entire file was transferred correctly. With a length of 128 bits inadvertent collisions are unlikely (however, see Exercise 15.11).

Detection of exact duplicates through these hash values is sufficient to handle many common sources of duplication, even though pages will match only if they are byte-for-byte the same. Pages mirrored across multiple sites, such as the Java documentation, may be identified in this way. Many sites will return the same "Not Found" page for every invalid URL. Some URLs that contain a user or session id may represent the same content regardless of its value. Ideally, exact duplicates should be detected during the crawling processing. Once a mirrored page is detected, other mirrored pages linked from it can be avoided.

From the perspective of a user, two pages may be considered duplicates because they contain essentially the same material even if they are not byte-for-byte copies of one another. To detect these near-duplicates, pages may be canonicalized into a stream of tokens, reducing their content to a standard form much as we do for indexing. This canonicalization usually includes the removal of tags and scripts. In addition we may remove punctuation, capitalization, and extraneous white space. For example, the HTML document of Figure 8.1 (page 278) might be canonicalized to:

william shakespeare wikipedia the free encyclopedia william shakespeare william shakespeare baptised 26 April 1564 died 23 April 1616 was an english poet and playwright he is widely regarded as the...

After canonicalization a hash function may be applied to detect duplicates of the remaining content.

However, near-duplicates often contain minor changes and additions, which would not be detected by a hash value over the entire page. Menus, titles, and other boilerplate may differ. Material copied from one site to another may have edits applied. Detecting these near-duplicates requires that we compare documents by comparing the substrings they contain. For example, a newswire article appearing on multiple sites will have a large substring (the news story) in common, but other parts of the pages will differ.

The degree to which a page is a copy of another may be measured by comparing the substrings they have in common. Consider a newswire story appearing on two sites; the page on the first site is 24 KB in size and the page on the second site is 32 KB, after canonicalization. If the story itself has a size of 16 KB, then we might compute the similarity of the two pages in terms of this duplicate content as

$$\frac{16 \text{ KB}}{24 \text{ KB} + 32 \text{ KB} - 16 \text{ KB}} = 40\%.$$

Thus, the news story represents 40% of the combined content of the pages.

Broder et al. (1997) describe a method to permit the computation of content similarity and the detection of near-duplicates on the scale of the Web. Their method extracts substrings known as *shingles* from each canonicalized page and compares pages by measuring the overlap between these shingles. We provide a simplified presentation of this method; full details can be found in Broder et al. (1997) and in related papers (Henzinger, 2006; Bernstein and Zobel, 2005; Charikar, 2002).

The shingles of length w from a page (the w-shingles) consist of all substrings of length w tokens appearing in the document. For example, consider the following three lines from *Hamlet*:

#1: To be, or not to be: that is the question
#2: To sleep: perchance to dream: ay, there's the rub
#3: To be or not to be, ay there's the point

The first two lines are taken from the standard edition of Shakespeare's works used throughout the book. The last is taken from what may be a "pirated" copy of the play, reconstructed from memory by a minor actor.[11]

---

[11] `internetshakespeare.uvic.ca/Library/SLT/literature/texts+1.html` (accessed Dec 23, 2009)

After canonicalization we have the following 2-shingles for each line, where the shingles have been sorted alphabetically and duplicates have been removed:

#1: be or, be that, is the, not to, or not, that is, the question, to be

#2: ay there, dream ay, perchance to, s the, sleep perchance, the rub, there s, to dream, to sleep

#3: ay there, be ay, be or, not to, or not, s the, the point, there s, to be

For this example we use $w = 2$. For Web pages $w = 11$ might be an appropriate choice (Broder et al., 1997).

Given two sets of shingles A and B, we define the *resemblance* between them according to the number of shingles they have in common

$$\frac{|A \cap B|}{|A \cup B|}. \tag{15.30}$$

Resemblance ranges between 0 and 1 and indicates the degree to which A and B contain duplicate content. To simplify the computation of resemblance, we calculate a hash value for each shingle; 64-bit hash values are usually sufficient for this purpose (Henzinger, 2006). Although the range of a 64-bit value is small enough that the Web is likely to contain different shingles that hash to the same value, pages are unlikely to contain multiple matching shingles unless they contain duplicate content. For the purpose of our example we assign 8-bit hash values arbitrarily, giving the following sets of shingle values:

#1: 43, 14, 109, 204, 26, 108, 154, 172

#2: 132, 251, 223, 16, 201, 118, 93, 197, 217

#3: 132, 110, 43, 204, 26, 16, 207, 93, 172.

A Web page may consist of a large number of shingles. One way of reducing this number is to eliminate all but those that are equal to 0 mod m, where $m = 25$ might be appropriate for Web data (Broder et al., 1997). Another approach is to keep the smallest s shingles. Resemblance is then estimated by comparing the remaining shingles. For our example we are following the first approach with $m = 2$, leaving us with the even-valued shingles:

#1: 14, 204, 26, 108, 154, 172

#2: 132, 16, 118

#3: 132, 110, 204, 26, 16, 172.

For this example it is easy to make pairwise comparisons between the sets of shingles. However, for billions of Web documents pairwise comparisons are not feasible. Instead, we construct tuples consisting of pairs of the form

⟨ *shingle value, document id* ⟩

and sort the pairs by shingle value (essentially constructing an inverted index). For our example this gives the following tuples:

⟨14, 1⟩, ⟨16, 2⟩, ⟨16, 3⟩, ⟨26, 1⟩, ⟨26, 3⟩ ⟨108, 1⟩, ⟨110, 3⟩, ⟨118, 2⟩, ⟨132, 2⟩, ⟨132, 3⟩, ⟨154, 1⟩, ⟨172, 1⟩, ⟨172, 3⟩, ⟨204, 1⟩, ⟨204, 3⟩.

Our next step is to combine tuples with the same shingle value to create tuples of the form

⟨ *id1, id2* ⟩,

where each pair indicates that the two documents share a shingle. In constructing these pairs we place the lower-valued document identifier first. The actual shingle values may now be ignored because there will be one pair for each shingle the documents have in common. For our example we have the following pairs:

⟨2, 3⟩, ⟨1, 3⟩, ⟨2, 3⟩, ⟨1, 3⟩, ⟨1, 3⟩.

Sorting and counting gives triples of the form

⟨ *id1, id2, count* ⟩.

For our example these triples are

⟨1, 3, 3⟩, ⟨2, 3, 2⟩.

From these triples we may estimate the resemblance between #1 and #3 as

$$\frac{3}{6+6-3} = \frac{1}{3},$$

and the resemblance between #2 and #3 as

$$\frac{2}{3+6-2} = \frac{2}{7}.$$

The resemblance between #1 and #2 is 0.

15.7 Summary

Although this chapter is long and covers a wide range of topics, three factors occur repeatedly: scale, structure, and users.

- The Web contains an enormous volume of material on all topics and in many languages, and is constantly growing and changing. The scale of the Web implies that for many queries there are large numbers of relevant pages. With so many relevant pages, factors such as novelty and quality become important considerations for ranking. The same query will mean different things to different users. Maintaining an accurate and appropriate index for millions of sites requires substantial planning and resources.

- The structure represented by HTML tags and links provides important features for ranking. Link analysis methods have been extensively explored as methods for determining the relative quality of pages. The weighting of terms appearing in titles and anchor text may be adjusted to reflect their status. Without links, Web crawling would be nearly impossible.

- User experience drives Web search. Search engines must be aware of the range of interpretations and intent underlying user queries. Informational queries require different responses than navigational queries, and search engines must be evaluated with respect to their performance on both query types. Clickthroughs and other implicit user feedback captured in search engine logs may be analyzed to evaluate and improve performance.

15.8 Further Reading

A Web search engine is a mysterious and complex artifact that undergoes constant tuning and enhancement by large teams of dedicated engineers and developers. In this chapter we have covered only a small fraction of the technology underlying Web search.

The commercial importance of Web search and Web advertising is now significant enough that a large community of search engine marketing and search engine optimization (SEO) companies have grown around it. These SEOs advise Web site owners on how to obtain higher rankings from the major engines by means both fair and (occasionally) foul. Members of this community often blog about their work, and the technical tidbits appearing in these blogs can make for fascinating reading. A good place to start is the Search Engine Roundtable.[12] The personal blog of Matt Cutts, the head of Google's Webspam team, is another good entry point.[13]

---

[12] www.seroundtable.com
[13] www.mattcutts.com

The first Web search engines appeared in the early 1990s, soon after the genesis of the Web itself. By the mid-1990s commercial search services, such as Excite, Lycos, Altavista, and Yahoo!, were handling millions of queries per day. A history of these early search engines may be found at Search Engine Watch, a site that has tracked the commercial aspects of search engine technology since 1996.[14] Along with the content-based features discussed in Part III, these early engines incorporated simple link-based features — for example, using a page's in-degree as an indicator of its popularity (Marchiori, 1997).

15.8.1 Link Analysis

By the late 1990s the importance of static ranking and link analysis was widely recognized. In 1997 Marchiori outlined a link analysis technique that foreshadowed the intuition underlying PageRank. In the same year Carrière and Kazman (1997) presented a tool for exploring the linkage relationships between Web sites.

On 15 April 1998, at the 7th World Wide Web Conference in Brisbane, Australia, Brin and Page presented their now-classic paper describing the basic PageRank algorithm and the architecture of their nascent Google search engine (Brin and Page, 1998). In papers published soon afterwards, they and their colleagues built upon this work, describing foundational algorithms for personalized PageRank and Web data mining (Brin et al., 1998; Page et al., 1999). While Brin and Page were creating PageRank (and the Google search engine), Kleinberg independently developed the HITS algorithm and presented it at the 9th Annual Symposium on Discrete Algorithms in January 1998 (Kleinberg, 1998, 1999). A paper co-authored by Kleinberg, extending HITS to accommodate anchor text, was presented at the 7th World Wide Web Conference on the same day as Brin and Page's paper (Chakrabarti et al., 1998). Together the work of Brin, Page, and Kleinberg engendered a flood of research into link analysis techniques.

Bharat and Henzinger (1998) combined HITS with content analysis. They also recognized the problems that tightly connected communities cause for HITS and suggested the solution that Lempel and Moran (2000) later developed into SALSA. Rafiei and Mendelzon (2000) extended PageRank along the lines of SALSA to determine the topics for which a page is known (its "reputation"). Davidson (2000) recognized that some links should be assigned lower weights than others and trained a classifier to recognize links arising from commercial relationships rather than solely from merit. Cohn and Chang (2000) applied *principal component analysis* (PCA) to extract multiple eigenvectors from the HITS matrix. A number of other authors explore efficient methods for computing personalized and topic-oriented PageRank (Haveliwala, 2002; Jeh and Widom, 2003; Chakrabarti, 2007).

Ng et al. (2001a,b) compare the stability of HITS and PageRank, demonstrating the role of PageRank's jump vector and suggesting the addition of a jump vector to HITS. Borodin et al. (2001) provide a theoretical analysis of HITS and SALSA and suggest further improvements.

---

[14] searchenginewatch.com/showPage.html?page=3071951 (accessed Dec 23, 2009)

Richardson and Domingos (2002) describe a query-dependent version of PageRank in which the random surfer is more likely to follow links to pages related to the query. Kamvar et al. (2003) present a method for accelerating the computation of PageRank.

More recently, Langville and Meyer (2005, 2006) provide a detailed and readable survey of the mathematics underlying PageRank and HITS. Bianchini et al. (2005) explore further properties of PageRank. Craswell et al. (2005) discuss the extension of BM25F to incorporate static ranking. Baeza-Yates et al. (2006) generalize the role of the jump vector and replace it with other damping functions to create a family of algorithms related to PageRank. Najork et al. (2007) compare the retrieval effectiveness of HITS and basic PageRank, both alone and in combination with BM25F, illustrating the limitations of basic PageRank. In a related study Najork (2007) compares the retrieval effectiveness of HITS and SALSA, finding that SALSA outperforms HITS as a static ranking feature.

Gyöngyi et al. (2004) present a link analysis technique called *TrustRank* for identifying Web spam. A related paper by Gyöngyi and Garcia-Molina (2005) provides a general overview and discussion of the Web spam problem. In addition to link analysis techniques, content-oriented techniques such as the e-mail spam filtering methods described in Chapter 10 may be applied to identify Web spam. The AIRWeb[15] workshops provide a forum for the testing and evaluating methods for detecting Web spam as part of a broader theme of adversarial IR on the Web.

Golub and Van Loan (1996) is the bible of numerical methods for matrix computations. They devote two long chapters to the solution of eigenvalue problems, including a thorough discussion of the power method.

15.8.2 Anchor Text

Anchor text was used as a ranking feature in the earliest Web search engines (Brin and Page, 1998). Craswell et al. (2001) demonstrate its importance in comparison to content features. Robertson et al. (2004) describe the incorporation of anchor text into the probabilistic retrieval model. Hawking et al. (2004) present a method for attenuating weights for anchor text, adjusting term frequency values when anchor text is repeated many times.

15.8.3 Implicit Feedback

Joachims and Radlinski (2007) provide an overview of methods for interpreting implicit feedback; Kelly and Teevan (2003) provide a bibliography of early work. Dupret et al. (2007), Liu et al. (2007), and Carterette and Jones (2007) all discuss the use of clickthroughs for Web search evaluation. Agichtein et al. (2006b) learn relevance judgments by combining multiple browsing and clickthrough features. Qiu and Cho (2006) present a method for determining a user's interests from clickthroughs, thus allowing search results to be personalized to reflect these interests.

---

[15] airweb.cse.lehigh.edu

15.8.4   Web Crawlers

A basic architecture for a Web crawler is described by Heydon and Najork (1999). Olston and Najork (2010) provide a recent and thorough survey of the area.

The problem of optimizing the refresh policy of an incremental crawler has been studied by several groups (Edwards et al., 2001; Wolf et al., 2002; Cho and Garcia-Molina, 2003; Olston and Pandey, 2008). Dasgupta et al. (2007) examine the trade-offs between visiting new URLs and revisiting previously crawled pages. Pandey and Olston (2008) consider the impact of new pages on search results. Chakrabarti et al. (1999) describe focused crawlers that are dedicated to crawling pages related to a specific topic. Little has been published regarding the efficient implementation of priority queues for Web crawlers, but Yi et al. (2003) provide a possible starting point for investigation.

Broder et al. (1997) introduced shingles as a method for detecting near-duplicates. Henzinger (2006) experimentally compared this method with a competing method by Charikar (2002) and introduced a combined algorithm that outperforms both. Bernstein and Zobel (2005) used a version of shingling to evaluate the impact of near-duplicates on retrieval effectiveness.

15.9   Exercises

Exercise 15.1   Compute basic PageRank for the following Web graphs. Assume $\delta = 3/4$.

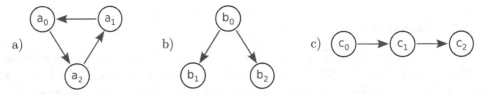

Exercise 15.2   Compute basic PageRank for the following Web graph. Assume $\delta = 0.85$.

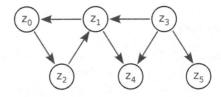

Exercise 15.3   Given Equations 15.9 and 15.10, show that for all $n \geq 0$

$$\sum_{\alpha \in \Phi} r^{(n)}(\alpha) \ = \ N.$$

Exercise 15.4 Compute extended PageRank for the follow matrix and jump vector in Equation 15.12 (page 525). Assume $\delta = 0.85$.

Exercise 15.5 Show that the transition matrix M' (page 531) is aperiodic for any Web graph.

Exercise 15.6 Suggest additional sources of information, beyond those listed on page 525, that might be enlisted when setting the follow matrix and jump vector

Exercise 15.7 Compute the co-citation matrix $A = W^T W$ and the bibliographic coupling matrix $H = WW^T$ for the adjacency matrix W in Equation 15.24 (page 533).

Exercise 15.8 Compute the authority vector $\vec{a}$ and hub vector $\vec{h}$ for the adjacency matrix W in Equation 15.24 (page 533).

Exercise 15.9 Langville and Meyer (2005) suggest the following example to illustrate the convergence properties of HITS. Compute the authority vector $\vec{a}$ for the following adjacency matrix, starting with the initial estimate $\vec{a}^{(0)} = \langle 1/2, 1/2, 1/2, 1/2 \rangle^T$.

$$
W = \begin{pmatrix} 0 & 0 & 0 & 0 \\ 1 & 0 & 0 & 0 \\ 1 & 0 & 0 & 0 \\ 0 & 1 & 1 & 0 \end{pmatrix} \tag{15.31}
$$

Recompute the authority vector $\vec{a}$ starting with the initial estimate $\vec{a}^{(0)} = \langle 1/\sqrt{3}, 1/3, 1/3, 2/3 \rangle^T$.

Exercise 15.10 View the `robots.txt` file on well-known Web sites. Are any pages or crawlers disallowed? Why?

Exercise 15.11 The MD5 algorithm is known to be insecure. Given an MD5 value for a string, it is possible to construct a different string that gives the same value. How could this vulnerability be exploited by a malicious site to cause problems for a Web search service? Search this topic and suggest possible solutions.

Exercise 15.12 Search the term "Google bombing". Suggest ways in which a search engine might cope with this problem.

Exercise 15.13 (project exercise) Using the technique described by Bharat and Broder (1998), as updated by Gulli and Signorini (2005), estimate the size of the indexable Web.

Exercise 15.14 (project exercise) Build a "crawler trap", which generates dynamic context to make a Web site appear much larger than it really is (billions of pages). The trap should generate random pages, containing random text (Exercise 1.13) with random links to other random pages in the trap. URLs for the trap should have seeds for a random number generator embedded within them, so that visiting a page will consistently give the same contents.

Warning: Deploying the trap on a live Web site may negatively impact search results for that site. Be cautious. Ask for permission if necessary. If you do deploy the trap, we suggest that you add a `robots.txt` entry to steer well-behaved crawlers away from it.

15.10 Bibliography

Agichtein, E., Brill, E., and Dumais, S. (2006a). Improving Web search ranking by incorporating user behavior information. In *Proceedings of the 29th Annual International ACM SIGIR Conference on Research and Development in Information Retrieval*, pages 19–26. Seattle, Washington.

Agichtein, E., Brill, E., Dumais, S., and Ragno, R. (2006b). Learning user interaction models for predicting Web search result preferences. In *Proceedings of the 29th Annual International ACM SIGIR Conference on Research and Development in Information Retrieval*, pages 3–10. Seattle, Washington.

Baeza-Yates, R., Boldi, P., and Castillo, C. (2006). Generalizing PageRank: Damping functions for link-based ranking algorithms. In *Proceedings of the 29th Annual International ACM SIGIR Conference on Research and Development in Information Retrieval*, pages 308–315. Seattle, Washington.

Bernstein, Y., and Zobel, J. (2005). Redundant documents and search effectiveness. In *Proceedings of the 14th ACM International Conference on Information and Knowledge Management*, pages 736–743. Bremen, Germany.

Bharat, K., and Broder, A. (1998). A technique for measuring the relative size and overlap of public Web search engines. In *Proceedings of the 7th International World Wide Web Conference*, pages 379–388. Brisbane, Australia.

Bharat, K., and Henzinger, M. R. (1998). Improved algorithms for topic distillation in a hyper-linked environment. In *Proceedings of the 21st Annual International ACM SIGIR Conference on Research and Development in Information Retrieval*, pages 104–111. Melbourne, Australia.

Bianchini, M., Gori, M., and Scarselli, F. (2005). Inside PageRank. *ACM Transactions on Internet Technology*, 5(1):92–128.

Borodin, A., Roberts, G. O., Rosenthal, J. S., and Tsaparas, P. (2001). Finding authorities and hubs from link structures on the World Wide Web. In *Proceedings of the 10th International World Wide Web Conference*, pages 415–429. Hong Kong, China.

Brin, S., Motwani, R., Page, L., and Winograd, T. (1998). What can you do with a Web in your pocket? *Data Engineering Bulletin*, 21(2):37–47.

Brin, S., and Page, L. (1998). The anatomy of a large-scale hypertextual Web search engine. In *Proceedings of the 7th International World Wide Web Conference*, pages 107–117. Brisbane, Australia.

Broder, A. (2002). A taxonomy of Web search. *ACM SIGIR Forum*, 36(2):3–10.

Broder, A. Z., Glassman, S. C., Manasse, M. S., and Zweig, G. (1997). Syntactic clustering of the Web. In *Proceedings of the 6th International World Wide Web Conference*, pages 1157–1166. Santa Clara, California.

Büttcher, S., Clarke, C. L. A., and Soboroff, I. (2006). The TREC 2006 Terabyte Track. In *Proceedings of the 15th Text REtrieval Conference*. Gaithersburg, Maryland.

Carrière, J., and Kazman, R. (1997). WebQuery: Searching and visualizing the Web through connectivity. In *Proceedings of the 6th International World Wide Web Conference*, pages 1257–1267.

Carterette, B., and Jones, R. (2007). Evaluating search engines by modeling the relationship between relevance and clicks. In *Proceedings of the 21st Annual Conference on Neural Information Processing Systems*. Vancouver, Canada.

Chakrabarti, S. (2007). Dynamic personalized PageRank in entity-relation graphs. In *Proceedings of the 16th International World Wide Web Conference*. Banff, Canada.

Chakrabarti, S., Dom, B., Raghavan, P., Rajagopalan, S., Gibson, D., and Kleinberg, J. (1998). Automatic resource list compilation by analyzing hyperlink structure and associated text. In *Proceedings of the 7th International World Wide Web Conference*. Brisbane, Australia.

Chakrabarti, S., van den Burg, M., and Dom, B. (1999). Focused crawling: A new approach to topic-specific Web resource discovery. In *Proceedings of the 8th International World Wide Web Conference*, pages 545–562. Toronto, Canada.

Charikar, M. S. (2002). Similarity estimation techniques from rounding algorithms. In *Proceedings of the 34th Annual ACM Symposium on Theory of Computing*, pages 380–388. Montreal, Canada.

Cho, J., and Garcia-Molina, H. (2000). The evolution of the Web and implications for an incremental crawler. In *Proceedings of the 26th International Conference on Very Large Data Bases*, pages 200–209.

Cho, J., and Garcia-Molina, H. (2003). Effective page refresh policies for Web crawlers. *ACM Transactions on Database Systems*, 28(4):390–426.

Chung, C., and Clarke, C. L. A. (2002). Topic-oriented collaborative crawling. In *Proceedings of the 11th International Conference on Information and Knowledge Management*, pages 34–42. McLean, Virginia.

Clarke, C. L. A., Agichtein, E., Dumais, S., and White, R. W. (2007). The influence of caption features on clickthrough patterns in Web search. In *Proceedings of the 30th Annual International ACM SIGIR Conference on Research and Development in Information Retrieval*, pages 135–142. Amsterdam, The Netherlands.

Clarke, C. L. A., Scholer, F., and Soboroff, I. (2005). The TREC 2005 Terabyte Track. In *Proceedings of the 14th Text REtrieval Conference*. Gaithersburg, Maryland.

Cohn, D., and Chang, H. (2000). Learning to probabilistically identify authoritative documents. In *Proceedings of the 17th International Conference on Machine Learning*, pages 167–174.

Craswell, N., and Hawking, D. (2004). Overview of the TREC 2004 Web Track. In *Proceedings of the 13th Text REtrieval Conference*. Gaithersburg, Maryland.

Craswell, N., Hawking, D., and Robertson, S. (2001). Effective site finding using link anchor information. In *Proceedings of the 24th Annual International ACM SIGIR Conference on Research and Development in Information Retrieval*, pages 250–257. New Orleans, Louisiana.

Craswell, N., Robertson, S., Zaragoza, H., and Taylor, M. (2005). Relevance weighting for query independent evidence. In *Proceedings of the 28th Annual International ACM SIGIR Conference on Research and Development in Information Retrieval*, pages 416–423. Salvador, Brazil.

Cucerzan, S., and Brill, E. (2004). Spelling correction as an iterative process that exploits the collective knowledge of Web users. In *Proceedings of the Conference on Empirical Methods in Natural Language Processing*, pages 293–300.

Dasgupta, A., Ghosh, A., Kumar, R., Olston, C., Pandey, S., and Tomkins, A. (2007). The discoverability of the Web. In *Proceedings of the 16th International World Wide Web Conference*. Banff, Canada.

Davidson, B. D. (2000). Recognizing nepotistic links on the Web. In *Proceedings of the AAAI-2000 Workshop on Artificial Intelligence for Web Search*, pages 23–28.

Dupret, G., Murdock, V., and Piwowarski, B. (2007). Web search engine evaluation using clickthrough data and a user model. In *Proceedings of the 16th International World Wide Web Conference Workshop on Query Log Analysis: Social and Technological Challenges*. Banff, Canada.

Edwards, J., McCurley, K., and Tomlin, J. (2001). An adaptive model for optimizing performance of an incremental Web crawler. In *Proceedings of the 10th International World Wide Web Conference*, pages 106–113. Hong Kong, China.

Golub, G. H., and Van Loan, C. F. (1996). *Matrix Computations* (3rd ed.). Baltimore, Maryland: Johns Hopkins University Press.

Gulli, A., and Signorini, A. (2005). The indexable Web is more than 11.5 billion pages. In *Proceedings of the 14th International World Wide Web Conference*. Chiba, Japan.

Gyöngyi, Z., and Garcia-Molina, H. (2005). Spam: It's not just for inboxes anymore. *Computer*, 38(10):28–34.

Gyöngyi, Z., Garcia-Molina, H., and Pedersen, J. (2004). Combating Web spam with TrustRank. In *Proceedings of the 30th International Conference on Very Large Databases*, pages 576–584.

Haveliwala, T., and Kamvar, S. (2003). *The Second Eigenvalue of the Google Matrix*. Technical Report 2003-20. Stanford University.

Haveliwala, T. H. (2002). Topic-sensitive PageRank. In *Proceedings of the 11th International World Wide Web Conference*. Honolulu, Hawaii.

Hawking, D., and Craswell, N. (2001). Overview of the TREC-2001 Web Track. In *Proceedings of the 10th Text REtrieval Conference*. Gaithersburg, Maryland.

Hawking, D., Upstill, T., and Craswell, N. (2004). Toward better weighting of anchors. In *Proceedings of the 27th Annual International ACM SIGIR Conference on Research and Development in Information Retrieval*, pages 512–513. Sheffield, England.

Henzinger, M. (2006). Finding near-duplicate Web pages: A large-scale evaluation of algorithms. In *Proceedings of the 29th Annual International ACM SIGIR Conference on Research and development in Information Retrieval*, pages 284–291. Seattle, Washington.

Heydon, A., and Najork, M. (1999). Mercator: A scalable, extensible web crawler. *World Wide Web*, 2(4):219–229.

Ivory, M. Y., and Hearst, M. A. (2002). Statistical profiles of highly-rated Web sites. In *Proceedings of the SIGCHI Conference on Human Factors in Computing Systems*, pages 367–374. Minneapolis, Minnesota.

Jansen, B. J., Booth, D., and Spink, A. (2007). Determining the user intent of Web search engine queries. In *Proceedings of the 16th International World Wide Web Conference*, pages 1149–1150. Banff, Canada.

Jeh, G., and Widom, J. (2003). Scaling personalized Web search. In *Proceedings of the 12th International World Wide Web Conference*, pages 271–279. Budapest, Hungary.

Joachims, T., Granka, L., Pan, B., Hembrooke, H., and Gay, G. (2005). Accurately interpreting clickthrough data as implicit feedback. In *Proceedings of the 28th Annual International ACM SIGIR Conference on Research and Development in Information Retrieval*, pages 154–161. Salvador, Brazil.

Joachims, T., and Radlinski, F. (2007). Search engines that learn from implicit feedback. *IEEE Computer*, 40(8):34–40.

Jones, R., Rey, B., Madani, O., and Greiner, W. (2006). Generating query substitutions. In *Proceedings of the 15th International World Wide Web Conference*, pages 387–396. Edinburgh, Scotland.

Kamvar, S. D., Haveliwala, T. H., Manning, C. D., and Golub, G. H. (2003). Extrapolation methods for accelerating PageRank computations. In *Proceedings of the 12th International World Wide Web Conference*, pages 261–270. Budapest, Hungary.

Kellar, M., Watters, C., and Shepherd, M. (2007). A field study characterizing web-based information-seeking tasks. *Journal of the American Society for Information Science and Technology*, 58(7):999–1018.

Kelly, D., and Teevan, J. (2003). Implicit feedback for inferring user preference: A bibliography. *ACM SIGIR Forum*, 37(2):18–28.

Kleinberg, J. M. (1998). Authoritative sources in a hyperlinked environment. In *Proceedings of the 9th Annual ACM-SIAM Symposium on Discrete Algorithms*, pages 668–677. San Francisco, California.

Kleinberg, J. M. (1999). Authoritative sources in a hyperlinked environment. *Journal of the ACM*, 46(5):604–632.

Langville, A. N., and Meyer, C. D. (2005). A survey of eigenvector methods of Web information retrieval. *SIAM Review*, 47(1):135–161.

Langville, A. N., and Meyer, C. D. (2006). *Google's PageRank and Beyond: The Science of Search Engine Rankings*. Princeton, New Jersey: Princeton University Press.

Lawrence, S., and Giles, C. L. (1998). Searching the World Wide Web. *Science*, 280:98–100.

Lawrence, S., and Giles, C. L. (1999). Accessibility of information on the Web. *Nature*, 400:107–109.

Lee, U., Liu, Z., and Cho, J. (2005). Automatic identification of user goals in Web search. In *Proceedings of the 14th International World Wide Web Conference*, pages 391–400. Chiba, Japan.

Lempel, R., and Moran, S. (2000). The stochastic approach for link-structure analysis (SALSA) and the TKC effect. *Computer Networks*, 33(1-6):387–401.

Liu, Y., Fu, Y., Zhang, M., Ma, S., and Ru, L. (2007). Automatic search engine performance evaluation with click-through data analysis. In *Proceedings of the 16th International World Wide Web Conference Workshop on Query Log Analysis: Social and Technological Challenges*, pages 1133–1134. Banff, Canada.

Marchiori, M. (1997). The quest for correct information on the Web: Hyper search engines. In *Proceedings of the 6th International World Wide Web Conference*. Santa Clara, California.

Metzler, D., Strohman, T., and Croft, W. (2006). Indri TREC notebook 2006: Lessons learned from three Terabyte Tracks. In *Proceedings of the 15th Text REtrieval Conference*. Gaithersburg, Maryland.

Najork, M., and Wiener, J. L. (2001). Breadth-first search crawling yields high-quality pages. In *Proceedings of the 10th International World Wide Web Conference*. Hong Kong, China.

Najork, M. A. (2007). Comparing the effectiveness of HITS and SALSA. In *Proceedings of the 16th ACM Conference on Information and Knowledge Management*, pages 157–164. Lisbon, Portugal.

Najork, M. A., Zaragoza, H., and Taylor, M. J. (2007). HITS on the Web: How does it compare? In *Proceedings of the 30th Annual International ACM SIGIR Conference on Research and Development in Information Retrieval*, pages 471–478. Amsterdam, The Netherlands.

Ng, A. Y., Zheng, A. X., and Jordan, M. I. (2001a). Link analysis, eigenvectors and stability. In *Proceedings of the 17th International Joint Conference on Artificial Intelligence*, pages 903–910. Seattle, Washington.

Ng, A. Y., Zheng, A. X., and Jordan, M. I. (2001b). Stable algorithms for link analysis. In *Proceedings of the 24th Annual International ACM SIGIR Conference on Research and Development in Information Retrieval*, pages 258–266. New Orleans, Louisiana.

Ntoulas, A., Cho, J., and Olston, C. (2004). What's new on the Web?: The evolution of the web from a search engine perspective. In *Proceedings of the 13th International World Wide Web Conference*, pages 1–12.

Olston, C., and Najork, M. (2010). Web crawling. *Foundations and Trends in Information Retrieval*.

Olston, C., and Pandey, S. (2008). Recrawl scheduling based on information longevity. In *Proceedings of the 17th International World Wide Web Conference*, pages 437–446. Beijing, China.

Page, L., Brin, S., Motwani, R., and Winograd, T. (1999). *The PageRank Citation Ranking: Bringing Order to the Web*. Technical Report 1999-66. Stanford InfoLab.

Pandey, S., and Olston, C. (2008). Crawl ordering by search impact. In *Proceedings of the 1st ACM International Conference on Web Search and Data Mining*. Palo Alto, California.

Qiu, F., and Cho, J. (2006). Automatic identification of user interest for personalized search. In *Proceedings of the 15th International World Wide Web Conference*, pages 727–736. Edinburgh, Scotland.

Rafiei, D., and Mendelzon, A. O. (2000). What is this page known for? Computing Web page reputations. In *Proceedings of the 9th International World Wide Web Conference*, pages 823–835. Amsterdam, The Netherlands.

Richardson, M., and Domingos, P. (2002). The intelligent surfer: Probabilistic combination of link and content information in PageRank. In *Advances in Neural Information Processing Systems 14*, pages 1441–1448.

Richardson, M., Prakash, A., and Brill, E. (2006). Beyond PageRank: Machine learning for static ranking. In *Proceedings of the 15th International World Wide Web Conference*, pages 707–715. Edinburgh, Scotland.

Rivest, R. (1992). *The MD5 Message-Digest Algorithm*. Technical Report 1321. Internet RFC.

Robertson, S., Zaragoza, H., and Taylor, M. (2004). Simple BM25 extension to multiple weighted fields. In *Proceedings of the 13th ACM International Conference on Information and Knowledge Management*, pages 42–49. Washington, D.C.

Rose, D. E., and Levinson, D. (2004). Understanding user goals in web search. In *Proceedings of 13th International World Wide Web Conference*, pages 13–19. New York.

Spink, A., and Jansen, B. J. (2004). A study of Web search trends. *Webology*, 1(2).

Upstill, T., Craswell, N., and Hawking, D. (2003). Query-independent evidence in home page finding. *ACM Transactions on Information Systems*, 21(3):286–313.

Wolf, J. L., Squillante, M. S., Yu, P. S., Sethuraman, J., and Ozsen, L. (2002). Optimal crawling strategies for Web search engines. In *Proceedings of the 11th International World Wide Web Conference*, pages 136–147. Honolulu, Hawaii.

Yi, K., Yu, H., Yang, J., Xia, G., and Chen, Y. (2003). Efficient maintenance of materialized top-k views. In *Proceedings of the 19th International Conference on Data Engineering*, pages 189–200.

16 XML Retrieval

The representation of documents in XML provides an opportunity for information retrieval systems to take advantage of document structure by returning individual document components when appropriate. In response to a user query an XML information retrieval system might return a mixture of paragraphs, sections, articles, bibliographic entries and other elements. This facility is of particular benefit when a collection contains very long documents, such as manuals or books, and the user should be directed to the most relevant portions of these documents.

This chapter completes a thread of ideas relating to document structure that runs throughout the book. We initiated this thread in Chapter 1, which introduced a simplified view of XML through a collection of Shakespearean plays, including *Macbeth* (see Figure 1.2 on page 10). This collection served as a running example throughout Chapter 2 and as an occasional example in later chapters. In Section 2.1.3 we introduced an approach to supporting lightweight structure through inverted indices, which we extended and formalized in Section 5.2. In Section 8.7 we incorporated structure into the probabilistic model by weighting terms according to the structural elements in which they appear. For example, terms appearing in a title or abstract might receive a higher weight than terms appearing in an appendix or footnote. In Chapter 15 we explored the role of anchor text and link structure in Web search.

In this chapter we substantially extend our view of XML and XML information retrieval. Section 16.1 discusses essential aspects of XML that were ignored or avoided in previous chapters, particularly the recursive structure of XML documents and the inclusion of attributes in tags. Section 16.2 continues this discussion by examining XML retrieval from a database perspective. It introduces the XPath query language, which may be used to retrieve a set of XML elements that satisfy specified criteria. XPath fills the role with respect to XML retrieval that the Boolean algebra fills with respect to basic document retrieval, by allowing us to select a subset of elements that may then be subjected to further processing, such as ranking. Our discussion also covers a variant of XPath, the NEXI query language, which is specifically intended to address issues associated with XML IR. In addition, the section briefly introduces the XQuery language, which provides sophisticated facilities for querying and manipulating XML documents.

Many of the languages described in these sections, including XPath, XQuery, and XML itself, are standards of the World Wide Web Consortium (W3C) the international standards body for many Web technologies. The W3C publishes the official definitions for these technologies, which are available through its Web site.[1]

---

[1] www.w3.org

The third through fifth sections of the chapter parallel Parts II, III, and IV of the book: Section 16.3 examines indexing and query processing methods; Section 16.4 discusses ranking; Section 16.5 covers evaluation. Our discussion of indexing and query processing builds on the lightweight structure of Section 5.2.

Our discussion of ranked retrieval and evaluation is set in the context of the Initiative for the Evaluation of XML Retrieval (INEX[2]). Since 2002 INEX has provided a TREC-like experimental forum for presenting and evaluating technologies for information retrieval over collections of documents encoded in XML. Roughly 100 groups from industry and academe participate in INEX annually. Until 2006 INEX used a collection of magazine and journal articles taken from the publications of the IEEE Computer Society. Since 2006 INEX has worked with an XML collection developed from articles in the English-language Wikipedia. The NEXI language was created as part of the INEX effort.

XML retrieval is a broad topic with a strong connection to traditional database research, and there are many views as to what constitutes the essential aspects of the area. Although major database vendors now incorporate support for XML into their products, the role of XML from an IR perspective has not yet solidified. As a result, when compared with previous chapters, this chapter is flavored as more of an introductory overview than as an in-depth tutorial.

16.1   The Essence of XML

Figure 16.1 shows a portion of a journal article represented in XML. The figure illustrates several aspects of XML that were not covered in previous chapters. The document begins with an XML *declaration*, which indicates that it follows version 1.0 of the XML standard and that its contents are encoded in UTF-8:

```
<?xml version="1.0" encoding="UTF-8"?>
```

Each element begins with a start tag of the form `<name>` and ends with an end tag of the form `</name>`. XML start tags may contain one or more attributes of the form

  attribute = *value*.

In the figure the article tag contains attributes supplying bibliographic information:

```
<article journal="IEEE TKDE" volume="9" number="2" year="1997">
```

---

[2] www.inex.otago.ac.nz

```
<?xml version="1.0" encoding="UTF-8"?>
<article journal="IEEE TKDE" volume="9" number="2" year="1997">
   <!-- Foundational paper on inverted index compression -->
   <header>
       <title>Text Compression for Dynamic Document Databases</title>
       <author>Alistair Moffat</author>
       <author>Justin Zobel</author>
       <author>Neil Sharman</author>
       <abstract><p>For compression of text databases...</p>...</abstract>
   </header>
   <body>
       <section number="1">
          <title>Introduction</title>
          <p>Modern document databases contain vast quatities of text...</p>
          <p>There are good reasons to compress the text...</p>
          ...
       </section>
       <section number="2">
          <title>Reducing memory requirements</title>
          <p>In this section we assume a static text collection...</p>...
          <section number="1">
             <title>Method A</title>
             <p>The first method considered for choosing which words...</p>...
          </section>
       </section>
       ...
   </body>
</article>
```

Figure 16.1   A journal article encoded in XML.

The section tag contains an attribute specifying its number:

```
<section number="2">
```

Attribute values must be surrounded by either single quotes or double quotes. Tags may also be of the form *<name/>*. This form (not illustrated in the figure) is called an *empty-element tag*. Empty-element tags are essentially equivalent to a start tag immediately followed by an end tag (*<name></name>*). Empty-element tags have no content but may have attributes.

XML documents may also include comments that start with the string "`<!--`" and end with the string "`-->`". In the figure a comment provides a brief review of the paper. When an XML document is created or updated by an application or tool, it is not unusual for that software to include a comment indicating the software's name and version number. Comments are neither content nor structure. Tools for parsing and processing XML are not required to make comments visible, and it may not be appropriate to retain comments in documents for indexing and retrieval purposes.

XML elements must nest. Overlapping elements are not permitted. In contrast to this rule, the region algebra of Section 5.2 allows overlap. In practice, so does HTML, at least to a limited extent. For example, consider the HTML fragment

```
<p> Simple <b>example...<p>
<p> ...illustrating <em>overlapping</b> tags in </em> HTML. </p>
```

Although technically this fragment is not valid HTML, its intent is perfectly clear. Most browsers would handle it correctly, rendering it as

> Simple **example...**
> **...illustrating *overlapping* tags in** HTML.

The requirement for XML elements to nest can make it awkward to capture document structure that is not strictly hierarchical (Hockey, 2004). For example, in the extract from *Macbeth* shown in Figure 1.2, lines 6 and 8 both have multiple speakers. The XML encoding in Figure 1.3 on page 12 splits these lines to maintain the required hierarchical structure while ignoring the (arguably more significant) poetic structure. The following encoding better reflects the poetic structure of line 8:

```
<SPEECH>
  <SPEAKER>First Witch</SPEAKER>
    <LINE>Where the place?
</SPEECH>
<SPEECH>
  <SPEAKER>Second Witch</SPEAKER>
                            Upon the heath.</LINE>
</SPEECH>
```

Unfortunately, this encoding is not well-formed XML.

Although XML does not support overlapping elements, it does support recursive structure. As illustrated in Figure 16.1, sections may contain sections that contain sections, and so on. This recursive structure allows us to create subsections and subsubsections as appropriate, without the need to predefine a maximum depth for nesting.

The XML standard defines the notion of a *well-formed document*. Along with other requirements a well-formed document must obey the formatting rules for tags, attributes, and comments outlined above.

An important feature of XML is the ability to provide *structural metadata* that places constraints on the content of a well-formed XML document. These constraints may require certain elements to contain other certain elements. For example, all journal articles may be required to include both a header and a body. A set of allowed attributes may be specified for each element, with some attributes being required and others being optional. For example, an article may be required to have attributes specifying a journal and a year, and may be allowed to have additional attributes specifying a volume and issue number. Further restrictions may be placed on attribute values. For example, section numbers may be restricted to the natural numbers. When structural metadata is provided for an XML document, a retrieval system can take advantage of it to optimize query processing.

There are two standards for specifying structural metadata for XML. The first, called a *document type definition* or *DTD*, is the older and simpler of the two. It is concerned primarily with the structural organization of XML documents — how elements must nest and which attributes they may possess. The second, called *XML Schema*, allows complex types to be defined for elements and attributes. DTDs were inherited from the older SGML standard upon which XML is based. XML Schema is a newer invention intended to address the limitations of DTDs. Any constraint that can be expressed by a DTD can be expressed in XML Schema, but not vice versa.

16.1.1   Document Type Definitions

Figure 16.2 presents a DTD consistent with the journal article in Figure 16.1. For simplicity the DTD includes only the elements and attributes shown in that figure. In reality a DTD for journal articles would need to include elements for citations, footnotes, figures, tables, captions, lists, equations, appendices, and similar structures.

The DTD starts with a declaration indicating that it adheres to version 1.0 of the XML standard. Despite its cryptic appearance the remainder of the DTD is more or less a context-free grammar describing how elements nest and what attributes each may contain. Each ELEMENT declaration defines a rule in the grammar. For example, the declaration

```
<!ELEMENT article (header, body)>
```

indicates that an article element contains two child elements: a header and a body. In turn the header consists of a title, one or more authors, and an optional abstract:

```
<!ELEMENT header (title, author+, abstract?)>
```

```
<?xml version="1.0"?>
<!ELEMENT article (header body)>
<!ATTLIST article journal CDATA #REQUIRED>
<!ATTLIST article volume  CDATA #IMPLIED>
<!ATTLIST article number  CDATA #IMPLIED>
<!ATTLIST article year    CDATA #REQUIRED>
<!ELEMENT header (title, author+, abstract?)>
<!ELEMENT body (section+)>
<!ELEMENT title (#PCDATA)>
<!ELEMENT author (#PCDATA)>
<!ELEMENT section (title, p*, section*)>
<!ATTLIST section number CDATA #REQUIRED>
<!ELEMENT abstract (p)>
<!ELEMENT p (#PCDATA)>
```

Figure 16.2   A (partial) DTD for journal articles.

A question mark ("?") after an element name indicates that the element is optional. A plus sign ("+") after an element name indicates that the element occurs one or more times. An asterisk ("∗") after an element name indicates that the the element occurs 0 or more times.

One potentially confusing aspect of a DTD is that the order of elements is not specified by an ELEMENT declaration. In a header the title, authors, and abstract may appear in any order. It is perfectly acceptable to have the abstract appear first in the header, followed by an author, followed by the title, followed by another two authors. For historical reasons inherited from SGML, specifying order is not possible in an XML DTD.

The declaration for a title indicates that it contains only text:

```
<!ELEMENT title (#PCDATA)>
```

The notation "#PCDATA" stands for "parsed character data", which is essentially ordinary text. Attributes are declared by ATTLIST declarations. The following declaration indicates that sections have a required attribute providing the section number:

```
<!ATTLIST section number CDATA #REQUIRED>
```

The attribute has type "CDATA", indicating that it consists of ordinary text. We might wish to indicate that its value should be a natural number, but such type constraints cannot be expressed in a DTD.

Why is ordinary text called "#PCDATA" in an element declaration but "#CDATA" in an attribute declaration? The answer has to do with details of parsing XML, which are beyond the scope

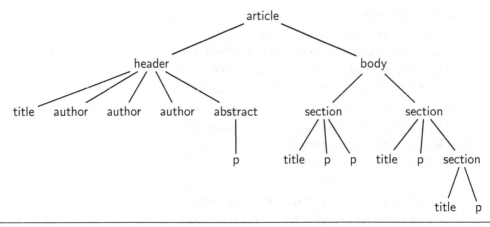

Figure 16.3   Tree structure of the XML document shown in Figure 16.1.

of this book. Although the basic concept of a DTD as a context-free grammar is relatively straightforward, a thorough presentation and discussion of DTDs could fill a chapter on its own.

To associate a DTD with a document, a *document type declaration* must be included in the document. Although the DTD can appear directly in the type declaration, it is usually more convenient to place the DTD in a separate file and reference it through its file name. In this way multiple documents can easily share a DTD. For example, the DTD in Figure 16.2 might be stored in the file "`article.dtd`". The following type declaration would then be added as the second line of the document in Figure 16.1, immediately after the XML declaration:

```
<!DOCTYPE article SYSTEM "article.dtd">
```

16.1.2   XML Schema

XML Schema provides powerful type mechanisms for elements and attributes. We provide only a brief outline of XML Schema; a thorough presentation and discussion could fill a book on its own (van der Vlist, 2002). At the core of XML Schema is a large number of built-in *primitive types* including integers, floating point numbers, dates, times, durations, and URLs. *Derived types* place additional restrictions on these primitive types. For example, we might place a minimum length requirement on strings representing journal names. *Complex types* combine primitive types, derived types, and other complex types to provide types for elements. For example, the ordering of elements in an article and its header might be specified by a complex type, which might further restrict the values of its volume attribute and number attribute to the natural numbers, and the value of its year attribute to years.

16.2   Paths, Trees, and FLWORs

Since XML elements must nest, they may be viewed as a tree. Figure 16.3 illustrates the tree structure of the document in Figure 16.1. The tree represents only the portion of the document included in that figure; the remainder has been omitted for clarity and simplicity. Although the figure does not include them, the document's text (i.e., its `#PCDATA`) may be viewed as a set of leaf nodes attached to the elements that contain them. Attributes also may be viewed as leaf nodes attached to their corresponding elements.

Perhaps because an XML document is naturally viewed as a tree, XML retrieval is often framed as a tree-matching or path-matching problem. This view is the one taken by the principal XML query languages, including XPath, NEXI, and XQuery.

16.2.1   XPath

XPath provides a standard notation for specifying sets of elements and other nodes in XML documents. The W3C finalized and published the initial version of XPath (version 1.0) in November 1999.[3] The second version of XPath (version 2.0) was finalized and published in conjunction with the first version of the new XQuery standard in January 2007.[4] As a result of a desire to have XPath 2.0 form a strict subset of XQuery, XPath 2.0 does not maintain full backward compatibility with XPath 1.0. Fortunately, these incompatibilities are mostly related to the details of the underlying data models and need not concern us for the simple examples given in this chapter.

XPath provides expressions, called *path expressions*, to specify sets of document elements and other nodes. The simplest path expression is just a list of element names separated by the slash character. For example, the path expression

```
/article/body/section
```

specifies the set of all top-level sections in an article's body. Similarly, the path expression

```
/article/body/section/section
```

specifies the set of all second-level sections (subsections). The path expression

```
/article/body/section/title
```

specifies all top-level section titles. This notation deliberately resembles the notation used for specifying the path components of URLs and file paths in UNIX-derived operating systems.

---

[3] `www.w3.org/TR/xpath`

[4] `www.w3.org/TR/xpath20`

In addition to path expressions, XPath supports a full range of arithmetic, logical, and string expressions, and provides a large collection of built-in functions. This support allows XPath to be incorporated into other languages, filling the role of a general-purpose expression language for those languages. Such languages include XQuery and the stylesheet language XSL, another W3C standard. XPath 1.0 also provides an operator for merging sets of elements, which is extended in XPath 2.0 with support for other set operations.

Predicates may be included in path expressions to specify values for attributes and for the positions of elements. For example, the path expression

```
/article/body/section[2]
```

specifies the second section in document order. The path expression

```
/article/body/section[@number=2]
```

specifies top-level sections numbered with an attribute value of 2 (which is the same element as in the previous example). Predicates also may reference the content of elements and attributes. The path expression

```
/article/body/section[contains(./title,"memory requirements")]
```

specifies sections containing the string "memory requirements" in their titles, where the period in "./title" indicates the current node. It is also possible to "skip" elements in a path by using what is known as *descendant-or-self notation*, which is indicated by a double slash ("//"). For example, the path expression

```
/article//section
```

specifies *all* sections in an article regardless of nesting or depth. The path expression

```
//section/title
```

specifies all section titles.

The examples above do little more than touch upon the complexities of path expressions. Along with the features illustrated above, XPath provides a bewildering collection of additional notations for navigating among ancestors, siblings, and descendants.

16.2.2   NEXI

XPath does not support ranked retrieval. Like the Boolean algebra of Section 2.2.3 and the region algebra of Section 5.2, XPath has exact-match semantics. That is, a path expression specifies a set of nodes that exactly match the criteria specified by the expression. In particular the `contains` function in an XPath expression performs an exact string match. For example, the path expression

```
//article//section[contains(.,"compression codes")]
```

requires the string "compression codes" to appear literally in a matching section. XPath provides no way to specify a ranked set of paragraphs *about* compression codes.

Working in the context of INEX, Trotman and Sigurbjörnsson (2004) created a variant of XPath called NEXI (Narrowed Extended XPath I) to address this limitation. NEXI narrows path expressions to a subset of those included in XPath while providing extensions in support of ranked retrieval.

Because exact containment of elements may be less critical in IR applications, NEXI supports only the descendant-or-self notation ("//") for paths. To specify ranked retrieval NEXI replaces the `contains` function with `about`. A ranked list of article sections about compression codes would be requested by the path expression

```
//article//section[about(.,"compression codes")]
```

NEXI accommodates both strict and loose interpretations of path expressions. Under a strict interpretation the solution set for the above expression would include only sections from articles. Under a loose interpretation the structural information is treated as a hint regarding the user's requirements: The path expression indicates that the user prefers article sections, but the system is free to return other elements, such as paragraphs. When ranking elements the system must balance the content of elements against the structural hints provided by the user to determine overall relevance.

NEXI allows path elements to be combined with the Boolean operators "and" and "or". For example, the path expression

```
//article[about(.//p,"compression codes") and about(.//author, Moffat)]
```

requests a ranked list of articles written by Moffat that contain paragraphs about compression codes. NEXI uses quotes only for phrases, so "Moffat" is not quoted in this expression. NEXI also permits wildcards in path expressions, which are indicated by an asterisk ("*"). For example, the path expression

```
//section//*[about(.,"compression codes")]
```

requests a ranked list of elements about compression codes that are contained in sections.

Although NEXI is not an official W3C standard, it is widely accepted within the XML IR community. Outside this community NEXI is still relatively unknown, a situation that may change as XML IR gains wider usage.

16.2.3 XQuery

We conclude this section with a brief glimpse at the XQuery language. XQuery (also called XML Query) substantially extends XPath with facilities for manipulating and transforming XML documents. Notably, XQuery allows expressions to dynamically construct XML, so that the output of an expression is itself XML. XQuery expressions operate over ordered sequences of nodes and values. Each node and value in a sequence must have a type associated with it, with XML Schema providing the type system.

At the heart of XQuery is the *FLWOR expression* (pronounced "flower"), which is an acronym for `for`, `let`, `where`, `order` by and `return`. The expansion of this acronym lists the parts of a FLWOR expression and hints at its operation. FLWOR expressions provide a mechanism for creating, filtering, sorting, and iterating over sequences. Analogously to the `select` statement in SQL, FLWOR expressions can compute joins across multiple XML documents.

To illustrate FLWOR expressions we adapt an example from the XQuery standard.[5] Assume we have a bibliography of plays encoded in XML as follows:

```
<bib>
  <play>
    <author>Shakespeare</author>
    <title>Hamlet</title>
    <year>1599</year>
  </play>
  <play>
    <author>Beckett</author>
    <title>Waiting For Godot</title>
    <year>1949</year>
  </play>
  <play>
    <author>Shakespeare</author>
    <title>Macbeth</title>
    <year>1603</year>
  </play>
  <play>
    <author>Stoppard</author>
    <title>Rosencrantz and Guildenstern Are Dead</title>
    <year>1966</year>
  </play>
</bib>
```

---

[5] `www.w3.org/TR/xquery`

```
<works>
{
    for $a in fn:distinct-values($bib/play/author)
    order by $a
    return
        <playwright>
            <name> {$a} </name>
            <plays>
            {
                for $p in $bib/play[author = $a]
                order by $p/title
                return $p/title
            }
            </plays>
        </playwright>
}
</works>
```

Figure 16.4   An XQuery FLWOR expression.

The FLWOR expression in Figure 16.4 reorganizes this data by creating a list of playwrights, each accompanied by a list of his plays. The example consists of two nested expressions. The outer expression constructs a list of authors; the inner expression constructs a list of plays for a single author. Executing this expression over the bibliography above (bound to the variable $bib) generates the following output:

```
<works>
    <playwright>
        <name>Beckett</name>
        <plays>
            <title>Waiting For Godot</title>
        </plays>
    </playwright>
    <playwright>
        <name>Shakespeare</name>
        <plays>
            <title>Hamlet</title>
            <title>Macbeth</title>
        </plays>
    </playwright>
```

```
<playwright>
  <name>Stoppard</name>
  <plays>
    <title>Rosencrantz and Guildenstern Are Dead</title>
  </plays>
</playwright>
</works>
```

Heavily influenced by theoretical database and programming language research, XQuery possesses complex formal semantics and static typing. Its learning curve is steep. Surprisingly, given the effort and complexity underlying the type system, static typing is optional. An implementation is free to choose how types are enforced: either statically before a query is executed or dynamically by throwing type errors during execution. Hybrid approaches are also permitted.

16.3 Indexing and Query Processing

Indexing and query processing for XML pose two significant problems that are not easily handled by the region algebra of Section 5.2. First, elements may nest recursively. The solution to the expression

```
//section/section
```

includes all sections contained in another section, regardless of nesting or depth. Although the solution could be represented as a set of intervals, some nesting in others, it cannot be represented as a GC-list. XPath query processing strategies must handle this recursion properly. Second, XPath expressions may specify direct containment relationships. The solution to the expression

```
/article/body/section/p
```

includes only paragraphs directly contained in top-level sections, not those contained in subsections or subsubsections. On the other hand, unlike the region algebra, XPath has no requirement for overlapping structure. Elements must nest, and we may treat documents as trees.

To accommodate recursive structure and direct containment, we extend our inverted list ADT (page 33) so that each element of a postings list becomes a tuple containing three values: a start position, an end position, and a depth in the tree:

(start, end, depth)

Unlike the region algebra the start and end tags of elements do not have separate postings lists but share a combined postings list. For an element the start position in the tuple indicates the position of the start tag, and the end position indicates the position of the end tag. For other tokens, such as words, the start and end positions are equal, indicating the position of the token. The tuples in these extended postings lists are ordered by start position.

For example, returning to the inverted index for *Macbeth* in Figure 2.1 (page 34), the extended postings list for plays becomes

$$\{(3, 40508, 1),\ (40511, 75580, 1),\ \ldots,\ (1234602, 1271504, 1)\}.$$

In this postings list the depth is always 1, because plays occur only as topmost elements, but the depth need not be the same for all tuples in a postings list. For example, the extended postings list for speeches is

$$\{(312, 470, 4),\ (471, 486, 4),\ \ldots,\ (506542, 506878, 3),\ \ldots,\ (1271273, 1271498, 4)\}.$$

Speeches usually occur at depth 4, nested in a scene of an act of a play, but may appear at depth 3 in the prologue of a play. The postings list for "witch" is

$$\{(1598, 1598, 6),\ (27555, 27555, 6),\ \ldots,\ (432149, 432149, 4),\ \ldots,\ (1245276, 1245276, 6)\}.$$

A witch may occur as a speaker at depth 6 or in a list of personae at depth 4. To accommodate this extension the four methods of our inverted list ADT are modified as follows:

first(*term*)	returns the first tuple for the given *term*
last(*term*)	returns the last tuple for the given *term*
next(*term, current*)	returns the first tuple starting after the *current* position
prev(*term, current*)	returns the last tuple starting before the *current* position

For example,

first("⟨PLAY⟩") = (3, 40508, 1)
last("⟨SPEECH⟩") = (1271273, 1271498, 4)
next("⟨SPEECH⟩", 400) = (471, 486, 4)
prev("witch", 20000) = (1598, 1598, 6)

This modified inverted index may be combined with knowledge taken from structural metadata to efficiently solve XPath expressions. For example, the code in Figure 16.5 solves the path expression

```
//section//section
```

over a journal article like that in Figure 16.1. From the DTD in Figure 16.2 we see that sections are recursive, and thus the path expression may have a nonempty solution set. Rather than explicitly identifying all sections containing sections, we note that the only sections that form

```
1    (u, v, d) ← first("⟨section⟩")
2    (u′, v′, d′) ← next("⟨section⟩", u)
3    while u < ∞ do
4        if v′ < v then
5            report the interval [u′,v′]
6            (u′, v′, d′) ← next("⟨section⟩", u′)
7        else
8            (u, v, d) ← (u′, v′, d′)
```

Figure 16.5   Code to solve the path expression `//section//section`.

```
1    (u, v, d) ← first("⟨section⟩")
2    while u < ∞ do
3        (u′, v′, d′) ← next("⟨p⟩", u)
4        while v′ < v do
5            if d′ = 4 then
6                report the interval [u′,v′]
7            (u′, v′, d′) ← next("⟨p⟩", u′)
8        (u, v, d) ← next("⟨section⟩", v)
```

Figure 16.6   Code to solve the path expression `/article/body/section/p`.

a part of the solution set are those that do not appear at the topmost level. Thus, the code processes each top-level section in turn and reports all the sections that are contained within it, regardless of depth.

On line 1 the first section is stored in the tuple (u, v, d). This section must be a top-level section because its starting position has the lowest value. On line 2 the first candidate section, which may be an element of the solution set, is stored in the tuple (u', v', d'). The loop over lines 3 to 8 checks each candidate section in turn, determining if it is contained in the current top-level section. If so, it is reported on line 5. If not, it becomes the new top-level section on line 8. Reporting a section may involve displaying it to a user or, more likely, storing it for further processing. Note that depth values are not required in order to compute the solution.

The use of depth values is illustrated by the code in Figure 16.6, which provides a solution to the path expression

`/article/body/section/p`.

From the DTD we see that sections are only contained within article bodies, making it unnecessary to explicitly consider articles and bodies when evaluating this path expression. To satisfy the path expression, a paragraph in the solution set must be contained directly in a top-level section. From the DTD, we see that such a paragraph must lie at depth 4. Beginning with the first top-level section (line 1), the code iterates over the top-level sections, reporting the paragraphs at depth 4 contained in each (lines 2 to 8). To advance from one top-level section to another, the method call on line 8 skips lower-level sections by indexing beyond the end of the current top-level section. Lines 4 to 7 iterate over the paragraphs contained in the current top-level section, reporting a paragraph only if it appears at depth 4 (lines 5 to 7).

16.4   Ranked Retrieval

Ranked retrieval for XML may be viewed as two distinct problems distinguished by the types of queries supported. First, we may view XML IR as ranking elements with respect to a query expressed as a term vector, just as standard document retrieval ranks documents with respect to a term vector. For example, given the term vector $\langle$ "text", "compression" $\rangle$, the IR system returns a ranked list of elements ordered according to their probability of relevance to this query.

Under the second view queries are expressed as path expressions in a language such as NEXI. Elements are ranked by considering both content and structure. The structure specified by the query may be interpreted either as a strict filter or more loosely as a hint. When interpreted as a filter, only elements exactly matching the structure indicated by the path expression are included in the result list. When interpreted loosely, the IR system must strike a balance between the potentially competing requirements of structure and content. Consider the path expression

```
/article/body/section[about(./title,"memory requirements")].
```

When interpreted strictly, the IR system is constrained to return only top-level sections, ranked according to the relevance of their titles to the topic of memory requirements. When interpreted loosely, the IR system may give preference to sections over other elements and give greater weight to query terms occurring in their titles, but it is free to return subsections, subsubsections, paragraphs and other elements.

In the jargon of INEX the problem of ranking elements according to term vector is called a *content-only task*, or CO task. The problem of filtering and ranking elements according to a path expression is called a *content-and-structure task*, or CAS task. Queries for CO tasks may be treated as a special case of CAS queries. Given a term vector $\langle t_1, t_2, \ldots, t_n \rangle$ for a CO task, we may view it as equivalent to the CAS query

```
//*[about(.,"t₁ t₂ tₙ")] .
```

Although many ranking methods for CAS queries have been proposed in the research literature, the problem is still poorly understood, and none of the proposed methods has emerged as the clear winner. One simple but reasonable method for handling CAS queries is to treat structure and content separately, through a two-step retrieval process. As the first step the path expression is applied as a filter restricting the results to a subset of the elements. In this first step the path expression's **about** functions are ignored, with all elements being treated as equally relevant to any topic. In the second step a query vector is constructed from the terms appearing in the **about** functions. The elements selected in the first step are then ranked according to this term vector. For example, given the path expression

```
/article/body/section[about(./title,"memory requirements")],
```

the first step would create a set of top-level sections and the second step would rank these sections according to the term vector ⟨"memory", "requirements"⟩. The structural constraint in the **about** function (./title) might be honored by the ranking function or might be ignored. Similarly, for the path expression

```
//article[about(.//p,"compression codes") and about(.//author, Moffat])],
```

the method would rank articles according to the term vector ⟨"compression", "codes", "moffat"⟩. Although this simple method may ignore some aspects of a CAS query, such as the separate author and paragraph constraints in the previous example, no other method has been shown to produce consistently better performance. The problem remains open for further research.

In the remainder of Section 16.4 we focus on the CO task. As with CAS queries, many ranking methods for CO queries have been proposed in the literature and tested at INEX. Although many of these methods have merit, none has been shown to consistently outperform the simple approach of ranking individual elements by using a standard ranking formula, such as BM25. Under this approach, elements are treated as if each is a separate document. Document ranking methods are then applied to this collection of elements.

When applying document ranking techniques to a collection of elements, several problems immediately arise. First, a fragment of text may belong to several different elements. For example, a fragment of text contained in the journal article of Figure 16.1 may form part of a paragraph, a subsection, a section, the body, and the article itself. If each of these elements is considered to be a separate "document" for retrieval purposes, this repetition may distort term and document statistics. Second, the nesting of these elements (called "overlap" in INEX jargon) can lead to excessive redundancy in the search results. If a paragraph is highly relevant, then the subsection, section, body, and article that contain it may also be highly relevant, but it may not be useful to report all of these elements individually in the result list. Finally, not all element types are suitable as retrieval results. Some elements, such as paragraphs and sections, may be reasonably presented to a user, but others are not appropriate. For example, a section title by itself may be much less useful to the user than the section that contains it.

16.4.1 Ranking Elements

If we consider our collection to consist of XML elements treated as separate documents for ranking purposes, a specific term occurrence may be contained in several different elements. For example, consider the term "method" occurring in the first paragraph of Section 2.1 of the document in Figure 16.1 ("The first method considered..."). This term occurrence may be viewed as part of a paragraph, a subsection, a section, a body, and an article. If we view each of these elements as a separate document, the term appears five times in the "collection".

Table 16.1   Top ranking elements for the query ⟨"text", "index", "compression", "algorithms"⟩ over the INEX collection of IEEE magazine and journal articles. IDF values were computed by treating each article as a document.

BM25 Score	Document Identifier	Element
32.000923	/co/2000/ry037.xml	/article[1]/body[1]
31.861366	/co/2000/ry037.xml	/article[1]
31.083460	/co/2000/ry037.xml	/article[1]/body[1]/section[2]
30.174324	/co/2000/ry037.xml	/article[1]/body[1]/section[5]
29.420393	/tk/1997/k0302.xml	/article[1]
29.250019	/tk/1997/k0302.xml	/article[1]/body[1]/section[1]
29.118382	/tk/1997/k0302.xml	/article[1]/body[1]
29.075621	/co/2000/ry037.xml	/article[1]/body[1]/section[3]
28.417294	/tk/1997/k0302.xml	/article[1]/body[1]/section[6]
28.106693	/tp/2000/i0385.xml	/article[1]
27.761749	/co/2000/ry037.xml	/article[1]/body[1]/section[7]
27.686905	/tk/1997/k0302.xml	/article[1]/body[1]/section[3]
27.584927	/tp/2000/i0385.xml	/article[1]/body[1]
27.273247	/co/2000/ry037.xml	/article[1]/body[1]/section[4]
27.186977	/tp/2000/i0385.xml	/article[1]/body[1]/section[1]
27.072521	/tk/1997/k0302.xml	/article[1]/body[1]/section[3]/section[1]
26.992224	/co/2000/ry037.xml	/article[1]/body[1]/section[5]/section[1]
...	...	...

When applying standard relevance ranking techniques in the context of XML information retrieval, term-frequency statistics may be computed for each element independently (Mass and Mandelbrod, 2004). For a given element e we compute its term-frequency value $f_{t,e}$ as the number of times the term t occurs in the element e. Although the same term occurrence may be contained in multiple elements, for the purposes of computing term frequencies it may be treated as a different occurrence in each element that contains it.

Most ranking techniques also require global statistics, such as inverse document frequency, computed over the collection as a whole. Such global statistics should not be computed as if each element is an independent document. It is not appropriate to compute inverse document frequency under the assumption that a given term is repeated in all of the elements that contain it, because the number of elements that contain a term depends solely on the structural arrangement of the original XML (Vittaut et al., 2004; Kekäläinen et al., 2004). Instead, we choose a subset of the elements such that each term occurrence is contained in exactly one of the elements in this subset. For example, the subset might consist of all article elements. Inverse document frequency and other global statistics may then be computed over this subset.

Table 16.2   Top ranking elements from Table 16.1 after overlap removal.

BM25 Score	Document Identifier	Element
32.000923	/co/2000/ry037.xml	/article[1]/body[1]
29.420393	/tk/1997/k0302.xml	/article[1]
28.106693	/tp/2000/i0385.xml	/article[1]
. . .	. . .	. . .

Using these conventions for computing term frequency and inverse document frequency, we may then apply standard ranking formulae to rank elements. Table 16.1 shows the top ranking elements for INEX topic number 162 ("Text and Index Compression Algorithms") over the INEX collection of IEEE magazine and journal articles. In this example the original INEX markup has been modified to make it consistent with the DTD in Figure 16.2. The first column lists BM25 scores; the second column lists document identifiers; the third column lists elements within those documents. All elements are drawn from only three documents. The document /tk/1997/k0302.xml is the journal article shown in Figure 16.1.

16.4.2   Overlapping Elements

As illustrated by Table 16.1, the direct application of a standard relevance ranking technique to a set of XML elements can produce a list in which the top ranks are dominated by structurally related elements. A highly scoring section is likely to contain several highly scoring paragraphs and to be contained in a highly scoring article. If each of these elements is presented as a separate result, the user may waste considerable time reviewing and rejecting redundant content.

One possible solution is to report only the highest-scoring element along a given path in the tree, and to remove from the lower ranks any element containing it or contained within it. Table 16.2 shows the outcome of this approach on the ranked list of Table 16.1. All but three elements are eliminated. Of the remaining elements, two are full articles and one is an article body. The predominance of larger elements, such as articles, is not unusual for this method when it is applied to the INEX collections. Due to their source, many of the articles in the INEX collections are narrow in focus and are not long, often less than ten thousand words in length. As a result full articles often rank highly, depending on the topic.

In addition, the practice of reporting only one solution along a given path destroys some of the possible benefits of XML IR. For example, an outer element may contain a substantial amount of information that does not appear in an inner element, but the inner element may be heavily focused on the query topic and provide a short overview of the key concepts. In such cases it is reasonable to report elements that contain, or are contained in, higher-ranking elements. Even when an entire book is relevant, a user may still wish to have the most important paragraphs identified, to guide her reading and to save time (Fuhr and Großjohann, 2001; Clarke, 2005).

16.4.3 Retrievable Elements

Although an XML IR system may potentially retrieve any element, many elements may not be appropriate retrieval results. This is usually the case when elements contain very little text (Kamps et al., 2004). For example, a section title containing only the query terms may receive a high score from a ranking algorithm but alone will be of limited value to a user, who may prefer the actual section. Other elements may reflect the document's physical rather than logical structure, such as font changes, which may have little or no meaning to a user. An effective XML IR system must return only those elements that have sufficient content to be usable and can stand alone as independent objects (Pehcevski et al., 2004; Mass and Mandelbrod, 2003). Standard document components such as paragraphs, sections, subsections, and abstracts often meet these requirements; titles, italicized phrases, and similar elements often do not.

16.5 Evaluation

The evaluation of XML IR systems extends the effectiveness measures presented in Chapter 12. In extending these measures we must address the same concerns as we did when considering ranking methods in the previous section, particularly the issue of overlap.

16.5.1 Test Collections

To date, INEX represents the only large-scale evaluation effort directed toward XML IR. Until 2006 the main collection at INEX consisted of over 12,000 articles taken from the IEEE Computer Society's magazines and journals between 1995 and 2002. Figure 16.1 provides an example of a typical document from this collection (although the markup used in the INEX collection is slightly different). The collection has a total size of roughly 500MB. In 2006 a larger collection was developed from Wikipedia articles. This new collection consists of more than 600,000 English-language articles and has a total size of more than 4GB. Denoyer and Gallinari (2006) describe the creation and organization of this collection. In recent years a third collection has been developed and used for a limited set of INEX experiments. This collection consists of more than 50,000 out-of-copyright books and has a total size of more than 50GB (Wu et al., 2008).

The creation of topics and judgments at INEX has always been a cooperative effort of the participants. Each participating group creates two or three topics, which are collected and reviewed by the INEX organizers. After the topic set is finalized, the organizers distribute it to the groups, who return ranked lists of XML elements to the organizers. Judging pools are created from the submitted runs. Using a judging interface supplied by the organizers, participants judge the pools for the topics they contributed. On the basis of these judgements the organizers compute effectiveness measures that then become the official results.

16.5.2   Effectiveness Measures

Overlap causes considerable problems with retrieval evaluation, and the INEX organizers and participants have wrestled with these problems since INEX's inception (Kazai and Lalmas, 2006). Although notable progress has been made, these problems are still not fully solved. In addition, because XML information retrieval is concerned with locating those elements that provide complete coverage of a topic while containing as little extraneous information as possible, simple "relevant" versus "not relevant" judgments for individual elements are not sufficient. Several attempts have been made to develop measures that satisfy the requirements of XML IR while retaining a tractable judging process.

In one approach the INEX organizers adopted two dimensions for relevance assessment (Piwowarski and Lalmas, 2004). Each element is judged independently with respect to these dimensions. The first dimension, the *exhaustivity* dimension, reflects the degree to which an element covers the topic. The second dimension, the *specificity* dimension, reflects the degree to which an element is focused on the topic. A four-point scale is used on both dimensions. Thus, a (3,3) element is highly exhaustive and highly specific, a (1,3) element is marginally exhaustive and highly specific, and a (0,0) element is not relevant.

Efforts were then made to adapt existing effectiveness measures to use these two-dimensional judgments. One attempt, used at early INEX conferences, is a version of the mean average precision (MAP) measure described in Section 2.3. This version of MAP is adjusted by various *quantization functions* to give different weights to different elements, depending on their exhaustivity and specificity values. For example, a *strict quantization* function gives a weight of 1 to (3,3) elements and a weight of 0 to all others. This variant is essentially the standard MAP value, with (3,3) elements treated as "relevant" and all other elements treated as "not relevant". Other quantization functions are designed to give partial credit to elements that are "near misses" due to a lack of exhaustivity and/or specificity. Both the *generalized quantization* function and the *specificity-oriented generalization* (sog) function credit elements "according to their degree of relevance" (Kazai et al., 2004), with the second function placing greater emphasis on specificity.

Unfortunately, this version of MAP does not penalize overlap. In particular, both the generalized and the sog quantization functions can give credit to elements even when (3,3) elements containing them are reported at higher ranks. To address this problem Kazai et al. (2004) and Kazai and Lalmas (2006) developed an *XML cumulated gain* measure called XCG, which extends the nDCG measure of Section 12.5.1. The XCG measure compares the cumulated gain of a ranked list with an ideal gain vector. This ideal gain vector is constructed from the relevance judgments by eliminating overlap and retaining only the best element along a given path. Thus, the XCG measure rewards retrieval runs that avoid overlap.

At more recent INEX conferences assessors have made relevance judgments by highlighting the relevant parts of articles. When judging a ranked list of elements, recall may be computed as the fraction of highlighted text retrieved, and precision may be computed as the fraction of retrieved text that is highlighted.

16.6   Further Reading

XML is a prominent Web standard with importance far beyond the boundaries of information retrieval. A large and growing set of applications uses XML for data storage and interchange. For example, XML is the primary document format for both Microsoft Office 2007 and the OpenOffice productivity suite. Most major database vendors now provide support for XML through extensions to their traditional relational DB offerings. Introductions to XML are available at all levels, from the basic (Tittel and Dykes, 2005) to the professional (Evjen et al., 2007).

During the late 1990s, database researchers developed and evaluated a number of proposals for XML query languages, most notably the Lorel language from Stanford (Abiteboul et al., 1997), the YATL language from INRIA (Cluet et al., 2000), and the Quilt language (Chamberlin et al., 2000). Within a few years this research had coalesced into a preliminary standard for XQuery, although version 1.0 of the standard was not finalized until 2007.[6] Melton and Buxton (2006) provide a readable and detailed explanation of XPath, XQuery, and other methods for querying XML.

The XQuery 1.0 standard does not include facilities for updating XML documents. These were added through the XQuery Update Facility 1.0, released by the W3C in August 2008.[7] Recently the W3C has proposed recommendations for "Full Text" extensions to XQuery and XPath.[8] These recommendations include extensive facilities for keyword and Boolean search along with limited support for element ranking.

Efficiently solving path expressions requires specialized indexing. Al-Khalifa et al. (2002) describe a *structural index* for efficient pattern matching between queries and document trees. Zhang et al. (2001) propose methods for solving a subset of path expressions in the context of a traditional relational database system. Bruno et al. (2002) substantially extend this work, describing algorithms to support the pattern matching of a small query tree (called a *twig*) against a much larger tree representing the XML document collection. Their algorithms, which they call *holistic twig joins*, represent the foundational methods for solving path expressions through the use of inverted lists. Our extended ADT for inverted lists, which we presented in Section 16.3, is based upon their data structures.

Much of subsequent research on solving path expressions builds upon the holistic twig join algorithms. Jiang et al. (2003) present methods for improving the efficiency of holistic twig joins. Kaushik et al. (2004) combine holistic twig joins with structural joins to take better advantage of available structural information. Lu et al. (2005) suggest additional algorithmic improvements and extensions for holistic twig join processing. Gottlob et al. (2005) explore

---

[6] www.w3.org/TR/xquery

[7] www.w3.org/TR/xquery-update-10

[8] www.w3.org/TR/xpath-full-text-10/

beyond tree matching, taking into account the detailed semantics of XPath queries. Zhang et al. (2006) propose feature-based indexing of document substructures as a method for quickly identifying a set of candidate answers for a path expression.

In the database community ranked retrieval is often called "top-k" retrieval. Theobald et al. (2008) describe index structures and query processing for top-k retrieval over XML and other semi-structured data, including support for the proposed XML Full-Text extension. Trotman (2004) presents another proposal for index structures for ranked retrieval over XML and other structured documents.

Research into XML IR has been greatly accelerated through the efforts of the INEX organizers and participants.[9] Ongoing activities at INEX have now expanded beyond basic retrieval tasks to explore topics such as entity ranking, question answering, data mining, passage retrieval, and link analysis. Recent INEX proceedings should be consulted for a detailed picture of current research work (Fuhr et al., 2007, 2008).

Other XML IR research has addressed a wide range of issues with a particular focus on the trade-offs between content and structure. Amer-Yahia et al. (2005) describe and evaluate efficient query processing methods for XML IR that account for both content and structure over heterogeneous collections. Kamps et al. (2006) examine how best to express queries that reference both structure and content. Lehtonen (2006) considers problems associated with XML IR over heterogeneous collections. Chu-Carroll et al. (2006) propose an XML-based query language for semantic search over XML collections. Amer-Yahia and Lalmas (2006) provide a short survey of XML IR research covering up to 2006.

Work continues on evaluation methodologies for XML IR. Kazai et al. (2004) provide a detailed exposition of the overlap problem in the context of INEX retrieval evaluation and propose a number of potential evaluation measures. Further information on exhaustivity and specificity can be found in Piwowarski and Lalmas (2004), who provide a detailed rationale for these concepts. Kazai and Lalmas (2006) provide a careful analysis of the application of the nDCG measure to the problem of XML IR evaluation. Piwowarski et al. (2008) provide a thorough discussion of XML IR evaluation, summarizing many of the lessons learned at INEX. Ali et al. (2008) develop a framework for XML IR evaluation that considers the user's probable browsing history when accounting for the impact of overlap.

An ideal XML IR test collection should perhaps be less homogeneous than the two main INEX collections: the IEEE collection and the Wikipedia collection. For both collections a single DTD describes all the articles that the collection contains. The articles in these collections are similar in size. Each small enough to be read in its entirety in a short period of time. An ideal test collection for XML would consist of a wider variety of documents with differing sizes and differing DTDs. Such a collection would include books and other long documents as well as shorter articles. In future years it is possible that the newer XML book collection may evolve to meet these requirements (Wu et al., 2008; Koolen et al., 2009).

---

[9] www.inex.otago.ac.nz

16.7   Exercises

Exercise 16.1 Create a DTD consistent with the structure of Shakespearean plays, as illustrated in Figure 1.3.

Exercise 16.2 The path expression `/article/body/section/p` may be solved without considering depth by modifying lines 5–7 of Figure 16.6 to skip paragraphs contained in subsections. Write this modified algorithm. Is your version more efficient than the version shown in Figure 16.6?

Exercise 16.3 Write an algorithm to solve the expression `/article/body/section/section`, assuming the DTD of Figure 16.2 and the inverted index ADT described in Section 16.3.

Exercise 16.4 Write an algorithm to solve the expression `/article/body/section[2]`, assuming the DTD of Figure 16.2 and the inverted index ADT described in Section 16.3.

16.8   Bibliography

Abiteboul, S., Quass, D., McHugh, J., Widom, J., and Wiener, J. (1997). The Lorel query language for semistructured data. *International Journal on Digital Libraries*, 1(1):68–88.

Al-Khalifa, S., Jagadish, H. V., Patel, J. M., Wu, Y., Koudas, N., and Srivastava, D. (2002). Structural joins: A primitive for efficient XML query pattern matching. In *Proceedings of the 18th IEEE International Conference on Data Engineering*, pages 141–152.

Ali, M. S., Consens, M. P., Kazai, G., and Lalmas, M. (2008). Structural relevance: A common basis for the evaluation of structured document retrieval. In *Proceedings of the 17th ACM Conference on Information and Knowledge Management*, pages 1153–1162. Napa, California.

Amer-Yahia, S., Koudas, N., Marian, A., Srivastava, D., and Toman, D. (2005). Structure and content scoring for XML. In *Proceedings of the 31st International Conference on Very Large Data Bases*, pages 361–372. Trondheim, Norway.

Amer-Yahia, S., and Lalmas, M. (2006). XML search: Languages, INEX and scoring. *SIGMOD Record*, 35(4):16–23.

Bruno, N., Koudas, N., and Srivastava, D. (2002). Holistic twig joins: Optimal XML pattern matching. In *Proceedings of the 2002 ACM SIGMOD International Conference on Management of Data*, pages 310–321. Madison, Wisconsin.

Chamberlin, D., Robie, J., and Florescu, D. (2000). Quilt: An XML query language for heterogeneous data sources. In *Proceedings of WebDB 2000 Conference*, pages 53–62.

Chu-Carroll, J., Prager, J., Czuba, K., Ferrucci, D., and Duboue, P. (2006). Semantic search via XML fragments: A high-precision approach to IR. In *Proceedings of the 29th Annual International ACM SIGIR Conference on Research and Development in Information Retrieval*, pages 445–452. Seattle, Washington.

Clarke, C. L. A. (2005). Controlling overlap in content-oriented XML retrieval. In *Proceedings of the 28th Annual International ACM SIGIR Conference on Research and Development in Information Retrieval*, pages 314–321. Salvador, Brazil.

Cluet, S., Siméoni, J., and De Voluceau, D. (2000). YATL: A functional and declarative language for XML. Bell Labs, Murray Hill, New Jersey.

Denoyer, L., and Gallinari, P. (2006). The Wikipedia XML corpus. *ACM SIGIR Forum*, 40(1):64–69.

Evjen, B., Sharkey, K., Thangarathinam, T., Kay, M., Vernet, A., and Ferguson, S. (2007). *Professional XML (Programmer to Programmer)*. Indianapolis, Indiana: Wiley.

Fuhr, N., and Großjohann, K. (2001). XIRQL: A query language for information retrieval in XML documents. In *Proceedings of the 24th Annual International ACM SIGIR Conference on Research and Development in Information Retrieval*, pages 172–180. New Orleans, Louisiana.

Fuhr, N., Kamps, J., Lalmas, M., and Trotman, A., editors (2008). *Focused Access to XML Documents: Proceedings of the 6th International Workshop of the Initiative for the Evaluation of XML Retrieval*, volume 4862 of *Lecture Notes in Computer Science*. Berlin, Germany. Springer.

Fuhr, N., Lalmas, M., Malik, S., and Szlávik, Z., editors (2005). *Advances in XML Retrieval: Proceedings of the 3rd International Workshop of the Initiative for the Evaluation of XML Retrieval*, volume 3493 of *Lecture Notes in Computer Science*. Berlin, Germany. Springer.

Fuhr, N., Lalmas, M., and Trotman, A., editors (2007). *Proceedings of the 5th International Workshop of the Initiative for the Evaluation of XML Retrieval*, volume 4518 of *Lecture Notes in Computer Science*.

Gottlob, G., Koch, C., and Pichler, R. (2005). Efficient algorithms for processing XPath queries. *ACM Transactions on Database Systems*, 30(2):444–491.

Hockey, S. (2004). The reality of electronic editions. In Modiano, R., Searle, L., and Shillingsburg, P. L., editors, *Voice, Text, Hypertext: Emerging Practices in Textual Studies*, pages 361–377. Seattle, Washington: University of Washington Press.

Jiang, H., Wang, W., Lu, H., and Yu, J. X. (2003). Holistic twig joins on indexed XML documents. In *Proceedings of the 29th International Conference on Very Large Data Bases*, pages 273–284. Berlin, Germany.

Kamps, J., de Rijke, M., and Sigurbjörnsson, B. (2004). Length normalization in XML retrieval. In *Proceedings of the 27th Annual International ACM SIGIR Conference on Research and Development in Information Retrieval*, pages 80–87. Sheffield, England.

Kamps, J., Marx, M., de Rijke, M., and Sigurbjörnsson, B. (2006). Articulating information needs in XML query languages. *ACM Transactions on Information Systems*, 24(4):407–436.

Kaushik, R., Krishnamurthy, R., Naughton, J. F., and Ramakrishnan, R. (2004). On the integration of structure indexes and inverted lists. In *Proceedings of the 2004 ACM SIGMOD International Conference on Management of Data*, pages 779–790. Paris, France.

Kazai, G., and Lalmas, M. (2006). eXtended cumulated gain measures for the evaluation of content-oriented XML retrieval. *ACM Transactions on Information Systems*, 24(4):503–542.

Kazai, G., Lalmas, M., and de Vries, A. P. (2004). The overlap problem in content-oriented XML retrieval evaluation. In *Proceedings of the 27th Annual International ACM SIGIR Conference on Research and Development in Information Retrieval*, pages 72–79. Sheffield, England.

Kekäläinen, J., Junkkari, M., Arvola, P., and Aalto, T. (2004). TRIX 2004 — Struggling with the overlap. In *Proceedings of INEX 2004*, pages 127–139. Dagstuhl, Germany. Published in LNCS 3493, see Fuhr et al. (2005).

Koolen, M., Kazai, G., and Craswell, N. (2009). Wikipedia pages as entry points for book search. In *Proceedings of the 2nd ACM International Conference on Web Search and Data Mining*.

Lehtonen, M. (2006). Preparing heterogeneous XML for full-text search. *ACM Transactions on Information Systems*, 24(4):455–474.

Lu, J., Ling, T. W., Chan, C. Y., and Chen, T. (2005). From region encoding to extended Dewey: On efficient processing of XML twig pattern matching. In *Proceedings of the 31st International Conference on Very Large Data Bases*, pages 193–204. Trondheim, Norway.

Mass, Y., and Mandelbrod, M. (2003). Retrieving the most relevant XML components. In *Advances in XML Retrieval: Proceedings of the 3rd International Workshop of the Initiative for the Evaluation of XML Retrieval*, number 3493 in Lecture Notes in Computer Science, pages 53–58. Berlin, Germany: Springer.

Mass, Y., and Mandelbrod, M. (2004). Component ranking and automatic query refinement for XML retrieval. In *Proceedings of INEX 2004*, pages 53–58. Dagstuhl, Germany. Published in LNCS 3493, see Fuhr et al. (2005).

Melton, J., and Buxton, S. (2006). *Querying XML*. San Francisco, California: Morgan Kaufmann.

Pehcevski, J., Thom, J. A., and Vercoustre, A. (2004). Hybrid XML retrieval re-visited. In *Proceedings of INEX 2004*, pages 153–167. Dagstuhl, Germany. Published in LNCS 3493, see Fuhr et al. (2005).

Piwowarski, B., and Lalmas, M. (2004). Providing consistent and exhaustive relevance assessments for XML retrieval evaluation. In *Proceedings of the 13th ACM Conference on Information and Knowledge Management*, pages 361–370. Washington, D.C.

Piwowarski, B., Trotman, A., and Lalmas, M. (2008). Sound and complete relevance assessment for XML retrieval. *ACM Transactions on Information Systems*, 27(1):1–37.

Theobald, M., Bast, H., Majumdar, D., Schenkel, R., and Weikum, G. (2008). Topx: Efficient and versatile top-k query processing for semistructured data. *The VLDB Journal*, 17(1):81–115.

Tittel, E., and Dykes, L. (2005). *XML for Dummies* (4th ed.). New York: Wiley.

Trotman, A. (2004). Searching structured documents. *Information Processing & Management*, 40(4):619–632.

Trotman, A., and Sigurbjörnsson, B. (2004). Narrowed Extended XPath I (NEXI). In *Proceedings of INEX 2004*. Dagstuhl, Germany. Published in LNCS 3493, see Fuhr et al. (2005).

van der Vlist, E. (2002). *XML Schema: The W3C's Object-Oriented Descriptions for XML*. Sebastopol, California: O'Reilly.

Vittaut, J., Piwowarski, B., and Gallinari, P. (2004). An algebra for structured queries in Bayesian networks. In *Proceedings of INEX 2004*, pages 100–112. Dagstuhl, Germany. Published in LNCS 3493, see Fuhr et al. (2005).

Wu, H., Kazai, G., and Taylor, M. (2008). Book search experiments: Investigating IR methods for the indexing and retrieval of books. In *Proceedings of the 30th European Conference on Information Retrieval Research*, pages 234–245.

Zhang, C., Naughton, J., DeWitt, D., Luo, Q., and Lohman, G. (2001). On supporting containment queries in relational database management systems. In *Proceedings of the 2001 ACM SIGMOD International Conference on Management of Data*, pages 425–436. Santa Barbara, California.

Zhang, N., Özsu, M. T., Ilyas, I. F., and Aboulnaga, A. (2006). FIX: Feature-based indexing technique for XML documents. In *Proceedings of the 32nd International Conference on Very Large Data Bases*, pages 259–270. Seoul, South Korea.

VI Appendix

A   Computer Performance

The chapters in Part II of this book list performance numbers for various techniques related to inverted indices. To put these numbers into the right context, we give a brief overview of some important aspects of computer performance and provide a summary of the key performance characteristics of the computer system that was used to conduct the experiments described in this book (see Table A.1).

IR systems, like most database systems, spend a large fraction of their time moving data from one part of the computer to another. Their performance is determined largely by two factors: locality of data access and pipelined execution.

Data locality, in this context, means sequential versus random access. An example of a sequential data-access pattern is the term-at-a-time query processing strategy for disjunctive queries described in Section 5.1.2. An example of random data access is the sort-based dictionary from Section 4.2, which realizes lookup operations by means of binary search. Regardless of whether we store the index in memory or on disk, performance is usually improved. We rearranged the data so as to facilitate sequential access.

Pipelined execution is a feature of modern microprocessors that allows the CPU to begin executing instruction I_{n+1} while still working on instruction I_n. In order for this to be possible, the CPU needs to know the address of I_{n+1} before it is done with I_n. This can be tricky if I_n is a branch instruction (i.e., an "IF" statement).

A.1   Sequential Versus Random Access on Disk

For hard disk drives, the difference between sequential and random access is obvious, given that we first have to tell the drive's read head to position itself above the data before they can be read. This positioning operation involves two phases. In the first phase the read head is positioned over the disk track that contains the data (*seek latency*). In the second phase we wait for the disk to spin into the right location so that the data we want to read are directly under the head (*rotational latency*).

The average rotational latency depends on the hard drive's rotational velocity. If the disk spins at 7200 revolutions per minute (rpm), one rotation takes $1/120$ sec ≈ 8.3 ms. In order to read a piece of data from a random location on disk, on average we have to wait half a rotation — approximately 4.2 ms.

Table A.1 Key performance characteristics of the computer system used for the experiments described in this book. The system is equipped with two hard disk drives, arranged in a RAID-0 (striping). All disk operations in the indexing/retrieval experiments from Part II were carried out on the RAID-0.

CPU	
Model	1× AMD Opteron 154, 2.8 GHz
Data cache	64 KB (L1), 1024 KB (L2)
TLB cache	40 entries (L1), 512 entries (L2)
Execution pipeline	12 stages
Disk	
Total size	2× 465.8 GB
Average rotational latency	4.2 ms (7000 rpm)
Average seek latency	8.6 ms
Average random access latency	12.8 ms ($\approx$ 36 million CPU cycles)
Sequential read/write throughput (single disk)	45.5 MB/sec
Sequential read/write throughput (RAID-0)	87.4 MB/sec
Memory	
Total size	2048 MB
Random access latency	75 ns ($\approx$ 210 CPU cycles)
Sequential read/write throughput	3700 MB/sec

The average seek latency for index operations depends on the size of the index. A smaller index covers fewer disk tracks, and the disk head needs to travel less between subsequent read operations. For example, although the hard drive used in our experiments has an average random access latency of roughly 12.8 ms (seek latency: 8.6 ms; rotational latency: 4.2 ms), the average lookup latency in our dictionary interleaving experiments for the GOV2 collection (Table 4.4 on page 116) was only 11.4 ms — because the index covered only around 13% of the disk.[1]

A.2   Sequential Versus Random Access in RAM

For main memory the difference between sequential and random access is not quite as obvious, and the fact that we often refer to main memory as *random access memory* suggests that the difference, if it exists, is likely to be negligible. However, this is not the case.

---

[1] Note, however, that the file system (**ext3**) did not make any strong guarantees regarding the contiguity of the index on disk. It is quite likely that the index was not strictly contiguous and that an even lower latency could have been achieved if its contiguity has been enforced.

Data transfers between the CPU and main memory are sped up through the use of caches. In this context the two most relevant caches are the following:

- The **data cache**. This cache sits between the CPU and main memory and holds a copy of recently used data. It is arranged in *cache lines*, in which a single line typically holds 64 bytes of data. A cache line represents the granularity with which the cache communicates with the computer's main memory. If a process reads a single byte of data from RAM, the whole cache line is loaded into the cache, so that subsequent operations, involving other bytes within the same line, will be faster.

  The data cache is usually not a single cache but a hierarchy of caches referred to as level-1 (L1), level-2 (L2), and so forth. The L1 cache, at the top of the hierarchy, is the fastest, but also the smallest, among these caches.

- The **translation lookaside buffer (TLB)**. Essentially all modern microprocessors support virtual memory, wherein the address under which a process accesses a given piece of data (its *virtual address*) is different from the address at which it is actually stored in main memory (its *physical address*). The translation between virtual and physical addresses is realized through the *page table*; the granularity of the translation is a *page*, usually 4 or 8 KB.

  In a naïve implementation of virtual memory, each memory access requires two physical operations — one for the page table (translating the virtual address into a physical address) and the other for the actual data access. To avoid the resulting performance degradation, processors employ a special cache, the TLB, which holds copies of recently accessed page table entries.

Cache misses, both data and TLB misses, are quite expensive and can easily consume several dozen CPU cycles. In the worst case a memory access can trigger a data cache miss as well as a TLB miss. For the computer used in our experiments, such a double miss carries a penalty of roughly 75 ns, enough time to read almost 300 bytes sequentially.

It is worth pointing out that many random-access index operations cause combined data/TLB cache misses. This is one of the reasons why the grouping technique from Section 6.4 not only reduces the size of the search engine's dictionary but also improves its lookup performance (see Table 6.12 on page 220), as it decreases the number of random memory accesses in the binary search phase of each dictionary lookup.

A.3   Pipelined Execution and Branch Prediction

Pipelined execution has been a standard technique in CPU design since at least the mid-1980s, when Intel launched its i386 family of microprocessors. The basic idea is that a given machine instruction never utilizes all components of the CPU at the same time. Therefore, by pipelining the individual stages of the execution, utilization and overall performance can be improved.

Consider a simplistic three-stage pipeline:

1. **Fetch**. The instruction is loaded into the CPU either from main memory or from a cache.
2. **Decode**. The instruction's in-memory representation is translated into microcode that can be executed by the CPU.
3. **Execute**. The processor executes the instruction and updates the affected CPU registers and memory locations.

If we run a linear program without any branch instructions, then all three stages of the pipeline can be kept busy at all times. However, if one of the instructions currently in the pipeline, say I_n, is a branch instruction, then the processor does not know the location of the following instructions I_{n+1} and I_{n+2} and thus cannot load them before it has executed I_n. The pipeline is *stalled*.

Modern processors address this problem by employing a technique called *branch prediction*, in which they try to predict, based on past branching behavior, whether the IF case or the ELSE case of a given branch instruction will be invoked. Based on this prediction, they speculatively load the following instructions into the pipeline. In case of a misprediction, the work carried out for I_{n+1} and I_{n+2} has to be discarded and different instructions have to be loaded into the CPU, leaving the pipeline partially empty.

Prediction accuracy is usually well above 90%, but can be much lower for certain types of operations. You may remember the γ code from Section 6.3.1. A naïve decoder for this code would process the unary part of each codeword by inspecting the compressed bit sequence, one bit at a time, until it encounters the first $\bar{1}$ bit, roughly along the following lines:

```
1   bitPos ← 0
2   for i ← 1 to n do
3       k ← 1
4       while bitSequence[bitPos] = 0 do
5           bitPos ← bitPos + 1
6           k ← k + 1
7       fetch the next k bits in order to decode the current codeword
8       bitPos ← bitPos + k
```

The conditional jump in line 2 is unproblematic because the processor quickly learns that it should not break out of the loop (assuming that n is large). The branch in line 4, however, is more complicated to predict. Consider an encoded postings sequence in which the unary component of the γ code is 1 (i.e., bit sequence $\bar{1}$) for half the postings and 2 (i.e., bit sequence $0\bar{1}$) for the other half. Then the CPU will go from line 4 to line 5 about one-third of the time, and to line 8 two-thirds of the time. The optimal strategy is always to predict a branch (i.e., to assume that $bitSequence[bitPos]$ is $\bar{1}$). It leads to a misprediction rate of 33%.

For the simplistic three-stage pipeline from before, a misprediction rate of 33% does not seem too bad. However, the execution pipelines of modern microprocessors consist of a dozen or more stages, and repeated mispredictions can reduce the processor's execution rate substantially. Table-driven decoding (page 208) decreases the number of branch mispredictions and should usually be preferred over bit-by-bit decoding procedures.

Index

Printed in the United States
by Baker & Taylor Publisher Services